# Tribunal Practice and Procedure

*third edition*

2 New York Street
Manchester
M1 4HJ

Edward Jacobs is one of the founding judges of the Upper Tribunal, assigned to the Administrative Appeals Chamber. He was previously a Child Support and Social Security Commissioner. Edward Jacobs is author of *Child Support: the legislation* (CPAG) and a contributing editor to *Jowitt's Dictionary of English Law* (Sweet and Maxwell).

Available as an ebook at www.lag.org.uk/ebooks

The purpose of the Legal Action Group is to promote equal access to justice for all members of society who are socially, economically or otherwise disadvantaged. To this end, it seeks to improve law and practice, the administration of justice and legal services.

# Tribunal Practice and Procedure

THIRD EDITION

Edward Jacobs

Legal Action Group
2014

This edition published in Great Britain 2014
by LAG Education and Service Trust Limited
3rd floor, Universal House, 88–94 Wentworth Street, London E1 7SA
www.lag.org.uk

Second edition 2011
First edition 2009

British Library Cataloguing in Publication Data
a CIP catalogue record for this book is available from the British Library.

Crown copyright material is produced with the permission of the Controller of
HMSO and the Queen's Printer for Scotland.

This book has been produced using Forest Stewardship Council
(FSC) certified paper. The wood used to produce FSC certified
products with a 'Mixed Sources' label comes from FSC certified
well-managed forests, controlled sources and/or recycled
material.

Print ISBN    978 1 908407 45 0
ebook ISBN    978 1 908407 46 7

Typeset by Regent Typesetting, London
Printed in Great Britain by Hobbs the Printers, Totton, Hampshire

To Jill

# Foreword to the third edition

Lord Justice Sullivan, Senior President of Tribunals

I am delighted to be able to extend a warm welcome to the third edition of this invaluable guide to the tribunals system established under the 2007 Act. Since the second edition was published in 2011, the Property Chamber has joined the First-tier Tribunal, the jurisdictions of the Chambers comprising the First-tier Tribunal have steadily increased as new rights of appeal have been created, and the Upper Tribunal's judicial review function has been greatly expanded. A legal system which is having to cope with large numbers of litigants in person has much to learn from the practice and procedure adopted by tribunals, as described in this work. I am sure that it will not be too long before we need a fourth edition!

Sir Jeremy Sullivan
Senior President of Tribunals
October 2014

# Foreword to the first edition

Lord Justice Carnwath, Senior President of Tribunals

I am pleased to have this opportunity to write the foreword to this timely work. The Tribunal Reform programme began with the ground-breaking Report of Sir Andrew Leggatt in 2001. He drew attention to the important role that tribunals play in the UK justice system, accounting for more than 500,000 cases a year. He called for radical overhaul of a system which had grown up in a piecemeal and illogical way so as to create 'a system that is independent, coherent, professional, cost-effective and user-friendly'. It should have 'a collective stand to match that court system and collective power to fulfil the needs of users in the way that it was originally intended'. The Upper Tribunal was to be a very important part of the new structure, providing a unified appeal route to replace the 'hotchpotch' of different appeal procedures applying to different tribunals under the previous law. He also called for the harmonisation of the disparate sets of rules governing different tribunals.

The general thrust of his recommendations was accepted by government in 2004. In due course it led to the creation of a Tribunal Service in 2006 as part of what is now the Ministry of Justice, and to the enactment of a flexible legislative framework in the Tribunal, Courts & Enforcement Act 2007.

Since then the pace of reform has gathered pace. I was formally appointed Senior President in November 2007. A year later on 'T-Day' (3 November 2008), the First-tier and Upper Tribunals were created and the first Chambers established: the Social Entitlement, Health, Education and Social Care, and War Pensions Chambers at the First-tier level, and the Administrative Appeals Chamber in the Upper Tribunal. In April we were joined by the tax jurisdictions and in June by the Lands Tribunal. The General Regulatory Chamber will follow in two stages in September 2009 and January 2010, and the asylum and immigration jurisdictions in February 2010. The Tribunals Procedure Committee has made great steps towards the Leggatt goal of harmonising the Rules by providing new sets of Rules for all Chambers, conforming to a common model with appropriate variations to reflect the needs of different jurisdictions. All this has been achieved without significant disruption to the day-to-day work of tribunals. I am proud to have been involved in what has been a remarkable co-operative achievement by judges and administrators working together.

These structural changes mean nothing unless they bring with them gains in terms of improved access to justice and improved substantive coherence for the legal framework within which tribunals operate. Edward Jacobs' new work seems destined to make a major contribution to the latter objective. His 'structured approach' to the procedure and practice of tribunals emphasises what is shared by the components of the new system rather than their differences. I am particularly pleased to note the valuable quotations from judgments relating to different tribunals which help to illustrate the underlining principles. I look forward to using the work as a ready handbook and guide to the new tribunals world.

Robert Carnwath
Senior President of Tribunals
August 2009

# Preface

In the three and a half years since the previous edition, the tribunal system has continued to expand. It has absorbed more tribunals by creating a Property Chamber in the First-tier Tribunal with appeals to the Lands Chamber of the Upper Tribunal. The transfer of judicial review cases from the High Court has significantly increased the work of the Immigration and Asylum Chamber of the Upper Tribunal, continuing the practice of transferring cases from the High Court. And new jurisdictions continue to be added to the General Regulatory Chamber of the First-tier Tribunal and to the Administrative Appeals and the Tax and Chancery Chambers of the Upper Tribunal.

As in previous editions, the text is generally applicable to all jurisdictions, but I have usually cited only the rules of procedure that apply to the Upper Tribunal other than the Lands Chamber, identifying the equivalent rules for other Chambers in the footnotes. I have also continued to follow my previous practice of adopting terminology appropriate to England, leaving readers to read 'permission' as 'leave' in Northern Ireland, 'costs' as 'expenses' in Scotland and so on.

As part of the preparation of this edition, I have the read the entire text. Despite that, I have probably missed some errors and have, no doubt, incorporated new ones. I am grateful to readers who have pointed out mistakes in the past and I encourage all readers to do so in the future.

The text is up-to-date as of late September 2014, but the references to the rules of procedure incorporate changes to 20 October 2014, including the new rules for the Immigration and Asylum Chamber of the First-tier Tribunal.

Edward Jacobs
October 2014

# Contents

# Table of cases

# Table of statutes

# Table of statutory instruments

# Table of European legislation

# Abbreviations

| | |
|---|---|
| Article 6 | Article 6 of the European Convention on Human Rights |
| Commissioner | Social Security and Child Support Commissioners and their predecessors. Other Commissioners, such as Commissioners of Tax, are identified as such |
| CPR | Civil Procedure Rules |
| Decision-maker | Officer authorised to make public law decisions for a body, such as a Government Department or local authority |
| GRC Rules | Tribunal Procedure (First-tier Tribunal) (General Regulatory Chamber) Rules 2009 |
| HESC Rules | Tribunal Procedure (First-tier Tribunal) (Health, Education and Social Care Chamber) Rules 2008 |
| IAC Rules | Tribunal Procedure (First-tier Tribunal) (Immigration and Asylum Chamber) Rules 2014 |
| Lands Rules | Tribunal Procedure (Upper Tribunal) (Lands Chamber) Rules 2010 |
| PC Rules | Tribunal Procedure (First-tier Tribunal) (Property Chamber) Rules 2013 |
| R(IB) 2/04 | References in this form are to decisions of the Commissioners reported before 2010 |
| SEC Rules | Tribunal Procedure (First-tier Tribunal) (Social Entitlement Chamber) Rules 2008. |
| Tax Rules | Tribunal Procedure (First-tier Tribunal) (Tax Chamber) Rules 2009. |
| TCEA | Tribunals, Courts and Enforcement Act 2007 |
| UTR | Tribunal Procedure (Upper Tribunal) Rules 2008 |
| WPAFC Rules | Tribunal Procedure (First-tier Tribunal) (War Pensions and Armed Forces Compensation Chamber) Rules 2008 |

# CHAPTER 1

# Introduction to the tribunal system

*continued*

# Introduction

1.1      This book is about tribunals, what they are and how they work. It covers all aspects, except for the substantive law applied by tribunals.

1.2      Tribunals are exclusively judicial bodies that operate in a way which distinguishes them from other courts. As a word, tribunal has a long history, but only as a synonym for a court. It is still used in that sense, for example in article 6. However, tribunal as a distinct form of judicial body and as a word to convey that concept is a twentieth century innovation. The oldest citation of the modern use of the word in the *Oxford English Dictionary*, 2nd edn, 1989, is from the Military Service Act 1916.

1.3      There have long been bodies that were similar in many ways to what we now call a tribunal; their use proliferated in the nineteenth century.[1] But they were not exclusively judicial, as this role was secondary to their administrative functions. They went by a variety of names, often Commission or Commissioner. They may still not be extinct. The housing benefit review boards were too closely linked, both in structure[2] and practice, to their local authorities to be independent judicial bodies, but were only replaced by an appeal to a judicial tribunal in 2001.

1.4      Tribunals emerged as exclusively judicial bodies in the twentieth century with the local pension committee under the Old Age Pensions Act 1908 and the umpire under the National Insurance Act 1911. Since then there has been increasing recognition of their judicial status, that status has been enhanced, and tribunals have developed their own distinctive identity. Their development and the attitude of successive Governments to them can be traced in the reports of the three general public enquiries that have considered tribunals.[3]

1.5      The first inquiry was by the Donoughmore Committee, which reported in 1932.[4] It was set up in part to consider the safeguards that were required on judicial and quasi-judicial decisions in order to secure the constitutional principle of the supremacy of the law. The committee considered tribunals in this context, distinguishing between tribunals that were independent of Ministerial influence, which it called Specialised Courts of Law, and those that were not, although it admitted that the difference was one of degree not kind.[5] The committee recognised the value of tribunals,[6] but with the focus set by its terms of reference, it was concerned not with the internal working of tribunals but with the circumstances in which they were established and the safeguards on their use. As to the former, the Committee recommended that judicial decisions should be left to the ordinary

---

1   Their history is traced by Chantal Stebbings in *Legal Foundations of Tribunals in Nineteenth Century England*, Cambridge, 2006.

2   *R (Bewry) v Norwich City Council* [2002] HRLR 2, a decision of the Administrative Court, and *Tsfayo v United Kingdom* (application no: 60860/00) November 14, 2006, ECtHR.

3   There have been numerous committees with more limited terms of reference.

4   *The Report of the Committee on Ministers' Powers* Cmd. 4060 (1932).

5   *The Report of the Committee on Ministers' Powers* Cmd. 4060 (1932), Section III, paras 5–7.

6   *The Report of the Committee on Ministers' Powers* Cmd. 4060 (1932), Section III, para 10.

courts of law. Tribunals should be established only on special grounds and if their advantages over the ordinary courts were beyond question.[7] And when they were used, the Committee recommended that the rules of natural justice be observed and the courts be given power to ensure that they acted only within their powers.[8] The concerns that led to the Committee being established, its discussion and its recommendations all show a concern, at the level of constitutional theory, about the developing use of tribunals.

1.6    A quarter of a century later either these concerns had been allayed or tribunals were accepted as an inevitable feature regardless of them. The focus now turned to their status and the details of their operation rather than their constitutional position. The Franks Committee, which reported in 1957,[9] was set up in part to consider the constitution and working of statutory tribunals. This Committee endorsed the value of tribunals but was not concerned to limit their use. Rather the focus was on their judicial nature, the standards they must attain and the supervision they required. It based its recommendations around three principles of openness, fairness and impartiality:

> In the field of tribunals openness appears to us to require the publicity of proceedings and knowledge of the essential reasoning underlying the decisions; fairness to require the adoption of a clear procedure which enables the parties to know their rights, to present their case fully and to know the case which they have to meet; and impartiality to require the freedom of tribunals from the influence, real or apparent, of Departments concerned with the subject-matter of their decision.[10]

1.7    Consistently with the requirement of impartiality, the Committee rejected the official evidence that 'tribunals should properly be regarded as part of the machinery of administration, for which the Government must retain a close and continuing responsibility' in favour of the view that 'tribunals should be properly regarded as machinery provided by Parliament for adjudication rather than as part of the machinery of administration.'[11] The committee made a series of recommendations on the constitution of tribunals, their procedure and control over particular decisions by appeal and judicial review. It also recommended more general supervision through two Councils on Tribunals (one for England and Wales, the other for Scotland) in order to keep under review the constitution and procedures of tribunals. This proposal led to the Tribunals and Inquiries Act 1958 under which the Council on Tribunals was given powers in respect of many, but not all, tribunals. This Act was replaced by the Tribunals and Inquiries Act 1992.

---

7   *The Report of the Committee on Ministers' Powers* Cmd. 4060 (1932), Section III, paras 9 and 10.

8   *The Report of the Committee on Ministers' Powers* Cmd. 4060 (1932), Section III, para 11.

9   *The Report of the Committee on Administrative Tribunals and Enquiries* Cmnd. 218 (1957).

10   *The Report of the Committee on Administrative Tribunals and Enquiries* Cmnd. 218 (1957), para 42.

11   *The Report of the Committee on Administrative Tribunals and Enquiries* Cmnd. 218 (1957) at para 40.

1.8      By the end of the century the focus had changed again. The terms of reference to the inquiry led by Sir Andrew Leggatt, which reported in 2001,[12] accepted statutory tribunals as judicial bodies and directed attention to issues of efficiency and effectiveness. Leggatt's key recommendation was that tribunals should be freed from their relationship with a sponsoring department and be brought within a single coherent structure with uniform powers for tribunals and rights of appeal for the parties.

1.9      The idea of systematic reform was not new. It had been proposed without success by Professor Robson to the Donoughmore Committee,[13] picked up by Professor Wade[14] and repeated by Professor Robson to the Franks Committee, which rejected his proposal that would have brought system to appeals against administrative decisions.[15]

1.10      Sir Andrew Leggatt's report was followed in 2001 by a consultation paper and then, in 2004, by a White Paper on *Transforming Public Services: Complaints, Redress and Tribunals.*[16] This proposed a co-ordinated approach to administrative justice. There followed administrative action and legislation, but the vision of the White Paper has only been partly realised. Administratively, a Tribunals Service was established, as a companion to the Courts Service. Beginning in April 2006, tribunals began to be moved from their sponsoring departments into the Department for Constitutional Affairs, now the Ministry of Justice. And their administrations, although they remained separate, were co-ordinated under the new Tribunals Service. In terms of legislation, the Tribunals, Courts and Enforcement Act (TCEA) was passed in 2007. This established a First-tier Tribunal and an Upper Tribunal and made common provision for the powers of, and appeal rights to and from, those tribunals. Finally, the Council on Tribunals was replaced by the Administrative Justice and Tribunals Council, which was itself abolished in 2013.

1.11      In April 2011, the Tribunals Service merged with Her Majesty's Courts Service to form Her Majesty's Courts and Tribunals Service. This administrative merger has in turn led to greater judicial integration and assimilation between the courts and tribunals through the Lord Chief Justice's power of deployment under the Courts and Crime Act 2013 s21.

1.12      The current priority is to find ways of reconciling the political aspiration for devolution and the practical problems of operating jurisdictions that apply across national boundaries within the United Kingdom.

---

12   *Tribunals for Users – One System, One Service.*

13   *The Report of the Committee on Ministers' Powers* Cmd. 4060 (1932), Section III, para 19.

14   'Quasi–Judicial' and its Background (1949) 10 CLJ 216 at 217.

15   *The Report of the Committee on Administrative Tribunals and Enquiries* Cmnd. 218 (1957) at paras 120–123.

16   Cm 6243.

# Nature of a tribunal

## What a tribunal is

1.13   Tribunal is used in a general sense and in a specific sense. In its general sense, it covers all bodies, including courts, that determine the legal position of the parties before them. In its specific sense, it is used to distinguish one particular class of judicial body from the rest.

1.14   Lord Dilhorne captured this distinction in *Attorney-General v BBC*[17] when he said 'While every court is a tribunal, the converse is not true'.[18]

1.15   There is no general definition of what constitutes a tribunal in this specific sense and of its distinctive features. Referring to that sense in *Royal Aquarium and Summer and Winter Garden Society Ltd v Parkinson*,[19] Fry LJ expressed the opinion that '. . . that word has not, like the word "court", an ascertainable meaning in English law'.[20]

1.16   The reason for this is simply that there is no need for a general definition. The proper classification of a body as a tribunal always arises in a particular legal context. That context may affect the answer, so that a body may be a court for one purpose and a tribunal for another. For example, a particular body may be a tribunal for the purposes of article 6, but a court for the purposes of the Contempt of Court Act 1981.

1.17   The tribunals with which this book is concerned may be defined by a combination of characteristics relating to their method of creation, their purpose, the scope of their jurisdiction and powers, their membership, their procedures, and their relationship with the parties to proceedings before them. A tribunal in this sense is a body created by statute.[21] Its purpose is to determine a person's legal position in respect of a private law dispute or a public law entitlement, whether initially, on appeal or on judicial review.[22] It is given only a narrow and limited jurisdiction. But that jurisdiction is conferred generally and is not limited to an individual case. The members are likely to be expert in the jurisdiction; they are not limited to lawyers and may include others with relevant knowledge and experience. The procedures are likely to be relatively simple and user-friendly. Finally, it is independent of the parties to the proceedings. In other words, the tribunal is an expert, independent standing statutory body, available to deal with all those cases within its jurisdiction and easily accessible by users.

1.18   This does not mean that these features are unique to tribunals. Court judges may, for example, be just as expert in their jurisdiction as tribunal judges. Nor does it mean that all tribunals exhibit these features. The

---

17  [1981] AC 303.

18  [1981] AC 303 at 340.

19  [1892] 1 QB 431.

20  [1892] 1 QB 431 at 446.

21  Lords Guest and Devlin in *United Engineering Workers' Union v Devanayagam* [1968] AC 356 at 382–383.

22  A tribunal may have an original jurisdiction, an appellate jurisdiction, a judicial review jurisdiction or a combination. The Upper Tribunal has appellate jurisdiction under, for example, TCEA s11, a judicial review jurisdiction under TCEA s15, and an original jurisdiction in the case of forfeiture under the Forfeiture Act 1982.

Competition Appeal Tribunal, for example, does not operate procedures that are designed to make it readily accessible by those without legal assistance. What it does mean is that tribunals are bodies in which these features are likely to occur in combination.

1.19    In the past, a tribunal's powers were always[23] subject to the one limitation identified by Hale LJ in *R v Secretary of State for the Home Department ex p Saleem:*[24]

> Their determinations are no less binding than those of the ordinary courts: the only difference is that tribunals have no direct powers of enforcement and, in the rare cases where this is needed, their decisions are enforced in the ordinary courts.[25]

However, the Upper Tribunal has the powers of the High Court (TCEA s25).

1.20    The label given to a body is not decisive. Some bodies are called tribunals and are tribunals for the purposes of this book. Other bodies bear different names, but are nonetheless tribunals within the above definition. A body that is called a court may even be within the definition. The former National Industrial Relations Court would have been a tribunal for this purpose.

1.21    A tribunal may be made a superior court of record by statute. The Upper Tribunal is so designated by TCEA s3(5), as is the Employment Appeal Tribunal by section 20(3) of the Employment Tribunals Act 1996.

1.22    This does not mean that the principles covered in this book are unique to tribunals as here defined. They are derived from principles that apply to all judicial bodies and many of the cases cited relate to the courts. The principles also apply to the occasional inquiries that are set up by the government outside the authority of any particular statute, whether or not the Tribunals of Inquiry (Evidence) Act 1921 applies. And they may be appropriate to domestic tribunals, which owe their existence to contract.

## How a tribunal operates

1.23    If the issue of definition were all that distinguished tribunals from courts, it would scarcely be worth making. However, there are features that characterise tribunals apart from definitional factors. Tribunals may be distinguished from courts by their membership and their procedures. These characteristics are not unique to tribunals, but to the particular features that are likely to be present in relation to tribunals. The same features may also be present in court proceedings. If they are, it is likely that the courts will adopt similar approaches.[26]

1.24    Some of the features that distinguish a tribunal from a court are recognised in TCEA. Section 2(3) imposes on the Senior President a duty to

---

23  At least in England and Wales. The employment tribunal in Scotland has power to enforce its own decisions.

24  [2001] 1 WLR 443.

25  [2001] 1 WLR 443 at 457.

26  See Chancery Modernisation Review: Final Report (2013), chapter 9 of which deals with litigants in person.

have regard to particular features in carrying out the functions of that office:

- tribunals should be accessible;
- their proceedings should be fair and handled quickly and efficiently;
- their members should be expert in the subject-matter or law with which the tribunal is concerned; and
- innovative methods of resolving disputes should be developed.

The requirements of accessibility, fairness and efficiency mirror the same requirements for the civil justice system under section 1(3) of the Civil Procedure Act 1997.

1.25    And section 22(4) of TCEA sets the objectives for the rules of procedure:

- that justice is done;
- that the tribunal system is accessible and fair;
- that proceedings are handled quickly and efficiently;
- that the rules are both simple and simply expressed; and
- that the rules where appropriate confer on members responsibility for ensuring that proceedings before the tribunal are handled quickly and efficiently.

1.26    Before dealing with individual features of the operation of tribunals, there is a general point to make about the language that is sometimes used in relation to tribunals. The language in which the distinctive features of tribunal procedure are described can give an inaccurate impression. The procedure before tribunals may be said to be informal and inquisitorial, but these statements must not be taken too literally. It is also said that the strict rules of evidence do not apply, but this gives no indication of how tribunals approach fact-finding. Language such as this is not descriptive of how tribunals operate. It conveys something of what tribunals are not rather than what they are. It is used to differentiate tribunals from courts, to distance tribunals from the procedures appropriate to court proceedings.

## Accessibility[27]

1.27    Ease and convenience of use is an important feature of tribunals. As Lord Reading CJ said of the Income Tax Commissioners in *R v Bloomsbury Income Tax Commissioners*:[28]

> The exigencies of the State require that there should be a tribunal to deal expeditiously and at comparatively little expense with all such questions and to decide them finally, reserving always to the individual the right to have the Commissioners' decisions on points of law reviewed by the Courts.[29]

1.28    This was repeated by the Donoughmore Committee on *Ministers' Powers*:[30]

---

27  Accessibility for disabled people was addressed by the former Council on Tribunals in its *Making Tribunals Accessible to Disabled People* (2002).

28  [1915] 3 KB 768.

29  [1915] 3 KB 768 at 784.

30  Cmd. 4060 (1932).

We recognise that such Ministerial Tribunals have much to recommend them. In cases where justice can only be done if it is done at a minimum cost, such Tribunals, which are likely to be cheaper to the parties, may on this ground be preferred to the ordinary Courts of Law. In addition they may be more readily accessible, freer from technicality, and – where relief must be given quickly – more expeditious. They possess the requisite expert knowledge of their subject – a specialised Court may often be better for the exercise of a special jurisdiction. Such Tribunals may also be better able at least than the inferior Courts of Law to establish uniformity of practice.[31]

1.29    This description was in turn endorsed by the Franks Committee on *Administrative Tribunals and Enquiries*:[32]

38. We agree with the Donoughmore Committee that tribunals have certain characteristics which often give them advantages over the courts. These are cheapness, accessibility, freedom from technicality, expedition and expert knowledge of their particular subject.

1.30    The same view underpins the entire approach of Sir Andrew Leggatt in his *Review of Tribunals*:[33]

It should never be forgotten that tribunals exist for users, not the other way round. No matter how good tribunals may be, they do not fulfil their function unless they are accessible by the people who want to use them, and unless the users receive the help they need to prepare and present their cases.[34]

1.31    And the Council on Tribunals[35] identified accessibility as one of its standards for tribunals.[36]

1.32    The courts and tribunals have been sensitive to the difficulties of parties who are either unrepresented or who lack legal representation. This has been necessary in order to render effective the proceedings that statute has made available. It has also, given the tribunal context, been necessary in order to ensure that the proceedings are fair under the principles of natural justice and article 6.

1.33    Accessibility has in part been attributable to, or found its expression in, the features considered below. These approaches now have to be applied and developed under TCEA. The first duty of the Senior President is to have regard to the need for tribunals to be accessible (TCEA s2(3)(a)). This feature of the tribunal system is given more concrete expression in the requirement for the rules of procedure to ensure that the tribunal is accessible and that the rules are simple and simply expressed (TCEA s22(4)(b) and (d)). And individual tribunals are required to apply the overriding objective in determining and operating their procedure.[37] UTR r2(2) is illustrative:[38]

---

31   Section III, para 10.
32   Cmnd. 218 (1957).
33   *Tribunals for Users – One System, One Service* (2001).
34   *Tribunals for Users – One System, One Service* (2001), para 6.
35   Replaced by the Administrative Justice and Tribunals Council.
36   *Tribunals for Users – One System, One Service* (2001), para 6.
37   See para 3.22.
38   See also: GRC Rules r2(2); HESC Rules r2(2); IAC Rules r2(2); Lands Rules r2(2); PC Rules r3(2); SEC Rules r2(2); Tax Rules r2(2); WPAFC Rules r2(2).

> (2) Dealing with a case fairly and justly includes–
>
> . . .
>
> > (b) avoiding unnecessary formality and seeking flexibility in the proceedings;
> > (c) ensuring, so far as practicable, that the parties are able to participate fully in the proceedings;
> > (d) using any special expertise of the Upper Tribunal effectively; . . .

1.34   Fees can also inhibit access to a tribunal. A fee for initiating proceedings may be imposed. But it must be imposed directly by statute or under an appropriate statutory enabling power.[39] And it must not operate to abrogate the right of access to justice. As Laws LJ explained in giving the judgment of the Court of Appeal in *R v Lord Chancellor ex p Witham*: 'Access to the courts is a constitutional right; it can only be denied by the government if it persuades Parliament to pass legislation which specifically – in effect by express provision – permits the executive to turn people away from the court door'.[40] This reasoning is equally applicable to tribunals as it is to courts.

## Speed

1.35   This is part of accessibility. It is embodied in the Senior President's duty under TCEA s2(3)(b)(ii) to have regard to the need for proceedings to be handled quickly. However, as Sir Andrew Leggatt noted 'Speed should not be an end in itself. It should follow from obedience to the watchwords which should inform every tribunal: informality, simplicity, efficiency, and proportionality.'[41]

1.36   Speed has to be balanced, or reconciled, with the Senior President's duty in section 2(3)(b)(i) to ensure that proceedings are fair. It must not be attained at the cost of failing to provide a fair hearing. That would render the decision liable to be set aside, which would length the total time taken.

1.37   The duty to ensure that proceedings are handled quickly does not apply directly to individual cases. It is imposed on the Senior President and not on the tribunal hearing a case. And it operates through general policy and through practice directions rather than decisions in particular cases.

1.38   TCEA s22(4) is more significant in individual cases. It requires the rules of procedure to secure specified objectives. Two are relevant to the speed of proceedings:

> (c) that proceedings before the First-tier Tribunal or Upper Tribunal are handled quickly and efficiently,
>
> . . .
>
> (e) that the rules where appropriate confer on members of the First-tier Tribunal, or Upper Tribunal, responsibility for ensuring that proceedings before the tribunal are handled quickly and efficiently.

1.39   Resources will always have an impact on speed. The more hearings that can be held, the more quickly cases can be heard. To some extent, speed can

---

39   TCEA s42 contains an appropriate power.
40   [1998] QB 575 at 586.
41   *Tribunals for Users – One System, One Service* (2001), para 31.

be achieved through general procedures. For example: the absence of formal pleading and discovery stages reduces the time that a case would take compared to a court. And to some extent speed can be achieved through efficiency measures. For example, effective listing can ensure that time is not wasted and cases are heard as quickly as possible. However, there is a limit to the effect that these measures can have. The rules of procedure and practice directions must have an impact in individual cases if the duty is to prove effective in practice.

## The law of evidence

1.40 Tribunals are generally not bound by the strict rules of evidence. This allows greater flexibility in the evidence that they receive. For example: expert evidence before a court must at least conform to a minority but respected body of opinion within the profession. That limitation does not apply in a tribunal.[42]

## The bridging function

1.41 In all forms of legal proceedings, there is a bridge to be crossed between the lay parties and the court or tribunal. The lay parties know the facts, but do not known the law or, therefore, which facts are relevant. The court or tribunal knows the law, but not the facts within the parties' knowledge. If the parties are represented competently (but not necessarily by a lawyer), this bridge is crossed in the pre-hearing work undertaken by the representatives. They obtain the relevant facts by inquiry of the parties and present only those that are relevant. In the case of tribunals, it is less likely than in a court that this work will be done by representatives before the hearing. It therefore devolves, in whole or in part, to the tribunal itself.

1.42 This leads tribunals[43] to adopt two approaches to help them in this task: the enabling approach and the inquisitorial approach. They are complementary. The enabling approach is concerned with the attitude to the parties. The inquisitorial approach is concerned with the evidence and issues. These approaches may require a greater degree of intervention by, and assistance from, the tribunal than is usual in the courts.[44]

1.43 The proper approach is a matter of duty for the tribunal, not a matter of choice. Originally, it was based in the requirement of natural justice and of article 6. Under TCEA, it is also based in the overriding objective. Every party before a tribunal has a right to be heard and the tribunal must ensure that that right is effective. As the Commissioner explained in *R(I) 6/69*:[45]

> But the broad general principle is that a claimant has a right to be heard and that a tribunal has a corresponding duty not only to ensure that he is aware

---

42 See further chapter 10 below.
43 And courts in which the bridging function has not been performed by representatives. This is increasingly so even in the High Court.
44 On which see *Jones v National Coal Board* [1957] 2 QB 55.
45 *R(I) 6/69* at [7].

of this right but also to assist him, by such means as may be appropriate in any particular case, to exercise it.

## Enabling approach

1.44    Tribunals are expected to take an enabling approach. There is no express legal requirement that they do so, but it is an aspect of accessibility (TCEA ss2(3)(a) and 24(2)(b)). And the overriding objective requires that, as far as practicable, the parties must be able to participate fully in the proceedings: see for example UTR r2(2)(c).

1.45    This approach requires the tribunal to try to create a framework for proceedings that allows parties who are inexperienced with the procedures involved to give of their best in an unfamiliar setting. This is achieved through appropriate application of the tribunal's powers under its rules of procedure, the explanations given to the parties, the manner in which the hearing is conducted and the atmosphere that is created. Members are selected who have an aptitude for this approach and it is reinforced by training.

1.46    Professor Kathleen Bell found that this was the approach that the appellants wanted in the former Supplementary Benefit Appeal Tribunals:

> . . . members should play an active and *enabling* role towards the appellant by showing sympathetic understanding of his problem, by listening, asking relevant questions, drawing him out and generally helping him sort out his case. They were able to distinguish this enabling role from that of an advocate.[46]

She recommended that tribunal members should be made aware of:

> . . . appellants' expectations of the tribunal and their concept of it as a body which will play an active and *enabling* role towards them through the medium of a rather informal but thorough exploration of the case.[47]

1.47    Sir Andrew Leggatt recommended[48] that the enabling approach should be taken, especially in those tribunals that involved public law entitlement:

> . . . tribunals have developed different ways of assisting unrepresented parties, in particular when the encounter is between citizen and state,[49] and departments are represented by an official or an advocate who is familiar with the law, the tribunal and its procedures. In these circumstances, tribunal chairmen may find it necessary to intervene in the proceedings more than might be thought proper in the courts in order to hold the balance between the parties, and enable citizens to present their cases. All the members of a tribunal must do all they can to understand the point of view, as well as the case, of the citizen. They must be alert for factual or legal aspects of the case which appellants may not bring out, adequately or at all, but which have a bearing on the possible outcomes. It may also be necessary on occasion to intervene to protect a witness or party, to avoid proceedings becoming too confrontational. The balance is a delicate one,

---

46  *Research Study on Supplementary Benefit Appeal Tribunals – Review of Main Findings: Conclusions: Recommendations* (1975), p18.

47  *Research Study on Supplementary Benefit Appeal Tribunals – Review of Main Findings: Conclusions: Recommendations* (1975), p22.

48  *Tribunals for Users – One System, One Service* (2001).

49  The reasoning also applies if someone is involved who is not a citizen, as for example in an immigration or asylum case.

and must not go so far on any side that the tribunal's impartiality appears to be endangered.

We are convinced that the tribunal approach must be an enabling one: supporting the parties in ways which give them confidence in their own abilities to participate in the process, and in the tribunal's capacity to compensate for the appellants' lack of skills or knowledge . . .[50]

1.48　As these quotations make clear, the enabling approach is particularly appropriate for an unrepresented party.

1.49　As part of the enabling approach, tribunals adopt processes and procedures that are less complicated and more informal than those that are typically associated with courts. This is part of the overriding objective.[51] This is not to say that courts cannot operate relatively simple processes and procedures or that they are inevitably formal. The point is that there is a range of simplicity and formality and that tribunals are typically at the more user-friendly end of the spectrum.

1.50　The expectations of the parties and their ability to use the forms and procedures also reflects the difficulties they may experience without assistance. In *Burns International Security Services (UK) Ltd v Butt*,[52] the Employment Appeal Tribunal decided that:

It seems to us that in the field of industrial relations where application forms are frequently completed by individual employees without professional assistance a technical approach is particularly inappropriate . . .

It was pointed out in *Cocking v Sandhurst (Stationers) Ltd* [1974] ICR 650 that the rules did not require that the complaint as presented should be free of all defects and should be in the form in which it finally came before the tribunal for adjudication. The purpose of the rules is to ensure that the parties know the nature of the respective cases which are made against them.[53]

1.51　This approach is not limited to the employment tribunal and the Employment Appeal Tribunal. The courts also took the same approach in cases involving planning law and the Rent Act 1968.[54] The Commissioners took the same approach.[55] This approach may be inherent in the rules of procedure (especially rr2 and 5–7).[56] There is a limited express power in respect of some forms of application,[57] but the approach has been applied more widely.[58]

1.52　However, in the war pensions case of *R (Clancy) v Secretary of State for Defence*,[59] Davis J decided that it was too late to rely on the substance of an application, if the appropriate form has not been used and the proceedings had been disposed of in accordance with that form.

---

50　*Tribunals for Users – One System, One Service* (2001), paras 7.4–7.5.
51　See UTR r2(2)(b) and its equivalents in the other rules.
52　[1983] ICR 547.
53　[1983] ICR 547 at 550–551.
54　See the authorities cited in *Burns International* [1983] ICR 547.
55　*R(I) 15/53* at [4]; *R(I) 50/56* at [18].
56　*R(RB) v First-tier Tribunal (Review)* [2010] UKUT 160 (AAC) at [10].
57　GRC Rules r45; HESC Rules r50; IAC Rules r36; Lands Rules r58; PC Rules r56; SEC Rules r41; Tax Rules r42; UTR r48; WPAFC Rules r39.
58　*LS v Lambeth LBC* [2010] UKUT 461 (AAC) at [94].
59　[2006] EWHC 3333 (Admin).

1.53   The enabling approach in action is exemplified by *R(I) 6/69*. The Commissioner set out the proper approach for a tribunal to take:

> It is the tribunal's duty to afford every claimant a reasonable opportunity of addressing them, of calling or adducing evidence, and of calling attention to any points or matters which he thinks should be taken into consideration. He must also be afforded a reasonable opportunity to reply to any submissions or arguments adverse to his case made on behalf of the Secretary of State. This means something more than a mere passive willingness to accede to a request, should one be made to address the tribunal; it involves a degree of active assistance and encouragement. How much assistance and encouragement is required will necessarily vary from case to case and from claimant to claimant. Some unrepresented claimants are unable to express themselves clearly or unable to distinguish between what is relevant and what is irrelevant. In many such cases the tribunal can do little more than invite answers to questions.[60]

But this simplicity and informality is not uncontrolled. There are limits to which it is permissible or appropriate.

1.54   For some purposes, formal attention to the correct procedures is necessary. So in *Sivanandan v Enfield LBC*,[61] the Court of Appeal decided that an employment tribunal is required formally to dismiss a claim if it is withdrawn in order to pursue a remedy elsewhere. Wall LJ emphasised the need in such circumstances for 'a clear procedural discipline'.[62]

1.55   Even if a lesser degree of formality than that used in courts is appropriate, the proceedings must not be so informal that all aspects of a case are not considered. The purpose of the enabling approach is to enhance the quality of the decision-making; it must not be used to impede it. As Pill LJ explained in the context of a planning appeal in *Dyason v Secretary of State for the Environment*:[63]

> A relaxed hearing is not necessarily a fair hearing. The hearing must not become so relaxed that the rigorous examination essential to the determination of difficulty questions may be diluted.[64]

1.56   Informality of approach should not deprive a party of a right, such as the right to question witnesses.[65]

1.57   Nor should it be allowed to prejudice or embarrass a party's presentation of a case. The recalling of witnesses in an employment tribunal was considered by the Employment Appeal Tribunal in *Aberdeen Steak Houses Group plc v Ibrahim*.[66] Wood J said:

> It is possible for informality to go too far and it is important for parties appearing before any judicial body, and for their legal advisers in preparing for trial, to know the rules normally to be applied during that hearing. It is important that there should be consistency. It is also important that any

---

60   *R(I) 6/69* at [7].
61   [2005] EWCA Civ 10; (2005) *Times* 20 January.
62   [2005] EWCA Civ 10 at [122].
63   (1998) 75 P&CR 506.
64   (1998) 75 P&CR 506 at 512.
65   *R(I) 13/74* at [9].
66   [1988] ICR 550.

sudden change from that norm should not present a party with an embarrassing situation from which a feeling of unfairness may arise.[67]

## Inquisitorial approach

1.58    In many jurisdictions, the tribunal will take an inquisitorial approach.[68] There is no express legal requirement that they do so, but it is an aspect of accessibility (TCEA ss2(3)(a) and 24(2)(b)). And the overriding objective requires that, as far as practicable, the parties must be able to participate fully in the proceedings: see for example UTR r2(2)(c).

1.59    This approach requires a tribunal to be actively involved in identifying the issues and obtaining relevant evidence at the hearing.[69] This may be done by identifying the issues that arise, by explaining what is relevant to the parties, by questioning them or by a mixture of these techniques. However it is done, it has two aspects. First, the issues aspect: it ensures that relevant issues are identified. Second, the investigative aspect: it ensures that those issues are properly investigated and considered. Both aspects blend with the enabling approach.

1.60    What is required in a particular case is dictated by a combination of the nature of the parties, of the proceedings and of the issues. It arises in part from the non-contentious role of public parties to the proceedings, who are concerned only with the correct application of the law,[70] from the need to protect the public interest,[71] and from the enabling approach, which recognises that lay parties may not be and need not be represented. Such factors can apply even if the tribunal is deciding a dispute between the parties or to vindicate a right claimed by a party.[72] Individually and collectively, they make it inappropriate to follow an adversarial approach.

1.61    This in turn makes it inappropriate for there to be cross-examination as practised in courts. The courts see this as essential to the fact-finding process. As Viscount Sankey LC explained in *Mechanical and General Inventions Co Ltd and Lehwess v Austin and the Austin Motor Co Ltd*:[73]

> Cross-examination is a powerful and valuable weapon for the purpose of testing the veracity of a witness and the accuracy and completeness of his story.[74]

1.62    By taking an inquisitorial approach, a tribunal compensates for this lack of a rigorous challenge by each party of the other's case, thereby ensuring a fair hearing for all the parties to the proceedings. As Pill LJ explained in

---

67  [1988] ICR 550 at 558.

68  This is not universal,as circumstances differ between jurisdictions: *Secretary of State for the Home Department v MN and KY* [2014] UKSC 30 at [25].

69  It is not unique to tribunals. *Re J (Paternity: Welfare of Child)* [2007] 1 FLR 1064 at [11] is an example of a court in a case involving a child contemplating raising an issue of its own motion.

70  *R (Starling) v Child Support Commissioners* [2008] EWHC 1319 (Admin) at [31]–[33].

71  As explained by Diplock LJ in *R v Deputy Industrial Injuries Commissioner ex p Moore* [1965] 1 QB 456 at 486.

72  *Browning v Information Commissioner and DBIS* [2013] UKUT 236 (AAC) at [60] and [65].

73  [1935] AC 346.

74  [1935] AC 346 at 359, quoting the Master of the Rolls in the Court of Appeal.

*Dyason v Secretary of State for the Environment*[75] in the context of a planning appeal:

> If cross-examination disappears, the need to examine propositions in that way does not disappear with it. . . . The absence of an accusatorial procedure places an inquisitorial burden upon an Inspector.[76]

1.63   The need for an inquisitorial approach may also arise from the nature of the proceedings. If a court is under a duty to make a decision on the basis of all the facts and circumstances of the case, the judge has a duty to obtain the necessary evidence regardless of the wishes of the parties. *Miller v Miller*[77] concerned relief proceedings ancillary to a divorce. In the Court of Appeal, Thorpe LJ referred[78] to the 'trial judge's obligation to investigate whatever he conceives relevant and necessary to enable him to discharge his statutory duty' in those proceedings and explained that as a consequence 'Ancillary relief proceedings are quasi-inquisitorial and the judge is never confined by what the parties elect to put in evidence or by whatever they may agree to exclude from evidence.' An inquisitorial approach is likewise required if the tribunal is under a duty to consider whether to make a particular order.[79]

1.64   The nature of the issues will determine the extent to which the public interest may require a tribunal to investigate a case. In *R (Starling) v Child Support Commissioners*,[80] the court was concerned with an appeal in a child support case. Collins J identified a public interest in: (i) the possibility that the person with care would have to depend on social security benefits if the correct amount of maintenance was not identified; and (ii) the welfare of the children.[81]

1.65   To the extent that the approach is based on the abilities of the parties and their representatives to present a case, it is flexible. Its operation depends on the extent to which the parties are informed participants in the proceedings, whether they are represented and, if so, the quality of that representation. Either or both of the aspects of the inquisitorial approach (the issues aspect and the investigative aspect) may be required, depending on the circumstances. And the extent to which they have to be applied may differ.

1.66   In *R(I) 6/69*, the Commissioner related the inquisitorial approach to the need to make the right to be heard effective:

> How much assistance and encouragement is required will necessarily vary from case to case and from claimant to claimant . . . But the broad general principle is that the claimant has a right to be heard and that a Tribunal has a corresponding duty not only to ensure that he is aware of this right but also to assist him, by such means as may be appropriate in any particular

75   (1998) 75 P&CR 506.
76   (1998) 75 P&CR 506 at 512.
77   [2006] 1 FLR 151.
78   [2006] 1 FLR 151 at [24].
79   See also *Tameside & Glossop Acute Services NHS Trust v Thompstone* [2008] 2 All ER 553 at [52].
80   [2008] EWHC 1319 (Admin).
81   [2008] EWHC 1319 (Admin) at [32].

case, to exercise it. The fact that a tribunal is master of its own procedure makes it the more urgent that this principle should be observed.[82]

Accordingly, for an inarticulate, unrepresented and uninformed claimant, both aspects may apply.

1.67    If the claimant is represented by solicitors and counsel before both the First-tier Tribunal and the Upper Tribunal, neither aspect may apply. As Mummery LJ said in *Jeleniewicz v Secretary of State for Work and Pensions*:[83]

> In this case the Claimant was represented by solicitors and counsel both before the Appeal Tribunal and the Commissioner. It was proper and reasonable for the Commissioner to proceed on the basis that the claimant's legal representatives had supplied him with all the information relevant to questions that he had to decide and that the submissions made to him by counsel were based on the available information and were directed to the relevant provisions of the Directive and the 2000 Regulations.

1.68    And in *Chandra v Care Standards Tribunal*,[84] the deputy judge held that, as both parties were represented before the tribunal by counsel, it was their responsibility, and not that of the tribunal, to call the authors of a report that was in evidence.[85]

1.69    If a party's representative is not professional, experienced or even competent, the investigative aspect but not the issues aspect may apply. In *Kumchyk v Derby City Council*,[86] the Employment Appeal Tribunal dealt with this issue in the course of discussing the circumstances in which a point could be taken for the first time before the Appeal Tribunal:

> It is well established in these tribunals [industrial tribunals, now employment tribunals], and we hope in this appeal tribunal, that where the representation is a non-professional representation, or possibly even where it is an inexperienced professional representation (if such a thing can be conceived), in listening to an argument put forward by an advocate or evaluating a point of law put forward by an advocate, the tribunal will be as helpful as possible, perhaps by itself refining and improving the argument, perhaps by suggesting to the advocate that the argument might be put in a different or more favourable fashion, something of that sort. But we think it is very far from the duty or indeed the practice of the chairman of industrial tribunals that they should be expected to introduce into the case issues that do not figure in the presentation on the one side or the other side, at any rate in normal circumstances . . .[87]

1.70    However, the inquisitorial approach is not completely excluded for parties who have access to expert legal advice. In *Krasniqi v Secretary of State for the Home Department*,[88] the appellant to the Asylum and Immigration Tribunal was the Secretary of State. The Court of Appeal decided that the Tribunal, whose jurisdiction depended on there being a point of law, was entitled 'to extract a point of law from nebulously expressed grounds of

82  *R(I) 6/69* at [7].
83  [2008] EWCA Civ 1163 at [31]; reported as *R(IS) 3/09*.
84  [2008] EWHC 2833 (Admin).
85  [2008] EWHC 2833 (Admin) at [17].
86  [1978] ICR 1116.
87  [1978] ICR 1116 at 1123.
88  [2006] EWCA Civ 391; (2006) *Times* 20 April.

appeal, or in exceptional cases to identify for itself an obvious issue of law which the appellant had missed'.[89] Sedley LJ described this as 'a potentially benign power' and remarked that the Secretary of State ought to be less in need of this kind of assistance than a good many applicants who lacked expert legal advice.[90]

1.71    Even in a case in which the inquisitorial approach applies to its fullest extent, there are limits to it. There may be statutory limits on the extent to which the tribunal may or must take the initiative.[91] And this approach does not relieve the parties of their responsibilities of obtaining and presenting evidence; nor can it be used to relieve them of the cost involved in doing so.[92]

## Tribunal membership

1.72    The Senior President is under a duty to have regard to the needs for members of a tribunal to be expert in the subject matter or law of the cases they decide (s2(3)(c)). And the overriding objective requires that any special expertise of the tribunal must be used effectively: see for example UTR r2(2)(d).

1.73    Not being a court allows those with appropriate non-legal skills to participate directly in the decision-making as members of the tribunal rather than as assessors or witnesses.[93] This helps to make tribunals more accessible to the parties by reducing the need to rely on legal representation and making it easier to allow representation by other specialists.

1.74    A tribunal with a narrow jurisdiction is by definition specialist. Tribunals with wider jurisdiction achieve the same effect through assigning panel members to particular jurisdictions and ticketing them for particular areas of work. This specialisation of the members enhances the quality of their decisions and the potential speed of clearance.

1.75    Members may be appointed to a tribunal for their expertise or they may acquire or enhance it as a result of their membership. A tribunal that appoints members with particular knowledge, experience or expert may be an expert tribunal or a specialist tribunal.[94] An expert tribunal is one that is entitled to rely on its own expertise to reach conclusions independently of and, in appropriate cases, in contradiction of the evidence. In *R v Medical Appeal Tribunal (North Midland Region) ex p Hubble*,[95] Diplock J described the function of a medical appeal tribunal as being 'to use their own expertise to reach their own expert conclusions upon the matters of medical fact and opinion involved'.[96] A specialist tribunal is one that is not

---

89   [2006] EWCA Civ 391 at [19].
90   [2006] EWCA Civ 391 at [19].
91   See chapter 4.
92   Although there may be a statutory power to do so. See Social Security Act 1998 s20.
93   Lord Hope and Baroness Hale in *Gillies v Secretary of State for Work and Pensions* [2006] 1 WLR 781 at [22] and [36].
94   'Expert tribunal' is an established expression; 'specialist tribunal' is not.
95   [1958] 2 QB 228.
96   [1958] 2 QB 228 at 241.

so entitled, but is entitled to use its knowledge and experience in questioning the witnesses and assessing the evidence.[97]

1.76    Specialisation is not without its dangers. A tribunal can become isolated from the mainstream of jurisprudence, applying principles in a way that is out of step with other comparable areas of law. For example: the Commissioners were much more likely to find that a tribunal's facts and reasons were inadequate than the Employment Appeal Tribunal, while the latter was far more likely than the Commissioners to find that a tribunal was biased. One potential advantage of the Upper Tribunal is that these differences can be eliminated.

## Rights of audience

1.77    It is consistent with ease of access to tribunals that they do not have limited rights of audience. In other words, a party may be represented by anyone regardless of qualifications. This allows representation by professionals from disciplines other than law, such as accountants or social workers. It allows representation by specialists in the relevant area of law who do not hold legal practitioner qualifications. And it allows representation by anyone else selected by the party as suitable to present, or help to present, a case to a tribunal.

1.78    There is no control over those who may represent except in immigration, which is subject to control because of the perceived abuse by representatives.

## Non-contentious public parties

1.79    If the tribunal has jurisdiction over statutory decisions by public bodies, the public body itself is unlikely to be a contentious party to the proceedings. Its only concerns are to ensure that the facts are correctly found and that the law is properly interpreted and applied.

1.80    In *R v Lancashire County Council ex p Huddleston*,[98] the Court of Appeal was concerned with a local authority's decision on a student grant. Sir John Donaldson MR put the status of the local authority in the proceedings in the context of public law which had:

> ... created a new relationship between the courts and those who derive their authority from the public law, one of partnership based on a common aim, namely the maintenance of the highest standards of public administration.[99]

The result was this:

> The analogy is not exact, but just as the judges of the inferior courts when challenged on the exercise of their jurisdiction traditionally explain fully what they have done and why they have done it, but are not partisan in their own defence, so should be the public authorities.[100]

---

97  *R(M) 1/93* at [9].
98  [1986] 2 All ER 941.
99  [1986] 2 All ER 941 at 945.
100  [1986] 2 All ER 941 at 945.

1.81   In *R v Deputy Industrial Injuries Commissioner ex p Moore*,[101] Diplock LJ said of the position of the decision-maker dealing with entitlement to a social security benefit:

> . . . a claim by an insured person to benefit is not strictly analogous to a *lis inter partes*. Insurance tribunals form part of the statutory machinery for investing claims, that is, for ascertaining whether the claimant has satisfied the statutory requirements which entitle him to be paid benefit out of the fund. In such an investigation, neither the insurance officer nor the Minister (both of whom are entitled to be represented before the insurance tribunal) is a party adverse to the claimant.[102]

1.82   In *Commissioners of Inland Revenue v Sneath*,[103] Lord Hanworth MR said of the position of a surveyor on an appeal against an income tax assessment:

> There is no interest in the surveyor, except to bring before the Court all facts relevant to the assessment. The decision does not enure in his favour unless he is to be treated as representing the taxpayers at large, exclusive of the one upon whom the assessment in question is made.[104]

1.83   Similarly a rating valuation officer was described by Lord Radcliffe in *Society of Medical Officers of Health v Hope*[105] as:

> . . . a neutral official charged with the statutory and recurring duty of bringing into existence a valuation list and maintaining its contents in correct and legal form.[106]

1.84   And in *R (JF) v London Borough of Croydon and the Special Educational Needs Tribunal*,[107] Sullivan J said of the tribunal:

> Although the proceedings are in part adversarial because the Authority will be responding to the parents' appeal, the role of an education authority as a public body at such a hearing is to assist the Tribunal by making all relevant information available. Its role is not to provide only so much information as will assist its own case. At the hearing, the Local Education Authority should be placing all of its cards on the table, including those which might assist the parents' case.[108]

## Co-operative decision-making

1.85   The rules of procedure require the parties to co-operate. UTR r2(4) is illustrative:[109]

> (4) Parties must–
>     (a) help the Upper Tribunal to further the overriding objective; and
>     (b) co-operate with the Upper Tribunal generally.

101 [1965] 1 QB 456.
102 [1965] 1 QB 456 at 486. The courts took the same approach to the position of the insurance officer at the stage of the claim: see *R v Medical Appeal Tribunal (North Midland Region) ex p Hubble* [1958] 2 QB 228 at 240.
103 [1932] 2 KB 362.
104 [1932] 2 KB 362 at 382.
105 [1960] AC 551.
106 [1960] AC 551 at 565. See also Lord Edmund–Davies in *Attorney-General v BBC* [1981] AC 303 at 350–351.
107 [2006] EWHC 2368 (Admin).
108 [2006] EWHC 2368 (Admin) at [11].
109 See also: GRC Rules r2(4); HESC Rules r2(4); IAC Rules r2(4); Lands Rules r2(4); PC Rules r3(4); SEC Rules r2(4); Tax Rules r2(4); WPAFC Rules r2(4).

1.86   These rules give legislative form to a principle of co-operation that was developed by the courts and tribunals. The authorities remain relevant to the interpretation and application of this duty in the rules of procedure.

### Between the parties

1.87   Co-operation is a characteristic of decision-making by some public bodies. However, its significance is not confined to those bodies. It also affects appellate decision-making in tribunals in two ways. First, it affects the allocation between the parties of responsibility for producing evidence. Second, it affects the way that the tribunal approaches the burden of proof on the evidence produced.

1.88   In *Kerr v Department for Social Development*,[110] Baroness Hale emphasised the responsibility on both parties to co-operate in providing the information necessary for a decision. She set out the adjudication procedures on a claim for a social security benefit and noted that it was common ground that the decision-maker had power to make inquiries.[111] She continued:

> What emerges from all this is a co-operative process of investigation in which both the claimant and the department play their part. The department is the one which knows what questions it needs to ask and what information it needs to have in order to determine whether the conditions of entitlement have been met. The claimant is the one who generally speaking can and must supply that information. But where the information is available to the department rather than the claimant, then the department must take the necessary steps to enable it to be traced.[112]

1.89   This approach has, as yet, been little developed. In *Kerr*, the information required for the claimant's case either could not be obtained by the claimant or was not so readily available. It is not clear how far Baroness Hale's reasoning extends beyond this. Nor is it clear to what extent her reasoning depends on the statutory provisions. The statutory provisions considered in that case have now been supplemented by more detailed provisions that put a greater responsibility on claimants for benefit. In *Secretary of State for the Home Department v MN and KY*,[113] an asylum case, Lord Carnwath identified an obligation on the Secretary of State to produce evidence to show that expert evidence was reliable. His reasoning is consistent with *Kerr*, although he did not cite that decision on this issue.

1.90   The principle in *Kerr* is not limited to imposing a duty on public bodies. Nor is it limited to the initial stage of establishing entitlement. In *Jeleniewicz v Secretary of State for Work and Pensions*,[114] the Court of Appeal held:

> First, as to the process adopted by the Commissioner on the hearing of the appeal, there was no error of law. As Baroness Hale observed in *Kerr* at paragraph 62 the claimant is the person who, generally speaking, can and

---

110   [2004] 1 WLR 1372.
111   *R v Secretary of State for Social Services ex p Child Poverty Action Group* [1990] 2 QB 540.
112   [1990] 2 QB 540 at [62].
113   [2014] UKSC 30 at [32].
114   [2008] EWCA Civ 1163 at [30]; reported as *R(IS) 3/09*.

must supply the information needed to determine whether the conditions of entitlement have been met. A similar point was made by Lord Hope in his speech (paragraph 16) when he said that facts which may be reasonably within the claimant's knowledge are for the claimant to supply at each stage of the inquiry. In my judgment, this is as true in determining whether the conditions of entitlement have ceased to be satisfied as it is when determining whether the conditions have been satisfied.

### Between the parties and the tribunal

1.91   A duty of co-operation derives from the public status of a party and the nature of the proceedings. In *R v Lancashire County Council ex p Huddleston*,[115] the Court of Appeal was concerned with judicial review of a local authority's decision on a student grant. Sir John Donaldson MR described those proceedings as being:

> ... a process which falls to be conducted with all the cards face upwards on the table and the vast majority of the cards will start in the authority's hands.[116]

Although this case concerned judicial review, the reasoning applies equally to an appeal. The Privy Council considered the *Huddleston* case in *Marshall v Deputy Governor of Bermuda*.[117] It analysed the so-called duty of candour, but noted its limits. Lord Phillips explained:

> Each of the cases in which Lord Donaldson made these statements involved a decision taken by a public authority that related to and adversely affected an individual. Care must be taken when applying Lord Donaldson's statements to judicial review proceedings in relation to acts of public authorities that do not involve any exercise of discretion. Furthermore those statements apply to the situation where it is not possible for the court to assess the merits of an issue that has been raised unless the public authority against whom the claim is brought furnishes the court with information which it alone is in a position to provide. They should not be relied upon to transfer to the respondent the onus of proving matters which a claimant is under a duty and in a position to prove.[118]

1.92   Co-operation may also derive from the nature of the rule or principle that the tribunal has to apply. If a tribunal is required to take account of all the circumstances of a case relevant to an issue, the parties are under a duty to provide the tribunal with the information that is required. In *Jenkins v Livesey*,[119] the House of Lords was concerned with the ancillary relief provisions of the Matrimonial Causes Act 1973. The relevant provisions required the court to have regard to all the circumstances of the case in making financial orders consequent upon a divorce. Lord Brandon explained that:

> ... in proceedings in which parties invoke the exercise of the court's powers under sections 23 and 24, they must provide the court with the information about all the circumstances of the case, including, inter alia, the particular matters so specified. Unless they do so, directly or indirectly, and ensure

---

115  [1986] 2 All ER 941.
116  [1986] 2 All ER 941 at 945.
117  [2010] UKPC 9.
118  [2010] UKPC 9 at [29].
119  [1985] AC 424.

that the information provided is correct, complete and up-to-date, the court is not equipped to exercise, and therefore lawfully and properly exercise, its discretion in the manner ordained by section 25(1).[120]

1.93 The case management approach to proceedings may also require the parties to co-operate procedurally.[121]

## Pressures for change

1.94 The nature of tribunals and their procedure is not constant. It has changed over time. From the 1980s, tribunals became more independent and their members were better trained. From the 1990s, the increase in the number of salaried judges allowed for more, and more effective, case management. From around 2000, there was, anecdotally, a more legalistic approach in some tribunals. This increasingly professional approach collided with greater professionalism among non-lawyer representatives. They proliferated and sought a greater role in the hearing, although they have not always accepted the correlative responsibility.

1.95 The increased case management and legalism among the judiciary and the demand for greater involvement by representatives have yet to be reconciled, in theory and practice, with the traditional enabling and inquisitorial approaches of some tribunals. Under TCEA, these pressures for change will have to be released under the constraints imposed by the duties of expert decision-making and accessibility that are imposed on the Senior President and, thereby, ultimately on tribunals.

## Judicial nature of a tribunal

### Judicial

1.96 This word is ambiguous, as pointed out by Lopes LJ in *Royal Aquarium and Summer and Winter Garden Society Ltd v Parkinson*:[122]

> The word 'judicial' has two meanings. It may refer to the discharge of duties exercisable by a judge or by justices in court, or to administrative duties which need not be performed in court, but in respect of which it is necessary to bring to bear a judicial mind – that is, a mind to determine what is fair and just in respect of the matters under consideration.[123]

This section is concerned with 'judicial' in the former sense.

1.97 Judicial independence is a constitutional principle that derives from the wider principles of the rule of law and the separation of powers. As an instance of the rule of law, it means that the judiciary make their decisions independent from any influence or control. As an instance of the separation of powers, it focuses on freedom from influence or control by the State. Such influence or control might be systemic and directed at the legal system generally or individual and directed at a particular judge.

120 [1985] AC 424 at 436–437.
121 See chapter 7 below.
122 [1892] 1 QB 431.
123 [1892] 1 QB 431 at 452.

1.98        The importance of judicial independence in a modern democracy has
been given international recognition.[124] At a national level, section 3 of the
Constitutional Reform Act 2005 contains a statutory guarantee of continued independence for the judiciary. Section 3(5) and (6) contains specific
duties in furtherance of that independence:

> 3(5) The Lord Chancellor and other Ministers of the Crown must not seek to
>      influence particular judicial decisions through any special access to the
>      judiciary.
>   (6) The Lord Chancellor must have regard to–
>       (a) the need to defend that independence;
>       (b) the need for the judiciary to have the support necessary to enable
>           them to exercise their functions;
>       (c) the need for the public interest in regard to matters relating to the
>           judiciary or otherwise to the administration of justice to be properly
>           represented in decisions affecting those matters.

The duties in subsection (6) are reflected in the Lord Chancellor's oath
under section 6A of the Promissory Oaths Act 1868, inserted by section 17
of the 2005 Act.

1.99        There is a limited, but not exhaustive, definition of 'judiciary' in the
2005 Act. TCEA s1 extends that statutory definition, and paragraph 66 of
Schedule 8 amends the 2005 Act to include members appointed to the
Upper Tribunal and First-tier Tribunal. The amendment does not include
transferred-in judges. This omission may not matter, as all tribunal judiciary may come within the general meaning of judiciary.

1.100       Of more significance to the parties before a tribunal is article 6, which
provides that the tribunal must be independent. This may be enforced
under the Human Rights Act 1998 by a party to proceedings who alleges
a violation of the Convention right. If the State is a party to the proceedings, the other party is also protected by the requirement, also embodied
in article 6, that the tribunal must be impartial between the parties.

1.101       The appointments system could allow the State to influence judges
through selection and promotion. This was largely removed from political
control by the creation of the Judicial Appointments Commission under
the 2005 Act. This protection does not operate within the tribunal system
under TCEA. The initial appointment to a tribunal is made by the Commission, but allocation to particular chambers or to jurisdictions or areas
of work within chambers is not handled by the Commission. Instead, it is
dealt with by assignment, ticketing and judicial assistance.

1.102       Pressure can be put on the judiciary through their salaries. It has been
recommended that there should be specific legal provision to ensure that
judicial salaries increase at least by the cost of living[125] and that judicial
salaries and benefits should be set by an independent body and their value

---

124 By the United Nations in the *Basic Principles on the Independence of the Judiciary*; by
    the Council of Europe in article 6(1) of the *European Convention on Human Rights
    and Fundamental Freedoms*; by the Commonwealth Parliamentary Association in
    the *Commonwealth (Latimer House) Principles on the Three Branches of Government*
    (agreed in 1998 and approved in 2003).
125 The Consultative Council of European Judges in Opinion No 1 (2001) on standards
    concerning the independence of the judiciary and irremovability of judges, at
    para 62.

maintained.[126] Parliament has not gone so far. It has provided a statutory guarantee not to reduce salaries of court judiciary by amendment under Schedule 3 to the 2005 Act. This provides no protection against pay freezes or erosion by inflation. It has not been extended to tribunal judiciary, although clause 20 of the draft Constitutional Renewal Bill contained a provision that would have remedied this. The Senior Salaries Review Body makes annual recommendations on judicial salaries, but the Government need not accept them.

1.103    The relationship between a tribunal and its sponsoring Department can create the appearance that the tribunal is not independent. And if the sponsoring Department has the power to make rules of procedure for the tribunal, it may create rules that favour the Department. TCEA deals with both. Section 35 allows the Lord Chancellor to assume, solely or jointly, responsibility for a tribunal. It also prevents any exercise of this power being revoked. Section 36 gives the Lord Chancellor control over the power to make rules of procedure. This may be transferred to the Lord Chancellor or to the Tribunal Procedure Committee. This section only applies to scheduled tribunals, which do not include employment tribunals.

1.104    TCEA creates one potential interference with individual judicial independence. Section 23(1) gives the Senior President power to issue practice directions and section 23(6) envisages that they may include guidance on the application or interpretation of the law. This will have to be reconciled with the independence of the tribunal judiciary and the tribunal's duty to interpret and apply the law.

## Is a tribunal judicial?

1.105    This question can only be answered in a particular context, because the question only arises in a particular context. The enquiry is related to the questions of what a tribunal is and what distinguishes it from a court.

1.106    The question has arisen in a number of contexts. The following analysis is based on those contexts. It sets out the general tests that have been applied by the courts and the different factors that the courts have considered in applying those tests. The significance of each of those factors can only be determined in the context of the other factors in the case and of the general test that the court applied. The factors and their interrelation can be analysed, but ultimately, the decision in each case is, as Lord Edmund-Davies said in *Attorney-General v BBC*,[127] 'largely a matter of impression'.[128]

---

126 The Commonwealth Parliamentary Association in the *Commonwealth (Latimer House) Principles on the Three Branches of Government*, p18.
127 [1981] AC 303.
128 [1981] AC 303 at 351.

## Do statements made by a tribunal attract absolute privilege in defamation?

1.107   This issue arose in *Copartnership Farms v Harvey-Smith*.[129] The court had to decide whether comments made by a member of a Military Local Tribunal were protected by absolute privilege for the purposes of an action in defamation. The function of the tribunal was to consider exemptions from military service. Sankey J held that the statements were protected. He described the issue as 'whether the tribunal on the occasion is a tribunal which acts in a manner similar to that in which Courts of justice act.'[130] He did not consider it decisive that:[131]

a)  the members were appointed by a non-judicial authority;
b)  the tribunal could not administer an oath, especially as its decisions affected a party's status and penalties attached to false statements made to the tribunal;
c)  the tribunal had power to hear all or part of a case in private;
d)  only those members present throughout the proceedings were en-titled to vote;
e)  the chairman had a casting vote; and
f)  a Government Department could intervene in the proceedings.

The judge concluded that the legislation had provided 'the tribunal with certain powers which possibly Courts of justice have not.'[132]

1.108   The issue was the same in *Addis v Crocker*,[133] which concerned a Disciplinary Committee under the Solicitors Act 1957. The Court of Appeal held that statements made were protected by absolute privilege. It was not decisive that:[134] (a) the hearings were held in private, with only the findings and decision announced publicly; and (b) that there might also be a criminal liability.

1.109   Both courts took account of the fact that the decisions of the tribunals affected the status of one of the parties.

1.110   In *Collins v Henry Whiteway and Co Ltd*[135] Horridge J refused to extend this privilege to the Court of Referees under the Unemployment Insurance Act 1920. This body decided issues on referral by an insurance officer. If the officer did not agree with the Court's recommendation, the issue could be referred to an umpire. The judge said:

> It is not a body deciding between the parties, nor does its decision affect criminally or otherwise the status of an individual . . .

> The Court of Referees is merely discharging administrative duties which need not be performed in Court, but in respect of which it is necessary to bring to bear a judicial mind.[136]

129  [1918] 2 KB 405.
130  [1918] 2 KB 405 at 408.
131  [1918] 2 KB 405 at 409–414.
132  [1918] 2 KB 405 at 414.
133  [1961] 1 QB 11.
134  [1961] 1 QB 11 at 23–28.
135  [1927] 2 KB 378.
136  [1927] 2 KB 378 at 383.

## Does the tribunal exercise the judicial power of the state?

1.111   This issue is particularly relevant in those jurisdictions that apply a strict separation of powers between the legislature, the executive and the judiciary.

1.112   In *Shell Company of Australia v Federal Commissioner of Taxation*,[137] the Privy Council had to decide whether an Australian Board of Review for income tax purposes was exercising the judicial power of the State. This issue determined whether its members had to be appointed for life. The Council decided that the Board was not exercising judicial power. It adopted a definition of 'judicial power' given by Griffith CJ:

> ... the words 'judicial power' as used in s71 of the Constitution mean the power which every sovereign authority must of necessity have to decide controversies between its subjects, or between itself and its subjects, whether the rights relate to life, liberty or property. The exercise of this power does not begin until some tribunal which has power to give a binding and authoritative decision (whether subject to appeal or not) is called upon to take action.[138]

The Council then listed five factors which were not sufficient to show that a tribunal was a court:[139] (a) the tribunal gives a final decision; (b) it hears witnesses on oath; (c) two or more contending parties appear before it; (d) it gives decisions that affect the rights of subjects; and (e) matters are referred to it by another body.

1.113   The minority of the Privy Council in *United Engineering Workers' Union v Devanayagam*[140] analysed the position of a president of a Ceylonese Labour Tribunal in terms of judicial power. The issue was whether a president of a Labour Tribunal was a judicial officer. This depended on whether the president's chief function was to exercise the judicial power of the State.[141] The status of the president determined whether appointments were made by the Judicial Service Commission or the Public Service Commission. The minority decided that the president was a judicial officer. They emphasised these features:[142]

> (a) the Tribunal could only act when there was a controversy;
> (b) it gave a binding and authoritative decision;
> (c) its powers came from the State, not the parties;
> (d) it acted in conformity with principle;
> (e) which was reinforced by a right of appeal on questions of law;
> (f) the Tribunal would establish a set of principles that would develop from its discretionary power to make orders that were just and equitable; and
> (g) it dealt with existing rights, rather than conferring new rights for the future.

In contrast the majority commented that:

> The holder of a judicial office exercises judicial power, but the fact that some judicial power is exercised does not establish that the office is judicial.[143]

---

137  [1931] AC 275.
138  [1931] AC 275 at 295–296.
139  [1931] AC 275 at 297.
140  [1968] AC 356.
141  [1968] AC 356 at 380.
142  [1968] AC 356 at 382–388.
143  [1968] AC 356 at 368.

## Does the member hold judicial office?

1.114   In *United Engineering Workers' Union v Devanayagam*,[144] the majority decided that the president of a Labour Tribunal was not a judicial officer. They defined the test as being whether the issues that the Tribunal had to decide made it desirable for the presidents to have the same qualifications as those in other courts. The majority based its decision on a combination of factors. Two that seem to have been particularly significant were that: (a) the tribunal was not limited to determining legal rights; and (b) it was empowered to make any decision that was just and equitable. The fact that there was a right of appeal to a court on questions of law was not decisive.[145]

1.115        In a pair of cases, the Privy Council considered the same issue in respect of a Ceylonese commissioner and the members of the Board of Review for the purposes of imposing a penalty for late disclosure of income tax. It decided that they were not judicial officers. In *Ranaweera v Wickramasinghe*,[146] in respect of a commissioner, the Council set out this test:

> . . . where the resolution of disputes by some executive officer can be properly regarded as being part of the execution of some wider administrative function entrusted to him, then he should be regarded as still acting in an administrative capacity, and not as performing some different and judicial function.[147]

In *Ranaweera v Ramachandran*,[148] it decided that the same was true of the Board of Review, although Lord Diplock dissented.

## Does the tribunal have power to enforce its decisions?

1.116   This is not essential in order for a tribunal to be a court.[149]

## Does the law of contempt apply to proceedings?

1.117   *Attorney-General v BBC*[150] illustrates the variety of ways in which the status of a body can be analysed and the impossibility of isolating the court's analysis of the judicial character of a tribunal from the context of the particular issue. The issue for the House of Lords was whether a local valuation court was an inferior tribunal for the purposes of contempt. Viscount Dilhorne decided that the local valuation court was a court, but one that discharged administrative functions.[151] Lord Salmon decided that the local valuation court was not a type of body that needed the protection of the law of contempt.[152] Lord Edmund-Davies made a detailed analysis of

---

144 [1968] AC 356.
145 [1968] AC 356 at 376.
146 [1970] AC 951.
147 [1970] AC 951 at 959.
148 [1970] AC 962.
149 *R (H) v Secretary of State for the Home Department* [2004] 2 AC 253 at [26].
150 [1981] AC 303.
151 [1970] AC 951 at 338 and 339–340.
152 [1970] AC 951 at 344.

the various factors suggested as determinative, finding that some were against the local valuation court being an inferior court: (a) the fact that it was not bound by the rules of evidence; (b) it had no power to summon the attendance of witnesses or to order the production or inspection of documents; and (c) the members could rely on their own knowledge. But, in the end, he admitted that the test was largely one of impression.[153] Lord Fraser decided that the court had administrative functions, while emphasising the importance of convenience, certainty and freedom of expression in defining the scope of contempt.[154] Lord Scarman concentrated on the purpose of the court, which was essentially administrative, and decided that it was not appropriate to extend the protection of contempt to such a body.[155]

1.118    In *Peach Grey & Co v Sommers*,[156] the issue was whether the Divisional Court of Queen's Bench had jurisdiction to punish for contempt in proceedings before an industrial tribunal.[157] This depended on whether the tribunal was an inferior court. The Court decided that it was. Rose LJ set out factors that were not decisive:[158]

a) the tribunal was not a court of record;
b) its awards were enforced in the county court and its costs were taxed there;
c) it was not bound to observe the strict rules of evidence, although it did so in practice;
d) conciliation proceedings were available; and
e) the rights of audience were not limited to lawyers.

He then set out factors suggestive that the tribunal was a court:[159]

f) (it was established by Parliament;
g) it had a legally qualified chairman appointed by the Lord Chancellor and panel members appointed by the Secretary of State for Employment;
h) it sat in public;
i) it decided cases that affected the rights of subjects;
j) it had power to compel witnesses to attend, to administer the oath, strike out pleadings, allow amendments and order discovery;
k) the parties could be legally represented;
l) it had rules of procedure for giving evidence and making submissions;
m) it could award costs;
n) it had a duty to give reasons for decision;
o) an appeal on law lay to the Employment Appeal Tribunal and then to the Court of Appeal.

---

153 [1970] AC 951 at 347–351.
154 [1970] AC 951 at 353.
155 [1970] AC 951 at 359–362.
156 [1995] ICR 549.
157 Now an employment tribunal.
158 [1995] ICR 549 at 557.
159 [1995] ICR 549 at 557.

1.119   In *Pickering v Liverpool Daily Post and Echo Newspapers plc*,[160] the House of
Lords decided that the law of contempt applied to a mental health review
tribunal. Lord Bridge gave two reasons.[161] The first was that the tribunal
was expressly mentioned in section 12(1)(b) of the Administration of Justice Act 1960, which dealt with contempt. The other was that the tribunal
exercised the power of the State. The latter point relied on the reasoning
of Lord Donaldson MR, which noted that since 1983 the tribunal no longer
made recommendations that could be accepted or rejected but decisions
that were binding as to the patient's liberty.[162]

1.120   Peter Gibson LJ in *Bache v Essex County Council*[163] accepted that a representative's conduct could in an extreme case amount to contempt before
an employment tribunal.[164]

## Does the law of perjury apply to proceedings?

1.121   Perjury can be committed by swearing falsely before a tribunal. In *R v
Tomlinson*,[165] the Court of Crown Cases Reserved held that perjury could
be committed by giving false evidence to a local marine board. Cockburn
CJ explained why:

> The inquiry was before a tribunal invested with judicial powers, and
> enabled to inquire on oath, and pass a sentence affecting the status of the
> person accused. It would be highly inconvenient if false swearing upon
> such an inquiry did not amount to perjury. It would be fatal to the person
> accused, if he were not to have protection against witnesses who came to
> swear falsely.[166]

## Is the tribunal administrative rather than judicial?

1.122   A tribunal that applies policy as well as law is administrative[167] rather than
judicial. As is a tribunal that allows members to vote despite not being
present throughout the whole of the proceedings.[168]

## Is the tribunal quasi-judicial?

1.123   According to Lords Guest and Devlin in *United Engineering Workers' Union
v Devanayagam*,[169] a person who is not a judicial officer but who has to
exercise judicial power of the State is acting quasi-judicially.[170]

---

160  [1991] 2 AC 370.
161  [1991] 2 AC 370 at 417.
162  [1991] 2 AC 370 at 380–381.
163  [2000] 2 All ER 847.
164  [2000] 2 All ER 847 at 853.
165  (1866) LR 1 CCR 49.
166  (1866) LR 1 CCR 49 at 53–54.
167  Lord Simonds in *Labour Relations Board of Saskatchewan v John East Ironworks* [1949]
     AC 134 at 149.
168  Sankey J in *Copartnership Farms v Harvey-Smith* [1918] 2 KB 405 at 413.
169  [1968] AC 356.
170  [1968] AC 356 at 380.

## Administrative and judicial decision-making

1.124   The courts have distinguished between judicial and administrative decision-making. In *Karanakaran v Secretary of State for the Home Department*,[171] the Court of Appeal drew this distinction in deciding that a decision-maker dealing with an asylum claim was not constrained by the rules of evidence.

## Superior court of record

1.125   TCEA s3(5) provides that the Upper Tribunal is a superior court of record. And section 25 confers on the Upper Tribunal the same powers, rights, privileges and authority as the High Court in relation to the attendance and examination of witnesses, the production and inspection of documents, and all other matters incidental to the Upper Tribunal's functions. Equivalent provision is made for the Employment Appeal Tribunal by sections 20(3) and 29(2) of the Employment Tribunals Act 1996.

1.126   A superior court of record has three characteristics.[172] First, it is presumed to act within its powers unless the contrary is shown. In practice, this is unlikely to be of significance, as the Upper Tribunal's jurisdiction is entirely statutory. Second, its decisions have effect as precedents for lower tribunals. Third, it has power to punish for contempt.[173]

1.127   The Upper Tribunal has decided that it has power to punish for contempt in Scotland, although there is no Scottish concept equivalent to a superior court of record.[174]

1.128   The Upper Tribunal has disciplinary power over solicitors, but not over non-legal representatives.[175]

## Specialism

1.129   Tribunals are inevitably specialised. The Senior President has the duty under TCEA s2(3)(c) to have regard to the need for members to be expert in the subject matter of, or the law to be applied in, their tribunal. This may be because the members are appointed to the tribunal on account of their knowledge, experience or expertise relevant to the tribunal's jurisdiction. Or it may be because the members acquire, through training and experience, familiarity with the particular legal and factual issues that arise before the tribunal. Or a combination of both. Ultimately, the specialism derives from the tribunal's limited jurisdiction or the assigning and ticketing within its jurisdiction. The specialism will inevitably relate to the relevant law. But it may also involve other relevant areas, such as medical or financial.

---

171  [2000] 3 All ER 449.
172  *R (Cart) v Upper Tribunal* [2010] 1 All ER 908 at [75].
173  See also *CB v Suffolk County Council* [2010] UKUT 413 (AAC) at [22].
174  *MR v CMEC and DM* [2009] UKUT 283 (AAC) at [14]–[15].
175  *B v Home Office* [2012] 4 All ER 276 at [146]–[147].

1.130    Specialisation exposes the judges and members to a greater number and variety of cases than would be possible in the general courts. They are thereby able to develop case-law more quickly than the courts could and to base their decisions on a range of experience (of evidence, circumstances and argument) that would not be available in isolated or individual cases.

1.131    The courts respect this specialism,[176] but have also controlled the use that can be made of it.

## Respect for specialism

1.132   The Court of Appeal and the Supreme Court may have to consider the degree of respect that should be given to a tribunal's specialism at two stages: at the permission stage or on an appeal. The two stages are not separate in practice, as the respect to be shown on an appeal will be relevant to whether permission should be given.

### Deference at the permission stage

1.133   An appeal to the Court of Appeal in second appeals from the county court and High Court is governed by section 55(1) of the Access to Justice Act 1999. An appeal only lies if the appeal would raise an important point of principle or practice or there is some other compelling reason. These criteria did not apply to tribunals, but they were applied as a matter of practice following the judgment of Hale LJ in *Cooke v Secretary of State for Social Security*[177] to appeals from second-tier appellate tribunals.[178] TCEA s13(6) and (6A) provides for the same additional criteria to be applied to the Upper Tribunal. This is narrower than the test which applies to other appeals, which is whether there is a real prospect of success or some other compelling reason. The effect is to treat the tribunals who are covered by those provisions[179] equally with the courts rather than afford particular respect to tribunals on account of their specialism.

### Deference on an appeal

1.134   The courts and higher tribunals may be required to respect the decisions of a tribunal simply because the legal structure requires it. As Lord Radcliffe explained in *Edwards v Bairstow*,[180] referring to the General Commissioners:

> As I see it, the reason why the courts do not interfere with commissioners' findings or determinations when they really do involve nothing but questions of fact is not any supposed advantage in the commissioners of greater experience in matters of business or any other matters. The reason is simply that by the system that has been set up the commissioners are the first

176  See for example the comments of Lords Hope and Walker (both dissenting) in *Autologic Holdings plc v Inland Revenue Commissioners* [2005] 1 WLR 52 at [60] and [78] respectively.

177  [2002] 3 All ER 279 at [14]–[18].

178  The Social Security and Child Support Commissioners, the Employment Appeal Tribunal, the Immigration Appeal Tribunal and the Lands Tribunal.

179  For the cases in which these additional criteria do not apply, see chapter 4.

180  [1956] AC 14.

tribunal to try an appeal, and in the interests of the efficient administration of justice their decisions can only be upset on appeal if they have been positively wrong in law.[181]

To do otherwise would risk turning an appeal on law into an appeal on fact.[182]

1.135 The courts also make realistic assumptions that a tribunal is familiar with and applies basic legal concepts, like the burden and standard of proof.[183] They are also not easily satisfied that a tribunal failed to take account of a matter that was not expressly mentioned[184] or that a tribunal has failed to apply correctly its self-direction on the law.[185]

1.136 The respect with which this section is concerned is additional to these considerations and is based on the special knowledge, experience or expertise of a tribunal in its particular jurisdiction. It applies both on judicial review and on appeal and both to issues of substantive law and to discretionary decisions on procedural matters.[186] It applies both to an established legislative scheme[187] and, where the tribunal is appropriately constituted, to a newly established scheme.[188] It is, though, doubtful whether this professed respect for specialism is always reflected in the courts' decisions.

1.137 The senior courts have said that they should respect: the way in which a tribunal acting as a specialist fact-finder conducted its business within the area of its expertise;[189] findings of fact made by an expert and specialist tribunal in an area where court judges have no expertise;[190] findings of mixed fact and law made by specialist judges;[191] the Upper Tribunal's assessment of proportionality;[192] the Upper Tribunal's assessment of the adequacy of reasons given by the First-tier Tribunal;[193] consistent lines of authority at Upper Tribunal level.[194]

---

181 [1956] AC 14 at 38.
182 Carnwath LJ in *IBA Healthcare Ltd v Office of Fair Trading* [2004] ICR 1364 at [96], quoting Lord Radcliffe in *Edwards v Bairstow* [1956] AC 14; *BBC v Sugar (No 2)* [2010] 1 WLR 2278 at [27]; *MA (Somalia) v Secretary of State for the Home Department* [2011] 2 All ER 65 at [45].
183 Wilson J in *Re P (Witness Summons)* [1997] 2 FLR 447 at 455 and the Commissioner in *R(SB) 5/81* at [7].
184 *MA (Somalia) v Secretary of State for the Home Department* [2010] UKSC 49 at [45].
185 *MA (Somalia) v Secretary of State for the Home Department* [2010] UKSC 49 at [46].
186 Robert Walker LJ in *Jones v Governing Body of Burdett Coutts School* [1999] ICR 38 at 47.
187 *AH (Sudan) v Secretary of State for the Home Department* [2008] AC 678 at [30].
188 *Secretary of State for Defence v Duncan and McWilliams* [2009] EWCA Civ 1043 at [119]–[120].
189 *Secretary of State for Work and Pensions v Cattrell* [2011] EWCA Civ 572 at [23].
190 *Napp Pharmaceutical Holdings Ltd v Director General of Fair Trading* [2002] 4 All ER 376 at [34].
191 *Secretary of State for Work and Pensions v R (MM and DM)* [2013] EWCA Civ 1565 at [65].
192 *Obrey, Snodgrass and Shadforth v Secretary of State for Work and Pensions* [2013] EWCA Civ 1584 at [13]–[18].
193 *PK (Congo) v Secretary of State for the Home Department* [2013] EWCA Civ 1500 at [22] and [25].
194 *R v National Insurance Commissioners ex p Stratton* [1979] QB 361 at 368, 369 and 374; *Presho v Chief Adjudication Officer* [1984] AC 310 at 319–320.

## The basis for deference

1.138   This approach has been justified on a variety of reasoning. In *R v Preston Supplementary Benefits Appeal Tribunal ex p Moore*,[195] Lord Denning MR reasoned from the lack of a right of appeal:[196]

> The courts should not enter into a meticulous discussion of the meaning of this or that word in the Act. They should leave the tribunals to interpret the Act in a broad and reasonable way, according to the spirit and not to the letter: especially as Parliament has given them a way of alleviating any hardship. The courts should only interfere when the decision of the tribunal is unreasonable in the sense that no tribunal acquainted with the ordinary use of language could reasonably reach that decision: see *Cozens v Brutus* [1973] AC 854, 861. Nevertheless, it has to be realised that the Act has to be applied daily by thousands of officers of the commission: and by 120 appeal tribunals. It is most important that cases raising the same points should be decided in the same way. There should be uniformity of decision. Otherwise grievances are bound to arise. In order to ensure this, the courts should be ready to consider points of law of general application . . .

> In short, the court should be ready to lay down the broad guidelines for tribunals. But no further. The courts should not be used as if there was an appeal to them. Individual cases of particular application must be left to the tribunals.[197]

1.139   In *Bromley LBC v Special Educational Needs Tribunal*,[198] Sedley LJ derived the same approach from the intention behind the legislation:

> Until the welcome setting up of the special educational needs tribunals by the Education Act 1993, challenges to LEAs' statements [of special educational needs] could be made only on questions of law by way of judicial review. . . . Unlike the High Court, it is a specialist tribunal with a lawyer chairman and lay members chosen for their knowledge and experience (see s 334(2) [of the Education Act 1996] and the Special Educational Needs Tribunal Regulations 1995, SI 1995/3113, reg 3). In my view this restructuring has jurisprudential implications. Where previously the parent's only resort from the local education authority was to the court, which had therefore to do its best to construe the statutory language in so far as construction was an appropriate exercise, there is now interposed a specialist tribunal whose remit is not necessarily the same. In particular, where a court has to limit itself to the interpretation of terms of legal art and the setting of outer limits to the meaning of ordinary words in their statutory context, the tribunal is empowered to take a much closer look at the content of the LEA's statement. Indeed for many purposes it stands in the LEA's shoes, re-evaluating the available information in order if necessary to recast the statement. But in carrying out this function it also has a supervisory role – to interpret and apply the relevant law. Where the law is expressed in words which, while not terms of legal art, have a purpose dictated by – and therefore a meaning coloured by – their context, it is clearly Parliament's intention that particular respect should be paid to the tribunal's conclusions. By virtue of s 11 of the Tribunals and Inquiries Act 1992 the High Court retains an appellate jurisdiction which undoubtedly requires it to intervene where an error of

---

195  [1975] 1 WLR 624.

196  The decisions of the tribunal could only be challenged by way of what is now known as judicial review.

197  [1975] 1 WLR 624 at 631–632.

198  [1999] 3 All ER 587.

law or jurisdiction or due process can be shown; but the area of expert judgment bounded by the High Court's jurisdiction is large. This is so both because the nature of the subject matter of appeals to and from SENT makes it appropriate and because the statutory scheme requires it.[199]

1.140 In *R v National Insurance Commissioner ex p Stratton*,[200] Lord Denning MR derived his approach from the expertise of the judges:

> These commissioners are judges ... They give hundreds of decisions on points of law regarding the interpretation of the regulations. They know just how they work.[201]

> I venture to suggest that we should proceed on this principle: if a decision of the commissioners has remained undisturbed for a long time, not amended by regulation, nor challenged by certiorari [judicial review], and has been acted upon by all concerned, it should normally be regarded as binding. The High Court should not interfere with it save in exceptional circumstances, such as where there is a difference of opinion between commissioners: see *R v National Insurance Commissioner ex p Michael* [1977] 1 WLR 109. A recent decision may be less binding. It may be brought before the High Court with the very object of getting a ruling on a difficult point. The Department itself should do it, if need be. Then the High Court can and should do whatever the justice of the case requires.[202]

Bridge LJ was more limited in his statement of the authority of the decisions which the court was considering. His reasoning was based on longevity linked with implied legislative approval. He said:

> In view of the time for which those decisions have stood unchallenged and of the terms of the new regulation as amended in 1971 which appear to give them legislative approbation it would no doubt be wrong to say that the decision should now be overruled, nor were we invited to take this course by either counsel in argument.[203]

1.141 This approach was confirmed by the House of Lords (now replaced by the Supreme Court). In *Presho v Insurance Officer*,[204] Lord Brandon cited the comments of Lord Denning and Bridge LJ with approval and said that it was one of the 'important considerations' in support of his reasoning in that case that it:

> ... accords with that which has been adopted since 1926 by a substantial number of social security commissioners (or their earlier equivalents) after the expression concerned had first appeared in this class of legislation in 1911.[205]

1.142 In *Cooke v Secretary of State for Social Security*,[206] Hale LJ emphasied that the courts would not know the wider statutory context in which a tribunal made its decision:

199 [1999] 3 All ER 587 at 594.
200 [1979] QB 361.
201 [1979] QB 361 at 368.
202 [1979] QB 361 at 369. The references to the High Court are explained by the fact that, at the time, there was no appeal from a Commissioner's decision and the only recourse was to apply to the High Court for what is now known as judicial review.
203 [1979] QB 361 at 374.
204 [1984] AC 310.
205 [1984] AC 310 at 319–320.
206 [2002] 3 All ER 279.

It is also important that such appeal structures have a link to the ordinary court system, to maintain both their independence of government and the sponsoring department and their fidelity to the relevant general principles of law. But the ordinary courts should approach such cases with an appropriate degree of caution. It is quite probable that on a technical issue of understanding and applying the complex legislation the social security commissioner will have got it right. The commissioners will know how that particular issue fits into the broader picture of social security principles as a whole. They will be less likely to introduce distortion into those principles. They may be better placed, where it is appropriate, to apply those principles in a purposive construction of the legislation in question. They will also know the realities of tribunal life. All this should be taken into account by an appellate court when considering whether an appeal will have a real prospect of success.[207]

1.143   In *Obrey, Snodgrass and Shadforth v Secretary of State for Work and Pensions*,[208] the Court of Appeal based its reasoning in part on its power to decide where the line between issues of fact and law should be drawn, relying on the decision of the Supreme Court in *R (Jones) v First-tier Tribunal (Social Entitlement Chamber)*.[209]

### The limits to deference

1.144   This approach is flexible enough to allow a court to intervene when a tribunal has made a material error of law.[210] In *Cockburn v Chief Adjudication Officer* and *Secretary of State for Social Security v Fairey (aka Halliday)*,[211] Lord Slynn said:

> It is obviously sensible that the rulings of the commissioners and the practice of administering the scheme which they have laid down and which have been followed over many years should not lightly be interfered with. But if the Court of Appeal, and even more so if your Lordships' House, is satisfied that wrong distinctions have been drawn as a matter of principle which ought not to be followed they are entitled to say so.[212]

And in *Hinchy v Secretary of State for Work and Pensions*,[213] Baroness Hale said:

> . . . if the specialist judiciary who do understand the system and the people it serves have established consistent principles, the generalist courts should respect those principles unless they can clearly be shown to be wrong in law.

207  [2002] 3 All ER 279 at [16]. See also *AH (Sudan) v Secretary of State for the Home Department* [2008] AC 768 at [30].
208  [2013] EWCA Civ 1584 at [14] and [30].
209  [2013] 2 AC 48.
210  *BBC v Sugar (No 2)* [2010] 1 WLR 2278 at [27].
211  [1997] 1 WLR 799.
212  [1997] 1 WLR 799 at 814.
213  [2005] 1 WLR 967 at [49]. See also Lord Hoffmann at [30].

1.145 There is no basis for respect if: there are divergent views, whether at the same level[214] or between tiers;[215] the senior courts are as able as the Upper Tribunal to identify an error of law;[216] the issue is one of general law or general principle;[217] the issue is a hard-edged point of statutory interpretation that has caused difficulty to the Upper Tribunal.[218]

### The role of the Upper Tribunal

1.146 The deference due to a specialist tribunal does not affect the role of the Upper Tribunal in providing specialist guidance on issues of law arising in the First-tier Tribunal.[219]

## Use of specialist knowledge or expertise

1.147 If a tribunal makes use of the specialist knowledge or expertise of a panel member in a way that is decisive, it may have to make that known to the parties. In *Butterfield and Creasy v Secretary of State for Defence,*[220] Park J said:

> There is a potential problem if a medical member of a tribunal is the only person present with specialist medical knowledge, and he perceives a possible medical objection to the appellant's case, particularly an objection which has not been taken in advance by the Secretary of State and of which the appellant has not had prior notice. If the medical member believes that there is such an objection, plainly he must say so. He is a member of the Tribunal because of his medical expertise, and if he thinks that his medical expertise is relevant in some specific way which has not otherwise been pointed out, he must draw on it in the course of the hearing and the tribunal's deliberations. I do not for a moment suggest that the medical member of the tribunal should in some way suppress his personal expertise and reactions to medical issues which arise. However, if the point which concerns him is a new one and might in itself be decisive, it does seem to me that fairness requires that it be explained to the appellant or to the appel-lant's representative, and that the appellant should be given a realistic opportunity to consider it. In some cases, though I hope not many, this may require the offer of an adjournment, however inconvenient and irksome that may be.

214 Lord Denning MR and Roskill LJ in *R v National Insurance Commissioner ex p Michael* [1977] 1 WLR 109 at 112 and 115; *Chandler v Secretary of State for Work and Pensions* [2008] 1 FLR 638 at [22].

215 *AP (Trinidad and Tobago) v Secretary of State for the Home Department* [2011] EWCA Civ 551 at [25] and [50]. In *OH (Serbia) v Secretary of State for the Home Department* [2008] EWCA Civ 694 at [19], Wilson LJ said that deference only applies at the interface between a non-specialist court and a specialist tribunal. That case concerned the internal reconsideration within the single Asylum and Immigration Tribunal, but the reasoning is equally applicable between tiers of the present tribunal system and is consistent with the approach in AP.

216 *AP (Trinidad and Tobago) v Secretary of State for the Home Department* [2011] EWCA Civ 551 at [25] and [50].

217 Lord Denning MR in *R v National Insurance Commissioner ex p Michael* [1977] 1 WLR 109 at 112.

218 *R (Mahmoudi) v London Borough of Lewisham* [2014] EWCA Civ 284 at [14].

219 *AP (Trinidad and Tobago) v Secretary of State for the Home Department* [2011] EWCA Civ 551 at [46] and [50].

220 [2002] EWHC 2247 (Admin) at [14].

## Powers of judicial review

1.148 The courts do not allow specialist tribunals that have judicial review powers to operate those powers differently from the courts on account of their
specialism. In *IBA Healthcare Ltd v Office of Fair Trading*,[221] the Court of
Appeal considered the scope of judicial review as applied under statute by
the Competition Appeal Tribunal. The tribunal had decided that the principles were different on the ground that, unlike the Administrative Court,
it was not a non-specialist court considering the decision of a specialist
decision-maker, but a tribunal specialist in the area of decision-making.
The Court of Appeal held that the ordinary principles of judicial review
applied regardless of the specialism of the reviewing tribunal.[222]

## Tribunal system and judiciary

1.149 Under TCEA it is possible, for the first time, to talk of a tribunal system.
Before TCEA, there were numerous individual tribunals for particular
jurisdictions. In some jurisdictions, there was a dedicated appeal structure of tribunals. And the Council on Tribunals had oversight of most
tribunals. But there was no overall system.

1.150 As a result of TCEA, that has changed. There is now a system, albeit
not a comprehensive one. In effect, TCEA provides a constitutional settlement for tribunals and their judiciary. Responsibility is divided between
the Lord Chief Justice and the Senior President of Tribunals.

1.151 The tribunal system created by TCEA consists of three structures.
Section 3 created two new tribunals: a First-tier Tribunal and an Upper
Tribunal. Although they are separate, they may sit together. This allows,
for example, an appeal to the First-tier Tribunal and judicial review proceedings in the Upper Tribunal to be heard by the same panel.[223]Each
tribunal is divided into chambers, each of which must have one or two
Chamber Presidents (s7). The members and functions of some tribunals
were immediately transferred into the Upper Tribunal or the First-tier Tribunal, as appropriate.[224] Other tribunals were brought into the structure
later. The rest remain outside the structure. TCEA also provided for the
transfer of ministerial functions for particular tribunals to the Lord Chancellor and for rule making powers to be transferred to the Lord Chancellor
(s35) or the Tribunal Procedure Committee (s36).

1.152 Alongside the First-tier Tribunal and the Upper Tribunal, the structure
for employment[225] remains as before.

---

221 [2004] ICR 1364.
222 [2004] ICR 1364 at [51]–[53].
223 As in *Reed Employment plc v the Commissioners for Her Majesty's Revenue and Customs*
[2010] UKFFT 596 (TC).
224 Under TCEA s30 and Sch 6.
225 The Employment Tribunals Act 1996. For procedure in employment tribunals and
the Employment Appeal Tribunal, see Jeremy McMullen, Rebecca Tuck and Betsan
Criddle, *Employment Tribunal Procedure – A User's Guide to Tribunals and Appeals*
(3rd edn, LAG, 2004).

1.153    These three structures are united under a Senior President (s2(1)). Section 2(3) is a key provision, setting out the factors to which the Senior President must have regard in performing the office:

> (3) A holder of the office of Senior President of Tribunals must, in carrying out the functions of that office, have regard to–
> (a) the need for tribunals to be accessible,
> (b) the need for proceedings before tribunals–
> (i)  to be fair, and
> (ii) to be handled quickly and efficiently,
> (c) the need for members of tribunals to be experts in the subject-matter of, or the law to be applied in, cases in which they decide matters, and
> (d) the need to develop innovative methods of resolving disputes that are of a type that may be brought before tribunals.

## The First-tier Tribunal

1.154    The First-tier Tribunal is organised into seven Chambers:

- the General Regulatory Chamber
- the Health, Education and Social Care Chamber;
- the Immigration and Asylum Chamber;
- the Property Chamber;
- the Social Entitlement Chamber;
- the Tax Chamber; and
- the War Pensions and Armed Forces Compensation Chamber.

### The General Regulatory Chamber

1.155    The functions of this Chamber are allocated by article 3 of the First-tier Tribunal and Upper Tribunal (Chambers) Order 2010. It has jurisdiction over all functions relating to:

> (a) proceedings in respect of the decisions and actions of regulatory bodies which are not allocated to the Health, Education and Social Care Chamber or to the Tax Chamber;
> (b) matters referred to the First-tier Tribunal under Schedule 1D to the Charities Act 1993; and
> (c) the determination of remuneration for carrying mail-bags in a ship or aircraft.

### The Health, Education and Social Care Chamber

1.156    The functions of this Chamber are allocated by article 4 of the First-tier Tribunal and Upper Tribunal (Chambers) Order 2010. It has jurisdiction over all functions relating to:

> (a) an appeal against a decision related to children with special educational needs;
> (b) a claim of disability discrimination in the education of a child;
> (c) an application or an appeal against a decision or determination related to work with children or vulnerable adults;
> (d) an appeal against a decision related to registration in respect of the provision of health or social care;

(e) an application in respect of, or an appeal against a decision related to, the provision of health care or health services;

(f) an appeal against a decision related to registration in respect of social workers and social care workers;

(g) an appeal against a decision related to the provision of childcare;

(h) an appeal against a decision related to an independent school or other independent educational institution;

(i) applications and references by and in respect of patients under the provisions of the Mental Health Act 1983 or paragraph 5(2) of the Schedule to the Repatriation of Prisoners Act 1984.

## The Immigration and Asylum Chamber

1.157   The functions of this Chamber are allocated by article 5 of the First-tier Tribunal and Upper Tribunal (Chambers) Order 2010. It has jurisdiction over all functions related to immigration and asylum matters, except those allocated to the General Regulatory and Social Entitlement Chambers.

## The Property Chamber

1.158   The functions of this Chamber are allocated by article 5A of the First-tier Tribunal and Upper Tribunal (Chambers) Order 2010. It has jurisdiction over all functions relating to:

(a) a reference by the Chief Land Registrar and any other application, matter or appeal under the Land Registration Act 2002;

(b) proceedings under any of the enactments referred to in section 6A(2) of the Agriculture (Miscellaneous Provisions) Act 1954 or the Hill Farming Act 1946;

(c) housing etc, under the Housing Act 2004;

(d) leasehold property;

(e) residential property;

(f) rents;

(g) the right to buy;

(h) applications and appeals under the Mobile Homes Act 1983.

## The Social Entitlement Chamber

1.159   The functions of this Chamber are allocated by article 6 of the First-tier Tribunal and Upper Tribunal (Chambers) Order 2010. It has jurisdiction over all functions in relation to appeals:[226]

(a) in cases regarding support for asylum seekers, failed asylum seekers, persons designated under section 130 of the Criminal Justice and Immigration Act 2008, or the dependants of any such persons;

(b) in criminal injuries compensation cases;

(c) regarding entitlement to, payments of, or recovery or recoupment of payments of, social security benefits, child support, vaccine damage payments, health in pregnancy grant and tax credits, with the exception of–

(i) appeals under section 11 of the Social Security Contributions (Transfer of Functions, etc.) Act 1999 (appeals against decisions of Her Majesty's Revenue and Customs);

226 By limiting the allocation to appeals, the Order fails to cover references of applications for a departure direction or a variation under the Child Support Act 1991.

(ii) appeals in respect of employer penalties or employer information penalties (as defined in section 63(11) and (12) of the Tax Credits Act 2002);

(iii) appeals under regulation 28(3) of the Child Trust Funds Regulations 2004;

(d) regarding saving gateway accounts with the exception of appeals against requirements to account for an amount under regulations made under section 14 of the Saving Gateway Accounts Act 2009;

(e) regarding child trust funds with the exception of appeals against requirements to account for an amount under regulations made under section 22(4) of the Child Trust Funds Act 2004 in relation to section 13 of that Act;

(f) regarding payments in consequence of diffuse mesothelioma;

(g) regarding a certificate or waiver decision in relation to NHS charges;

(h) regarding entitlement to be credited with earnings or contributions;

(i) against a decision as to whether an accident was an industrial accident.

### The Tax Chamber

1.160    The functions of this Chamber are allocated by article 7 of the First-tier Tribunal and Upper Tribunal (Chambers) Order 2010. It has jurisdiction over all functions, except those functions allocated to the Social Entitlement Chamber or to the Tax and Chancery Chamber of the Upper Tribunal, related to an appeal, application, reference or other proceeding in respect of:

(a) a function of the Commissioners for Her Majesty's Revenue and Customs or an officer of Revenue and Customs;

(b) the exercise by the Serious Organised Crime Agency of general Revenue functions or Revenue inheritance tax functions (as defined in section 323 of the Proceeds of Crime Act 2002);

(c) the exercise by the Director of Border Revenue of functions under section 7 of the Borders, Citizenship and Immigration Act 2009;

(d) a function of the Compliance Officer for the Independent Parliamentary Standards Authority.

### The War Pensions and Armed Forces Compensation Chamber

1.161    The functions of this Chamber are allocated by article 8 of the First-tier Tribunal and Upper Tribunal (Chambers) Order 2010. It has jurisdiction over all functions relating to appeals under the War Pensions (Administrative Provisions) Act 1919 and the Pensions Appeal Tribunals Act 1943.

## The Upper Tribunal

1.162    TCEA s3(5) confers on the Upper Tribunal the status of a superior court of record.

1.163    TCEA s25 gives the Upper Tribunal the same powers, rights, privileges and authority as the High Court in respect of the attendance and examination of witnesses, the production and inspection of documents, and all other matters incidental to the Upper Tribunal's functions. The same powers are conferred on the Employment Appeal Tribunal (by section 29(2) of the Employment Tribunals Act 1996) and the Crown Court (by section 45 of the Senior Courts Act 1981). This does not include the power to give a vexatious litigant permission to commence or defend proceedings. That power can only be exercised by the High Court itself.[227]

1.164   In *Trinity Mirror plc*,[228] the Court of Appeal decided that a matter was incidental to the jurisdiction of the Crown Court 'only when the powers to be exercised relate to the proper despatch of the business before it'.[229]

1.165   The Upper Tribunal is organised into four Chambers:[230]

- the Administrative Appeals Chamber;
- the Immigration and Asylum Chamber of the Upper Tribunal;
- the Tax and Chancery Chamber;
- the Lands Chamber.

1.166   The Lord Chancellor has power under TCEA ss32, 33 and 34 to provide for appeals to the Upper Tribunal against decisions of tribunals whose functions in relation to Wales, Scotland and Northern Ireland are otherwise outside the structure created by TCEA. This power is exercised by amendments to the relevant legislation in the Transfer of Tribunal Functions Order (for statutes) and the Consequential Provisions Order (for secondary legislation) that effect the transfer of jurisdictions into the TCEA structure.

1.167   If there is a doubt or dispute as to which chamber has jurisdiction in a particular matter, the Senior President may allocate the matter to the most appropriate chamber.[231]

## The Administrative Appeals Chamber

1.168   The functions of this Chamber fall into three categories: appellate, judicial review and referral.

1.169   The appellate function is allocated by article 10(a) of the First-tier Tribunal and Upper Tribunal (Chambers) Order 2010. It has jurisdiction over all functions relating to an appeal:

(i)   against a decision made by the First-tier Tribunal, except an appeal assigned to the Tax and Chancery Chamber or the Immigration and Asylum Chamber of the Upper Tribunal;

(ii)   under section 5 of the Pensions Appeal Tribunals Act 1943 (assessment decision) against a decision of the Pensions Appeal Tribunal in Northern Ireland established under paragraph 1(2) of Schedule 1 to the Pensions Appeal Tribunals Act 1943;[232]

(iii)   against a decision of the Pensions Appeal Tribunal in Scotland established under paragraph 1(2) of Schedule 1 to the Pensions Appeal Tribunals Act 1943;[233]

(iv)   against a decision of the Mental Health Review Tribunal for Wales established under section 65 of the Mental Health Act 1983;

(v)   against a decision of the Special Educational Needs Tribunal for Wales;

227   *IB v Information Commissioner* [2011] UKUT 370 (AAC), [2012] AACR 26.
228   [2008] 2 All ER 1159.
229   [2008] 2 All ER 1159 at [30].
230   Article 9 of the First-tier Tribunal and Upper Tribunal (Chambers) Order 2010.
231   Article 14 of the First-tier Tribunal and Upper Tribunal (Chambers) Order 2010.
232   In Northern Ireland, entitlement appeals are heard by the Social Security Commissioners, while assessment appeals are heard by the Upper Tribunal.
233   This covers both entitlement and assessment decisions.

(vi) under section 4 of the Safeguarding Vulnerable Groups Act 2006 (appeals);

(vii) transferred to the Upper Tribunal from the First-tier Tribunal under Tribunal Procedure Rules, except an appeal allocated to the Tax and Chancery Chamber by article 13(1)(e);

(viii) against a decision in a road transport case.[234]

1.170 The judicial review function is allocated by article 10(b) of the First-tier Tribunal and Upper Tribunal (Chambers) Order 2010. It has jurisdiction over all functions relating to an application, except one allocated to another chamber by article 11(c), (d) or (e), 12(c) or 13(g), for the Upper Tribunal:

(i) to grant the relief mentioned in section 15(1) of the Tribunal, Courts and Enforcement Act 2007 (Upper Tribunal's 'judicial review' jurisdiction);

(ii) to exercise the powers of review under section 21(2) of that Act (Upper Tribunal's 'judicial review' jurisdiction: Scotland).

1.171 The referral jurisdiction is allocated by article 10(c), (d) and (e) of the First-tier Tribunal and Upper Tribunal (Chambers) Order 2010. It has jurisdiction over all functions relating to:

(c) a matter referred to the Upper Tribunal by the First-tier Tribunal–

(i) under section 9(5)(b) of the Tribunals, Courts and Enforcement Act 2007 (review of decision of First-tier Tribunal), or

(ii) under Tribunal Procedure Rules relating to non-compliance with a requirement of the First-tier Tribunal,

except where the reference is allocated to another chamber by article 11(b) or 13(1)(f);

(d) a determination or decision under section 4 of the Forfeiture Act 1982;

(e) proceedings, or a preliminary issue, transferred under Tribunal Procedure Rules to the Upper Tribunal from the First-tier Tribunal, except those allocated to the Lands Chamber by article 12(cc) or to the Tax and Chancery Chamber by article 13(1)(e).

## The Immigration and Asylum Chamber of the Upper Tribunal

1.172 The jurisdiction of this Chamber is allocated by article 11 of the First-tier Tribunal and Upper Tribunal (Chambers) Order 2010. It has jurisdiction over all functions related to:

(a) an appeal against a decision of the First-tier Tribunal made in the Immigration and Asylum Chamber of the First-tier Tribunal;

(b) a matter referred to the Upper Tribunal under section 9(5)(b) of the Tribunals, Courts and Enforcement Act 2007 or under Tribunal Procedure Rules by the Immigration and Asylum Chamber of the First-tier Tribunal;

(c) an application for the Upper Tribunal to grant relief mentioned in section 15(1) of the Tribunals, Courts and Enforcement Act 2007 (Upper Tribunal's 'judicial review' jurisdiction), or to exercise the power of review under section 21(2) of that Act (Upper Tribunal's 'judicial review' jurisdiction: Scotland), which is made by a person who claims to be

---

234 This expression is not defined. According to the explanatory note to the First-tier Tribunal and Upper Tribunal (Chambers) (Amendment) Order 2012, it is intended to cover appeals against decisions of the traffic commissioners and appeals against decisions made by the Department of the Environment in Northern Ireland. This is how the expression is defined by UTR r1(3).

a minor from outside the United Kingdom challenging a defendant's assessment of that person's age;

(d) an application for the Upper Tribunal to exercise the powers of review under section 21(2) of the Tribunals, Court and Enforcement Act (Upper Tribunal's 'judicial review' jurisdiction: Scotland), which relates to a decision of the First-tier Tribunal mentioned in paragraph (a);

(e) an application for the Upper Tribunal to grant relief mentioned in section 15(1) of the Tribunals, Courts and Enforcement Act 2007 (Upper Tribunal's 'judicial review' jurisdiction), which is designated as an immigration matter–

(i) in a direction made in accordance with Part 1 of Schedule 2 to the Constitutional Reform Act 2005 specifying a class of case for the purposes of section 18(6) of the Tribunals, Courts and Enforcement Act 2007; or

(ii) in an order of the High Court in England and Wales made under section 31A(3) of the Senior Courts Act 1981, transferring to the Upper Tribunal an application of a kind described in section 31A(1) of that Act.

## The Lands Chamber

1.173　The jurisdiction of this Chamber is allocated by article 12 of the First-tier Tribunal and Upper Tribunal (Chambers) Order 2010. It has:

(a) all functions related to–

(i) compensation and other remedies for measures taken which affect the ownership, value, enjoyment or use of land or water, or of rights over or property in land or water;

(ii) appeals from decisions of–

(aa) the First-tier Tribunal made in the Property Chamber other than appeals allocated to the Tax and Chancery Chamber by article 13(h);

(ab) leasehold valuation tribunals in Wales, residential property tribunals in Wales, rent assessment committees in Wales, the Agricultural Land Tribunal in Wales or the Valuation Tribunal for Wales;

(ac) the Valuation Tribunal for England;

(iii) the determination of questions of the value of land or an interest in land arising in tax proceedings;

(iv) proceedings in respect of restrictive covenants, blight notices or the obstruction of light;

(b) the Upper Tribunal's function as arbitrator under section 1(5) of the Lands Tribunal Act 1949;

(c) an application for the Upper Tribunal to grant the relief mentioned in section 15(1) of the Tribunals, Courts and Enforcement Act 2007 (Upper Tribunal's 'judicial review' jurisdiction) which relates to a decision of a tribunal mentioned in sub-paragraph (a)(ii);

(cc) any case which may be transferred under Tribunal Procedure Rules to the Upper Tribunal from the Property Chamber of the First-tier Tribunal in relation to functions listed in article 5A(c) to (h);

(d) any other functions transferred to the Upper Tribunal by the Transfer of Tribunal Functions (Lands Tribunal and Miscellaneous Amendments) Order 2009.

## The Tax and Chancery Chamber

1.174 The functions of this Chamber fall into three categories: appellate, judicial review and referral.

1.175 The jurisdiction of this Chamber is allocated by article 13 of the First-tier Tribunal and Upper Tribunal (Chambers) Order 2010. It has jurisdiction over all functions relating to:

    (a) an appeal against a decision of the First-tier Tribunal made–
        (i) in the Tax Chamber;
        (ii) in the General Regulatory Chamber in a charities case;
    (b) a reference or appeal in respect of–
        (i) a decision of the Financial Services Authority;
        (ii) a decision of the Bank of England;
        (iii) a decision of a person related to the assessment of any compensation or consideration under the Banking (Special Provisions) Act 2008;
        (iv) a determination or dispute within the meaning of regulation 14(5) or 15 of the Financial Services and Markets Act 2000 (Contribution to Costs of Special Resolution Regime) Regulations 2010;
    (c) a reference in respect of a decision of the Pensions Regulator;
    (d) an application under paragraph 50(1)(d) of Schedule 36 to the Finance Act 2008;
    (e) proceedings, or a preliminary issue, transferred to the Upper Tribunal under Tribunal Procedure Rules–
        (i) from the Tax Chamber of the First-tier Tribunal;
        (ii) from the General Regulatory Chamber of the First-tier Tribunal in a charities case;
    (f) a matter referred to the Upper Tribunal under section 9(5)(b) of the Tribunals, Courts and Enforcement Act 2007 or under Tribunal Procedure Rules relating to non-compliance with a requirement of the First-tier Tribunal–
        (i) by the Tax Chamber of the First-tier Tribunal;
        (ii) by the General Regulatory Chamber of the First-tier Tribunal in a charities case;
    (g) an application for the Upper Tribunal to grant the relief mentioned in section 15(1) of the Tribunals, Courts and Enforcement Act 2007 (Upper Tribunal's 'judicial review' jurisdiction), or to exercise the powers of review under section 21(2) of that Act (Upper Tribunal's 'judicial review' jurisdiction: Scotland), which relates to–
        (i) a decision of the First-tier Tribunal mentioned in paragraph (1)(a)(i) or (ii);
        (ii) a function of the Commissioners for Her Majesty's Revenue and Customs or an officer of Revenue and Customs, with the exception of any function in respect of which an appeal would be allocated to the Social Entitlement Chamber;
        (iii) the exercise by the Serious Organised Crime Agency of general Revenue functions or Revenue inheritance tax functions (as defined in section 323 of the Proceeds of Crime Act 2002), with the exception of any function in relation to which an appeal would be allocated to the Social Entitlement Chamber;
        (iv) a function of the Charity Commission, or one of the bodies mentioned in sub-paragraph (b) or (c);
    (h) an appeal against a decision of the First-tier Tribunal made in the Property Chamber in a case mentioned in article 5A(a).

1.176    Article 13(2) provides:

> (2) In this article 'a charities case' means an appeal or application in respect of a decision, order or direction of the Charity Commission, or a reference under Schedule 1D of the Charities Act 1993.

## Judicial review in the Upper Tribunal

1.177    For England and Wales, the Lord Chief Justice has issued two practice directions. *Practice Direction (Upper Tribunal: Judicial Review Jurisdiction)*[235] orders:

1. The following direction takes effect in relation to an application made to the High Court or Upper Tribunal on or after 3 November 2008 that seeks relief of a kind mentioned in section 15(1) of the Tribunals, Courts and Enforcement Act 2007 ('the 2007 Act').
2. The Lord Chief Justice hereby directs that the following classes of case are specified for the purposes of section 18(6) of the 2007 Act--
   a. Any decision of the First-tier Tribunal on an appeal made in the exercise of a right conferred by the Criminal Injuries Compensation Scheme in compliance with section 5(1) of the Criminal Injuries Compensation Act 1995 (appeals against decisions on review); and
   b. Any decision of the First-tier Tribunal made under Tribunal Procedure Rules or section 9 of the 2007 Act where there is no right of appeal to the Upper Tribunal and that decision is not an excluded decision within paragraph (b), (c), or (f) of section 11(5) of the 2007 Act.
3. This Direction does not have effect where an application seeks (whether or not alone) a declaration of incompatibility under section 4 of the Human Rights Act 1998.
4. This Direction is made by the Lord Chief Justice with the agreement of the Lord Chancellor. It is made in the exercise of powers conferred by section 18(6) of the 2007 Act and in accordance with Part 1 of Schedule 2 to the Constitutional Reform Act 2005.

*Practice Direction (Upper Tribunal: Judicial Review Jurisdiction) (No 2)*[236] orders:

1. The Lord Chief Justice hereby specifies the following class of case for the purposes of section 18(6) of the Tribunals, Courts and Enforcement Act 2007: applications calling into question a decision of the Secretary of State not to treat submissions as an asylum claim or a human rights claim within the meaning of Part 5 of the Nationality, Immigration and Asylum Act 2002 wholly or partly on the basis that they are not significantly different from material that has previously been considered.
2. An application also falls within the class specified in para 1 if, in addition to calling into question a decision of the sort there described, it challenges (i) a decision or decisions to remove (or direct the removal of) the applicant from the United Kingdom; or (ii) a failure or failures by the Secretary of State to make a decision on submissions said to support an asylum or human rights claim; or both (i) and (ii); but not if it challenges any other decision.
3. This direction takes effect on 17 October 2011 in relation to applications made on or after that date to the High Court or Upper Tribunal for

---

235  [2009] 1 WLR 327.
236  [2012] 1 WLR 16.

judicial review or for permission to apply for judicial review that seek relief of a kind mentioned in section 15(1) of the 2007 Act.

4. For the avoidance of doubt, (i) a case which has been transferred under this direction continues to fall within the specified class of case and the Upper Tribunal has the function of deciding the application, where, after transfer, additional material is submitted to the Secretary of State for decision but no decision has been made upon that material; (ii) this direction does not have effect where an application seeks a declaration of incompatibility under section 4 of the Human Rights Act 1998, or where the applicant seeks to challenge detention.

5. This direction is made by the Lord Chief Justice with the agreement of the Lord Chancellor. It is made in the exercise of powers conferred by section 18(6)(7) of the 2007 Act and in accordance with Part 1 of Schedule 2 to the Constitutional Reform Act 2005.

1.178   In addition, cases may be transferred from the Administrative Court to the Upper Tribunal on an individual basis.

## Judges

1.179   Judges become judges of the Upper Tribunal or First-tier Tribunal in three ways: (i) by transfer-in; (ii) by appointment; and (iii) by virtue of holding another office. There is equivalent provision for other members. Transfer-in is appropriate when the function of a tribunal is transferred into the Upper Tribunal or First-tier Tribunal. Appointments are governed by Schedule 3 to TCEA; selection is made through the Judicial Appointments Commission. Other officeholders are specified in TCEA ss4–6.

1.180   A judge is authorised to decide matters within a jurisdiction by assignment, ticketing and judicial assistance. Within the Upper Tribunal and First-tier Tribunal, judges are assigned to a chamber and ticketed for jurisdictions within that chamber. They may provide judicial assistance to other tribunals.[237]

1.181   Decisions are occasionally made by judges who are not authorised to do so. Their decisions are valid, provided that they believed that they held an appropriate appointment to hear the case and were sitting in the appropriate tribunal in order to do so.[238]

1.182   Judges may be salaried or fee-paid. Salaried judges are not allowed to engage in practice. They may work full-time or part-time. The latter are paid the appropriate proportion of the full-time salary. Fee-paid judges are allowed to engage in practice and are paid a fee for each session.

---

237  For example: Employment Tribunals Act 1996 s5D, inserted by TCEA Sch 8 para 8.
238  *Baldock v Webster* [2006] QB 315.

## Death of judge

1.183   A judge may die before the hearing is complete or while the decision is still in discussion.

1.184   If a judge dies before the hearing is complete, another judge may take over and read the evidence already given.[239] This is so even if the judge was sitting with assessors or colleagues,[240] or if the facts are in dispute.[241] In one case, the new judge even read the previous judge's notes on the demeanour of witnesses, albeit with the agreement of the parties.[242]

1.185   In *Coleshill v Lord Mayor, Aldermen and Citizens of the City of Manchester*, Scrutton LJ doubted whether a different judge could take over a case that was part heard.[243] That case involved a jury. His comments have been distinguished on that basis[244] and never applied to cases that do not involve a jury.

1.186   If one member of a panel dies while the decision is still in discussion, the position depends on whether the members were agreed on the outcome. If they were, the decision stands as that of the majority,[245] provided that a majority decision is possible. If they were not, the decision does not stand, at least where the dissenting and deceased member was the presiding judge.[246]

1.187   The death of a judge after the decision has been announced does not affect the decision, at least in criminal cases.[247]

## Titles

1.188   The Senior President has specified the title by which judges and other members of the First-tier Tribunal and the Upper Tribunal are known.

1.189   All judges of the Upper Tribunal are known as Upper Tribunal Judges.

1.190   Salaried judges of the First-tier Tribunal are known as Tribunal Judges. If they have district or regional responsibilities, they are known as District Tribunal Judges or Regional Tribunal Judges. The lead judge in a jurisdiction is known as Principal Judge followed by the jurisdiction in brackets. Fee-paid judges of the First-tier Tribunal are known as Deputy Tribunal Judges.

1.191   The Senior President, Chamber Presidents and Deputy Chamber Presidents use their title followed by SP, CP or DCP.

1.192   When a judge is referred to in a decision, the first reference uses the full title. Thereafter, only Judge is used.

1.193   Non-legal members use their usual style.

---

239  Evans-Lombe J in *R (Hitch) v Income Tax Special Commissioners* [2005] 1 WLR 1651.
240  *Re British Reinforced Concrete Engineering Co Ltd's Application* (1929) 45 TLR 186 at 187.
241  Karminski J in *The Forest Lake* [1968] P 270 at 273.
242  *The Hopemount* (1943) 75 Ll LR 94 at 96.
243  [1928] 1 KB 776 at 786.
244  MacKinnon J in *In re British Reinforced Concrete Engineering Co Ltd's Application* (1929) 45 TLR 186 at 187.
245  *R v Greater Manchester Valuation Panel ex p Shell Chemicals UK Ltd* [1982] QB 255.
246  *R v Department of Health ex p Bhaugeerutty* (1998) *Times* 1 May.
247  *R v Coates* [2004] 1 WLR 3043.

## The future

1.194 The basic structure of the tribunals is now complete. A number of smaller jurisdictions have yet to be brought within the structure. It is likely that the Employment Appeal Tribunal and the employment tribunal will remain outside the Upper Tribunal and First-tier Tribunal structure for the time being.

# CHAPTER 2

# Jurisdiction

*continued*

2.1 Jurisdiction is central to the operation of all tribunals. They must act only within the jurisdiction that is conferred on them by legislation and, in doing so, they must exercise only the powers conferred on them.

## The nature of 'jurisdiction'

2.2 Jurisdiction is used with two meanings: a general meaning and a particular meaning.

2.3 In its general meaning, it has a narrow, strict sense and a wider sense. In the narrow sense, it means the tribunal's authority to deal with particular types of case. In the wider sense, it means the powers that the tribunal may exercise when exercising its jurisdiction in the narrow sense.

2.4 In its particular meaning, it refers to two matters: whether the proceedings have been properly brought and whether the tribunal was properly constituted to decide the case.

2.5 Whether proceedings have been properly brought may raise issues relating to permission to proceed,[1] the time within which proceedings were brought,[2] and whether a party has a particular status.[3] These are all preliminary matters that may have to be decided before the tribunal is entitled to enter upon the task of making a decision that fulfils its ultimate function. These matters are preliminary to the tribunal's exercise of its jurisdiction in the strict sense, but not necessarily preliminary to the tribunal beginning to consider the case. Ideally they should be considered at the outset, but they have to be decided whenever they arise.

2.6 Unfortunately, the law does not have terms of art, or even generally accepted language, to distinguish these differences of use. If it did, it would assist in precision of thought and analysis and reduce the opportunity for confusion. In *Carter v Ahsan*,[4] Sedley LJ distinguished between constitutive and adjudicative jurisdiction:

> By constitutive jurisdiction I mean the power given to a judicial body to decide certain classes of issue. By adjudicative jurisdiction I mean the entitlement of such a body to reach a decision within its constitutive jurisdiction.[5]

This captures the distinction between the narrow and wider senses of the general meaning of jurisdiction, but it has not been adopted.

2.7 In this book, jurisdiction is generally used in its narrow, strict meaning. This section deals with the general meaning of jurisdiction. The particular meaning is dealt with below.[6]

---

1 *Re Taylor (a bankrupt)* [2007] Ch 150 at [56]; *Seal v Chief Constable of South Wales Police* [2007] 1 WLR 1910, distinguished in *Adorian v Metropolitan Police Commissioner* [2009] 4 All ER 227.

2 *Rogers v Bodfari (Transport) Ltd* [1973] ICR 325; Rimer J in *Carter v Ahsan* [2005] ICR 1817 at [70]; and *R(I) 7/94* at [31]. But not a limitation period barring a remedy rather than extinguishing a right: see the distinction drawn by Sir John Donaldson P in *Secretary of State for Employment v Atkins Auto Laundries Ltd* [1972] 1 WLR 507 at 512; *Seal* [2007] 1 WLR 1910 at [6].

3 *R (R) v Mental Health Review Tribunal* (2006) *Times* 4 January.

4 [2005] ICR 1817.

5 [2005] ICR 1817 at [16].

6 See paras 2.50 onwards.

2.8    The vagueness of language can lead to confusion in citation, if not in analysis. Authorities on one meaning of jurisdiction are not relevant to the other. But this does not stop them being confused. *Chessington World of Adventures Ltd v Reed*[7] is an example. Morison J was there dealing with an alleged inherent procedural power to make a restricted reporting order (jurisdiction in the wider sense), but cited a passage[8] from *Secretary of State for Employment v Mann*[9] that dealt with substantive law (jurisdiction in the narrow sense).

2.9    The vagueness of the language can leave it unclear whether some matters are jurisdictional and, if they are, in what sense. This is true of the temporal and geographical limits within which the tribunal must function.

2.10   The temporal limit of a tribunal's power determines the time in respect of which the tribunal has authority. This issue will always arise when a tribunal is created or abolished. It also arises every time there is a change in the tribunal's jurisdiction under other heads. It is usually considered in the context of the retrospective effect of legislation.

2.11   There are two geographical limits of a tribunal's power. One limit depends on the location of events, persons or property. The tribunal's authority may be limited to a particular country or area of a country where the events took place, property is located there or a person is present. The geographical limit may represent the area of authority of the legal system of which the tribunal system is a part[10] or it may be a lesser area. The limit may apply to the tribunal system as a whole, particular tribunals within a system, or both.

2.12   The other geographical limit depends on a person's connection with that geographical area. The connection may be based on nationality, domicile or residence.[11] Residence may be actual, ordinary or habitual.

## The strict meaning of jurisdiction

2.13   The factors that define the type of case that the tribunal exists to decide were identified by Diplock LJ in *Garthwaite v Garthwaite*:[12]

> In its narrow and strict sense, the 'jurisdiction' of a validly constituted court connotes the limits which are imposed on its power to hear and determine issues between persons seeking to avail themselves of its process by reference (i) to subject-matter of the issue, or (ii) to the persons between whom the issue is joined, or (iii) to the kind of relief sought, or any combination of these factors.[13]

---

7   [1998] IRLR 56.
8   [1998] IRLR 56 at 62.
9   [1996] ICR 197 at 204.
10   Confusingly, the geographical area covered by a legal system is also known as a jurisdiction.
11   The habitual residence of the parties is expressly referred to as a jurisdictional issue in section 44 of the Child Support Act 1991.
12   [1964] P 356.
13   [1964] P 356 at 387.

## The exclusivity principle

2.14 A provision that purports to oust the jurisdiction of the courts will be inter-preted strictly.[14] This does not apply if the courts have never had any juris-diction to be ousted.[15] Nor does it apply if there is an effective alternative to court proceedings.[16] One alternative is a tribunal.

2.15 The courts will not allow a party to bring court proceedings if the proper venue for the substance of the dispute is a tribunal. The courts accept and respect the autonomy of the tribunal within its jurisdiction.[17] This principle dates at least to the decision of the House of Lords in *Barraclough v Brown*.[18] The case concerned entitlement to expenses relating to the removal of a sunken vessel. Under the terms of the legislation, these expenses could be recovered in a court of summary jurisdiction. An action was brought in the High Court for a declaration on the right to the expenses. The House decided that it was not permissible to take the advantage conferred by a statute without using the means provided by the statute for enforcement (such as a tribunal).[19] The legislation did not create the expenses as a debt recoverable in normal civil proceedings. They could only be recovered in a court of summary jurisdiction. By implication, the legislation provided that no other court had jurisdiction.[20]

2.16 This decision was followed and applied to tax legislation by the Court of Appeal in *Argosam Finance Co Ltd v Oxby (Inspector of Taxes)*[21] and re-affirmed by the House of Lords in *Autologic Holdings plc v Inland Revenue Commissioners*.[22] In the latter case, the tax paying company had sought to obtain declarations and relief from the courts instead of appealing against the assessment of tax to the Special Commissioners. The House held that the court proceedings were in substance an appeal, an indirect way of obtaining what was available through the statutory appeal, and a way of sidestepping the statutory procedure.[23]

2.17 This principle does not prevent parties using court proceedings by con-sent to decide a matter that relates to the basis of the tribunal's jurisdic-tion, but is preliminary to it and suitable for decision without being too closely related to the tribunal's jurisdiction.[24]

2.18 Ultimately, the exclusivity principle is a principle of interpretation, not a rule of law. This has two consequences. First, the same result may be obtained, without reference to the exclusivity principle, simply by

---

14 Lord Reid in *Anisminic v Foreign Compensation Commission* [1969] 2 AC 149 at 170.

15 *A v B (Investigatory Powers Tribunal: jurisdiction)* [2010] 1 All ER 1149 at [22].

16 Lord Nicholls in *Farley v Secretary of State for Work and Pensions (No 2)* [2006] 1 WLR 1817 at [18].

17 Lord Wilberforce in *Anisminic v Foreign Compensation Commission* [1969] 2 AC 149 at 208.

18 [1897] AC 615.

19 [1897] AC 615 at 620 per Lord Herschell.

20 [1897] AC 615 at 622 per Lord Watson.

21 [1965] Ch 390.

22 [2006] 1 AC 118.

23 [2006] 1 AC 118 at [12], [13] and [23] per Lord Nicholls.

24 *Autologic Holdings plc v Inland Revenue Commissioners* [2006] 1 AC 118 at [14] per Lord Nicholls, relying on Lord Wilberforce in *Vandervell Trustees Ltd v White* [1971] AC 912 at 939–940. Lord Nicholls emphasised that this gave the court a discretion at [15].

interpretation of the relevant legislation.[25] Second, the exclusivity principle is subject to contrary provision.

2.19   The relationship between a tribunal's jurisdiction and judicial review requires separate consideration. The availability of judicial review cannot be removed by implication. It must be removed expressly and clearly. However, judicial review is a discretionary remedy, so that the High Court may refuse permission if the tribunal provides an adequate alternative remedy.

2.20   In *A v B (Investigatory Powers Tribunal: jurisdiction)*,[26] the Supreme Court held that there was no scope for a judicial review in addition to the tribunal's jurisdiction under section 65(2)(a) of the Regulation of Investigatory Powers Act 2000.

## Determining a tribunal's jurisdiction

2.21   A tribunal has jurisdiction to determine whether it has jurisdiction in particular circumstances.[27] It is treated as deciding any issue of jurisdiction, even if it does not do so expressly and the issue is not raised by the parties.[28] Under UTR r8(2)(a) and its equivalents, the tribunal is under a duty to strike out proceedings if it does not have jurisdiction. This duty, if it is valid, deprives the tribunal of the power to decide the issue. See chapter 12.

2.22   If the tribunal deals expressly with the issue itself, it may do so as a preliminary issue.[29] But if the matter may be better tested elsewhere, it may be more appropriate for the tribunal to adjourn to allow this to be done.[30] This is consistent with the exclusivity principle.

2.23   An issue of jurisdiction may be raised by any party to the proceedings at any stage.[31] The tribunal is under a duty to take any jurisdictional point on its own initiative, even if the issue is not raised by the parties.[32] A tribunal must ensure that it has jurisdiction to make its decision, but it need not seek out an alternative jurisdiction on which it can make a decision.[33]

2.24   On appeal, the Upper Tribunal has power to determine the First-tier Tribunal's jurisdiction and so on up the judicial hierarchy.[34]

---

25   As in *R v Davey* [1899] 2 QB 301 and *Farley v Child Support Agency* [2006] UKHL 31 at [18].

26   [2010] 1 All ER 1149.

27   *R v Fulham, Hammersmith and Kensington Rent Tribunal ex p Zerek* [1951] 2 QB 1.

28   *Boudhiba v Central Examining Court No 5 of the National Court of Justice, Madrid* [2007] 1 WLR 124 at [15]. An issue of jurisdiction is always raised by an appeal for the purposes of provisions such as section 12(8)(a) of the Social Security Act 1998: see chapter 4.

29   *Potts v IRC* (1982) 56 TC 25 at 35 and Rimer J in *Carter v Ahsan* [2005] ICR 1817 at [70].

30   Devlin J in *R v Fulham, Hammersmith and Kensington Rent Tribunal ex p Zerek* [1951] 2 QB 1 at 13–14.

31   Buxton LJ in *Carter v Ahsan* [2005] ICR 1817 at [82].

32   Rimer J and Buxton LJ in *Carter v Ahsan* [2005] ICR 1817 at [75] and [82].

33   *B v R* [2010] 1 FLR 563 at paras [33] and [37].

34   Lord Denning MR in *Arsenal Football Club Ltd v Ende* [1977] QB 100 at 116.

2.25　　The factors relevant to a tribunal's jurisdiction may be readily apparent from the information provided when the proceedings were commenced or they may require further consideration of evidence and argument. They may have to be objectively present or the tribunal may be given the power, expressly or by implication, to decide for itself whether the factor exists.[35]

2.26　　A tribunal must not accept jurisdiction that has purportedly but wrongly been conferred on it. It must disregard any decision that does so, even if it has not been set aside.[36] It cannot leave the issue to be dealt with on judicial review, because that is not an exclusive means of remedying an excess of jurisdiction.[37] This is subject to the rules of precedent. The earlier decision must be accepted if binding.

## The scope of the tribunal's jurisdiction

2.27　　A tribunal is a statutory body. It has only the jurisdiction that is conferred on it by statute.[38] It may be conferred directly by statute or in delegated legislation. Jurisdiction can only be conferred in delegated legislation under the authority of an appropriate enabling statutory provision. A power enabling the making of procedural provisions is not sufficient.[39]

2.28　　The extent of a tribunal's jurisdiction is, therefore, a matter of statutory interpretation. The ordinary principles apply.[40] There are no special rules relevant to jurisdiction. In particular, there is no rule that a tribunal may remedy an apparently obvious omission from its jurisdiction under the guise of interpretation.[41] However, in *OFCOM v Morrissey and the Information Commissioner*,[42] the Upper Tribunal accepted for the purposes of argument that there was a presumption that a tribunal could decide a public law issue in the context of a case on private law rights, but held that it did not cover a challenge to the reasonableness of a decision.[43]

---

35　Sedley LJ in *Carter v Ahsan* [2005] ICR 1817 at [21].

36　*R(I) 14/65* at [7] and *R(AF) 1/09* (leave given outside maximum time allowed); *R(I) 7/94* at [30]–[31] (application to set aside a decision made outside the prescribed time); *R(SB) 1/95* at [12]–[13] (late appeal accepted on an invalid application); *Akewushola v Secretary of State for the Home Department* [2000] 1 WLR 2295 at 2302 (previous decision set aside by chairman without power to do so); *Carter v Ahsan* [2005] ICR 1817 at [75] (Court of Appeal decision overruling Employment Appeal Tribunal decision on scope of appeal before employment tribunal).

37　Willes J in *Mayor and Aldermen of the City of London v Cox* (1867) LR 2 HL 239 at 262–263; *R v Judge Pugh ex p Graham* [1951] 2 KB 623.

38　Lord Atkin in *Evans v Bartlam* [1937] AC 473 at 480.

39　See chapter 3.

40　For example: *Horizon Recruitment Ltd v Vincent* [2010] ICR 491 (whether employment tribunal with jurisdiction over an agreement had jurisdiction to decide whether it was an enforceable agreement).

41　*Pendragon plc v Jackson* [1998] ICR 215.

42　[2011] UKUT 116 (AAC).

43　[2011] UKUT 116 (AAC) at [47].

2.29    Jurisdiction cannot be extended by the consent of the parties,[44] whether given positively or by acquiescence,[45] or by estoppel by representation.[46] By parity of reasoning, it cannot be restricted by consent. Nor can the tribunal waive a lack of jurisdiction as an irregularity.

2.30    However, it may be that the parties can, by agreeing on an issue of fact relevant to the tribunal's power to hear the case, ensure that the tribunal has jurisdiction. Sedley LJ discussed this possibility in *Clark v Clark Construction Initiatives Ltd*:[47]

> I would therefore dismiss this appeal. In doing so, however, I record my own doubt whether the duration of the claimant's employment was in truth a jurisdictional issue. The point has not been argued. But while it is trite law that the statutory remit of a tribunal cannot be enlarged by consent or by silence (see *British Midland Airways v Lewis* [1978] ICR 782), whether any one case lies within or outside the tribunal's jurisdiction is typically a mixed question of fact and law. If the parties disagree about whether there was a full year's employment before dismissal, the tribunal's decision on the point will determine whether it has jurisdiction. If they agree that there was, their agreement will ordinarily determine jurisdiction, not by enlarging the statutory remit but by bringing themselves within it. In the latter situation there may be no jurisdictional issue permitting intervention of the tribunal's own motion. The House of Lords in *Carter v Ahsan* [2008] ICR 82 (cf [2005] ICR 1817) has considered this restricted concept of jurisdiction; and while, as I stress, it has not been an issue before us, attention may need in other cases to be paid to it.

2.31    A tribunal cannot decline jurisdiction that it has, even if it considers that it would be inappropriate to exercise it. In *Kapur v Kapur*,[48] Bush J said:

> ... if a court has jurisdiction, as I understand the law, there is no way in which the court could decline jurisdiction on the ground of hardship, apparent unfairness or any other ground.[49]

2.32    Whether a matter is a jurisdictional one is determined by its substance rather than the language used in the legislation and there is reluctance to invalidate proceedings for failure to comply with a procedural requirement.[50]

2.33    The limited scope of a tribunal's jurisdiction can give rise to boundary issues with related jurisdictions of other tribunals or the courts. For example: the respective roles of the family courts and the Special

---

44  Lords Reid and Hodson in *Essex County Council v Essex Incorporated Congregational Church Union* [1963] AC 808 at 820–821 and 828; Woolf LJ in *R v Secretary of State for Social Services ex p CPAG* [1990] 2 QB 540 at 556; *Rydqvist v Secretary of State for Work and Pensions* [2002] 1 WLR 3343.

45  Peter Gibson LJ in *Aparau v Iceland Frozen Foods plc* [2000] ICR 341 at 353.

46  Lords Reid and Hodson in *Essex County Council v Essex Incorporated Congregational Church Union* [1963] AC 808 at 820–821 and 828; Lord Wilberforce in *Secretary of State for Employment v Globe Elastic Thread Co Ltd* [1980] AC 506 at 519; Lord Hoffmann in *Watt (formerly Carter) v Ahsan* [2008] AC 696 at [30].

47  [2009] ICR 718 at [14]. *Carter v Ahsan* [2008] ICR 82 (cf [2005] ICR 1817) has considered this restricted concept of jurisdiction; and while, as I stress, it has not been an issue before us, attention may need in other cases to be paid to it.

48  [1984] FLR 920.

49  [1984] FLR 920 at 922.

50  Lord Bingham in *Seal v Chief Constable of South Wales Police* [2007] 1 WLR 1910 at [7].

Educational Needs and Disability Tribunal[51] and the jurisdictions of the employment tribunal and the county court.[52]

2.34 A tribunal has no inherent jurisdiction in its strict meaning. However, it may have implied or inherent powers in the wider meaning. These powers are sometimes referred to in terms of a tribunal's jurisdiction. It is in this sense that a tribunal is sometimes said to have inherent jurisdiction. This use is best avoided in order to prevent confusion.

## Issue estoppel

2.35 Lord Hoffmann explained the position of issue estoppel in *Watt (formerly Carter) v Ahsan:*[53]

> Although estoppel in pais and estoppel *per rem judicatam* share the word estoppel, they share very little else. The former is based upon a policy of giving a limited effect to non-contractual representations and promises while the latter is based upon the altogether different policy of avoiding relitigation of the same issues. It is easy to see why parties should not be able to agree to confer upon a tribunal a jurisdiction which Parliament has not given it. And if they cannot do this by contract, it would illogical if they could do it by non-contractual representations or promises. But when a tribunal has decided that it does have jurisdiction, the question of whether this decision is binding at a later stage of the same litigation, or in subsequent litigation, involves ... quite different issues about fairness and economy in the administration of justice.
>
> Issue estoppel arises when a court of competent jurisdiction has determined some question of fact or law, either in the course of the same litigation (for example, as a preliminary point) or in other litigation which raises the same point between the same parties ...

2.36 Issue estoppel is subject to the court's discretion to allow an issue to be re-opened if there are special circumstances that require this in order to prevent an injustice.[54]

2.37 The principles of issue estoppel may be modified or overridden by statutory provision.[55]

## The practical significance of jurisdiction

2.38 The significance of matters of jurisdiction has reduced over the years under two pressures. First, the scope of judicial review has widened, allowing review of matters that were not formerly regarded as jurisdictional. Second, the difficulties of drawing the distinctions between the concepts employed by the cases to distinguish between jurisdictional and other matters have become apparent.

---

51 This was analysed by Munby J in *X County Council v DW, PW and SW* [2005] 2 FLR 508.
52 Buxton LJ in *Carter v Ahsan* [2005] ICR 1817 at [87].
53 [2008] AC 696 at [30]–[31].
54 Lord Keith in *Arnold v Westminster Bank plc* [1991] 2 AC 93 at 109; Lord Hoffmann in *Watt (formerly Carter) v Ahsan* [2008] AC 696 at [34].
55 Such as Social Security Act 1998 s17 and Child Support Act 1991 s46A.

2.39     For practical purposes, jurisdiction is significant for five purposes. First a tribunal is under a duty to investigate its jurisdiction. Second, it may not waive a lack of jurisdiction as an irregularity. Third, the parties cannot establish jurisdiction by consent, acquiescence, waiver or estoppel. Fourth, the tribunal has no authority to deal with parties, issues or remedies that are outside its jurisdiction. Fifth, a tribunal may be prepared to exercise its discretion to re-open an issue of jurisdiction that has already been decided between the parties.

## Validity of decision for purposes of founding an appeal

2.40    Although a decision-maker or a tribunal may have made a decision that it was not allowed by law to make, the decision is valid for the purposes of an appeal.[56]

## The validity of secondary legislation

2.41    Legislation may be primary or secondary. Primary legislation is made by Parliament in statutes or Acts of Parliament. Secondary legislation is made under the delegated authority of primary legislation. Regulations relating to the substantive law to be applied by tribunals will almost certainly have been made by a minister. However, it may have been subject to scrutiny by Parliament in two ways. It may have been confirmed by an affirmative resolution or it may have been subject to a negative resolution procedure, under which it is laid before Parliament and is valid unless there is a vote against it.

2.42    The significance of the distinction between primary and secondary legislation is that secondary legislation is not valid unless it is authorised by primary legislation. Decision-makers and tribunals have jurisdiction to decide whether or not secondary legislation was authorised by primary legislation.[57] It is an error of law for a tribunal to apply secondary legislation that was made without authority.

### The enabling powers

2.43    If there is a challenge to the validity of secondary legislation, the tribunal must identify the relevant enabling power. The powers under which the legislation is made are set out at the beginning of the legislation. The list used to end with a mop-up provision including 'all other powers enabling in that behalf', but this does not cover every possibility. It only does so if that power was expressly relied on or had to be relied on to authorise the legislation.[58]

2.44    Some enabling powers are compulsory[59] and have to be implemented. Most enabling powers are not compulsory and do not have to

---

56  See *Calvin v Carr* [1980] AC 574; *London and Clydeside Estates Ltd v Aberdeen District Council* [1980] 1 WLR 182; *Re Gale dec'd* [1966] Ch 236; *R(I) 9/63* at [20]–[22].

57  *Chief Adjudication Officer v Foster* [1993] AC 754.

58  *Vibixa Ltd v Komori UK Ltd* [2006] 1 WLR 2472.

59  For example: Child Support Act 1991 s22(4)(b).

be implemented. But a failure to make secondary legislation, even commencement provisions, may be the subject of judicial review.

2.45 Enabling powers may be relatively broad or narrow in their terms. Secondary legislation may fall outside the terms of a narrow enabling provision but within the terms of a wider provision. In those circumstances, the secondary legislation is valid.[60] The limitations on the narrower provision do not control the scope of the wider provision.

2.46 The secondary legislation may be based on the combined effect of a number of different enabling powers. In these circumstances, it is not necessary to maintain a strict separation between the powers, unless there is a compelling reason to do so.[61]

### Interpretation

2.47 Having identified the enabling provisions, the tribunal must interpret the enabling power and the secondary legislation. If possible, a tribunal must interpret secondary legislation in a way that renders it valid. This includes, where appropriate, taking account of the Human Rights Act 1998 to interpret both the enabling power and the secondary legislation.

### Unauthorised provisions

2.48 Secondary legislation is not authorised in these circumstances:

- if it was made by an incorrect procedure: *Howker v Secretary of State for Work and Pensions;*[62]
- if it is not authorised by the enabling power as interpreted: *Chief Adjudication Officer v Foster;*[63]
- if it was not a rational exercise of the enabling power: *O'Connor v Chief Adjudication Officer;*[64]
- if it is in conflict with statutory rights under primary legislation: *R v Secretary of State for Social Security ex p Joint Council for the Welfare of Immigrants.*[65]

### The wider meaning of jurisdiction

2.49 In *Garthwaite v Garthwaite,*[66] Diplock LJ distinguished the narrow sense from the wider sense of the word. He described this sense in this passage:

In its wider sense it embraces also the settled practice of the court as to the way in which it will exercise its power to hear and determine issues which fall within its 'jurisdiction' (in the strict sense), or as to the circumstances in which it will grant a particular kind of relief which it has 'jurisdiction' (in the strict sense) to grant, including its settled practice to refuse to exercise such powers or to grant such relief in particular circumstances.[67]

---

60 *R v Secretary of State for Social Security ex p Rouse* (1993) *Times* 1 February.
61 Lord Hope in *Banks v Chief Adjudication Officer* [2001] 1 WLR 1411 at [43].
62 [2003] ICR 405.
63 [1993] AC 754.
64 [1999] 1 FLR 1200.
65 [1997] 1 WLR 275.
66 [1964] P 356.
67 *Garthwaite v Garthwaite* [1964] P 356 at 387.

This passage is influenced by the issue before the court. The wider sense of the term may be expressed as covering the powers that a tribunal has to further the exercise of its jurisdiction. These powers may be express, implied or inherent.[68]

## Validity of actions, notices and decisions

### Terminology

2.50   Actions, notices and decisions may all be defective. The issue may arise in connection with an appeal, referral, set aside or review. For convenience, this section refers only to decisions and appeals.

### Invalidity and its significance

2.51   The issue is what effect the defect has. Two questions arise. First, was the decision invalid? Second, what are the consequences? Specifically, is it of any effect until it is set aside?

2.52   Generally it is not necessary to distinguish invalidity from any other ground on which a decision may be set aside on appeal. However, there are exceptions. For example: if a decision is found to be invalid on appeal, the tribunal must either declare the decision invalid or replace the decision with its own. This latter course will only be possible if the tribunal has both jurisdiction and the necessary information to do so.[69] Also, void actions cannot be validated retrospectively.[70]

### Logic and convenience

2.53   In identifying those decisions that are invalid and determining the consequences of invalidity, the law has had to strike a balance between logic and practicality. Logically, a decision is only valid if all the conditions necessary for it to be made have been satisfied. However, that would produce the result that any defect would render a decision invalid, regardless of its significance or of the impact it has had. The law seeks to avoid this by distinguishing between decisions that were not validly made and those that were validly made but defective. This distinction is illustrated by two similar cases involving attempts by local authorities to recover overpayments of housing benefit from landlords of the benefit claimant.

2.54   In *Warwick District Council v Freeman*,[71] the authority had decided that benefit had been overpaid to the claimant and invoiced the landlord. When the landlord asked for a review, the local authority replied that the procedure did not apply to landlords and sued for payment in the county court. The Court of Appeal held that there was no basis for the local authority's civil action to recover the overpayment, because the authority

---

68   See chapter 3.
69   *R(U) 3/88* at [10]–[12].
70   *Re Taylor (a bankrupt)* [2007] Ch 150 at [70].
71   (1994) 27 HLR 616.

'did not go through the proper process for so doing so as to entitle them to take action in the county court'.[72]

2.55 In *Haringey London Borough Council v Awaritefe*,[73] the authority had also sued the landlord in the county court. The landlord's defence was that the notification of the decision was defective. The Court of Appeal distinguished *Freeman* as a case in which the notification procedures had not been followed at all. *Awaritefe*, in contrast, was a case in which the procedures had been followed, but defectively. In those circumstances, the test to be applied was whether the landlord had suffered 'substantive harm' or 'significant prejudice'. (The members of the Court clearly regarded those terms as interchangeable.) If so, there had not been substantial compliance with the notification provisions. If not, there had been substantial compliance. On the facts of that case, there had been no prejudice.

2.56 The distinction between decisions that are invalid and those that are valid but defective has produced some fine distinctions. Moreover, the cases do not always refer to other lines of authority, still less explain how they are to be reconciled.

2.57 A decision is presumed to be valid in the absence of evidence to the contrary.[74]

## Validity for the purpose of ruling on validity

2.58 All decisions, even if invalid, retain sufficient status to allow an appeal.[75] And in those cases in which invalid decisions may simply be ignored, they have sufficient status to allow proceedings to be brought for them to be set aside.[76]

## Validity of Upper Tribunal decision and directions

2.59 The First-tier Tribunal must accept the validity of a decision and directions of the Upper Tribunal, even if it considers that they were made without jurisdiction.[77]

## Decisions made in other proceedings

2.60 The starting point is that a decision made in separate proceedings must be accepted as validly made until it is set aside. There may, or may not, be a statutory provision that that decision is final or conclusive.

2.61 In *Isaacs v Robertson*,[78] the Privy Council decided that:

> . . . an order made by a court of unlimited jurisdiction ... must be obeyed unless and until it has been set aside by the court.[79]

72  (1994) 27 HLR 616 at 621.
73  (1999) 32 HLR 517.
74  Carnwath LJ in *Secretary of State for Work and Pensions v Menary-Smith* [2006] EWCA Civ 1751 at [53].
75  See: *Calvin v Carr* [1980] AC 574 at 589–591; *London and Clydeside Estates Ltd v Aberdeen District Council* [1980] 1 WLR 182; *Re Gale dec'd* [1966] Ch 236; *R(I) 9/63* at [20]–[22].
76  Diplock LJ in *Harkness v Bell's Asbestos and Engineering Ltd* [1967] 2 QB 729 at 736.
77  *Nesbitt (David John Edwards)'s Application* [2013] NIQB 111.
78  [1985] AC 97.
79  [1985] AC 97 at 101. See also *R(H) 1/07*.

The same principle applies if the order was made by a court of limited jurisdiction.[80] It applies even if the order was made without jurisdiction.[81]

2.62        The Privy Council in *Isaacs* disapproved of the distinction between void and voidable orders,[82] but approved what Romer LJ said in *Hadkinson v Hadkinson*:[83]

> It is the plain and unqualified obligation of every person against, or in respect of whom, an order is made by a court of competent jurisdiction, to obey it unless and until that order is discharged. The uncompromising nature of this obligation is shown by the fact that it extends even to cases where the person affected by an order believes it to be irregular or even void. 'A party who knows of an order, whether null and void, regular or irregular, cannot be permitted to disobey it . . . It would be most dangerous to hold that the suitors, or their solicitors, could themselves judge whether an order was null and void – whether it was regular or irregular. That they should come to the court and not take upon themselves to determine such a question: that the course of a party knowing of an order, which was null and irregular and who might be affected by it was plain. He should apply to the court that it might be discharged. As long as it existed it must not be disobeyed.' (*per* Lord Cottenham LC in *Chuck v Cremer* (1846) Cooper temp. Cottenham 205, 338).[84]

The same applies to an undertaking. In *Johnson v Walton*,[85] Lord Donaldson MR said:

> . . . when an injunctive order is made or when an undertaking given, it operates until it is revoked on appeal or by the court itself, and it has to be obeyed whether or not it should have been granted or accepted in the first place.[86]

2.63        The decisions of the Commissioners were to the same effect.[87]

2.64        A collateral challenge is permissible, but only in limited circumstances. An example was *Boddington v British Transport Police*.[88] In that case, a person convicted of an offence was allowed to challenge the validity of the byelaw that created the offence. It is not clear whether the byelaw was void or voidable.[89] The key consideration was that the person concerned would not otherwise have had a fair opportunity to challenge the validity of the byelaw.[90]

2.65        Despite these authorities, there are recognised but limited circumstances in which a decision can be treated as invalid.

80  *Director of Public Prosecutions v T* [2001] 1 WLR 209.
81  Wall LJ in *Re B (Court's Jurisdiction)* [2004] 2 FLR 741 at [68]. In that case, the court lacked jurisdiction because the child who was the subject of the residence order in question was not habitually resident in England.
82  [1985] AC 97 at 102–103.
83  [1952] P 285 at 288.
84  For an example of the principle in operation, see *Re Gale dec'd* [1966] Ch 237.
85  [1990] 1 FLR 350.
86  [1990] 1 FLR 350 at 352.
87  *R(I) 9/63* at [20]–[22].
88  [1999] 2 AC 143.
89  [1999] 2 AC 143 at 164.
90  *Director of Public Prosecutions v T* [2007] 1 WLR 209 at [26].

## Power to entertain proceedings

2.66 A decision is invalid if there was, in the circumstances, no power to entertain or embark upon the proceedings that led to it. This may arise in two circumstances. First, the proceedings may never have been commenced. Second, the proceedings may already have been concluded.

2.67 Both circumstances were considered by the Tribunal of Commissioners in *R(I) 7/94*. In that case, tribunal A had decided an appeal. Tribunal B refused to set that decision aside, but it was later set aside by tribunal C and the case was reheard by tribunal D. The issue for the Tribunal of Commissioners was whether tribunal D had jurisdiction. This turned on whether tribunal C had power to embark on the further proceedings to set aside the decision made by tribunal A. The Commissioners decided that it did not and that tribunal D should have decided that it had no power to decide the appeal again. The power to consider the application to set aside had been exhausted, because: (i) there had been a valid application by a prescribed person; (ii) the application had not already have been determined; when (iii) a properly constituted tribunal (tribunal B) had sat and considered the application; and (iv) then decided the application.[91]

2.68 The Tribunal of Commissioners did not refer to the authorities that decide that a decision of a court is binding until quashed. Instead, it relied on a tribunal's duty to ensure that it has jurisdiction.[92] It also justified its power to go behind the decision of tribunal C by reference to its power to decide on the validity of secondary legislation:

> If Commissioners may, incidentally to determining the issue before them, pronounce on the validity of provisions in regulations, so must they be able to pronounce on the validity of decisions of other administrative bodies.[93]

The appeal tribunal was not, of course, an administrative body. The decision was made by a judicial body and, although it was not subject to an appeal, it was subject to judicial review.

2.69 It is also possible that the Tribunal of Commissioners was influenced by the fact that a decision under the set aside power was a determination rather than a decision. This was the analysis relied on by the Commissioner in *R(I) 14/65*. The Commissioner decided that he was not bound by a grant of leave to appeal out of time, which the tribunal had no power to do. He described the extension of time as having 'no meaning'.[94] Unlike the Tribunal of Commissioners, he considered the authorities on the validity of decisions, but distinguished them:

> But the grant, or refusal to grant, leave to appeal is not as it seems to me, a 'decision' in the sense that a person's substantive rights are thereby determined; rather is it a determination as to the manner in which those rights are to be decided.[95]

However, in principle this should not be relevant, as the decision was subject to judicial review.

---

91  *R(I) 7/94* at [30].
92  *R(I) 7/94* at [27].
93  *R(I) 7/94* at [25].
94  *R(I) 14/65* at [7].
95  *R(I) 14/65* at [6].

2.70    If the issue is whether any proceedings have ever been commenced, the focus is on the contents of the application and the person who made it. For example: in *R(SB) 1/95*, a tribunal chairman had extend the time for appealing against a decision. (As with decisions under the set aside power, the decision to extend time was not subject to an appeal.) The application had identified the date of that decision as 1991 instead of 1970. The appeal was then heard by an appeal tribunal. The Commissioner decided that the tribunal had no jurisdiction. The decision to extend time was invalid, because the application did not comply with the requirement to identify the decision under appeal.

2.71    If the issue is whether proceedings have already been concluded, the focus is on the tribunal and its constitution. In *R v Secretary of State for the Home Department ex p Choudhary*,[96] an immigration officer had stamped a passport with indefinite leave to remain. The Court of Appeal decided that stamp was 'clearly invalid', as the officer had no power to put the stamp on the passport or to give indefinite leave.[97] And in *Akewushola v Secretary of State for the Home Department*,[98] the Immigration Appeal Tribunal dismissed an appeal, but the chairman purported to set aside its decision. When the case came on for rehearing, the new Immigration Appeal Tribunal decided that it did not have jurisdiction. This was confirmed by the Court of Appeal on the grounds that: (i) the rules governing the tribunal did not authorise a chairman to set aside a decision and (ii) there was no power for a tribunal to review its own decisions unless authorised by statute. This deprived the second tribunal of any jurisdiction whether or not 'a purported decision plainly made without power can be ignored or must first be quashed by the High Court'.[99] In other words, the tribunal had no jurisdiction even if the setting aside order remained valid until quashed.[100]

## No decision made

2.72    It is possible that the decision under appeal is so lacking in the key elements required that it has never been taken. The circumstances in which this might occur were considered by the Tribunal of Commissioners in *R(IB) 2/04*. The Tribunal referred to the possibility that 'there may be some decisions of the Secretary of State which have so little coherence or connection to legal powers that they do not amount to decisions at all', but it did 'not consider it would be helpful here to seek to identify characteristics which might lead to that conclusion in a particular case'.[101]

2.73    If an appeal is lodged against a decision that has not been made, the tribunal's only powers are to strike out the case or to declare that it has no jurisdiction on that ground.

---

96  [1978] 1 WLR 1177.
97  [1978] 1 WLR 1177 at 1182 D–E and F–G.
98  [2000] 1 WLR 2295.
99  [2000] 1 WLR 2295 At 2302 in the penultimate para in Sedley LJ's judgment.
100  See also *R v West* [1964] 1 QB 15.
101  *R(IB) 2/04* at [72].

## Decision made but not notified

2.74 In *R (Anufrijeva) v Secretary of State for the Home Department*,[102] the House of Lords decided that a decision did not have legal effect until it was communicated. But this does not mean that an uncommunicated decision is ineffective for all purposes.[103] For example: in *R(U) 7/81* a Tribunal of Commissioners held that failure to notify a decision in accordance with a statutory requirement did not render the decision invalid.[104]

2.75 As to the form in which notification must be made, the Tribunal of Commissioners in *R(U) 7/81* considered notification under section 100(2) of the Social Security Act 1975, which required notification in writing of a decision and the reasons for it. The Tribunal decided:

> Also we do not consider that notification of a Computer Centre decision must necessarily take the form of an exact copy of the original; indeed that would be confusing to many persons. But there must be accurate disclosure in clearly intelligible terms of the effect of the decision, and of course the reasons for it must be supplied to the person concerned.[105]

2.76 These decisions are consistent with the effect produced by UTR r7(1) and equivalent provisions. See chapter 7.

## Decision made on invalid grounds

2.77 A decision is not invalid just because it was made on invalid grounds.

2.78 This arises if a tribunal has power to make a form of decision on limited grounds and makes a decision in that form but on other grounds. This was considered by the Tribunal of Commissioners in *R(I) 7/94*. The social security appeal tribunal had power to set aside a tribunal's decision only on procedural grounds. The Tribunal said that a decision to set aside would not be invalid just because it was made on other grounds that were outside the tribunal's power.[106]

## Decision made in error of law

2.79 A decision is not invalid merely because it contains an error of law.

## Decisions made without due process

2.80 A decision is not invalid just because there was unfairness in the procedure that led to it. In *R(I) 7/94*, the Tribunal of Commissioners said that a breach of natural justice 'however gross' did not render a decision invalid.[107] However, in *CGU International Insurance plc v AstraZeneca Insurance Co Ltd*[108] the Court of Appeal said that an unfairness could be

102 [2004] 1 AC 604 at [26].
103 [2004] 1 AC 604, per Lord Millett at [39].
104 *R(U) 7/81* at [21].
105 *R(U) 7/81* at [21].
106 *R(I) 7/94* at [32].
107 *R(I) 7/94* at [32].
108 (2006) *Times* 3 November.

such a substantial defect as to invalidate the decision. This was in the context of the Court of Appeal's residual power to set aside a refusal of leave to appeal from an arbitration.

## Failure to apply the procedure correctly

2.81   In the case of procedural requirements, the trend of authorities has been to focus on the effects of the defect rather than on its nature, and on the impact on those affected rather than on its significance for the essence of the decision. This has at least three consequences. First, the validity of a decision can only be decided in retrospect, once its effects are known. Second, the decision may be valid as against one party or for one purpose, but not against another party or for another purpose. Third, in order to decide the validity of a decision, it may be necessary to balance the competing interests of the persons concerned.

2.82   *R (P) v Haringey London Borough Council*[109] is a good illustration of this approach to invalidity. The case concerned notification of a decision not to reinstate a pupil who had been excluded from a school. The judge held:

> The notices, though defective, are not so defective as not to comply substantially with the legal requirement of notifying the claimant of his right to appeal and are not invalid. Considering the facts, and the absence of any waiver, the consequences which flow from the defects are not critical in this case. If, however, the notices had been given in a form which had misled P's mother into thinking that she had more time to appeal than in fact she had, then the position might have been different.[110]

2.83   Many authorities have analysed this issue in terms of whether he decision made was 'void', 'voidable' and 'nullity'. They have been disapproved on the ground that the terms can only be understood as stating the consequence of a judicial determination rather than the basis for it.[111]

2.84   For a long time, the effect of a failure to comply with a provision depended on whether it was 'mandatory' and 'directory'. Compliance with a mandatory provision was essential to validity, whereas a failure to comply with a directory provision was regarded as a mere irregularity that did not affect the validity of what had been done.

2.85   This distinction was disapproved on the ground that mandatory and directory were not rigid categories but points on a spectrum of non-compliance.[112] They were replaced by a test of whether there had been 'substantial compliance' with the provision.[113]

---

109  [2009] ELR 49.

110  [2009] ELR 49 at [19].

111  Lord Diplock in *Hoffmann-La Roche & Co AG v Secretary of State for Trade and Industry* [1975] AC 295 at 366. The context was the validity of a statutory instrument rather than a decision, but the point is valid for all public law contexts. However, Lord Diplock's historical explanation for the terms is probably not correct.

112  Lord Hailsham in *London and Clydeside Estates Ltd v Aberdeen District Council* [1980] 1 WLR 182 at 189–190.

113  Lord Woolf MR in *R v Secretary of State for the Home Department ex p Jeyeanthan* [2000] 1 WLR 354 at 362.

2.86       This test was in turn replaced by the House of Lords in *R v Soneji*.[114] The test now depends on statutory interpretation. Lord Steyn summarised the law:

> ... the rigid mandatory and directory distinction, and its many technical refinements have outlived their usefulness. Instead, ... the emphasis ought to be on the consequences of non-compliance, and posing the question whether Parliament can fairly be taken to have intended total invalidity. That is how I would approach what is ultimately a question of statutory construction.[115]

However, Lord Carswell said that there might still be some value in the concept of substantial performance.[116]

2.87       The House of Lords has confirmed the importance of a proper analysis of the governing statute, which may indicate the effect of non-compliance and thereby render irrelevant any consideration of the consequences of non-compliance.[117]

2.88       The significance of the failure is determined in the context of the case as a whole. In *R v Sekhon*,[118] Lord Woolf CJ said that the issue in that case was:

> ... the type of issue that courts regularly are required to determine when engaged in case management. The strict compliance with procedural requirements relating to issues of this nature would not normally be expected to go to jurisdiction. The provisions tell the judge the order in which he must deal with matters and the considerations he must have in mind. Any default by the judge can be satisfactorily dealt with on appeal when it is to be expected that the court would examine the circumstances and not focus on technicalities. The issue would be what did justice require having regard to the Parliamentary code.[119]

2.89     The particular issue of failure to comply with rules of procedure is discussed in chapter 7.

## Ordinary and habitual residence

2.90     Every legal system requires parties to have some form of connection with the country before they are allowed access to the courts and tribunals. The form of that connection varies from one area of law to another. Residence is a common connecting factor, of which ordinary and habitual residence are regular variants.

### Ordinary and habitual

2.91     The House of Lords has said that neither of these expressions is a term of art. In *Levene v Inland Revenue Commissioners*,[120] Lord Warrington said so of

114 [2005] 4 All ER 321.
115 [2005] 4 All ER 321 at [23].
116 [2005] 4 All ER 321 at [63].
117 *R v Clarke* [2008] 2 All ER 665.
118 [2003] 1 WLR 1655.
119 [2003] 1 WLR 1655 at [37].
120 [1928] AC 217 at 232.

'ordinary residence'. And in *Re J (A Minor) (Abduction: Custody Rights)*,[121] Lord Brandon said the same of 'habitual residence'. As they are not terms of art, the expressions have their ordinary meanings.

2.92        It is not surprising that the authorities on ordinary and habitual residence are often used interchangeably. However, as ordinary words, their meaning may vary according to the statutory context and purpose.[122] Whether this is so is an issue of law.[123] For example:

- in the context of the Children Act 1989 ordinary residence fulfils 'specific administrative and jurisdictional purposes' and is not to be equated with habitual residence;[124]
- for purposes like founding jurisdiction, it may be necessary that a person must always be ordinarily or habitually resident somewhere.[125]

2.93    It is possible that the context may have the effect that ordinary residence and habitual residence are synonymous. In *Ikimi v Ikimi*,[126] the Court of Appeal considered these terms in defining the divorce jurisdiction. Thorpe LJ said:

> It seems to me that, having traced the origins of the shift in language from 'ordinarily' to 'habitually', precisely the same meaning must be given to each in determining the bounds of this court's divorce jurisdiction. In his speech in the case of *Nessa v Chief Adjudication Officer* [1999] 1 WLR 1937, 1941C–F Lord Slynn left open the question as to whether the two adverbs are always synonymous. But it seems to me plain that they must be so in this field. I am further of the opinion that it is essential that the same meaning be given to 'habitually' wherever it appears in family law statutes. I would not however necessarily make the same extension to the Hague Convention which is an international instrument, the construction of which is settled and developed within the wider field of international jurisprudence.[127]

And in *Mark v Mark*,[128] counsel conceded that the concepts were interchangeable, relying on *Ikimi*.

2.94        As concepts, the House of Lords has accepted that there is a common core of meaning, despite possible differences in the context. In *Nessa v Chief Adjudication Office*,[129] Lord Slynn said of these expressions:

> There is an overlap between the meaning of 'ordinary' and 'habitual' residence and one is sometimes defined in terms of the other . . . I am not satisfied, but it is unnecessary to decide, that they are always synonymous. Each may take a shade of meaning from the context and the object and purpose of the legislation. But there is a common core of meaning which makes it

---

121  [1990] 2 AC 562 at 578.

122  Baroness Hale in *Mark v Mark* [2006] 1 AC 98 at [15].

123  Lord Hoffmann in *Moyna v Secretary of State for Work and Pensions* [2003] 1 WLR 1929 at [24].

124  Wall J in *Re G (Adoption: Ordinary Residence)* [2003] 2 FLR 944 at 951–952.

125  Lord Slynn in *Nessa v Chief Adjudication Officer* [1999] 1 WLR 1937 at 1942.

126  [2002] Fam 72.

127  [2002] Fam 72 at [31].

128  [2006] 1 AC 98 at [3].

129  [1999] 1 WLR 1937.

relevant to consider what has been said in cases dealing with both ordinary and habitual residence.[130]

## Meaning

2.95 In *Shah v Barnet London Borough Council*,[131] Lord Scarman set out the elements of ordinary residence:

> Unless, therefore, it can be shown that the statutory framework or the legal context in which the words are used requires a different meaning, I unhesitatingly subscribe to the view that 'ordinarily resident' refers to a man's abode in a particular place or country which he has adopted voluntarily and for settled purposes as part of the regular order of his life for the time being, whether of short or of long duration.[132]

He explained that the test depends:

> . . . more upon the evidence of matters susceptible of objective proof than upon evidence as to state of mind.[133]

2.96 Whether or not ordinary or habitual residence has been established is an issue of fact[134] that involves an element of judgment in assessing the overall effect of the relevant factors. So, on an appeal on a point of law, the only issue is whether the tribunal's decision was within the bounds of reasonable judgment.[135]

2.97 In *Nessa v Chief Adjudication Officer*,[136] Lord Slynn gave examples of the factors that are relevant to whether habitual residence has been established:

> It is a question of fact to be decided on the date when the determination has to be made on the circumstances of each case whether and when that habitual residence has been established. Bringing possessions, doing everything necessary to establish residence before coming, having a right of abode, seeking to bring family, 'durable ties' with the country of residence or intended residence, and many other factors have to be taken into account.[137]

2.98 Another relevant factor is whether it is possible to identify where the person has lived in the country in question. The Court of Appeal explained the significance of this in *Re Brauch (A Debtor) ex p Britannic Securities and Investments Ltd*.[138] Goff LJ said:

> . . . whether you can say where the debtor was staying during the alleged period of residence or whether you cannot is part of the factors which have to be weighed in determining this question of fact, but I am satisfied that

130 [1999] 1 WLR 1937.
131 [1983] 2 AC 309.
132 [1983] 2 AC 309 at 343–344.
133 [1983] 2 AC 309 at 344.
134 Lord Brandon in *Re J (A Minor) (Abduction: Custody Rights)* [1990] 2 AC 562 at 578. For a comparison with the EC test of habitual residence, see *L-K v K (No 2)* [2007] 2 FLR 729.
135 Lord Hoffmann in *Moyna v Secretary of State for Work and Pensions* [2003] 1 WLR 1929 at [25].
136 [1999] 1 WLR 1937.
137 [1999] 1 WLR 1937 at 1942.
138 [1978] Ch 316.

it is not right to say that you cannot find ordinary residence unless you can specify the place or places at which it has taken place.[139]

Buckley LJ emphasised the relevant issue:

> If the evidence satisfies the court that the debtor has lived in England for a sufficiently substantial period in a manner or for a reason inconsistent with his presence in the country being of a purely transitory character, I can see no reason why the court should be precluded from finding that he ordinarily resided here ... merely because the evidence does not disclose where in England he was living.[140]

2.99    This passage makes the point that the reason for the residence may be of evidentiary value in showing that it was for a settled purpose. In *Kapur v Kapur*,[141] Bush J considered that education was the party's settled purpose for being in the United Kingdom. In *Shah v Barnet London Borough Council*,[142] Lord Scarman included this in a longer list of possibilities:

> Education, business or profession, employment, health, family or merely love of the place spring to mind. And there may be many others.[143]

Later he explained how the evidentiary value of the evidence could vary according to the circumstances:

> A man's settled purpose will be different at different ages. Education in adolescence or early adulthood can be as settled a purpose as a profession or business in later years.[144]

2.100   The length of residence that is necessary in order to establish ordinary or habitual residence depends on the circumstances of the case. In *Nessa v Chief Adjudication Officer*,[145] Lord Slynn said:

> The requisite period is not a fixed period. It may be longer where there are doubts. It may be short ...[146]

2.101   For those who have previously been ordinarily or habitually resident, it is possible to resume that residence immediately on return. Lord Slynn said:

> There may indeed be special cases where the person concerned is not coming here for the first time, but is resuming an habitual residence previously had ... On such facts the adjudication officer may or of course may not be satisfied that the previous habitual residence has been resumed. This position is quite different from that of someone coming to the United Kingdom for the first time.[147]

2.102   Ordinary residence excludes residence that is extraordinary or abnormal. In *R (A) v Secretary of State for Health*,[148] the Court of Appeal held that failed asylum seekers were not ordinarily resident for the purpose of entitlement to free NHS treatment. Ward LJ explained:

---

139 [1978] Ch 316 at 332–333.
140 [1978] Ch 316 at 337.
141 [1984] FLR 920 at 923.
142 [1983] 2 AC 309.
143 [1983] 2 AC 309 at 344.
144 [1983] 2 AC 309 at 344.
145 [1999] 1 WLR 1937.
146 [1999] 1 WLR 1937 at 1943.
147 [1999] 1 WLR 1937 at 1943.
148 [2010] 1 WLR 279.

The words are to be given their ordinary meaning. Asylum seekers are clearly resident here but is the manner in which they have acquired and enjoy that residence ordinary or extraordinary? Normal or abnormal? Were they detained, then no-one would suggest they were ordinarily resident in the place of their detention. While they are here under sufferance pending investigation of their claim they are not, in my judgment, ordinarily resident here. Residence by grace and favour is not ordinary. The words must take some flavour from the purpose of the statute under consideration and, as I have set out above, the purpose of the National Health Act is to provide a service for the people *of* England and that does not include those who ought not to be here. Failed asylum seekers ought not to be here. They should never have come here in the first place and after their claims have finally been dismissed they are only here until arrangements can be made to secure their return, even if, in some cases, like the unfortunate YA, that return may be a long way off.[149]

2.103   The need for residence to be voluntary will only be relevant if the person concerned is being detained. That detention may be lawful or unlawful. It will be lawful if the person is in custody or in hospital by reason of mental or physical health. It will be unlawful if the person has, for example, been forced to move to a country as a member of someone's family or household. According to Lord Scarman in *Shah v Barnet London Borough Council*,[150] the lack of consent is relevant because:

> Enforced presence . . . may be so overwhelming a factor as to negative the will to be where one is.[151]

2.104   However, in *Re MacKenzie, MacKenzie v Attorney-General*,[152] Morton J decided that a woman who had been detained in a lunatic asylum for 54 years had become ordinarily resident in the United Kingdom as a result of that residence. There is a hint in the reasoning that the judge believed that, under the relevant legislation, the claimant had to be ordinarily resident somewhere.[153] If this decision is sound, it is authority that in exceptional circumstances the fact of prolonged residence displaces the need for the residence to be voluntary.

2.105   It is possible that this case would be decided differently today, as a person who has been detained may not be resident. The Court of Appeal has decided that a person who has been detained in prison[154] or, by analogy, under the Mental Health Act 1983 is not resident.

2.106   Ordinary or habitual residence can only be established once the person is resident.[155] A person can only establish residence in a country by being physically present there.[156] However, that presence need not be continuous.[157]

149  [2010] 1 WLR 279 at [61].
150  [1983] 2 AC 309.
151  [1983] 2 AC 309 at 344.
152  [1940] 4 All ER 310.
153  [1940] 4 All ER 310 at 317.
154  *HR (Portugal) v Secretary of State for the Home Department* [2009] EWCA Civ 371; (2009) *Times* 15 June.
155  *Re M (Abduction: Habitual Residence)* [1996] 1 FLR 887 at 895 and 896.
156  *Re A (Wardship: Habitual Residence)* [2007] 1 FLR 1589 at [33].
157  *Re M (Abduction: Habitual Residence)* [1996] 1 FLR 887 at 895 and 896.

2.107    Absence is not necessarily inconsistent with retaining ordinary or habitual residence. What matters is whether the circumstances of the absence show that they are inconsistent with the person establishing or maintaining that residence in a particular place. In appropriate circumstances, an absence may be sufficient to show that the person has abandoned ordinary or habitual residence on the day of departure.[158] A person's intention to return is relevant, but not decisive. In *R v Lancashire County Council ex p Huddleston*,[159] a family left England intending to return. They were kept abroad by the father's employment for 13 years. When the daughter returned to attend university, the local authority decided that she was not ordinarily resident. The Court of Appeal decided that the local authority was entitled to come to that conclusion. It is possible that on these facts today the daughter would have been found to have resumed her ordinary residence immediately on return.[160]

2.108    The habitual residence of a child may be determined by the parent or parents who have parental responsibility for the child. Usually, the child and the person with parental responsibility will have the same habitual residence.[161] It is possible for one parent to change a child's habitual residence unilaterally, although this depends on a factual enquiry tailored to the circumstances of the individual case.[162] The child's state of mind may be relevant, depending on their age and maturity.[163]

## Lawfulness of residence

2.109    In *Mark v Mark*,[164] the House of Lords decided that it is irrelevant for the purpose of the concepts of ordinary and habitual residence whether the person's presence in this country is lawful. However, it may be relevant in three ways.

2.110    First, the statutory context may require this to be implied as a qualification. This is unlikely in tax and divorce jurisdiction cases,[165] but likely in the context of immigration cases.[166]

2.111    Second, even if the person's presence does not have to be lawful as a matter of statutory construction, it may be relevant as evidence of lack of ordinary or habitual residence.[167]

2.112    Third, it may be relevant to whether the residence is ordinary or extraordinary.[168]

158  Lord Brandon in *Re J (A Minor) (Abduction: Custody Rights)* [1990] 2 AC 562 at 578.
159  [1986] 2 All ER 941.
160  See Lord Slynn in *Nessa v Chief Adjudication Officer* [1999] 1 WLR 1937 at 1943.
161  *Re J (A Minor) (Abduction: Custody Rights)* [1990] 2 AC 562.
162  *Re H (Jurisdiction)* [2014] EWCA Civ 1101.
163  *In re LC (Children)* [2014] 2 WLR 124.
164  [2006] 1 AC 98.
165  [2006] 1 AC 98 per Baroness Hale at [31] and [36].
166  [2006] 1 AC 98 at [32].
167  [2006] 1 AC 98 at [36]. Lord Hope said at [13] that a person's lawful presence was relevant to their intention to remain, but not to whether they were actually present here. This was in relation to domicile rather than habitual residence, but the same reasoning may apply.
168  *R (A) v Secretary of State for Health* [2010] 1 WLR 279.

# Finality

2.113 Finality[169] and certainty are legitimate aims of legal policy.[170] However, in public law consistency is also an important consideration[171] that may conflict.

2.114 Finality is secured by a variety of means. For example: estoppel; abuse of process; merger; abuse of power; legitimate expectation; legislative provision; time limits; and the nature of the decision-making process. Judge Richardson summarised the law on estoppel and abuse of process in *Verdin v Harrods Ltd*:[172]

> Firstly, where a cause of action has been determined in litigation between two parties, as a general rule that cause of action cannot be raised again in subsequent litigation between them. The technical term for this principle is cause of action estoppel. Secondly, where an issue has been determined in litigation between two parties, as a general rule that issue cannot be raised again in subsequent litigation between two parties. The technical term for this principle is issue estoppel. Thirdly, even where a cause of action or issue has not been determined in prior litigation between two parties, there may be circumstances in which it would be an abuse of process for the cause of action or issue to be raised between them. The categories of abuse of process are not closed. There may be an abuse of process if a party seeks to litigate an issue which should have been raised in earlier proceedings. There may be an abuse of process if a party seeks to litigate an issue which has been decided in a test case by which it was understood he would be bound.

## Time limits

2.115 There will almost always be an express limit on the time within which proceedings may be initiated. If there is, it operates in effect as a bar on raising the issue in those proceedings and to that extent provides for finality. However, the legislation may allow a challenge by other means. For example: the decision-maker may have power to change the tribunal's decision.[173]

2.116 A time limit must comply with article 6. This requires that a party must have access to a tribunal. That right is violated if sufficient time is not allowed. The issue was considered by the Court of Appeal on an application for permission to appeal in *Denson v Secretary of State for Work and*

---

169 Finality as used here includes, but is wider than, estoppel. It has been suggested that finality should be used instead of estoppel on the ground that it is clearer – see *Cross and Tapper on Evidence*, 10th edn, LexisNexis, p95 n89. However, here finality is used in its broader sense. Legislation may distinguish between finality and conclusiveness. For example: Social Security Act 1998 s17(1) provides that a decision is final on the issue of entitlement or payment that it covers, while s17(2) provides that findings of fact and determinations within it are conclusive for the purpose of other decisions.

170 *Denson v Secretary of State for Work and Pensions* reported as *R(CS) 4/04* at [24]. For convenience, reference throughout the remainder of this section will be to finality only.

171 See chapter 14.

172 [2006] ICR 396 at [24].

173 For example: see the decision-maker's powers under regulation 6 of the Social Security and Child Support (Decisions and Appeals) Regulations 1999.

*Pensions.*[174] The Court was concerned with the time for appealing to a tribunal in a child support case. The legislation allowed 28 days with the possibility of extension for cause to a maximum of 13 months. The Court decided that limiting the period in which an appeal could be made pursued the aim of certainty and finality, which was a legitimate aim, and that the time period allowed was proportionate to that aim.[175]

## Issues that have been, or could have been, decided already

2.117   Most decisions are final when taken and communicated. Some are provisional. An instance of this is a conditional discharge of a patient in a mental health case. This is ordered on the basis that the patient can be satisfactorily treated and supervised in the community, provided the conditions of discharge are satisfied. It is treated as provisional only. If it turns out that the conditions cannot be met, the tribunal is entitled to substitute a different decision.[176]

2.118   It is necessary to distinguish three lines of authority. One deals with civil law cases, a second with public law cases and a third with cases decided by an inquisitorial procedure.

### Civil law cases[177]

2.119   The finality of the decision in proceedings or of a conclusion on an issue within a decision is governed by estoppel. There are different varieties of estoppel; some are rules of evidence, others rules of policy. The variety relevant to this issue is known by the Latin tag of *res judicata*. The principles of res judicata are not rules of evidence. They are rules of policy that bring finality to litigation.[178]

2.120   As between the parties to a case and their privies,[179] the outcome decision of a case is binding. This is because the cause of action is merged into the judgment and ceases to exist.[180] This extends to issues that could have been, but were not, raised in the earlier proceedings.

2.121   The parties are also bound by the court's conclusions on issues that are the component parts of the cause of action. However, this is applied less rigidly than estoppel of the outcome of a cause of action. Diplock LJ explained this in *Mills v Cooper*:[181]

> . . . a party to civil proceedings is not entitled to make, as against the other party, an assertion, whether of fact or of the legal consequences of facts, the correctness of which is an essential element in his cause of action or

---

174   *R(CS) 4/04.*

175   At [24]–[26].

176   *R (H) v Secretary of State for the Home Department* [2004] 2 AC 253.

177   This includes criminal law.

178   Diplock LJ in *Mills v Cooper* [1967] 2 QB 459 at 469. Accordingly, UTR r15(2) and its equivalents do not apply.

179   One party may be privy to another by blood, title or interest. For convenience, no further reference is made to privies in this section.

180   Diplock LJ in *Thoday v Thoday* [1964] P 181 at 197. A former employee's cause of action in the county court for wrongful dismissal merges with the judgment of an employment tribunal on wrongful dismissal: *Fraser v HLMAD Ltd* [2006] ICR 1395.

181   [1967] 2 QB 459.

defence, if the same assertion was an essential element in his previous cause of action or defence in civil proceedings between the same parties or their predecessors in title and was found by a court of competent jurisdiction in such previous civil proceedings to be incorrect, unless further material which is relevant to the correctness of the assertion and could not by reasonable diligence have been adduced by that party in the previous proceedings has since become available to him.[182]

2.122 As between different parties, sections 11 and 12 of the Civil Evidence Act 1968 apply, but only for courts and those tribunals to which the strict rules of evidence apply.[183] Section 11 deals with convictions. It provides that a conviction is evidence that the accused committed that offence. The relevant provisions are:

(1) In any civil proceedings the fact that a person has been convicted of an offence by or before any court in the United Kingdom or by a court-martial there or elsewhere shall (subject to subsection (3) below) be admissible in evidence for the purpose of proving, where to do so is relevant to any issue in those proceedings, that he committed that offence, whether he was so convicted upon a plea of guilty or otherwise and whether or not he is a party to the civil proceedings; but no conviction other than a subsisting one shall be admissible in evidence by virtue of this section.

(2) In any civil proceedings in which by virtue of this section a person is proved to have been convicted of an offence by or before any court in the United Kingdom or by a court-martial there or elsewhere–

(a) he shall be taken to have committed that offence unless the contrary is proved; and

(b) without prejudice to the reception of any other admissible evidence for the purpose of identifying the facts on which the conviction was based, the contents of any document which is admissible as evidence of the conviction, and the contents of the information, complaint, indictment or charge-sheet on which the person in question was convicted, shall be admissible in evidence for that purpose.

(3) Nothing in this section shall prejudice the operation of section 13 of this Act or any other enactment whereby a conviction or a finding of fact in any criminal proceedings is for the purposes of any other proceedings made conclusive evidence of any fact.

2.123 The conviction is only evidence of guilt. It is not evidence of other matters that are not necessarily involved in the offence. Apart from subsection (3), there is no provision that the fact of conviction is conclusive for later proceedings. In other words, its probative worth has to be assessed in the context of the evidence as a whole.

2.124 Section 12 deals with findings of adultery and paternity. The former are unlikely to be relevant to a tribunal, but the latter may. The previous finding is evidence of paternity, but is not conclusive.

2.125 If neither the principles of res judicata nor sections 11 and 12 of the Civil Evidence Act 1968 apply, a finding of fact in one proceeding in not admissible as evidence in later proceedings.[184] The reason is that the

---

182 [1967] 2 QB 459 at 468–469. See also Lord Keith in *Arnold v National Westminster Bank plc* [1991] 2 AC 93 at 104 and 109.

183 See the definition in Civil Evidence Act 1968 s18(1).

184 *Secretary of State for Trade and Industry v Bairstow* [2004] Ch 1 at [15]–[27].

finding represents the opinion of the fact-finder and that opinion is not relevant evidence in other proceedings.[185] This is, of course, subject to statutory provision that makes a finding of fact relevant, or even conclusive,[186] for other purposes. And UTR r15(2)(a) and its equivalents allow a tribunal to admit evidence that would otherwise be inadmissible.

2.126     However, even between different parties in separate civil proceedings, the court may refuse to allow findings in the earlier proceedings to be challenged if that would be an abuse of the process of the court.[187] The principles were set out by Sir Andrew Morritt V-C in *Secretary of State for Trade and Industry v Bairstow*:[188]

> (a) A collateral attack on an earlier decision of a court of competent jurisdiction may be but is not necessarily an abuse of the process of the court.
> (b) If the earlier decision is that of a court exercising a criminal jurisdiction then, because of the terms of ss11 to 13 Civil Evidence Act 1968, the conviction will be conclusive in the case of later defamation proceedings but will constitute *prima facie* evidence only in the case of other civil proceedings. . . .
> (c) If the earlier decision is that of a court exercising a civil jurisdiction then it is binding on the parties to that action and their privies in any later civil proceedings.
> (d) If the parties to the later civil proceedings were not parties to or privies of those who were parties to the earlier proceedings then it will only be an abuse of the process of the court to challenge the factual findings and conclusions of the judge or jury in the earlier action if (i) it would be manifestly unfair to a party to the later proceedings that the same issues should be relitigated or (ii) to permit such relitigation would bring the administration of justice into disrepute.[189]

Public law defences in private law cases require a different approach. The tribunal may allow them to be raised again if the circumstances warrant it.[190]

## Public law cases

2.127     The principles of estoppel can apply to public law cases.[191] In *Thrasyvoulou v Secretary of State for the Environment*,[192] the House of Lords was concerned with a second enforcement notice issued by a local authority against the owner of premises. The owner had successfully appealed against a previous enforcement notice on the same grounds. The House of Lords decided that the local authority could not raise the issue again. Lord Bridge set out the test for whether the principles of estoppel applied to public law cases:

---

185  See also chapter 10.
186  Social Security Act 1998 s17(2) is an example.
187  An application on this ground was rejected by the Court of Appeal in *Simms v Conlon* [2007] 3 All ER 802.
188  [2004] Ch 1.
189  [2004] Ch 1 at [38].
190  *Barber v Croydon LBC* [2010] HLR 26.
191  But see the comments of Lord Hoffmann in *R v East Sussex County Council ex p Reprotech (Pebsham) Ltd* [2003] 1 WLR 348 at [35], quoted below, on the usefulness of estoppel in public law.
192  [1990] 2 AC 273.

In principle they must apply equally to adjudications in the field of public law. In relation to adjudications subject to a comprehensive self-contained statutory code, the presumption, in my opinion, must be that where the statute has created a specific jurisdiction for the determination of any issue which establishes the existence of a legal right, the principle of *res judicata* applies to give finality to that determination unless an intention to exclude that principle can properly be inferred as a matter of construction of the relevant statutory provisions.[193]

2.128    The courts and the Upper Tribunal have recognised the relevance of a statutory code. In *Staffordshire County Council v Barber*,[194] the Court of Appeal held that a later industrial (now employment) tribunal could not consider a fresh claim on the same issue. In so deciding, the court took account of the tribunal's power to review its own decisions in the interests of justice.[195] In *White v Aldridge QC and the London Borough of Ealing*,[196] the Court of Appeal held that it was not necessary to consider whether estoppel applied in a Special Educational Needs Tribunal in view of its power to strike out cases that were frivolous or vexatious. And in *RC v CMEC and WC*,[197] the Upper Tribunal took account of the effects on estoppel of a statutory decision-making framework: see the section on 'Inquisitorial proceedings' below at para 2.144.

2.129    If estoppel does apply, the issue may arise whether there is privity of interest between different Secretaries of State. The issue arose in *R (Nahar) v Social Security Commissioners*.[198] The factual issue was whether the claimant was married. The immigration authorities decided that she was, but the social security authorities decided that she was not. The Commissioner refused leave to appeal and the claimant sought a judicial review. Munby J dismissed the application. His reason was:

> I am satisfied that there can here be no issue estoppel. In my judgment there is neither identity of parties nor any sufficient privity of interest as between the Entry Clearance Officer and/or the Secretary of State for the Home Department on the one hand and the Secretary of State for Work and Pensions on the other hand. On that simple but fundamental ground the claimant's case must fail insofar as it is based on issue estoppel.[199]

2.130    In addition to estoppel, the nature of the decision or the decision-making process may provide for finality or limit the scope of finality.

2.131    As to the nature of the decision, this may be more limited in public law case than in a civil one. A civil law case is likely to deal with an issue for all time. A decision on, say, criminality or negligence is definitive between the parties. This is also possible in a public law case. But it is also possible that the outcome in a public law case is limited to a particular application, basis (like a claim for a particular social security benefit) or period (like a tax year).

193 [1990] 2 AC 273 at 289.
194 [1996] ICR 379.
195 [1996] ICR 379 at 392.
196 [1999] ELR 150.
197 [2009] UKUT 62 (AAC).
198 [2002] 1 FLR 670.
199 [2002] 1 FLR 670 at [51].

2.132    If the proceedings deal with a particular application, basis or period, the tribunal's findings of fact and conclusions of law will not, subject to contrary provision, be binding in respect of a different application, basis or period. They may also be limited to a particular claim or application. For example: a decision based on the credibility of a party is not binding in a later case in which the party appears as a witness.[200]

2.133    One reason for this is that the tribunal had no jurisdiction over any other application, basis or period.[201] The proceedings are initiated in respect of a particular application, issue or period. That, in turn, limits the jurisdiction of the tribunal and the extent to which its decision is binding. The tribunal may have to decide an issue, but it only has jurisdiction to do that in the context of the particular case. It does not have a general jurisdiction to decide the issue once and for all time. The House of Lords dealt with this point in *Society of Medical Officers of Health v Hope*.[202] The House was there concerned with a decision by a local valuation court in respect of a particular year of assessment. Referring to the valuation court's limited jurisdiction, Lord Radcliffe said:

> For that limited purpose it is a court with a jurisdiction competent to produce a final decision between the parties before it: but it is not a court of competent jurisdiction to decide general questions of law with that finality which is needed to set up the estoppel *per rem judicatam* that arises in certain contexts from legal judgments.[203]

2.134    This was also the view of the Privy Council in *Caffoor v Commissioners of Income Tax, Colombo*.[204] The issue was whether a decision made in one year of assessment was binding as to that issue in later years. The Council decided that it was not. Lord Radcliffe said:

> . . . it is not the status of the tribunal itself, judicial or administrative, that forms the determining element for estoppel in cases of this kind but the limited nature of the question that is within the tribunal's jurisdiction.[205]

2.135    A second reason for this result is that the decision-makers and the public bodies for whom they act are not contentious parties.[206] So, unlike in most litigation, there is no dispute between the parties. There is only an issue to be resolved.[207] Even if the public body is not itself a party to the proceedings, there is no real dispute. *Boulter v The Justices of Kent*[208] was a case involving an application before the justices for a licence in respect of a public house. Lord Herschell said:

200  *Ocampo v Secretary of State for the Home Department* [2006] EWCA Civ 1276, reported in (2006) *Times* 27 October as *GO (Colombia) v Secretary of State for the Home Department*.

201  Lord Radcliffe in *Society of Medical Officers of Health v Hope* [1960] AC 551 at 565–566.

202  [1960] AC 551.

203  [1960] AC 551 at 563–564.

204  [1961] AC 584. The Council refused to follow its earlier decision in *Hoystead v Commissioner of Taxation* [1926] AC 155.

205  [1961] AC 584 at 599. See also *Matalan Retail Ltd v Commissioners of Revenue and Customs* [2009] EWHC 2046 (Ch), (2009) *Times* 21 October.

206  Lord Radcliffe in *Society of Medical Officers of Health v Hope* [1960] AC 551 at 563–565.

207  See chapter 1.

208  [1897] AC 556.

There is, in truth, no *lis*, no controversy *inter partes*, and no decision in favour of one of them against the other, unless, indeed, the entire public are regarded as the other party . . .[209]

2.136 A third reason producing the same result is that, if a statutory duty is involved, the application of a statutory duty cannot be abrogated by estoppel. In *Society of Medical Officers of Health v Hope*,[210] the House of Lords was concerned with a valuation for rating purposes by a valuation officer. Lord Keith said:

. . . a public officer in the position of the respondent [the valuation officer] cannot be estopped from carrying out his duties under the statute.[211]

2.137 And in *Commissioners of Inland Revenue v Brooks*,[212] Lord Parker said:

. . . where there is a statutory provision requiring an estimate to be made for a statutory purpose and by a statutory authority, the principle of estoppel cannot be invoked to render the provision nugatory in cases where such principle might otherwise have applied.[213]

2.138 Of course, none of this prevents a decision in one proceedings being relevant in later proceedings. For example: a decision on an issue in respect of one tax year may be a cogent factor in determining the same point in a later year.[214] Indeed, it may be improper to argue for a different result in the absence of new evidence or circumstances. For example: a tribunal's decision to discharge a patient is a decision on a particular application. There is no legislation that prevents an immediate application for readmission. Nevertheless, the House of Lords has decided that an application for re-admission must be based on fresh facts not known to the tribunal.[215]

2.139 The decision-making process may also provide for or limit the scope of finality.

2.140 It is not permissible to have more than one decision governing the same issue for the same period. As the Tribunal of Commissioners explained in *R(I) 9/63*:

. . . it is not legally possible to have two decisions by different boards or tribunals on an identical question relating to the same period, which conflict with each other. Nor indeed is it convenient to have two decisions even to the same effect, since if one were reviewed there would then be a conflict.[216]

2.141 A decision, once finally made, cannot be changed except with legislative authority, regardless of whether or not there has been reliance or detrimental reliance. *Re 56 Denton Road, Twickenham*[217] concerned a decision

---

209 [1897] AC 556 at 569.
210 [1960] AC 551.
211 [1960] AC 551 at 568.
212 [1915] AC 478.
213 [1915] AC 478 at 491–492. See also *Maritime Electric Co Ltd v General Dairies Ltd* [1937] AC 610 at 620.
214 Lord Hanworth MR in *Commissioners of Inland Revenue v Sneath* [1932] 2 KB 362 at 384.
215 *R (von Brandenburg) v East London and The City Mental Health NHS Trust* [2004] 2 AC 280.
216 *R(I) 9/63* at [18].
217 [1953] Ch 51.

by the War Damage Commission on the damage to a property. The Commission first made a preliminary decision. Then it changed it in a way that was more favourable to the owner. Finally it attempted to revert to its original decision. The court held that the second decision, the one most favourable to the owner, was final and irrevocable. Vaisey J accepted the proposition that:

> ... where Parliament confers upon a body such as the War Damage Commission the duty of deciding or determining any question, the deciding or determining of which affects the rights of the subject, such decision or determination made and communicated in terms which are not expressly preliminary or provisional is final and conclusive, and cannot in the absence of express statutory power or the consent of the person or persons affected be altered or withdrawn by the body.[218]

The judge went on to say that this principle 'ought not to be denied its proper force and effect' whether or not the owner had altered her position in reliance on the Commission's decision.[219]

2.142    Legislation may provide that a decision is final subject to permissible challenges.[220] An express provision on finality does not bar a claim for a judicial review.[221] That wording is not sufficient to prevent a claim for negligence against a decision-maker.[222]

2.143    The legislation may provide for a decision, or its continuing operation, to be affected by a decision of a court, of a tribunal (including the tribunal that made the decision)[223] or of a decision-maker.[224]

## Inquisitorial proceedings

2.144    In *R(I) 9/63*, a Tribunal of Commissioners (whose proceedings were inquisitorial) said that estoppel did not directly apply to tribunals, but that they proceeded by analogy.[225] This statement was never developed by the Commissioners.

2.145    In *Thoday v Thoday*,[226] Diplock LJ said that estoppel did not apply to proceedings that were inquisitorial:

> 'Estoppel' merely means that, under the rules of the adversary system of procedure upon which the common law of England is based, a party is not allowed, in certain circumstances, to prove in litigation particular facts or matters which, if proved, would assist him to succeed as plaintiff or defendant in an action. If the court is required to exercise an inquisitorial function and may inquire into facts which the parties do not choose to prove, or would under the rules of the adversary system be prevented from proving, this is a function to which the common law concept of estoppel is alien. It may well be a rational rule to apply in the exercise of such an inquisitorial

---

218  [1953] Ch 51 at 56–57.
219  [1953] Ch 51 at 57.
220  Social Security Act 1998 s17(1) is an example.
221  *R v Medical Appeal Tribunal ex p Gilmore* [1957] 1 QB 574.
222  *Jones v Department of Employment* [1989] QB 1.
223  For example: UTR r47.
224  For example: Social Security and Child Support (Decisions and Appeals) Regulations 1999 regs 4 and 6.
225  [1964] P 181 at [24].
226  [1964] P 181.

function to say that if a court having jurisdiction to do so has once inquired into the truth of a particular allegation of fact and reached a decision thereon, another court of co-ordinate jurisdiction in the exercise of its own discretion should not re-embark upon the same inquiry, but should accept the decision of the first court. But this is a different concept from estoppel as hitherto known in English law.[227]

2.146   Diplock LJ's suggestion has been considered and developed in cases involving children, in which the proceedings are inquisitorial. In *Re B (Minors) (Care Proceedings: Issue Estoppel)*,[228] the court reviewed the family law cases. Those cases had refused to apply the rigid rules of estoppel, preferring Diplock LJ's discretionary approach. Hale J set out some of the factors that had to be balanced in cases under the Children Act 1989: the interests of finality, the importance of the issue in the earlier proceedings, and the likelihood that a different outcome would be reached in the later proceedings.[229]

2.147   This was applied more widely in cases involving children by the Court of Appeal in *White v Aldridge QC and the London Borough of Ealing*.[230] Butler-Sloss LJ said:

> In cases with an inquisitorial element, the approach, as Diplock LJ explained, is not the same as in strict common-law litigation. Since the court has its own function to perform to arrive at the right result, independent of the submissions of the parties, it has to adopt a degree of flexibility to an application to strike out or to refuse to hear evidence on certain issues. But the underlying principle not to relitigate the same issue twice applies in all cases of an inquisitorial nature including Children Act cases.[231]

2.148   Hale J's analysis has been adapted to child support proceedings, which are subject to a statutory decision-making framework. In *RC v CMEC and WC*,[232] the Upper Tribunal said:

> Hale J's advice needs some adjustment for application in the child support scheme. Tribunals must make the best findings they can on the information and evidence available to them. The information may include findings made by previous tribunals and family courts. The significance of those findings will depend on their reliability and relevance. In assessing their reliability, tribunals must consider: (i) the evidence on which they were based; (ii) the nature of the fact-finding process (for example, whether the parent was subject to cross-examination); and (iii) the evidence now available. If there is no evidence to the contrary, tribunals may be entitled to conclude that the findings previously made are sufficient and reliable in the child support context. Whether or not this is so will depend on their relevance in the particular case. In assessing the relevance of previous findings, tribunals must consider: (iv) the facts that are relevant to the issue before the tribunal; (v) the precision with which they have to be found in order to apply the legislation; (vi) whether the previous findings relate, or can be related by other evidence, to the time now in issue; and (vii) the extent to

---

227  [1964] P 181 at 197.
228  [1997] Fam 117.
229  [1997] Fam 117 per Hale J at 128–129.
230  [1999] ELR 150.
231  [1999] ELR 150 at 157.
232  [2009] UKUT 62 (AAC).

which the issues in the previous proceedings affected the evidence that was obtained or the facts that were found.[233]

## Issues covered by an inquiry

2.149    The report of an inquiry is admissible on the findings of fact and on the conclusions reached, for example on a person's suitability for particular work, but it is not binding on a tribunal, provided the tribunal explains why and in what respects it differs in its findings or conclusions.[234]

## Statements and promises

2.150    Statements or promises made by a party outside litigation may prevent that party taking a different position in litigation. This is covered by estoppel by representation and promissory estoppel. They are not dealt with here.[235] These principles are not applicable to the acts, statements and promises of a public authority.

2.151        It is not possible to prevent a public authority from enforcing a duty. In *Maritime Electric Co Ltd v General Dairies Ltd*,[236] the Privy Council was concerned with a case in which a public utility company considerably underbilled a customer for electricity supplied. The Council held that the utility company was not bound by this mistake. Lord Maugham said:

> . . . where, as here, the statute imposes a duty of a positive kind, not avoidable by the performance of any formality, for the doing of the very act which the plaintiff seeks to do, it is not open to the defendant to set up an estoppel to prevent it. This conclusion must follow from the circumstance that an estoppel is only a rule of evidence which in certain circumstances can be invoked by a party to an action; it cannot therefore avail in such a case to release the plaintiff from an obligation to obey such a statute, nor can it enable the defendant to escape from a statutory obligation of such a kind on his part. It is immaterial whether the obligation is onerous or otherwise to the party suing. The duty of each party is to obey the law.[237]

2.152    Nor is it possible to prevent a public authority from exercising a discretion in a particular way. In *Southend-on-Sea Corporation v Hodgson (Wickford) Ltd*,[238] the Divisional Court of Queen's Bench was concerned with a local authority's enforcement notice in respect of work carried on at premises without planning permission. The defence to this was that an officer of the local authority has stated in advance that the work did not involve a change of use and so did not require permission. Accordingly, it was argued that the local authority could not exercise its discretion to issue an enforcement notice. The Court rejected this argument. Lord Parker CJ said:

> I can see no logical distinction between a case ... of an estoppel being sought to be raised to prevent the performance of a statutory duty and one where it is sought to be raised to hinder the exercise of a statutory discretion. After

233 [2009] UKUT 62 (AAC) at [57].
234 Leveson J in *Secretary of State for Education and Skills v Mairs* [2005] ICR 1714.
235 See books on estoppel and evidence.
236 [1937] AC 610.
237 [1937] AC 610 at 620.
238 [1962] 1 QB 416.

all, in a case of discretion there is a duty under the statute to exercise a free and unhindered discretion.[239]

This line of authority is now subject to the developing law on legitimate expectation.

2.153    It is not possible to require a public authority to act outside its powers. In *Minister of Agriculture and Fisheries v Matthews*,[240] the Divisional Court of King's Bench was concerned with the validity of a lease purportedly granted by the Ministry. Cassels J held that the Ministry could not be stopped from denying the validity of the lease on the grounds that it had no power to grant it. He said:

> ... the plaintiff [the Minister] is a statutory and not an actual person and can, therefore, only perform the acts which he is empowered to perform.[241]

2.154    Legitimate expectation cannot be relied on to require a public body to act contrary to statute.[242]

2.155    However, it is possible to hold a public authority to a decision that is subject to a technical irregularity. So in *Wells v Minister of Housing and Local Government*,[243] the plaintiff was informed by a local authority that permission was not required for a particular use of their land. The plaintiff did not formally apply for a determination whether the use would involve development. However, the Court of Appeal held that the local authority's letter was effective as a determination. Lord Denning MR said:

> Now I know that a public authority cannot be estopped from doing its public duty, but I do think that it can be estopped from relying on technicalities; and this is a technicality to be sure. ... I take the law to be that a defect in procedure can be cured, and an irregularity can be waived, even by a public authority, so as to render valid that which would otherwise be invalid.[244]

This principle was accepted by the courts, although it only applied to the benefit of a party who had relied detrimentally on the public authority's statement or action.[245]

2.156    However, in *R (Reprotech (Pebsham) Ltd) v East Sussex County Council*,[246] the House of Lords left open whether *Wells* was correctly decided.[247] More to the point, Lord Hoffmann, with whom all the other Law Lords agreed, said:

> It is true that in early cases such as the *Wells* case ... Lord Denning MR used the language of estoppel in relation to planning law. At that time the public law concepts of abuse of power and legitimate expectation were undeveloped and no doubt the analogy of estoppel seemed useful. ... It seems to me that in this area, public law has already developed whatever

239 [1962] 1 QB 416 at 423–424.
240 [1950] 1 KB 148.
241 [1950] 1 KB 148 at 153.
242 *R v Secretary of State for Education and Employment ex p Begbie* [2000] 1 WLR 1115 at 1125 and 1132; *R (Nadarajah) v Secretary of State for the Home Department* (2005) *Times* 14 December.
243 [1967] 1 WLR 1000.
244 [1967] 1 WLR 1000 at 1007.
245 *Norfolk County Council v Secretary of State for the Environment* [1973] 1 WLR 1400.
246 [2003] 1 WLR 348.
247 [2003] 1 WLR 348 per Lord Hoffmann at [30].

is useful from the moral values which underlie the private law concept of estoppel and the time has come for it to stand upon its own two feet.[248]

2.157   The full implications of this approach for planning law, for other areas of public law and for the effect of previous decisions in litigation have not developed.

2.158      Legislation may make specific provision.[249]

248  [2003] 1 WLR 348 at [35].
249  For example: Nationality, Immigration and Asylum Act 2002 s96.

# CHAPTER 3

# Procedure

*continued*

## Principles of procedural justice

3.1   Courts and tribunals have always needed rules of procedure to govern their proceedings. Those rules were not chosen randomly. They were chosen because they were internally consistent and appropriate to the types of case and to the nature of the proceedings involved. They also, no doubt, reflected the preferences of those who made them. The modern approach is to have general principles and consistency of provisions across jurisdictions.

3.2   Over the past 100 years, basic principles of procedural justice have been developed and recognised. In any modern system of procedure, these principles describe, explain, justify, control the content of, and govern the application of the specific rules of procedure. All the principles set out below are consistent with, and provide considerations relevant to the application of, the overriding objective and the duty to co-operate.

3.3   Viewed broadly, there have been four stages to the development. At first, the courts imposed minimum judicial control over tribunals. Next, principles appropriate to tribunals were identified and developed separately from the courts. Then, general principles were developed for court procedure. Finally, those principles were adopted and adapted for tribunals.

## The essential features of judicial decision-making

3.4   The courts applied the most basic principles of procedural justice to tribunals: they had to comply with the principles of natural justice and to act only within their powers. This was the first focus for procedural justice: the judge's approach to the proceedings in an individual case. These principles reflect or embody basic characteristics of judicial decision-making: that the parties must be given the chance to put their sides of a case and the judge must decide objectively under and according to law.

3.5   The Donoughmore Committee on *Ministers' Powers*, which reported in 1932,[1] considered that these were sufficient safeguards for the tribunals of the time.[2]

## Effective access

3.6   This assumed that the parties were before the tribunal and able to participate in the proceedings. Those assumptions were not necessarily valid for the types of case that come before tribunals. Tribunals responded to this by developing a second focus for procedural justice: the parties, especially lay parties. They developed procedures and approaches that increased the chances of effective access for lay parties, whether represented or not.[3] Again, the focus is on the individual case.

3.7   The approach developed by the tribunals was bolstered by Professor Kathleen Bell's *Research Study on Supplementary Benefit Appeal Tribunals*, which was published in 1975. This considered the approach of the tribunal

---

1   Cmd. 4060 (1932).
2   Section III para 11.
3   This is now an aspect of article 6.

to the parties and the atmosphere in the hearing, recommending the enabling approach towards the parties.[4]

## Systemic considerations

3.8  Professor Bell's study exemplified the approach of identifying the principles underlying the disparate practices of different tribunals, building on best practice and leading the way in the development of new principles. In doing so, a new focus was added beyond the individual case: the requirements of the tribunal system as a whole, including the efficient use of public funds and the appropriate allocation of resources between cases.

## General principles

3.9  It was natural that these three component features of procedural justice – the essential nature of the judicial functions, effective access and systemic considerations – should be embodied in a wider analysis that identified the unifying and underlying general principles of procedural justice.

### The Franks Committee

3.10  The Franks Committee on *Administrative Tribunals and Enquiries*, which reported in 1957,[5] went beyond basic protection for the parties and based its recommendations around three principles appropriate in the context of tribunals – openness, fairness and impartiality:

> In the field of tribunals openness appears to us to require the publicity of proceedings and knowledge of the essential reasoning underlying the decisions; fairness to require the adoption of a clear procedure which enables the parties to know their rights, to present their case fully and to know the case which they have to meet; and impartiality to require the freedom of tribunals from the influence, real or apparent, of Departments concerned with the subject-matter of their decision.[6]

### The Woolf Report

3.11  In his report on *Access to Justice*,[7] Lord Woolf identified the principles on which a system of civil justice should be based:

> The system should:
> (a) be *just* in the results it delivers;
> (b) be *fair* in the way in treats litigants;
> (c) offer appropriate procedures at a reasonable *cost*;
> (d) deal with cases with reasonable *speed*;
> (e) be *understandable* to those who use it;
> (f) be *responsive* to the needs of those who use it;
> (g) provide as much *certainty* as the nature of particular cases allows; and
> (h) be *effective*: adequately resourced and organised.[8]

---

4  *Review of Main Findings: Conclusions: Recommendations* (1975) pp18 and 22. See chapter 1.
5  Cmnd 218 (1957).
6  Cmnd 218 (1957) at para 42.
7  HMSO 1996.
8  *Access to Justice*, HMSO, 1996, Section 1, para 1.

3.12   He then described the features of a system based on those principles. Shorn of their supporting paragraphs, the features were:[9]

- litigation will be avoided wherever possible;
- litigation will be less adversarial and more co-operative;
- litigation will be less complex;
- the timescale of litigation will be shorter and more certain;
- the cost of litigation will be more affordable, more predictable, and more proportionate to the value and complexity of individual cases;
- parties of limited financial means will be able to conduct litigation on a more equal footing;
- there will be clear lines of judicial and administrative responsibility for the civil justice system;
- the structure of the courts and the deployment of judges will be designed to meet the needs of litigants;
- judges will be deployed effectively so that they can manage litigation in accordance with the new rules and protocols;
- the civil justice system will be responsive to the needs of litigants.

3.13   This found legislative expression in the requirement of section 1(3) of the Civil Procedure Act 1997 that: 'The power to make Civil Procedure Rules is to be exercised with a view to securing that the civil justice system is acces-sible, fair and efficient'.

3.14   Lord Woolf's principles were developed for the courts, but they had the potential to be extended to tribunals.

### The Bowman Report

3.15   The Committee chaired by Sir Jeffery Bowman investigated appeals, following and building on the Woolf proposals. In chapter 2 of its *Review of the Court of Appeal (Civil Division)* of September 1997, it set out a number of general principles governing appeals:

- a civil appeal should be dealt with in ways which reflect the principles which Lord Woolf recommended the civil justice system should meet;
- an appeal should not be seen as an automatic further stage in a case;
- an individual who has grounds for dissatisfaction with the outcome of his or her case should always be able to have the case looked at by a higher court so that it can consider whether there appears to have been an injustice and, if so, allow an appeal to proceed;
- an appeal process should ensure that, so far as is practical, uncertainty and delay are reduced to a minimum;
- there is a private and a public purpose of appeals in civil cases: the private purpose is to correct an error, unfairness or wrong exercise of discretion which has led to an unjust result. The public purpose is to ensure public confidence in the administration of justice and, in appropriate cases, to:
  - clarify and develop the law, practice and procedure; and
  - help maintain the standards of first instance courts and tribunals;

---

9  *Access to Justice*, HMSO, 1996, Section 1, para 9.

- appeals should always be dealt with in ways that are proportionate to the grounds of complaint and the subject matter of the dispute;
- more than one level of appeal cannot normally be justified except in restricted circumstances where there is an important point of principle or practice or one which for some other special reason should be considered by the Court of Appeal.

3.16 As with Lord Woolf's principles, these principles were developed for the courts, but they had the potential to be extended to tribunals.

## The Leggatt Report

3.17 Sir Andrew Leggatt, in the report that followed his *Review of Tribunals*,[10] identified:

> ... the watchwords which should inform every tribunal: informality, simplicity, efficiency, and proportionality.[11]

3.18 That deceptively simple analysis paved the way for adapting to the tribunal context the general principles that had been developed for the courts. That task was made easier by the proposal that there should be a coherent structure for tribunals to replace the separate tribunals for each jurisdiction.

## The Council on Tribunals

3.19 Shortly after the Leggatt Report was published, the Council on Tribunals[12] published a detailed *Framework of Standards for Tribunals*.[13] These ranged from the most basic constitutional principles, like independence, to the most practical, like payment of expenses:

> **Standard 1: Tribunals should be independent and provide open, fair and impartial hearings**
> a) Tribunals should be free to reach decisions according to law without influence (actual or perceived) from the body or person whose decision is being challenged or appealed, or from anyone else.
> b) Judicial officers should be independent.
> c) Appointments to judicial office should take account of the diversity of our society, and the composition of tribunals should be monitored to inform those making appointments.
> d) Tribunal hearings should be open and fair.
>
> **Standard 2: Tribunals should be accessible to users and focus on the needs of users**
> a) Potential users of the tribunal should be given access to information about its services.
> b) Procedural Rules should be short, clear, simple, and up to date.
> c) Forms should be short and simple.
> d) The papers required by the tribunal should be proportionate and appropriate to the issues at stake.
> e) Tribunals should provide users with clear information about how their case will be handled.

10 *Tribunals for Users – One System, One Service* (2001).
11 *Tribunals for Users – One System, One Service* (2001) at para 31.
12 Subsequently replaced by the Administrative Justice and Tribunals Council, which has itself now been abolished.
13 2002, updated in 2006.

f)  A complaints policy and procedure should be in place in relation to the performance of both judiciary and administration, and should be publicised to users.

g)  Tribunals should establish and publish a clear policy on the payment of travelling expenses.

h)  Tribunals should establish and publish a clear policy on equal treatment and continuously monitor compliance.

**Standard 3: Tribunals should offer cost effective procedures and be properly resourced and organised**

a)  Judicial resources should be managed to provide a good service, and to ensure that individuals sit often enough to maintain knowledge and skills.

b)  Standards for judicial behaviour and performance should be set and monitored.

c)  Cases should be heard, and a final decision given, within a reasonable period.

d)  Programmes of induction and refresher training should be provided for tribunal chairs, members and administrative staff.

e)  Appropriate levels of administrative and clerical support should be provided for the proper conduct of tribunal hearings.

f)   Standards for hearing venues and for service and performance should be set and monitored in consultation with users.

g)  Appropriate planning, budgeting and monitoring procedures should be in place.

h)  Where relevant, tribunals should work with first tier decision-makers and/or second tier tribunals continuously to improve the 'end to end' experience for the user (e.g. to ensure the whole appeals process is completed in a reasonable time).

## Under TCEA

3.20   These principles are distilled for the tribunal system in the duties of the Senior President and in the objectives of the rules of procedure. TCEA s2(3) contains the core of the Senior President's duties:

(3) A holder of the office of Senior President of Tribunals must, in carrying out the functions of that office, have regard to–

(a) the need for tribunals to be accessible;

(b) the need for proceedings before tribunals–

(i)  to be fair; and

(ii) to be handled quickly and efficiently;

(c) the need for members of tribunals to be experts in the subject-matter of, or the law to be applied in, cases in which they decide matters; and

(d) the need to develop innovative methods of resolving disputes that are of a type that may be brought before tribunals.

The Senior President is only under a duty to have regard to the factors listed, but those factors are stated as unqualified needs. And their nature gives an imperative to the duty to have regard to them.

3.21   TCEA s22(4) sets the objectives for the rules of procedure:

(4) Power to make Tribunal Procedure Rules is to be exercised with a view to securing–

(a) that, in proceedings before the First-tier Tribunal and Upper Tribunal, justice is done;

(b) that the tribunal system is accessible and fair;

(c) that proceedings before the First-tier Tribunal or Upper Tribunal are handled quickly and efficiently;

(d) that the rules are both simple and simply expressed; and

(e) that the rules where appropriate confer on members of the First-tier Tribunal, or Upper Tribunal, responsibility for ensuring that proceedings before the tribunal are handled quickly and efficiently.

The language of 'with a view to securing' repeats section 1(3) of the Civil Procedure Act 1997. But the reality is that, as with CPR, these provisions set the agenda for the Rules Committee in making rules of procedure.

## The overriding objective and the duty to co-operate[14]

3.22 These two concepts are central to the modern approach to procedural justice. They embody and give effect to the general principles identified by Lord Woolf, Sir Andrew Leggatt and the Council on Tribunals. And in turn those principles inform the way that those concepts are applied.

3.23 The overriding objective concerns the tribunal's attitude to the proceedings and the parties, both individually and systemically. The essence of a tribunal's procedure is to deal with cases fairly and justly. It is not necessary for legislation so to provide and it does not. Rather it recognises this and identifies it as the overriding objective of the rules of procedure. This elevates the rules above being rules for their own sake. It gives them a purpose and provides that they must be interpreted and applied to achieve that end. In keeping with the common law approach, this is achieved through principles of interpretation and through the balancing of factors relevant in a particular case rather than by creating rights and duties.

3.24 However, the overriding objective does affect the substance of procedural justice. The legislation specifies some of the features that allow a case to be dealt with fairly and justly. It thereby gives substance to the vague but important concept of justice. It does not replace the practice of itemising individual manifestations of justice in tribunals' practices and rules of procedure; this continues. Instead, it goes beyond them, identifies the unifying and underlying principles, and elevates them to an overriding position.

3.25 The duty to co-operate defines the attitude of the parties and their representatives[15] to the proceedings and to each other. They must help the tribunal to further the overriding objective and co-operate with the tribunal generally. The rules impose that duty in terms rather than recognising it as a feature of tribunal procedure. The effect of the duty is to make the tribunal and the parties partners in a common enterprise of ensuring that the proceedings are conducted smoothly and that the rules of procedure are operated to fulfil their purpose rather than for tactical, partisan advantage.

---

14 See below at para 3.102 onwards.

15 *Geveran Trading Co Ltd v Skjevesland* [2003] 1 WLR 912 at [37].

## Procedural and substantive justice

3.26   In theory, substantive and procedural justice are separate. Substantive justice is the aim of judicial proceedings; procedural justice is the means to achieving it.[16] In operation, they are not so distinct.[17] The rules of procedure may increase or reduce the chances of the parties' securing what they regard as substantive justice, as the following examples show.

3.27   Any aspect of procedure that enhances access to the judicial process increases the chances that the party will secure substantive justice.

3.28   Any aspect of procedure that limits the amount of time or money that a party may devote or expect others to devote to a case reduces the chances that the party will secure substantive justice. It is no longer possible to say as Bowen LJ said in *Cropper v Smith*[18] that: 'Courts do not exist for the sake of discipline, but for the sake of deciding matters in controversy'. It is now recognised that matters in controversy must be decided in a context of discipline. That discipline relates to matters of cost and time.

3.29   As to cost, as Knight Bruce V-C recognised in *Pearse v Pearse*:[19] 'Truth, like all good things, may be loved unwisely – may be pursued too keenly – may cost too much.'

3.30   And time spent on one case may be to the detriment of other cases and of the system as a whole.

3.31   In an individual case, time spent on a claim for disability living allowance under the special rules that apply to the terminally ill may prevent an award being made during the claimant's life-time and a delay in a child's statement of special educational needs may have an impact on the child's education in the meantime.

3.32   Beyond the individual case, in a world of limited administrative and judicial resources the time spent on one case is time that cannot be devoted to another and time wasted on one case is time lost to other cases. Before CPR, Lord Roskill noted in *Ashmore v Corporation of Lloyds*.[20]

> Litigants are not entitled to the uncontrolled use of a trial judge's time. Other litigants await their turn. Litigants are only entitled to so much of the trial judge's time as is necessary for the proper determination of the relevant issues.[21]

Lord Woolf MR repeated this warning under CPR in *Biguzzi v Rank Leisure plc*[22] in the context of whether to strike out a case:

> . . . the courts are not confined to considering the relative positions of the parties. They have to take into account the effect of what has happened on the administration of justice generally. That involves taking into account the effect of the court's ability to hear other cases if such defaults are allowed to occur.[23]

---

16  Collins MR in *In the Matter of an Arbitration between Coles and Ravenshear* [1907] 1 KB 1 at 4.
17  Lord Phillips in *Secretary of State for the Home Department v AF (No 3)* [2010] 2 AC 269 at [60].
18  (1884) 26 Ch D 700 at 710.
19  (1846) 63 ER 950 at 957.
20  [1992] 1 WLR 446.
21  [1992] 1 WLR 446 at 448.
22  [1999] 1 WLR 1926.
23  [1999] 1 WLR 1926 at 1933.

3.33    The requirement of a decision within a reasonable time under article 6 recognises that it is permissible and necessary to limit the time devoted to an individual case.

3.34    The result is that, on the modern approach, there is no contrast or conflict between substantive and procedural justice. Procedure exists to assist in achieving substantive justice and substantive justice can only be attained in the context of procedural justice. But procedural justice constrains the extent to which substantive justice can be realised and thereby helps to define what substantive justice in law means. Substantive justice has no meaning in law once separated from the procedure that provides the only context in which it can exist.

## Sources of procedural provisions

### Practice and procedure

3.35    Practice and procedure are usually used interchangeably or as a composite expression. It is, therefore, usually unnecessary to distinguish between them. In this book, procedure is generally used.

3.36    Practice may also be used in a more limited sense to refer to the way in which a tribunal is accustomed to operate in respect of matters that are not governed by any rule of law or procedure. For example: it may refer to the layout of and seating arrangements in the tribunal room, the order and manner of addressing the tribunal, and whether the decision is given on the day. It is used in this sense to describe practice directions that are not issued under statutory authority.

### Sources

3.37    The practice and procedure of the First-tier Tribunal and the Upper Tribunal are governed by TCEA, rules of procedure, other delegated legislation, practice directions, practice statements, directions and the tribunal's control over its own procedure. There may also be powers and duties that are not expressed in the rules of procedure.

### Rules of procedure

3.38    Rules of procedure are essential for the conduct of judicial business.[24] A tribunal's procedure is how it operates. The rules govern the commencement, conduct and disposal of proceedings. In *Harding v Wealands*,[25] Sir William Aldous said that the natural meaning of 'procedure' was:

> . . . the mode or rules used to govern and regulate the conduct of the court's proceedings.[26]

---

24  Collins MR in *In the Matter of an Arbitration between Coles and Ravenshear* [1907] 1 KB 1 at 4.

25  [2005] 1 WLR 1539.

26  [2005] 1 WLR 1539 at [86]. For a discussion of the scope of procedure in the context of a drafting error, see *Steele v Mooney* [2005] 1 WLR 2819.

3.39    The purpose of rules of procedure was explained by Lord Woolf CJ in *R v Sekhon*[27] as being:

> . . . to provide a convenient and just machinery enabling the court to exercise its jurisdiction.[28]

In *The Bramble Bush: the classic lectures to law and law schools*,[29] Karl Llewellyn said of the rules of procedure:

> . . . convenience, efficiency and fairness are their aim. . . . they tend to degenerate into red tape.[30]

Nowadays, the overriding objective applies to prevent that degeneration.[31]

3.40    Rules of procedure differ from the substantive rules that the tribunal has to apply. They deal not with what the tribunal does, but with how it does it. As Lush LJ put it in *Poyser v Minors*.[32]

> 'Practice' in its larger sense – the sense in which it was obviously used in that Act [the County Courts Act 1856], like 'procedure' which is used in the Judicature Acts, denotes the mode of proceeding by which a legal right is enforced, as distinguished from the law which gives or defines the right, and which by means of the proceeding the Court is to administer the machinery as distinguished from its product.[33]

## The enabling power

3.41    A tribunal's rules of procedure may be contained in a statute or made under the authority delegated by an enabling power contained in a statute. Rules made under delegated authority must be made within the scope of that authority and are invalid if they are not. Tribunals have jurisdiction to decide whether their rules are authorised by statute.[34]

3.42    The enabling power must be interpreted in the light of its purpose. As counsel put it to the Court of Appeal in *FP (Iran) v Secretary of State for the Home Department*,[35] an enabling power to regulate access to justice does not include a power to deny access. In that case, the court held that a rule was unlawful because it effectively denied a party the right to be heard.

3.43    Some matters are outside the scope of an enabling power on procedure.

3.44    *Fundamental rights.* Rules governing fundamental rights in the administration of justice are not matters of procedure. For example: rules that remove the right to trial by jury[36] or the confidentiality between solicitor and client on which legal professional privilege is based[37] are not authorised procedural powers.

---

27  [2003] 1 WLR 1655.
28  [2003] 1 WLR 1655 at [21].
29  Oxford University Press 2008.
30  Oxford University Press 2008 at pp20–21.
31  See below at para 3.103 onwards.
32  (1881) 7 QBD at 329.
33  (1881) 7 QBD at 333.
34  See chapter 2.
35  [2007] EWCA Civ 13; (2007) *Times* 26 January at [21].
36  *Safeway Stores plc v Tate* [2001] QB 1120.
37  *General Mediterranean Holdings SA v Patel* [2000] 1 WLR 272.

3.45   *Jurisdiction.* A power to make rules of procedure does not include the power to affect jurisdiction.[38] Accordingly, as the right of appeal is a matter of jurisdiction, a procedural enabling power cannot take away a right of appeal[39] or create a new one.[40] Nor can it authorise an extension of a tribunal's jurisdiction.[41]

3.46   *Evidence.* The rules of evidence are not part of the rules of procedure, although the rules relating to disclosure of evidence, the attendance of witnesses and the manner of giving evidence are.[42] This is subject to provision to the contrary as in TCEA Sch 5 para 10(2), which allows rules of procedure to modify any rules of evidence provided for elsewhere.

3.47   As the scope of an enabling power is a matter of interpretation, these limitations are subject to provision to the contrary. In the case of interference with a fundamental right, such a provision would have to be sufficiently clear to be effective.

## Rules of procedure under TCEA

3.48   Section 22 of TCEA provides for rules governing the practice and procedure of the First-tier Tribunal and the Upper Tribunal.

3.49   These are made by the Tribunal Procedure Committee (s22(2)). They are made under section 22(3) and Schedule 5 with a view to securing the objectives listed in section 22(4):

(a) that, in proceedings before the First-tier Tribunal and Upper Tribunal, justice is done;
(b) that the tribunal system is accessible and fair;
(c) that proceedings before the First-tier Tribunal or Upper Tribunal are handled quickly and efficiently;
(d) that the rules are both simple and simply expressed;[43] and
(e) that the rules where appropriate confer on members of the First-tier Tribunal, or Upper Tribunal, responsibility for ensuring that proceedings before the tribunal are handled quickly and efficiently.

3.50   The membership of the Tribunal Procedure Committee is governed by Part 2 of Schedule 5 (s22(3)).

3.51   As the rules of procedure are delegated legislation, tribunals cannot vary them by their decisions,[44] except to the extent that the rules themselves allow for this.

---

38  Diplock LJ in *Garthwaite v Garthwaite* [1964] P 356 at 395.
39  Lord Reading CJ and Shearman and Sankey JJ in *The King v Tribunal of Appeal under the Housing Act 1919* [1920] 3 KB 334 at 342, 343 and 346.
40  Lord Westbury LC in *Attorney-General v Sillem* (1864) 11 ER 1200 at 1208.
41  Diplock LJ in *Garthwaite v Garthwaite* [1964] P 356 at 395.
42  Adrian Zuckerman, *Civil Procedure*, 2nd edn, Thomson Sweet & Maxwell, 2006, para 1.45.
43  The aim of simplicity in both content and expression is also a requirement of CPR under section 2(7) of the Civil Procedure Act 1997.
44  *Bovale Ltd v Secretary of State for Communities and Local Government* [2009] 3 All ER 340 at [27(i)].

3.52     Tribunals should rely on the rules of procedure and should not import provisions of the CPR into their proceedings.[45]

## The nature of the rules

3.53    The rules will take one of four forms: a duty (such as the duty to give reasons), a power (such as the power to withdraw), a discretion (such as the discretion whether to hold a hearing), or a default provision (such as most time limits, which are subject to the power to extend time).

## Other delegated legislation

3.54    Not all procedural provisions are within the powers of the Tribunal Procedure Committee. They may also be made under Regulations or Orders.

## Retrospective changes to the rules of procedure

3.55    If the change is to the interpretation of the rule rather than to the rule itself, the normal approach to case-law applies and the rule is treated as if it had always had that meaning. So, the new interpretation applies in all cases.

3.56     If the rule is amended or a new rule is introduced, two questions arise. First, is there an express or clear provision governing its application to existing proceedings? Ideally, there should be a savings or transitional provision. Often there is not and the second question arises: what does fairness require?[46] This is the modern test that has replaced the former test of whether the provision was procedural (and retrospective) or substantive (and not retrospective). The usual answer is that it is fair to apply changes to procedural provisions in ongoing proceedings.[47]

## Powers and duties outside the express rules

3.57    Modern rules of procedure cover many eventualities that are likely to occur. However, it is impossible to make specific provision for every thing that may happen. Some matters are within the tribunal's power to regulate its own procedure. For example: the sequence of submissions at an oral hearing are within the control of the tribunal. This aside and in the absence of such a provision, it may be impossible to interpret the rules to include a particular power. In *Khan v Heywood and Middleton Primary Care Trust,*[48] the Court of Appeal held that there was no power for an employment tribunal to reinstate proceedings that had been withdrawn. Brooke LJ explained:

---

45  *R (Howes) v Child Support Commissioners* [2008] 1 FLR 1691 at [39]; *CB v Suffolk County Council* [2010] UKUT 413 (AAC) at [22].

46  Lord Mustill in *L'Office Cherifien des Phosphates v Yamashita – Shinnihon Steamship Co Ltd* [1994] 1 AC 486 at 525.

47  As in *Attorney-General v Vernazza* [1960] AC 965. In this respect, they resemble rules of policy such as the immigration rules rather than rules of substantive law: *Odelola v Secretary of State for the Home Department* [2009] 1 WLR 1230.

48  [2007] ICR 24.

... the ET [employment tribunal] is a creature of statute and its procedure is specifically governed by the 2004 Regulations. It is much used by litigants in person. Its procedures are governed by what is meant to be an informal, but clearly understood code. Thus, while at first blush, and particularly given the tight time-limits for instituting proceedings, it might seem sensible to have a procedure by means of which a litigant who had mistakenly withdrawn a claim should be allowed to revive it, I am satisfied that, for such a procedure to exist, it would need to be set out expressly in the rules. I therefore regard the absence of any such express provision in the rules as important.[49]

This certainly applies if the rules make adequate provision.[50]

3.58    However, a tribunal may have additional powers or duties. The possibility that a tribunal may have procedural powers that are not expressly set out may be recognised in legislation. So TCEA Sch 5 para 15 provides that any rule allowing a decision to be corrected or set aside is additional to any such power that is exercisable apart from the rules.

3.59    There are a variety of techniques by which a tribunal may acquire additional powers and duties. They are not mutually exclusive.

### Supplementing the legislation

3.60    One approach is to recognise openly that the terms of the legislation are being supplemented. This is not common. But in *Wiseman v Borneman*,[51] Lord Reid was open in acknowledging that the courts supplemented procedural legislation, albeit cautiously and consistently with the legislative scheme, as justice required. He said:

> For a long time the courts have, without objection from Parliament, supplemented procedure laid down in legislation where they have found that to be necessary for this purpose. But before this unusual power is exercised it must be clear that the statutory procedure is insufficient to achieve justice and that to require additional steps would not frustrate the apparent purpose of the legislation.[52]

3.61    And in *Local Government Board v Arlidge*,[53] Lord Haldane LC said:

> ... what that procedure is to be in detail must depend on the nature of the tribunal. ... When ... Parliament entrusts it with judicial duties, Parliament must be taken, in the absence of any declaration to the contrary, to have intended it to follow a procedure which is its own, and is necessary if it is to be capable of doing its work efficiently.[54]

3.62    The decision of the Divisional Court of Queen's Bench in *R v Kensington and Chelsea Rent Tribunal ex p Macfarlane*[55] may be an example. A party to the proceedings alleged that he had not received a notice from the tribunal that it would inspect his premises. When the tribunal could not gain entry,

---

49  [2007] ICR 24 at [70].
50  *Lynch v East Dunbartonshire Council* [2010] ICR 1094 at [48] (further claims in respect of the same matter could be adjourned or struck out).
51  [1971] AC 297.
52  [1971] AC 297 at 308.
53  [1915] AC 120.
54  [1915] AC 120 at 132.
55  [1974] 1 WLR 1486.

it decided not to entertain the case. Its rules contained no power to set aside the decision in these circumstances.[56] However, the Court held that it had power to re-open the case. Lord Widgery CJ said:

> . . . the disappointed party . . . can go back to the tribunal, explain why he did not attend, and the tribunal will then have the jurisdiction if it thinks fit to reopen the matter and to reconsider its decision in the light of representations made by the absent party.[57]

3.63    As that passage makes clear, the tribunal has a power to re-open the case, but not a duty. That power must not be exercised too freely but, if there is an application, the court decided that the tribunal was under a duty to consider it. Lord Widgery said:

> It was the tribunal's duty on the receipt of that application from the applicant to consider whether they would allow the case to be re-opened, and I would stress that tribunals must be very firm in the view which they take about this kind of case. There must be no question of absent parties taking no action over a period of months, and then coming back to the tribunal with some story of having been ill or being in South America when the hearing occurred. Tribunals must be satisfied before they reopen a case that there is a good argument on the merits for giving the absent party a chance to be heard, that he has got a real and reasonable excuse, that he had to be given a further chance and that, in considering whether he ought to be given a further chance to be heard, due regard must be had to the other party to the proceedings and to any third parties who may have acted upon the tribunal's decision on the assumption that it was right and to be sustained.[58]

This case was one in which a party had not received notice, was thereby disadvantaged and applied to the tribunal to reopen his case. Although Lord Widgery's reasoning is not limited to these circumstances, the decision has not been developed, probably because tribunals are likely to have legislative power dealing with this and other possibilities. As a result, the scope of the power and the need for an application are both open issues.

## Background rules

3.64    Another analysis is that the rules of procedure exist against a background of general rules that apply by operation of law. These general rules include the principles of natural justice and article 6.[59] The rules of procedure replace those general rules in so far as they apply. But in so far as the rules of procedure are silent, the general rules continue to apply.

---

56  A party must have notice of a hearing in order for the hearing to be fair. There is authority that there is no breach of natural justice if the tribunal itself is not at fault. If notice is sent but not received, the tribunal is not at fault. See below at para 3.153 onwards. The tribunal, though, may have a power to set aside its decision in these circumstances. However, this is only a power and does not amount to a breach of natural justice or render the tribunal's decision wrong in law if it declines to exercise the power.

57  [1974] 1 WLR 1486 at 1493.

58  [1974] 1 WLR 1486 at 1493.

59  For a fuller discussion of the relationship between these principles and the rules of procedure, see below at para 3.164 onwards.

3.65    Sir Jocelyn Simon P espoused this approach in *Qureshi v Qureshi*[60] In that case, no rules had been made for an arbitration council to sit abroad. However, Sir Jocelyn said:

> Where a legislative authority by an enactment setting up a tribunal or other body envisages rules to be made governing the procedure of such tribunal or body, and no such rules are made, the tribunal or body is not necessarily thereby disabled from performing its function. In such case the tribunal or body acts effectively provided it acts in accordance with natural justice and to promote the objective with which it was set up, and possibly by analogy with the procedural rules prescribed for comparable tribunals or bodies.[61]

### Inherent powers

3.66    Courts have inherent powers.[62] In *Connelly v Director of Public Prosecutions*,[63] Lord Morris justified and explained the scope of these powers by reference to their purpose:

> There can be no doubt that a court which is endowed with a particular jurisdiction has powers which are necessary to enable it to act effectively within such jurisdiction. I would regard them as powers which are inherent in its jurisdiction. A court must enjoy such powers in order to enforce its rules of practice and to suppress any abuses of its process and to defeat any attempted thwarting of its process.[64]

3.67    In *Bremer Vulkan Schiffbau und Maschinenfabrik v South India Shipping Corporation Ltd*,[65] Lord Diplock linked this with the court's power to regulate its own procedure:

> The High Court's power to dismiss a pending action for want of prosecution is but an instance of a general power to control its own procedure so as to prevent its being used to achieve injustice. Such a power is inherent in its constitutional function as a court of justice. . . .
>
> The power to dismiss a pending action for want of prosecution in cases where to allow the action to continue would involve a substantial risk that justice could not be done is thus properly described as an 'inherent power' the exercise of which is within the 'inherent jurisdiction' of the High Court. It would I think be conducive to legal clarity if the use of these two expressions were confined to the doing by the court of acts which it needs must have power to do in order to maintain its character as a court of justice.[66]

3.68    In *Chessington World of Adventures Ltd v Reed*,[67] Morison J said that employment tribunals had no inherent jurisdiction.[68] In the context, he must have

---

60  [1972] Fam 173.
61  [1972] Fam 173 at 196.
62  These powers are discussed in detail by I.H. Jacob, 'The Inherent Jurisdiction of the Court' [1970] *Current Legal Problems* 23 and M.S. Dockray, 'The Inherent Jurisdiction to Regulate Civil Proceedings' (1997) 113 LQR 120.
63  [1964] AC 1254.
64  [1964] AC 1254 at 1301. See also Tuckey LJ in *R (Roberts) v Parole Board* [2005] QB 410 at [32], linking the power to use a specially appointed advocate to the Board's status as a court for the purpose of Convention rights. If this is correct, all tribunals that are covered by article 6(1) have the inherent powers of a court.
65  [1981] AC 909.
66  [1981] AC 909 at 977.
67  [1998] IRLR 56.
68  [1998] IRLR 56 at 62.

intended to refer to inherent procedural powers. However, this comment
was not essential to the decision and is not soundly based in authority,
because the case cited in support deals with substantive (not procedural)
jurisdiction.[69]

3.69    In *R v Assessment Committee of Saint Mary Abbotts, Kensington*,[70] the
Court of Appeal decided that the committee did not have any power to
regulate its own procedure because it was not 'a court or a tribunal exercising judicial functions in the legal acceptation of the terms'.[71] However,
the court recognised that the committee 'would have some discretion, and
might refuse to hear a manifestly improper person as agent' of an objec-
tor.[72] The implication is that if a tribunal does exercise judicial functions,
it has power over its own procedure.

3.70    The courts have recognised that tribunals have some specific inherent
powers. In *Akewushola v Secretary of State for the Home Department*,[73] the
Court of Appeal recognised that they have the power to correct accidental
mistakes in their decisions.[74] And in *R v Industrial Tribunal ex p Cotswold
Collotype Co Ltd*,[75] the Divisional Court of Queen's Bench decided that a
tribunal had inherent power to direct a rehearing before a differently constituted tribunal if the members were unable to agree on a decision.[76]

3.71    A Commissioner relied on tribunals' power to control their own procedure as a basis for inherent powers to set aside their own decisions on
procedural grounds.[77] However, in *Akewushola v Secretary of State for the
Home Department*,[78] the Court of Appeal decided that tribunals did not
have power to rescind or review their decisions. Sedley LJ said:

> . . . I do not think that, slips apart, a statutory tribunal – in contrast to a
> superior court – ordinarily possesses any inherent power to rescind or
> review its own decisions. Except where the High Court's jurisdiction is
> unequivocally excluded by privative legislation, it is there that the power of
> correction resides.[79]

Sedley LJ linked his reasoning to the statutory nature of a tribunal. However, this is not decisive. As Morison J pointed out in the Employment
Appeal Tribunal in *Chessington World of Adventures Ltd v Reed*,[80] the Court
of Appeal is statutory, but it has inherent jurisdiction.[81] His lordship did
not analyse the origin of an inherent power, but appeared to relate it to the
judicial oath of a High Court judge.[82]

---

69  See the discussion in chapter 2.
70  [1891] 1 QB 378.
71  [1891] 1 QB 378 per Lord Esher MR at 382.
72  [1891] 1 QB 378 per Lord Esher MR at 383.
73  [2000] 1 WLR 2295.
74  [2000] 1 WLR 2295 per Sedley LJ at 2301.
75  [1979] ICR 190.
76  Lord Widgery CJ at 193, relying on *Fussell v Somerset Justices Licensing Committee*
    [1947] KB 276.
77  *R(U) 3/89* at [4] and [5] of the Appendix to the decision.
78  [2000] 1 WLR 2295.
79  [2000] 1 WLR 2295 at 2301.
80  [1998] IRLR 56.
81  [1998] IRLR 56 at 61.
82  [1998] IRLR 56 at 61.

3.72    Whatever the correct jurisprudential basis, a tribunal has no power of review even if the practice of review has been accepted by the public body affected.[83]

3.73    In *O'Keefe v Southampton City Council*,[84] the Employment Appeal Tribunal decided that tribunals have no inherent power to strike out.

3.74    And in *R (Harpers Leisure International Ltd) v Guildford Borough Council*,[85] Charles J decided that tribunals have no inherent power to stay for an abuse of process.

3.75    The extent to which tribunals have other inherent powers is undecided. However, TCEA s25 gives the Upper Tribunal the same powers as the High Court in respect of all other matters incidental to the Upper Tribunal's functions. This may include the Court's inherent powers.

3.76    In *MR v CMEC and DM*,[86] a Scottish panel of the Upper Tribunal decided that it had the inherent power of the Court of Session 'to compel parties to a cause to produce documents which may have a bearing on the issue between them'. It also held that it had power to commit for contempt for failure to comply with a direction.[87] This is also a feature of a supreme court of record.[88]

3.77    The relationship between rules of procedure and inherent powers was analysed by the Court of Appeal in *Raja v Van Hoogstraten (No 9)*.[89]

> The position pre-CPR, therefore, was that the inherent powers of the court could not be invoked to do something which was inconsistent with a rule. Thus, if a rule gave a wide discretion to the court to decide whether or not to make a particular order, the court could not exercise its inherent powers to make such an order *ex debito justitiae* as if it had no discretion, or a discretion which could only be exercised one way in accordance with the rules.

> The same position has obtained since the introduction of the CPR. The CPR are a 'new procedural code with the overriding objective of enabling the court to deal with cases justly' (r1.1(1)). There is no doubt that the court continues to have the inherent jurisdiction to regulate the conduct of civil litigation: see section 19(2)(b) of the Supreme Court Act 1981. The existence of the inherent jurisdiction is also implicitly acknowledged by CPR 3.1(1) which provides that the list of powers in that rule 'is in addition to. . . any powers it may otherwise have'.

> In our judgment, therefore, where the subject-matter of an application is governed by rules in the CPR, it should be dealt with by the court in accordance with the rules and not by exercising the court's inherent jurisdiction. There is no point in exercising the court's inherent jurisdiction if that would involve adopting the same approach and would lead to the same result as an application of the rules. And it would be wrong to exercise the inherent jurisdiction of the court to adopt a different approach and arrive at a different outcome from that which would result from an application of the rules.[90]

83  *R (Secretary of State for Defence) v President of the Pensions Appeal Tribunal* (2004) *Times* 27 February.

84  [1988] ICR 419 at 422.

85  (2009) *Times* 14 August.

86  [2009] UKUT 283 (AAC) at [11].

87  [2009] UKUT 283 (AAC) at [14]–[15].

88  See chapter 1.

89  [2009] 1 WLR 1143.

90  [2009] 1 WLR 1143 at [76]–[78].

## Implied powers

3.78   If a power is not inherent, it may be implied. Lord Selborne recognised this possibility in *Spackman v Plumstead Board of Works*:[91]

> No doubt in the absence of special provisions as to how the person who is to decide is to proceed, the law will imply no more than that the substantial requirements of justice shall not be violated.[92]

3.79   So did Lord Bridge in *Lloyd v Mahon*:[93]

> ... the courts will not only require the procedure prescribed by the statute to be followed, but will readily imply so much and no more to be introduced by way of additional procedural safeguards as will ensure the attainment of fairness.[94]

3.80   There are some circumstances in which it is essential to imply a provision to fill an omission in the rules of procedure. An obvious example is a time limit. So in *Qureshi v Qureshi*,[95] Sir Jocelyn Simon P said that in the absence of an express provision a reasonable time must be allowed.[96] Another example is the use of an interpreter, identified by Sedley LJ in *Akewushola v Secretary of State for the Home Department*.[97]

3.81   Any implied power must be consistent with the statutory enabling provisions. It is not possible to imply a power that could not have been conferred expressly because of the lack of a suitable enabling provision. Any implied power must also be consistent with the provisions of the rules of procedure. As these are increasingly detailed in their provision and wide in their coverage of issues, it may be difficult to justify implying provisions that may have been deliberately excluded.

## The relationship between inherent and implied powers

3.82   Finding an inherent power and implying a power are different legal techniques. In *Golder v United Kingdom*,[98] the European Court of Human Rights employed both techniques. The case concerned article 6. The Court decided that the right of access to a court was inherent in this,[99] but that the language allowed limitations to be implied.[100] This suggests two distinctions. One is that a power is inherent if it is of the nature of, or a precondition for the existence of, the right of access, whereas a power is implied as a consequence of that right. The other is that finding an inherent power concentrates on identifying the nature of and ensuring the effectiveness of the right, whereas implying a power concentrates on, or is limited by, the possibilities of the language in which the right is expressed.

---

91   (1885) 10 App Cas 229.
92   (1885) 10 App Cas 229 at 240.
93   [1987] AC 625.
94   [1987] AC 625 at 703.
95   [1972] Fam 173.
96   [1972] Fam 173 at 196.
97   [2000] 1 WLR 2295 at 2301.
98   (1975) 1 EHRR 524.
99   (1975) 1 EHRR 524 at [36].
100   (1975) 1 EHRR 524 at [38].

3.83 This analysis is consistent with *Stefan v General Medical Council*,[101] in which the Privy Council referred to implication as an issue of language.[102] It is also consistent with *Chessington World of Adventures Ltd v Reed*.[103] An implication would not extend the scope of express provisions in the rules of procedure, but Morison J there left open the possibility that in exceptional circumstances an inherent power might be wider than a carefully defined legislative provision:

> If, as I believe, Parliament has weighed the circumstances in which it would be appropriate to make a gagging order, it would be difficult to justify resorting to an inherent jurisdiction to extend those circumstances. . . . Simply because I cannot at the moment rule out the possibility that there might be some special case which might call for an application of the court's inherent jurisdiction, I am not prepared to hold that it would never be appropriate for the court to make a gagging order beyond those circumstances . . .[104]

3.84 However, in *Akewushola v Secretary of State for the Home Department*,[105] Sedley LJ emphasised that the breadth of the coverage of the rules of procedure was an impediment to finding an inherent power.[106]

## Practice directions

3.85 Courts have inherent jurisdiction to make practice directions, provided they are consistent with any rules of court or relevant statutory provisions.[107]

3.86 Practice directions that are not issued pursuant to statute are not strictly law.[108]

3.87 TCEA s23 provides for practice directions governing the practice and procedure of the First-tier Tribunal and the Upper Tribunal. The potential scope of a practice direction is the same as that of rules of procedure under section 22. As they are statutory, they may be challenged on the ground that their content was not authorised by the enabling power.[109]

3.88 A practice direction may be given by the Senior President or by a Chamber President (s23(1) and (2)).

3.89 If the direction is given by the Senior President, it requires the approval of the Lord Chancellor (s23(4)). If it is given by a Chamber President, it requires the approval of both the Senior President and the Lord Chancellor (s23(5)).

3.90 For some directions, the Lord Chancellor is not required to give approval and does not have to be consulted. This applies for directions on

---

101 [1999] 1 WLR 1293.
102 [1999] 1 WLR 1293 at 1297.
103 [1998] IRLR 56.
104 [1998] IRLR 56 at 61–62.
105 [2000] 1 WLR 2295.
106 [2000] 1 WLR 2295 at 2301.
107 *Langley v North West Water Authority* [1991] 1 WLR 697 at 709; *Bovale Ltd v Secretary of State for Communities and Local Government* [2009] 3 All ER 340 at [10]. A local practice was held to be in conflict with a rule of court in *The Cashmere* (1890) 15 PD 121 at 123.
108 *Hume v Somerton* (1890) 25 QBD 239 at 243.
109 As in *R (Ewing) v Department for Constitutional Affairs* [2006] 2 All ER 993.

the application or interpretation of the law or the making of decisions by members of the First-tier Tribunal or Upper Tribunal (s23(6)).[110]

3.91    For other directions, the Lord Chancellor is not required to give approval but must be consulted. This applies for directions setting the criteria by which members of the First-tier Tribunal and Upper Tribunal may be chosen to decide particular categories of matter (s23(7)).

3.92    Rules of procedure may refer to practice directions (paragraph 17 of Schedule 5).

3.93    As practice directions may only be made by specified persons, tribunals cannot vary them by their decisions,[111] except to the extent that the practice directions themselves allow for this. For this purpose, a practice direction is something issued as a practice direction and does not include a decision that happens to contain guidance or directions.[112]

3.94    In *Godwin v Swindon Borough Council*[113] May LJ said that under CPR practice directions are subordinate to the rules and 'at best a weak aid to the interpretation of the rules themselves'. There is nothing in the Civil Procedure Act 1997 that so provides.[114] However, the conclusion may be justified under TCEA on the ground that rules and practice directions are made by different bodies and, perhaps, by the fact that the rules are made by a broader-based body after wider consultation.

## Practice statements

3.95    There is no express statutory authority for practice statements. The power to issue these is inherent in the nature and function of the office as Senior President.

3.96    The Senior President has mainly used these statements to exercise the powers to delegate functions to staff and to prescribe the composition of tribunals. It may be that a failure to comply with these statements is an error of law. However, the Senior President has also issued a statement on records of proceedings. The status of a statement such as this has yet to be established.

3.97    The title suggests that a practice statement is descriptive of the practice that is in fact followed rather than prescriptive of what it should be. However, that is not how it is used under TCEA.

---

110  There is equivalent provision in s5(5) of the Civil Procedure Act 1997 as substituted by para 6 of Sch 2 to the Constitutional Reform Act 2005.

111  *Bovale Ltd v Secretary of State for Communities and Local Government* [2009] 3 All ER 340 at [27].

112  [2009] 3 All ER 340 at [40]–[44].

113  [2002] 1 WLR 997 at [11].

114  May LJ referred to para 6 of Sch 1, which is the equivalent of para 17 of Schedule 5 to TCEA. However, that does not so provide. Para 6 was analysed by Sullivan J in *R (Ewing) v Department for Constitutional Affairs* [2006] 2 All ER 993 at [13] as recognising and referring to the court's inherent power. That reasoning need not, and perhaps cannot, apply under TCEA, as section 23 contains an express power to make practice directions.

## Directions

3.98 Under the rules of procedure, tribunals have power to regulate their own procedure[115] and to give directions in relation to the conduct or disposal of proceedings.[116] There is specific provision for the procedure relating to directions.[117]

3.99 The exercise of these case management powers in a particular case does not involve the making of a practice direction, which could only be made by the persons authorised under the legislation.[118] In principle, the position is the same for case management directions issued in standard form for a particular class of case.

3.100 If there is a gap in the rules of procedure or practice directions, tribunals have power to fill gaps through their regulation of their own procedure, at least pending the making of rules or the giving of a practice direction.[119]

## Guidance

3.101 It is permissible for tribunals to issue guidance that is confined to explaining how tribunals interpret and apply their rules of procedure and practice directions.[120]

# Overriding objective and co-operation

## The overriding objective

3.102 The rules of procedure lay down an overriding objective. UTR r2 is illustrative:[121]

> (1) The overriding objective of these Rules is to enable the Upper Tribunal to deal with cases fairly and justly.
> (2) Dealing with a case fairly and justly includes–
> > (a) dealing with the case in ways which are proportionate to the importance of the case, the complexity of the issues, the anticipated costs and the resources of the parties;
> > (b) avoiding unnecessary formality and seeking flexibility in the proceedings;

---

115 See: UTR r5(1); GRC Rules r5(1); HESC Rules r5(1); IAC Rules r4(1); Lands Rules r5(1); PC Rules r6(1); SEC Rules r5(1); Tax Rules r5(1); WPAFC Rules r5(1).

116 See: UTR r5(2); GRC Rules r5(2); HESC Rules r5(2); IAC Rules r4(2); Lands Rules r5(2); PC Rules r6(2); SEC Rules r5(2); Tax Rules r5(2); WPAFC Rules r5(2).

117 See: UTR r6; GRC Rules r6; HESC Rules r6; IAC Rules r5; Lands Rules r6; PC Rules r7SEC Rules r6; Tax Rules r6; WPAFC Rules r6.

118 *Bovale Ltd v Secretary of State for Communities and Local Government* [2009] 3 All ER 340 at [24].

119 *Bovale Ltd v Secretary of State for Communities and Local Government* [2009] 3 All ER 340 at [41].

120 *Bovale Ltd v Secretary of State for Communities and Local Government* [2009] 3 All ER 340 at [36].

121 See also: GRC Rules r2; HESC Rules r2; IAC Rules r2; Lands Rules r2; PC Rules r2; SEC Rules r2; Tax Rules r2; WPAFC Rules r2. The CPR equivalent is r1.1–1.2.

    (c) ensuring, so far as practicable, that the parties are able to participate fully in the proceedings;

    (d) using any special expertise of the Upper Tribunal effectively; and

    (e) avoiding delay, so far as compatible with proper consideration of the issues.

(3) The Upper Tribunal must seek to give effect to the overriding objective when it–

    (a) exercises any power under these Rules; or

    (b) interprets any rule or practice direction.

## The function of the overriding objective

3.103 Lord Woolf explained the reason and function of the overriding objective in his report on *Access to Justice*:

> Every word in the rules should have a purpose, but every word cannot sensibly be given a minutely exact meaning. Civil procedure involves more judgment and knowledge than the rules can directly express. In this respect, rules of court are not like an instruction manual for operating a piece of machinery. Ultimately their purpose is to guide the court and the litigants towards the just resolution of the case. Although the rules cannot offer detailed directions for the technical steps to be taken, the effectiveness of those steps depends upon the spirit in which they are carried out. That in turns depends on an understanding of the fundamental purpose of the rules and of the underlying system of procedure.[122]

3.104 Tribunals are judicial bodies and, as such, should deal with proceedings in a way that is fair and just. As Lord Donaldson MR said in *R v Leicester City Justices ex p Barrow*,[123] 'Fairness ... is fundamental to all court proceedings'[124] and 'Any unfairness ... strikes at the roots of justice.'[125] Accordingly, the overriding objective does not, and need not, stipulate the function of tribunal procedure. What it does is to identify the function of the rules with the essential nature of judicial procedure and provides for them to be interpreted and applied in a way that furthers that function. It does not necessarily dictate the outcome. What it does is to provide a framework for argument, analysis and decision-making.

## A general principle of fairness

3.105 The overriding objective recognises but does not establish fairness as an essential component of the judicial process. This is shown by the cases in which the courts use the same criteria when the overriding objective does not apply.[126] Judges even refer to the overriding objective in circumstances in which the rules of procedure are not engaged. Accordingly, the Court of Appeal has described as an 'economic and efficient approach, in line with the overriding objective' for a witness to give evidence on just one

---

122 *Access to Justice*, Chapter 20, para 10.
123 [1991] 2 QB 260.
124 [1991] 2 QB 260 at 285.
125 [1991] 2 QB 260 at 290.
126 *Igwemma v Chief Constable of Greater Manchester Police* [2002] QB 1012 at [34].

occasion.[127] And the Employment Appeal Tribunal has treated the overriding objective as relevant when a tribunal is considering whether to change a decision after it was announced orally but before it was promulgated.[128]

## Fairly and justly

3.106　The rules do not distinguish between the concepts of fairly and justly. They may be used as a composite expression. A clue to a possible distinction is found in the case-law on unemployment benefit. The Commissioners decided that whether an employer had just cause to leave employment voluntarily involved a compromise between the rights of the employee and the interests of the community.[129] Building on that, fairness focuses on the interests of the parties, while justice takes account of wider consideration.

## Interpreting and applying rules of procedure

3.107　The tribunal must seek to give effect to the overriding objective whenever it interprets a rule or exercises a power under the rules. Exercising a power covers both (i) considering whether to exercise it and (ii) actually exercising it. The wording of rule 2(3)(a) may appear to apply only to (ii). However, that would significantly reduce the scope and, therefore, the effectiveness of the provision. This can be avoided by taking account of the overriding objective in interpreting itself so that it covers both (i) and (ii).

3.108　The duty to give effect to the overriding objective is not absolute. It recognises that the language may not allow the rules to be interpreted or applied to achieve the objective.[130] Subject to that, it ensures that every application or interpretation is informed by the purpose of the rules.[131]

3.109　The rules give examples of what is involved in dealing with a case fairly and justly. They reflect the duties on the Senior President under TCEA s2(3) and of the Tribunal Procedure Committee under TCEA s22(4). They are not exhaustive and depend on the individual circumstances of the case for their operation. Nevertheless, they guide the tribunal in understanding the essence of the tribunal's procedure. Statements of the overriding objective may differ slightly in the factors they include. To that extent, the differences are not of practical significance, as the factors are not exhaustive. However, the overall tone of the statements can indicate significant differences. For example: the focus of CPR r1.1 is on expedition and efficiency, whereas the rules of procedure under TCEA focus more on access and participation.

3.110　One effect of the overriding objective is that it is possible for the rules to make more general provision than would otherwise be the case, leaving it to the balancing exercise under the overriding objective to adjust their application to particular circumstances.

127 *Salford Royal NHS Foundation Trust v Roldan* [2010] ICR 1457 at [69].
128 *CK Heating Ltd v Doro* [2010] ICR 1449 at [10] and [14].
129 *R(U) 20/64* at [8].
130 *Vinos v Marks & Spencer plc* [2001] 3 All ER 784 at [26].
131 *Totty v Snowden* [2002] 1 WLR 1384 at [34].

3.111    Full participation in the proceedings is an essential element of the overriding objective. This is similar to the requirement of equality of arms under article 6.[132] The inquisitorial and enabling approaches contribute to satisfying the provision.[133]

3.112    Full participation under rule 2(2)(c) may require that a witness participate by video link.[134] But it does not require that each side be allowed the same number of expert witnesses.[135]

## Interpreting practice directions

3.113    The relevance of the overriding objective to practice directions is limited.

3.114    First, tribunals must seek to give effect to the overriding objective in interpreting practice directions.[136] But the overriding objective that must be given effect is that the purpose of the rules of procedure is to enable the tribunal to deal with cases fairly and justly. It does not provide an overriding objective for the practice directions themselves.

3.115    Second, the overriding objective does not extend to the exercise of a power under a practice direction.

3.116    Third, the duty to co-operate (see below) is tied in part to the overriding objective. To that extent, the duty in respect of practice directions is limited.

3.117    These differences are a consequence of the limited scope of the rule-making authority given to the Tribunal Procedure Committee. Although it is responsible for making the rules of procedure (TCEA s22), it has no responsibility for practice directions, which can only be made by the Senior President of Tribunals or a Chamber President (TCEA s23).

## TCEA, practice statements and substantive law

3.118    There is no provision for an overriding objective in the interpretation or application of TCEA itself, practice statements or the substantive law that the tribunal has to apply.

## The duty to co-operate

3.119    The rules require the parties to co-operate with the tribunal and each other in furthering the overriding objective and generally. UTR r2(4) is illustrative:[137]

> (4) Parties must–
>> (a) help the Upper Tribunal to further the overriding objective; and
>> (b) co-operate with the Upper Tribunal generally.

---

132  See below at para 3.210 onwards.
133  See chapter 1.
134  *Rowland v Bock* [2002] 4 All ER 370 at [9].
135  *Kirkman v Euro Exide Corporation (CMP Batteries Ltd)* (2007) *Times* 6 February.
136  UTR r2(3)(b). The duty of parties to co-operate generally is not a feature of CPR.
137  See also: GRC Rules r2(4); HESC Rules r2(4); IAC Rules r2(4); Lands Rules r 2(4); PC Rules 3(4); SEC Rules r2(4); Tax Rules r2(4); WPAFC Rules r2(4). The CPR equivalent is r1.3.

3.120  For example: the parties must notify the tribunal when they have settled issues in order to save time spent in preparing a case or the need for an oral hearing.[138]

3.121  Co-operation is a duty, not an exhortation. Failure to comply requires the tribunal to consider what action to take under UTR r7 and its equivalents. This is discussed below.

3.122  Representatives act for the parties. Inevitably, they are constrained by the duties imposed on the parties. Accordingly, this duty applies to representatives as it does to the parties themselves.[139] The extent to which a party is held responsible for the failings of a representative is considered below.

3.123  By co-operating with the tribunal, the parties must inevitably co-operate with each other. In this way, the furthering of the overriding objective becomes a collective enterprise.

3.124  This changes the culture of proceedings. The parties are entitled to retain their separate stances on the substantive issues, but should work co-operatively on procedural matters. Directions issued by the tribunal may assist the parties in understanding what this requires in a particular case.[140]

3.125  In *Bache v Essex County Council*, Mummery LJ explained some of what is involved in co-operation:

> Just as the tribunal is under a duty to behave fairly, so are the parties and their representatives. The tribunal is accordingly entitled to require the parties and their representatives to act in a fair and reasonable way in the presentation of their evidence, in challenging the other side's evidence and in making submissions. The ruling of the tribunal on what is and is not relevant and on what is the fair and appropriate procedure ought to be respected even by a party and his representative who do not agree with a ruling.[141]

## Representatives

3.126  Two issues arise in respect of representatives.

3.127  First, what duties do they owe to the tribunal? This will be worked out in the context of rule 2(4) and its equivalents.

3.128  Second, to what extent must a party take the consequences of the failings of a representative? This was discussed by the Court of Appeal in *BR (Iran) v Secretary of State for the Home Department*.[142]

> The other general issue is that, as the present cases all too graphically show, delay of whatever sort will often have to be laid at the door of legal advisers. In ordinary private litigation, both before and after the introduction of the Civil Procedure Rules, a party has attributed to him, and is responsible for, the action or inaction of his lawyers: see *Training in Compliance Ltd v Dewse* [2001] CP Rep 46, para 66, per Peter Gibson LJ, cited with approval by Arden LJ in *FP(Iran) v Secretary of State for the Home Department* [2007]

---

138  *Red River UK Ltd v Skeikh* (2009) *Times* 6 May.
139  *Geveran Trading Co Ltd v Skjevesland* [2003] 1 WLR 912 at [37].
140  *RC v CMEC and WC* [2009] UKUT 62 (AAC) at [58].
141  [2000] ICR 313.
142  [2007] 1 WLR 2278 at [18].

EWCA Civ 13 at 80. But, as Arden LJ went on to urge, considerations in asylum cases are different. And that view was underlined, as a matter of ratio, by Sedley LJ at para 45 of the same case, where he adopted the observation of Lord Denning MR in *R v Immigration Appeal Tribunal ex p Mehta* [1975] 1 WLR 1087 that it is no consolation to tell a person that she can sue her solicitor for his mistake if the mistake is about to lead to her removal from this country; and, *a fortiori*, if the removal is to a condition of persecution.

3.129   However, this does not meant that the courts do not take account of the fact that the fault was that of the party's representative. In *Flaxman-Binns v Lincolnshire County Council*,[143] the Court of Appeal was concerned with an application to lift a stay on a stale claim. The Court said:

> The fact that the delay was attributable to fault on the part of his solicitor rather than fault on the part of the plaintiff is a factor which weighs in the plaintiff's favour . . .[144]

In *Royal Bank of Scotland v Craig*,[145] the Court of Appeal held that the judge had been wrong to refuse to adjourn when a party had been left without representation as a result of mismanagement by his original counsel. In *Short v Birmingham City Council*,[146] Tugendhat J was concerned with a delay in appealing. He said that, although the major part of the delay was attributable to the claimant's legal advisers, it was not intentional and had not prejudiced the administration of justice or the respondents.[147] In *Jurkowska v Hlmad Ltd*,[148] the Court of Appeal, despite having reservations, confirmed a judge's decision to extend time by 33 minutes when a relevant document was not provided by a solicitor who had not realised the document existed. And in *Newcastle City Council v Marsden*,[149] the Employment Appeal Tribunal held that the normal requirement of finality in litigation was outweighed by three factors: (i) the tribunal had been misled; (ii) by the plain misconduct of a representative; (iii) without prejudice to the other party.

3.130   This approach is in line with the approach taken in limitation of actions where the failings of a representative are not visited on the party *as a matter of law*.[150] However, see below the discussion of the refusal to allow issues to be raised or arguments to be made that a representative failed to raise or make.[151]

---

143 [2004] 1 WLR 2232.
144 [2004] 1 WLR 2232 at [41].
145 (1997) 94 (39) LS Gaz 39.
146 [2005] HLR 6.
147 [2005] HLR 6 at [12].
148 [2008] ICR 841.
149 [2010] ICR 743 at [19].
150 *Corbin v Penfold Metallising Co Ltd* (2000) *Times* 2 May.
151 At para 4.96 below.

## Human rights

3.131 Usually an appropriate use of the overriding objective will avoid any potential violation of a party's Convention rights under the Human Rights Act 1998.[152]

3.132 The rules of procedure are legislation. As such, the tribunal is subject to the duty under section 3(1) of the Human Rights Act that it must, so far as it is possible, read and give effect to them in a way that is compatible with Convention rights.

3.133 A Convention right can, therefore, supplement the overriding objective when it cannot alone produce a compatible result. For example: in *Goode v Martin*[153] the Court of Appeal used section 3(1) to allow it to read words into the CPR that it could not otherwise have justified.[154]

3.134 However, as Lord Woolf MR explained in *Daniels v Walker*,[155] representatives must 'take a responsible attitude as to when it is right to raise a Human Rights Act point'.[156]

## Previous authorities

3.135 The authorities that were decided before the new procedural regime began are no longer necessarily decisive.[157] But as Rimer LJ remarked in *Jurkowska v Hlmad Ltd*:[158]

> ... dealing with cases justly requires that they be dealt with in accordance with recognised principles. Those principles may have to be adapted on a case by case basis to meet what are perceived to be the special or exceptional circumstances of a particular cases. But they at least provide the structure on the basis of which a just decision can be made. ... Nothing less should be expected from a developed system of civil law.

3.136 Accordingly, the existing authorities may remain relevant in two ways. First, the principles may remain valid under the new regime. For example: in *Hertfordshire Investments Ltd v Bubb*,[159] the Court of Appeal decided that the principles for the admission of fresh evidence continued to apply and in *Newcastle City Council v Marsden*,[160] the Employment Appeal Tribunal recognised finality of litigation as a principle that would be of particular relevance. Second, the authorities may indicate factors that are relevant in applying the new regime. For example: in *Albon (trading as NA Carriage Co) v Naza Motor Trading Sdn Bhd (No 5)*,[161] Lightman J set out

---

152 Lord Woolf MR in *Daniels v Walker* [2000] 1 WLR 1382 at 1386.

153 [2002] 1 WLR 1828.

154 [2002] 1 WLR 1828 at [41]–[42]. See also Toulson J in *General Mediterranean Holdings SA v Patel* [2000] 1 WLR 272 at 295–296.

155 [2000] 1 WLR 1382.

156 [2000] 1 WLR 1382 at 1386.

157 Lord Woolf MR in *Biguzzi v Rank Leisure plc* [1999] 1 WLR 1926 at 1932.

158 [2008] ICR 841 at [19].

159 [2000] 1 WLR 1828. See also *Flynn v Scouigall* [2004] 1 WLR 3069 at [24]; *Parsons v George* [2006] 1 WLR 3264 at [41].

160 [2010] ICR 743 at [19].

161 [2008] 1 WLR 2380.

old authorities on when an adjournment should be given on account of the illness of a witness, but said:

> In my judgment however the exercise of the court's discretion whether to grant an adjournment is governed, not by these authorities, but by the terms of the CPR and in particular the overriding objective set out in CPR r1.1. No doubt considerations held critical in the authorities cited are relevant, but not decisive.[162]

## Acting judicially

3.137   The tribunal must act judicially. This has two aspects.

3.138   First, acting judicially refers to the personal manner and behaviour of the members of the tribunal and their interpersonal skills. In this sense, it refers to matters that do not affect the outcome of the proceedings. If the tribunal as a whole or any of its members is deficient in this respect, the appropriate recourse is by way of complaint.

3.139   Second, acting judicially refers to the manner in, and basis on, which the tribunal makes its decision. If the tribunal is deficient in this respect, the appropriate recourse is by way of appeal or judicial review.

3.140   These two aspects may overlap. For example: a racist comment is the proper subject of a complaint and may show that one of the parties did not have a fair hearing.

3.141   In *Royal Aquarium and Summer and Winter Garden Society Ltd v Parkinson*,[163] Fry LJ said that acting judicially required that the proceedings were:

> . . . conducted with the fairness and impartiality which characterize proceedings in Courts of justice, and are proper to the function of a judge.[164]

3.142   Other judges have spelt out what this involves. The essence of this requirement is that the tribunal must act in accordance with the principles of natural justice[165] and the Convention rights of the parties, especially article 6. Lord Diplock treated the duty of a tribunal to act rationally on material of probative value as part of the requirements of natural justice.[166]

3.143   In *R (Starling) v Child Support Commissioners*,[167] Collins J held that a tribunal exercising a child support jurisdiction was entitled to raise an issue on its own initiative, despite the fact that it had not been considered by the decision-maker or raised by any of the parties to the appeal, provided that the tribunal dealt with the issue fairly. He described something of what fairness required:

> I should add this in dealing with the question of fairness. Where a tribunal raises an issue of its own motion such as this it is obviously important

---

162 [2008] 1 WLR 2380 at [18].

163 [1892] 1 QB 431.

164 [1892] 1 QB 431 at 447, cited with approval by Lord Dilhorne in *Attorney-General v BBC* [1981] AC 303 at 340.

165 Lord Parker CJ in *R v The Medical Appeal Tribunal (Midland Region) ex p Carrarini* [1966] 1 WLR 883 at 887.

166 *Mahon v Air New Zealand Ltd* [1984] AC 808 at 820–821.

167 [2008] EWHC 1319 (Admin).

that the appellant is not put at a disadvantage and that the chairman of the tribunal does not take on the mantle of a party and descend into the arena. Of course he is entitled to test the evidence given by the appellant, to raise issues which he considers to be important and to point perhaps in the direction against the approach adopted by the appellant. But he must take care not to appear to be acting in a way which suggests that he has taken over the role of a party rather than staying in his role as chairman.[168]

3.144   A tribunal must not act capriciously or arbitrarily.[169] It must act according to law,[170] although without stifling judicial creativity.[171] Judges must respect their oath and may not opt out of hearings if they disapprove of the law.[172] The tribunal must act with scrupulous fairness.[173] It must act impartially and independently.[174] And the members must give their undivided attention to the hearing.[175] Such comments are no more than examples of the need for proceedings to be fair.

3.145   A judge should only communicate with parties or their representatives in identical terms and in a form that produces a record of the exchanges.[176]

3.146   A tribunal must exercise a discretion with due regard to the purpose for which it was conferred.[177] A discretion must also be exercised according to common sense and justice.[178] And must not be exercised 'subjectively or at whim or by rigid rule of thumb, but in a principled manner in accordance with reason and justice'.[179]

3.147   The exercise of a judicial power or duty cannot be delegated,[180] without statutory authority. For circumstances in which delegation is authorised under TCEA, see chapter 7.

## Fairness

3.148   Procedural fairness is an essential attribute of the judicial function. It is guaranteed by the common law principles of natural justice, article 6 and the overriding objective. The purpose of fairness is to enhance the quality of the decision taken, to show respect for the parties and to comply with the rule of law.[181]

168   [2008] EWHC 1319 (Admin) at [43].
169   Farwell J in *Hinckley and South Leicestershire Permanent Benefit Building Society v Freeman* [1941] Ch 32 at 39.
170   *R(U) 7/81* at [8].
171   Lord Judge CJ in a talk on *Judicial Independence and Responsibilities* given to the 16th Commonwealth Law Conference at Hong Kong on April 9, 2009.
172   *McClintock v Department of Constitutional Affairs* [2008] IRLR 29.
173   Henriques J in *R (M) v Inner London Crown Court* [2003] 1 FLR 994 at [45].
174   Stanley Burton J in *Berg v IML London Ltd* [2002] 1 WLR 3271 at [13].
175   *R v Marylebone Magistrates Court ex p Joseph* (1993) *Times* 7 May.
176   *Constantinou v Wilmot-Josife* [2010] 2 FLR 1449 at [17].
177   Lord Bingham in *South Bucks District Council v Porter* [2003] 2 AC 558 at [29].
178   Bowen LJ in *Gardner v Jay* (1885) 29 ChD 50 at 58.
179   *United Arab Emirates v Abdeighafar* [1995] ICR 65 at 70.
180   *Barnard v National Dock Labour Board* [1953] 2 QB 18; Lord Parker CJ in *R v Governor of Brixton Prison ex p Enahoro* [1963] 2 QB 455 at 465–466.
181   *Osborn v The Parole Board* [2013] UKSC 61 at [64]–[71].

3.149    On appeal, the issue is whether the procedure was fair, not whether the tribunal was entitled to consider that its procedure was fair.[182] Sedley LJ explained the correct approach in *Terluk v Berezovsky*:[183]

> ... the test to be applied to a decision on the adjournment of proceedings is not whether it lay within the broad band of judicial discretion, but whether, in the judgment of the appellate court, it was unfair.

3.150    However:[184]

> ... the question whether a procedural decision was fair does not involve a premise that in any given forensic situation only one outcome is ever fair.

3.151    A tribunal must act judicially. The right to fairness is an essential aspect of that requirement. As Henriques J said in *R (M) v Inner London Crown Court*,[185] judges:

> ... must act on all relevant evidence before them ... and reach a rational judgment. For my part, a requirement that they act with scrupulous fairness would add nothing. That is a standard to which all judges and justices should aspire in all their functions.

3.152    Fairness is often expressed as the right to a fair hearing. However, an oral hearing is not necessarily required. The principles apply whether or not the case is decided at an oral hearing and at all stages of the proceedings.

## The sources of the right to fairness

3.153    The right to fairness is governed by common law principles and by Convention rights, principally under article 6.[186] They are not identical. As Lord Hope noted in *R (West) v Parole Board*:[187]

> The right to a fair hearing under this article [6(1)] carries with it some ancillary rights that are not usually regarded as part of the general right to procedural fairness in common law. The right to a hearing within a reasonable time and the right to legal assistance of one's own choosing, for example, are expressly guaranteed by art 6.[188]

However, as the common law and the Convention right are so similar, there is little point in distinguishing between the authorities.

### Natural justice

3.154    Natural justice is nowadays defined in terms of procedural fairness. It is a compendious way of referring to the approach to procedure required of those who exercise a judicial function.[189]

---

182  *Osborn v The Parole Board* [2013] UKSC 61 at [65].
183  [2010] EWCA Civ 1345 at [18].
184  [2010] EWCA Civ 1345 at [20]. See also at [27].
185  [2003] 1 FLR 994 at [45].
186  If article 6 does not apply, procedural saafeguards may arise under article 8: *IR (Sri Lanka) v Secretary of State for the Home Department* [2012] 1 WLR 232.
187  [2005] 1 WLR 350.
188  [2005] 1 WLR 350 at [41].
189  Geoffrey Lane LJ in *R v Board of Visitors of Hull Prison ex p St Germain (No 2)* [1979] 1 WLR 1401 at 1408.

3.155    In *R v Deputy Industrial Injuries Commissioner ex p Moore*,[190] Diplock LJ said:

> Where, as in the present case, a personal bias or *mala fides* on the part of the deputy commissioner is not in question, the rules of natural justice which he must observe can, in my view, be reduced to two. First, he must base his decision on evidence, whether a hearing is requested or not. Secondly, he must fairly listen to the contentions of all persons who are entitled to be represented at the hearing.[191]

3.156    However, this statement is too narrow in that it excludes a number of features of natural justice that contribute to fairness. Dyson LJ included these in his definition in *AMEC Capital Projects Ltd v Whitefriars City Estates Ltd*:[192]

> The common law rules of natural justice or procedural fairness are two-fold. First, the person affected has the right to prior notice and an effective opportunity to make representations before a decision is made. Second, the person affected has the right to an unbiased tribunal. These two requirements are conceptually distinct.[193]

3.157    The effectiveness to which Dyson LJ referred includes knowledge of the other party's case. As Lord Denning explained for the Privy Council in *Kanda v Government of the Federation of Malaysia*:[194]

> If the right to be heard is to be a real right which is worth anything, it must carry with it a right in the accused man to know the case which is made against him. He must know what evidence has been given and what statements have been made affecting him: and then he must be given a fair opportunity to correct or contradict them.[195]

3.158    The right to make representations is not unlimited. It is confined to matters that affect the parties' rights. As Dyson LJ explained in *AMEC Capital Projects Ltd v Whitefriars City Estates Ltd*:[196]

> The reason for the common law right to prior notice and an effective opportunity to make representations is to protect parties from the risk of decisions being reached unfairly. But it is only directed at decisions which can affect parties' rights. Procedural fairness does not require that parties should have the right to make representations in relation to decisions which do not affect their rights, still less in relation to 'decisions' which are nullities and which cannot affect their rights.

### Analogous principle

3.159    Natural justice does not include failings by a party or by the party's representative. This was decided by the House of Lords in *Al-Mehdawi v Secretary of State for the Home Department*.[197] Lord Bridge said:

---

190 [1965] 1 QB 456.
191 [1965] 1 QB 456 at 487–488.
192 [2005] 1 All ER 723.
193 [2005] 1 All ER 723 at [14].
194 [1962] AC 322.
195 [1962] AC 322 at 337.
196 [2005] 1 All ER 723 at [41].
197 [1990] 1 AC 876.

... a party to a dispute who has lost the opportunity to have his case heard through the default of his own advisers to whom he has entrusted the conduct of the dispute on his behalf cannot complain that he has been the victim of a procedural impropriety or that natural justice should be denied to him . . .[198]

3.160   In *Al-Mehdawi*, the House recognised the existence of a principle by analogy with natural justice. This is based on the suppression of information by one of the parties to the proceedings to the detriment of another.[199] In *R v Criminal Injuries Compensation Board ex p A*,[200] the House took a similar approach, based on objective unfairness,[201] to a failure by the police to disclose information to the Criminal Injuries Compensation Board. This was based on the police's close co-operation with the Board. The principle will cover anyone who has a co-operative role in relation to the tribunal.[202]

3.161       The present status of *Al-Mehdawi* is uncertain. According to Arden LJ in *FP (Iran) v Secretary of State for the Home Department*,[203] it probably applies to civil litigation in which the court has to consider the interests of all the parties in order to deal with the case justly. But it does not apply to asylum cases. In *Haile v Immigration Appeal Tribunal*,[204] the Court of Appeal distinguished the case, and had regard to 'the wider interests of justice', suggesting that *Al-Mehdawi* might need to be reconsidered in the light of *ex p A*.[205] And in *FP (Iran)*, Sedley LJ said that there was no general principle of law which fixed a party with the procedural errors of a representative.[206]

3.162       A party may be able to rely on four other powers to deal with the type of case covered by *Al-Mehdawi*.

3.163       First, the rules of procedure require the parties to co-operate with the tribunal.[207] Suppression by a party of relevant information is likely to be a breach of that duty.

3.164       Second, the tribunal has an express power to set aside its own decision.[208]

3.165       Third, the circumstances may give rise to a mistake of fact that amounts to an error of law under *E and R v Secretary of State for the Home Department*.[209] This happened in *MM (unfairness; E & R) Sudan*,[210] in which the Secretary of State had failed to pass to the presenting officer or the tribunal a letter from the solicitor of the asylum seeker. The absence of that letter affected the reasoning of the First-tier Tribunal.

198 [1990] 1 AC 876 at 898.

199 [1990] 1 AC 876 per Lord Bridge at 896.

200 [1999] 2 AC 330.

201 [1999] 2 AC 330 per Lord Slynn at 345.

202 See the discussion of co-operative decision-making in chapter 1.

203 [2007] EWCA Civ 13: (2007) *Times* 26 January at [80].

204 [2002] INLR 283.

205 [2002] INLR 283 per Simon Brown LJ at [26].

206 [2002] INLR 283 at [46].

207 See chapter 3.

208 See chapter 15.

209 [2004] QB 1044

210 [2014] UKUT 0105 (IAC).

3.166 Fourth, there are old authorities that, in the absence of an express power, a tribunal may have power to re-open a case in order to prevent injustice. For example: in *R v Kensington and Chelsea Rent Tribunal ex p MacFarlane*,[211] a party to the proceedings before the tribunal did not receive notice of the hearing. The Divisional Court held that the tribunal had the power to reopen the case if a party did not receive a notice or for some other reason could not attend. It is clear from the reasoning that this is not a duty, so that there is no breach of natural justice if the tribunal declines to reopen the case, and that this power is not exercised just for the asking but only in limited circumstances.[212] It is doubtful if this line of authorities is still of any legal or practical significance.

3.167 As to legal significance, the cases arose at a time when the rules of procedure were not as detailed and comprehensive as they are today. Any such power would have to be consistent with the statutory scheme of procedure for the tribunal[213] and that is now unlikely. Moreover, the modern view is that a tribunal has no inherent powers other than to correct accidental mistakes in its decision.[214]

3.168 As to practical significance, the express power to set aside will usually be sufficient to cover any eventualities that would be caught by these cases.

## No fault

3.169 There are conflicting authorities on whether there can be a breach of natural justice without any fault by the parties, the tribunal or its administration.[215]

## Article 6(1)

3.170 Article 6(1) of the European Convention on Human Rights and Fundamental Freedoms provides:

> *Right to a fair trial*
> 1. In the determination of his civil rights and obligations or of any criminal charge against him, everyone is entitled to a fair and public hearing within a reasonable time by an independent and impartial tribunal established by law. Judgment shall be pronounced publicly but the press and public may be excluded from all or part of the trial in the interest of morals, public order or national security in a democratic society, where the interests of juveniles or the protection of the private life of the parties so require, or to the extent strictly necessary in the opinion of the court in special circumstances where publicity would prejudice the interests of justice.
> 2. Everyone charged with a criminal offence shall be presumed innocent until proved guilty according to law.

---

211 [1974] 1 WLR 1486.
212 [1974] 1 WLR 1486 per Lord Widgery CJ at 1493.
213 Lord Reid in *Wiseman v Borneman* [1971] AC 297 at 308.
214 Sedley LJ in *Akewushola v Secretary of State for the Home Department* [2000] 1 WLR 2295 at 2301.
215 *KH v CMEC* [2012] UKUT 329 (AAC) at [24] is an example of the Upper Tribunal finding a breach of natural justice in such circumstances.

3. Everyone charged with a criminal offence has the following minimum rights:
   (a) to be informed promptly, in a language which he understands and in detail, of the nature and cause of the accusation against him;
   (b) to have adequate time and facilities for the preparation of his defence;
   (c) to defend himself in person or through legal assistance of his own choosing or, if he has not sufficient means to pay for legal assistance, to be given it free when the interests of justice so require;
   (d) to examine or have examined witnesses against him and to obtain the attendance and examination of witnesses on his behalf under the same conditions as witnesses against him;
   (e) to have the free assistance of an interpreter if he cannot understand or speak the language used in court.

3.171   In practice, tribunals are mainly concerned with article 6(1). But the remaining provisions of the article may be relevant for two reasons. First, some proceedings or aspects of proceedings before tribunals may be criminal for the purposes of article 6. Second, the other provisions may provide guidance to the tribunal on similar issues in civil proceedings.

## The relationship between fairness and procedural legislation

3.172   The rules of procedure give expression to the requirement for fairness by making specific provision for the eventualities that may occur in relation to proceedings. The more comprehensive the rules of procedure are in their coverage and the more specific they are in their content, the less the scope for the operation of the common law principles or the Convention right.

3.173   What happens if there is a conflict between the right to fairness and an express rule of procedure? This may be resolved in favour of fairness by the interpretative approach of the common law, the Human Rights Act and the overriding objective. To the extent that it cannot, the rules of procedure must be applied regardless of any unfairness they may cause.

### Natural justice

3.174   Natural justice may be relevant both to the interpretation of procedural legislation and to its application.

3.175   Legislation must, if possible, be interpreted in a way that is compatible with those principles. This applies both to the rules of procedure and to their enabling provisions. There is a presumption that the principles of natural justice apply unless there is provision otherwise. In *Fairmount Investments Ltd v Secretary of State for the Environment*,[216] Lord Russell said:

> For it is to be implied, unless the contrary appears, that Parliament does not authorise by the Act the exercise of powers in breach of the principles of natural justice, and that Parliament does by the Act require, in the particular procedures, compliance with those principles.[217]

216 [1976] 1 WLR 1255.
217 [1976] 1 WLR 1255 at 1263.

3.176    And in deciding whether there is provision otherwise, the clarity of the language is relevant. As Megarry J said in *John v Rees*:[218]

> The more indefinite the language, the less apt it is to exclude the members' reasonable expectation of being accorded natural justice.[219]

3.177    The fact that legislation makes express provision for one class of case does not prevent the principles of natural justice producing the same effect for other classes. In *R (West) v Parole Board*,[220] Lord Bingham summarised the authorities:

> While s32 of the 1991 Act expressly provided for oral hearings in some classes of case, those classes did not include cases such as the present in which oral hearings were permitted but not required. That, it was submitted, represented a legislative choice. But the maxim expression *unius exclusio alterius* can seldom, if ever, be enough to exclude the common law rules of natural justice . . .

3.178    If legislation cannot be interpreted compatibly with natural justice, it must be implemented.[221] However, this is subject to two limitations. First, there may be greater freedom to interpret the legislation in order to be compatible with the equivalent article 6 Convention right than under the common law rules of interpretation. Second, it may be possible to require the legislation to be applied in a way that complies with natural justice.

3.179    Legislation may also replace natural justice by making equivalent provision. If it does so, it will usually make more specific provision. For example: legislation may provide, as does natural justice, that a party to the proceedings must have notice of the hearing, but it may make this right more precise by specifying a minimum period of notice, the contents of the notice, the method of service and so on.

3.180    Whether legislation is compatible or incompatible with natural justice, it must so far as possible be applied in a way that is compatible. In the case of discretions, this is achieved through the requirement that they must be exercised judicially. For example: a tribunal may be under a duty to exercise its discretion to adjourn if it has insufficient time in a hearing to deal properly with the case.[222]

### Convention right

3.181    Article 6(1) guarantees to every party to the proceedings a fair hearing. Section 3(1) of the Human Rights Act 1998 provides:

> (1) So far as it is possible to do so, primary legislation and subordinate legislation must be read and given effect in a way which is compatible with the Convention rights.

---

218  [1970] Ch 345.
219  [1970] Ch 345 at 401–402.
220  [2005] 1 WLR 350 at [29].
221  As in *MT (Algeria) v Secretary of State for the Home Department* [2008] 2 All ER 786 at [14]–[18].
222  As in *R v Thames Magistrates' Court ex p Polemis* [1974] 1 WLR 1371, where a summons was served on the foreign master of a ship at 10.30 am to appear in court at 2 pm and the ship was due to sail at 9 pm.

3.182   This means that the legislation must be interpreted and applied to ensure, so far as that is possible, that it does not conflict with article 6. This covers both the rules of procedure themselves and any enabling provision. The approach required by section 3(1) reinforces, and goes further than, the common law approach that legislation be interpreted, so far as the language allows, in a way that does not conflict with natural justice.

### The overriding objective

3.183   Under TCEA, the rules of procedure and practice directions are subject to the overriding objective. This operates in addition to the common law principles set out above. It is the overriding objective of the rules to enable a tribunal to deal with cases justly and fairly, which includes the right to fairness. A tribunal must 'seek to give effect to the overriding objective when it . . . interprets any rule or practice direction.' However, it may provide a lesser guarantee of procedural fairness in the event of a conflict than either the common law approach or the Human Rights Act.

3.184   As regards the common law approach, the overriding objective applies only to the rules of procedure and practice directions. It does not apply to the enabling provisions, which are subject to the common law approach. It is unclear to what extent, if at all, the duty under TCEA differs from the presumptive approach of the common law.

3.185   As regards the Human Rights Act, 'seek to give effect' gives the tribunal less scope for interpreting a provision than the duty under section 3(1) of the Human Rights Act to read and give effect to legislation in a way that is compatible with Convention rights 'so far as it is possible to do so'. It also applies, unlike the overriding objective, to enabling provisions.

## The nature of the right to fairness

3.186   Both the common law and the Convention right, like all the Convention rights, are more akin to a principle than a rule. In *Wilson v First County Trust Ltd (No 2)*,[223] Lord Rodger said:

> It is well recognised, however, that Convention rights are to be seen as an expression of fundamental principles rather than as a set of mere rules. In applying the principles the courts must balance competing interests.

3.187   So, even though the Convention right is in its terms absolute, it may be subject to restriction. But in keeping with the interpretation of the Convention generally, any restriction must satisfy specific criteria. They were set out by the European Court of Human Rights in *Ashingdane v United Kingdom*:[224]

> . . . the limitations applied must not restrict or reduce the access left to the individual in such a way or to such an extent that the very essence of the right is impaired. Furthermore, a limitation will not be compatible with Art 6(1) if it does not pursue a legitimate aim and if there is not a reasonable relationship of proportionality between the means employed and the aim sought to be achieved.

223  [2004] 1 AC 816 at [181].
224  (1985) 7 EHRR 528 at [57].

These conditions allow an appropriate procedural bar to bringing proceedings, such as a reasonable time limit or permission to appeal. But they prevent bars, even if drafted in terms of procedure, that effectively prevent reliance on the Convention right. Absolute time limits on commencing proceedings may be acceptable in some circumstances. In refusing permission to appeal to the Court of Appeal in *Curtis v Secretary of State for Work and Pensions*,[225] Buxton LJ commented that such a limit was more understandable in the case of an obligation owed by one citizen to another (like child support) than in cases of an obligation to pay by a public authority.[226] For lodging an appeal, six weeks was considered generous by Burton J in *Woodward v Abbey National plc*.[227]

3.188     Also, as a human right, the right must be applied to the substance and not to the form of the domestic law. In *Wilson v First County Trust Ltd (No 2)*,[228] Lord Nicholls said:

> Human rights conventions are concerned with substance, not form, with practicalities and realities, not linguistic niceties.

3.189     Both these points illustrated a more general principle, that the right to fairness must be interpreted and applied in a way that renders it effective.

## Process and substance

3.190     The right to fairness sets the minimum standard for resolving disputes about the existence of legal rights and obligations in domestic law, and about their interpretation and application in a particular case.

3.191     It is concerned with process. In *Matthews v Ministry of Defence*,[229] Lord Hoffmann referred to:

> . . . the underlying principle, which is to maintain the rule of law and the separation of powers . . .

And Lord Walker said:

> . . . art 6 is in principle concerned with the procedural fairness and integrity of a state's judicial system . . .[230]

3.192     As fairness is concerned with process, it follows that it is not concerned with the content of the rights and obligations themselves. The difference between a right or obligation and its enforcement is one of substance that is not determined by the terms in which the law is framed. In *Wilson v First County Trust Ltd (No 2)*,[231] Lord Nicholls said:

> Human rights conventions are concerned with substance, not form, with practicalities and realities, not linguistic niceties. The crucial question . . . is whether, as a matter of substance, the relevant provision of national law has the effect of preventing an issue which ought to be decided by a court from being so decided. The touchstone in this regard is the proper role of courts

---

225 [2006] EWCA Civ 1556.
226 [2006] EWCA Civ 1556 at [28].
227 [2005] ICR 1702 at [2].
228 [2004] 1 AC 816 at [35].
229 [2003] 1 AC 1163 at [29]. See also *Golder v United Kingdom* (1975) 1 EHRR 524 at [34].
230 [2003] 1 AC 1163 at [142].
231 [2004] 1 AC 816 at [35].

in a democratic society. A right of access to a court is one of the checks on the danger of arbitrary power.[232]

He defined the issue as whether the legislation in question was:

... encroaching on territory which ought properly to be the province of the courts in a democratic society.[233]

## The scope of the Convention right

### Determination

3.193   An interim measure, such as a suspension, is not determinative of civil rights or obligations. As such it is not within the scope of article 6, provided that no financial penalty is involved.[234]

### Civil right or obligation[235]

3.194   A civil right or obligation is an autonomous concept under the Convention.[236] That means that the proper classification of a right or obligation is determined by reference to the jurisprudence of the European Court of Human Rights.[237] It is not dictated by the classification used in domestic law. This approach was inevitable, given the variation between the legal classification systems of civil law countries.[238]

3.195       There must be a right in issue. This will not always be the case. In *Ali v Birmingham City Council*,[239] the Supreme Court held that a potential benefit was not a civil right if it depended on a series of evaluative judgments. In *R (V: a child) v Independent Appeal Panel for Tom Hood School*,[240] Silber J held that there was no arguable right involved in the permanent exclusion of a child from a particular school.

3.196       Although the Convention is concerned with civil and political rights, it has been extended in practice. It may include social and economic rights. In *Airey v Ireland*,[241] the Court said:

Whilst the Convention sets forth what are essentially civil and political rights, many of them have implications of a social or economic nature. The Court therefore considers ... that the mere fact that an interpretation of the Convention may extend into the sphere of social and economic rights should not be a decisive factor against such an interpretation; there is no water-tight division separating that sphere from the field covered by the Convention.

232  See also *Van Droogenbroeck v Belgium* (1982) 4 EHRR 443 at [38]; *R (Anderson) Secretary of State for the Home Department* [2003] 1 AC 837 at [13].
233  [2004] 1 AC 816 at [36].
234  *R (Malik) v Waltham Forest Primary Care Trust* [2006] ICR 1111 at [28]–[32].
235  For a comparison of these words in this context with the more general common law understanding, see the decision of the Privy Council in *Meerabux v Attorney-General . of Belize* [2005] 2 AC 513.
236  *König v Federal Republic of Germany* (1975) 2 EHRR 170 at [88].
237  *R (MK (Iran)) v Secretary of State for the Home Department* [2010] 4 All ER 892.
238  On which see Lord Goff's analysis in *Re State of Norway's Application (Nos 1 & 2)* [1990] 1 AC 723.
239  [2010] All ER 175.
240  (2009) *Times* 18 March.
241  (1979) 2 EHRR 305 at [26].

3.197 The scope of the Convention also covers some rights and obligations that would in some Continental countries be classified as part of administrative, rather than civil, law. This has compensated for the lack of a European Convention governing administrative rights and obligations, which was originally intended but never implemented.[242] The extended meaning given to this autonomous concept in areas of administrative law has been balanced by an acceptance that compliance with article 6(1) on a challenge to an administrative decision need not necessarily involve a right to challenge on the facts and merits rather than just the legality of the decision.[243]

3.198 Lord Hoffmann has suggested that the law may be close to this state: the administrative right or obligation is not civil for the purposes of the Convention, but the dispute whether the decision was lawful is concerned with civil rights or obligations.[244] Perhaps, the right to have an administrative decision made lawfully is a civil one.

3.199 Proceedings that do not involve a civil right are nonetheless within article 6 if they will be dispositive of, or if they may have a substantial effect on, proceedings that are.[245]

### A variable standard

3.200 The level of procedural protection under article 6 varies according to what is at stake in the proceedings.[246] It involves a balance between the rights of the parties and the public interest. But as an irreducible minimum every party has the right to sufficient information about the other party's evidential case to give effective instructions and, so far as possible, to refute that case.[247]

## Protective rights

3.201 Article 6 refers to a fair hearing. But this right would be rendered ineffective if it stood alone. In order to protect it, the European Court of Human Rights has identified additional, protective rights.

### Right of access[248]

3.202 The first protective right is an inherent right of access to a tribunal. In *Golder v United Kingdom*,[249] the Court held:

242 Lord Hoffmann in *Runa Begum v Tower Hamlets London Borough Council* [2003] 2 AC 430 at [28]–[30].

243 *Bryan v United Kingdom* (1995) 21 EHRR 342 at [47]; Lord Hoffmann in *R (Alconbury Developments Ltd) v Secretary of State for Environment, Transport and the Regions* [2003] 2 AC 295 at [87]; Lords Bingham and Hoffmann in *Runa Begum v Tower Hamlets London Borough Council* [2003] 2 AC 430 at [5] and [34].

244 Lord Bingham in *Runa Begum v Tower Hamlets London Borough Council* [2003] 2 AC 430 at [32] and [34].

245 *R (G) v Governors of X School* [2012] 1 AC 167. See also *Kulkarni v Milton Keynes NHS Foundation Trust* [2010] ICR 101.

246 *R (G) v Governors of X School* [2012] 1 AC 167 at [71].

247 *Bank Mellat v Her Majesty's Treasury* [2012] QB 91 at [18] and [21].

248 See also the discussion of deeming provisions in chapter 7.

249 (1975) 1 EHRR 524 at [36].

> . . . the right of access constitutes an element which is inherent in the right stated by Article 6(1). This is not an extensive interpretation forcing new obligations on the Contracting States: it is based on the very terms of the first sentence of Article 6(1) read in its context and having regard to the object and purpose of the Convention, a lawmaking treaty, and to general principles of law.

As the Court pointed out, if it were otherwise a State could dispense with courts altogether or for particular classes of case, which would be 'indissociable from a danger of arbitrary power'[250] and:

> The fair, public and expeditious characteristics of judicial proceedings are of no value at all if there are no judicial proceedings.[251]

However, the right of access is not unqualified:

> As this is a right which the Convention sets forth without, in the narrower sense of the term, defining, there is room, apart from the bounds delimiting the very content of any right, for limitations permitted by implication.[252]

Possible examples were 'minors and persons of unsound mind'.[253]

3.203    The restriction of access to the court was discussed by the Court of Appeal in *Cachia v Faluyi*:[254]

> The point arises in this way. The Convention gives these three children a right of access to a court to claim compensation for their loss of dependency following the death of their mother. Although the European Court of Human Rights recognises that the enactment of limitation periods represents the pursuit of a legitimate aim (see *Stubbings v United Kingdom* 23 EHRR 213, 227, paras 53–55), these claims were not statute-barred when this writ was issued in 1997.

> The European Court of Human Rights has also recognised the legitimacy of other restrictions on the right of access to a court that have been drawn to its attention from time to time. Cases involving vexatious litigants, persons under disability, and the striking out of actions for want of prosecution are obvious examples. A fuller list can be found in standard text-books on Article 6(1): see, for example, *Clayton and Tomlinson, The Law of Human Rights*, Vol 1, pp 640–1, para 11.191. The governing test, set out in the judgment of the ECtHR in *Ashingdane v United Kingdom* 7 EHRR 528, 546, para 57, and repeated often in later cases, is that such restrictions must not impair the essence of the right of access; they must have a legitimate aim, and the means used must be reasonably proportionate to the aim sought to be achieved.

3.204    Access to a tribunal involves more than mere acquiescence by the State. It must provide not only access, but effective access. So, in *FP (Iran) v Secretary of State for the Home Department*,[255] the Court of Appeal decided that a rule requiring a tribunal to hear a case even when a party was, without fault, unaware of the date of the hearing was unlawful as it arbitrarily denied the right to be heard. This approach will often overcome the

---

250  (1975) 1 EHRR 524 at [35].
251  (1975) 1 EHRR 524 at [35].
252  (1975) 1 EHRR 524 at [38].
253  (1975) 1 EHRR 524 at [39].
254  [2001] 1 WLR 1966 at [17]–[18].
255  [2007] EWCA Civ 13; (2007) *Times* 26 January. Arden LJ limited her judgment (at [61]–[74]) to the proposition that a right could not be taken away before it has been communicated to the person entitled to it.

limitation on the scope of natural justice identified by the House of Lords in *Al-Mehdawi v Secretary of State for the Home Department*.[256]

3.205 Access to a tribunal may involve a positive obligation. In *Airey v Ireland*,[257] the European Court held that:

> ... fulfilment of a duty under the Convention on occasion necessitates some positive action on the part of the State ... The obligation to secure an effective right of access to the courts falls into this category.

In this case, the Court held that this required the State to provide free legal aid.[258] However, it emphasised that this was not the only means by which access to a tribunal could be made effective:

> In certain eventualities, the possibility of appearing before a court in person, even without a lawyer's assistance, will meet the requirements of Article 6(1); there may even be occasions when such a possibility secures adequate access even to the High Court. Indeed, much must depend on the particular circumstances. ... but there are others such as, for example, a simplification of procedure. ... However, ... Article 6(1) may sometimes compel the State to provide for the assistance of a lawyer when such assistance proves indispensable for an effective access to court either because legal representation is compulsory ... or by reason of the complexity of the procedure or of the case.[259]

3.206 In *A v United Kingdom*,[260] the Court held that the availability of a conditional fee arrangement was sufficient to allow access, despite its novelty and the risk of costs, because the green form scheme allowed free advice and a chance to make an informed assessment of the risks of litigation.[261]

3.207 Proceedings may be fair despite the fact that a party is unaware that public funding for legal representation is available and is represented by another professional. For example: the Court of Appeal held in *Khan v Commissioners of Revenue and Customs*[262] that proceedings had been fair when a taxpayer who, in ignorance of his right to publicly funded legal representation, had been represented by an accountant.

3.208 In the tribunal context, there are a number of features that are likely to render the right of access effective without specific legal funding for the particular case: the nature of the procedures, a tribunal's enabling and inquisitorial approach, the neutral position of the public party and the availability of free advice and representation, such as that provided by welfare rights organisations. The duties of the Senior President under TCEA s2(3) and the statutory requirements for the tribunal's rules of procedure in TCEA s22(4) enhance the right of access for unrepresented parties.

3.209 On the effect of limited funding, see *DN v Greenwich London Borough Council*.[263]

---

256 [1990] 1 AC 876.
257 (1979) 2 EHRR 305 at [25].
258 (1979) 2 EHRR 305 at [24].
259 (1979) 2 EHRR 305 at [26].
260 (2003) 36 EHRR 917.
261 (2003) 36 EHRR 917 at [90]–[100].
262 [2006] EWCA Civ 89; (2006) *Times* 21 March.
263 [2005] LGR 597.

3.210   If a claimant lacks the mental capacity to take his case to a tribunal on appeal, it may be necessary for the State to provide for a form of referral to ensure access to an independent tribunal.[264]

3.211   The merits of a case are irrelevant if the issue of access to justice is raised, unless the case is plainly worthless.[265]

## Equality of arms

3.212   Equality of arms between the parties is an aspect of effective access. However, this must not be taken too literally. There is, for example, no need to allow both parties to call the same number of expert witnesses.[266]

3.213   Equality of arms requires knowledge of the proceedings and the chance to participate effectively in them. Accordingly, notice of proceedings properly served is necessary for the operation of equality of arms.[267] And, as the European Court of Human Rights explained in *Moser v Austria*:[268]

> The principle of equality of arms – one of the elements of the broader concept of a fair trial – requires that each party should be afforded a reasonable opportunity to present his or her case under conditions that do not place him or her at a substantial disadvantage vis-à-vis his or her opponent . . . Each party must be given the opportunity to have knowledge of and comment on the observations filed or evidence adduced by the other party . . .

3.214   This concept confirms and supports the basic requirements of natural justice and the inquisitorial and enabling approaches.[269]

## Material before the tribunal

3.215   A hearing cannot be fair if the parties are not shown the evidence before the tribunal and have a right to comment on it. It is the duty of the tribunal to ensure that all potentially relevant material is put to the parties.[270] The same documents should be before all the parties and the tribunal.[271] This is subject to provision to the contrary.[272]

3.216   A party who chooses not to attend a hearing cannot hear any evidence given at the hearing. By choosing not to attend, the party has waived this right.

3.217   The rules of procedure may provide for the handling of potentially harmful evidence, confidential information or the identity of a witness. It is consistent with fairness for witnesses to be granted anonymity.[273]

---

264  *R (H) v Secretary of State for Health* [2005] 1 WLR 1209. The House of Lords at [2006] 1 AC 441 decided that a referral system was not required under that particular legislation.

265  Sedley LJ in *FP (Iran) v Secretary of State for the Home Department* [2007] EWCA Civ 13 at [20]; (2007) *Times* 26 January.

266  *Kirkman v Euro Exide Corporation (CMP Batteries Ltd)* [2007] EWCA Civ 66; (2007) *Times* 6 February.

267  *Švenčionienė v Lithuania* [2009] 1 FLR 509.

268  [2007] 1 FLR 702 at [86].

269  See chapter 1.

270  *HAL v Finland* Application No 38267/97 judgment on 27 January 2004 at [44]–[47].

271  *Lloyds Bank plc v Cassidy* (2005) *Times* 11 January.

272  See chapter 10.

273  *R v Davis* [2006] 1 WLR 3130.

### Understanding proceedings

3.218 If a party has reduced capacity to understand the proceedings, whether by age or mental health, there are steps which a tribunal should take in order to ensure fairness. They were set out by Scott Baker LJ in *R (P) v West London Youth Court*:[274]

> It is apparent from the judge's judgment and Dr Marriott's evidence that there are indeed a number of steps that can be taken during the trial. These include: (i) keeping the claimant's level of cognitive functioning in mind; (ii) using concise and simple language; (iii) having regular breaks; (iv) taking additional time to explain court proceedings; (v) being proactive in ensuring the claimant has access to support; (vi) explaining and ensuring the claimant understands the ingredients of the charge; (vii) explaining the possible outcomes and sentences; (viii) ensuring that cross-examination is carefully controlled so that questions are short and clear and frustration is minimised.

### Understanding the consequences of decisions

3.219 A party to the proceedings may not understand the consequences of a decision. As a result, the party's consent may not be properly informed. For example: a party who has initiated an appeal but does not attend a hearing may not realise that the tribunal may make a decision that is more adverse than the one under appeal. The tribunal's failure to advise on this may amount to, or lead to, unfairness.[275]

### Interpreters

3.220 In *R(I) 11/63*, the Commissioner decided that it was not a requirement of natural justice to provide an interpreter for a claimant. It may be that the law has moved on since then. In principle, it should be a requirement in securing an equality of arms between the parties and, under article 6(3)(e), the provision of an interpreter is expressly required for criminal cases. In practice, the tribunal provides interpreters as required.

### Enforcement

3.221 The right to fairness would be undermined without a right to enforce the decision made. In *Hornsby v Greece*,[276] the Court said that article 6:

> . . . would be illusory if a Contracting State's domestic legal system allowed a final, binding judicial decision to remain inoperative to the detriment of one party. It would be inconceivable that Article 6 should describe in detail procedural guarantees afforded to litigants – proceedings that are fair, public and expeditious – without protecting the implementation of judicial decisions; to construe Article 6 as being concerned exclusively with access to a court and the conduct of proceedings would be likely to lead to situations incompatible with the principle of the rule of law which the Contracting States undertook to respect when they ratified the Convention. Execution of a judgment given by any court must therefore be regarded as

274 [2006] 1 WLR 1219 at [26].
275 Lord Denning MR and Roskill LJ in *Hanson v Church Commissioners for England* [1978] QB 823 at 833–834 and 837–838.
276 (1997) 24 EHRR 250 at [40].

an integral part of the 'trial' for the purposes of Article 6; moreover, the Court has already accepted this principle in cases concerning the length of proceedings.

3.222   However, national law may give no right to a particular party to be involved in the enforcement process. This was the position in *R (Kehoe) v Secretary of State for Work and Pensions*,[277] which concerned the enforcement of payments of child support maintenance. The House of Lords held that there was no violation in a parent with care being given no right to be involved in decisions on enforcement, which was a matter exclusively for the Secretary of State.

## The tribunal's relationship with the State

3.223   The independence of a tribunal is an aspect of the separation of powers. It must be free from influence by the State. The concern here is with the structure of the tribunal system, the appointment of members and the control over the tribunal's rules of procedure.

3.224   The power for a minister to issue directions to a tribunal does not prevent it being independent, provided that they are not mandatory and do no more than require the tribunal to take account of matters that are relevant in so far as appropriate.[278] However, the powers conferred on the Senior President of Tribunals and on Chamber Presidents is wider in that they envisage a practice direction on the application or interpretation of the law or on decision-making by members of the First-tier Tribunal or Upper Tribunal (TCEA s23(6)).

## The tribunal's attitude to the proceedings

3.225   This covers a number of aspects. The most fully developed is bias, but this is but one aspect of the attitude that is required of judges in the conduct of a hearing.

### Hearing both sides

3.226   Each party must know of the proceedings and the time and place of any hearing. The tribunal must allow a party to present a case. This entails allowing each party to know the other's case and any additional material that the tribunal may take into account, and giving them a chance to respond. This will usually require the tribunal to hear the evidence of the party's witnesses[279] and, perhaps, to question witnesses whose evidence is presented in hearsay form.[280]

3.227   This applies whether a party attends or not. A tribunal that hears a case cannot reject a party's case just because that party did not attend.[281] It may, in the circumstances of a case, be a breach of the requirement of fairness

---

277 [2006] 1 AC 42.

278 *R (Girling) v Parole Board* [2007] QB 783.

279 Geoffrey Lane LJ in *R v Board of Visitors of Hull Prison ex p St Germain (No 2)* [1979] 1 WLR 1401 at 1407–1408.

280 [1979] 1 WLR 1401 at 1410.

281 *London Borough of Southwark v Bartholomew* [2004] ICR 358.

to proceed in the absence of a party even if that course was authorised under the rules of procedure.[282]

3.228    This is subject to the tribunal's control over the proceedings to ensure, for example, that its time is used efficiently and not devoted to hearing irrelevant or repetitious evidence and argument.

### The tribunal's thinking

3.229   A tribunal may have to inform the parties of its provisional conclusions or doubts about a party's case in order to allow them to be dealt with. This is important for two reasons. First, the party may not realise that the tribunal is concerned about an issue. Second, the party may have evidence that is relevant to the issue and may be able to allay the tribunal's concerns.

3.230    A party must be taken to know that the tribunal is concerned with the issues raised by the proceedings and the tribunal need not explain to the parties whether or not they are inclined at any time to decide the issue one way or another.[283] However, issues may arise in the course of proceedings and without a party realising. In *R v Mental Health Review Tribunal ex p Clatworthy*,[284] Mann J said that if a tribunal 'desires to proceed on the basis of some point which has not been put before it and which on the face of the matter is not in dispute',[285] it must be put to the parties for comment. Otherwise, the need for disclosure will depend on the significance of the point to the outcome of the case. It is, though, good practice to put any points to the party affected, as there may be an answer that is not apparent to the tribunal.

### Concentration on proceedings

3.231   There cannot be fairness if a judge appears to be asleep during a hearing, for example as a result of having drunk alcohol.[286] But this may depend on the nature and stage of the proceedings at which this occurs.[287]

### Participation in the proceedings

3.232   Tribunals are entitled, and in furtherance of the inquisitorial and enabling approaches may be required, to keep the parties to matters relevant to the proceedings, to question them about their case and to ensure that the time for the hearing is used efficiently. As Davis J explained of the Pensions Appeal Tribunal in *R (Clancy) v Secretary of State for Defence*:[288]

> . . . Mr Clancy had complained that he had had, as it were, something of a rough time before the Tribunal – questions being shot at him and his representative, and in consequence a lack of coherence, as he claimed, in advancing his case was experienced. But that can reflect the nature of such

---

282  *GJ v Secretary of State for Work and Pensions, JG and SW* [2012] UKUT 447 (AAC).

283  May LJ in *Baron v Secretary of State for Social Services* reported as an Appendix to *R(M) 6/86*.

284  [1985] 3 All ER 699.

285  At 704.

286  *Stansbury v Datapulse plc* [2004] ICR 523.

287  *R v Betson and Cockran* (2004) *Times* 28 January.

288  [2006] EWHC 3333 (Admin) at [5].

Tribunal hearings. The Tribunal members are not expected to sit quietly and silently letting a party say whatever he likes, for as long as he likes, using whatever materials he likes, and I can see no complaint on that ground. I stress that Mr Clancy was assisted by a representative from the Royal British Legion.

3.233   Accordingly, the Commissioners decided that interrupting and questioning a claimant was not indicative of bias and was often intended to be helpful.[289]

## Detachment

3.234   In *London Borough of Southwark v Kofi-Adu*,[290] the Court of Appeal was concerned with a trial on a claim for possession in the course of which the judge had intervened excessively. Jonathan Parker LJ pointed out the importance of a judge remaining detached and said that loss of detachment 'may so hamper his ability properly to evaluate and weigh the evidence before him as to impair his judgment, and may *for that reason* render the trial unfair.'[291]

## Discourtesy

3.235   Tribunals have a duty to remain courteous with a party who appears without assistance.[292] Discourtesy by a tribunal to a representative or a party may render a hearing unfair by creating the impression that the representative or party is not being allowed effectively to put a case to a tribunal.[293]

## Bias

3.236   Bias affects the perception of fairness. Research has shown this to be so, whether or not the decision-maker is aware of it. [294]

3.237      The most comprehensive overview of the authorities on common law decisions on bias was undertaken by the Court of Appeal in *Locabail (UK) Ltd v Bayfield Properties Ltd.*[295] Its analysis was slightly modified by the House of Lords in *Porter v Magill*[296] in order to bring it into line with the jurisprudence under article 6(1).

3.238      Bias is a matter of jurisdiction, not discretion. It there is bias in any form, the tribunal must be differently constituted, regardless of any other consideration such as inconvenience to the parties, cost and delay.[297] However, chance remarks that appear to show bias must be considered objectively and in their context.[298] And an immediate apology about an

289  *R(S)* 4/82 at [27]; *R(SB)* 6/82 at [6].
290  [2006] EWCA Civ 281; (2006) *Times* 1 June.
291  [2006] EWCA Civ 281 at [146].
292  Wall LJ in *Re O (Children) (Hearing in Private: Assistance)* [2006] Fam 1 at [16].
293  *R v Hare* (2004) *Times* 16 December.
294  Joshua Greene, *Moral Tribes*, Atlantic Books, 2014, pages 84–85.
295  [2000] QB 451.
296  [2002] 2 AC 357.
297  *AWG Group Ltd v Morrison* [2006] 1 WLR 1163.
298  *National Assembly for Wales v Condron* (2006) *Times* 13 December.

inappropriate personal remark may remove any appearance of bias.[299] If the whole judiciary is affected, practicality overrides principle and someone has to decide the case.[300]

3.239 If bias is not established, the judge has a discretion not to sit in order to remove any genuine concern by one of the parties.

3.240 Bias is often alleged on appeal as part of an attack on the integrity of the judge. Such allegations may say more about the complainant than the judge. As Wall LJ commented in *Re Bradford; Re O'Connell:*[301]

> ... an intemperate and wholly unwarranted attack on the integrity of a judge for which there is no evidential basis and which derives only from the fact that the judge has rejected the appellant's case tells me more about the litigant than it does about the judge.

3.241 Bias in one member of a tribunal does not taint the others.[302] However, the tribunal's decision will only be valid if the tribunal remains properly constituted apart from the member affected.

3.242 There are three categories of bias: actual, presumed and subconscious. They require separate treatment.

## Actual bias

3.243 Actual bias occurs if a judge involved in a case is partial towards one of the parties or hostile towards another. This is usually avoided by selection of persons with the appropriate qualities to be judges of the tribunal, by the training given to them, and by the standard they apply to themselves.

3.244 There is an obvious difficulty in proving actual bias. The judge concerned is unlikely to admit it. And there is a limit to which that judge's attitude and motivation can be examined on an appeal. The most that an appellate body can do is to allow, or require, the judge a chance to comment on the allegations.

3.245 In practice, even if actual bias did occur, it is likely that the case will fall within one of the other categories of bias and be easier to establish under the terms of that category.

## Bias presumed from an interest in the outcome of the case

3.246 Judges must not have a personal interest that is sufficient to have influenced the outcome of the proceedings.[303] The interest may be financial, but is not so limited and may include the promotion of a cause.[304] It may be waived by the party who is presumed to be affected, provided the waiver is unequivocal and given in full knowledge of the relevant facts.[305]

---

299 *Reid v Chief Constable of Merseyside* (1996) *Times* 5 February.
300 *The Judges v Attorney-General for the Province of Saskatchewan* (1937) 53 TLR 464; *Panton v Minister of Finance* [2001] UKPC 33 at [16].
301 [2007] 1 FLR 530 at [9].
302 *ASM Shipping Ltd of India v Harris* (2007) *Times* 6 August.
303 *Locabail (UK) Ltd v Bayfield Properties Ltd* [2000] QB 451 at [10] and [14].
304 As in *R v Bow Street Metropolitan Stipendiary Magistrate ex p Pinochet Ugarte (No 2)* [2000] 1 AC 119.
305 *Locabail (UK) Ltd v Bayfield Properties Ltd* [2000] QB 451 at [15].

## Possibility of subconscious bias

3.247   The test for this type of bias was formulated by the House of Lords in *Porter v Magill*.[306] Lord Hope set out the correct approach:

> The court must first ascertain all the circumstances which have a bearing on the suggestion that the judge was biased. . . . The question is whether the fair-minded and informed observer, having considered the facts, would conclude that there was a real possibility that the tribunal was biased.

3.248   According to Baroness Hale in *Gillies v Secretary of State for Work and Pensions*:[307]

> The 'fair minded and informed observer' is probably not an insider (ie another member of the same tribunal system). Otherwise she would run the risk of having the insider's blindness to the faults that outsiders can so easily see. But she is informed. She knows the relevant facts. And she is fair minded.

3.249   Lord Hope spelt out some of the characteristics of the observer in *Helow v Secretary of State for the Home Department*:[308]

> The fair-minded and informed observer is a relative newcomer among the select group of personalities who inhabit our legal village and are available to be called upon when a problem arises that needs to be solved objectively. Like the reasonable man whose attributes have been explored so often in the context of the law of negligence, the fair-minded observer is a creature of fiction. Gender-neutral (as this is a case where the complainer and the person complained about are both women, I shall avoid using the word 'he'), she has attributes which many of us might struggle to attain to.
>
> The observer who is fair-minded is the sort of person who always reserves judgment on every point until she has seen and fully understood both sides of the argument. She is not unduly sensitive or suspicious, as Kirby J observed in *Johnson v Johnson* (2000) 201 CLR 488, 509, para 53. Her approach must not be confused with that of the person who has brought the complaint. The 'real possibility' test ensures that there is this measure of detachment. The assumptions that the complainer makes are not to be attributed to the observer unless they can be justified objectively. But she is not complacent either. She knows that fairness requires that a judge must be, and must be seen to be, unbiased. She knows that judges, like anybody else, have their weaknesses. She will not shrink from the conclusion, if it can be justified objectively, that things that they have said or done or associations that they have formed may make it difficult for them to judge the case before them impartially.
>
> Then there is the attribute that the observer is 'informed'. It makes the point that, before she takes a balanced approach to any information she is given, she will take the trouble to inform herself on all matters that are relevant. She is the sort of person who takes the trouble to read the text of an article as well as the headlines. She is able to put whatever she has read or seen into its overall social, political or geographical context. She is fair-minded, so she will appreciate that the context forms an important part of the material which she must consider before passing judgment.

---

306   [2002] 2 AC 357 at [102]–[103].
307   [2006] 1 WLR 781 at [39].
308   [2008] 1 WLR 2416 at [1]–[3].

3.250 The Court of Appeal in *Locabail (UK) Ltd v Bayfield Properties Ltd*[309] listed some circumstances in which there was or was not likely to be a possibility of subconscious bias:

> We cannot, however, conceive of circumstances in which an objection could be soundly based on the religion, ethnic or national origin, gender, age, class, means or sexual orientation of the judge. Nor, at any rate ordinarily, could an objection be soundly based on the judge's social or educational or service or employment background or history, nor that of any member of the judge's family; or previous political associations; or membership of social or sporting or charitable bodies; or Masonic associations; or previous judicial decisions; or extra-curricular utterances (whether in text books, lectures, speeches, articles, interviews, reports or responses to consultation papers); or previous receipt of instructions to act for or against any party, solicitor or advocate engaged in a case before him; or membership of the same Inn, circuit, local Law Society or chambers. . . . By contrast, a real danger of bias[310] might well be thought to arise if there were personal friendship or animosity between the judge and any member of the public involved in the case; or if the judge were closely acquainted with any member of the public involved in the case, particularly if the credibility of that individual could be significant in the decision of the case; . . . or if, for any other reason, there were real ground for doubting the ability of the judge to ignore extraneous considerations, prejudices and predilections and bring an objective judgment to bear on the issues before him.

3.251 Being a member of same chambers as a fee-paid judge is not indicative of bias.[311] The fact that a judge hearing a case and someone interested in the proceedings are both Freemasons is not decisive on the possibility of bias.[312]

3.252 The proper approach to the issue is to apply the principle and not to argue by analogy from other cases. As Lord Phillips MR explained in *R (PD) v West Midlands and North West Mental Health Review Tribunal*:[313]

> The natural reaction of the lawyer to any problem is to look for case precedent and this is true even where the issue is essentially one of fact. In such circumstances precedent can be helpful in focussing the mind on the relevant issues and producing consistency of approach. In a case such as the present, however, the search is for the reaction of the fair-minded and informed observer. The court has to apply an objective assessment as to how such a person would react to the material facts. There is a danger when applying such a test that citation of authorities may cloud rather than clarify perception. The court must be careful when looking at case precedent not to permit it to drive common sense out of the window.

---

309 [2000] QB 451 at [25].

310 The reference to danger of bias needs to be updated to a real possibility in line with *Porter v Magill* [2002] 2 AC 357.

311 *Birmingham City Council v Yardley* (2004) *Times* 9 December. The recorder in that case had informed the parties at the outset.

312 *R (Port Regis School Ltd) v North Dorset District Council* (2006) *Times* 14 April. The requirement that judicial appointees must disclose on appointment whether or not they are Freemasons was ended in 2009 following the decision of the European Court of Human Rights in *Grande Oriente d'Italia di Palazzo Giustiniani v Italy (No 2)* (Application 26740/02).

313 [2004] EWCA Civ 311 at [8].

3.253    Whether or not there would be the possibility of subconscious bias is not a matter for the judge's discretion.[314] The potential inconvenience, costs and delay are not relevant to the issue of recusal. [315]

## Judge's previous involvement[316]

3.254    The issue of recusal (whether or not a judge should withdraw from involvement in a case) depends on the facts and circumstances of the particular case.[317]

3.255    The test depends on the impression created by the circumstances of the case, not the particular constitutional arrangements involved. As Lord Rodger explained in *R (Al-Hasan) v Secretary of State for the Home Department:*[318]

> . . . art 6(1) does not require that a member state should comply with any theoretical constitutional concepts as such. The question is always simply whether the requirements of the convention are met in the particular case. Similarly, in a domestic law context, the question will turn, not on theoretical administrative or other concepts as such, but on whether the tribunal can be regarded as impartial and independent in the particular circumstances.

3.256    The Court of Appeal in *Locabail (UK) Ltd v Bayfield Properties Ltd*[319] gave some contrasting examples:

> . . . a real danger of bias[320] might well be thought to arise .. . if, in a case where the credibility of any individual were an issue to be decided by the judge, he had in a previous case rejected the evidence of that person in such outspoken terms as to throw doubt on his ability to approach such person's evidence with an open mind on any later occasion; or if on any question at issue in the proceedings before him the judge had expressed views, particularly in the course of the hearing, in such extreme and unbalanced terms as to throw doubt on his ability to try the issue with an objective judicial mind . . . The mere fact that a judge, earlier in the same case or in a previous case, had commented adversely on a party or witness, or found the evidence of a party or witness to be unreliable, would not without more found a sustainable objection.

3.257    The fact that a party to the proceedings has previously appeared before a member of a tribunal is not sufficient to show bias. In *Lodwick v London Borough of Southwark,*[321] Pill LJ said:

> A party cannot normally expect a judge to recuse himself because the judge has previously made adverse comments about him, in the course of a case or cases, though the circumstances of each situation will need specific consideration. Neither can parties assume or expect that findings adverse to a

---

314  *Morrison v AWG Group Ltd* [2006] EWCA Civ 6 at [20].
315  *Morrison v AWG Group Ltd* [2006] EWCA Civ 6 at [6] and [29].
316  See also chapter 4.
317  *Secretary of State for the Home Department v AF (No 2)* [2008] 2 All ER 67 at [23].
318  [2005] 1 WLR 688 at [4].
319  [2000] QB 451 at [25].
320  The reference to danger of bias needs to be updated to a real possibility in line with *Porter v Magill* [2002] 2 AC 357.
321  [2004] ICR 884 at [24].

party in one case entitled that party to a different judge or tribunal in a later case.

3.258 It is even possible for the same person to decide the same issue without there being any possibility of bias. In practice, the issue is most likely to arise when deciding on a successful appeal whether a case may be remitted for rehearing by the same tribunal.[322] In *AMEC Capital Projects Ltd v Whitefriars City Estates Ltd,*[323] the facts of the case were unusual in that the same person had been appointed as arbitrator to deal with the same issue twice. On the first occasion, he had had no jurisdiction to decide the issue, although he had done so. The Court of Appeal decided that there was no possibility of bias when he decided the same issue again, this time with jurisdiction. Dyson LJ said:

> In my judgment, the mere fact that the tribunal has previously decided the issue is not of itself sufficient to justify a conclusion of apparent bias. Something more is required. Judges are assumed to be trustworthy and to understand that they should approach every case with an open mind. The same applies to adjudicators, who are almost always professional persons. That is not to say that, if it is asked to redetermine an issue and the evidence and arguments are merely a repeat of what went before, the tribunal will not be likely to reach the same conclusion as before. It would be unrealistic, indeed absurd, to expect the tribunal in such circumstances to ignore its earlier decision and not to be inclined to come to the same conclusion as before, particularly if the previous decision was carefully reasoned. The vice which the law must guard against is that the tribunal may approach the rehearing with a closed mind. If a judge has considered an issue carefully before reaching a decision on the first occasion, it cannot sensibly be said that he has a closed mind if, the evidence and arguments being the same as before, he does not give as careful a consideration on the second occasion as on the first. He will, however, be expected to give such reconsideration of the matter as is reasonably necessary for him to be satisfied that his first decision was correct.[324]

3.259 Having specialist expertise relevant to the case is not indicative of bias[325] so long as the knowledge relates to the subject matter of the case and not to the particular facts of the case.[326] (Indeed, expertise is an advantage for a tribunal – see TCEA s2(3)(c).) However, there may be bias if the member is one of 'a close-knit group sharing an esprit de corps'.[327]

3.260 A party's own conduct that is capable of being regarded by an objective observer as likely to affront or antagonise the tribunal cannot be relied on to show that the tribunal may be biased. Judges are made of sterner stuff.[328]

322 *AMEC Capital Projects Ltd v Whitefriars City Estates Ltd* [2005] 1 All ER 723 at [19].
323 [2005] 1 All ER 723.
324 [2005] 1 All ER 723 at [20].
325 Lord Hope in *Gillies v Secretary of State for Work and Pensions* [2006] 1 WLR 781 at [23].
326 Baroness Hale in *Gillies v Secretary of State for Work and Pensions* [2006] 1 WLR 781 at [45].
327 Lord Rodger in *Gillies v Secretary of State for Work and Pensions* [2006] 1 WLR 781 at [33].
328 Lord Keith in *Re Lonrho plc* [1990] 2 AC 154 at 177–178; *Bennett v Southwark London Borough Council* [2002] ICR 881.

3.261    A party to the proceedings may waive the right to object to a particular member of a tribunal. This may be done in advance of or after the hearing. Delay in raising an objection may be taken as waiver. However, waiver is only effective if it is properly informed.[329] It is the duty of a representative to ensure that the party is properly informed of all matters relevant to the potential bias and its waiver.[330]

## Recusal – principle and good practice

3.262    There is a distinction between the principles that govern when a judge cannot sit (subject to the possibility of waiver) and good practice that governs when a judge may think it appropriate not to sit, perhaps after canvassing the views of the parties.

3.263    It is important to maintain this distinction so that judges are not required to recuse themselves when it would not be appropriate to do so. As the Court of Appeal pointed out in *Locabail (UK) Ltd v Bayfield Properties Ltd*,[331] a judge:

> ... would be as wrong to yield to a tenuous or frivolous objection as he would to ignore an objection of substance.

All the more so as it may allow parties to generate their own grounds for recusal.[332]

3.264    However, it is also important to allow judges to take account of genuine misgivings by the parties in order to maintain confidence in the judicial system. The courts have, therefore, recognised that judges have the power to recuse themselves in circumstances that do not require them to do so, but cause justifiable concern to the parties.

## When should an allegation of bias be raised?

3.265    An allegation should only be made if there is material that supports it. Instructions from a party alone are never sufficient to justify a representative in arguing that a judge may be biased.[333]

3.266    If allegations that the First-tier Tribunal was biased are made on appeal, it is relevant to consider why the issue was not raised at the time. By silence or delay in raising the issue, the party affected may be treated as having waived the right to fairness in that particular respect or the right to object on that ground. As the Court of Appeal said in *Locabail (UK) Ltd v Bayfield Properties Ltd*:[334]

> The greater the passage of time between the event relied on as showing a danger of bias[335] and the case in which the objection is raised, the weaker (other things being equal) the objection will be.

329  *Smith v Kvaerner Cementation Foundations Ltd* [2007] 1 WLR 370 at [26], [33] and [37].
330  [2007] 1 WLR 370 at [33].
331  [2000] QB 451 at [21].
332  *R(I) 42/59* at [28].
333  *Arab Monetary Fund v Hashim (No 8)* (1993) *Times* 4 May.
334  [2000] QB 451 at [25].
335  The reference to danger of bias needs to be updated to a real possibility in line with *Porter v Magill* [2002] 2 AC 357.

3.267   However, it is also relevant to consider whether it was reasonable in all the circumstances to raise the point at the hearing. This is the position both at common law and under the Convention right. In *Stansbury v Datapulse plc*,[336] the Court of Appeal said that it may not be reasonable, even for a legal representative, to raise an issue about the conduct of a tribunal that will, if it rejects the argument, hear and determine the case.[337]

3.268   There are cases in which the Court of Appeal has decided that an issue of bias should have been raised immediately and not after the complainant has taken the chance of a favourable outcome.[338] They depend on their own particular facts and do not lay down a general principle.

3.269   If the allegations involve issues of fact, such as what was said or done at the hearing below, these must be determined, even by a tribunal whose jurisdiction is limited to issues of law. This may involve asking the judge concerned to make a statement of the facts, but cross-examination or orders for disclosure are not appropriate.[339] Whether or not the judge was affected by bias is not a matter for evidence from the judge, but for assessment on appeal.[340]

3.270   However, it is permissible to consider first whether proceedings would have been fair even if the allegations were true.[341]

## Fairness when evidence or information is withheld

3.271   This is discussed in chapter 10.

## Fairness on appeal or judicial review

### When an appeal or judicial review is required

3.272   A decision may be made by a minister or an official of a public body who is not independent and impartial.[342] If so, article 6 confers a right to challenge before a tribunal that complies with the Convention right.[343] In this respect, the law reflects utilitarian considerations on the proper expenditure of public funds on dispute resolution.[344]

3.273   In setting the conditions that must be met, the European Court of Human Rights and the domestic courts have imposed a right to challenge an administrative decision, but without imposing a right to an inappropriate judicial oversight.[345]

---

336  [2004] ICR 523.

337  [2004] ICR 523 at [23]–[24].

338  *Birmingham City Council and Nott v Yardley* [2004] EWCA Civ 1756 at [27]–[31]; *Steadman-Byrne v Amjad* [2007] EWCA Civ 625 at [17].

339  *Locabail (UK) Ltd v Bayfield Properties Ltd* [2000] QB 451 at [18]–[19]; *R(I) 11/63* at [20]–[21].

340  [2000] QB 451 at [19].

341  *Stansbury v Datapulse plc* [2004] ICR 523 at [25].

342  See on this type of case and the different considerations for courts of the classic kind *R (Hammond) v Secretary of State for the Home Department* [2006] 1 AC 603.

343  *Albert and Le Compte v Belgium* (1983) 5 EHRR 533 at [29].

344  Lord Hoffmann in *Runa Begum v Tower Hamlets London Borough Council* [2003] 2 AC 430 at [42]–[44].

345  Lord Bingham in *Runa Begum v Tower Hamlets London Borough Council* [2003] 2 AC 430 at [5].

3.274    The body before whom a challenge is brought must have 'full jurisdiction'.[346] In practice, the issue turns on whether judicial review or an appeal is the more appropriate form of challenge. Judicial review is appropriate if only the legality of the decision is in issue. This is especially so if the case depends on a policy for which the minister is publicly accountable.[347] An appeal may be appropriate if the facts or merits of the decision are in issue. But judicial review may nonetheless be sufficient if the facts have been found by a decision-maker who was not independent but whose integrity is not open to legitimate doubt[348] – an example of attention to substance rather than to form.

3.275    In *R (Refugee Legal Centre) v Secretary of State for the Home Department*,[349] Sedley LJ drew a distinct between individual instances of unfairness and intrinsic unfairness in the decision-making process. Judicial review was not necessarily an appropriate remedy for the latter.

### When an appeal or judicial review is available

3.276    If a case has been determined by a tribunal that complies with article 6, the Convention does not require that the State must provide for a right to challenge that tribunal's decision on appeal. But if domestic law provides an appeal (or judicial review), that appeal is also subject to article 6.[350]

3.277    There is no general rule that an appeal cures any breach of natural justice in the tribunal below.[351]

## Reasonable time

3.278    Proceedings must not take more than a reasonable time. The principles governing what constitutes a reasonable time were summarised by the European Court of Human Rights in *Jevremović v Serbi*:[352]

> The court reiterates that the reasonableness of the length of proceedings must be assessed in the light of the circumstances of the case and having regard to the criteria laid down in the court's case law, in particular the complexity of the case, the conduct of the applicant and of the relevant authorities, as well as the importance of what is at stake for the applicant . . .
>
> Further, according to the court's established jurisprudence, a chronic backlog of cases is not a valid explanation for excessive delay, and the repeated re-examination of a single case following remittal may in itself disclose a serious deficiency in the respondent State's judicial system . . .
>
> Finally, the court notes that particular diligence is required in all cases concerning civil status and capacity . . . and that this requirement is additionally

---

346  *Albert and Le Compte v Belgium* (1983) 5 EHRR 533 at [29].

347  *R (Alconbury Developments Ltd) v Secretary of State for Environment, Transport and the Regions* [2003] 2 AC 295.

348  *R (Beeson) v Dorset County Council* [2004] LGR 92; *Runa Begum v Tower Hamlets London Borough Council* [2003] 2 AC 430.

349  [2005] 1 WLR 2219 at [7].

350  *Belgian Linguistic Case (No 2)* (1968) 1 EHRR 252 at [9].

351  *Calvin v Carr* [1980] AC 574.

352  [2008] 1 FLR 550 at [79]–[81].

reinforced in States where domestic law itself provides that certain kinds of cases must be resolved with particular urgency . . .

3.279 The primary responsibility for dealing with cases within a reasonable time rests on the relevant tribunal system, rather than on the parties to initiate procedures to ensure that it happens.[353]

3.280 Mummery LJ considered the factors that determines what constitutes a reasonable time in *Connex South Eastern Ltd v Bangs*:[354]

Article 6 does not lay down what is a reasonable time. It does not even attempt to identify any of the factors relevant to determining what is a reasonable time. The question obviously depends on all the circumstances of the particular case: the nature of the tribunal, its jurisdiction, constitution and procedures, the subject matter of the case, its factual and legal complexity and difficulty, the conduct of the tribunal and of the parties and any other special features of the situation in which delay has occurred.

3.281 A similar duty may exist in public law, at least as a matter of interpretation of the relevant legislation.[355]

## Compensation for delay

3.282 Section 8(1) of the Human Rights Act 1998 confers power to award damages or compensation as one of the remedies for a breach of a Convention right. This power is only conferred on a tribunal that has the power to award damages or compensation (s8(2)).

3.283 The power to award damages is subject to three statutory restrictions.

3.284 The first restriction is that financial compensation must be necessary in order to afford just satisfaction for the violation of the Convention right. In deciding whether this is necessary, all the circumstances of the case must be considered. These include the other remedies available and the consequences of any decision in respect of the violation (s8(3)).

3.285 The second restriction is that the tribunal must take account of the jurisprudence of the European Court of Human Rights in determining whether to award damages and, if so, their amount (s8(4)). But the domestic courts are free to depart from the jurisprudence, especially in order to ensure that the amount of the damages is appropriate for this country.[356]

3.286 The third restriction applies to a breach by a judicial act done in good faith. The only damages that may be awarded are those for compensation for a breach of article 5(5) of the Convention. Judicial acts are those of a court or tribunal, whether or not done on the instruction of a judge or member of a tribunal (s9(5)). Article 5 deals only with the right to liberty and security and will not be relevant to most tribunals. It provides:

*Right to liberty and security*
1. Everyone has the right to liberty and security of person. No one shall be deprived of his liberty save in the following cases and in accordance with a procedure prescribed by law:

353 *Mitchell and Holloway v United Kingdom* (2003) 36 EHHR 951 at [56].
354 [2005] ICR 763 at [2].
355 *R (MK (Iran)) v Secretary of State for the Home Department* [2010] 4 All ER 892 at [34].
356 Stanley Burnton J in *R (KB) v South London and South and West Region Mental Health Review Tribunal* [2004] QB 936 at [47].

(a) the lawful detention of a person after conviction by a competent court;

(b) the lawful arrest or detention of a person for non-compliance with the lawful order of a court or in order to secure the fulfilment of any obligation prescribed by law;

(c) the lawful arrest or detention of a person effected for the purpose of bringing him before the competent legal authority on reasonable suspicion of having committed an offence or when it is reasonably considered necessary to prevent his committing an offence or fleeing after having done so;

(d) the detention of a minor by lawful order for the purpose of educational supervision or his lawful detention for the purpose of bringing him before the competent legal authority;

(e) the lawful detention of persons for the prevention of the spreading of infectious diseases, of persons of unsound mind, alcoholics or drug addicts or vagrants;

(f) the lawful arrest or detention of a person to prevent his effecting an unauthorised entry into the country or of a person against whom action is being taken with a view to deportation or extradition.

2.  Everyone who is arrested shall be informed promptly, in a language which he understands, of the reasons for his arrest and of any charge against him.

3.  Everyone arrested or detained in accordance with the provisions of paragraph 1(c) of this Article shall be brought promptly before a judge or other officer authorised by law to exercise judicial power and shall be entitled to trial within a reasonable time or to release pending trial. Release may be conditioned by guarantees to appear for trial.

4.  Everyone who is deprived of his liberty by arrest or detention shall be entitled to take proceedings by which the lawfulness of his detention shall be decided speedily by a court and his release ordered if the detention is not lawful.

5.  Everyone who has been the victim of arrest or detention in contravention of the provisions of this Article shall have an enforceable right to compensation.

3.287    The approach to damages for a violation of article 6(1) was considered by the House of Lords in *R (Greenfield) v Secretary of State for the Home Department*.[357] The House decided that a finding that the right had been violated would usually provide just satisfaction without an award of damages. The exception was where there was a causal connection between the violation and a loss. An example is where the violation has affected the outcome of the case. In practice, the need for compensation may be avoided by directing a rehearing. The amount of any damages awarded should be in line with the figures used by the European Court of Human Rights. There is no power to award damages for delay under public law.[358]

## Prejudgment

3.288    Prejudging a case is always a breach of natural justice and the Convention right. However, prejudgment must be distinguished from a preview or a preliminary view.

---

357  [2005] 1 WLR 673.
358  *R (MK (Iran)) v Secretary of State for the Home Department* [2010] 4 All ER 892.

3.289   It is not only permissible for the tribunal to preview the case in preparation for a hearing, but desirable in order to ensure that the hearing is effective and conducted as efficiently as possible.

3.290   It is also permissible to come to a preliminary view, provided that the view is flexible and open to change.[359]

## Forms of proceedings

3.291   Cases come before a tribunal by way of proceedings. Proceeding before a tribunal is a way of determining a legal issue in respect of a person's rights or duties.

3.292   Legislation will provide for the form that proceedings before a tribunal may take. There are five possibilities: a claim, an application, an appeal, a judicial review and a referral.[360] The tribunal may also offer some alternative form of dispute resolution.

### Claim

3.293   A claim is the appropriate form of proceedings when a decision-maker has not made a decision that can be challenged. For example: an employee may make a claim against an employer for unfair dismissal to an employment tribunal.[361] There has been a decision in that case, but it was not made by a decision-maker acting in a public law capacity.

### Application

3.294   An application is the appropriate form of proceedings to ask a tribunal to check on a particular legal status, such as liability to detention on grounds of mental health. A request to a tribunal on a procedural matter is also often called an application.

### Appeal

3.295   An appeal is the appropriate form of proceedings to challenge the correctness of a decision that has the force of law. The decision may have been made by a decision-maker or by another tribunal. For example: a person who is subject to a deportation order may make an appeal to the Asylum and Immigration Tribunal against the order[362] and an employee may make an appeal to the Employment Appeal Tribunal against the decision of an employment tribunal.[363]

---

359   *Bolton Metropolitan Borough Council v Secretary of State for the Environment* (1994) *Times* 4 August. But see chapter 12 on making provisional findings of fact.
360   The legislation will specify the precise term used.
361   Employment Rights Act 1996 s111.
362   Nationality, Immigration and Asylum Act 2002 s82.
363   Employment Tribunals Act 1996 s21.

## Judicial review

3.296   Judicial review is the appropriate form of proceedings to challenge the lawfulness of a decision that has the force of law. The decision may have been made by a decision-maker or by another tribunal. Judicial review will usually be available if there is no provision for an appeal. For example: a person from whom a local authority is attempting to recover overpaid benefit may apply for a judicial review of the decision to enforce the liability.

## Referral or reference

3.297   These interchangeable terms are used to describe a variety of ways by which, without a claim, an appeal or a judicial review, an issue may be brought before a tribunal for decision.

## Relationship between appeal and judicial review

3.298   Appeal and judicial review are not mutually exclusive. The same decision may be subject to both, but this is exceptional.

## Relationship between appeal and referral

3.299   Appeals and referrals are not mutually exclusive. The same decision may be subject to both. And, depending on the interpretation of the legislation, a right of appeal may survive a referral.[364]

## Proceedings on procedural issues

3.300   Procedural issues may arise in respect of proceedings on a claim, application, appeal, judicial review or referral. They may relate to aspects of the procedure within those proceedings (when they are often called interlocutory issues) or to the decision given. These may be designated as separate proceedings or part of the original proceedings. It is unlikely that the difference will be of any practical significance.

## Alternative dispute resolution

3.301   Tribunals may occasionally operate an alternative form of dispute resolution. They may also refer parties to, and facilitate their use of, alternative dispute resolution that is available elsewhere.

## Ex gratia schemes

3.202   These are not part of the tribunal structure, but may provide an alternative recourse for a party. If an appropriate scheme is available, it should be used before resorting to judicial review.[365]

---

364 As in *R v Hughes (James)* (2009) *Times* 1 June.
365 *Humphries v Secretary of State for Work and Pensions* [2008] EWHC 1585 (Admin).

# CHAPTER 4

# Appeals

*continued*

*continued*

# Nature of an appeal

## What is an appeal?

4.1 According to Lord Westbury LC in *Attorney-General v Sillem* 'an appeal is the right of entering a superior Court, and invoking its aid and interposition to redress the error of the court below.'[1]

4.2 This is not sufficiently broad to cover all appeals; nor is it sufficient to distinguish between judicial review and appeal. As far as appeals are concerned, it deals only with appeals from one court to another. It omits appeals from a tribunal to a court and from a decision-maker to a court or tribunal. As far as judicial review[2] is concerned, it does not draw a distinction based on the scope of the challenge to a decision. On judicial review, the challenge is limited to three issues: whether the decision-maker had authority to make the decision; whether it was a permissible decision; and whether it was reached by a proper procedure. On an appeal, the challenge may relate to those issues, but it may also relate to the merits of the decision itself.

4.3 Lord Diplock gave a fuller definition in *Attorney-General v Ryan*:[3]

'Appeal' in the context of an ouster clause means re-examination by a superior judicial authority of both findings of fact and conclusions of law as to the legal consequences of those facts made by an inferior tribunal in the exercise of a jurisdiction conferred on it by statute to decide questions affecting the legal rights of others, and the substitution of the superior judicial authority's own findings of fact and conclusions of law for those of the inferior tribunal. In 'review' the function of the superior judicial authority is limited to re-examining the inferior tribunal's conclusions of law as to the legal consequences of the facts as they have been found by the inferior tribunal.[4]

4.4 Although better than Lord Westbury's, this definition is still not perfect. It distinguishes appeal from review. But it is limited by its context of ouster of jurisdiction clauses and confined to appeals from tribunals. It also covers appeals on both fact and law, whereas an appeal may be limited to issues of law. And it includes the power to substitute a decision rather than remit the case for a rehearing or reconsideration. This is a power that may be available on an appeal, but it is not of the essence of an appeal. It is also now permissible in judicial review.[5]

4.5 Put more accurately, an appeal is a challenge, authorised by statute and brought before a higher and judicial authority, to the correctness of a decision.[6]

---

1 (1864) 11 ER 1200 at 1209.

2 Review is also used to refer to a process by which decisions may be changed by a decision-maker or a tribunal at the same level or, in some circumstances, at a lower level. On the importance of maintaining the distinction between an appeal and a judicial review, see Lord Griffith in *R v Lord President of the Privy Council ex p Page* [1993] AC 682 at 694.

3 [1980] AC 718.

4 [1980] AC 718 at 730.

5 TCEA s17.

6 See the arguments of counsel and the decisions at first instance and in the Court of Appeal in *Furtado v City of London Brewery Company* [1914] 1 KB 152 and 709. And see *R(IS) 2/97* at [9]–[10] of the Appendix.

4.6     Not every such challenge is an appeal. This is a relatively modern concept in English legal development. The early law developed other techniques for avoiding error or for remedying it when it had occurred. The law
continues to develop those techniques. The extensive powers of a tribunal
over its own decisions are mentioned below when commenting on the
judgment of Stanley Burnton J in *Kataria v Essex Strategic Health Authority*.[7] The reconsideration procedure used by the Asylum and Immigration
Tribunal under the Asylum and Immigration (Treatment of Claimants
etc) Act 2004 is a particularly clear example. Accordingly, as a matter of
practice and practicality an appeal may not be necessary. Moreover, an
appeal is not essential in law, unless it is necessary in order to comply with
article 6.

4.7     Rix LJ explained part of what is involved in the process of an appeal in
*Compagnie Noga D'Importation et D'Exportation SA v Abacha*:[8]

> . . . it is the nature of the legal process that, once judgment has been ren-
> dered, analysis thereafter becomes clarified and refined, and citation of
> authority is applied to the findings made at first instance so as to illuminate
> that clarification and refinement of analysis of which I speak. But that is the
> function of the appeal process.

### Statutory

4.8     All appellate jurisdiction is statutory,[9] because the creation of a right of
appeal requires legislative authority.[10] So, an appeal lies only if it is conferred under a statute.[11] It must be conferred expressly;[12] it cannot be
conferred by implication.[13] But the use of the word 'appeal' is not essential;[14] the issue is one of interpretation.[15] There is no presumption that an
appeal is intended, even in order to comply with article 6.[16] But a decision
may be so analysed as to bring it within the scope of an appeal right in
order to comply with article 6.[17]

4.9     A power to make procedural provisions does not authorise providing
for an appeal. This follows from two considerations. First, the right to

---

7   [2004] 3 All ER 572.

8   [2001] 3 All ER 513 at [47].

9   Lord Atkin in *Evans v Bartlam* [1937] AC 473 at 480.

10  Lord Westbury LC in *Attorney-General v Sillem* (1864) 11 ER 1200 at 1207.

11  *Furtado v City of London Brewery Company* [1914] 1 KB 709 at 712.

12  Lord Halsbury LC in *Lane v Esdaile* [1891] AC 210 at 211; Arden LJ in *Secretary of State for Work and Pensions v Morina* [2007] 1 WLR 3033 at [46].

13  *R v Hanson* (1821) 106 ER 1027, *R v Stock* (1838) 112 ER 892; *Furtado v City of London Brewery* [1914] 1 KB 709 at 712; Lord St Leonards in *Attorney-General v Sillem* (1864) 11 ER 1200 at 1217.

14  Lord St Leonards in *Attorney-General v Sillem* (1864) 11 ER 1200 at 1218.

15  *Betterment Properties (Weymouth) Ltd v Dorset County Council* [2007] EWHC 365 (Ch) at [14]; (2007) *Times* 13 March. Lightman J held that the legislation in that case did not create an appeal. This was confirmed by the Court of Appeal: see [19]–[32] of the judgment of Lloyd LJ in [2008] EWCA Civ 22; (2008) *Times* 13 February.

16  Arden LJ in *Secretary of State for Work and Pensions v Morina* [2007] 1 WLR 3033 at [46]. One relevant factor is whether there is a time limit on commencing the procedure, although this is not essential: at [24].

17  As in *R(H) 3/05*.

appeal is a substantive right, not a matter of procedure.[18] Consequently, a power that authorises the making of procedural provision does not include the power to make provision relating to jurisdiction.[19] Second, as the right of appeal affects the jurisdiction both of the body from which the appeal lies and of the body to which it lies, it cannot be created as a matter of procedure by either one of them.[20]

4.10      It is for the person who alleges that statute confers a right of appeal to show that it does so.[21]

4.11      A power to make regulations to regulate the right of appeal does not authorise the removal of the right.[22] As Mummery LJ explained in *R v Secretary of State for the Home Department ex p Saleem*, it does cover:[23]

> time limits for appealing; setting procedures for the service of documents, including the determination of the adjudicator, by post on parties or their representatives; and putting upon parties the obligation to provide details of their address and to notify changes of address.[24]

4.12      A tribunal may have an express power to correct mistakes made by persons exercising one of its delegated functions. This power may also be implied as part of the tribunal's power over its own procedure.[25] However, this is not an appeal.

### Before a higher authority

4.13      The challenge must be made before a higher authority. So, the power for a lower authority to overturn a tribunal's decision, even on the ground that it was wrong, is not an appeal, because it is not before a higher authority. For the same reason, a power for a tribunal to overturn its own decisions is not an appeal. This applies whether the power is limited to procedural mistakes or covers substantive errors of fact or law.

4.14      In theory, there could be an appeal to a tribunal of the same level, but this would be surprising, unusual and inappropriate. Stanley Burnton J referred to this possibility in *Kataria v Essex Strategic Health Authority*:[26]

> Appeals to tribunals or courts of equal standing to the tribunal or court responsible for the original decision are rare, if known at all. It would be most unfortunate if a subsequent tribunal of equal standing to the first tribunal were required to hear and to rule on contentions that the first tribunal procedure had been unfair, that its discretions had been exercised unreasonably (e.g. that an adjournment should have been granted), that its

---

18   *Colonial Sugar Refining Co, Ltd v Irving* [1905] AC 369 at 372–373; Horridge and Shearman JJ in *Newman v Klausner* [1922] 1 KB 228 both at 231.

19   Lord Westbury LC in *Attorney-General v Sillem* (1864) 11 ER 1200 at 1208. See also chapter 3.

20   Lord Westbury LC in *Attorney-General v Sillem* (1864) 11 ER 1200 at 1208.

21   *Furtado v City of London Brewery* [1914] 1 KB 709 at 712.

22   *Tarr v Tarr* [1973] AC 254; *R v Secretary of State for the Home Department ex p Saleem* [2001] 1 WLR 443 at 459.

23   [2001] 1 WLR 443.

24   [2001] 1 WLR 443 at 452–453.

25   *Re Macro (Ipswich) Ltd* [1996] 1 WLR 145 at 154–155. The discussion refers to inherent power or jurisdiction, but the context suggests that the power is implicit or implied.

26   [2004] 3 All ER 572 at [27].

procedure had been irregular, or that any of its findings of fact or its decision was incorrect. It is most unlikely that Parliament intended this.

In fact, tribunals have powers to do all the things set out in that passage, although they are not labelled an appeal. Under TCEA, tribunals have power to set aside their own decisions on procedural grounds. They also have power to set aside their own decisions for error of law, with or without the agreement of all the parties. They may even have power to set aside a decision if the interests of justice so require,[27] although the context may limit this to procedural considerations.[28]

4.15     The appeal may lie from the decision of a tribunal lower in the hierarchy or from a decision-maker.

## Against a decision

4.16     The appeal must be against a decision. It may be limited to the final decision or it may include interlocutory decisions. But there must be a decision. So, a delay in making and a failure to make a decision cannot be challenged through a statutory appeal and are matters for judicial review.[29]

4.17     An appeal confers 'a right to a rehearing of the whole matter in dispute, the appellate tribunal not being confined to the particular reasons which have been given by the court below as the ground for their decision.'[30] This is subject to provision to the contrary.[31]

4.18     Although it is not sufficient to seek to challenge an aspect of the tribunal's reasoning as opposed to its decision,[32] an appeal may lie for a procedural error and this may include inadequate reasons. So, in practice, the inadequacy of the tribunal's reasons may make the decision itself wrong and so appealable.

4.19     In the case of the Upper Tribunal, the decision will usually be the decision of the First-tier Tribunal below. This has an impact on the exercise that is undertaken on the appeal. In *Gover v Propertycare Ltd*,[33] the Court of Appeal heard an appeal from a decision of the Employment Appeal Tribunal. Counsel argued that the issue for the Court was whether the decision of the employment tribunal, which had been the subject of the appeal to the Employment Appeal Tribunal, was correct. The Court rejected this. Buxton LJ explained why:

> As to authority, this court's jurisdiction to hear this appeal, coming as it does from a statutory tribunal, is only to be found in s37(1) of the Employment Tribunals Act 1996, which provides for an appeal *from the EAT* on a question of law only. I do not see how we can in any realistic sense be hearing an appeal from the EAT if we are only concerned with whether the ET was right. As to the business of this court, the assumption that we in effect repeat the exercise already performed by the expert EAT of reviewing the

27  For example: reg 43(1) quoted in *Kataria* at [9].
28  *R(U) 3/89* at [22]; *R(SB) 4/90* at [10].
29  *Commissioners for Her Majesty's Revenue and Customs v Mobilx Ltd* [2007] EWHC 1769 (Ch), reported as *Mobilx Ltd v Revenue and Customs Commissioners* (2007) *Times* 14 March.
30  Humphreys J in *Fulham Borough Council v Santilli* [1933] 2 KB 357 at 367.
31  Humphreys J in *Stepney Borough Council v Joffe* [1949] 1 KB 599 at 604–605.
32  *Lake v Lake* [1955] P 336.
33  [2006] ICR 1073.

decision of the ET tends in practice to impose on this court an exercise that is inappropriate both in its nature and in its extent.[34]

4.20    However, this is not always so. If there are successive appeals from a decision-maker, both of which are on a point of law, and the particular case is concerned with judicial review grounds, the focus in the second appeal is on the decision of the original decision-maker. This is the case in homelessness appeals. An appeal lies to the county court against the local authority's decision. The appeal is on a point of law, which includes judicial review grounds.[35] A further appeal lies to the Court of Appeal. On that second appeal, the focus is on the decision of the local authority, not of the county court judge. As Auld LJ explained in *Osmani v Camden London Borough Council*:[36]

> As Mr McGuire observed, the main focus of attention on a second appeal such as this should be on the decision of the Council rather than that of the country court judge on appeal from it. As I have said, the appeal lies only on a point of law, and, within the *Wednesbury* type formulation given by Lord Bingham,[37] matters of fact, discretion and judgment on such an issue are essentially matters for the local housing authority. Given the nature of the statutory scheme, which requires authorities administering it to determine on a case by case basis quite complex questions involving the weighing of policy issues and identification of priorities concerning the interests of others as well as those of any individual applicant, courts should tread wearily before interfering.

4.21    A party may be aware of a decision before it is actually made or promulgated and seek to appeal immediately. In *R(U) 3/85*, a Tribunal of Commissioners decided that in these circumstances '. . . the appeal was a continuing one to take effect as and when the relevant concrete decision was actually made'.[38]

### Correctness of the decision

4.22    The challenge must be made to the correctness of the decision as made. A power to revisit a decision on the ground that it is no longer appropriate in view of a change of circumstances is not an appeal, because it is not a challenge to the correctness of the decision as made. Under TCEA, it is a review.[39]

## When an appeal begins

4.23    An appeal begins as soon as it is lodged or permission is given, not when it is heard or the appellant attends the hearing.[40]

---

34    [2006] ICR 1073 at [8].

35    *Nipa Begum v Tower Hamlets London Borough Council* [2000] 1 WLR 306.

36    [2005] HLR 22 at [34].

37    In *Runa Begum v Tower Hamlets London Borough Council* [2003] 2 AC 430 at [7].

38    *R(U) 3/85* at 8.

39    UTR r47(2)(c).

40    *R v Income Tax Special Commissioners ex p Elmhirst* [1936] 1 KB 487.

## Classification of appeals

4.24   Appeals have been classified in different ways.

4.25      In *Quilter v Mapleson*,[41] Jessel MR distinguished between appeals strictly so called and appeals by way of rehearing:

> On an appeal strictly so called, such a judgment can only be given as ought
> to have been given at the original hearing; but on a rehearing such a judg-
> ment may be given as ought to be given if the case came at that time before
> the Court of first instance.[42]

4.26   However, this distinction does not identify the process involved in the
appeal. On an appeal strictly so called, it may be permissible to hear fresh
evidence[43] although that is more appropriate to a rehearing. And rehearing covers a range of procedures, as the Court of Appeal explained in *Jones
v Attorney-General*:[44]

> The problem plainly cannot be resolved by determining that the right of
> appeal . . . is by way of rehearing, for both an appeal from petty sessions to
> the Crown Court, which is in truth a new trial, and an appeal to the Court of
> Appeal, which has been called a rehearing on documents, are so described.
> We think that Mr. Vinelott was right when he said that there is a wide range
> of differing processes of appeal between these two extremes, and that in the
> absence of statutory provision or rules of court it is for the court to which an
> appeal lies to regulate its own procedure.[45]

4.27   In his report on *Access to Justice*, Lord Woolf classified appeals into broadly
three forms:[46] (i) the second hearing; (ii) the rehearing; and (iii) the review
of the outcome of the case. A second hearing involves the appellate body
hearing the case completely afresh as if there has been no earlier hearing.
Despite its form, this is an appeal.[47] It takes this form, because there is no
formal record of the proceedings[48] or if it is necessary in order to comply
with article 6.[49] The decision given replaces that given below.[50] This is so
whether the appeal is successful or not. In this form of appeal, the burden
of proof is as it was at the first hearing,[51] regardless of who initiated the
appeal. A rehearing differs from a second hearing in that the emphasis is
on whether the decision below was wrong rather than looking at the case
completely afresh as if there had been no earlier decision. The issues are
limited to the grounds of appeal. If the appeal is successful, the decision
given may replace that given below, although occasionally a case may be

---

41   (1882) 9 QBD 672.
42   (1882) 9 QBD 672 at 676. This was approved by the Privy Council in *Ponnamma v
     Arumogan* [1905] AC 383.
43   See chapter 10.
44   [1974] Ch 148.
45   [1974] Ch 148 at 161.
46   *Access to Justice*, HMSO, 1996, chapter 14, paras 32–34.
47   The form of proceeding is a matter of procedure and does not affect its nature as an
     appeal: Lord Goddard CJ in *Drover v Rugman* [1951] 1 KB 380 at 382. See also Russell
     LJ in *Stevens v Stevens* [1965] P 147 at 164.
48   *Drover v Rugman* [1951] 1 KB 380 at 382.
49   May LJ in *EI Du Pont De Nemours & Co v ST Dupont* [2006] 1 WLR 2793 at [96].
50   *R(I)* 9/63 at [18].
51   Lord Goddard CJ in *Drover v Rugman* [1951] 1 KB 380 at 382.

remitted for a fresh hearing. In a review of the outcome of a case, a successful appeal has the result that the case is remitted for rehearing. An appeal does not have to fall exactly within one of these perfect forms. It may represent a hybrid.[52]

4.28    In practice, the important issue is not the classification or label. There is no pre-determined list of possibilities. Nor do all appeals under the same label necessarily have the same features or features that are exclusive to that particular category.[53] Even in the case of a coherent modern code, it can be difficult to identify the practical significance of a particular classification. CPR are such a code, but in *Meadow v General Medical Council*[54] Auld LJ described the distinction drawn in CPR between a review and a rehearing as 'thin and variable according to the circumstances and needs of each case'.[55] And in *EI Du Pont De Nemours & Co v ST Dupont*,[56] May LJ described 'review' under CPR as involving 'a spectrum of appropriate respect depending on the nature of the decision of the lower court which is challenged.'[57]

4.29    The classification of an appeal into a particular category or under a particular label does not necessarily determine the tribunal's powers and duties. The correct approach is to focus on the specific issue raised rather than the classification of the type of appeal. As May LJ said in *EI Du Pont De Nemours & Co v ST Dupont*:[58]

> At this margin [between rehearing and review under CPR], attributing one label or the other is a semantic exercise which does not answer such questions of substance as arise in any appeal.

May LJ had listed some of these questions:

> Will the appeal court start all over again as if the lower court had never made a decision? Will the appeal court hear the evidence again? What weight is to be given to the decision of the lower court? Will the appeal court admit fresh evidence and, if so, upon what principles? To what extent and upon what principles will the appeal court interfere with the decision of the lower court?[59]

The answer to such questions is a matter of principle, not of discretion.[60] These and other issues are considered below at para 4.44 onwards.

---

52  For example: an appeal to the First-tier Tribunal in its social security jurisdiction is a second hearing but the Social Security Act 1998 s12(8)(a) gives the tribunal power to restrict itself to issues raised by the appeal.

53  Clarke LJ in *Assicurazioni Generali SpA v Arab Insurance Group* [2003] 1 WLR 577 at [8]–[13].

54  [2007] QB 462.

55  [2007] QB 462 at [128].

56  [2006] 1 WLR 2793.

57  [2006] 1 WLR 2793 at [94].

58  [2006] 1 WLR 2793 at [98].

59  [2006] 1 WLR 2793 at [85].

60  [2006] 1 WLR 2793 at [93].

4.30      Once the nature of an appeal and the tribunal's powers have been identified on the basis of the wording of the legislation, this may enter the tribunal's philosophy and survive changes in the wording of the legislation.[61]

## The purposes of an appeal

4.31   An appeal fulfils at least three functions.[62]

4.32      First, an appeal against a decision may be necessary as a matter of constitutional practice or law.

4.33      As a matter of constitutional practice, an appeal against an administrative decision has been described as the very essence of administrative decision-making in a free country[63] and, in the absence of an appeal, the decision should be open to review.[64]

4.34      As a matter of law, an appeal may be necessary in order to ensure a fair hearing under article 6. Whether or not this is so depends on whether, for the purposes of article 6, the decision-maker was independent and whether there was a hearing. If the decision-maker was not independent, an appeal is necessary. Otherwise, it is not; article 6 makes no provision for an appeal in every case.

4.35      Second, an appeal helps to ensure public confidence in the administration of the law, to clarify and develop the law, practice and procedures,[65] and to maintain the standards of the body from which the applies lies.

4.36      Third, an appeal allows wrong decisions to be corrected. This is primarily a matter of concern to the parties to the proceedings.[66]

4.37      In *Stepney Borough Council v Joffe*,[67] Lord Goddard CJ emphasised that the role of an appeal was limited to correcting error:

> It is constantly said (although I am not sure that it is always sufficiently remembered) that the function of a court of appeal is to exercise its powers when it is satisfied that the judgment below is wrong, not merely because it is not satisfied that the judgment was right.[68]

Lord Radcliffe made the same point in *Edwards v Bairstow*:[69] 'The court is not a second opinion, where there is reasonable ground for the first.'[70]

---

61  See the approach of the Tribunal of Commissioners in *R(IB) 2/04* at [19]–[25]. The Tribunal reasoned from past practice and authorities without referring to changes in the wording of the legislation and without considering first principles, which would have produced the same result by pointing to the lack of independence in the decision-makers.

62  See the Woolf Report on *Access to Justice*, HMSO, 1996, chapter 14, para 2, the Bowman Committee Report on *the Review of the Court of Appeal (Civil Division)*, 1997, chapter 2 paras 8–12 and Robert Thomas, *Administrative Justice and Asylum Appeals* (Hart 2011), pages 237–239.

63  Bowen LJ in *R v Justices of the County of London and the London County Council* [1893] 2 QB 476 at 492.

64  *R v Chancellor, Masters and Scholars of the University of Cambridge* (1723) 93 ER 698 at 702–703.

65  *Taylor v Lawrence* [2003] QB 528 at [26].

66  [2003] QB 528 at [26].

67  [1949] 1 KB 599.

68  [1949] 1 KB 599 at 603.

69  [1956] AC 14.

70  [1956] AC 14 at 38.

This distinction has been particularly significant when an appeal concerns an exercise of judgment. If the appellate body is entitled or required to exercise the judgment afresh, it is nonetheless entitled to take account of the way in which it was exercised below.

4.38 Appeals may also be used for other functions, depending on the needs of the parties and the First-tier Tribunal, as perceived by the Upper Tribunal. They may be used proactively to avoid future problems by providing guidance on matters of procedure or the gathering and assessment of evidence. And they may be used to achieve as much consistency as is possible in decisions involving particular issues of judgment.[71]

4.39 An appeal can be effective even if the tribunal's powers are limited and cannot correct mistakes with retrospective effect.[72] The tribunal may nonetheless identify those mistakes and ensure that they are corrected for the future.[73]

## Effectiveness

4.40 An appeal must be effective. The right of appeal is absolute and must not be interfered with. Accordingly, decision-makers and tribunals should not take any steps that would undermine the appeal process, even if they think the appeal is without merit.[74] Nor may they undermine the decision by administrative action.[75]

4.41 This is subject to provision to the contrary. For example: a decision may be set aside on review even while an appeal is proceeding and doing so excludes that decision from the right of appeal (TCEA ss11(5)(e) and 13(8)(e)).

## Multiple appeals

4.42 It is possible, although unusual, for an appeal to lie against the same decision under different provisions. Appeals in respect of tax penalties are an example. An appeal lies to the Upper Tribunal on any ground under section 100B(3) of the Taxes Management Act 1970. An appeal also lies to the Upper Tribunal under TCEA s11. This is limited to issues of law, but applying under this section allows the First-tier Tribunal to use its review powers.

4.43 If a party has a choice from multiple appeals, the choice that the party has made is determined on the documentation as a whole; a mistake in one part of the documents may be corrected elsewhere.[76]

---

71 See chapter 13 for further discussion of these functions.
72 *Vodafone Ltd v British Telecommunications plc* [2010] 3 All ER 1028 at [46].
73 *Vodafone Ltd v British Telecommunications plc* [2010] 3 All ER 1028 at [45].
74 *Lloyd-Davies v Lloyd-Davies* [1947] P 53.
75 *TB (Jamaica) v Secretary of State for the Home Department* (2008) *Times* 9 September.
76 *Mucelli v Government of Republic of Albania* [2009] 1 WLR 276 at [38].

## Scope of an appeal

4.44    This section deals with a number of related issues that determine the scope of an appeal. The heads under which the topic is discussed overlap. They may represent more the particular ways that the same or similar issues have been framed and analysed in different legislative contexts than differences of substance.

### The decision under appeal

4.45    An appeal lies against, or sometimes with respect to,[77] a decision. Usually, the tribunal only has jurisdiction to decide issues relating to that decision.[78]

4.46    The appeal may be limited to a final or outcome decision or it may include interlocutory decisions.[79] Under TCEA s11(1), an appeal lies to the Upper Tribunal on any point of law arising from any decision except an excluded decision. And under section 21(1) of the Employment Tribunals Act 1996, an appeal lies to the Employment Appeal Tribunal 'from any decision of, or arising in any proceedings before, an employment tribunal'.

4.47    The scope of the appeal may be extended by statute to include issues covered by other decisions on which that decision depends. For example: section 84(10) of the Value Added Tax Act 1994 deals with the possibility that a decision under appeal is dependent on an earlier decision that is not appealable. It authorises the tribunal to allow the appeal on the ground that it would have allowed an appeal against the earlier decision.

4.48    The right of appeal may cover all aspects of the decision or be more restricted. This may be expressly stated. Otherwise, it is a matter of interpretation. For example: in *Retarded Children's Aid Society Ltd v Barnet London Borough Council*,[80] the Court of Appeal decided that an appeal lay on the issue whether a residential home could be registered, but not in respect of the conditions imposed on registration. And in *Jones v Attorney-General*,[81] an appeal against an order of the Charity Commissioners was held to include an appeal against a report that was an essential step in the statutory process of making the order.[82]

4.49    The appeal may not be limited to the grounds on which the decision was based. For example: in *Joyce v Secretary of State for Health*,[83] a nurse was added to the list of persons considered unsuitable to work with vulnerable adults on the ground of misconduct by sleeping on duty. On appeal, the nurse argued that the tribunal could not take account of any other grounds on which the decision might have been based. Goldring J held

---

77    For example: Competition Act 1998 ss46(1) and 47(1).

78    *Re W (Permission To Appeal)* [2008] 1 FLR 406 at [21]–[22]. For examples, see *British Broadcasting Corporation v Sugar* [2009] 1 WLR 430 and *MS (Palestinian Territories) v Secretary of State for the Home Department* [2010] 1 WLR 1639.

79    See below at 4.172 onwards.

80    [1969] 2 QB 22.

81    [1974] Ch 148.

82    [1974] Ch 148 at 161.

83    [2009] 1 All ER 1025.

that the tribunal was not so limited for a number of reasons, including the purpose of the legislation, the language of the legislation, and the differing nature of the decisions taken by the nurse's employer, the Secretary of State and the tribunal.[84] Similarly, in *Tower MCashback LLP 1 v Revenue and Customers Commissioners*,[85] the Supreme Court held that the Commissioners were not limited to the reasons given in a closure notice.

4.50 The appeal may include issues that the decision-maker did not consider when making the decision. In *R (Starling) v Child Support Commissioners*,[86] the decision-maker had not considered whether an absent parent should be attributed with income as a result of working for an artificially reduced amount of earnings. The absent parent's solicitor argued that this issue was not within the decision under appeal, as the decision-maker had not been under a duty to consider it when making the decision. Collins J rejected that argument:

> However, the Secretary of State's decision was the assessment of the appropriate amount which should be regarded as the assessed income for the purpose of maintenance payments. It is against that decision that the appeal is brought. The fact that the Secretary of State did not have regard to a particular issue, a particular piece of evidence, in reaching his decision does not seem to me to mean that it is a matter which could not be dealt with by the tribunal on appeal. It is the decision as to correct amount which is the subject of the appeal. Thus the tribunal is seized of that issue: what is the correct amount?[87]

4.51 The power of a tribunal to consider issues that arise for the first time on the appeal is considered below.

## The permissible grounds for appeal

4.52 A ground of appeal is something that, if accepted, would lead to the decision under appeal being changed, rather than to a new decision on different evidence.[88]

4.53 The permissible grounds for appeal may be general or limited. A general appeal[89] allows a decision to be challenged on any grounds, whether related to the facts, the law or the merits (the application of the law to the facts, including the exercise of a judgment or discretion). A limited appeal restricts the grounds on which a decision may be challenged.

4.54 The permissible grounds of appeal may be stated more specifically in the legislation setting up a tribunal or in the tribunal's rules of procedure.[90] This may be achieved indirectly by specifying the form of procedure. For example: section 158(3) and (4) of the National Health Service Act

---

84  [2009] 1 All ER 1025 at [60]–[70].

85  [2011] 2 AC 457.

86  [2008] EWHC 1319 (Admin).

87  [2008] EWHC 1319 (Admin) at [3].

88  Arden LJ in *AS (Afghanistan) v Secretary of State for the Home Department* [2011] 1 WLR 385 at [30].

89  This is the expression used by the Franks Committee in *The Report of the Committee on Administrative Tribunals and Enquiries* Cmnd. 218 (1957) at para 105.

90  For example: Nationality, Immigration and Asylum Act 2002 s84 and, in substance, Value Added Tax Act 1994 s84(4ZA).

2006 provides that an appeal shall be by way of redetermination and that any decision may be made that could have been made. In effect, this provides for a general appeal.

4.55    The TCEA deals with appeals within the tribunal structure. The ground for appeal to the Upper Tribunal is restricted to 'any point of law arising from a decision made by the First-tier Tribunal, other than an excluded decision' (s11(1)). There is equivalent provision for an appeal from the Upper Tribunal to the Court of Appeal (s13(1)). The point of law may be a defect in the decision, in the reasoning on which the decision is based or in the procedure that led to the decision.

4.56    The TCEA does not provide for the grounds of an appeal on entry into the tribunal structure, whether the initial appeal is to the First-tier Tribunal or the Upper Tribunal. This is governed by the legislation governing the particular subject matter. The permissible ground of appeal may also be limited to whether the decision met specified criteria,[91] although this may depend on the context.[92]

4.57    If the grounds are not specified in the legislation, they have to be determined by interpretation of the relevant legislation and the nature of the proceedings. According to *Jones v Attorney-General*,[93] it may also be subject to the tribunal's control over its own procedure. The issue can be difficult.[94]

4.58    One consideration is whether the body from which the appeal lies satisfies article 6. If it does not, perhaps because the decision-maker is not independent or because there has not been a hearing, the appeal is likely to be general and take the form of a complete rehearing.[95]

4.59    Another consideration is whether the issues that might be raised are justiciable. If they are not, the appeal is likely to be limited to scrutiny of the decision on judicial review grounds.[96] This will be so even if a complete reconsideration is required on human rights grounds, for example if the decision-maker was not independent.

4.60    A further consideration is the nature of the decision made by the initial decision-maker. If that is merely an opinion rather than a binding conclusion, this will limit the appeal to the issue whether the decision-maker 'has made an error of principle or reached a conclusion that is clearly wrong'.[97] And an appeal against a decision that involves an assessment of risk may not allow a tribunal to substitute its own assessment of that risk.[98]

---

91  *Foley v Post Office* [2000] ICR 1283 (whether the employer acted reasonably or unreasonably).

92  Contrast *Post Office v Jones* [2001] ICR 805 at [29] and *Collins v Royal National Theatre Board Ltd* [2004] 2 All ER 851, interpreting the same words (whether the reasons for the decision were material and substantial) in different subsections.

93  [1974] Ch 148 at 161.

94  See the Court of Appeal's analysis of the Immigration and Asylum Act 1999 s65 and para 21 of Sch 4 in *Huang v Secretary of State for the Home Department* [2006] QB 1 at [24]–[26] and the House of Lords' decision at [2007] 2 AC 167.

95  This is the approach of CPR: *Score Draw Ltd v Finch* [2007] EWHC 462 (Ch); (2007) *Times* 9 April.

96  See the approach of the Tribunal of Commissioners in *R(H) 6/06* at [39]. This coincides with the line drawn by Stephen Toulmin in *The Uses of Argument* Cambridge 2003 at 162 as the limit beyond which rational argument is no longer possible.

97  *Re DLP Ltd's Patent* [2008] 1 All ER 839 at [22].

98  *Post Office v Jones* [2001] ICR 805 at [24].

## Incidental issues

4.61 In the absence of clear statutory provision to the contrary, a tribunal has power to deal with issues incidental to the permissible grounds of appeal. In *Revenue and Customs Commissioners v Vodafone 2,*[99] the Court of Appeal was concerned with paragraph 33 of Schedule 18 to the Finance Act 1998. This gave a company power to apply to the Commissioners to direct the Revenue to give a closure notice in an inquiry into the company. The paragraph provided that the application 'shall be heard and determined in the same way as an appeal.' It also provided that:

> The Commissioners hearing the application shall give a direction unless they are satisfied that an officer of Revenue and Customs has reasonable grounds for not giving a closure notice within a specified period.

The Revenue argued that the Commissioners' powers were limited to deciding whether the Revenue had reasonable grounds for not giving a closure notice. The Court rejected this argument and decided that the Commissioners had power to decide any incidental question of law arising on the application. This included making a reference to the European Court of Justice.

## The time for consideration

4.62 The issue here is whether the appeal has to be considered as at time of the events involved, at the date of the decision under appeal or at the time of the hearing.

4.63 The time for consideration is related to the evidence that may be considered. The relevant time may determine the evidence that may be taken into account or the circumstances that may be considered. Conversely, the nature of the appeal may determine whether fresh evidence may be heard on the appeal and this in turn may be relevant to the issues that can be considered by the tribunal.

4.64 This may be specified in the legislation. For example: section 12(8)(b) of the Social Security Act 1998 and equivalent provisions[100] prohibit the First-tier Tribunal from taking 'into account any circumstance not obtaining at the time when the decision appealed against was made.'[101] As the provision is concerned with circumstances rather than evidence, it is permissible for a tribunal to consider any evidence regardless of when it was produced, provided that it can be related to the relevant time.[102] Decisions

---

99  2006 STC 1530.

100  Child Support Act 1991 s20(7)(b), Child Support, Pensions and Social Security Act 2000 Sch 7 para 6(9)(b) and Pensions Appeal Tribunals Act 1943 s5B(b).

101  The courts have produced a similar result in cases of professional negligence resulting in loss of a chance to bring litigation, in which the liability of the negligent party has to be determined as at the time of the breach of duty. See *Charles v Hugh James Jones and Jenkins (a firm)* [2000] 1 WLR 1278 at 1288–1291; *Dudarec v Andrews* [2006] 1 WLR 3002.

102  *R(DLA) 2 and 3/01; Secretary of State for Defence v Rusling* [2003] EWHC 1359 QB at [71]–[72]; *Omar v City of Westminster* [2008] EWCA Civ 421; (2008) *Times* 25 March at 32].

based on the future likelihood of events are based on circumstances obtaining at the time when the decision is made.[103]

4.65    The legislation may make different provision for different types of case. For example: section 85 of the Nationality, Immigration and Asylum Act 2002 makes express provision for different classes of appeal. For some, the tribunal on appeal may consider evidence of any matter arising after the date of the decision under appeal (s85(4)). For others, the tribunal may only consider circumstances appertaining at the time of the decision under appeal (s85(5)). This differential treatment does not involve any violation of a Convention right, as a fresh claim may be brought in respect of new circumstances that the tribunal cannot consider.[104]

4.66    If the legislation is not explicit, its language may be sufficiently clear on the issue. In *Wandsworth London Borough Council v Randall*,[105] the Court of Appeal was concerned with a possession order against a tenant by succession under a periodic tenancy. The issue was whether the composition of the tenant's family had to be determined at the time he succeeded to the tenancy or at the time of the hearing. The Court decided that it was the latter. The language was clear in its context and there was nothing to show that Parliament could not have intended this meaning. And in *Albion Water Ltd v Dŵr Cymru Cyf*,[106] the Court of Appeal was concerned with an appeal to the Competition Appeal Tribunal and the scope of the tribunal's power to 'make any other decision which the OFT [Office of Fair Trading] could itself have made.' One issue was whether this authorised the tribunal to make a decision if the OFT could lawfully have done so at the time it made the decision under appeal or to make a decision if it could fairly do so at the time of the hearing on the material then available. The Court decided that it was the latter. It did so despite the statutory institutional structure with an appeal from the decision of the OFT and despite the fact that the tribunal did not have to follow the procedure laid down for the OFT.

4.67    Otherwise, the answer may be found, as a matter of interpretation, in the nature of the substantive issue or in the procedures that apply.

## Substantive issues

4.68    In assessing damages or compensation, the courts take account of evidence that was not before the judge whose decision is under appeal and of circumstances that have changed since that decision was made.[107]

---

103  *Secretary of State for Work and Pensions v Bhakta* [2006] EWCA Civ 65.
104  *AS (Somalia) v Entry Clearance Officer, Addis Ababa* (2008) *Times* 14 April and *AS (Somalia) v Secretary of State for the Home Department* [2009] UKHL 32; [2009] WLR 1385, although Lord Hope left open the possibility that its operation might, in an individual case, violate the Convention right under article 8.
105  [2008] 3 All ER 393.
106  [2009] 2 All ER 279.
107  See *Bwllfa and Merthyr Dare Steam Collieries (1891) Ltd v Pontypridd Waterworks Co* [1903] AC 426, as explained by Rimer LJ in *McDougall v Richmond Adult Community College* [2008] ICR 431.

4.69    This approach may also be taken if the issue is the fitness of a person to practice a profession.[108]

4.70    However, this does not apply to issues of liability. In *McDougall v Richmond Adult Community College*,[109] a case under the Disability Discrimination Act 1995, the issue was whether an impairment was likely to recur. The Court of Appeal decided that this had to be determined on the evidence available at the time of the alleged discrimination, because that was the date at which the employer had to decide how to act. Evidence that only became available later could not be taken into account. Whether a wrong had been committed had to be determined on the evidence available at the time the act occurred.

### Decision-making procedures

4.71    In *R v Social Fund Inspector ex p Lidicott*,[110] there had been a change in the legislation between the date of the original decision by the social fund officer and the date of the review of that decision by a social fund inspector. The legislation provided that on review the inspector had 'power to make any determination which a social fund officer could have made'. Sedley J analysed this language and held that it authorised the Secretary of State to direct inspectors to take account of changes after the date of the officer's decision.

4.72    In *R (McGinley) v Schilling*,[111] the issue was whether disablement for the purposes of a police officer's injury pension was determined at the time of the initial determination or later at the time of the referral to a medical referee. The Court of Appeal decided that it was to be determined at the later date. May LJ set out the factors pointing to this conclusion:[112] (a) the decision under appeal had not been made by an independent decision-maker; (b) it would be strange if the referee had to make a judgment on disablement at any earlier date; and (c) the governing legislation allowed additional evidence to be admitted on the appeal.

4.73    In *British Telecommunications plc v Office of Communications*,[113] the issue was whether the tribunal could consider fresh evidence that had not been before the decision-maker. The Court of Appeal decided that the tribunal had been entitled to admit the fresh evidence. In doing so, it took account of the tribunal's duty to decide whether the decision under appeal was right on the merits of the case and the tribunal was under a duty to have appropriate expertise available to it.

4.74    It does not, though, follow that the decision in a rehearing must always be made as at the date of the appeal rather than of the decision under appeal.

---

108  As in *Sheikh v Law Society* [2005] 4 All ER 717 at [15]. (The decision of the Court of Appeal at [2007] 3 All ER 183 does not affect this point.)
109  [2008] ICR 431.
110  (1995) *Times* 24 May.
111  [2005] ICR 1282.
112  [2005] ICR 1282 at [34]–[35].
113  [2011] 4 All ER 372.

4.75    In *R v Immigration Appeal Tribunal ex p Weerasuriya*,[114] the issue was whether an immigration appeal had to be decided as at the time of the Secretary of State's decision or as at the time of the appeal. Webster J decided that it was the former. He identified the issue as whether the 'appellate structure has to be regarded as an extension of the original administrative decision-making or whether it is to be regarded as simply a process for enabling that decision to be reviewed.'[115]

4.76    In contrast, in *Ravichandran v Secretary of State for the Home Department*,[116] the Court of Appeal decided that an asylum appeal has to be decided on the circumstances obtaining at the date of the appeal, because the appeal is an extension of the decision-making structure. The result, as explained by Laws LJ in *A(C) v Secretary of State for the Home Department*,[117] is that the tribunal 'must . . . decide what if any relief to grant in the light of the facts arising at the time it is considering the case.'[118]

4.77    In *Omar v City of Westminster*,[119] the issue was whether it was permissible to take account of a change of circumstances on a review of a homelessness decision by a local authority. The Court of Appeal analysed reviews in these cases according to whether or not the decision-making process was ongoing.[120] If the review is part of the decision-making process (eg if the person has accepted an offer of accommodation but challenges its suitability), it can take into account any change of circumstances down to the date of the review. But if the review is not part of the decision-making process (eg if the person has refused an offer of accommodation and the local authority has decided that it has discharged its duty towards that person), it is confined to the facts as they were at the time of the decision under review, whether or not they were known then.

4.78    *Boreh v London Borough of Ealing*[121] is an example of the latter. The local authority had offered the homeless claimant a property without any mention of adapting it to her needs. She refused and the local authority warned that it had discharged its duty to house her. The claimant asked for a review. The Court of Appeal held that the reviewing officer could not take account of a later offer to make suitable adaptations.[122]

4.79    In *R(S) 2/98*, a Tribunal of Commissioners confirmed that tribunals dealing with social security appeals had to deal with any issue that arose between the time the decision under appeal was made and the date of the hearing of the appeal. But in doing so they did not treat the tribunal as merely an extension of the original administrative decision-making. This

114 [1983] 1 All ER 195.
115 [1983] 1 All ER 195 at 201–202 approved by the Court of Appeal in *R v Immigration Appeal Tribunal ex p Kotecha* [1983] 1 WLR 487 at 492–493.
116 [1996] Imm AR 97 and (1996) IRA 97.
117 [2004] EWCA Civ 1165.
118 [2004] EWCA Civ 1165 at [15].
119 [2008] EWCA Civ 421; (2008) *Times* 25 March.
120 [2008] EWCA Civ 421 at [25].
121 [2009] 2 All ER 383.
122 [2009] 2 All ER 383 at [30].

approach was later reversed by section 12(8)(b) of the Social Security Act 1998.[123]

4.80 The approach to be taken by Housing Benefit Review Boards was unclear. In *R v City of Westminster ex p Mehanne*,[124] on judicial review at first instance the judge decided that the Board was required to consider the claimant's circumstances at the time of the hearing, not at the time of the local authority's decision. Unfortunately, he did not set out his reasoning, merely referring to the applicant's skeleton arguments, and on appeal the Court of Appeal[125] did not clarify the issue. But in *R v Housing Benefit Review Board of the London Borough of Waltham Forest ex p Iqbal*,[126] again on judicial review at first instance, the judge held that the Board could only take account of circumstances at the date of the local authority's decision. He was influenced by the express provision allowing the local authority to review its decision for a change of circumstances,[127] although he admitted that this interpretation did create anomalies.

## The evidence that may be considered

4.81 This may be determined by legislation, the time for consideration and the nature of the appeal.

4.82 The legislation may limit the evidence that may be taken into account. For example: regulation 13(2)(a) of the Education (Prohibition from Teaching or Working with Children) Regulations 2003 (repealed) provided that on appeal a tribunal might not take account of information that had not been before the Secretary of State.[128] The legislation may also make it clear that further evidence may be taken into account. For example: under the Charities Act 1993,[129] a tribunal must consider afresh the decision under appeal and take account of any new evidence that was not before the decision-maker.

4.83 The time as at which a decision has to be made may also limit the evidence that may be taken into account, as only evidence that relates to that time will be relevant.

4.84 The nature of the appeal may determine whether evidence may be heard on the appeal. Further evidence can be considered if the proceedings involve rehearing the issues afresh. And if there is no record of the evidence on which a decision was based and the reasons for it, the tribunal is practically compelled to decide the matter afresh.[130] The procedure usually followed by a particular tribunal may determine the nature of

123 See also: Child Support Act 1991 s20(7)(b); Child Support, Pensions and Social Security 2000 Sch 7 para 6(9)(b); and Pensions Appeal Tribunals Act 1943 s5B(b).
124 [1997] EWHC 1117 (Admin).
125 *R v City of Westminster Housing Benefit Review Board ex p Mehanne* [2000] 1 WLR 16.
126 [1997] EWHC 810 (Admin).
127 The Commissioner was not influenced by an equivalent provision in *R(SB) 1/82* at [9] and [12].
128 Discussed in *Secretary of State for Children, Schools and Families v Philliskirk* [2009] ELR 68.
129 Charities Act 1993 Sch 1C para 1(4), inserted by Charities Act 2006 Sch 4.
130 Edmund Davies LJ in *Sagnata Investments Ltd v Norwich Corporation* [1971] 2 QB 614 at 634; *Rushmoor Borough Council v Richards* (1996) *Times* 5 February; *Haw v City of Westminster Magistrates' Court* [2008] QB 888 at [25].

proceedings on any new appeal allocated to it. This was the approach of the Tribunal of Commissioners in *R(IB) 2/04*.[131] Rather than reasoning from basic principle, the Tribunal took an historical approach, despite the fact that it was dealing with a newly created appeal tribunal.[132] This approach may be difficult to apply in the tribunal structure under TCEA where, even within chambers, there may be divergent approaches to different types of case.

## Transcripts

4.85 The Upper Tribunal considered the use of transcripts of evidence in *HSW/2001/2010*:[133]

> First, the Upper Tribunal is entitled to all the evidence that was before the tribunal. That includes the oral evidence. There is no difference between providing copies of the documents that were before the tribunal and providing a transcript of the oral evidence and argument at the hearing. A transcript is not evidence of what was said at the hearing, it is the record of proceedings. No satellite issues can arise as are possible when the evidence is provided by witness statements.

> Second, the issues raised in a particular case may be such that the Upper Tribunal is able to decide the case without seeing all the evidence.

> Third, there is no formal procedure that has to be followed. There is no need for an application that a party be allowed to produce or rely on a transcript. The authorities cited by Mr McKendrick involved specific rules that applied in the High Court. There is no equivalent in the Tribunal Procedure (Upper Tribunal) Rules 2008 (SI No 2698).

> Fourth, the transcript may only be used in support of an argument that the tribunal made an error of law.

> Fifth, the other party must not be taken by surprise. Natural justice and the Convention right to a fair hearing require that all the parties have a reasonable time to prepare their cases.

> Sixth, the production of a transcript may be relevant in an application for costs.

## Issues raised by the parties

4.86 A tribunal is under a duty to deal with all the issues raised by a party that is within its jurisdiction,[134] unless its decision on one issue renders the others redundant. In this sense, the grounds set the agenda for the consideration by the tribunal.[135]

4.87 The tribunal is not limited to a literal reading of the issues as advanced by the party. It is entitled to extract an issue from grounds of appeal that

---

131 *R(IB) 2/04* at [19]–[25].

132 See also the reliance on the procedure on appeal to the High Court in *Haw v City of Westminster Magistrates' Court* [2008] QB 888 at [25].

133 *HSW/2001/2010* at [15]–[20].

134 See chapter 2 for a general discussion of jurisdiction.

135 Carnwath LJ in *Secretary of State for Work and Pensions v Menary-Smith* [2006] EWCA Civ 1751 at [39].

are nebulously expressed.[136] And it may do so even for the benefit of a decision-maker.[137]

4.88      The legislation may specify the stage of the proceedings at which, or the circumstances in which, an issue may be raised. The stage at which an issue may be raised in a social security case is governed by section 12(8)(a) of the Social Security Act 1998.[138] It provides that an appeal tribunal under that Act 'need not consider any issue that is not raised by the appeal'. In *R (Starling) v Child Support Commissioners*,[139] Collins J described the child support equivalent of this provision as 'the most ill drafted and obscure provision in the field of child support'.[140] It has been interpreted to mean that the issue must be raised at or before the hearing by one of the parties to the proceedings.[141]

## The tribunal's duty to consider other issues

4.89      In addition to the issues raised by the parties, a tribunal must investigate and, if appropriate, decide other obvious issues that have not been raised by any of the parties.[142]

4.90      Issues of jurisdiction always arise. As Morison J explained in the Employment Appeal Tribunal in *Sogbetun v Hackney London Borough Council*:[143]

> . . . a jurisdiction question arises regardless of whether the jurisdiction point has been previously spotted or simply abandoned or neglected.[144]

4.91      The legislation may identify the extent of a tribunal's duty to consider issues. So under section 12(8)(a) the Social Security Act 1998, a tribunal is not under a statutory duty to consider any issue that is not raised by the appeal.[145] However, the tribunal retains the power to do so. In *R(IB) 2/04*, a Tribunal of Commissioners decided that this power must be exercised judicially and in a way that ensured a fair hearing for all the parties to the proceedings.[146] The circumstances may be such that the only proper exercise of the power is to consider the issue. This will be so if the issue is obvious[147] or if it is in the public interest to raise it.[148]

---

136   *Krasniqi v Secretary of State for the Home Department* [2006] EWCA Civ 391 at [19]; (2006) *Times* 20 April.

137   [2006] EWCA Civ 391 at [18]–[19].

138   See also: Child Support Act 1991 s20(7)(a), the Child Support, Pensions and Social Security Act 2000 Sch 7 para 6(9)(a) and the Pensions Appeal Tribunals Act 1943 s5B(a).

139   [2008] EWHC 1319 (Admin).

140   [2008] EWHC 1319 (Admin) at [36].

141   *R(IB) 2/04* at [32].

142   See also para 4.214 onwards.

143   [1998] ICR 1264.

144   [1998] ICR 1264 at 1270. See further chapter 2.

145   There is equivalent provision in Child Support Act 1991 s20(7)(a), Child Support, Pensions and Social Security Act 2000 Sch 7 para 6(9)(a) and Pensions Appeal Tribunals Act 1943 s5B(a).

146   *R(IB) 2/04* at [32] and [93]–[94].

147   *Mooney v Secretary of State for Work and Pensions* 2004 SLT 1141 at [35] (also *R(DLA) 5/04*).

148   *R (Starling) v Child Support Commissioners* [2008] EWHC 1319 (Admin) at [31]–[33].

4.92     The provision was interpreted differently by the Court of Appeal in Northern Ireland in *Mongan v Department for Social Development*.[149] The Court decided that any issue that was within the tribunal's inquisitorial duty was raised by the appeal. The extent of this duty depended on the facts of the case. It did not require an exhaustive trawl through the evidence, but it did require a tribunal to deal with issues that were clearly apparent from the evidence.[150]

4.93     There is a difference between the approach of the Commissioners and the Court of Appeal.[151] On appeal on an issue of law, a tribunal would not go wrong on the Commissioners' approach if it exercised its power in a way that it was entitled to do, even if the Commissioner would have exercised it differently. However, on the Court of Appeal's approach the Commissioner would have to decide whether or not the tribunal was under a duty to consider the issue and would have no power to show any deference to the tribunal's judgment.

4.94     Subject to this, the slightly different interpretations of the legislation produce an effect that is broadly the same as the position that obtains apart from statute. So, before the introduction of the limit to the tribunal's inquisitorial duty in section 12(8)(a) of the Social Security Act 1998, the Tribunal of Commissioners in *R(SB) 2/83* decided that a tribunal did not have to take 'an uncanvassed factual point . . . in the absence of the most obvious and clear-cut circumstances.'[152] This is consistent with the way in which the courts have limited the duty of a tribunal to take an inquisitorial approach on an application for permission to appeal.

4.95     Apart from statute, the scope of the tribunal's duty to consider issues that have not been raised by the parties depends on the extent to which, and circumstances in which, a tribunal is required to be inquisitorial. In *Hooper v Secretary of State for Work and Pensions*,[153] the Court of Appeal considered but left open the issue of the extent to which a tribunal had to deal with issues that were not raised by the parties. Dyson LJ distinguished the case of *R v Secretary of State for the Home Department ex p Robinson*[154] on the ground that it applied to applications for permission to appeal, but suggested that the scope of a tribunal's inquisitorial duty might be limited by the statutory limits on its jurisdiction (in this case to errors of law).[155] Thomas LJ considered that the absence of any legal aid might be a relevant factor.[156] And Ward LJ preferred to leave the matter open without any comment.[157]

---

149  [2005] NICA 16, reported as *R3/05 (DLA)*.
150  [2005] NICA 16 at [14]–[18].
151  In *Hooper v Secretary of State for Work and Pensions* [2007] EWCA Civ 495, reported as *R(IB) 4/07* at [28], the Court of Appeal endorsed the approach in *Mongan*, but without being sufficiently specific to resolve the difference identified here.
152  *R(SB) 2/83* at [11].
153  [2007] EWCA Civ 495, reported as *R(IB) 4/07*.
154  [1998] QB 929. Discussed in chapter 4.
155  [1998] QB 929 at [44]–[45].
156  [1998] QB 929 at [59].
157  [1998] QB 929 at [61].

## The tribunal's power to consider other issues

4.96 A tribunal's power to raise issues of its own initiative is limited by the statutory scope of the appeal. This was considered by the Court of Appeal in *R (Walmsley) v Lane*.[158] The case concerned an appeal to a Parking and Traffic Adjudicator against a penalty charge. The legislation provided a list of grounds on which representations could be made to the charging authority. On appeal, the Adjudicator had a duty to consider representations on those grounds and power to 'give the charging authority concerned such directions as he considers appropriate'. The Adjudicator had dismissed the appeal, but on judicial review the judge had directed the authority to cancel the penalty charge notice, despite the fact that none of the specified grounds was satisfied.[159] The Court of Appeal held that this was not permissible. The power to give directions only arose if one of the specified grounds was established. That power could not be used to extend the scope of the appeal beyond those grounds. The Court noted that the authority had power under other provisions to take account of other factors.

4.97 The scope of the tribunal's power to deal with issues of its own initiative is also governed by the powers of the decision-maker, the nature of the appeal and the tribunal's powers on the appeal. The Commissioners used these factors to allow any issue to be considered that was within the purview of the original claim for benefit.[160]

4.98 A tribunal may deal on its own initiative with an issue that involves a point of general importance that concerns the State's compliance with its international obligations.[161]

## Issues raised for the first time

4.99 An issue may arise for the first time on an appeal for two reasons.

4.100 The first way is if the parties have not have raised it before.

4.101 In *R(F) 1/72*, the Commissioner decided that a local tribunal was entitled to take a point against the appellant claimant that had first been raised by the decision-maker on the appeal. The issue related to a provision different from that on which the decision had been based. However, the Commissioner held it could be considered as an appeal to the tribunal and to the Commissioner was 'a rehearing of the whole case'.[162]

4.102 And in *R(SB) 9/81*, the Commissioner decided that a tribunal had jurisdiction to consider any issues that were within the purview of the original claim for benefit. In that case, the issues had not been considered by the decision-maker and were not mentioned in the claimant's letter of appeal to the tribunal. They were first raised by her representative at the hearing before the tribunal. Nonetheless, the tribunal considered the

---

158 [2006] RTR 177.

159 [2005] RTR 370.

160 *R(F) 1/72* at [9], emphasising that the appeal was a rehearing of the whole case, and *R(SB) 9/81* at [9], emphasising the powers of the decision-maker and the tribunal.

161 *Bulale v Secretary of State for the Home Department* [2008] EWCA Civ 806; (2008) *Times* 25 July.

162 [2008] EWCA Civ 806 at [9].

issues and accepted the representative's argument. The Commissioner held that the tribunal was entitled to do so, emphasising that the tribunal and the Commissioner had power to substitute a decision that the decision-maker could and should have made.[163]

4.103    A party or a representative may not be allowed to raise points that could have been raised earlier. If a tribunal hears a case on appeal as if for the first time, there is no scope for limiting a party to points that have been made already. However, there is scope for this on further appeal to the Upper Tribunal or to a court. In the Court of Appeal in *Stanley Cole (Wainfleet) Ltd v Sheridan*,[164] Ward LJ said:

> The interests of justice do not demand that any shortcomings in a litigant in person's presentation of his or her case should be overcome by affording the litigant the indulgence of the chance to do better second time round.

And Buxton LJ said:

> True it is ... that Tribunals permit, even perhaps encourage, lay representation; but that gives no more licence than where professional advocates are engaged to attempts to reargue the case if on reflection the representative thinks that it could have been better put.[165]

4.104    The Court of Appeal may refuse to hear an appeal, even if permission has been granted. As Mummery LJ explained in *Office of Communications v Floe Telecom Ltd (in liquidation)*:[166]

> Permission to appeal has been granted, but that does not bind this court to decide an appeal which it ought not to decide.

The Court has used this power to refuse to hear appeals on grounds that were not put to the tribunal below. For example: in *Secretary of State for Work and Pensions v Hughes (A Minor)*,[167] the Court refused to hear an appeal in these circumstances despite the fact that the Commissioner had given permission to appeal.

4.105    However, the Court of Appeal does allow issues to be raised for the first time. In *Chief Adjudication Officer v Maguire*,[168] it dealt (as the only issue) with a point on which the adjudication officer had specifically made no submission to the Commissioner. It did not explain its decision to deal with the issue, other than to comment that 'this issue will literally govern thousands of other cases'.[169] And in *Campbell v South Northamptonshire District Council*,[170] the Court allowed counsel to raise a human rights issue that he had not put to the Commissioner.[171] It gave no reason for doing so.

4.106    It is difficult to discern any principle governing the choice of whether or not to allow a new issue to be raised.

163 [2008] EWCA Civ 806 at [9].
164 [2003] ICR 1449.
165 [2003] ICR 1449 at [46].
166 [2009] EWCA Civ 47 at [18]; (2009) *Times* 23 February.
167 [2004] EWCA Civ 16, reported as *R(DLA) 1/04*.
168 [1999] 1 WLR 1778.
169 [1999] 1 WLR 1778 at 1780.
170 [2004] 3 All ER 387.
171 [2004] 3 All ER 387 at [31].

4.107　　The second way in which an issue may arise for the first time on an appeal is as a result of the tribunal's conclusion on another issue. For example: if the decision under appeal was that there was no jurisdiction to decide the case and the tribunal decides that there was jurisdiction, the merits of the case will arise for the first time as a result of that conclusion. Depending on the governing legislation, the tribunal may limit its decision to the issue raised by the appeal, leaving the decision-maker to deal with other issues, or it may deal with those issues itself.[172]

4.108　　The legislation may make express provision prohibiting or authorising issues to be considered for the first time on an appeal. So, section 24(2) of the Child Support Act 1991 provides:

> (2) Where a question which would otherwise fall to be determined by the Secretary of State under this Act first arises in the course of an appeal to the Upper Tribunal, that tribunal may, if it thinks fit, determine the question even though it has not been considered by the Secretary of State.[173]

4.109　　The Commissioners interpreted such provisions as covering questions that were first identified during the appeal and not as limited to questions that only arose because of the course taken by the appeal. In *R(I) 4/75*, the Chief Commissioner described the discretion as a 'useful provision [that] should be liberally construed'.[174] Accordingly it is only excluded if the question has already been considered fully to the point where the decision-maker could have decided it.[175] A question does not arise until there is some doubt about it.[176] In practice, the effect of such a provision is little or no different from what would otherwise have been the scope of an appeal.

4.110　　In the absence of express provision, the issue depends on the form of the appeal and the powers of the tribunal.

4.111　　*R(U) 2/54* is an example of the approach taken by the Commissioners before there was any statutory power to deal with questions first arising. The claimant had been disqualified for unemployment benefit on the ground that she had left her employment voluntarily without just cause. The Commissioner commented that if the tribunal had decided that the claimant had not left voluntarily, it was entitled to determine whether she was disqualified on the ground that she had lost her employment through misconduct.[177] That ground for disqualification arose under the same legislative provision.

---

172　*R(IS) 2/08.*

173　This was previously the Child Support Act 1991 s24(8). A power to deal with questions first arising was conferred on tribunals in social security cases by the National Insurance Act 1965 s70A, which was inserted by the Social Security Act 1973 s84(6) and Sch 21 para 7. The provision was then consolidated, first as the Social Security Act 1975 s102 and then as the Social Security Administration Act 1992 s36. When the power was introduced, it did not at first apply to means tested benefits. It was later extended to them. This social security power was later abolished by the Social Security Act 1998 s86(2) and Sch 8.

174　*R(I) 4/75* at [12].

175　*CIS/807/1992* at [6].

176　*R v Westminster (City) London Borough Council Rent Officer ex p Rendall* [1973] QB 959 at 975–976.

177　[1973] QB 959 at [8].

## Arguments not put to the tribunal below

4.112   Whether an argument may be raised for the first time on appeal depends on the nature of the appeal.

4.113      If the appeal involves a complete reconsideration of the decision, any issue may be raised. As Payne J explained in *Blundell v Rimmer:*[178]

> It is, I think, clear on authority that the appeal from the district registrar is a rehearing of the application and that I am entitled to treat the matter as though it had come before me for the first time, and, moreover, that I am not fettered by the previous exercise of the district registrar's discretion although I should, of course, give to it the weight which it deserves. Authority for that proposition can be found in the speech of Lord Atkin in *Evans v Bartlam* [1937] AC 473, 478 . . .[179]

4.114   Otherwise, there is a discretion whether to allow the argument to be put. As Widgery LJ explained in *Wilson v Liverpool Corporation:*[180]

> It seems to me that this case is within the well-known rule of practice that if a point is not taken in the court of trial, it cannot be taken in the appeal unless that court is in possession of all the material necessary to enable it to dispose of the matter finally, without injustice to the other party, and without recourse to a further hearing below.
>
> . . . I recognise, as does Lord Denning MR, that being a rule of practice this rule contains an element of discretion.[181]

4.115   In *R (Child Support Agency) v Learad,*[182] the Administrative Court exercised its discretion to deal with an issue of law that might have a practical importance between the parents.

## Points not pursued

4.116   A point mentioned but not pursued is usually treated as abandoned. See *Adams v Mason Bullock (a Firm).*[183]

## Concessions

4.117   Concessions may or may not be appropriate. They are not appropriate or binding for the interpretation of documents[184] or legislation.[185]

4.118      If a concession is made, it remains binding unless it can be withdrawn. It may be withdrawn on appeal, if that can be done without prejudice to the other parties.[186]

---

178  [1971] 1 WLR 123.
179  [1971] 1 WLR 123 at 128.
180  [1971] 1 WLR 302.
181  [1971] 1 WLR 302 at 307.
182  [2008] 1 FLR 31 at [9]–[12].
183  (2005) *Times* 6 January.
184  Lord Diplock in *Bahamas International Trust Co Ltd v Threadgold* [1974] 1 WLR 1514 at 1525.
185  Lord Diplock in *Cherwell District Council v Thames Water Authority* [1975] 1 WLR 448 at 452.
186  *Davoodipanah v Secretary of State for the Home Department* [2004] EWCA Civ 106; (2004) *Times* 5 February at [22].

4.119    The tribunal is not obliged to accept a concession, especially if it contrary to its inquisitorial role, and it may be consistent with the decision-maker's non-partisan role to resile from a concession.[187]

## Appeals involving exercises of judgment

4.120    If the appeal is against a decision based on an exercise of judgment, the question arises whether the tribunal is limited to deciding if the judgment was exercised wrongly or is allowed or required to exercise the judgment afresh.

4.121    The approach to identifying the scope of the appeal in these cases was set out by Etherton J in *Banbury Visionplus Ltd v Revenue and Customs Commissioners*.[188] The position is this. The scope of the appeal may be made clear in the language of the statute that allows the appeal. In the absence of express provision, any limitation on the scope of the appeal must be apparent from the nature of the decision or the legislative context.[189]

4.122    The general approach of the courts has been that the judgment must be exercised afresh on appeal.[190] Otherwise, the right of appeal would be rendered illusory[191] or unduly restricted.[192]

4.123    However, there are cases in which this approach has not been taken. *John Dee Ltd v Customs and Excise Commissioners*[193] is an example. There it was permissible to require security 'Where it appears to the Commissioners requisite to do so for the protection of the revenue'. Statute provided for a general appeal 'with respect to . . . the requirement of security'. Neill LJ explained the Court of Appeal's decision:

> It seems to me that the 'statutory condition' . . . which the tribunal has to determine in an appeal . . . is whether it appeared to the commissioners requisite to require security. In examining whether that statutory condition is satisfied the tribunal will . . . consider whether the commissioners had acted in a way in which no reasonable panel of Commissioners could have acted or whether they had taken into account some irrelevant matter or had disregarded something to which they should have given weight. The tribunal may also have to consider whether the commissioners have erred on a point of law.[194]

One factor that influenced the decision in this case was that the tribunal was under no duty to protect the revenue; that statutory responsibility was imposed on the Commissioners.[195] It is not clear to what extent that factor affected the outcome.

---

187   *LC v Secretary of State for Work and Pensions* [2009] UKUT 153 (AAC).
188   [2006] STC 1568.
189   [2006] STC 1568 at [44].
190   As in *Secretary of State for Children, Schools and Families v Philliskirk* [2009] ELR 68 at [19].
191   Lord Goddard CJ in *Stepney Borough Council v Joffe* [1949] 1 KB 599 at 602.
192   Lord Parker CJ in *Godfrey v Bournemouth Corporation* [1969] 1 WLR 47 at 51.
193   [1995] STC 941, as explained in *Banbury Visionplus Ltd v Revenue and Customs Commissioners* [2006] STC 1568 at [39]–[44].
194   [1995] STC 941 at 952.
195   [1995] STC 941 at 952.

4.124    A fresh exercise of the judgment is also excluded if, exceptionally, a right of appeal is given against a decision that involves a discretion which is non-justiciable. This may be because the discretion involves a consideration of a number of unrelated factors with no indication, in the legislation or the context, of which were relevant. Or it may be because the discretion involves non-legal judgments on considerations of policy, finance or social matters. In these limited circumstances, the right of appeal does not allow a tribunal to substitute its exercise of discretion for that of the decision-maker. It is limited to challenges to the legality of the decision on judicial review grounds.[196]

4.125    If a discretion (or any other judgment) has to be exercised afresh on appeal, the way in which it was exercised below is not binding, but must be taken into account for whatever it is worth. As Lord Atkin explained in *Evans v Bartlam*:[197]

> ... where there is a discretionary jurisdiction given to the Court or judge the judge in Chambers is in no way fettered by the previous exercise of the Master's discretion. His own discretion is intended by the rules to determine the parties' rights: and he is entitled to exercise it as though the matter came before him for the first time. He will, of course, give the weight it deserves to the previous decision of the Master: but he is in no way bound by it.[198]

This approach is compatible with the tribunal's power to admit fresh evidence.[199]

4.126    A different approach must be taken if the issue is whether the exercise was wrong in law. The difference was emphasised by Griffiths LJ in *C M Van Stillevoldt BV v E L Carriers Inc*:[200]

> If I had to approach this matter by considering whether or not the registrar had erred in his approach to the exercise of his discretion because he had applied the wrong principles of law or had given a wholly erroneous weight to some matter or failed to take into account some other matter, I should unhesitatingly come to the conclusion that I could not interfere with his discretion; it appears to me that he has taken all the relevant matters into consideration. However, I have to exercise my own discretion in this case; and I have after some hesitation . . . come to the conclusion that the balance comes down on the other side to that chosen by the registrar.[201]

## Appeals from another tribunal on issues of fact

4.127    The proper approach to an appeal on an issue of fact was considered by the Court of Appeal in *Subesh v Secretary of State for the Home Department*.[202] The effect of this decision was conveniently summarised in *P v Secretary of State for the Home Department*:[203]

196  See the decision of the Tribunal of Commissioners in *R(H) 6/06* (especially at [24] and [39]) analysing the decision of an earlier Tribunal of Commissioners in *R(H) 3/04*.
197  [1937] AC 473.
198  [1937] AC 473 at 478.
199  *British Telecommunications plc v Office of Communications* [2011] 4 All ER 372 at [65].
200  [1983] 1 WLR 207.
201  [1983] 1 WLR 207 at 212.
202  [2004] Imm AR 112.
203  [2005] Imm AR 84.

a) The first instance decision is taken to be correct until the contrary is shown' (paragraph 44);

b) The appellant before the IAT [Immigration Appeal Tribunal], if he is to succeed, 'must persuade the appellate court or tribunal not merely that a different view of the facts from that taken below is reasonable and possible, but that there are objective grounds upon which the court ought to conclude that a different view is the right one ... The true distinction is between the case where the appeal court might *prefer* a different view (perhaps on marginal grounds) and one where it concludes that the process of reasoning and the application of the relevant law, *require* it to adopt a different view. The burden which an appellant assumes is to show that the case falls within this latter category' (paragraph 44, see also paragraphs 46 and 53);

c) This approach is not a function of jurisdiction but of the principle of finality of litigation (paragraphs 25, 26, 40 and 48);

d) This approach 'is not confined to appeals on disputed issues of fact which the judge below has resolved by reference to oral testimony' (paragraph 42);

e) It is a separate point to note that, 'pragmatically, the IAT (like any appeal court) will give due weight to the advantage that the Court below can be presumed to have obtained from the relevant oral testimony (paragraph 41) (see also paragraphs 37 and 46); and

f) The judgment in *Subesh* should not be read like a statute (paragraph 49).[204]

## Appeals from a decision-maker on issues of fact

4.128  The approach to appeals on fact from decision-makers[205] is different from that taken to appeals on fact from another tribunal. A decision-maker is not independent for the purposes of the Convention right in article 6. This indicates that a tribunal should be more willing to differ from the findings of fact on which a decision was based, than on appeal from a tribunal that does comply with that article.

## A fair hearing

4.129  If a tribunal deals with an issue of which the parties have not had notice, it must ensure a fair hearing at least for the party adversely affected by the issue.[206] Collins J explained something of what this involves in *R (Starling) v Child Support Commissioners:*[207]

> I should add this in dealing with the question of fairness. Where a tribunal raises an issue of its own motion such as this it is obviously important that the appellant is not put at a disadvantage and that the chairman of the tribunal does not take on the mantle of a party and descend into the

---

204  [2005] Imm AR 84 at [12]. The summary was taken from the argument of counsel for the Secretary of State.

205  For example: Safeguarding Vulnerable Groups Act 2006 s4(2)(b).

206  *R v Mental Health Review Tribunal ex p Clatworthy* [1985] 3 All ER 699 at 704; *R(IB) 2/04* at [32] and [93]–[94].

207  [2008] EWHC 1319 (Admin) at [43].

arena. Of course he is entitled to test the evidence given by the appellant, to raise issues which he considers to be important and to point perhaps in the direction against the approach adopted by the appellant. But he must take care not to appear to be acting in a way which suggests that he has taken over the role of a party rather than staying in his role as chairman.

## Precedent or jurisdictional fact

4.130   The jurisdiction of a decision-maker or a tribunal may depend on the existence of a fact. The legislation may provide that either (i) the fact must exist or (ii) the decision-maker or tribunal must be satisfied that it exists. (i) is a precedent fact; (ii) is not.

### Relevance

4.131   The distinction is not relevant if the tribunal is rehearing the case afresh, because it may then substitute its conclusion on the facts for that of the decision-maker.[208] The issue is only relevant on an appeal on an issue of law or on judicial review. If the fact is a precedent one, the tribunal on appeal must decide if the fact exists. If it is not, the tribunal must accept the finding made below unless it is perverse.[209]

### Drawing the distinction

4.132   The legislation may take one of two forms. It may take this form: 'If the facts are X, then consequence Y follows'. Alternatively, it may take this or comparable form: 'If the decision-maker is satisfied that the facts are X, then consequence Y follows'.

4.133        The former suggests a precedent fact;[210] the latter does not. However, the language has to be interpreted. If a fact is defined in wholly objective terms and defines the limit of a body's jurisdiction, it is likely to be a jurisdictional fact.[211]

## The judge's notes

4.134   These are only obtained if there is a conflict of fact about what happened or what was said before the judge.[212]

## Permission to appeal

4.135   Permission to appeal is one possible element of initiating proceedings; it justifies a separate section.

---

208  *R(IB) 2/04* at [25].
209  Lords Fraser and Scarman in *R v Secretary of State for the Home Department ex p Khera* [1984] AC 74 at 97 and 110.
210  *R (A) v Croydon LBC* [2009] UKSC 8, [2009] 1 FLR 1324 at [23].
211  *R (A) v Croydon LBC* [2009] UKSC 8, [2010] 1 All ER 469 at [29]–[32].
212  Sedley LJ in *McKee v Secretary of State for Work and Pensions* [2004] EWCA Civ 334 at [12] (refusing an application for permission to appeal).

4.136 An application for permission is a separate proceeding.[213] This is relevant to the scope of a decision to strike out or bar participation in proceedings.[214] It may also be of relevance for transitional provisions governing the transfer of proceedings to the First-tier Tribunal or Upper Tribunal.

## Terminology

4.137 'Permission' and 'leave' are synonymous. The former is the more modern term, although the latter is still used in Northern Ireland. This book uses permission, which is frequently used in practice even when a statute refers to leave, unless it is historically necessary to refer to leave.

4.138 The legislation will distinguish between someone who applies for permission to appeal and someone to whom permission has been given. They may be distinguished by title: an 'applicant' may describe someone who applies for permission; an 'appellant' may describe an applicant to whom permission has been given. The distinction is relevant under UTR, but without using distinguishing terminology. Under those Rules, 'applicant' is reserved for someone who initiates judicial review proceedings. 'Appellant' is used to designate both someone who applies for permission to appeal and someone to whom permission has been given. However, in this section, 'applicant' is used to refer to a person who has applied for permission to appeal.

4.139 Any party other than the person applying for permission is called the respondent.

4.140 The legislation may distinguish between an application that is unsuccessful on procedural grounds and an application that is unsuccessful on the merits. This distinction may be reflected in terminology. An application may be 'rejected' for procedural reasons, such as lateness, and 'refused' on the substantive merits. Under UTR, rejection is not used and the process is described as not admitting the appeal.

## Admitting an application and extending time

4.141 It may be necessary to consider whether to admit an application that was not admitted by the First-tier Tribunal or to extend the time for making the application.

4.142 An application may only be admitted if it is in the interests of justice to do so. UTR r21(7) provides:[215]

> (7) If the appellant makes an application to the Upper Tribunal for permission to appeal against the decision of another tribunal, and that other tribunal refused to admit the appellant's application for permission to appeal because the application for permission or for a written statement of reasons was not made in time–
> (a) the application to the Upper Tribunal for permission to appeal must include the reason why the application to the other tribunal for

---

213 *Harkness v Bell's Asbestos and Engineering Ltd* [1967] 2 QB 729 at 735 and 736.
214 *SL v Secretary of State for Work and Pensions and KL-D* [2014] UKUT 0128 (AAC) at [21]–[22].
215 See also Lands Rules r21(6).

permission to appeal or for a written statement of reasons, as the case may be, was not made in time; and

(b) the Upper Tribunal must only admit the application if the Upper Tribunal considers that it is in the interests of justice for it to do so.

4.143   Extending time depends on the tribunal's discretion under UTR r5(3)(a). This is discussed in chapter 7.

4.144   If permission is given out of time without time being extended, the grant is of no effect.[216]

4.145   It is permissible to shorten time for applying for permission to appeal to a higher tribunal or court and this may be desirable in order to bring finality to proceedings.[217]

## Applying too soon

4.146   A party may be aware of a decision before it is actually made or promulgated and apply for permission to appeal immediately. In *R(U) 3/85*, a Tribunal of Commissioners decided that an appeal lodged in these circumstances '. . . was a continuing one to take effect as and when the relevant concrete decision was actually made'.[218]

4.147   The same reasoning applies to applications for permission. However, it may be safer for a party to apply again when the decision has been made or promulgated rather than assume that the tribunal will take this approach.

## The need for permission to appeal

4.148   If an appeal does not lie as of right, permission is required before the case can proceed. If permission is required, it is a condition precedent to jurisdiction.[219] The grant or refusal of permission will always be discretionary.

4.149   The higher the case moves up the judicial hierarchy, the more likely it is that permission will be required. However, it is not essential in principle.

4.150   There may be no limit on the power to grant permission. It may be limited to specific issues, typically issues of law rather than fact. And it may be limited to specific circumstances; this is likely in the case of second appeals, which are discussed below.

4.151   If an appeal lies only on a point of law, permission will generally be required. Otherwise, it can be difficult to exclude appeals that relate only to issues of fact. However, it is possible to have an appeal on limited grounds without the need for permission.[220]

216  Kennedy LJ in *Lloyd Jones v T Mobile (United Kingdom) Ltd* [2003] EWCA Civ 1162 at [3].

217  Thorpe LJ in *Re P (Residence: Appeal)* [2008] 1 FLR 198 at [7].

218  *R(U) 3/85* at [8].

219  *Re Taylor (a bankrupt)* [2007] Ch 150 at [56].

220  As in *Banga (t/a Banga Travel) v Secretary of State for the Department of Transport* [2008] EWCA Civ 188; (2008) *Times* 29 January.

### Under TCEA

4.152   Permission is always required for an appeal to or from the Upper Tribunal (ss11(3) and 13(3)). It is discretionary.[221]

## The function of permission[222]

4.153   The function of permission is to deter or filter out cases that are frivolous, unnecessary or unmeritorious,[223] by scrutinising the grounds of dissatisfaction to see if they have sufficient merit.[224] It also operates as a protection for applicants who make ill-informed attempts at bringing an appeal. As Sedley LJ explained in the Court of Appeal in *Such v Secretary of State for the Home Department*:[225]

> . . . the preliminary application, which this is, is a valuable protection for a litigant against the risk of getting in too deep; getting, in other words, into this court without a real prospect of success on a point of law and finding herself liable for a very large sum of costs for the other side's representation.[226]

Finally, the permission filter allows the appellate court to use its time efficiently by devoting it to the most meritorious cases.

4.154   The Bowman Committee considered that the permission stage provided an opportunity for case management if permission were granted.[227] However, tribunals have power to give directions whether or not a case requires permission.[228]

## Who may apply?

### Definition

4.155   The persons who have the right of appeal are always limited. The personal scope of the right may be defined in a number of ways.

4.156   The person who was the subject of a decision by a decision-maker or a party to the proceedings before a tribunal will almost certainly have the benefit of any right of appeal that exists.

4.157   The personal scope of the right may also be defined by the effect that the decision has on a person or by the person's attitude to the decision.

221  *Short v Birmingham City Council* [2005] HLR 6 at [26].

222  See the 1997 Bowman Committee *Report on the Review of the Court of Appeal (Civil Division)*, chapter 3 paras 4–20.

223  Lord Halsbury LC in *Lane v Esdaile* [1891] AC 210 at 212; *Kemper Reinsurance Co v Minister of Finance* [2000] 1 AC 1 at 14.

224  Hale LJ in *R v Secretary of State for the Home Department ex p Saleem* [2001] 1 WLR 443 at 459.

225  [2006] EWCA Civ 711 at [10].

226  See also the comments of Sullivan J in *R (Davies) v Secretary of State for the Communities and Local Government* (2008) *Times* 15 October.

227  *Report on the Review of the Court of Appeal (Civil Division)*, chapter 3 para 7.

228  See chapter 7.

4.158   An example of the effect of a decision is where an appeal lies at the instance of a 'person aggrieved'. This is interpreted broadly. In *Arsenal Football Club Ltd v Ende*,[229] Lord Denning MR said:

> In former times those words were construed in a very restricted sense. But in modern times they have been extended to include any one who has a genuine grievance, relevant to the matter in hand, which is worthy of serious consideration. The only limitation that I would put upon them is that the complaint must not be frivolous or vexatious or irrelevant.[230]

4.159   An example of the person's attitude to a decision is where an appeal lies at the instance of a party who is 'dissatisfied with' a decision.[231] In *Esso Petroleum Co Ltd v Ministry of Labour*,[232] the Court of Appeal decided that this did not allow an appeal in respect of an issue that was not covered by a decision.[233] Nowadays, this omission might be considered as an error of law, provided that it was within the scope of the decision before the First-tier Tribunal.

4.160   Language such as 'dissatisfied with' is indicative that the decision must have been notified to the persons affected by it. In *R v Secretary of State for the Home Department ex p Saleem*,[234] Mummery LJ said of this wording:

> That expression is a clear and powerful indication that Parliament contemplated that the aggrieved party would, in the ordinary course of events, actually receive notification of the determination of his appeal by the adjudicator.[235]

4.161   The personal scope may also be defined by reference to a person's status[236] or by the interest that a person has in the case.

4.162   The right of appeal may be conferred personally or on behalf of someone else.[237] If the latter, the issue arises whether the right is conferred in that person's own right or only as representative of the other person.

## Under TCEA[238]

4.163   The TCEA does not deal with the right of appeal on entry into the system. Usually, this appeal will lie to the First-tier Tribunal, but in some cases the appeal will lie to the Upper Tribunal. This right of appeal is left to the creating legislation.

229  [1977] QB 100.
230  [1977] QB 100 at 116.
231  For example: Tribunals and Inquiries Act 1992 s11(1).
232  [1969] 1 QB 98.
233  [1969] 1 QB 98 per Lord Denning MR at 109–110.
234  [2000] 4 All ER 814.
235  [2000] 4 All ER 814 at 823.
236  For example: a parent of a child may appeal under Education Act 1996 ss325 and 326.
237  For example: Social Security and Child Support (Decisions and Appeals) Regulations 1999 reg 25. The fact that someone has the right to appeal does not mean that that person will necessarily become a party to the proceedings on the appeal, as it may be conferred not in their own capacity, but only as representative of someone who is unable to act.
238  For tribunals that are outside TCEA structure, a right of appeal lies on a point of law under the Tribunals and Inquiries Act 1992 s11.

4.164    The TCEA deals with the right of appeal from the First-tier Tribunal to the Upper Tribunal and from the Upper Tribunal to the Court of Appeal. The basic rule is that only a 'party to a case' may appeal (ss11(2) and 13(2)). However, the Lord Chancellor may by order make provision for a person to be treated as being, or not being, a party for this purpose (ss11(8) and 13(14)).[239] No order has been made under these provisions. In addition, other primary legislation may confer a right of appeal on someone who was not a party to the case.[240]

### Appeals by a successful party

4.165   A successful party may not appeal in order to obtain confirmation or clarification of a favourable decision from a higher court.[241]

4.166    Nor, as an appeal only lies against a decision or order, may a successful party appeal in order to challenge particular findings or aspects of the reasoning.[242] This is subject to the possibility that the legislation may extend the right of appeal to something other than the decision or order, as in *Jones v Attorney-General*.[243]

4.167    However, there are circumstances in which a successful party may appeal.

4.168    First, a public body which has been successful before a First-tier Tribunal may appeal the favourable decision if it would be in the interests of the claimant to do so.[244]

4.169    Second, it may be possible to separate the tribunal's decision into decisions on separate issues to allow a successful party (exceptionally) to challenge one aspect of the tribunal's reasoning. In *Secretary of State for Work and Pensions v Morina*,[245] the Court of Appeal allowed the Secretary of State to appeal against the decision of a Commissioner. The Commissioner had decided that he had jurisdiction over a particular class of decision, but had then dismissed the claimant's appeal. The Commissioner's decision could be analysed into two: (i) a decision that he had jurisdiction; and (ii) that the appeal failed on the merits. This allowed the Secretary of State to challenge decision (i). Maurice Kay LJ emphasised that the case raised 'a fundamental legal issue of jurisdiction' and that the approach would not be taken in the case of an attempt to challenge 'an immaterial finding of no general significance'.[246]

239  Presumably, these provisions displace the Court of Appeal's power to give permission to someone who had not been a party to the case below, as recognised in *R (George Wimpey UK Ltd) v Tewkesbury Borough Council* (2008) *Times* 25 February.

240  For example: in a housing benefit or council tax benefit case the Child Support, Pensions and Social Security Act 2000 Sch 7 para 8(2)(a) confers a right of appeal to Upper Tribunal on the Secretary of State and anyone affected by the decision-maker's decision; and in a child support case the Child Support Act 1991 s24(1) confers a right of appeal on the Secretary of State.

241  *R(I) 68/53* at [5].

242  *Lake v Lake* [1955] P 336.

243  [1974] Ch 148 at 161. See below.

244  *R(U) 6/88* at [5]–[6].

245  [2007] 1 WLR 3033.

246  [2007] 1 WLR 3033 at [10].

4.170   Third, a public body (and perhaps others affected) may be able to appeal in the public interest against a favourable decision if it contains unnecessary rulings that create uncertainty and are damaging to the body's functioning.[247]

4.171   In *Roger Bell v Information Commissioner and the Ministry of Justice*,[248] the Upper Tribunal decided that these were specific examples of a more general principle that a party who has an interest in doing so may pursue an appeal against a favourable decision. In that case, Mr Bell had obtained a favourable decision from the Commissioner, but the Ministry had exercised its right of appeal. The judge decided that Mr Bell had an interest in appealing in order to preserve the decision in his favour.[249] He also said that the First-tier Tribunal was under a duty to ensure that people in Mr Bell's position at least were properly informed of their options and might have to do more.[250]

## Against what decisions?

4.172   Unless the legislation provides otherwise, an appeal must be against a decision. Even when an appeal lies on an issue or question of law, and not on an error of law, it must still be an appeal *against* a decision. This is why, as a general principle, a successful party cannot bring an appeal; the party may have an issue or question on which to appeal, but there is nothing to appeal *against*.

4.173   The legislation will specify the decisions that are subject to appeal. It may simply refer to 'decision'. In that case, it will be a matter of interpretation whether particular types of decision fall within that description. For example: in *Secretary of State for Work and Pensions v Morina*,[251] disposals of purported appeals that were outside the absolute time limit for appealing or were otherwise outside the tribunal's jurisdiction were not decisions for the purposes of an appeal to a Commissioner. In *CHR/3855/2005*, a Tribunal of Commissioners decided that this decision applied also to discretionary decisions to extend the time for appealing.

4.174   And it is a matter of statutory interpretation whether particular matters are covered by the decision that is appealable. For example: in *Jones v Attorney-General*,[252] an appeal against an order of the Charity Commissioners was held to include an appeal against a report that was an essential step in the statutory process of making the order.

4.175   It is a matter of analysis whether the decision made falls within the statutory description. For example: in *R(H) 3/05*, a Tribunal of Commissioners interpreted a particular form of decision so as to bring it within the statutory description, thereby avoiding a violation of article 6. And in *Secretary of State for Work and Pensions v Morina*,[253] the Court of Appeal analysed

---

247  *Office of Communications v Floe Telecom Ltd (in liquidation)* [2009] EWCA Civ 47; (2009) *Times* 23 February.

248  [2012] UKUT 433 (AAC).

249  [2012] UKUT 433 (AAC) at [20].

250  [2012] UKUT 433 (AAC) at [21].

251  [2007] 1 WLR 3033.

252  [1974] Ch 148 at 161.

253  [2007] 1 WLR 3033.

a Commissioner's decision as including a decision on jurisdiction in order to allow the successful party to appeal in respect of that issue.

### Under TCEA – excluded decisions

4.176 Under TCEA, an appeal lies against all decisions, except excluded decisions.

4.177 An appeal lies to the Upper Tribunal against decisions of the First-tier Tribunal (s11(1)) and to the Court of Appeal against decisions of the Upper Tribunal (s13(1)), except excluded decisions. Section 11(5) provides:

> (5) For the purposes of subsection (1), an 'excluded decision' is–
>
> (a) any decision of the First-tier Tribunal on an appeal made in exercise of a right conferred by the Criminal Injuries Compensation Scheme in compliance with section 5(1)(a) of the Criminal Injuries Compensation Act 1995 (appeals against decisions on reviews);
>
> (b) any decision of the First-tier Tribunal on an appeal under section 28(4) or (6) of the Data Protection Act 1998 (appeals against national security certificate);
>
> (c) any decision of the First-tier Tribunal on an appeal under section 60(1) or (4) of the Freedom of Information Act 2000 (appeals against national security certificate);
>
> (d) a decision of the First-tier Tribunal under section 9–
>
> > (i) to review, or not to review, an earlier decision of the tribunal;
> >
> > (ii) to take no action, or not to take any particular action, in the light of a review of an earlier decision of the tribunal;
> >
> > (iii) to set aside an earlier decision of the tribunal;[254] or
> >
> > (iv) to refer, or not to refer, a matter to the Upper Tribunal;
>
> (e) a decision of the First-tier Tribunal that is set aside under section 9 (including a decision set aside after proceedings on an appeal under this section have been begun); or
>
> (f) any decision of the First-tier Tribunal that is of a description specified in an order made by the Lord Chancellor.

4.178 Section 11(5)(f) is subject to section 11(6)–(7). Those decisions are prescribed by the Appeals (Excluded Decisions) Order 2009:

> **Excluded decisions**
>
> 2  For the purposes of section 11(1) of the Tribunals, Courts and Enforcement Act 2007, a decision of the First-tier Tribunal under section 103 of the Immigration and Asylum Act 1999 (appeals) is an excluded decision.
>
> 3  For the purposes of sections 11(1) and 13(1) of the Tribunals, Courts and Enforcement Act 2007, the following decisions of the First-tier Tribunal or the Upper Tribunal are excluded decisions–
>
> (a) any decision under section 20(7), (8B) or (8G)(b) (power to call for documents of taxpayer and others), 20B(1B) or (6) (restrictions on powers under sections 20 and 20A) or 20BB(2)(a) (falsification etc. of documents) of the Taxes Management Act 1970;
>
> (b) any decision under section 35A(2) (variation of undertakings), 79A(2) (variation of undertakings) or 219(1A) (power to require information) of the Inheritance Tax Act 1984;

---

254 A decision refusing to set aside another decision is not an excluded decision. However, that other decision is subject to the right of appeal, so an appeal against the refusal to set aside would be of no value.

(c) any decision under section 152(5) (notification of taxable amount of certain benefits) or 215(7) (advance clearance by Board of distributions and payments) of the Income and Corporation Taxes Act 1988;

(d) any decision under section 138(4) of the Taxation of Chargeable Gains Act 1992 (procedure for clearance in advance);

(e) any decision under section 187(5) or (6) (returns and information) of, or paragraph 3(2) or 6(2) of Schedule 21 (restrictions on powers under section 187) to, the Finance Act 1993;

(f) any decision under paragraph 91(5) of Schedule 15 to the Finance Act 2000 (corporate venturing scheme: advance clearance);

(g) any decision under paragraph 88(5) of Schedule 29 to the Finance Act 2002 (gains and losses from intangible fixed assets: transfer of business or trade);

(h) any decision under paragraph 2, 4, 7, 9, 10, 11 or 24 of Schedule 13 to the Finance Act 2003 (stamp duty land tax: information powers);

(i) any decision under section 306A (doubt as to notifiability), 308A (supplemental information), 313B (reasons for nondisclosure: supporting information) or 314A (order to disclose) of the Finance Act 2004;

(j) any decision under section 697(4) of the Income Tax Act 2007 (opposed notifications: determinations by tribunal);

(k) any decision under regulation 10(3) of the Venture Capital Trust (Winding up and Mergers) (Tax) Regulations 2004 (procedure for Board's approval);

(l) any decision under regulation 5A (doubt as to notifiability), 7A (supplemental information), 12B (reasons for nondisclosure: supporting information) or 12C (order to disclose) of the National Insurance Contributions (Application of Part 7 of the Finance Act 2004) Regulations 2007.

## Under TCEA – decisions

4.179   There is no inherent power to bypass the prohibition on appealing against excluded decisions.[255]

4.180   In *LS v London Borough of Lambeth*,[256] a three-judge panel of the Upper Tribunal decided that an appeal lay against any decision of the First-tier Tribunal that was not an excluded decision.[257]

4.181   Although every decision is appealable, it will not generally be appropriate to give permission to appeal in respect of case management decisions. As the judge explained in *RM v St Andrew's Hospital*:[258]

> ... Appellate courts are supportive of these decisions and discourage appeals against them. They often have to be made with little time for analysis or reflection. Appeals can disrupt the proceedings, produce inefficiency and increase costs. They are capable of being used for tactical purposes. Ultimately, the judge dealing with the case is probably best placed to make a judgment on how best to proceed in the context of the proceedings.

255 *Riniker v University College London* [2001] 1 WLR 13.
256 [2010] UKUT 461 (AAC).
257 [2010] UKUT 461 (AAC) at [79]–[97].
258 [2010] UKUT 119 (AAC).

Challenges are best considered at the end of the proceedings, when it is possible to judge whether the decision adversely affected the outcome.[259]

4.182 Permission to appeal should be given if the decision involves a point of substance that requires an urgent challenge and speedy resolution.[260] *RM v St Andrew's Hospital*[261] was an example. It concerned the disclosure of information that was central to the patient's understanding of his condition and to his case before the First-tier Tribunal.

> On the spectrum of case management decisions, the non-disclosure order is more susceptible to scrutiny than most. The judge held a hearing and took time before issuing her reasons. The issue is severable from the routine management of the case. It is important and its effects can be anticipated: the patient's solicitors argue that they are unable to obtain his instructions on the real case for his continued detention. There is no question of tactical advantage being sought and it has been possible to deal with the appeal quickly.[262]

## To whom is the application made?

4.183 An application is always needed. A tribunal has no power to give permission on its own initiative. However, it may indicate to a party that it will give permission or even invite a party to apply.

4.184 It is unlikely that the power to grant permission will be given exclusively to the person or body from whom the appeal lies. It will either be given exclusively to the tribunal or court to whom the appeal lies or to both.

### Under TCEA

4.185 For an appeal to the Upper Tribunal, section 11(4) provides for permission to be given either by the First-tier Tribunal or the Upper Tribunal. There is no requirement in TCEA that an application must first be made to the First-tier Tribunal. However, this is required by UTR r21(2). As this is a requirement of the rules, it can be waived under rule 7(2)(a).[263] Doing so is in line with the avoidance of circuity of action by doing directly what can be achieved indirectly.[264]

4.186 For an appeal from the Upper Tribunal, section 13(4) provides for permission to be given by that tribunal or by the Court of Appeal. However, section 13(5) prohibits the making of an application to that court unless an application has first been made to the Upper Tribunal.

4.187 The power is vested in the tribunal or the court. It is not vested in a judge or member of the tribunal or court.

259 [2010] UKUT 119 (AAC) at [7].

260 *Re P and P (Care Proceedings: Appointment of Experts)* [2009] 2 FLR 1370 at [17].

261 [2010] UKUT 119 (AAC).

262 [2010] UKUT 119 (AAC) at [9].

263 *ZN, BB and JHS v London Borough of Redbridge* [2013] UKUT 0503 (AAC) at [14]–[17].

264 *Re Collard's Will Trusts* [1961] Ch 293, approved by the House of Lords in *Pilkington v Inland Revenue Commissioners* [1964] AC 612.

## What contribution may a respondent make?

4.188   The position of respondents to an application for permission to appeal was explained by the Court of Appeal in *Jolly v Jay*:[265]

> . . . a respondent should only file submissions at this early stage if they are addressed to the point that the appeal would not meet the relevant threshold test or tests, or if there is some material inaccuracy in the papers placed before the court. By this phrase we mean an inaccuracy which might reasonably be expected to lead the court to grant permission when it would not have done so if it had received correct information on the point.

> If, on the other hand, the respondent wishes to advance submissions on the merits of the appeal . . . the appropriate time for him to do so is at the appeal itself. In general it is not desirable that respondents should make submissions on the merits at the permission stage, because this may well lead to delay in dealing with the permission application and take up the resources of the appeal court unnecessarily.

> Respondents will not be prejudiced at the appeal itself by having refrained from filing or making submissions at the permission stage, since this is essentially a 'without notice' procedure . . .

> When an application for permission is to be determined on paper, any submission from the respondent must be in writing. Even in the event of an oral hearing a respondent should consider whether he can make his submission equally well in writing, particularly as he may not be allowed the costs of his attendance at the hearing.

4.189   This approach may require some modification in the case of tribunals, as the respondent's views may be relevant to the exercise of the tribunal's powers to set aside or review. They may also be useful if the application for permission raises a new issue, as they may be able to show that it has no merit.[266]

## How is the tribunal constituted?

4.190   This is governed by the Senior President's practice statements on constitution.

## Proportionate use of resources

4.191   The Upper Tribunal is required to deal with cases proportionately and the parties are required to co-operate with the tribunal in doing so.[267] This means that applicants should limit their applications for permission so that they can be dealt with in a reasonable time.

4.192   In *CMA CGM SA v Beteiligungs-KG MS 'Northern Pioneer' Schiffahrtsgesellschaft mbH & Co*, the Court of Appeal gave guidance on the amount of time that should be devoted to an application:[268]

---

265  [2002] EWCA Civ 277 at [44]–[47].
266  *R (H) v South London and Maudsley NHS Foundation Trust and Secretary of State for Justice* [2010] EWCA Civ 1273 at [37].
267  Under UTR r.2 and its equivalents.
268  [2003] 1 WLR 1015 at [23].

The statutory requirement that applications for permission to appeal should be paper applications unless the court otherwise directs must surely have been intended to simplify the procedure and to save the court's time. That requirement reflects the fact that the criteria for the grant of permission to appeal are clear-cut and easy to apply. They do not require the drawing of fine lines, nor will they usually give much scope for the court to require assistance in the form of submissions or advocacy . . . Any written submissions placed before the court in support of an application for permission to appeal from findings in an arbitral award should normally be capable of being read and digested by the judge within the half-hour that, under the old regime, used to be allotted for such applications.

4.193  This guidance assumes that the judge is familiar with the case; an Upper Tribunal Judge who deals with an application for permission to appeal against a decision of the First-tier Tribunal will not have seen the case before. It also assumes that the applicant is represented; that will not be so for many applicants to the Upper Tribunal.

## Initial, first and second appeals

4.194  Initial appeals are appeals from a decision-maker to a tribunal. First appeals are appeals from the first judicial decision to be made in a case. Second appeals are appeals from a second decision in a case by a higher tribunal. For example: an appeal from a decision-maker to the First-tier Tribunal is, in these terms, an initial appeal; the appeal from the First-tier Tribunal to the Upper Tribunal is a first appeal; and the appeal from the Upper Tribunal to the Court of Appeal is a second appeal.

4.195  This distinction is relevant to the criteria that govern the granting of permission. Second appeals are subject to more restrictive criteria than first appeals. An initial appeal may lie as of right without the need for permission.

## Criteria for granting permission to appeal

4.196  These criteria apply to all appeals. In principle, an application for permission may be determined either by reference to the likely outcome or to the importance of the issue raised. In practice, this means that permission may be granted in three circumstances.

4.197  First, permission may be granted if it is clear that the tribunal below went wrong. However, this may not be clear.

4.198  So second, permission may be granted if it is arguable that the tribunal below may have gone wrong in law. The threshold is whether there is a realistic, as opposed to a fanciful or unrealistic, prospect that the appeal will succeed.[269] This means success on the merits of the party's case, not just some procedural advantage.[270]

269  Lord Woolf MR in *Smith v Cosworth Casting Processes Ltd* [1997] 1 WLR 1538 at 1538 and *Swain v Hillman* [2001] 1 All ER 91 at 92. 'No realistic prospect of success' means the same, for practical purposes, as 'clearly unfounded': *R (YH) v Secretary of State for the Home Department* [2010] 4 All ER 448 at [10].

270  *Secretary of State for the Home Department v Makke* [2005] EWCA Civ 176 at [23]–[24] (reported as *R (Makke) v Secretary of State for the Home Department* (2005) *Times* 5 April, but not on this issue).

4.199   Third, even if the tribunal did not go wrong, it may be appropriate to give permission. This is a permissible use of the discretion associated with permission. It may be appropriate if the Upper Tribunal is bound by authority and an appeal is needed in order for the issue to be considered by a higher court.[271] It may also be appropriate in order to provide a precedent or guidance on an issue of law.[272] This is particularly useful for a tribunal that has the responsibility of ensuring the orderly development of a specific body of law. It may be that this basis for granting permission is only permissible if it is allowed by the wording of the legislation. It is permissible if the legislation allows an appeal on a question, point or issue of law.[273] But it may not be permissible if the legislation allows an appeal on an error of law.[274] The language of error suggests that permission can only be granted if there is at least the possibility of an error.

4.200   It is sometimes said that permission cannot be given if there is no error of law.[275] However, these comments must be read as subject to this third possibility.

## Limited permission

4.201   The First-tier Tribunal may give permission to appeal to the Upper Tribunal,[276] and the Upper Tribunal may give permission to appeal to the Court of Appeal,[277] on limited grounds. There is no express provision allowing the Upper Tribunal to give permission to appeal to itself on such grounds. However, it would be surprising if it did not have the power that is given to the First-tier Tribunal and the possibility of limited permission is recognised by UTR r22(4)(b). It is surely also permissible under the discretionary exercise of giving permission. In *RC v CMEC and WC*,[278] a two-judge panel confirmed a Commissioner's grant of limited leave, for which there was no express power. The subsequent litigation assumed the validity of that decision.[279]

4.202   It is important for the parties and the tribunal to know whether permission has been limited. The issue may arise in two ways.

271   *Beedell v West Ferry Printers Ltd* [2001] ICR 962.
272   Lord Woolf MR in *Smith v Cosworth Casting Processes Ltd* [1997] 1 WLR 1538 at 1538.
273   As does TCEA s11(1). This is wider than s12(1), which allows a decision of the First-tier Tribunal to be set aside only if it involved the making of an error on a point of law.
274   As Social Security Act 1998 s14(1) did. The potential significance of the difference in language is greater if both are used in the same statute. Contrast the wording of s14(1), which allowed an appeal to a Commissioner on the ground that the decision of the tribunal was erroneous in point of law, with s15(1), which allowed an appeal to the Court of Appeal on a question of law.
275   *R v The Social Security Commissioner and the Social Security Appeal Tribunal ex p Pattni* [1993] Fam Law 213.
276   See: GRC Rules r43(5); HESC Rules r47(5); IAC Rules r34(5); PC Rules r53(5); SEC Rules r39(5); Tax Rules r40(5); WPAFC Rules r37(5).
277   UTR r45(5); Lands Rules r56(5).
278   [2009] UKUT 62 (AAC).
279   It culminated in the Supreme Court in *R (Cart) v Upper Tribunal and R (MR (Pakistan)) v Upper Tribunal and Secretary of State for the Home Department* [2011] UKSC 28.

4.203  First, a party may wish to raise an issue that was not identified at the permission stage. This is what happened in *R(I) 12/62*. A medical appeal tribunal granted permission to the claimant to appeal on a specified ground. The Secretary of State supported the appeal on this ground and argued that it had also gone wrong in respect of the burden of proof. The Commissioner gave permission to raise this other issue in case it was necessary but without deciding between two competing views:

> The view is attractive that, once the case is before the Commissioner on one ground, it is for him to decide whether the decision of the tribunal is erroneous in point of law on any ground. On the other hand the only right of appeal is that created by the statute, which itself imposes the necessity of obtaining leave to appeal . . . The regulations make no provision for anything in the nature of a cross-notice, and it is well arguable that in the absence of express provision the obtaining of leave in this case by the Minister, followed by appealing, is necessary.[280]

In practice, the Commissioners allowed any party to raise any issue once permission had been given.

4.204  Second, an application may contain a number of grounds. The tribunal may give permission and refer to some of those grounds or give permission on a ground of its own. This is open to three interpretations. The tribunal may have given permission only on the ground mentioned. If so, it should have given reasons for refusing permission on the other grounds.[281] Or it may have given permission on the ground mentioned and on the other grounds in the application for which it has not expressly refused permission. Or it may have given permission generally so that any issue can be raised on the appeal, whether previously identified or not. Ideally, the tribunal should make expressly clear what form of permission has been given.

4.205  If the First-tier Tribunal gave permission on limited grounds, the appellant may apply to the Upper Tribunal to give permission on the other grounds. There is nothing to prevent this being done at any stage of the proceedings.

4.206  The rules on limited permission provide that the tribunal must give reasons for 'any' grounds on which it refuses permission.[282] That envisages that there may not be any grounds on which permission was refused. In other words, the tribunal may give permission on all the grounds in the application but limit the permission to those grounds.

4.207  Under the CPR, a party who has been given conditional permission may prefer not to accept the permission but rather to challenge the conditions. The party has three choices: (i) not pursue the appeal; (ii) rely on the permission and accept the conditions; or (iii) not rely on the permission, but apply to the Court of Appeal for permission afresh.[283] The position is different before the Upper Tribunal, because UTR r21(2) prevents an application for permission in those circumstances.

---

280  [2009] UKUT 62 (AAC) at [10].

281  See UTR r22(1).

282  UTR r45(5); GRC Rules r43(5); HESC Rules r47(5); IAC Rules r34(5); Lands Rules r56(5); PC Rules r53(5); SEC Rules r39(5); Tax Rules r40(5); WPAFC Rules r37(5).

283  *R (Medical Justice) v Secretary of State for the Home Department* [2011] 4 All ER 425.

4.208   In practice, the power to give permission on limited grounds may not
be of practical significance. In *DL-H v Devon Partnership NHS Trust*,[284] the
Upper Tribunal decided that an appeal was not limited to issues covered
by the grant of permission:

> I reject the argument that an appeal is necessarily limited to the grounds
> in the application on which permission was given and that further permis-
> sion is required to raise other grounds. The right of appeal is conferred by
> section 11 of the Tribunals, Courts and Enforcement Act 2007. It is discre-
> tionary and subject to the grant of permission. Permission is governed by
> the rules of procedure. The rules contain three provisions for restricting
> the scope of an appeal: (i) limited permission; (ii) the control of the issues
> on which the tribunal requires submissions; and (iii) the power to strike
> out a party's case. The rules confer power on the First-tier Tribunal to give
> permission only on limited grounds: rule 47(5) of the Tribunal Procedure
> (First-tier Tribunal) (Health, Education and Social Care Chamber) Rules
> 2008 (SI No 2699). The Upper Tribunal has equivalent power in respect
> of an appeal to the Court of Appeal on limited grounds: rule 45(5) of the
> Tribunal Procedure (Upper Tribunal) Rules 2008 (SI No 2698). There is no
> express power for the Upper Tribunal to give limited permission to appeal
> to itself. However, the rules envisage this possibility: rule 22(4)(b). This is,
> presumably, permissible without express authority and in the exercise of
> the tribunal's discretion. The rules must be interpreted and applied to give
> effect to the overriding objective under rule 2. As a matter of interpretation,
> it would not be fair and just to restrict the scope of an appeal to the grounds
> in the application on which permission was given. The rules apply to the
> whole of the work of the Upper Tribunal, not just mental health. The Sec-
> retary of State for Work and Pensions is the respondent to the vast majority
> of appeals before the Administrative Appeals Chamber and takes a neutral
> and objective approach to appeals, often identifying issues favourable to a
> claimant. It would not be desirable to hinder that approach, as many appel-
> lants are either not represented at all or not professionally represented.
> Mental health cases are different in that the patient is usually profession-
> ally represented. But it is not possible, as a matter of interpretation, to draw
> a distinction on that ground. That is a matter, if it is relevant at all, for the
> application of the rules. My interpretation does not allow a party complete
> freedom to raise additional grounds at will. The Upper Tribunal has ample
> power to control the issues that will be considered on an appeal. As well as
> the possibility of giving limited permission, rule 15(1)(a) authorises the tri-
> bunal to give directions as to the issues on which it requires submissions.
> In an extreme case, the tribunal may even strike out all or part of a party's
> case under rule 8(3). Those provisions should be sufficient to ensure that
> additional grounds are only considered if that would be fair and just.

## Conditional permission

4.209   There is no express power authorising either the First-tier Tribunal or
the Upper Tribunal to give permission to appeal subject to conditions.
However, this possibility is recognised by UTR r22(4)(b). In principle,
this should be possible as part of the discretionary exercise of giving

---

284 [2010] UKUT 102 (AAC) at [3].

permission, at least by the tribunal to whom the appeal lies. The most likely condition will relate to costs.[285]

4.210     In principle, conditions should only be attached by the court or tribunal to whom the appeal lies. If the tribunal below were to attach conditions, it would have no power to enforce them.

4.211     See above under Limited permission for a discussion of the options available to a party on whom conditions are imposed in a grant of permission.

### On grounds identified by the applicant

4.212     It is always good practice for an applicant to identify the grounds on which permission could be given. It is not sufficient for the person applying for permission to identify the part of the decision that is challenged. The person should identify the issues raised and the reasons supporting the challenge to the decision. If the appeal would be a second appeal, the application should show how the additional criteria are satisfied.[286] Legislation may specify the particulars that the applicant must include in the grounds for appeal.[287] However, this may be applied loosely for the benefit of parties who are unfamiliar with the procedures.[288]

4.213     It is irrational for a rule of procedure to prevent a party from amending grounds of appeal to include an arguable and potentially meritorious point.[289]

### On grounds not identified by the applicant

4.214     This issue is related to the scope of the tribunal's inquisitorial approach.[290]

4.215     In asylum cases, the courts have limited the tribunal's inquisitorial duty on an application for permission to obvious points. In *R v Secretary of State for the Home Department ex p Robinson*,[291] the Court of Appeal was concerned with an application for judicial review of a refusal by the Immigration Appeal Tribunal of permission to appeal against the decision of a special adjudicator. The Court said:

> Because the rules place an onus on the asylum-seeker to state his grounds of appeal, we consider that it would be wrong to say that mere arguability should be the criterion to be applied for the grant of leave in such circumstances. A higher hurdle is required. The appellate authorities should of course focus primarily on the arguments adduced before them, whether these are to be found in the oral argument before the special adjudicator or, so far as the tribunal is concerned, in the written grounds of appeal on

---

285  For example: the Court of Appeal may impose the condition that a Secretary of State pay the costs of an appeal that raises issues of general importance, such as the interpretation of legislation.

286  *Re N (A Child)* [2010] 1 FLR 454 at [69]–[72].

287  As it was in *Secretary of State for the Home Department v Makke* [2005] EWCA Civ 176, reported as *R (Makke) v Secretary of State for the Home Department* (2005) *Times* 5 April.

288  *R(I)15/53* at [4].

289  *AM (Serbia) v Secretary of State for the Home Department* (2007) *Times* 19 February.

290  See chapter 1.

291  [1998] QB 929.

which leave to appeal is sought. They are not required to engage in a search for new points. If there is readily discernible an obvious point of Convention law which favours the applicant although he has not taken it, then the special adjudicator should apply it in his favour, but he should be under no obligation to prolong the hearing by asking the parties for submissions on points which they have not taken but which could be properly categorised as merely 'arguable' as opposed to 'obvious'. Similarly, if when the tribunal reads the special adjudicator's decision there is an obvious point of Convention law favourable to the asylum-seeker which does not appear in the decision, it should grant leave to appeal. If it does not do so, there will be a danger that this country will be in breach of its obligations under the Convention. When we refer to an obvious point we mean a point which has a strong prospect of success if it is argued. Nothing less will do. It follows that leave to apply for judicial review of a refusal by the tribunal to grant leave to appeal should be granted if the judge is of the opinion that it is properly arguable that a point not raised in the grounds of appeal to the tribunal had a strong prospect of success if leave to appeal were to be granted.[292]

4.216   *P v Secretary of State for the Home Department*[293] is to similar effect. The case concerned an asylum seeker who had been subject to domestic violence. One issue was whether she would have been sufficiently protected by internal relocation in her home country. The Court of Appeal rejected an argument that the adjudicator should have raised and determined this issue on her own initiative. Lord Woolf CJ said:

> In our view this is to place an unnecessary and inappropriate burden upon the Adjudicator and the Appellant who appears before her. In the absence of evidence that suggests that there is an alternative location to which the Appellant could go where she would not be at risk from her husband, adjudicators cannot be expected to investigate such issues for themselves of their own initiative when they have not been raised by the Secretary of State.[294]

4.217   The approach in the asylum cases was applied to all tribunals by Scott Baker J in *R (Begum) v Social Security Commissioners*[295] on the ground that it would be confusing and without logic to apply different tests. As to what was obvious:

> The position is that mere arguability is not the test, a higher hurdle must be surmounted. The point must be obvious; that is one which would have a strong prospect of success were leave to be granted. An obvious point, it seems to me, is one that stands out and not one that can only be gleaned by a paper chase through various documents which may underlie the decision maker's decision. Accordingly, it will, in my judgment, ordinarily be difficult to bring a reasons challenge within such a category, unless the reasons are obviously deficient on their face.
>
> [The Commissioner] . . . is not obliged to look and see whether every finding unchallenged in the grounds of appeal is supported by the evidence. He is not obliged to embark on a paper chase or do a detailed analysis of

292 [1998] QB 929 at 945–946. The position may be different on an appeal: see *Hooper v Secretary of State for Work and Pensions* [2007] EWCA Civ 495 at [44]–[45], [59] and [61], reported as *R(IB) 4/07*, discussed above at para 4.93.

293 [2004] EWCA Civ 1640; (2004) *Times* 14 December.

294 [2004] EWCA Civ 1640 at [33].

295 [2002] EWHC 401 (Admin) at [19].

conflicting evidence where, for example, one witness's evidence was preferred to that of another.[296]

4.218 However, this restrictive approach does not apply if the issue involves a point of general importance, such as one that concerns the State's compliance with its international obligations.[297]

### On error of fact

4.219 Appeals that cover issues of fact usually lie as of right and do not require permission. The principles that apply when permission is required were set out by the Upper Tribunal in *JP v Standards Committee of Surrey County Council*.[298] Permission must not be given so freely as to subvert the filter function that permission serves. If the appeal is from a tribunal, the principles in *Subesh v Secretary of State for the Home Department*[299] apply. If the appeal is from a decision-maker, a more lenient approach is appropriate, as the evidence has not yet been considered judicially. There is a discretion to give permission to appeal even if there is little or no prospect of success on factual grounds, provided that the circumstances justify a judicial consideration of the decision.

## Criteria for granting permission for second appeals

4.220 In principle, once a judicial decision has been the subject of an appeal, access to a further appeal should be permissible only on restricted grounds. This is especially so if the first appeal was to a specialist tribunal. The criteria consider above must be satisfied, but subject to further conditions.

### Under TCEA

4.221 The TCEA s13(6) authorises restrictive conditions to be imposed for appeals from the Upper Tribunal. This power is exercised by article 2 of the Appeals from the Upper Tribunal to the Court of Appeal Order 2008, under which the Upper Tribunal may not grant permission to appeal to the Court of Appeal unless it:

> . . . considers that–
> (a) the proposed appeal would raise some important point of principle or practice; or
> (b) there is some other compelling reason for the relevant appellate court to hear the appeal.

This is equivalent to section 55(1) of the Access to Justice Act 1999, which applies to the court system. It applies in England, Wales and Northern Ireland. Section 13(6A) makes equivalent provision for Scotland.

4.222 The effect of this provision is that permission will only be given in exceptional cases and not merely because there is a real prospect of

296 [2002] EWHC 401 (Admin) at [20] and [31].
297 *Bulale v Secretary of State for the Home Department* (2008) *Times* 25 July.
298 [2011] UKUT 316 (AAC) at [11]–[22].
299 [2004] EWCA Civ 56, discussed under the Scope of an appeal above.

success.[300] It applies at the permission stage only and does not limit the scope of the appeal if permission is given.[301]

4.223    The 'important point of principle or practice' was discussed in *Uphill v BRB (Residuary) Ltd.*[302] It must be one that has not been decided; the correct application of an established principle is not within article 2.[303] And, however theoretically important, it must be one that will affect the outcome of the particular case.[304] If the case does raise an important point of principle or practice, it may be appropriate to give permission limited to that issue alone.[305] Care should be taken in giving permission on an issue that was not raised below; it may be appropriate to obtain the views of the other parties before doing so.[306] The point of principle or practice must not merely be important, but must be one that calls for the attention of the Court of Appeal and cannot be left to the specialist tribunal.[307]

4.224    The 'other compelling reason' was also discussed in *Uphill v BRB (Residuary) Ltd.*[308] It must involve something other than an important point of principle or practice.[309] The Court of Appeal went on to analyse when it would be satisfied:

(1) A good starting point will almost always be a consideration of the prospects of success. It is unlikely that the court will find that there is a compelling reason to give permission for a second appeal unless it forms the view that the prospects of success are very high. That will usually be a necessary requirement, although as we shall explain, it may not be sufficient to justify the grant of permission to appeal. This necessary condition will be satisfied where it is clear that the judge on the first appeal made a decision which is perverse or otherwise plainly wrong. It may be clear that the decision is wrong because it is inconsistent with authority of a higher court which demonstrates that the decision was plainly wrong. Subject to what we say at (3) below, anything less than very good prospects of success on an appeal will rarely suffice. In view of the exceptional nature of the jurisdiction conferred by CPR 52.13(2), it is important not to assimilate the criteria for giving permission for a first appeal with those which apply in relation to second appeals.[310]

(2) Although the necessary condition which we have mentioned at (1) is satisfied, the fact that the prospects of success are very high will not necessarily be sufficient to provide a compelling reason for giving permission

300  *Tanfern Ltd v Cameron-Macdonald* [2000] 1 WLR 1311 at [41]–[42].

301  *R (HS) v Upper Tribunal (Immigration and Asylum Chamber) and Secretary of State for the Home Department* [2012] EWHC 3126 (Admin) at [31]. This is now the position under CPR r 54.7A(7).

302  [2005] 1 WLR 2070.

303  [2005] 1 WLR 2070 at [18].

304  *R (H) v South London and Maudsley NHS Foundation Trust and Secretary of State for Justice* [2010] EWCA Civ 1273 at [41].

305  *R (H) v South London and Maudsley NHS Foundation Trust and Secretary of State for Justice* [2010] EWCA Civ 1273 at [36].

306  *R (H) v South London and Maudsley NHS Foundation Trust and Secretary of State for Justice* [2010] EWCA Civ 1273 at [37].

307  *PR (Sri Lanka) v Secretary of State for the Home Department* [2011] EWCA Civ 988 at [37].

308  [2005] 1 WLR 2070.

309  [2005] 1 WLR 2070 at [19].

310  [2005] 1 WLR 2070 at [24].

to appeal. An examination of all the circumstances of the case may lead the court to conclude that, despite the existence of very good prospects of success, there is no compelling reason for giving permission to appeal. For example, if it is the appellant's fault that the first appeal was dismissed, because he failed to refer to the authority of a higher court which demonstrates that the decision on the first appeal was wrong, the court may conclude that justice does not *require* this court to give the appellant the opportunity to have a second appeal. There is a reason for giving permission to appeal, but it is not compelling, because the appellant contributed to the court's mistake. On the other hand, if the authority of a higher court which shows that the decision on the first appeal was wrong post-dated that decision, then there might well be a compelling reason for giving permission for a second appeal.

(3) There may be circumstances where there is a compelling reason to grant permission to appeal even where the prospects of success are not very high. The court may be satisfied that there are good grounds for believing that the hearing was tainted by some procedural irregularity so as to render the first appeal unfair. Suppose, for example, that the judge did not allow the appellant to present his or her case. In such a situation, the court might conclude that there was a compelling reason to give permission for a second appeal, even though the appellant had no more than a real, as opposed to fanciful, prospect of success. It would be plainly unjust to deny an appellant a second appeal in such a case, since to do so might, in effect, deny him a right of appeal altogether.

4.225 The meaning of 'other compelling reason' was also considered by the Court of Appeal in *Re B (Residence: Second Appeal)*.[311] The court held that the fact that the decision was arguably plainly wrong was not of itself a compelling reason for giving permission. Nor was the fact that the decisions given at different levels below were in conflict. The court did, though, consider that it was possible that the impact of a decision on the welfare of a child could provide a compelling reason. And in *Hall v Hall*[312] Thorpe LJ said that 'the correction of manifest injustice must be a compelling reason'.[313]

4.226 In *R (Cart) v Upper Tribunal*,[314] Lord Dyson cautiously suggested two possible examples of compelling reasons that combine an error that is serious in its nature or impact with a high degree of certainty that the error can be established: '(i) a case where it is strongly arguable that the individual has suffered ... "a wholly exceptional collapse of fair procedure" or (ii) a case where it is strongly arguable that there has been an error of law which has caused truly drastic consequences.'[315] In *Eba v Advocate General for Scotland*,[316] Lord Hope (giving the judgment of the Court) gave two examples that set slightly stricter criteria than the criteria for a first appeal: 'where it was clear that the decision was perverse or plainly wrong or where, due to some procedural irregularity, the petitioner had not had a fair hearing at all.'[317]

---

311 [2009] 2 FLR 632 at [10]–[12] and [14].
312 [2008] 2 FLR 575.
313 [2008] 2 FLR 575 at [7].
314 [2012] 1 AC 663.
315 [2012] 1 AC 663 at [131].
316 [2012] 1 AC 710.
317 [2012] 1 AC 710 at [48].

4.227      The Court of Appeal reacted to these decisions in *PR (Sri Lanka) v Secretary of State for the Home Department.*[318] It decided that the scope of 'compelling reason' was a matter of judicial policy in the deployment of scare judicial resources at the higher levels. It was for the Court of Appeal to set the limits of the concept as the final arbiter of whether cases should progress as far as that Court. The views of the Supreme Court were persuasive, but no more. The Court adopted the approach in *Uphill*. It decided that the principles set out above applied regardless of the subject matter, with no special approach for cases involving international obligations, such as asylum and human rights. Compelling meant legally compelling, not emotionally or politically. The provenance of the case might be relevant to the application of these principles. Applying this approach to the Upper Tribunal, the Court noted that it was a specialist body, and that judges of the High Court and the Court of Appeal contributed to its standards by sitting as members as well as through judicial oversight in the senior courts. Cases involving international obligations did not form a special category as there was no international right to a second appeal. By the time the case was considered by the Court of Appeal, it would already have been decided twice, by the First-tier Tribunal and the Upper Tribunal. The issue was whether there was something that made a third consideration compelling.

4.228      The Administrative Court in turned reacted to the Court of Appeal's decision. In the cases of *R (Khan, Jassi, Olawoyin and R) v Secretary of State for the Home Department and the Upper Tribunal (Immigration and Asylum Chamber,*[319] Ouseley J laid down the principles that that Court would follow in applying *Cart* and *PR*. He began by emphasising that *PR* was binding in the Administrative Court and applied to all applications for permission to apply for judicial review of non-appealable decisions of the Upper Tribunal, not just refusals of permission to appeal. In future, there would be no excuse for applications to be framed in terms of the previous law. They should be made promptly, be short and focused, and be supported by only the minimum documentation necessary. The judge concluded by reminding parties of the Court's cost powers.

4.229      In *JD (Congo) v Secretary of State for the Home Department and the Public Law Project,*[320] the Court of Appeal considered what factors were relevant to the whether there was a compelling reason. It decided that although (i) the fact that the appellant had succeeded before the First-tier Tribunal but lost before the Upper Tribunal, (ii) the fact that the Upper Tribunal had re-made the First-tier Tribunal's adverse decision to the same effect, and (iii) the impact of the decision on the appellant were not of themselves compelling reasons, they were factors that could be taken into account when deciding whether a sufficiently serious legal basis for challenging the Upper Tribunal's decision existed.[321]

---

318  [2011] EWCA Civ 988.
319  [2011] EWHC 2763 (Admin). The judge authorised his judgment to be cited as an authority.
320  [2012] 1 WLR 3273.
321  [2012] 1 WLR 3273 at [23], [26] and [27].

4.230    If the Upper Tribunal has correctly applied an authority that is also binding on the Court of Appeal, it may be a compelling reason that a party should have the chance to apply to the Supreme Court for permission to challenge that decision.[322] However, it would have to be appropriate in the circumstances of the particular case to give permission on that ground.[323]

### Outside TCEA

4.231    The Appeals from the Upper Tribunal to the Court of Appeal Order 2008 and Rules of the Court of Session r41.57 are made under the authority of TCEA s13(6) and (6A). Those subsections only applies, by virtue of subs (7), to applications for permission to appeal against decisions made by the Upper Tribunal on appeal under s11. So the provisions do not apply to: appeals direct from a decision-maker, such as under the Safeguarding Vulnerable Groups Act 2006; judicial review; and references, such as under the Forfeiture Act 1982. An appeal to the Court of Appeal against decisions under these jurisdictions would not be a second appeal, so the restrictive approach does not apply.

4.232    In some cases, an appeal from the decision of the Upper Tribunal is a second appeal, but it is outside the scope of s13(6) or (6A) because the tribunal's jurisdiction is not based in s11. So the Order does not apply to: appeals against decisions of two Welsh tribunals (the Mental Health Review Tribunal for Wales and the Special Educational Needs Tribunal for Wales), and the Pensions Appeal Tribunals in Scotland and Northern Ireland. An appeal to the Court of Appeal against decisions under these jurisdictions would be a second appeal. For such cases, *Cooke v Secretary of State for Social Security*[324] applies. Hale LJ there said that permission should only be given to appeal against a Commissioner's decision on limited grounds equivalent to those that apply under the Order. A decision by the Upper Tribunal on a referral under s9(5)(b) is in form not a decision on an appeal, so the Order does not apply, but in substance it is equivalent to an appeal. Presumably, *Cooke* would apply.

4.233    It may be that the *Cooke* approach is not as wide as the Order. In *LA v Secretary of State for Work and Pensions and TVI*,[325] the Inner House of the Court of Session held that it does not include issues of general law, such as habitual residence.[326]

## Refusing permission to appeal

4.234    Even if the case is one in which permission to appeal could be given, it may be inappropriate to do so. This is possible on two grounds: materiality and discretion.

---

322  *Re D (Leave to Remove: Appeal)* [2010] 2 FLR 1605.
323  *Re D (Leave to Remove: Appeal)* [2010] 2 FLR 1605 at [35].
324  [2002] 3 All ER 279.
325  Unreported 25 March 2004.
326  Unreported 25 March 2004 at [5].

4.235    As to materiality, the Court of Appeal in *Secretary of State for the Home Department v Makke*[327] held that the test of a real prospect of success refers to ultimate success on the merits. Accordingly, permission may be refused if the tribunal's mistake did not affect the outcome. Likewise, if the ultimate outcome is unlikely to be different even on a rehearing. In *R v Secretary of State for Social Services ex p Connolly*,[328] the Court of Appeal was concerned with a refusal of permission by a Commissioner. The applicant had been refused judicial review of that refusal and had appealed against that decision to the Court of Appeal. Slade LJ said:

> If an applicant presents . . . an arguable, even substantially arguable point of law, it may still, in some circumstances, be open to the commissioner to refuse leave in the proper exercise of his discretion, for example, if he is satisfied that the point of law will have no effect on the final outcome of the case.[329]

4.236    This is consistent with the way that the law defines an error of law taking account of the impact of the error on the outcome of the proceedings. In *R (Iran) v Secretary of State for the Home Department*,[330] Brooke LJ set out the most common ways in which a tribunal may go wrong in law[331] and added:

> Each of these grounds for detecting an error of law contain the word 'material' (or 'immaterial'). Errors of law of which it can be said that they would have made no difference to the outcome do not matter . . .[332]

4.237    In *Holmes-Moorhouse v Richmond upon Thames London Borough Council*,[333] Lord Neuberger assembled some of the ways in which a decision could survive an error in its reasoning. He was referring to a decision by a decision-maker rather than by a tribunal, but the examples are equally applicable:

> . . . a decision can often survive despite the existence of an error in the reasoning advanced to support it. For example, sometimes the error is irrelevant to the outcome; sometimes it is too trivial (objectively, or in the eyes of the decision-maker) to affect the outcome; sometimes it is obvious from the rest of the reasoning, read as a whole, that the decision would have been the same notwithstanding the error;[334] sometimes, there is more than one reason for the conclusion, and the error only undermines one of the reasons; sometimes, the decision is the only one which could rationally have been reached. In all such cases, the error should not (save, perhaps, in wholly exceptional circumstances) justify the decision being quashed.[335]

4.238    As to discretion, the permission filter confers a discretion rather than imposes a duty. Accordingly, permission may be refused despite there

---

327    [2005] EWCA Civ 176 at [23]–[24], reported as *R (Makke) v Secretary of State for the Home Department* (2005) *Times* 5 April, but not on this issue.
328    [1986] 1 WLR 421.
329    [1986] 1 WLR 421 at 432.
330    [2005] EWCA Civ 982.
331    [2005] EWCA Civ 982 at [9]. This paragraph is quoted below at para 4.283.
332    [2005] EWCA Civ 982 at [10].
333    [2009] 1 WLR 413.
334    As in *Re C (Care Proceedings: Sexual Abuse)* [2009] 2 FLR 46 at [10].
335    [2009] 1 WLR 413 at [51].

being an arguable point in the case. This allows permission to be refused if the application identifies a point of law, but it has no merit or substance[336] or further litigation would be disproportionate.[337]

4.239 It will also be appropriate to refuse permission, despite an error, if the proceedings as a whole have become abstract. In *R (Begum) v Social Security Commissioners*,[338] Scott Baker J, after dealing with the circumstances in which the Commissioner had to take a point that had not been raised by the applicant, said:

> The fact that the untaken point was an obvious one and had a strong prospect of success is not in itself enough if, assuming the point had been taken, there were other grounds on which the Commissioner would have been entitled to refuse leave, for example, that the proceedings had become academic.[339]

## If the outcome was not affected

4.240 A tribunal has four possible responses if an application raises an issue that has not affected the outcome of the appeal.

4.241 The first is to refuse permission on the ground that, although the tribunal went wrong, the mistake was not material to the decision.

4.242 The second is to refuse permission on the ground that the tribunal made a mistake, but it is appropriate to exercise the discretion to refuse permission.

4.243 The distinction between these first two possibilities may be very fine. In most cases, one or other will be the appropriate response.

4.244 The third is to give permission to appeal in respect of the mistake made by tribunal regardless of the fact that it was not material, but then give a decision confirming the decision under appeal (TCEA s12(2)(a)). This allows the Upper Tribunal to deal with an issue that will benefit later tribunals.

4.245 The fourth is to give permission on the ground that, although the mistake did not affect the outcome, the circumstances merit a rehearing. This approach will only be appropriate in rare cases. For example: if racist remarks were made by the tribunal in a case in which the evidence was anyway against the party. A rehearing may be desirable in such a case to give what the party had a right to have, an unbiased consideration of the merits of the case for whatever they were worth.

## Reasons for decision

4.246 In order to comply with article 6 reasons must be given. They may be short, but they must be sufficiently clear not to leave the precise reason to conjecture.[340] It may not be appropriate or permissible for a judge who makes forthright comments on the merits when refusing permission to take part in subsequent proceedings.[341]

---

336 *R(I) 3/61.*
337 *Cook v Plummer* [2008] 2 FLR 989 at [13].
338 [2002] EWHC 401 (Admin) at [19].
339 [2002] EWHC 401 (Admin) at [22].
340 Peter Gibson LJ in *Hyams v Plender* [2001] 1 WLR 32 at [17].
341 *Bridle v Bridle* [2011] 1 FLR 1213 at [4].

4.247　　It is not permissible to challenge a tribunal's decision by reference to the reasons it gives for refusing permission to appeal.[342]

## Directions when permission is given

4.248　When permission is given, the Upper Tribunal may give directions to help focus the submissions of the parties on the key issues that arise. These do not necessarily imply that no other grounds may be considered.[343]

## Reconsideration

4.249　There is an express power to apply for reconsideration under UTR r22(3)–(5). It applies to: (a) decisions under GRC, HESC and Tax Rules; (b) decisions of the Mental Health Review Tribunal for Wales; (c) decisions of the Special Educational Needs Tribunal for Wales; and (d) decisions under section 4 of the Safeguarding Vulnerable Groups Act 2006. This only applies if:

- the Upper Tribunal (i) refuses permission to appeal, (ii) gives limited permission, or (iii) gives conditional permission; and
- did so without a hearing.

An application must be made within 14 days.

4.250　　Otherwise, there may be a general power to reconsider a decision on permission to appeal.[344] This is more likely to be appropriate in order to grant permission than to revoke a grant already made.

## Challenging permission decisions

### Appeal

4.251　The governing legislation may provide that an appeal does lie against a decision on permission, but it must do so expressly.[345] In the absence of an express provision, any risk of prejudice to the unsuccessful applicant may be alleviated in two ways. First, the application may have a double right to apply for permission both to the body against which the appeal lies and, if that is refused, to the body to whom the appeal lies. Second, the applicant may have a right to renew the application before the same tribunal, usually at an oral hearing following a refusal on a paper consideration.

4.252　　The governing legislation may expressly provide that an appeal does not lie against a decision on permission. TCEA ss11 and 13 do not include these decisions in the list of decisions that are excluded from appeal. In the absence of an express provision, the issue must be decided on the proper interpretation of the legislation. For example: the grant or refusal

---

342　*Albion Water Ltd v Dŵr Cymru Cyf* [2009] 2 All ER 279 at [67].

343　Lord Woolf MR in *Smith v Cosworth Casting Processes Ltd* [1997] 1 WLR 1538 at 1538–1539.

344　See chapter 15.

345　Lord Esher MR in *Re Housing of the Working Classes Act, 1890 ex p Stevenson* [1892] 1 QB 609 at 611.

of permission may not be a 'decision' in terms of the appeal provision.[346] This has been repeatedly affirmed.[347] Likewise, the context and language used to define the scope of the right of appeal may make it clear that a refusal to extend time for appealing is not appealable.[348]

4.253    Apart from express statutory authority, there is generally no right of appeal against a decision to grant or refuse permission.[349] This has been derived from the need to prevent the purpose of permission as a filter being subverted.[350] It has also been derived from the nature of the decision on permission as being final and conclusive.[351]

4.254    In *Rickards v Rickards*,[352] the Court of Appeal held that this reasoning does not apply to decisions whether to extend time for appealing.

4.255    It is only the decision on permission that is not appealable. The reasoning that excludes an appeal does not apply to any other order, such as a costs order, that is made at the same time.[353] However, permission would rarely be given.[354]

4.256    The Court of Appeal has twice said that a decision on permission might be appealable if no decision had ever been made at all, as a result of bias, whimsy, personal interest or, most likely, mischance.[355] In practice, such cases would probably be dealt with under a tribunal's powers of set aside or review and without the need for an appeal.

4.257    In *Samuda v Secretary of State for Work and Pensions and Harris*,[356] the Court of Appeal decided that there was no right of appeal against a decision by the Upper Tribunal refusing to set aside its refusal of permission to appeal. Unfortunately, the Court based its reasoning on the review

---

346  *R (Sinclair Investments (Kensington) Ltd) v Lands Tribunal* [2006] 3 All ER 650 at [23]; *Secretary of State for Work and Pensions v Morina* [2007] 1 WLR 3033 at [45] and [50]; and *R(I) 14/65* at [6]. This interpretation may be made easier if the grant or refusal of permission is referred to as a determination rather than a decision. In an adjudication context, these words are usually synonymous: Vaisey J in *Re 56 Denton Road, Twickenham* [1953] Ch 51 at 56. And the legislation may not use the terms consistently: Maurice Kay LJ in *Morina* at [40]. However, the particular legislative context may be clear. Contrast, for example, the use of 'determination . . . on an application for leave to appeal' in the Child Support Commissioners (Procedure) Regulations 1999 regs 13(1) and 26(1) (revoked) with 'decision . . . on an appeal' in reg 26(2).

347  See *Bland v Chief Adjudication Officer* [1983] 1 WLR 262; *Kuganathan v Chief Adjudication Officer* (1995) *Times* 1 March; *R v Secretary of State for Trade and Industry ex p Eastaway* [2000] 1 WLR 2222; *R (Sinclair Investments (Kensington) Ltd) v Lands Tribunal* [2006] 3 All ER 650.

348  As in *White v Chief Adjudication Officer* [1986] 2 All ER 905 and in *Secretary of State for Work and Pensions v Morina* [2007] 1 WLR 3033 at [37].

349  Access to Justice Act 1999 s54(4) expressly provides that there is no right of appeal in the court system.

350  *Lane v Esdaile* [1891] AC 210.

351  *Re Housing of the Working Classes Act, 1890 ex p Stevenson* [1892] 1 QB 609.

352  [1990] Fam 194.

353  *Riniker v University College London* [2001] 1 WLR 13 at [13].

354  *Clark (Inspector of Taxes) v Perks* [2001] 1 WLR 17 at [20].

355  *Aden Refinery Co Ltd v Ugland Management Co Ltd* [1987] QB 650 at 666; *Daisystar Ltd v Town & Country Building Society* [1992] 1 WLR 390 at 393–394.

356  [2014] 3 All ER 201. In *Grogan v Rochdale Metropolitan Borough Council* [2013] EWCA Civ 1347 at [2], Gloster LJ had assumed in Mrs Grogan's favour that there was a right of appeal, but refused permission in any event.

power under TCEA s10 rather than on the set aside power under UTR r43, which the tribunal had exercised.

### Correction or set aside

4.258   The test for granting permission to appeal is necessarily flexible and it is inappropriate to apply to have the order set aside at the substantive hearing of the appeal.[357] If the order is wrongly drawn, it is possible for it to be corrected, but an application to do so should be made at the earliest opportunity and not at the hearing.[358] Any other approach would result in 'satellite litigation, which . . . is particularly prone to be wasteful of time, money and judicial resources.'[359]

### Judicial review

4.259   If there is no right to appeal or to make another application, a decision on permission to appeal may be challenged by way of judicial review: see chapter 6.

4.260      In *R (Cart) v Upper Tribunal*[360] and *Eba v Advocate General for Scotland*,[361] the Supreme Court decided that an unappealable decision of the Upper Tribunal was susceptible to judicial review if one of the second appeal criteria was satisfied: (i) the case raises an important point of principle or practice; or (ii) there is another compelling reason for the case to be subject to review.

## Judges who refuse permission

4.261   There is no objection in principle to a judge who has refused permission to appeal sitting on the renewed application at an oral hearing[362] or on the appeal itself if permission is later given.[363] There may, though, be circumstances in the particular case that make this inappropriate.

# Issues of fact and law

## Issues of fact, law and judgment

4.262   An appeal is a process of reconsideration of a decision. The scope of the reconsideration that is required or allowed may be limited to particular aspects of the decision under appeal. Legislation may require or allow the appellate tribunal to accord varying degrees of respect to exercises of judgment involved in the decision. A common way of limiting the scope of an appeal is to confine it to issues, points or questions of law or to the

---

357   *Tradigrain SA v Intertek Testing Services (ITS) Canada Ltd* [2007] EWCA Civ 154 at [12] and [52]; (2007) *Times* 20 March.
358   [2007] EWCA Civ 154 per Moore-Bick LJ at [12].
359   [2007] EWCA Civ 154 per Laws LJ at [52].
360   [2012] 1 AC 663.
361   [2012] 1 AC 710.
362   *Khreino v Khreino* [2000] 1 FLR 578.
363   *Mahomed v Morris* (2000) *Times* 3 February.

ground that the tribunal's decision was erroneous or wrong in law. These expressions, and variants of them, are synonymous. Issues of law may be contrasted with issues of fact and issues of judgment.

4.263 Issues of fact are those that deal with matters such as who did what, when, where, why and how. However, an issue may be classified as one of fact purely for definitional reasons. There is a clear instance of this in section 4 of the Safeguarding Vulnerable Groups Act 2006. Section 4(2) allows for an appeal against a decision to include a person on a list of barred persons on the ground of a mistake of law or of material fact, but section 4(3) provides that 'the decision whether or not it is appropriate for an individual to be included in a barred list is not a question of law or fact'.

4.264 Issues of judgment are dealt with separately.[364]

4.265 A limit on appeals to matters of law is compatible with article 6.[365] Even if it were not, the language used will not be susceptible to interpretation under section 3(1) of the Human Rights Act 1998 to turn an appeal on law into an appeal on fact or law.[366]

4.266 In *R (Mukarkar) Secretary of State for the Home Department*,[367] the Court of Appeal considered the effect of a change in the permissible grounds of appeal. Previously an appeal lay on any ground, but this was amended to limit appeals to errors of law. Carnwath LJ commented that the Government should show restraint in bringing appeals on issues of fact in the outstanding cases to which the previous law still applied.

4.267 As legislation distinguishes between issues of law and fact on appeal, the difference must be respected. But in practice the difference is not of great significance in determining the scope of the tribunal's jurisdiction.

4.268 In practice, an appeal on law covers many grounds that involve or relate to issues of fact and judgment. And an appeal on any ground may be restricted by the respect that is shown on appeal for findings of fact and exercises of judgment, and there may be a restriction on the circumstances in which fresh or further evidence can be adduced.

4.269 The practical significance is apparent if permission is required. If an appeal lies on law only, the limitation helps to deter appeals based on a dispute over the facts. Representatives may try to present disputes over facts as issues of law and unrepresented parties may not understand the difference. But the limitation does reduce the number of applications for permission and provides an easy formulation under which those that are made inappropriately can be refused. But if an appeal lies on any ground, more applications are made and the task of operating the permission filter is more difficult. So the significance lies in the size and management of the workload at the application stage.

4.270 Of greater significance in practice is the difference between those appeals that involve a complete reconsideration of the issues in the case and

---

364 See para 4.358.
365 Mummery LJ in *Connex South Eastern Ltd v Bangs* [2005] ICR 763 at [43].
366 [2005] ICR 763 at [43].
367 (2006) *Times* 16 August.

those that require an error to be identified in the decision under appeal.[368] The latter are more likely to require permission than the former.

4.271    The meaning of error of law is not wider when a right under an international convention is involved.[369]

## The disciplined approach to issues of law

4.272   Lord Wilberforce set out the line that has to be drawn in *Anisminic v Foreign Compensation Commission*[370] when he remarked of the function of courts:

> . . . just as their duty is to attribute autonomy of decision of action to the tribunal within the designated area, so, as the counterpart to this autonomy, they must ensure that the limits of that area which have been laid down are observed . . .

4.273   If a tribunal's jurisdiction is, by statute, limited to issues of law, it is not appropriate for the range of issues of law to be extended. In *Varndell v Kearney & Trecker Marwin Ltd*,[371] Eveleigh LJ said:

> We must not strive to create a body of judge-made law supplementing the law as laid down in the Employment Protection (Consolidation) Act 1978. The Act itself provides quite enough law in all conscience and it is not part of the judicial function to increase the potential area of appeal, which is given by section 136 and is only on a point of law, by increasing the numbers of points of law governing the determination of a case.[372]

4.274   The House of Lords made the same point in relation to issues of judgment in *Piglowska v Piglowski*.[373] Lord Hoffmann cautioned that:

> An appellate court should resist any temptation to subvert the principle that they should not substitute their own discretion for that of the judge by a narrow textual analysis which enables them to claim that he misdirected himself.[374]

4.275   And in *Re J (A Child) (Custody Rights: Jurisdiction)*,[375] the House of Lords warned that the extent of interference on appeal must not be such that it effectively removes any element of discretion from the tribunal below. Baroness Hale said:

> Too ready an interference by the appellate court, particularly if it always seems to be in the direction of one result rather than the other, risks robbing the trial judge of the discretion entrusted to him by the law. In short, if trial judges are led to believe that, even if they direct themselves impeccably on the law, make findings of fact which are open to them on the evidence, and are careful . . . in their evaluation and weighing of the relevant factors, their decisions are liable to be overturned unless they reach a particular

---

368  See above at para 4.27.
369  This argument was put in *MT (Algeria) v Secretary of State for the Home Department* [2008] QB 533 at [96] and rejected at [113].
370  [1969] 2 AC 149 at 208.
371  [1983] ICR 683.
372  [1983] ICR 683 at 695.
373  [1999] 1 WLR 1360.
374  [1999] 1 WLR 1360 at 1372.
375  [2006] 1 AC 80.

conclusion, they will come to believe that they do not in fact have any choice or discretion in the matter.[376]

4.276 Similarly, issues of fact must not be admitted under the guise of issues of law.[377] In *Krasniqi v Secretary of State for the Home Department*,[378] Sedley LJ advised that appellate tribunals should be 'rigorous in letting only issues of law go through to the second stage'.[379] Chadwick LJ agreed, adding that he wished to 'endorse his observations as to the need for rigour in identifying, with an appropriate degree of precision, which among the issues an applicant may seek to raise on an appeal are truly issues of law fit for consideration by an appellate tribunal.'[380]

4.277 Despite these warnings, there does appear to be a tendency for appellate tribunals to seek, if not strive, to extend the scope of their jurisdiction, either in individual cases or generally. In this, the tribunals are helped by the element of flexibility in the scope of issues of law and the potential for stating issues in different ways.[381]

4.278 The reality is that a judge is usually able to find an error of law in any case, sometimes easily, sometimes only with difficulty. The issue may seem to be not so much whether the decision involves an error of law, as whether the judge believes that something should be done about it. Judges do not articulate the factors that motivate them and may not even be conscious of them. This is significant for the way that applications for permission to appeal are presented. They may be more effective in cases where an error of law is not readily apparent if they try to influence the judge's instinct in favour of identifying an error on which to give permission.

## A general definition of an issue of law?

4.279 It is impossible to categorise, let alone list, every form that an issue of law may take. Any attempt at a comprehensive list or all embracing formula is doomed to failure by reason of its generality.

4.280 In *Mountview Court Properties Ltd v Devlin*,[382] Bridge J commented that an appeal on a point of law only lay if 'the decision . . . is itself vitiated by reason of the fact that it has been reached by an erroneous process of legal reasoning':[383]

> But this begs the question of where the line is drawn between legal and factual reasoning. It is also inadequate to account for those procedural matters that are issues of law, such as the adequacy of a tribunal's reasoning.

4.281 An issue, error or point of law is widely defined for the purposes of an appeal that involves a decision of a public body. In *Nipa Begum v Tower*

---

376 [2006] 1 AC 80 at [12].
377 *MA (Somalia) v Secretary of State for the Home Department* [2010] UKSC 49.
378 [2006] EWCA Civ 391; (2006) *Times* 20 April.
379 [2006] EWCA Civ 391 at [10].
380 [2006] EWCA Civ 391 at [41].
381 On the flexibility of the standard for adequacy of reasons see below at para 4.484 onwards.
382 (1970) 21 P & CR 689.
383 (1970) 21 P & CR 689 at 695 and 696.

*Hamlets London Borough Council*,[384] Auld LJ considered the meaning of 'point of law' 'as a matter of the plain meaning'[385] of the words and concluded that it:

> . . . includes not only matters of legal interpretation, but also the full range of issues which would otherwise be the subject of an application to the High Court for judicial review, such as procedural error and questions of vires,[386] to which I add, also of irrationality and (in)adequacy of reasons.[387]

4.282   It is also possible to rely on judicial review grounds by way of challenge to the validity of a decision by a public body in defence of a private law action by that body.[388]

4.283   Although it is impossible to list every form in which an issue of law can arise, Brooke LJ gave a useful list in *R (Iran) v Secretary of State for the Home Department*,[389] where he set out the most common ways in which a tribunal may make an error of law:

> When the court gave this guidance in *Subesh*, it was aware that it would not be of any relevance to an appellate regime in which appeals were restricted to points of law. It may be convenient to give a brief summary of the points of law that will most frequently be encountered in practice:
> i) Making perverse or irrational findings on a matter or matters that were material to the outcome ('material matters');
> ii) Failing to give reasons or any adequate reasons for findings on material matters;
> iii) Failing to take into account and/or resolve conflicts of fact or opinion on material matters;
> iv) Giving weight to immaterial matters;
> v) Making a material misdirection of law on any material matter;
> vi) Committing or permitting a procedural or other irregularity capable of making a material difference to the outcome or the fairness of the proceedings;
> vii) Making a mistake as to a material fact which could be established by objective and uncontentious evidence, where the appellant and/or his advisers were not responsible for the mistake, and where unfairness resulted from the fact that a mistake was made.
> Each of these grounds for detecting an error of law contain the word 'material' (or 'immaterial'). Errors of law of which it can be said that they would have made no difference to the outcome do not matter.

The different strategies available if a mistake is not material are discussed at para 4.217 onwards.

4.284   Perhaps a better way than listing the grounds of error of law is to define those matters that are not issues of law. One way of describing those issues is that they are those issues of judgment relating to facts or

---

384  [2000] 1 WLR 306.
385  [2000] 1 WLR 306 at 312. His lordship dealt with the issue later as a matter of the policy of the legislation (s204 of the Housing Act 1996) at 314–315.
386  Whether a provision in subordinate legislation is authorised by primary legislation.
387  [2000] 1 WLR 306 at 313. See also: Lord Denning MR in *Ashbridge Investments Ltd v Minister of Housing and Local Government* [1965] 1 WLR 1320 at 1326; Lord Templeman in *Re Preston* [1985] AC 835 at 862; Lord Hope in *RB (Algeria) v Secretary of State for the Home Department* [2010] 2 AC 110 at [216].
388  See the Court of Appeal in *Cannock Chase District Council v Kelly* [1978] 1 WLR 1 and the House of Lords in *Wandsworth London Borough Council v Winder* [1985] AC 461.
389  [2005] EWCA Civ 982 at [9]–[10].

procedure over which it is permissible to differ. But even this requires a judgment on what is permissible in a particular case, on which appellate judges may properly differ. It is at best descriptive of which issues are treated as ones of law rather than prescriptive of what those issues should be. The approach of Lord Carnwath in *R (Jones) v First-tier Tribunal (Social Entitlement Chamber)*[390] allows a court or tribunal to decide as a matter of policy the issues in respect of which a difference of view is legitimate.[391]

4.285    The following is an attempt at a systematic and classified list of the main issues of law that are likely to arise. Inevitably, there is some overlap.

## Issues of mixed fact and law

4.286    These are issues in which matters of fact and law are entwined. They must first be disentangled, as only the matters of law may be subject to the right of appeal.[392]

## Power to hear the case

4.287    The tribunal must have power to hear the case. This involves considering the jurisdiction of the tribunal itself, the appointment or ticketing of its members, and whether the individual case has been properly brought before the tribunal.

4.288    A tribunal makes an error of law if it acts outside its jurisdiction in the sense of the scope of its authority over issues, parties or remedies. This is covered in chapter 2.

4.289    A tribunal may make an error of law if it is not properly constituted. For example: the tribunal may not be properly constituted according to the relevant practice statement.[393] Or one of its members may not be authorised to sit at all or to hear the particular case or type of case.[394]

4.290    Finally, a tribunal makes an error of law if the individual case has not been properly brought before the tribunal.[395] This includes issues of notice and whether the case has been correctly listed for oral or paper hearing.

4.291    For the purposes of founding jurisdiction, an appeal against a decision is valid even though that decision was one which a decision-maker or a tribunal was not allowed by law to make.[396] Otherwise, the validity of the decision could only be determined on judicial review.

---

390  [2013] 2 AC 48 at [41]–[47]. See also Davis LJ's approach to issues of evaluation in *R (Evans) v Her Majesty's Attorney-General and the Information Commissioner* [2013] 3 WLR 1631 at [107]–[109].

391  In *Commissioners for Her Majesty's Revenue and Customs v Fairford Group plc* [2014] UKUT 0329 (TCC) at [28] considered that this did not apply to appeals against case management decisions.

392  *MT (Algeria) v Secretary of State for the Home Department* [2008] QB 533 at [97].

393  *De Haney v Brent MIND* [2004] ICR 348.

394  Lord Hope in *Gillies v Secretary of State for Work and Pensions* [2006] 1 WLR 781 at [6].

395  See chapter 2.

396  See *London and Clydeside Estates Ltd v Aberdeen District Council* [1980] 1 WLR 182 and *Re Gale dec'd* [1966] Ch 236. See also the decision of the Tribunal of Commissioners in *R(I) 9/63* at [20]–[22].

## Evidence

4.292   A tribunal cannot make an error of law by failing to consider evidence that was not before it.[397] However, it may make an error of law in some related way. For example: it may fail to obtain evidence in pursuance of its inquisitorial duty or to grant an adjournment for the evidence to be obtained.

4.293   A tribunal makes an error of law if it refuses to hear or to take account of evidence that is admissible on the issues in dispute.

4.294   The tribunal may also make an error of law in its assessment of the evidence and making its findings of fact. See below.

## Mistakes in the findings of fact

### Findings involving an exercise of judgment

4.295   The finding of facts usually[398] involves an exercise of judgment by the tribunal.[399] This exercise is accorded the same deference on appeal as other exercises of judgment.[400] Accordingly, a mistake as to a finding a fact that is in dispute is of itself not an error of law.[401] In *AJ (Cameroon) v Secretary of State for the Home Department*,[402] the Court of Appeal deprecated the 'misuse of factual arguments, sometimes amounting to little more than nuance, and often points of small detail, as a basis for assaulting the legality of a decision'.[403]

4.296   However, a tribunal may make an error of law in making its findings in a number of ways.

4.297   First, a tribunal may make an error of law if there is no evidence at all to justify a finding of fact.

4.298   Second, a tribunal makes an error of law if it does not make its findings in a rational way. It may have approached the exercise incorrectly in principle.[404] For example: it may have decided which evidence it preferred by reference to the number of witnesses called by each party or failed to consider the evidence as a whole.[405] Or the tribunal may have used irrational criteria. For example: it may have rejected evidence because the witness was disrespectful to the tribunal. Finally, it may have misunderstood the evidence.[406] This is likely to lead a tribunal to take account of an irrelevant consideration.[407]

4.299   Third, a tribunal makes an error of law if a finding cannot be justified rationally on the evidence.[408] This is sometimes described as a perverse

---

397  *R(S) 1/88* at [3].
398  See below for cases in which no exercise of judgment is involved.
399  See below at para 4.373 onwards.
400  On which see below.
401  *Inland Revenue Commissioners v George* (2003) *Times* 9 December. For mistake by finding a fact that is uncontroverted, see below.
402  [2007] EWCA Civ 373.
403  [2007] EWCA Civ 373 per Laws LJ at [22].
404  *AA v NA (Appeal: Fact-finding)* [2010] 2 FLR 1173 at [15].
405  See chapter 12.
406  *Hossack v General Dental Council* (1997) *Times* 22 April.
407  *Hampshire County Council v JP* [2009] UKUT 239 (AAC) at [32].
408  *Southall v General Medical Council* [2010] 2 FLR 1550 at [47].

finding. This is a finding that no tribunal acting rationally could have made. Every finding for which there is no evidence is perverse.

4.300     The perversity may lie in the tribunal's overall conclusion, an individual finding of fact, or its assessment of credibility.[409]

4.301     There must be an overwhelming case to support a conclusion that a tribunal's decision was perverse.[410] This is especially so of an argument that a conclusion on credibility is perverse.[411]

4.302     Fourth, the tribunal may make an error of law if it acts on information or material that is not put to the parties for comment.[412]

4.303     Fifth, the tribunal makes an error of law if it does not adequately explain how it made its findings. This is an aspect of adequacy of reasons.[413]

### Inferences

4.304 These are covered separately.[414] They always involve an issue of judgment. A tribunal makes an error of law if it draws an inference that was not supported by the evidence.

### Reasonableness

4.305 Reasonableness is sometimes said to be an issue of fact. This means that it is treated in the same way as a fact when an appeal is limited to issues of law. Reasonableness is not determined as the objective of a factual enquiry. It may involve such an enquiry, but it always involves the exercise of judgment. It is merely a specific example of an issue of judgment over which it is permissible to differ.[415]

4.306 In *Cresswell v Hodgson*,[416] Singleton LJ said 'when there has been an appeal to this court on that question of reasonableness it has been said time and again that it is really a question of fact'.[417]

4.307     This means that there are limited grounds on which a conclusion on reasonableness may be challenged:

i) if it is 'perverse or unreasonable';[418]

ii) if the tribunal misdirected itself 'by omitting some point of substance or by taking account of something which should not properly have been considered';[419] and

iii) if the tribunal applies a rigid rule instead of the more open standard of reasonableness.[420]

---

409 Mummery LJ in *Connex South Eastern Ltd v Bangs* [2005] ICR 763 at [43].
410 *Elmbridge Housing Trust v O'Donoghue* (2004) *Times* 24 June.
411 Mummery LJ in *Connex South Eastern Ltd v Bangs* [2005] ICR 763 at [43].
412 See chapter 3.
413 On which see below at para 4.389 onwards.
414 See chapter 11.
415 See above. See also Beldam LJ in *Chief Adjudication Officer v Upton* unreported 10 March 1997.
416 [1951] 2 KB 92.
417 [1951] 2 KB 92 at 96. See also: *R(SB) 6/88* at [15].
418 Brandon LJ in *Wall's Meat Co Ltd v Khan* [1979] ICR 52 at 60.
419 Sir Raymond Evershed MR in *Darnell v Millwood* [1951] 1 All ER 88 at 90.
420 See the decision of the Court of Appeal in *Marley (UK) Ltd v Anderson* [1996] ICR 728 as explained by the Employment Appeal Tribunal in *Tyne and Wear Autistic Society v Smith* [2005] ICR 663 at [35].

## Proportionality

4.308   Like reasonableness, proportionality is an issue of fact. This does not mean that it is not subject to scrutiny by the courts, but any challenge to the assessment of proportionality must be brought under a recognised head of error of law.[421]

## Risk and chance

4.309   These are matters of fact. In *MT (Algeria) v Secretary of State for the Home Department*,[422] the Court of Appeal referred to the assessment of the risk that a person might be tortured if removed to another country:

> But that process is all part of the fact-finding process. That process of assessment is quite different from, and plays a quite different role from, for instance, the assessment that the court has to make, based on found facts, of whether the defendant acted negligently: which is a matter of legal judgment, and not just a question of what is going to happen in certain circumstances in the future.[423]

## Foreign law

4.310   Foreign law has to be proved by evidence and found as a fact.

## Findings not involving an exercise of judgment – uncontroverted fact

4.311   The circumstances in which a mistake on uncontroverted fact is an error of law were set out by the Court of Appeal in *E and R v Secretary of State for the Home Department*.[424] Speaking for the Court, Carnwath LJ said:

> In our view, the time has now come to accept that a mistake of fact giving rise to unfairness is a separate head of challenge in an appeal on a point of law, at least in those statutory contexts where the parties share an interest in co-operating to achieve the correct result . . . Without seeking to lay down a precise code, the ordinary requirements for a finding of unfairness are . . . First, there must have been a mistake as to an existing fact, including a mistake as to the availability of evidence on a particular matter. Secondly, the fact or evidence must have been 'established', in the sense that it was uncontentious and objectively verifiable. Thirdly, the appellant (or his advisers) must not been have been responsible for the mistake. Fourthly, the mistake must have played a material (not necessarily decisive) part in the Tribunal's reasoning.

4.312   This has been treated as an example of a perverse finding rather than as a separate head of error of law.[425] However, it is accepted as a separate head of error of law, although the Court of Appeal in *MT (Algeria) v Secretary of State for the Home Department*[426] warned:

---

421   As in *A v Secretary of State for the Home Department* [2005] 2 AC 68 at [44], where Lord Bingham held that the reasons given by the tribunal had not supported its conclusion.

422   [2008] QB 533.

423   [2008] QB 533 at 109.

424   [2004] QB 1044 at [66].

425   Ward LJ in *Braintree District Council v Thompson* [2005] EWCA Civ 178 at [19].

426   [2008] QB 533 at [69].

We certainly caution against the use of this principle to turn what is a simple error of fact in to an error of law by asserting some new fact which is itself contentious.

## Legislation and case-law

4.313   A tribunal makes an error of law if it does not apply the correct law. If the law is found in legislation, the tribunal must interpret it correctly. This may involve an issue of law or an issue of fact.[427] If it is found in case-law, it must analyse the decisions properly. This always involves an issue of law.

### Validity of secondary legislation

4.314   A tribunal makes an error of law if it applies secondary legislation that was not authorised by primary legislation. The House of Lords decided in *Chief Adjudication Officer v Foster*[428] that tribunals and decision-makers have power to decide whether secondary legislation is authorised. In *T-Mobile (UK) Ltd and Telefónica 02 UK Ltd v Office of Communications*,[429] Jacob LJ said:

> It is not the function of a statutory tribunal to impugn statutory instruments or regulations made pursuant to statutory powers. Challenges to these are classically matters for JR . . .[430]

However, that must be read in its context. As a general proposition, it is contrary to *Foster*.

4.315   A decision is also erroneous in law if it violates a party's Convention right under the Human Rights Act 1998.

### Law not drawn to the parties' attention

4.316   A tribunal may make an error of law if it relies on legislation or authorities that were not cited by the parties and not drawn to the parties' attention so that they could make submissions on them. Ward LJ explained the test to be applied in *Stanley Cole (Wainfleet) Ltd v Sheridan*.[431] There are two requirements, both of which must be satisfied in order to render the proceedings unfair.

4.317   The first requirement is that the provision or authority must be significant to the outcome of the proceedings. There will not be a mistake in law:

> . . . simply because a judge (and for present purposes that includes the tribunal) cites in his or her judgment decided cases which had not been referred to in the course of the hearing. Judicial research would be stultified if that were so and if the parties had to be given the opportunity to address each and every case eventually set out in the judgment.[432]

---

427  On interpretation as an issue of fact or law, see below.
428  [1993] AC 754.
429  [2009] 1 WLR 1565.
430  [2009] 1 WLR 1565 at [51].
431  [2003] ICR 1449.
432  [2003] ICR 1449 at [29].

... the authority must be shown to be central to the decision and not peripheral to it. It must play an influential part in shaping the judgment. If it is of little or no importance and serves only to underline, amplify or give greater emphasis to a point that was explicitly or implicitly addressed in the course of the hearing, then no complaint can be made. If the point of the authority was so clear that a party could not make any useful comment in explanation, then it matters not that the authority was not mentioned.

Thus it seems to me, the authority must alter or affect the way the issues have been addressed to a significant extent so that it truly can be said by a fair-minded observer that the case was decided in a way which could not have been anticipated by a party fixed with such knowledge of the law and procedure as it would be reasonable to attribute to him in all the circumstances. There is, however, an important caveat. This is not intended to be an all-encompassing test. It is, in my judgment, impossible to lay down a rigid rule as to where the boundaries of procedural irregularity lie, or when the principles of natural justice are to apply, or what makes a hearing unfair. Everything depends on the subject matter and the facts and circumstances of each case.[433]

4.318   The second requirement is that the way in which the proceedings were conducted must have produced 'substantial prejudice' or 'material injustice'.[434]

## Interpretation

4.319   The interpretation of documents is an issue of law. This applies to statutes,[435] court orders[436] and other documents like deeds and contracts.[437]

4.320   In *Brutus v Cozens*,[438] Lord Reid distinguished between issues of fact and law in the meaning of language:

The meaning of an ordinary word of the English language is not a question of law. The proper construction of a statute is a question of law. If the context shows that a word is used in an unusual sense the court will determine in other words what that unusual sense is ... It is for the tribunal which decides the case to consider, not as law but fact, whether in the whole circumstances the words of the statute do or do not as a matter of ordinary usage of the English language cover or apply to the facts which have been proved. If it is alleged that the tribunal has reached a wrong decision then there can be a question of law but only of a limited character. The question would normally be whether their decision was unreasonable in the sense that no tribunal acquainted with the ordinary use of language could reasonably reach that decision.[439]

---

433 [2003] ICR 1449 at [31]–[33].

434 [2003] ICR 1449 at [34].

435 And so not the proper subject for a concession: *Cherwell District Council v Thames Water Authority* [1975] 1 WLR 448 at 452.

436 *R v Evans (Dorothy)* (2004) *Times* 10 December.

437 *Global Plant Ltd v Secretary of State for Health and Social Security* [1972] 1 QB 139 at 154. And so it is not the proper subject of a concession: *Bahamas International Trust Co Ltd v Threadgold* [1974] 1 WLR 1514 at 1525.

438 [1973] AC 854.

439 [1973] AC 854 at 861.

Lord Hoffmann explained this passage in *Moyna v Secretary of State for Work and Pensions*:[440]

> Lord Reid was here making the well-known distinction between the meaning of a word, which depends upon conventions known to the ordinary speaker of English or ascertainable from a dictionary, and the meaning which the author of an utterance appears to have intended to convey by using that word in a sentence. The latter depends not only upon the conventional meanings of the words used but also upon syntax, context and background. The meaning of an English word is not a question of law because it does not in itself have any legal significance. It is the meaning to be ascribed to the intention of the notional legislator in using that word which is a statement of law. It is because of the nature of language that, in trying to ascertain the legislator's meaning, it is seldom helpful to make additions or substitutions in the actual language he has used.
>
> ... What this means in practice is that an appellate court with jurisdiction to entertain appeals only on questions of law will not hear an appeal against such a decision unless it falls outside the bounds of reasonable judgment.[441]

4.321   So, the meaning of individual words is not an issue of law. This is because words in isolation have no legal significance. They take their meaning from their syntax, context and background. The meaning of words in their context is an issue of law. Once the meaning of words has been determined, the application of that meaning to the facts found by a tribunal will only involve an issue of law if the tribunal's conclusion is outside the bounds of reasonable judgment.

## Judgment

4.322   The nature of an exercise of judgment, including discretions, is considered separately.[442] The issue here is when an exercise of judgment will be erroneous in law.

### How an exercise of judgment may be erroneous in law

4.323   A tribunal makes an error of law if it fails to exercise a judgment when required. For example: it may fail to consider whether to adjourn when a party fails to attends an oral hearing.

4.324       An exercise of judgment will be erroneous in law in three circumstances: (a) if the tribunal took the wrong approach in law; (b) if the tribunal acted on the wrong material; and (c) if the tribunal went wrong in exercising its judgment.[443]

4.325       A tribunal may take the wrong approach in law in two ways. (i) It may misdirect itself on the law. For example: it may misplace the burden of proof. (ii) It may also go wrong in principle. For example: it may disregard

---

440   [2003] 1 WLR 1929.

441   [2003] 1 WLR 1929 at [24]–[25].

442   See below at para 4.373 onwards.

443   Lord Woolf MR in *AEI Rediffusion Music Ltd v Phonographic Performance Ltd* [1999] 1 WLR 1507 at 1523. The same approach applies to case management issues: Chadwick LJ in *Royal & Sun Alliance Insurance plc and Smith v T&N Ltd* [2002] EWCA Civ 1964 at [38]; *Grupo Torras SA v Al Sabah (No 2)* (1997) *Times* 17 April.

a principle that governs the exercise of a discretion.[444] There are no special rules for cases involving the welfare of children.[445]

4.326    A tribunal may act on the wrong material if it has not taken into account the correct parcel of considerations. It may have (i) overlooked a relevant consideration or (ii) taken account of an irrelevant consideration. This does not mean that a tribunal must set out every factor that it took into consideration in its reasons for decision.[446] But the reasons must at least identify the point or points that the tribunal considered decisive.[447]

4.327    The application of judgment to the parcel of considerations is known as the 'balancing exercise'.[448] A tribunal makes an error of law if it comes to a conclusion that it is not entitled to reach on the material before it.[449]

4.328    Judgment must always be exercised judicially, which limits the factors that may or must be taken into account. In some cases, the legislation sets out factors that must or must not be taken into account.[450]

4.329    A decision on reasonableness, which is an issue of fact, involves an exercise of judgment and may be erroneous in law on that basis.[451]

### Deference for the balancing exercise

4.330    If an appeal relates to the balancing exercise, the appellate tribunal will show deference to the exercise of judgment by the tribunal below. As Lord Radcliffe remarked in *Edwards v Bairstow*:[452]

> The court is not a second opinion, where there is reasonable ground for the first.[453]

4.331    This is not always observed, as Lord Carswell noted in *Director of Public Prosecutions v Collins*:[454]

> . . . the reports of cases before appellate tribunals are strewn with instances in which the courts have reminded themselves of the importance of resisting the temptation to interfere too lightly with the findings of a lower court to which a decision has been entrusted, and have then proceeded to yield to that very temptation . . . Appellate tribunals should pay more than lip service to that principle and when they do reverse them they should be clear on what basis they do so . . .

444  For example: the principles applicable if it sought to raise on appeal a point that was not raised below – Robert Walker LJ in *Jones v Governing Body of Burdett Coutts School* [1999] ICR 38 at 47.

445  Lord Fraser in *G v G* [1985] 1 WLR 647 at 651.

446  Tucker LJ *Redman v Redman* [1948] 1 All ER 333 at 334–335.

447  Holman J in *B v B (Residence Order: Reasons for Decision)* [1997] 2 FLR 602 at 606.

448  Bridge J in *Re F (A minor) (Wardship: Appeal)* [1976] Fam 238 at 266.

449  On which see below.

450  For example: reg 21 of the Child Support (Variations) Regulations 2000 lists factors that must be taken into account or disregarded when determining whether it would be just and equitable to agree to a variation in the calculation of a non–resident parent's liability for child support maintenance.

451  For example: Sir Raymond Evershed MR in *Darnell v Millwood* [1951] 1 All ER 88 at 90.

452  [1956] AC 14.

453  [1956] AC 14 at 38.

454  [2006] 1 WLR 2223 at [18].

4.332　There are two reasons for this deference. The first reason is that it is of the essence of an exercise of judgment that different tribunals may properly reach a different conclusion on the same facts.[455] The second, and supplementary, reason applies if the tribunal has particular expertise. If it does, an appellate body should take this into account in deciding whether the tribunal made an error of law.[456] However, this consideration has less relevance if the appellate body also has access to the same expertise.[457]

4.333　This deference is not based on a limit to the tribunal's appellate jurisdiction. In *Secretary of State for the Home Department v Rehman*,[458] the House of Lords was concerned with a decision of the Special Immigration Appeals Commission. The Commission was given an express power to exercise a discretion differently from the Secretary of State. Nonetheless, deference was appropriate. Lord Hoffmann explained why by reference to the basis of the deference due to the Secretary of State's judgment:[459]

> I emphasise that the need for restraint is not based upon any limit to the commission's appellate jurisdiction. The amplitude of that jurisdiction is emphasised by the express power to reverse the exercise of a discretion. The need for restraint flows from a commonsense recognition of the nature of the issue and the differences in the decision-making processes and responsibilities of the Home Secretary and the commission.[460]

4.334　The degree of deference varies according to the nature of the standard that is being applied. As Hoffmann LJ explained in *Re Grayan Building Services Ltd*:[461]

> . . . the standards applied by the law in different contexts vary a great deal in precision and generally speaking, the vaguer the standard and the greater the number of factors which the court has to weight up in deciding whether or not the standard has been met, the more reluctant an appellate court will be to interfere with the trial judge's decision.[462]

4.335　Lord Carnwath, the first Senior President, has said that this flexibility should allow the Upper Tribunal to give guidance on issues of fact in order to bring consistency of approach on the scope of legal categories.[463] And the House of Lords in *Tandon v Trustees of Spurgeons Homes*[464] held that the issue in that case – the classification of premises as a house – 'must not, save within narrow limits, be treated by the courts as a question of fact:

455　Asquith LJ in *Bellenden v Satterthwaite* [1948] 1 All ER 343 at 345.

456　Sedley LJ in *Bromley London Borough Council v Special Educational Needs Tribunal* [1999] 3 All ER 587 at 594.

457　See Lord Radcliffe's comments downplaying the value of the knowledge of business matters held by the General Commissioners for Income Tax in *Edwards v Bairstow* [1956] AC 14 at 38.

458　[2002] 1 All ER 122.

459　[2002] 1 All ER 122 at [58].

460　[2002] 1 All ER 122 at [57], Lord Hoffmann emphasised that the deference due would vary with the circumstances.

461　[1995] Ch 241. See also *Moyna v Secretary of State for Work and Pensions* [2003] 1 WLR 1929 at [27] and *Lawson v Serco Ltd* [2006] ICR 250 at [34].

462　[1995] Ch 241 at 254.

463　*R (Jones) v First-tier Tribunal (Social Entitlement Chamber)* [2013] 2 AC 48 at [41]–[47].

464　[1982] AC 755 at 767.

for the variations of judicial response could well be such as to give rise to unacceptable, even unjust, differences between one case and another.'

4.336   The issue on appeal is not how the appellate tribunal would have exercised the judgment,[465] it is whether the tribunal below made an error of law in its exercise. Accordingly, the appellate tribunal will not consider how it would have exercised the judgment.[466] This approach is not affected by the Human Rights Act 1998.[467]

4.337   The deference is particularly strong if the exercise of judgment was made on the basis of witnesses seen and heard by the tribunal below[468] or involved an assessment of credibility.[469] These factors may have affected: (i) the findings of primary fact; (ii) the inferences of fact drawn from those facts; or (iii) the application of the legal standard to those facts. The degree of deference shown is greater to (i) than to (ii) and (iii); the courts consider that they are as able as the trial judge to draw inferences or apply standards on the basis of the primary facts found.[470]

4.338   This appellate deference is limited to the balancing exercise. It does not cover other ways in which an exercise of judgment may be erroneous in law. For example: it does not extend to whether particular considerations were relevant to the exercise of the discretion. As Arden LJ in *Teinaz v Wandsworth London Borough Council*:[471]

> ... it is for the appellate tribunal to determine what considerations are relevant to the question at issue. It does not defer to the inferior tribunal in the selection or identification of these considerations. Second, unless permission is given for fresh evidence to be adduced on appeal, the appellate tribunal makes this determination on the factual material before the inferior tribunal.

4.339   The circumstances in which a balancing exercise will be erroneous in law have been expressed differently. To take a representative selection, judges have said that there is an error of law if the outcome was wrong,[472] or plainly wrong,[473] or plainly and obviously wrong,[474] or could not reasonably have been reached on the facts of the case,[475] or could not have been reached on the facts by a tribunal that was properly advised and acting reasonably.[476] But these are in essence different ways of expressing the

465  Viscount Simon LC in *Charles Osenton and Co v Johnson* [1942] AC 130 at 138.
466  Lord Widgery CJ in *Global Plant Ltd v Secretary of State for Health and Social Security* [1972] 1 QB 139 at 155.
467  *Biji v General Medical Council* (2001) *Times* 24 October.
468  Bridge LJ in *Re F (a minor) (wardship: appeal)* [1976] 1 All ER 417 at 439–440.
469  Baroness Hale in *Re J (A Child) (Custody rights: Jurisdiction)* [2006] 1 AC 80 at [10]. And see above on the difficulty of showing perversity in a finding on credibility.
470  Viscount Simonds and Lord Morton in *Benmax v Austin Motor Co Ltd* [1955] AC 370 at 373–374 and 374.
471  [2002] ICR 1471 at [40].
472  Lord Denning MR in *Ward v James* [1966] 1 QB 273 at 293.
473  Baroness Hale in *Re J (A Child) (Custody rights: Jurisdiction)* [2006] 1 AC 80 at [12].
474  Lord Bridge in *George Mitchell (Chesterhall) Ltd v Finney Lock Seeds Ltd* [1983] 2 AC 803 at 816.
475  Arnold P in *R v Birmingham Juvenile Court ex p S* [1984] Fam 93 at 97–98 and Lord Hailsham in *Simmons v Pizzey* [1979] AC 37; [1977] 2 All ER 432 at 59.
476  Woolf J in *Crake v Supplementary Benefits Commission* [1982] 1 All ER 498 at 451.

test set out by Lord Fraser in *G v G*:[477] whether the tribunal's exercise of judgment 'exceeded the generous ambit within which a reasonable disagreement is possible'.[478] This restricts the powers on appeal. Nonetheless, this formulation allows greater freedom to overturn the exercise of a discretion than if a court were reviewing the exercise of an administrative discretion.[479]

### Consistency in the balancing exercise

4.340　Complete consistency between tribunals in their exercise of the balancing exercise is impossible. However, if there are clear differences of opinion among tribunals on the significance to be given to particular considerations, it is appropriate for an appellate tribunal to provide guidance.[480]

### How an error of law may be shown

4.341　The error may appear expressly in the tribunal's reasons or its existence may be inferred from the decision reached.[481]

4.342　On appeal, the tribunal's exercise of judgment must generally be assessed on the information and evidence before the tribunal. As Arden LJ explained in *Teinaz v Wandsworth London Borough Council*,[482] a case involving a discretion to adjourn, '. . . unless permission is given for fresh evidence to be adduced on appeal, the appellate tribunal makes this determination on the factual material before the inferior tribunal'.[483]

### How an error of law may not be shown

4.343　It is not possible to show that an exercise of judgment involved an error of law by reasoning from analogy from other cases, because the nature of the exercise is not compatible with reasoning by analogy.[484]

4.344　Nor is it possible to show an error of law by pointing to the possibility of a different decision. Whenever the circumstances are such that a balancing exercise has to be undertaken in order to exercise a judgment, it is inevitable that there will be at least two possible decisions. The fact that a judge could reasonably have exercised the judgment differently merely emphasises the nature of the task and does not of itself show that there may have been an error of law.[485]

---

477　[1985] 1 WLR 647.

478　[1985] 1 WLR 647 at 652. In *Meadow v General Medical Council* [2007] QB 462, Auld LJ said at [125]: 'I doubt whether the adverbial emphasis of "clearly" adds anything logically or legally to an appellate court's characterisation of the decision below as "wrong"'.

479　*Re F (A Minor) (Wardship: Appeal)* [1976] Fam 238, in which the majority rejected Stamp LJ's view at 429–430; Lord Bridge in *G v G* [1985] 1 WLR 647 at 656.

480　Lords Diplock and Salmon in *Birkett v James* [1978] AC 297 at 317 and 326, approving the approach in *Ward v James* [1966] 1 QB 273.

481　Lord Denning MR in *Ward v James* [1966] 1 QB 273 at 293.

482　[2002] ICR 1471.

483　[2002] ICR 1471 at [40].

484　*Nancollas v Insurance Officer* [1985] 1 All ER 833 at 835. See also chapter 13.

485　*R v B (Judicial discretion)* (2008) *Times* 22 May.

4.345    In *R (Evans) v Her Majesty's Attorney-General and the Information Commissioner*,[486] Davis LJ said that a decision involving an evaluation, as opposed to a discretion, did not fit the classic division between issues of fact, law and mixed fact and law.[487]

## Grounds for judicial review

4.346    Every ground for judicial review is an issue of law for the purposes of an appeal on a point of law.[488] However, it is preferable to avoid the language of judicial review. In *John Dee Ltd v Customs and Excise Commissioners*,[489] the Court of Appeal recommended that tribunals should not refer to *Wednesbury* principles because the context in which they were formulated could lead to confusion.

## Procedural matters

### Breach of rules of procedure

4.347    The significance of breach of rules of procedure is dealt with in chapter 3.

### Fairness

4.348    This is the subject of the principles of natural justice[490] and article 6. These are dealt with in chapter 3.[491]

4.349    It has been said that this is a right that arises separately from the outcome of the proceedings. Even if the outcome has been upheld on appeal, the parties were nonetheless entitled to fairness in the proceedings which might have come to different findings of fact.[492] However, this is not easy to reconcile with the modern emphasis on the materiality of an error of law.

### Delay

4.350    This is additional to the right to a hearing within a reasonable time.[493] Delay may justify a court intervening while the delay is running,[494] imposing some sanction or criticism for the tribunal or its administration,[495] or awarding damages from the State.[496] But the issue here is the effect of the

---

486  [2013] 3 WLR 1631.

487  [2013] 3 WLR 1631 at [109].

488  Auld LJ in *Nipa Begum v Tower Hamlets London Borough Council* [2000] 1 WLR 306 at 313; Lord Templeman in *Re Preston* [1985] AC 835 at 862; and Carnwath LJ in *E and R v Secretary of State for the Home Department* [2004] QB 1044 at [40]–[43].

489  [1995] STC 941 at 950 and 952.

490  Lord Hope in *Gillies v Secretary of State for Work and Pensions* [2006] 1 WLR 781 at [6].

491  See para 3.150 onwards.

492  *Stansbury v Datapulse plc* [2004] ICR 523.

493  Lord Hope in *Porter v Magill* [2002] 2 AC 357 at [108] and Mummery LJ in *Connex South Eastern Ltd v Bangs* [2005] ICR 763 at [2].

494  Sedley LJ in *McKee v Secretary of State for Work and Pensions* [2004] EWCA Civ 334 at [9] (refusing an application for permission to appeal).

495  *Kwamin v Abbey National plc* [2004] ICR 841 at [12].

496  Mummery LJ in *Connex South Eastern Ltd v Bangs* [2005] ICR 763 at [43].

delay on the decision as between the parties. The question is: has the delay affected the decision or its reasons? If it has not, there is no reason why one of the parties should bear the consequences. Nor does delay necessarily justify a rehearing, which could of course compound the delay.[497]

4.351    Delay in proceedings[498] may arise at three stages.

4.352    The first stage at which delay may occur is before the case is heard. At this stage, the issue is whether the evidence was still obtainable and reliable.[499]

4.353    The second stage at which delay may occur is between the hearing and the decision. The dangers of delay were set out by Mummery LJ in *Connex South Eastern Ltd v Bangs:*[500]

> The likely effects of delayed decision-making, which can be serious, are relevant in determining what is a reasonable time. A tribunal's delay prolongs legal uncertainty and postpones finality. It increases anxiety in an already stressful situation. It may cause injustice. A claimant in the right is wrongly kept out of his remedy and a defendant in the right has to wait longer than is reasonable for the allegations and claims against him to be rejected. It is self evident that delay may also have a detrimental effect on the quality and soundness of the decision reached.[501] This is more likely to occur where the decision turns less on the interpretation and application of the law than on the resolution of factual disputes, on which the tribunal has heard contradictory oral evidence from witnesses.[502] Excessive delay may seriously diminish the unique advantage enjoyed by the tribunal in having seen and heard the witnesses give evidence and may impair its ability to make an informed and balanced assessment of the witnesses and their evidence.

4.354    Delay can also undermine the loser's confidence in the decision.[503]

4.355    The significance of delay depends on whether the appeal lies on any grounds or on an issue of law. For appeals on any ground, the issues were considered by the Privy Council in *Cobham v Frett.*[504] Lord Scott said:

> In their Lordships' opinion, a legitimate basis on which the Court of Appeal could assert the right to disagree with the judge's evaluation of the evidence and of the witnesses was absent. It can be easily accepted that excessive delay in delivery of a judgment may require a very careful perusal of the judge's findings of fact and of his reasons for his conclusions in order to ensure that the delay has not caused injustice to the losing party. It will be important to consider the quality of the judge's notes, not only of the evidence but also of the parties' submissions. In the present case the judge's notes were comprehensive and of high quality. As to demeanour, two things can be said. First, in their Lordships' collective experience, a judge re-reading his notes of evidence after the elapse of a considerable period of time can expect, if the notes are of the requisite quality, his impressions of the witnesses to be revived by the rereading. Second, every experienced judge . . . is likely to

497  *Kwamin v Abbey National plc* [2004] ICR 841 at [12].

498  For delay in commencing proceedings and the legal techniques by which it is minimised, see chapter 2.

499  *Boodhoo v Attorney-General of Trinidad and Tobago* [2004] 1 WLR 1489.

500  [2005] ICR 763 at [3]–[4].

501  See also *Boodhoo v Attorney-General of Trinidad and Tobago* [2004] 1 WLR 1489.

502  Including the assessment of credibility, on which see *Sambasivam v Secretary of State for the Home Department* (1999) *Times* 10 November.

503  *Sambasivam v Secretary of State for the Home Department* (1999) *Times* 10 November.

504  [2001] 1 WLR 1775.

make notes as the trial progresses recording his impression being made on him by the witnesses. Notes of this character would not, without the judge's permission or special request being made to him, form part of the record of an appeal. They might be couched in language quite unsuitable for public record. In the present case delay, with a consequent dimming of the judge's recollection of the evidence and of the witnesses demeanour, was not a ground of appeal. In these circumstances it is, in their Lordships' opinion, impermissible to conclude from the fact of a 12-month delay that the judge had a difficult task, let alone an 'impossible' one . . . in remembering the demeanour of witnesses.

In their Lordships' opinion, if excessive delay, and they agree that 12 months would normally justify that description, is to be relied on in attacking a judgment, a fair case must be shown for believing that the judgment contains errors that are probably, or even possibly, attributable to the delay. The appellate court must be satisfied that the judgment is not safe and that to allow it to stand would be unfair to the complainant.'[505]

4.356   For appeals on an issue of law, the position is different. In *Connex South Eastern Ltd v Bangs*,[506] Mummery LJ explained:

There are serious objections to transplanting the 'wrong/unsafe decision' approach from an ordinary civil appeal to an appeal from the decision of an employment tribunal, where the right to appeal is confined by statute to questions of law. To do so would, in my view, enable appellants to challenge facts found by a tribunal, whose decision on the facts or on the claims could not be characterised as perverse. This would circumvent the policy of s 21(1) of the 1996 Act to confine tribunal appeals to questions of law. As I shall explain, this result is not justified by the 1998 Act or by article 6 of the Convention.

4.357   The basic position is that a delay at this stage is a matter of fact, not law.[507] Accordingly, it cannot found an appeal on a matter of law. However, there are two circumstances in which the delay or its effect may involve an issue of law.[508] First, it may cause the decision to be perverse, either in its overall conclusion, on specific matters of material fact, or on its assessment of credibility.[509] Second, it may involve a serious procedural error or material irregularity. This will involve an issue of law if it deprived a party to the proceedings of the substance of that party's right to fairness in the proceedings and if it would be unfair or unjust to allow the decision to stand.[510]

4.358   The third stage at which delay may occur is between the decision and the giving of reasons. The delay may call into question whether the reasons could be reconstructed.[511] However, it is appropriate to allow the author of the reasons the opportunity to explain how the reasons were reconstructed.

---

505  [2001] 1 WLR 1775 at 1783–1784.

506  [2005] ICR 763 at [42].

507  [2005] ICR 763 at [43].

508  Outside the context of a statutory appeal, delay may give rise to a right to damages from the state for delay: [2005] ICR 763 at [43].

509  [2005] ICR 763 at [43].

510  [2005] ICR 763 at [43].

511  *Nash v Chelsea College* [2001] EWHC 538 (Admin).

### Record of proceedings

4.359   An inaccuracy or uncertainty in the record of evidence may make the tribunal's decision erroneous in law. Whether or not it does so is determined on the circumstances as a whole. In *De Silva v Social Security Commissioner*,[512] the tribunal's chairman was under a duty to make a record of proceedings. The appellant argued that the chairman's record was wrong and that this had led the tribunal into error. Latham LJ analysed the evidence and the tribunal's reasons and concluded that the record was not inaccurate as alleged. He said:

> . . . although I accept that a failure to make a proper record of the hearing could result in sufficient prejudice for it to amount to an error of law, that is not this case. The wording of the answer supports the assertion in the written decision as to the provenance of the answer. I am quite satisfied that there is therefore no uncertainty prejudicial to the appellant.[513]

4.360   In *R(DLA) 3/08*, a Tribunal of Commissioners decided that there was an error of law if the absence of a record of proceedings resulted in a real possibility of unfairness or injustice.[514] This may depend on the extent to which evidence of what took place at the tribunal can be obtained from other sources.

## Decision

4.361   A tribunal must act within its jurisdiction, and its decision must be expressed in terms that are capable of being implemented, based on the correct law, and not perverse.

### Jurisdiction

4.362   This is covered in chapter 2.

4.363       A tribunal must not act outside its jurisdiction or purport to exercise powers within its jurisdiction that it does not have.

4.364       It should be obvious that a tribunal must not make a decision which it knows is outside its powers, even with the intention of forcing an uncooperative party to participate in the proceedings.[515]

4.365       A tribunal must not refuse to exercise its jurisdiction. In *MS (Ivory Coast) v Secretary of State for the Home Department*,[516] the claimant appealed to the Asylum and Immigration Tribunal against the refusal of leave to remain. She relied on article 8 of the European Convention on the basis that she had an outstanding application for contact with her children. The Secretary of State argued that no removal directions had been given and would not be given pending the determination of the application for contact. Relying on that concession, the tribunal decided that the claimant's article 8 rights were sufficiently protected and dismissed her appeal. The Court of Appeal decided that the tribunal should have decided whether, on

---

512  [2001] EWCA Civ 539.
513  [2001] EWCA Civ 539 at [13].
514  *R(DLA) 3/08* at [27]–[28].
515  *Hall v Hall* [2008] 2 FLR 575.
516  [2007] EWCA Civ 133; (2007) *Times* 27 March.

the facts at the time of the hearing, her removal would have violated her rights. If so, the tribunal should have decided that she be given leave to remain.

4.366   If a tribunal acts in part outside its jurisdiction, it may be possible to severe and disregard that part of its decision.[517] However, the decision remains valid until set aside.[518]

### Implementation

4.367   In order to be implemented, a decision must be complete, comprehensible, and not self-contradictory.

4.368   What is necessary to make a decision complete depends on the subject matter of the decision. It includes matters like the date from which it becomes effective, the period for which it is operative, any amounts of money involved, and precisely what has to be done in order to implement or comply with the decision. It may be permissible to leave arithmetical matters to the decision-maker, subject to a liberty to restore in the event of a dispute.

4.369   A decision may also be incomplete if it fails to deal with every issue is in dispute, within its jurisdiction, and essential to its decision. As a matter of good practice, the decision should deal with every issue, however hopeless. But as a matter of law, a decision is not erroneous in law merely because it fails to refer to those hopeless points.[519]

### Perversity

4.370   A decision is perverse if it one that no tribunal, properly instructed on the law, was entitled to make. This may be because there was only one decision that the tribunal was entitled to make on its findings of fact and the law. Or it may be because this was not one of a number of decisions that it was entitled to make on those facts and the law. An argument on this ground must be particularised, so that the other party can deal with it, and be overwhelming in order to be successful.[520] This is especially so in respect of challenges to a tribunal's assessment of credibility.[521]

## Alternative dispute resolution

4.371   The rules of procedure provide that tribunals should inform the parties about appropriate alternative methods for the resolution of their dispute and, if the parties wish and it is compatible with the overriding objective, facilitate their use.[522] The rules of procedure are worded as an exhortation, not a command. A failure to comply is not an error of law.

---

517  *R(M) 1/98* at [3].
518  *R(I) 9/63* at [20]–[22].
519  *Srimanoharan v Secretary of State for the Home Department* (2000) *Times* 29 June.
520  Mummery LJ in *Yeboah v Crofton* (2002) *Times* 20 June.
521  Mummery LJ in *Connex South Eastern Ltd v Bangs* [2005] ICR 763 at [43].
522  See chapter 6.

## Adequate reasons

4.372 This may be treated as an example of a procedural matter. But the range of issues involved justifies separate coverage. The adequacy of reasons, the consequences of inadequacy and the effects of delay in providing reasons are dealt with below at para 4.389 onwards.

# Issues of judgment

4.373 An issue of judgment is one on which difference of opinion is both possible and legitimate. In some cases, difference of opinion is possible but not legitimate. For example: statutes and documents may be interpreted differently, as may case-law, but there is in law only one correct interpretation.

4.374 Issues of judgment were described by Lord Diplock in *Birkett v James*[523] as:

> ... decisions which involve balancing against one another a variety of relevant considerations upon which opinions of individual judges may reasonably differ as to their relative weight in a particular case.[524]

4.375 This description identifies the essential features. The conclusion involves taking into account a number of factors. The significance of each factor must be assessed in the context of all of the others. The task of assessing the overall significance of the factors in combination is so complex that it is inevitable that there may be legitimate scope for differences of opinion.

4.376 It is of the nature of an exercise of judgment that a tribunal has to explain how it was exercised.[525]

4.377 A tribunal may have to exercise judgment in four different circumstances.

4.378 First, the tribunal may have to analyse evidence.[526]

4.379 Second, the tribunal may have to make a finding of compound fact.[527] This is a finding that involves the overall effect of a number of constituent facts, each of which has to be analysed in the context of all the other facts. For example: whether a couple are living in the same household depends on the combined effect of a number of facts about the way they have organised their living arrangements.

4.380 Third, the tribunal may have to apply a standard to the circumstances of the case. For example: the standard of proportionality or reasonableness.

4.381 Fourth, the tribunal may have to exercise a power or discretion, including a case management power.

523 [1978] AC 297.
524 [1978] AC 297 at 317.
525 Wall LJ in *Cunliffe v Fielden* [2006] Ch 361 at [23]. See further para 4.464.
526 See chapter 12.
527 Jessel MR in *Erichsen v Last* (1881) 8 QBD 414 at 416.

4.382    The exercise of judgment in these different circumstances may involve different processes. As the Court of Appeal noted in *MT (Algeria) v Secretary of State for the Home Department*:[528]

> That assessment of proportionality is far different from the fact-finding exercise with which we are concerned in the present case.

## Discretion and other exercises of judgment

4.383    Discretion is used in two senses.

### The narrow sense of discretion

4.384    The essence of a discretion in its narrow and strict sense is that the decision-maker has a choice. For example: what procedure should a tribunal adopt at a hearing? In the circumstances of the case and on the material before the tribunal, there may only be one proper answer. But there may well be a range of different and more or less appropriate answers. The choice must be made judicially. But there is a choice.

4.385    This is different from the other ways in which a tribunal may have to exercise judgment. They do not involve a choice. Different tribunals might analyse the same facts differently. For the individual tribunal the facts may be difficult to analyse. The tribunal may be 'in two minds'. But the tribunal cannot simply chose one or the other decision as a matter of preference, even a judicially exercised preference.

4.386    The distinction was recognised in *R (Fisher) v English Nature*,[529] where Lightman J said of a statutory provision that it 'affords scope for judgment: it affords no scope for discretion'.[530] And in *Runa Begum v Tower Hamlets London Borough Council*,[531] where Lord Walker said of the process under the legislation dealing with homeless persons: '. . . it is apparent that the process involves some important elements of official discretion, and also issues which (although not properly described as involving the exercise of discretion) do call for the exercise of evaluative judgment'.

4.387    It was spelt out in more detail by the Court of Appeal in *R v Chalkley*[532] when commenting on the nature of a decision whether to admit evidence:

> . . . the task of determining (in)admissibility under section 78 [of the Police and Criminal Evidence Act 1984] does not strictly involve an exercise of discretion. It is to determine whether the admission of the evidence 'having regard to all the circumstances, including the circumstances in which the evidence was obtained . . . would have such an adverse effect on the fairness of the proceedings that the court ought not to admit it'. If the court is of that view, it cannot logically 'exercise a discretion' to admit the evidence, despite the permissive formula in the opening words of the provision that it 'may refuse' to admit the evidence in that event.[533]

---

528 [2008] QB 533 at [101].
529 [2004] 1 WLR 503.
530 [2004] 1 WLR 503 at [18].
531 [2003] 2 AC 430.
532 [1998] QB 848.
533 [1998] QB 848 at 874. The test for admitting or excluding evidence under the rules of procedure is different: see chapter 10.

## The wide sense of discretion

4.388    Discretion in its wide and looser sense means any exercise of judgment. For example: in *Birkett v James*,[534] Lord Diplock used discretion to describe decisions on interlocutory issues requiring the balancing of considerations.[535]

4.389    However, this use is not consistent. In the context of a decision on abuse of process, Lord Diplock disavowed its use in *Hunter v Chief Constable of West Midlands Police*,[536] despite his comment in *Birkett v James*, whereas the Court of Appeal used the word in *R v Chalkley*.[537] The Competition Tribunal has said that this use is better avoided and considered that 'the more correct concept is one of a margin of judgment or evaluation of the facts'.[538]

4.390    This wide use of discretion is dangerous in that it may mislead tribunals into believing that all forms of judgment involve, and therefore allow, a conscious choice. The better view is that the other forms of judgment are not discretions, although it may be appropriate for an appellate body to take the same approach to all exercises of judgment, whether discretions or not.[539]

4.391    Whether or not a judgment involves a discretion is not merely a matter of semantics. The proper classification may have a significance. For example: a discretion must be exercised in a way that is compatible with a party's Convention rights, but an exercise of judgment that does not involve a discretion does not. In *Campbell v South Northamptonshire District Council*,[540] the issue for the Court of Appeal was whether a decision on entitlement to housing benefit discriminated against the claimants in respect of their religious beliefs. The Court held that it did not. Peter Gibson LJ said:

> . . . If the tribunal were given a discretion, then it is not disputed that that discretion must be exercised comformably with the convention. However, it is plain that reg 7(1)(a) [of the Housing Benefit (General) Regulations 1987] gives neither the local authority nor the tribunal any discretion at all. What has to be decided is a pure question of fact as to whether or not the tenancy agreements are or are not on a commercial basis.[541]

534  [1978] AC 297.

535  [1978] AC 297 at 317. See also Lord Keith in *Devon County Council v George* [1989] AC 573 at 604 (whether something was necessary to facilitate attendance at school); Henry LJ in *Storer v British Gas plc* [2000] 1 WLR 1237 at [24] (issues of fact and degree). The scope for difference of view is shown in the description of a decision on abuse of process.

536  [1982] AC 529 at 536.

537  [1998] QB 848 at 874.

538  *UniChem Ltd v Office of Fair Trading* [2005] 2 All ER 440 at [172]. See also the Court of Appeal in *R v Clark* (2007) *Times* 29 October.

539  See Lord Bridge in *George Mitchell (Chesterhall) Ltd v Finney Lock Seeds* [1983] 2 AC 803 at 815.

540  [2004] 3 All ER 387.

541  [2004] 3 All ER 387 at [60].

## Types of discretion

4.392   A discretion may be unfettered or structured. The difference is the extent to which legislation guides the exercise of the discretion. A discretion may be wholly unfettered, wholly structured, or part and part.

4.393   No discretion conferred on a tribunal is entirely free. Even a discretion, such as the procedure to be followed at a hearing, has 'to be exercised judicially, and in accordance with what is just and proper'.[542]

4.394   It must also be exercised for the purpose for which it was given.

4.395   If it is structured, it may be restricted or guided. If it is restricted, legislation will specify factors that must not be taken into account. If it is guided, legislation will provide a list of factors that are relevant. The list may or may not be exhaustive. A discretion may be limited in a combination of both ways.[543]

4.396   If a tribunal exercises a discretion in a particularly unusual way, it is bound to give reasons.[544]

4.397   There is sometimes a preference for procedural discretions that are unfettered rather than structured. This is based on the belief that this allows the tribunal greater freedom of action. However, structured procedural discretions have advantages:

- the legislative guidance assists consistency both for the same judge over time and between judges;
- the criteria guide the tribunal in investigating facts and circumstances relevant to the discretion;
- they also assist the parties and their representatives to gather and present information of the relevant facts and circumstances, supported by argument directed to the criteria for decision;
- by making clear to the parties the matters that will be considered as relevant by the judge, they can avoid the need for an oral hearing on the exercise of the discretion.[545]

4.398   In short, a structured procedural discretion enhances the quality of decision-making. It seldom restricts the decision-maker's freedom of action unreasonably.

## Exercising judgment in practice

4.399   The process of decision-making that involves assessing the combined effect of a number of separate factors has been analysed by Richard A Posner, an experienced Federal appellate judge from the United States, in *How Judges Think*.[546] On his analysis, this involves a two stage process. The first stage is intuitive:

542  Megarry V-C in *Re Salmon (dec'd)* [1981] Ch 167 at 175.

543  For example: reg 21(1) of the Child Support (Variations) Regulations 2000 provides guidance for the exercise of the discretion whether a variation of child support maintenance would be just and equitable, whereas reg 21(2) restricts it.

544  Robert Walker LJ in *Jones v Governing Body of Burdett Coutts School* [1999] ICR 38 at 47.

545  On the relevance of this to the need for an oral hearing, see Lord Bingham in *R (West) v Parole Board* [2005] 1 WLR 350 at 35.

546  Harvard, 2008.

Because the unconscious mind has greater capacity than the conscious mind, the knowledge accessible to intuition is likely to be vast . . . When a decision depends on several factors, you may do better by using your intuition than by trying to evaluate consciously each factor separately and combining the evaluation to form an ultimate conclusion. The costs of consciously processing the information may be so high that intuition will enable a more accurate as well as a speedier decision than analytical reasoning would.[547]

There is no alternative to the use of intuition, because the working memory available to the conscious mind has too small a capacity to cope with the multitude of combinations involved.[548]

4.400    The second stage in Posner's process is to attempt to explain the decision analytically as a check on error:

The judicial opinion can best be understood as an attempt to explain how the decision, even if (as is most likely) arrived at on the basis of intuition, could have been arrived at on the basis of logical, step-by-step reasoning. That is a check on the errors to which intuitive reasoning is prone, because of its compressed, inarticulate character . . .[549]

4.401    The process of decision-making that involves assessing the reasonableness of an action or decision has been analysed by Aharon Barak, who was the President of the Supreme Court of Israel, in *The Judge in a Democracy*.[550] On his analysis, reasonableness is determined by the objective for which the standard is applied:

The concept of reasonableness assumes a pluralistic outlook, which recognizes the existence of a number of appropriate considerations and wishes to balance them by giving the 'appropriate' weight to the internal relations between them . . . the 'appropriate' weight of the relevant considerations is determined according to their power to advance the objectives which lie at the foundation of the act (or decision) whose reasonableness is being tested.[551]

## Deference under the Human Rights Act 1998

4.402    The issue of proportionality arises in respect of some of the Convention rights under the Human Rights Act 1998. The extent to which the courts will show respect or deference[552] to a decision-maker varies. In *Huang v Secretary of State for the Home Department*,[553] the Court of Appeal distinguished the circumstances in which it applies. It applies to judgments on the formation of policy or where for practical reasons the courts are not in a position to arrive at an autonomous decision.[554] It does not apply to

---

547  RA Posner, *How Judges Think*, Harvard, 2008, p108, footnotes omitted.

548  Philip Johnson-Laird, *How We Reason*, Oxford, 2006, chapter 5.

549  RA Posner, *How Judges Think*, Harvard, 2008, p110, footnote omitted.

550  Aharon Barak, *The Judge in a Democracy*, Princeton, 2006.

551  Aharon Barak, *The Judge in a Democracy*, Princeton, 2006, p69, quoting from his decision in *Ganor v Attorney-General*.

552  This term was in vogue for a time, but was disapproved by Lord Hoffmann in *R (ProLife Alliance) v BBC* [2004] 1 AC 185 at [75] on the ground that it suggested servility or gracious concession, which were inappropriate to the rule of law.

553  [2006] QB 1.

554  [2006] QB 1 at [52]–[53].

decisions on the application of the policy.[555] Laws LJ explained the proper approach on an appeal:

> If the policy perpetrates an apparent violation of a Convention right so that the government must demonstrate proportionality, the court will not be satisfied merely upon it being shown that a reasonable decision-maker might consider the policy proportionate. It will required a substantial reasoned justification of the policy in the light of the discipline inherent in this kind of case ... The difference between this approach and *Wednesbury* is plain to see. *Wednesbury* review consigned the relative weight to be given to any relevant factor to the discretion of the decision-maker. In the new world, the decision-maker is obliged to accord decisive weight to the requirements of pressing social need and proportionality.[556]

4.403    On appeal in *Huang*,[557] the House of Lords distinguished between deference and the ordinary judicial task of assessing the overall effect of competing considerations.


## Adequacy of reasons

4.404    Adequacy of reasons is principally relevant to the Upper Tribunal, which has to decide if the decision of the First-tier Tribunal involved an error on a point of law. The Court of Appeal accords respect to that tribunal's assessment of adequacy.[558] Adequacy is only relevant as the minimum standard for a tribunal's reasons. It is not the standard to which tribunals should aspire.[559]

4.405    The principles that govern the adequacy of reasons are of general application. However, it has been inevitable that case-law for each different tribunal has developed separately.[560] One benefit of the Upper Tribunal is that the common principles that apply across jurisdictions can be identified.


### The need for reasons

4.406    Reasons are essential to any decision taken by a tribunal in relation to proceedings. This follows from the nature of the decision as a judicial one. If a decision is taken without reasons, it is arbitrary and thereby not judicial.

4.407    But this does not mean that reasons have to be given to the parties or that a decision will be defective in law if they are not given when required.

4.408    The legislation may require a tribunal to give reasons for its decision. For the position under TCEA see chapter 14.


555  [2006] QB 1 at [55]–[56].

556  [2006] QB 1 at [54].

557  [2007] 2 AC 167 at [16].

558  *PK (Congo) v Secretary of State for the Home Department* [2013] EWCA Civ 1500 at [22] and [25].

559  On this see chapter 14.

560  See: *R (H) v Ashworth Special Hospital Authority* [2003] 1 WLR 127; *R (TS) v Angela Bowen (Chair of SENDIST) and Solihull Metropolitan Borough Council* [2009] EWHC 5 (Admin); *R v Criminal Injuries Compensation Board ex p Cook* [1996] 1 WLR 1037.

4.409    The law may impose a duty to give reasons in the absence of an express requirement. The techniques by which this is done were set out by the Privy Council in *Stefan v General Medical Council*:[561]

> This may arise through construction of the statutory provisions as a matter of implied intention. Alternatively it may be held to exist by operation of the common law as a matter of fairness.[562]

## The value of reasons

4.410    In *Flannery v Halifax Estate Agencies Ltd*,[563] the Court of Appeal gave a dual rationale of the need for reasons:

> The duty [to give reasons] is a function of due process, and therefore of justice. Its rationale has two principal aspects. The first is that fairness surely requires that the parties – especially the losing party – should be left in no doubt why they have won or lost. This is especially so since without reasons the losing party will not know . . . whether the court has misdirected itself, and thus whether he may have an available appeal on the substance of the case. The second is that a requirement to give reasons concentrates the mind; if it is fulfilled, the resulting decision is much more likely to be soundly based on the evidence than if it is not.[564]

4.411    In *English v Emery Reimbold & Strick Ltd*,[565] the Court of Appeal gave other reasons:

> While a constant refrain is that reasons must be given in order to render practicable the exercise of rights of appeal, a number of other justifications have been advanced for the requirement to give reasons. These include the requirement that justice must not only be done but be seen to be done. Reasons are required if decisions are to be acceptable to the parties and to members of the public . . . [T]he requirement to give reasons concentrates the mind of the judge and it has even been contended that the requirement to give reasons serves a vital function in constraining the judiciary's exercise of power . . . The function that judgments play under the common law in setting precedents for the future has also been identified as one of the justifications for the requirement to give reasons . . .
>
> We would put the matter at its simplest by saying that justice will not be done if it is not apparent to the parties why one has won and the other has lost.[566]

4.412    The reasoning in this case has been applied to tribunals by *Burns v Royal Mail Group plc (formerly Consignia plc)*.[567]

---

561 [1999] 1 WLR 1293.

562 [1999] 1 WLR 1293 at 1297.

563 [2000] 1 WLR 377.

564 [2000] 1 WLR 377 at 381. And, on the value to the decision-maker or tribunal, *R v Higher Education Funding Council ex p Institute of Dental Surgery* [1994] 1 WLR 242 at 256.

565 [2002] 1 WLR 2409 at [15]–[16].

566 See also: *Tramountana Armadora SA v Atlantic Shipping Co SA* [1978] 2 All ER 870 at 872; *R (O'Brien) v Independent Assessor* (2003) *Times* 5 May. The Employment Appeal Tribunal has emphasised that giving reasons helps to focus the decision-maker's attention on the factors that are relevant to decision: *Sogbetun v Hackney London Borough Council* [1998] ICR 1264 at 1270.

567 [2004] ICR 1103.

4.413    There is a tension between the most fundamental purpose of reasons and their use by the Upper Tribunal. The reasons exist to explain to the loser why the tribunal made the decision that it did. If the loser was the lay claimant, the reasons should ideally be written in terms that the claimant can understand. However, there is a risk that the Upper Tribunal will interpret the language used as indicating how the tribunal directed itself in law. This subverts the function that the primary reasons fulfil. The reasons became a letter to the Upper Tribunal rather than a letter to the claimant. And the terms of that letter may not be easily understandable by most lay parties.

## Representative's duty

4.414    A representative is under a duty to draw to the tribunal's attention any alleged deficiency in the reasoning and any query or ambiguity.[568] However, this is only possible if the reasons are given before the decision is promulgated, which is unlikely in a tribunal.

## The use of authorities

4.415    Authorities on adequacy must be used with care. Decisions on adequacy of reasons are relevant only for the principles they establish. Statements made in a particular context must be read as illustrations of the principles and not taken out of context as establishing further principles.[569] Moreover, the principles may depend on the standard of reasons required. For example: a decision on the standard for summary reasons[570] may not be relevant in other cases.

## The standard of reasons

4.416    The essential requirements for a judicial decision were set out by Sedley LJ in *Clark v Clark Construction Initiatives Ltd*:[571]

> The skeleton argument . . . is devoted to a single issue: whether the Lincoln employment tribunal has departed from the universal obligation of judicial tribunals to give reasons which are candid, intelligible, transparent and coherent . . . For my part I accept that these are qualities which litigants and the public are entitled to expect in all reasoned judgments.

> Candour, a subjective quality, is what Crewe CJ was describing when he spoke in the *Earl of Oxford's Case* (1626) Collins 190 of the covenant he had made with himself 'not to let affection press upon judgment'. It is echoed in the judicial oath to do justice without affection or ill-will. Intelligibility and coherence, which are objective and therefore justiciable qualities, may be achieved in a variety of ways. Transparency, a devalued word but one which is central to this appeal, means here that properly drawn reasons should make it possible for the reader to find sources, especially but not only sources of law, which are referred to but not recited.

---

568  *Re M (a Child) (Non-accidental injury: Burden of proof)* (2008) *Times* 16 December.
569  *H v East Sussex County Council* [2009] ELR 161.
570  Such as *H v East Sussex County Council* [2009] ELR 161.
571  [2009] ICR 718 at [5]–[6].

4.417   In *Flannery v Halifax Estate Agencies Ltd*,[572] the Court of Appeal was more specific on the standard required for transparency:

> The rule is the same [in all cases]: the judge must explain *why* he has reached his decision. The question is always, what is required of the judge to do so; and that will differ from case to case. Transparency should be the watchword.[573]

4.418   This is usually expressed as requiring the reasons to be adequate. In *Re Poyser and Mills' Arbitration*,[574] Megaw J said:

> Parliament provided that reasons shall be given, and in my view that must be read as meaning that proper, adequate, reasons must be given.[575]

4.419   In *South Bucks District Council v Porter*,[576] the House of Lords was concerned with a challenge to the adequacy of the reasons given in a planning decision. Lord Brown summarised the law as follows. This applies with appropriate modification, to decisions of tribunals.

> It may perhaps help at this point to attempt some broad summary of the authorities governing the proper approach to a reasons challenge in the planning context. Clearly what follows cannot be regarded as definitive or exhaustive nor, I fear, will it avoid all need for future citation of authority. It should, however, serve to focus the reader's attention on the main considerations to have in mind when contemplating a reasons challenge and if generally its tendency is to discourage such challenges I for one would count that a benefit.
>
> The reasons for a decision must be intelligible and they must be adequate. They must enable the reader to understand why the matter was decided as it was and what conclusions were reached on the 'principal important controversial issues', disclosing how any issue of law or fact was resolved. Reasons can be briefly stated, the degree of particularity required depending entirely on the nature of the issues falling for decision. The reasoning must not give rise to a substantial doubt as to whether the decision-maker erred in law, for example by misunderstanding some relevant policy or some other important matter or by failing to reach a rational decision on relevant grounds. But such adverse inference will not readily be drawn. The reasons need refer only to the main issues in the dispute, not to every material consideration. They should enable disappointed developers to assess their prospects of obtaining some alternative development permission, or, as the case may be, their unsuccessful opponents to understand how the policy or approach underlying the grant of permission may impact upon future such applications. Decision letters must be read in a straightforward manner, recognising that they are addressed to parties well aware of the issues involved and the arguments advanced. A reasons challenge will only succeed if the party aggrieved can satisfy the court that he has genuinely been substantially prejudiced by the failure to provide an adequately reasoned decision.[577]

572 [2000] 1 WLR 377.

573 [2000] 1 WLR 377 at 382. See also Griffiths LJ in *Eagil Trust Co Ltd v Pigott-Brown* [1985] 3 All ER 119 at 122.

574 [1964] 2 QB 467.

575 [1964] 2 QB 467 at 478. This statement was approved by the House of Lords in *Westminster City Council v Great Portland Estates plc* [1985] AC 661 at 673.

576 [2004] 1 WLR 1953.

577 [2004] 1 WLR 1953 at [35]–[36].

4.420  The prejudice must be measured against the value of reasons, as set out above.

4.421  It is sometimes said that the reasons must explain to one party why that party's case was not successful.[578] However, the Court of Appeal has also expressed this requirement in terms not of the party but of the body to which an appeal lies.[579] This removes the personal equation from the understanding and imposes an objective standard for reasons.

4.422  Adequacy is not perfection. The Upper Tribunal and courts are tolerant of the practicalities of writing reasons. In *B v B (Residence Order: Reasons for Decision)*,[580] Holman J explained why courts took account of the problems in delivering an unreserved judgment:

> ... a judgment is not to be approached like a summing-up. It is not an assault course. Judges work under enormous pressure of time and other pressures, and it would be quite wrong for this court to interfere simply because an ex tempore judgment given at the end of a long day is not as polished as it might otherwise be.[581]

4.423  This refers to the difficulties facing judges in courts when giving judgment on the spot. If a tribunal gives written reasons later, the pressure, and therefore the tolerance, may be less. All the more so if the tribunal only has to give reasons on request and is not required to provide them in every case. However, the courts have been tolerant even if a tribunal has a chance to provide written reasons. In *Shamoon v Chief Constable for the Royal Ulster Constabulary*,[582] Lord Hope said:

> It has also been recognised that a generous interpretation ought to be given to a tribunal's reasoning. It is to be expected, of course, that the decision will set out the facts. That is the raw material on which any review of its decision must be based. But the quality which is to be expected of its reasoning is not that to be expected of a High Court judge. Its reasoning ought to be explained, but the circumstances in which a tribunal works should be respected. The reasoning ought not to be subjected to an unduly critical analysis.[583]

4.424  And in *R (Jones) v First-tier Tribunal (Social Entitlement Chamber)*,[584] Lord Hope said:

> The appellate court should not assume too readily that the tribunal misdirected itself just because not every step in its reasoning is fully set out in it.[585]

---

578  For example: *R(A) 1/72* at [8]; Donaldson LJ in *Union of Construction, Allied Trades and Technicians v Brain* [1981] ICR 542 at 551; Ward LJ in *Re G (a Child) (Care proceedings: Placement for Adoption)* (2005) *Times* 1 August.

579  Brooke LJ in *R (Iran) v Secretary of State for the Home Department* (2005) *Times* 19 August.

580  [1997] 2 FLR 602.

581  [1997] 2 FLR 602 at 606.

582  [2003] ICR 337.

583  [2003] ICR 337 at [59].

584  [2013] 2 AC 48.

585  [2013] 2 AC 48 at [25].

## The standard in operation

4.425 There are many decisions in which the courts have indicated, in the context of the case, factors which are or are not relevant to adequacy. In *Bassano v Battista*,[586] Arden LJ explained how adequacy of reasons is determined on appeal:

> . . . the appellate court will examine the documents and evidence before the judge to see what the issues before him were and what the evidence was. In other words, this court will look to see whether the judge's reasons, even if not expressed in terms or expressed clearly, can be deduced from those documents and the evidence. If the reasons are ones that can be deduced from those documents and the evidence, and if the judge's findings of fact were ones which he was entitled to make having regard to those documents and that evidence, this court will not accede to a challenge to the judgment on the grounds of insufficiency of reasons.

### Reasons not rationalisation

4.426 The reasons must represent the reasons that led the tribunal to its decision. A rationalisation after the event is not sufficient.[587] In practice, however, it may not be possible to tell whether the reasons given were really those that influenced the tribunal.

### Reasons and conclusions

4.427 A mere statement of a conclusion is not adequate. As Mann J said of the reasons given by the mental health review tribunal in *R v Mental Health Review Tribunal ex p Clatworthy*:[588]

> I do not regard the reasons given by this tribunal as satisfactory . . . The reasons alone are a bare traverse of a circumstance in which discharge could be contemplated.[589]

### Reasons for reasons

4.428 A tribunal has to give reasons for its decision. It need not go further and give reasons for those reasons. This principle was stated by Parker LJ in *R v Secretary of State for the Home Department ex p Swati*.[590] That case concerned notification by an immigration officer. The illustrations given of the principle[591] may reflect that context and appear to allow a mere statement of a ground for refusal of entry. The principle stands, but more would be required of a tribunal.

---

586 [2007] EWCA Civ 370 at the second paragraph numbered [44].
587 Latham J in *S (a Minor) v Special Educational Needs Tribunal* [1995] 1 WLR 1627 at 1637.
588 [1985] 3 All ER 699.
589 [1985] 3 All ER 699 at 703.
590 [1986] 1 WLR 477 at 491.
591 [1986] 1 WLR 477 at 490.

### Resources

4.429   The adequacy of reasons cannot be affected by the workload or other limitations on the tribunal's time. As Dyson LJ explained in *R (H) v Ashworth Special Hospital Authority*:[592]

> If tribunals do not have the time and back-up resources that they need to discharge their statutory obligation to provide adequate reasons, then the time and resources must be found. I absolutely reject the submission that reasons which would be inadequate if sufficient resources were available may be treated as adequate simply because sufficient resources are not available. Either the reasons are adequate or they are not, and the sufficiency of resources is irrelevant to that question. The adequacy of reasons must be judged by reference to what is demanded by the issues which call for decision. What is at stake in these cases is the liberty of detained patients on the one hand, and their safety as well as that of other members of the public on the other hand. Both the detained persons and members of the public are entitled to adequate reasons.

### Length and detail

4.430   The length and detail required will depend on the case. There is, though, no reason in principle why reasons should be as detailed as a judgment.[593] *Crake v Supplementary Benefits Commission*[594] was concerned with the reasons of a Supplementary Benefits Appeal Tribunal. Woolf J said:

> It has got to be borne in mind, particularly with tribunals of this sort, that they cannot be expected to give long and precise accounts of their reasoning; but a short and concise statement in clear language should normally be possible which fairly indicates to the recipient why his appeal was allowed or dismissed . . .[595]

### Interlocutory decisions

4.431   Reasons for interlocutory decisions can usually be fairly short.[596]

### The context

4.432   Reasons are read in their context. This allows other material to be taken into account when deciding on their adequacy. In *Crake v Supplementary Benefits Commission*,[597] Woolf J decided that the tribunal's reasons in one of the cases were adequate. He took account of the reasons themselves, together with the chairman's record of proceedings and of the Commission's handbook to which the reasons referred.[598]

---

592   [2003] 1 WLR 127 at [76].
593   Carnwath LJ in *IBA Healthcare Ltd v Office of Fair Trading* [2004] ICR 1364 at [104].
594   [1982] 1 All ER 498.
595   [1982] 1 All ER 498 at 506.
596   *Carpenter v Secretary of State for Work and Pensions* [2003] EWCA Civ 33, reported as *R(IB) 6/03*; *KP v Hertfordshire County Council* [2010] UKUT 233 (AAC) at [28].
597   [1982] 1 All ER 498.
598   [1982] 1 All ER 498 at 508.

## Comprehensiveness

4.433 A tribunal's reasons need not deal with every piece of material in evidence.[599] Nor need a tribunal's reasons deal with every point that was raised in the case. This applies generally to the tribunal's reasons. In *Mountview Court Properties Ltd v Devlin*,[600] the Divisional Court was concerned with the reasons given by a rent assessment committee. Lord Parker CJ said:

> ... reasons are not deficient merely because every process of reasoning is not set out. I further think that reasons are not insufficient merely because they fail to deal with every point raised before the committee at the hearing.[601]

4.434 More examples appear in the following sections.

### Issues and submissions

4.435 The reasons must cover issues and submissions raised by the parties. In *Flannery v Halifax Estate Agencies Ltd*,[602] the Court of Appeal said:

> ... where the dispute involves something in the nature of an intellectual exchange, with reasons and analysis advanced on either side, the judge must enter into the issues canvassed before him and explain why he prefers one case over the other.[603]

4.436 But it is not necessary to deal with every issue or submission. In *Re Poyser and Mills' Arbitration*,[604] Megaw J limited the extent of the duty:

> The reasons that are set out must be reasons which not only will be intelligible, but which deal with the substantial points that have been raised.[605]

4.437 If a tribunal deals with one issue in a way that renders another redundant, its reasons need not deal with the redundant issue.[606]

4.438 In *Bolton Metropolitan District Council v Secretary of State for the Environment*,[607] Lord Lloyd in the House of Lords gave a more detailed statement of what was required in a planning dispute:

> What the Secretary of State must do is to state his reasons in sufficient detail to enable the reader to know what conclusion he has reached on the 'principal important controversial issues'. To require him to refer to every material consideration, however insignificant, and to deal with every argument, however peripheral, would be to impose an unjustifiable burden.[608]

This passage identifies the importance of the issues to the parties as a determinative factor in whether they should be dealt with in the reasons.

4.439 A party who was not present at the hearing will not be familiar with the arguments and issues as they developed. A fuller explanation will be

---

599 Laws LJ in *AJ (Cameroon) v Secretary of State for the Home Department* [2007] EWCA Civ 373 at [15].
600 (1970) 21 P&CR 689 at 692.
601 (1970) 21 P&CR 689 at 692.
602 [2000] 1 WLR 377.
603 [2000] 1 WLR 377 at 382.
604 [1964] 2 QB 467.
605 [1964] 2 QB 467 at 478.
606 *Post Office v Lewis* (1997) *Times* 25 April.
607 (1996) 71 P&CR 309.
608 (1996) 71 P&CR 309 at 314.

needed for a party in that position. Even a party who opted not to attend is entitled to adequate reasons.

### Self-evident reasons

4.440   Some reasons are self-evident. If they are, they do not have to be stated. In *Eagil Trust Co Ltd v Pigott-Brown*,[609] Griffiths LJ explained:

> ... if it be that the judge has not dealt with some particular argument but it can be seen that there are grounds on which he could have been entitled to reject it, this court should assume that he acted on those grounds unless the appellant can point to convincing reasons leading to a contrary conclusion ...[610]

This case, and the authority relied on, dealt with decisions by a judge in chambers or on costs.[611] But the reasoning applies, though with less leeway allowed to the judge, to all reasons. It follows from the need to test adequacy in the context of the evidence before the tribunal and the submissions of the parties.[612]

### Competence

4.441   Tribunals do not have to refer to well known principles of law, like the standard and burden of proof.[613] They are assumed to know these unless their reasons show otherwise.

4.442   This is but an example of the wider principle that judges are assumed to know how to perform their functions and which matters should be taken into account, unless the contrary is shown.[614] However, if the case is difficult or finely balanced, it may be necessary for a tribunal to show how it dealt with each relevant factor, such as those in a relevant statutory checklist.[615]

### Hopeless cases

4.443   The reasons required in hopeless cases may be quite short, especially if the appeal is limited to an issue of law.[616]

### The addressees

4.444   The law sets an objective standard for the adequacy of reasons. The standard is sometimes expressed in personal terms, that the party who has lost must be told why. However, the courts do not employ a personal equation that takes account of the difficulties that a particular party may have in understanding the reasons. In *R (Iran) v Secretary of State for the Home*

---

609   [1985] 3 All ER 119.
610   [1985] 3 All ER 119 at 122.
611   *English v Emery Reimbold & Strick Ltd* [2002] 1 WLR 2409 at [30].
612   *English v Emery Reimbold & Strick Ltd* [2002] 1 WLR 2409 at [26]. See also [13], citing a decision of the European Court of Human Rights.
613   See Wilson J in *Re P (Witness Summons)* [1997] 2 FLR 447 at 455 and the Commissioner in *R(SB) 5/81* at [7].
614   Lord Hoffmann in *Piglowska v Piglowski* [1999] 1 WLR 1360 at 1372.
615   *Re G (Children)* [2006] 2 FLR 629 at [40].
616   *Green v Half Moon Bay Hotel* [2009] UKPC 23 at [11] and [13].

*Department*,[617] Brooke LJ expressed the need for adequacy not for the individual parties but for the body to which an appeal lies. And in *English v Emery Reimbold & Strick Ltd*,[618] the Court of Appeal decided that reasons were adequate after hearing an explanation by counsel.[619]

4.445 However, the addressee of the reasons may be relevant for at least two reasons.

4.446 First, the knowledge of the parties may justify an explanation that is less detailed than would otherwise be required. In *Carpenter v Secretary of State for Work and Pensions*,[620] Laws LJ said of a tribunal's short reasons for refusing an adjournment:

> It seems to me important to recognise that the brief reference given by the tribunal itself in the decision notice to the refusal to adjourn, though in one sense a statement which could be regarded as more of a conclusion than a reason, was addressed to a tutored audience. Everyone involved in the case knew the short summary of facts which I have just repeated . . .[621]

4.447 And in *Derby Specialist Fabrication Ltd v Burton*,[622] Keene J speaking for the Employment Appeal Tribunal said:

> . . . it must be borne in mind that the extended reasons of an employment tribunal are directed towards parties who know in detail the arguments and issues in the case. The tribunal's reasons do not need to be spelt out in the detail required were they to be directed towards a stranger to the dispute.

4.448 Nevertheless, the reasons must be adequate, as Dyson LJ explained in *R (H) v Ashworth Special Hospital Authority*:[623]

> I do not accept that the 'informed audience' point can properly be relied on to justify as adequate a standard of reasoning in tribunals which would not be regarded as adequate in a judgment by a judge. It does not follow that tribunals are obliged to produce decisions which are as long as judgments by a judge often tend to be. Far from it. A brief judgment is no less likely to be adequately reasoned than a lengthy one.

4.449 Second, the fact that the addressee is not represented and lacks understanding of the proceedings may impose a duty that the reasons be fuller. As the Privy Council said in *Green v Half Moon Bay Hotel*:[624]

> If an appeal is hopeless, very short oral reasons given by an appellate court may be sufficient. But especially when the appellant is a litigant in person putting forward a case on which he has very strong feelings, the Court (even if it considers that his case is hopeless and his strong feelings are misguided) should say enough to make clear to the litigant why his appeal has failed. In this case it might have been helpful for the Court to spell out to Mr Greene that his statutory right of appeal was limited to issues of law and that all his complaints seem to have concentrated on matters of fact. It might also have been helpful and saved time if, when the Court realised

617 (2005) *Times* 19 August.
618 [2002] 1 WLR 2409.
619 [2002] 1 WLR 2409 at [57].
620 *R(IB)* 6/03.
621 *R(IB)* 6/03 at [29]. See also: *R v Mental Health Review Tribunal ex p Booth* [1998] COD 203 at 204; *Derby Specialist Fabrication Ltd v Burton* [2001] ICR 833 at [32].
622 [2001] ICR 833 at [32].
623 [2003] 1 WLR 127 at [79].
624 [2009] UKPC 23 at [11].

that Mr Greene was asking for written reasons, some written reasons, how-ever brief, had been prepared and made available to him in order to explain why the appeal had been dismissed.

4.450   The issue is one of balance. All courts and tribunals assume certain know-ledge and understanding when giving their reasons. For example: courts do not routinely explain the nature of precedent or the status of legislation. The issue on an appeal is the extent to which the tribunal may assume knowledge and understanding of the evidence and arguments in the case.

### Evidence of fact

4.451   The tribunal must make relevant findings of fact. But must the tribunal explain why it made them?

4.452   If an appeal lies only on an issue of law, there are limited circum-stances in which an appeal can be allowed on the basis of the tribunal's analysis of the evidence. In *Alexander Machinery (Dudley) Ltd v Crabtree*,[625] the Employment Appeal Tribunal said:

> Whilst there can be no appeal from findings of fact, the absence of evidence to support a particular finding is an error of law. Similarly a finding of fact or refusal to find a fact will involve an error of law if the finding or refusal is a conclusion which no tribunal, properly directing itself, could reach on the basis of the evidence which had been given and accepted by it. I stress the word 'accepted' because it is important that tribunals, in reaching find-ings of fact, should set out in substance what evidence they do or do not accept.[626]

4.453   This was confirmed by the Court of Appeal in *Varndell v Kearney & Trecker Marwin Ltd*.[627] Eveleigh LJ said:

> It seems to me that the arguments put forward on behalf of the employees in effect require, not a statement of reasons, but an analysis of the facts and arguments on both sides, with reasons for rejecting the arguments of the employees and reasons for accepting the facts relied upon in support of the tribunal's conclusion. This is not necessary. The tribunal said that they found as a fact that clause 4 was observed. It is admitted that there was evidence to support this finding and indeed the whole conclusion. There is no right of appeal on a question of fact, so of what use, generally speaking, is it to have a detailed recitation of the evidence? A conclusion of fact with which this court or the appeal tribunal might disagree, provided it is justifi-able on the evidence, gives rise to no ground of appeal. I therefore see no obligation upon the tribunal to state the facts in detail.[628]

In the context, the arguments referred to are those relating to the analysis of the evidence and the findings of fact. And the reference in the final sentence to there being no duty to 'state' the facts in detail refers to a state-ment of why they were found, not to a statement of what they were.

---

625  [1974] ICR 120.
626  [1974] ICR 120 at 122.
627  [1983] ICR 683.
628  [1983] ICR 683 at 693.

4.454 The Court drew attention to the fact that the decision of the industrial tribunal[629] in the *Alexander Machinery* case was wrong in law, because it had given no reasons for its award of compensation.[630] The Employment Appeal Tribunal had referred the case back to the industrial tribunal giving guidance on the further findings that must be made and explained. But the Tribunal's directions 'are no more than general guidelines and they are not rules of law'.[631]

4.455 Even under these general statements, there are circumstances in which a tribunal's reasons will not be adequate unless they explain how findings of fact were made. For example: without an explanation it may not be apparent, either to the parties or on appeal, how a particular finding was derived from the evidence, or that the tribunal relied (permissibly) on its personal knowledge in making a finding.

4.456 It is doubtful whether the general statements quoted from the cases accurately reflect the law. There are numerous statements in the authorities that suggest that tribunals do have to explain how they made their findings. For example: in *Re B (Appeal: Lack of Reasons)*,[632] Thorpe LJ said:

> I would say that the essential test is: does the judgment sufficiently explain what the judge has found and what he has concluded as well as the process of reasoning by which he has arrived at his findings, and then his conclusion?[633]

4.457 If an explanation is required, the authorities recognise that there are limits on the explanation that can be given. In *Flannery v Halifax Estate Agencies Ltd*,[634] the Court of Appeal suggested that in some circumstances it may be sufficient to state that one witness was believed rather than another:

> . . . when the court, in a case without written documents depending on eye-witness accounts is faced with two irreconcilable accounts, there may be little more to say other than the witnesses for one side were more credible . . .[635]

Later this was stated more generally:

> Where there is a straightforward factual dispute whose resolution depends simply on which witness is telling the truth about events which he claims to recall, it is likely to be enough for the judge (having, no doubt, summarised the evidence) to indicate simply that he believes X rather than Y; indeed there may be nothing more else to say.[636]

4.458 These statements may set too low a standard. It must surely be possible to indicate why the evidence of one witness was preferred to that of another.

---

629 Now an employment tribunal.

630 [1974] ICR 120: see Eveleigh LJ's analysis at 694.

631 Eveleigh LJ in *Varndell v Kearney & Trecker Marwin Ltd* [1983] ICR 683 at 694.

632 [2003] 2 FLR 1035.

633 [2003] 2 FLR 1035 at [11].

634 [2000] 1 WLR 377.

635 [2000] 1 WLR 377 at 381.

636 [2000] 1 WLR 377 at 382.

In *English v Emery Reimbold & Strick Ltd*,[637] the Court of Appeal suggested a higher standard:[638]

> . . . the judgment must enable the appellate court to understand why the judge reached his decision. This does not mean that every factor which weighed with the judge in his appraisal of the evidence has to be identified and explained. But the issues the resolution of which were vital to the judge's conclusion should be identified and the manner in which he resolved them explained. It is not possible to provide a template for this process. It need not involve a lengthy judgment. It does require the judge to identify and record those matters which were critical to his decision. If the crucial issue was one of fact, it may be enough to say that one witness was preferred to another because the one manifestly had a clearer recollection of the material facts or the other gave answers which demonstrated that his recollection could not be relied upon.

4.459   *Re F (Contact: Lack of Reasons)*[639] is an example of this more stringent approach. Hedley J, in the lead judgment for the Court of Appeal, expressed 'particular concern' at the absence of any explanation why the judge had not believed the evidence of two witnesses or how the judge had dealt with the controversial issue of supposed inconsistencies in their evidence.[640]

4.460   If a tribunal rejects the factual case presented, it need not consider whether there is another explanation favourable to the party. In *AJ (Cameroon) v Secretary of State for the Home Department*,[641] an asylum seeker gave an explanation of how he had come by scars on his body. The tribunal rejected his account and Laws LJ said:

> I do not consider, for my part, that the AIT [Asylum and Immigration Tribunal] was bound to make particular findings as to how, in their view, the appellant came by his injuries. The burden of proof was on him. The AIT rejected the case he put forward. They were not obliged to look for some different or modified case that might be in his favour. Such an exercise anyway would necessarily have been speculative, and for that reason inapt and unhelpful.[642]

## Expert evidence of opinion

4.461   In *English v Emery Reimbold & Strick Ltd*,[643] the Court of Appeal set out the standard when dealing with a conflict in expert evidence:

> Bingham LJ in *Eckersley v Binnie* (1987) 18 Con LR 1 at 77–78 . . . said that 'a coherent reasoned opinion expressed by a suitably qualified expert should be the subject of a coherent reasoned rebuttal'. That does not mean that the judgment should contain a passage which suggests that the judge has applied the same, or even a superior, degree of expertise to that displayed by the witness. He should simply provide an explanation as to why he has accepted the evidence of one expert and rejected that of another. It may be that the evidence of one or the other accorded more satisfactorily with facts found by the judge. It may be that the explanation of one was more

637  [2002] 1 WLR 2409.
638  [2002] 1 WLR 2409 at [19].
639  [2007] 1 FLR 65.
640  [2007] 1 FLR 65 at [17].
641  [2007] EWCA Civ 373.
642  [2007] EWCA Civ 373 at [11].
643  [2002] 1 WLR 2409.

inherently credible than that of the other. It may simply be that one was better qualified, or manifestly more objective, than the other. Whatever the explanation, it should be apparent from the judgment.[644]

4.462   A tribunal may reject expert evidence, even if it is the only, or the unanimous, expert evidence. However, it must have a basis in the evidence for doing so and must explain why it rejected the evidence.[645]

4.463   The standard of reasons required will vary according to the expertise of the tribunal. To adopt the distinction drawn by Waller LJ in *H v East Sussex County Council*,[646] 'the rejection of unchallenged technical evidence of an expert where the tribunal has no expertise in the area with which the evidence is concerned' will require a fuller explanation than 'the rejection of expert evidence providing opinion on the very point which that expert tribunal has to decide'.[647]

### Issues of judgment[648]

4.464   It can be difficult to explain the complex mental process involved in reaching a judgment. In some cases, once the facts are set out the conclusion reached is self-evident. However, in most cases some explanation is required so that the decision is open to scrutiny on appeal. As Wall LJ explained in *Cunliffe v Fielden*:[649]

> In my judgment, the proper exercise of a judicial discretion requires the judge to explain how he has exercised it. This is the well known 'balancing exercise'. The judge has not only to identify the factors he has taken into account, but to explain why he has given more weight to some rather than to others. Either a failure to undertake this exercise, or for it to be impossible to discern from the terms of the judgment that it has been undertaken, vitiates the judicial conclusion, which remains unexplained.

4.465   The practical importance of a lack of reasons was explained in, and exemplified by, *B v B (Residence Order: Reasons for Decision)*.[650] The Court of Appeal was there concerned with a dispute between parents over who should have a residence order for their child. The recorder had listed the factors he had taken into account, but not explained how he had analysed them. Holman J said of the recorder's judgment:

> . . . clearly an appellate court is only able to assess whether the court below has failed to take into account relevant matters or has inappropriately taken into account irrelevant matters, if that court does set out its reasons with sufficient detail and clarity to make clear the facts upon which it has relied, and the matters which is has taken into account in exercising its discretion.[651]

644 [2002] 1 WLR 2409 at [10].
645 Butler-Sloss LJ in *Re B (Care: Expert Witness)* [1996] 1 FLR 667 at 674; Charles J in *A County Council v K, D and L* [2005] 1 FLR 851 at [58].
646 [2009] ELR 161.
647 [2009] EWCA Civ 249 at [18].
648 See para 4.373 onwards.
649 [2006] Ch 361 at [12].
650 [1997] 2 FLR 602.
651 [1997] 2 FLR 602 at 606.

4.466  The courts have said that it is possible to give reasons for making value judgments on matters such as character. In *R v City of London Corporation ex p Matson*,[652] Swinton Thomas LJ said of the assessment of a person's suitability to be an alderman:

> I do not believe that any adverse assessment involves the articulation of inexpressible value judgments.[653]

4.467  The same is true for issues that involve the application of medical expertise.[654]

4.468  It is not necessary to set out every factor that the tribunal took into account. This would be expecting too much and this difficulty is recognised by the law. In *Redman v Redman*,[655] Tucker LJ said:

> I desire to emphasise as strongly as I can that the fact that a judge or commissioner does not set out every one of the reasons which actuate him in coming to his decision will not be sufficient to support an argument in this court that he has not applied his mind to the relevant considerations . . .[656]

4.469  Nor is a detailed analysis of the factors required. It should be sufficient to set out the key factors that influenced the tribunal in reaching its judgment. In *B v B (Residence Order: Reasons for Decision)*,[657] Holman J said of the judge's judgment that was under appeal:

> . . . a single extra sentence in the judgment, just identifying the point or points which in the end the recorder regarded as decisive, might have been all that was needed.[658]

4.470  If a value judgment is exercised in an unusual way, the reason must be given. In *Jones v Governing Body of Burdett Coutts School*,[659] the Court of Appeal was concerned with the exercise of a discretion to allow argument on new points of law before the Employment Appeal Tribunal. Robert Walker LJ dealt with the issue in general terms: 'if any court or tribunal exercises its discretion in a particularly unusual manner it is bound to give reasons'.[660]

### Proportionality

4.471  This is an instance of an issue of judgment, but with some adaptation of the approach. It was considered by the Court of Appeal in *Coates v South Bucks District Council*.[661] Lord Phillips MR said:

> In my judgment there is one cardinal rule. The judge's reasons should make clear to the parties why he has reached his decision. Where he has had to balance competing factors it will usually be possible to explain why he has concluded that some have outweighed others. Even where the

---

652  [1997] 1 WLR 765.
653  [1997] 1 WLR 765 at 783.
654  *Stefan v General Medical Council* [1999] 1 WLR 1293 at 1304.
655  [1948] 1 All ER 333.
656  [1948] 1 All ER 333 at 334.
657  [1997] 2 FLR 602.
658  [1997] 2 FLR 602 at 606.
659  [1999] ICR 38.
660  [1999] ICR 38 at 47.
661  [2004] EWCA Civ 1378.

competition is so unequal that the factors speak for themselves it is desirable to say so.[662]

And Neuberger LJ set out the criteria on which an appellate court will interfere with the exercise of a judge's discretion and said:

> Where as here an issue of proportionality arises, because a Convention right is involved, an appellate court must be particularly careful when scrutinising the judgment. However, in such a case, there will usually be room for more than one conclusion on the evidence and arguments put before the judge. While it would be wrong to equate the decision in such a case with the exercise of a discretion, it will normally involve the balancing of various competing factors, which is primarily the function of the Judge. I do not accept the notion that, in every such case, an appellate court should review such a balancing exercise on a 'right or wrong' basis, so that it is entitled, indeed, I think it would follow, obliged, to carry out that exercise afresh itself.

> I believe that my view is consistent with the approach of Lord Bingham of Cornhill in the leading English case concerning the exercise of the court's powers in a case such as this, *South Bucks District Council v Porter* [2003] 2 AC 558. In particular, at [37] of his speech, he referred to the assessment of proportionality, and said that it was 'in all essentials the task which the court is in any event required by domestic law to carry out', when applying the normal yardstick of an SIC 'justice and convenience' in connection with the grant of an injunction, i.e. when the court is exercising its discretion. However, I would accept that the band, or margin, of acceptability accorded to the Judge will be, at least often, narrower on a question of proportionality, than on one of discretion. To put the point in more practical terms, an appellate court should often be reluctant to interfere with a decision turning on proportionality, than with one which only turns on discretion.[663]

## Where no explanation is required

4.472 The above discussion shows that there are some cases in which a tribunal is not expected to explain how it made a finding or why it preferred particular evidence. These cases are limited and fall into two categories: (i) cases in which an explanation is not possible; and (ii) cases in which an explanation is possible but not required.[664]

4.473 Cases in category (i) are those in which it is impossible either to identify the particular factors that have influenced the tribunal (such as the nuances in the witness's delivery of the evidence) or to excavate the mental process of analysis (such as a complex issue of judgment).[665]

4.474 Cases in category (ii) are rare. But there is some authority that they include, at least so far as summary reasons are concerned, cases in which an expert tribunal has had to chose between conflicting opinion within its expertise.[666]

---

662  [2004] EWCA Civ 1378 at [7].

663  [2004] EWCA Civ 1378 at [42]–[43].

664  This classification is similar to that of Stephen Toulmin in *The Uses of Argument*, Cambridge, 2003, pp223–226.

665  *S (A Minor) v Special Educational Needs Tribunal* [1995] 1 WLR 1627 at 1636.

666  As in *H v East Sussex County Council* [2009] ELR 161.

## Irrelevant issues

4.475    If particular facts or issues are irrelevant given the way that the tribunal deals with the case, it is not necessary to deal with them in the reasons. In effect, those issues become of abstract interest only.[667]

4.476    In *Eagil Trust Co Ltd v Pigott-Brown*,[668] Griffiths LJ set the duty to give reasons in the context of the decision given by the court: 'It is sufficient if what he says shows the parties and, if need be, the Court of Appeal the basis on which he has acted.'[669]

4.477    This applies even if the issue that becomes irrelevant is the main argument of one of the parties to the proceedings.[670]

## Inconsistent decisions

4.478    A tribunal may have to decide afresh an issue that was previously determined by another tribunal in separate proceedings. For example: the same issue of fact may arise in respect of a later period of claim for a benefit. If the tribunal at the later hearing is not bound by the conclusion of the earlier tribunal and comes to a different conclusion, it is not necessary for it to explain specifically why. It is sufficient for the later tribunal to explain why it made the decision that it did on the evidence.[671]

## Procedural discretion

4.479    The standard required of reasons varies. In *Eagil Trust Co Ltd v Pigott-Brown*,[672] Griffiths LJ said of a judge's duty to give reasons:

> . . . the particularity with which he is required to set them out must depend on the circumstances of the case before him and the nature of the decision he is giving.[673]

4.480    One group of decisions in which a tribunal need not give reasons is those involving the exercise of some procedural discretions. For example: a chairman need not explain why one order of procedure is being followed rather than another. In *Capital and Suburban Properties Ltd v Swyche*,[674] Buckley LJ set out the approach and indicated its limit:

> There are some sorts of interlocutory applications, mainly of a purely procedural kind, upon which a judge exercising his discretion on some such question as whether a matter should be expedited or adjourned or extra time be allowed for a party to take some procedural step, or possibly whether relief by way of injunction should be granted or refused, can properly make

---

667  See chapter 7.
668  [1985] 3 All ER 119.
669  [1985] 3 All ER 119 at 122.
670  The Court of Appeal in *The Post Office v Lewis* (1997) *Times* 25 April.
671  Roskill LJ in *R v National Insurance Commissioner ex p Viscusi* [1974] 1 WLR 646 at 658–659. See chapter 14 for a fuller discussion and *Higgins v France* (1998) 27 EHRR 703 at [43], discussed below.
672  [1985] 3 All ER 119.
673  [1985] 3 All ER 119 at 122.
674  [1976] Ch 319.

an order without giving reasons. This, being an application involving questions of law, is in my opinion clearly not such a case.[675]

4.481 But if the discretion is exercised in a particularly unusual manner, the tribunal must give reasons.[676]

### Packages of reasons

4.482 Sometimes there is a flaw in one or some, but not all, of the reasons given by a tribunal for its decision. In *De Silva v Social Security Commissioner*,[677] the Court of Appeal held that a mistake in one of the examples given in support of one of a number of reasons rendered the tribunal's reasons inadequate. In *HK v Secretary of State for the Home Department*[678] and without reference to *De Silva*, the Court of Appeal took a different approach. Neuberger LJ explained:[679]

> Of course, as Jacob LJ said in argument, the issue cannot be resolved simply by asking how many of the Tribunal's reasons survive. The issue has to be determined partly by reference to the probative value of those reasons, both in absolute terms and by comparison with the rejected reasons, and objectively, but also subjectively, in the sense of seeing what weight the tribunal gave to the various reasons it gave. The issue also has to be determined bearing in mind the overall picture including reasons which a tribunal would have had, but which were not expressed. An example would be the impression made by a witness (a factor which is not, in my view, high in the hierarchy of cogency, especially in an asylum case which will normally involve an appellant from a very different cultural background from that of the Tribunal).[680]

### Reasons actually given

4.483 Tribunals do not necessarily limit their reasons to what is required in law. If a tribunal gives reasons that are not required, they may nonetheless indicate that the tribunal went wrong in law. Such indications cannot be ignored. There is no immunity for a tribunal in respect of reasons beyond the legal requirement.

## The flexibility of the standard

4.484 The standard of adequacy requires the court or Upper Tribunal to make a value judgment. This allows sufficient flexibility for adjustment to the standard, either generally or in an individual case.

4.485 Generally, this flexibility allows the Upper Tribunal to adjust the standard it applies to the adequacy of reasons given by the First-tier Tribunal in order to take account of the general standard of reasons that are given at that level. If the Upper Tribunal is generally satisfied with the standard of

---

675 [1976] Ch 319 at 325–326.
676 See above.
677 [2001] EWCA Civ 539.
678 [2006] EWCA Civ 1037.
679 [2006] EWCA Civ 1037 at [46].
680 See also Lord Neuberger in *Holmes-Moorhouse v Richmond upon Thames London Borough Council* [2009] 1 WLR 413 at [51].

reasons, it may be forgiving of deficiencies in individual cases. But if it is not generally satisfied with the standard, it may set a higher standard as a way of correcting the general deficiency.

4.486    In an individual case, the flexibility allows the Upper Tribunal the opportunity of identifying a deficiency in the reasons as an error of law in order to give effect to its sense that something has gone wrong in the case such that a reconsideration of the facts or of their application is appropriate.

## The consequence of failing to give adequate reasons

4.487    The predominant view is that inadequacy of reasons is, of itself, an error of law. Sir John Donaldson, the President of the National Industrial Relations Court, set this proposition in the context of the function of reasons. In *Norton Tool Co Ltd v Tewson*,[681] he referred to an industrial tribunal's duty to assess compensation for unfair dismissal and said:

> But it is a corollary of the discretion conferred upon the tribunals that it is their duty to set out their reasoning in sufficient detail to show the principles upon which they have proceeded ... Were it otherwise, the parties would in effect be deprived of their right of appeal on questions of law. No great elaboration is required and the task should not constitute a burden. Indeed, the need to give reasons may well assist in the process of properly making the discretionary assessment of damages.[682]

And in *Alexander Machinery (Dudley) Ltd v Crabtree*,[683] he said:

> The basis of this proposition is that in the absence of reasons it is impossible to determine whether or not there has been an error of law. Failure to give reasons therefore amounts to a denial of justice and is itself an error of law.[684]

4.488    This approach has also been taken by the Court of Appeal. In *Flannery v Halifax Estate Agencies Ltd*,[685] Henry LJ summarised the Court's reasons for directing a new trial:

> ... this judge was under a duty to give reasons and did not do so. Without such reasons, his judgment is not transparent, and we cannot know whether the judge had adequate or inadequate reasons for the conclusion he reached.[686]

This approach did not assume that the reasons accurately reflected the judge's incomplete reasoning. It was directly based on the inadequacy of the reasons:

> It should not be assumed that the court that (for whatever reason) failed to give reasons had no reasons. Here, for example, it seems likely that the judge believed he had said enough. In that we differ from him.[687]

---

681  [1973] 1 WLR 45.
682  [1973] 1 WLR 45 at 49.
683  [1974] ICR 120.
684  [1974] ICR 120 at 122.
685  [2001] 1 WLR 377.
686  [2001] 1 WLR 377 at 383.
687  [2001] 1 WLR 377 at 383.

4.489　There was previously a conflict of view. Some cases treated inadequacy of reasons as an error of law,[688] whilst others took the view that an inadequacy in the reasons was merely evidence of an error in the tribunal's approach to the case.[689] Woolf J attempted to update and reconcile the authorities in *Crake v Supplementary Benefits Commission*.[690] He distinguished those cases in which legislation provided for a decision to be quashed if the reasons given for it were inadequate.[691] Otherwise, it was likely that inadequate reasons would indicate some error of law in the tribunal's approach to the decision.[692] However, this reconciliation was difficult to sustain, especially as the tribunal in *Crake* was under a duty to provide a written statement of its reasons for decision. It was quickly distinguished in the social security context[693] and the fiction that the reasons reflected the tribunal's approach to the case was not adopted in *Flannery*.

4.490　However, the inadequacy of reasons does not necessarily mean that a rehearing is appropriate. Depending on the terms of the tribunal's powers on an appeal, it may be possible to substitute a decision to the same effect without a rehearing or simply to dismiss the appeal. In the Court of Appeal in *Carpenter v Secretary of State for Work and Pensions*,[694] Laws LJ said of a possible failure to give reasons for refusing to adjourn:

> If it is clear that the adjournment was in fact refused for good reason, but the expression of that good reason was insufficient and failed to fulfil applicable legal standards, that failure would not, in my judgment, of itself necessarily justify this court in allowing the appeal. The legal defect constituted by the tribunal's failure to express sufficient reasons would, or at least might, be remedied by this court declaring that the reasons were in truth legally insufficient, even though the appeal were dismissed. Such an approach would be in line with the Strasbourg jurisprudence within which the European Court of Human Rights has often said that its declaration of a particular position, without any further relief being granted, sufficiently vindicates whatever is the Convention right in question.[695]

## Summary reasons

4.491　Some rules of procedure require that tribunals give only summary reasons. For example: regulation 55(3) of the Special Educational Needs Tribunal for Wales Regulations 2012 requires a tribunal to provide 'a statement of the reasons (in summary form) for the tribunal's decision'.

4.492　Summary form may set a less demanding standard than the usual test of adequacy. In *H v East Sussex County Council*,[696] Waller LJ said:

> Summary reasons should not contain a fully comprehensive analysis or spell out every step in the reasoning or deal with every conceivable point;

---

688　Megaw J in *Re Poyser and Mills Arbitration* [1964] 2 QB 467 and *Givaudan & Co Ltd v Minister of Housing and Local Government* [1967] 1 WLR 250.

689　*Mountview Court Properties Ltd v Devlin* (1970) 21 P&CR 689.

690　[1982] 1 All ER 498.

691　[1982] 1 All ER 498 at 507.

692　[1982] 1 All ER 498: see 507–508 for his reasoning.

693　*R(SB) 11/92* at [13]–[14].

694　[2003] EWCA Civ 33, reported as *R(IB) 6/03*.

695　[2003] EWCA Civ 33, reported as *R(IB) 6/03* at [12].

696　[2009] ELR 161.

their purpose (as Donaldson LJ put it [in *UCATT v Brain* [1981] IRLR 225 at 227]) is to tell the parties in broad terms why they lost or won.[697]

On that basis, there is little if any difference between the standards for summary reasons and other reasons.

4.493    The rules of procedure under TCEA do not permit summary reason. However, they may provide that reasons need only be provided on request[698] or that they may be dispensed with by consent.[699]

## Supplementary reasons

4.494   A deficiency in a tribunal's reasons may become apparent at three stages. It may appear when the reasons are given but before the decision is promulgated. Or it may appear when an application is made for permission to appeal. Or it may appear on an appeal or judicial review. There is power at each of these stages for the reasons to be supplemented. At whatever stage they are provided, the additional reasons fulfil three functions. They allow the appellate tribunal or court to exercise its jurisdiction. They will show whether the tribunal's reasons for its decision were adequate. And they may show that in a discretion jurisdiction[700] it is not appropriate to grant relief.[701]

4.495    The principles apply both to adversarial jurisdictions and inquisitorial jurisdictions.[702]

### Before promulgation

4.496   If the reasons are given before the decision is promulgated, the parties may invite the tribunal to supplement its reasons.[703] There is limited scope for this in a tribunal, as the reasons will often be given either as part of the decision when it is promulgated or provided later.

### After promulgation

4.497   The following sections deal with the power to supplement reasons after promulgation. A three-judge panel of the Upper Tribunal has decided that these authorities are inconsistent with the review power under of TCEA s9.[704] They are retained as they are relevant to tribunals that have no review power.

---

697  [2009] EWCA Civ 249 at [19].

698  See SEC Rules r34(3).

699  See: UTR r40(3); GRC Rules r37(2); HESC Rules r29(2); Lands Rules r51(3); SEC Rules r32(2); Tax Rules r34(2). There is no equivalent power in the IAC Rules.

700  Judicial review is discretionary.

701  Hutchison LJ in *R v Westminster City Council ex p Ermakov* [1996] 2 All ER 302 at 313 and 316(4).

702  Arden LJ in *Re T (Contact: Alienation: Permission to Appeal)* [2003] 1 FLR 531 at [40].

703  Arden LJ in *Re T (Contact: Alienation: Permission to Appeal)* [2003] 1 FLR 531 at [41]; Thorpe LJ in *Re B (Appeal: Lack of Reasons)* [2003] 2 FLR 1035 at [5].

704  *JS v Secretary of State for Work and Pensions* [2013] UKUT 100 (AAC) at [2]–[3].

## On application for permission to appeal

4.498  If the decision has been promulgated, the reasons may be supplemented on an application for permission to appeal, at the judge's own initiative, at the request of the parties, or at the invitation of the appellate body.[705] This may avoid the need for an appeal.[706] But the power must be exercised appropriately. In *Brewer v Mann*,[707] the Court of Appeal analysed the authorities and said:

> ... where a judge has received no request from the parties to reconsider his judgment or add to his reasons, and has not demonstrated the need in conscience to revisit his judgment, but on the contrary has received grounds of appeal and an application for permission to appeal on the basis of the alleged inadequacies of his judgment, then it would be most unwise for him to rewrite his judgment (other than purely editorially) and it would take the most extraordinary reasons, if any, to justify such a course on his part. It is also plain to us that this was not the case of a short judgment on a straightforward issue where an appeal might be avoided if the judge supplied further reasoning which had been requested of him.[708]

## On appeal or judicial review

4.499  Once a decision has been promulgated, there may also be power to direct, or at least request and allow, a tribunal to supplement its reasons. This is a case management power, the exercise of which will be treated with respect on a further appeal.[709]

4.500  Under TCEA, the rules of procedure allow the Upper Tribunal to direct the First-tier Tribunal below to supplement the terms of its decision. UTR r5(3)(n) provides that the Upper Tribunal may:

> require any person, body or other tribunal whose decision is the subject of proceedings before the Upper Tribunal to provide reasons for the decision, or other information or documents in relation to the decision or any proceedings before that person, body or tribunal.

4.501  The Upper Tribunal has refused to use this power rather than to remit the case for a rehearing after deciding that the tribunal's reasons were inadequate.[710]

4.502  According to the Court of Appeal in *Hatungimana v Secretary of State for the Home Department*,[711] a power to obtain supplementary reasons only arises from provisions such as this and, in the absence of such a provision, the power cannot be exercised. This appears to overlook CPR 52.10.2(b), which allows the High Court on a statutory appeal to refer any issue back for determination.[712]

---

705 *English v Emery Reimbold & Strick Ltd* [2002] 1 WLR 2409 at [25].

706 *Re A (a child) (Duty to seek reasons)* (2007) *Times* 16 October.

707 [2012] EWCA Civ 246.

708 [2012] EWCA Civ 246 at [31].

709 *Barke v SEETEC Business Technology Centre Ltd* [2005] ICR 1373 at [49].

710 *CT v Secretary of State for Defence* [2009] UKUT 167 (AAC) at [40]–[41].

711 [2006] EWCA Civ 231 at [4]–[8]; (2006) *Times* 2 March.

712 *Adami v Ethical Standards Officer of the Standards Board for English* (2005) *Times* 2 December.

4.503    Apart from any specific provision, there is power to direct[713] or invite[714] a tribunal to provide or supplement its reasons. It is used on an appeal by remission of the case.[715] It is also used on judicial review, although more restrictively.[716] It may be used to require a tribunal to give reasons under what used to be called an order of mandamus.[717] And it may be used to protect the court's jurisdiction to grant what used to be called certiorari in the case of error of law on the face of the record. Otherwise, if the tribunal does not provide a record, or an adequate record, it would thereby protect its decision from judicial review. As Lord Denning MR explained in *R v Medical Appeal Tribunal ex p Gilmore*:[718] 'It seems to me that the tribunal cannot, by failing to find the material facts, defeat an application for certiorari. The court has always had power to order an inferior tribunal to complete the record.'[719]

4.504    The power has also been used by the Employment Appeal Tribunal.[720] It was disapproved in *Reuben v Brent London Borough Council*[721] on the ground that the employment tribunal was *functus officio* once its decision had been promulgated. But this was held to be wrong in *Barke v SEETEC Business Technology Centre Ltd*.[722]

4.505    In *Hicks v Russell Jones and Walker (a firm)*,[723] the Court of Appeal decided that, pending an appeal, the Court could refer a case back to a judge to make further findings of fact, supplementary to the original judgment, on an issue that might be relevant on the appeal. This power would only be exercised exceptionally and if the judge was agreeable.[724] The Court relied in part on the terms of an express power in CPR.

4.506    Supplementary reasons may be used on appeal as a way of overcoming an invalid attempt to correct a tribunal's decision or reasons.[725]

4.507    In *Brisset v Brisset*,[726] the Court of Appeal emphasised that additional information about a tribunal's reasons should only be obtained formally through the use of these powers and not by more informal contact such as may exist between the judges of the Upper Tribunal and the First-tier Tribunal. Wilson LJ said that judges at different levels had to maintain a Chinese wall between themselves in relation to pending appeals.[727] Jacob

---

713  As in *Mountview Court Properties Ltd v Devlin Properties* (1970) 21 P&CR 689 at 693.

714  As in *Barke v SEETEC Business Technology Centre Ltd* [2005] ICR 1373 at [29].

715  Lord Parker CJ in *Mountview Court Properties Ltd v Devlin Properties* (1970) 21 P&CR 689 at 693.

716  *Barke v SEETEC Business Technology Centre Ltd* [2005] ICR 1373 at [35]–[40].

717  Lord Parker CJ in *Mountview Court Properties Ltd v Devlin Properties* (1970) 21 P&CR 689 at 693.

718  [1957] 1 QB 574. Lord Denning MR also suggested that this power could be used on an appeal in *R v Deputy Industrial Injuries Commissioner ex p Howarth* reported as an Appendix to *R(I) 14/68*.

719  [1957] 1 QB 574 at 582–583.

720  *Yusuf v Aberplace Ltd* [1984] ICR 850 at 853–854.

721  [2000] ICR 102.

722  [2005] ICR 1373 at [25]–[28].

723  [2008] 2 All ER 1089.

724  [2008] 2 All ER 1089 at [15] and [25].

725  *Bone v Newham London Borough Council* [2008] ICR 923.

726  [2009] EWCA Civ 679.

727  [2009] EWCA Civ 679 at [11].

LJ said that 'what a judge cannot do is get involved in the appeal process itself'.[728] And Sedley LJ said:

> The collegiality which is an essential part of judicial life cannot be allowed to intrude into the forensic space which necessarily separates lower tribunals from those with oversight of their decisions.[729]

## Limitations

4.508 According to the Court of Appeal in *Barke v SEETEC Business Technology Centre Ltd,*[730] the power should not be used sparingly or restrictively.[731] It may be used to obtain reasons that elucidate the reasons that have been given or to supplement them in order to deal with matters that have been omitted.[732] However, they will be treated with scepticism if they change the reasons that have been given. Supplementary reasons must be the reasons that led to the decision and not a later rationalisation[733] or an attempt to deal with issues that the tribunal did not in fact consider. In *Barke*, the Court of Appeal warned of this risk:

> ... there are dangers in asking the original tribunal for further reasons where the ground of appeal is inadequacy of reasoning. It will not be appropriate where the inadequacy of reasoning is on its face so fundamental that there is a real risk that supplementary reasons will be reconstructions of proper reasons, rather than the unexpressed actual reasons for the decision. Nor will it be appropriate where there have been allegations of bias (unless, perhaps, where these are manifestly unfounded). The employment appeal tribunal should always be alive to the danger that an employment tribunal might tailor its response to a request for explanations or further reasons (usually subconsciously rather than deliberately) so as to put the decision in the best possible light.[734]

4.509 Supplementary reasons are of no value if the tribunal could not realistically be expected to recall its reasoning. In *Flannery v Halifax Estate Agencies Ltd,*[735] the Court of Appeal considered that it would not be realistic to expect the judge to reconstitute his reasons more than a year after the hearing. Nor should supplementary reasons be sought if they would require further analysis that would be incompatible with the reasons already given.[736]

4.510 If the remedy sought is discretionary and the reasons given were manifestly flawed, it will seldom be possible to avoid relief by providing supplementary reasons.[737]

728 [2009] EWCA Civ 679 at [24].

729 [2009] EWCA Civ 679 at [29].

730 [2005] EWCA Civ 578.

731 [2005] EWCA Civ 578 at [43].

732 See the directions given by the National Industrial Relations Court (replaced by the Employment Appeal Tribunal) in *Alexander Machinery (Dudley) Ltd v Crabtree* [1974] ICR 120 at 122 and by the Court of Appeal in *Re B (Appeal: Lack of Reasons)* [2003] 2 FLR 1035 at [15].

733 *R v Parole Board ex p Gittens* (1994) *Times* 3 February.

734 [2005] EWCA Civ 578 at [19].

735 [2000] 1 WLR 377 at 383.

736 *Re M-W (Care proceedings: expert evidence)* [2010] 2 FLR 46 at [47].

737 Hutchison LJ in *R v Westminster City Council ex p Ermakov* [1996] 2 All ER 302 at 316(4) and Collins J in *R v Lambeth London Borough Council Housing Benefit Review Board ex p Harrington* (1996) *Times* 10 December.

## Procedure

4.511  If a tribunal is required or invited to provide supplementary reasons, there should be liberty for the parties to apply for this request to be varied or discharged.[738]

### Duty to provide reasons at the time of decision

4.512  The above authorities do not apply if a decision-maker is under a statutory duty to give reasons in, or annexed to, its decision, but it is an open question whether this factor is relevant in the case of a tribunal's decision.[739]

### Cross-examination

4.513  The members of a tribunal that provides supplementary reasons cannot be cross-examined about them.[740]

### Dealing with an omitted issue

4.514  The Court of Appeal has also taken account of reasons given by a judge on an issue that was omitted from the original judgment and the subject of later argument.[741] This avoided the expense of a rehearing.

## Reasons for refusing permission to appeal

4.515  It is not permissible to challenge a tribunal's decision by reference to the reasons it gives for refusing permission to appeal.[742]

## Reasons under article 6

4.516  There is no express requirement in article 6(1) that a tribunal must give reasons for its decision. However, the Strasbourg jurisprudence has held that there is a requirement.

4.517      The law under article 6(1) is very similar to domestic law. However, it is appropriate to consider it separately for two reasons. First, cases which are not governed by article 6(1) must still be determined solely under the domestic law. Second, the Privy Council has suggested that the Human Rights Act 1998 may provide the impetus for a reconsideration of domestic law towards a general duty to give reasons.[743]

4.518      The basic test is linked to the underlying rationale for the requirement to give reasons. This was explained in *Hadjianastassiou v Greece*:[744]

> The national courts must, however, indicate with sufficient clarity the grounds on which they based their decision. It is this, *inter alia*, which

738  *Barke v SEETEC Business Technology Centre Ltd* [2005] ICR 1373 at [49].

739  *Barke v SEETEC Business Technology Centre Ltd* [2005] ICR 1373 at [37], although in *VK v Norfolk County Council* (2005) *Times* 6 January, the High Court decided that reasons could not be substantially supplemented in these circumstances.

740  *Barke v SEETEC Business Technology Centre Ltd* [2005] ICR 1373 at [39].

741  *Roche v Chief Constable of Greater Manchester Police* (2005) *Times* 10 November.

742  *Albion Water Ltd v Dŵr Cymru Cyf* [2009] 2 All ER 279 at [67].

743  *Stefan v General Medical Council* [1999] 1 WLR 1293 at 1301.

744  (1992) 16 EHRR 219.

makes it possible for the accused to exercise usefully the rights of appeal available to him.[745]

4.519 However, this does not require a tribunal to deal with every issue or argument raised in the proceedings. In *Van de Hurk v The Netherlands*,[746] the Court explained that:

> Article 6(1) obliges courts to give reasons for their decisions, but cannot be understood as requiring a detailed answer to every argument. Nor is the European Court called upon to examine whether arguments are adequately met. Making a general assessment, the Court does not find that the judgment of the Industrial Appeals Tribunal is insufficiently reasoned.[747]

4.520 The extent of the duty to give reasons depends on the circumstances of the case. In *Ruiz Torija v Spain*,[748] the Court said:

> The extent to which this duty to give reasons applies may vary according to the nature of the decision. It is moreover necessary to take into account, *inter alia*, the diversity of the submissions that a litigant may bring before the courts and the differences existing in the Contracting States with regard to statutory provisions, customary rules, legal opinion and the presentation and drafting of judgments. That is why the question whether a court has failed to fulfil the obligation to state reasons, deriving from Article 6 of the Convention, can only be determined in the light of the circumstances of the case.[749]

4.521 A relevant factor is the significance of the issues raised. In *Helle v Finland*,[750] the Court said:

> The notion of a fair procedure requires that a national court which has given sparse reasons for its decisions, whether by incorporating the reasons of a lower court or otherwise, did in fact address the essential issues which were submitted to its jurisdiction and did not merely endorse without further ado the findings reached by a lower court. This requirement is all the more important where a litigant has not been able to present his case orally in the domestic proceedings.[751]

4.522 An issue is obviously essential for this purpose if it would be decisive. In *Ruiz Torija v Spain*,[752] the Court held that the domestic court should have given 'a specific and express reply' to a limitation argument that would have been decisive.[753]

4.523 An explanation is also required if a tribunal takes a different approach in one of a series of related cases.[754]

4.524 The reasoning of the European Court accepts that the reason for a decision may be apparent without explanation. See its consideration of

---

745 (1992) 16 EHRR 219 at [33].
746 (1994) 18 EHRR 481.
747 (1994) 18 EHRR 481 at [61].
748 (1994) 19 EHRR 553.
749 (1994) 19 EHRR 553 at [29].
750 (1997) 26 EHRR 159.
751 (1997) 26 EHRR 159 at [60].
752 (1994) 19 EHRR 553.
753 (1994) 19 EHRR 553 at [30].
754 *Higgins v France* (1998) 27 EHRR 703 at [43].

whether 'silence . . . can reasonably be construed as an implied rejection' in *Ruiz Torija v Spain*[755] and *Hiro Balani v Spain*.[756]

## Delay in providing reasons

4.525    See *Nash v Chelsea College*,[757] discussed at paragraph 4.343.

## Tribunals and Inquiries Act 1992 s10

4.526    This is a default provision that applies to those tribunals that are specified in Schedule 1 to the Act. It applies only in the absence of legislative provision as to the giving of reasons.[758]

4.527    For those tribunals that are subject to the duty, it arises only on request made on or before the decision is given or notified.[759] The section does not specify who may or may not request reasons. There is a clue in section 10(3). This provides that the tribunal may refuse to furnish a statement to 'a person not primarily concerned with the decision if of the opinion that to furnish it would be contrary to the interests of any person primarily concerned'. Obviously the parties to the proceedings may request a statement. But it is unclear who else may make a request.

4.528    The duty to furnish a statement is imposed on the tribunal,[760] not on the presiding judge. But in practice it is likely that that judge will discharge the duty.

4.529    The tribunal's duty is to furnish a statement of the reasons for the decision.[761] As the reasons have to be those for the decision, they must be the tribunal's reasons and not just the reasons of the judge writing the statement. The reasons may be provided orally or in writing.[762]

4.530    The statement may be refused, or the contents restricted, on grounds of national security.[763]

4.531    There is power for the Lord Chancellor and the Lord Advocate, after consulting the Council on Tribunals, to exempt decisions of a particular tribunal or decisions of a particular description from the duty under section 10.[764] The power does not extend to any duty to give reasons other than section 10.

## Reasons and the tribunal's record

4.532    Section 10(6) of the Tribunals and Inquiries Act 1992 provides that a statement of the reasons for a tribunal's decision is part of that decision and, as

755  (1994) 19 EHRR 553 at [30].
756  (1994) 19 EHRR 566 at [28].
757  [2001] EWHC 538 (Admin).
758  Tribunals and Inquiries Act 1992 s10(5)(a).
759  Tribunals and Inquiries Act 1992 s10(1).
760  Tribunals and Inquiries Act 1992 s10(1).
761  Tribunals and Inquiries Act 1992 s10(1).
762  Tribunals and Inquiries Act 1992 s10(1).
763  Tribunals and Inquiries Act 1992 s10(2).
764  Tribunals and Inquiries Act 1992 s10(7)–(8).

such, is incorporated in the record. This applies to all statements, whether given under section 10 of the Act or any other legislative provision.

4.533     This was significant for the purposes of certiorari when it lay on the ground of error on the face of the record. However, that head of review has now subsumed into wider grounds of judicial review and is no longer of practical significance.

# Referrals

# Nature of a referral

## Types of referral

5.1   A referral[1] is a means by which a case is brought before a tribunal. As a form of initiating proceedings, they are not unique to tribunals.[2]

5.2   There are various types of referral. They may broadly be divided into three categories: those that initiate proceedings; those that enforce proceedings in another tribunal; and those that are purely a formal step in proceedings.

## Referrals that initiate proceedings

5.3   These referrals may be made in exercise of a power or a duty. They may be made by another tribunal, by a decision-maker or someone closely connected with the decision-maker, by a public body, or by an official.

5.4   In one type, a person or body that has jurisdiction to decide a case alternatively has power to pass it higher up the hierarchy of decision-making. The transfer of the case from one level of decision-making to the other is the referral. It is a permissible abdication of the responsibility for making a decision. The referral may be made by a decision-maker to a tribunal. For example: the Secretary of State may refer an application for a child support variation to the First-tier Tribunal.[3] The referral may also be made by one tribunal to another. For example: following a review, the First-tier tribunal may refer a matter to the Upper Tribunal.[4] This referral does not require the permission of the Upper Tribunal or the consent of any Chamber President.

5.5   In a second type, an issue may arise that is outside the jurisdiction of the person or body before whom it arises and has to be transferred to a decision-maker who has jurisdiction. That may be a tribunal. This differs from the first type in that the referral here is in exercise of a duty, not a power, as the person or body has no jurisdiction to decide the issue. There is no abdication of the responsibility for making a decision. For example: the Secretary of State must refer to the Upper Tribunal the issue whether a claimant may be relieved from forfeiture of the benefit of another's national insurance contributions as a result of having caused the death of that person.[5] Also: if a decision-maker objects to the appeal being treated as made in time, it must be referred to the First-tier Tribunal under rule 23(7) of the SEC Rules.

---

1   Referral and reference are interchangeable. Both are found in legislation. Here the former is used. Confusingly, UTR r1(3) defines 'reference' as including an appeal in a financial services case.

2   For example: National Health Service Reform and Health Care Professionals Act 2002 s29(4), although s 29(8) then refers to the proceedings as an appeal. This provision was discussed in *Council for the Regulation of Health Care Professionals v General Medical Council and Saluja* [2007] 1 WLR 3094.

3   Child Support Act 1991 s28D(1)(b).

4   TCEA s9(5)(b). The procedure before the Upper Tribunal is governed by Lands Rules r45 and UTR r26A. Previously a medical appeal tribunal had power to refer a question of law to a Commissioner under the Social Security Act 1975 s112(4).

5   UTR r26 under the Forfeiture Act 1982 s4.

5.6 In a third type, the decision-maker, or someone closely connected with the decision-maker, may refer a decision that has been made to a tribunal for reconsideration. Like the first type but unlike the second, the referral here is in exercise of a power, not a duty. And like the second type but unlike the first, there is no abdication of the responsibility of making a decision; it has already been made. For example: under previous legislation an assessment of disablement for benefit purposes could be referred to a medical appeal tribunal for reconsideration.[6]

5.7 In a fourth type, a public body or official is given the power to refer a question to a tribunal for consideration. For example: the Attorney-General may refer a question to the Upper Tribunal or First-tier Tribunal.[7]

5.8 In a fifth type, a public body or official is under a duty to refer a question to a tribunal for consideration. For example: the case of a recalled mental patient must be referred to the First-tier Tribunal.[8]

## Transfer of cases

5.9 Tribunals have the case management power to transfer cases to another court or tribunal under UTR r5(3)(k) and its equivalents.[9] In addition, the First-tier Tribunal has some specific powers of transfer. Under Tax Rules, a complex case can be transferred to the Upper Tribunal (r28). And under WPAFC Rules, a case can be transferred to Scotland or Northern Ireland if the appellant was resident outside the United Kingdom when the appeal was lodged and there is a good reason for the transfer, such as a closer connection with one of those jurisdictions (r19). This power is necessary because the Pensions Appeal Tribunals for Scotland and Northern Ireland retain their separate existence.

5.10 The procedure before the Upper Tribunal on a transfer is governed by Lands Rules r45 and UTR r26A.

5.11 Although transfers and referrals are treated differently under the rules of procedure, they are, in substance, equivalent.

## Referrals for enforcement by another tribunal

5.12 Paragraph 10(3) of Schedule 5 TCEA provides an enabling power for the First-tier Tribunal to refer to the Upper Tribunal a failure to comply with a direction on the attendance and examination of witnesses or the production and inspection of documents. Rule 7(3) of the HESC Rules is illustrative of the provision made under that authority:[10]

6 Under the Social Security Administration Act 1992 s46(3), now repealed. The referral was by an adjudication officer, although the decision referred was not made by an adjudication officer.

7 Charities Act 1993 Sch 1D para 2, inserted by the Charities Act 2006 Sch 4.

8 Mental Health Act 1983 ss66(4) and 75(1)(a). This procedure complies with the European Convention on Human Rights and Fundamental Freedoms: *R (Rayner) v Secretary of State for Justice* [2009] 1 WLR 310. For other referrals under the 1983 Act, see ss67, 68 and 71.

9 GRC Rules r5(3)(k); HESC Rules r5(3)(k); IAC Rules r4(2)(k); Lands Rules r55(3)(k); PC Rules r6(3)(n); SEC Rules r5(3)(k); Tax Rules r5(3)(k); WPAFC Rules r5(3)(k).

10 See also: GRC Rules r7(3); IAC Rules r6(3); PC Rules r8(5); SEC Rules r7(3); Tax Rules r7(3); WPAFC Rules r7(3).

(3) The Tribunal may refer to the Upper Tribunal, and ask the Upper Tribunal to exercise its power under section 25 of the 2007 Act in relation to, any failure by a person to comply with a requirement imposed by the Tribunal –

(a) to attend at any place for the purpose of giving evidence;
(b) otherwise to make themselves available to give evidence;
(c) to swear an oath in connection with the giving of evidence;
(d) to give evidence as a witness;
(e) to produce a document; or
(f) to facilitate the inspection of a document or any other thing (including any premises).

5.13   On a referral, the Upper Tribunal is able to exercise its enforcement powers under TCEA s25, which are the same as those of the High Court.

## Referrals that are a formal step in proceedings

5.14   This is not a separate way of beginning proceedings, but merely an administrative stage in making an appeal. An appeal may be lodged with one body that has to refer it to a tribunal for decision. For example: an appeal against a certificate of recoverable benefit must be referred to the First-tier Tribunal.[11]

5.15   If the body fails to refer the case to the tribunal, it may nonetheless have jurisdiction. In *R(H) 1/07*, the Commissioner was concerned with an appeal in a housing benefit case. Under the legislation, it was lodged with the local authority which had to refer it to the tribunal. The local authority had failed to refer the case. The Commissioner held that the tribunal had jurisdiction despite the local authority's failure to take this administrative step.

5.16   If the tribunal does not have jurisdiction without a referral, the remedy for failure to refer is judicial review. A practical alternative is to alert the tribunal, which may be able to ensure that the referral is made.

## Obligation to provide a referral system

5.17   There is, generally, no obligation to provide for a system for referral. Exceptionally, there may be. In *R (H) v Secretary of State for Health*, the Court of Appeal[12] decided that if a claimant lacked the mental capacity to take his case to a tribunal on appeal, it might be necessary for the State to provide for a form of referral to ensure access to an independent tribunal. However, on appeal the House of Lords[13] decided that this was not necessary under the Mental Health Act 1983.

## Scope of a referral

5.18   This has not been considered in the case-law.

---

11  Social Security (Recovery of Benefits) Act 1997 s12(1).
12  [2005] 1 WLR 1209.
13  [2006] 1 AC 441.

5.19    The scope of a referral will be determined by the legislation under which it is made. This may be further limited, if the legislation allows, by the terms of the reference to the tribunal. Usually, the reference will be limited to a live issue, but the legislation may provide that it also covers issues that may arise in the future.[14]

14  As does Forfeiture Act 1982 s4(1E).

# CHAPTER 6

# Other forms of procedure

# Judicial review

6.1   Judicial review is a means by which the High Court ensures that decisions are lawfully made within the authority conferred on the decision-making body.

## Judicial review in the Upper Tribunal in England and Wales

6.2   For judicial review generally, see Jonathan Manning, Sarah Salmon and Robert Brown *Judicial Review Proceedings.*[1]

6.3   The Lord Chief Justice has issued two directions transferring particular classes of case to the Upper Tribunal. They are set out in chapter 1. Otherwise, judicial review cases are transferred to the Upper Tribunal on a case by case basis. The proceedings before the Upper Tribunal are governed by UTR Part 4.

6.4   The Upper Tribunal should not slavishly follow the procedure for judicial review proceedings in the Administrative Court.[2]

6.5   In *R (Z) v Croydon London Borough Council,*[3] the Court of Appeal transferred an age assessment case to the Upper Tribunal. Sir Anthony May P explained why and the procedure that would be followed:

> The Administrative Court does not habitually decide questions of fact on contested evidence and is not generally equipped to do so. Oral evidence is not normally a feature of judicial review proceedings or statutory appeals. ... Transfer to the Upper Tribunal is appropriate because the judges there have experience of assessing the ages of children from abroad in the context of disputed asylum claims. If an age assessment judicial review claim is started in the Administrative Court, the Administrative Court will normally decide whether permission should be granted before considering whether to transfer the claim to the Upper Tribunal. The matter could be transferred for permission also to be considered, but the Administrative Court should not give directions for the future conduct of the case after transfer, and in particular should not direct a rolled-up hearing in the Upper Tribunal.[4]

The Court rejected the argument that transfer was not appropriate in view of the applicant's vulnerable personal circumstances.[5]

## Judicial review in the Upper Tribunal in Scotland

6.6   There are no mandatory transfers of judicial review applications to the Upper Tribunal in Scotland. All judicial review proceedings must be commenced in the Court of Session.[6] There is a limited discretion to transfer cases under the Act of Sederunt (Transfer of Judicial Review Applications

---

1  3rd edition, Legal Action Group, 2013.
2  *Reed Employment plc v Commissioners for Her Majesty's Revenue and Customs* [2010] UKFTT 596 (TC) at [35].
3  [2011] PTSR 748.
4  [2011] PTSR 748 at [31].
5  [2011] PTSR 748 at [32].
6  *EF v Secretary of State for Work and Pensions* [2009] UKUT 92 (AAC).

from the Court of Session) 2008 (SSI 2008 No 357). Only those applications that fall exclusively within it may be transferred to the Upper Tribunal.[7]

## Judicial review of the Upper Tribunal

6.7 For the susceptibility of the Upper Tribunal to judicial review, see chapter 1.

## The grounds for judicial review

6.8 Lord Diplock listed the grounds on which judicial review lies in *Council for the Civil Service Unions v Minister for the Civil Service*:[8]

> Judicial review has I think developed to a stage today when without reiterating any analysis of the steps by which the development has come about, one can conveniently classify under three heads the grounds upon which administrative action is subject to control by judicial review. The first ground I would call 'illegality', the second 'irrationality' and the third 'procedural impropriety'. That is not to say that further development on a case by case basis may not in course of time add further grounds. I have in mind particularly the possible adoption in the future of the principle of 'proportionality' which is recognised in the administrative law of several of our fellow members of the European Economic Community . . .
>
> By 'illegality' as a ground of judicial review I mean that the decision-maker must understand correctly the law that regulates his decision-making power and must give effect to it . . .
>
> By 'irrationality' I mean what can now be succinctly referred to as '*Wednesbury* unreasonableness' (*Associated Provincial Picture Houses Ltd v Wednesbury Corporation* [1948] 1 KB 223). It applies to a decision that is so outrageous in its defiance of logic or of accepted moral standards that no sensible person who had applied his mind to the question to be decided could have arrived at it . . .
>
> I have described the third head as 'procedural impropriety' rather than failure to observe the basic rules of natural justice or failure to act with procedural fairness towards the person who will be affected by the decision. This is because susceptibility to judicial review under this head covers also failure by an administrative tribunal to observe rules of procedure that are expressly laid down in the legislative instrument by which its jurisdiction is conferred, even where such failure does not involve any denial of natural justice.

This is to some extent out-of-date but it provides a convenient indication of the core principles of judicial review.

---

7   Note by Lord Hodge in the *Petition of Sharon Currie* [2009] CSOH 145, in which the application alleged an error of law. Lord Hodge's reasoning can be read as meaning that a challenge to a procedural decision for an error of law that is not of a procedural nature (such as a lack of jurisdiction) would be outside the scope of mandatory transfers. In other words, the Act of Sederunt applies only to challenges on procedural grounds rather than to challenges of procedural decisions. A discretionary transfer was not possible, as the case involved a devolved matter – criminal injuries compensation.

8   [1985] AC 374 at 410–411.

## Illegality

6.9   If the decision-maker or tribunal has jurisdiction over a dispute but declines or fails to adjudicate, that decision is illegal in Lord Diplock's sense and subject to judicial review.[9] Likewise, if the decision-maker or tribunal has no jurisdiction, but does adjudicate.[10] Other errors of law are also subject to judicial review,[11] provided that they are relevant to the decision.[12] However, those other errors are not subject to judicial review if the decision of the decision-maker or tribunal is final and conclusive. It is more likely that a decision of a court will be held to be final and conclusive than that of a decision-maker or a tribunal.[13]

## Judicial review by specialist tribunal

6.10  The principles of judicial review are the same whether they are applied by the Administrative Court or by a specialist tribunal. In *Office of Fair Trading v IBA Healthcare Ltd*,[14] the Court of Appeal considered the scope of judicial review as applied under statute by the Competition Appeal Tribunal. The tribunal had decided that the principles were different on the ground that, unlike the Administrative Court, it was not a non-specialist court considering the decision of a specialist decision-maker, but a tribunal specialist in the area of decision-making. The Court of Appeal held that the ordinary principles of judicial review applied regardless of the specialism of the reviewing tribunal.[15]

## Judicial review and appeal

6.11  The Upper Tribunal set out the differences between an appeal and a judicial review in *LS v London Borough of Lambeth*:[16]

> Most importantly, the Upper Tribunal's power to substitute its own decision for a decision of the First-tier Tribunal that has been found to be erroneous on a point of law is far more limited in judicial review proceedings than its power to re-make the First-tier Tribunal's decision in appellate proceedings (compare section 17 of the 2007 Act with section 12). Also of importance is the fact that there is a power to award costs against an unsuccessful party in judicial review proceedings but no power to award costs in an appeal from the Social Entitlement Chamber of the First-tier Tribunal (see rule 10 of the Tribunal Procedure (Upper Tribunal) Rules 2008 (SI 2008/2698)). There are other distinctions between the procedures. Judicial review proceedings are more cumbersome than appellate procedures because they involve the tribunal as a party, even though the tribunal rarely takes any active part. Also, judicial review proceedings do not give

---

9  Lord Browne-Wilkinson in *R v Lord President of the Privy Council ex p Page* [1993] AC 682 at 698.
10  [1993] AC 682 per Lord Browne-Wilkinson at 698.
11  [1993] AC 682 per Lord Browne-Wilkinson at 701.
12  [1993] AC 682 per Lord Browne-Wilkinson at 702.
13  [1993] AC 682 per Lords Griffiths and Browne-Wilkinson at 693 and 703.
14  [2004] ICR 1364.
15  [2004] ICR 1364 at [51]–[53].
16  [2010] UKUT 461 (AAC).

the First-tier Tribunal an opportunity to review its decision under section 9 of the 2007 Act. Finally, the statutory provisions governing the grant of remedies in the event of a successful appeal under the 2007 Act differ from the combination of statutory provisions and common law principles which govern the grant of remedies on an application for judicial review – whether in the High Court in England and Wales, in the High Court in Northern Ireland, in the Court of Session by petition to its supervisory jurisdiction, or in the Upper Tribunal.[17]

6.12  Judicial review and appeal are not mutually exclusive. Their relationship was considered by the Court of Appeal in *R v Chief Constable of the Merseyside Police ex p Calveley*.[18] Sir John Donaldson MR explained the relationship in terms of the discretionary nature of judicial review, saying that if there was a right of appeal: 'the court, in the exercise of its discretion, will very rarely make this remedy [judicial review] available in these circumstances'.[19]

6.13  Glidewell LJ summarised the exception to the usual refusal to grant judicial review: 'Judicial review in such a case should only be granted in exceptional circumstances'.[20]

6.14  And May LJ warned against allowing the exception to displace the rule:

> . . . one must guard against granting judicial review in cases where there is an alternative appeal route, merely because it may be more effective and convenient to do so.[21]

> Although judicial review can provide an effective, convenient and relatively swift remedy, it should only be granted, particularly where the basis of the application is merely delay in taking the necessary proceedings, where this can properly be described as amounting to an abuse of process.[22]

6.15  In practice, judicial review is likely to be pursued only if an appeal does not lie. There are at least two reasons. First, the scope of judicial review is more limited than that of appeal. Second, every ground for judicial review is a ground of appeal, even if appeal is limited to issues of law.[23] The presence of such an appeal is an indication that the legislative purpose is to direct cases to the statutory procedure rather than to the Administrative Court.[24]

6.16  Judicial review will be the only remedy available if there is no appeal against a decision.

6.17  The Upper Tribunal may hear an appeal and a judicial review as part of the same proceedings. It may even sit jointly with the First-tier Tribunal to hear an appeal to that tribunal and a judicial review in the Upper

---

17  [2010] UKUT 461 (AAC) at [81].
18  [1986] QB 424.
19  [1986] QB 424 at 433; *BX v Secretary of State for the Home Department* (2010) *Times* 14 June.
20  [1986] QB 424 at 440.
21  [1986] QB 424 at 437.
22  [1986] QB 424 at 439.
23  Lord Templeman in *Re Preston* [1985] AC 835 at 862. See also chapter 4.
24  Mummery LJ in *R (Davies) v Financial Services Authority* [2004] 1 WLR 185 at [31].

Tribunal.[25] This ensures that the evidence heard on the appeal is available in the judicial review proceedings.

## Judicial review of decisions of the First-tier Tribunal

6.18    The scope of the right to appeal to the Upper Tribunal is so wide that there is little need for judicial review, except for those decisions excluded from the right of appeal. However, if judicial review is sought of a decision of the First-tier Tribunal, that tribunal is the respondent and may make submissions. It is, though, inappropriate for that tribunal to make submissions on the merits of its decision, particularly with there is another party with an interest in opposing the application.[26]

6.19        An application for judicial review of a review decision of the First-tier Tribunal is unlikely to succeed, as those decisions involve a substantial element of judgment or discretion.[27]

## Judicial review of decisions on permission to appeal

6.20    The Administrative Court and the Court of Appeal have limited the scope of judicial review in these cases. The following discussion is additional to the authorities following the decision of the Supreme Court in *R (Cart) v Upper Tribunal*,[28] which are discussed in chapter 4.

### The basic principle

6.21    The basic principle is based on respect for a statutory scheme of appeals and a need to ensure the effectiveness and coherence of the scheme. This was the approach taken by the Court of Appeal in *R (Sivasubramaniam) v Wandsworth County Court*.[29] The scheme there involved appeals with leave from a district judge to a circuit judge and from that judge to the Court of Appeal. The circuit judge refused leave and judicial review was sought. The Court connected the existence of a coherent statutory scheme for appeals with the basic principles on which judicial review is available:

> . . . judicial review is customarily refused as an exercise of judicial discretion where an alternative remedy is available. Where Parliament has provided a statutory appeal procedure it will rarely be appropriate to grant permission for judicial review. The exceptional case may arise because the statutory procedure is less satisfactory than the procedure of judicial review. Usually, however, the alternative procedure is more convenient and judicial review is refused.
>
> We believe that these general principles apply with particular force in the context of the applications before us. Under the 1999 Act, and the rules pursuant to it, a coherent statutory scheme has been set up governing appeals at all levels short of the House of Lords. One object of the scheme is to ensure that, where there is an arguable ground for challenging a decision

25  *Reed Employment plc v Commissioners for Her Majesty's Revenue and Customs* [2010] UKFTT 596 (TC) at [41].

26  *R (RB) v First-tier Tribunal* (Review) [2010] UKUT 160 (AAC) at [14].

27  *R (RB) v First-tier Tribunal* (Review) [2010] UKUT 160 (AAC) at [30].

28  [2012] 1 AC 663.

29  [2003] 1 WLR 475.

of the lower court, an appeal will lie, but to prevent court resources being wasted by the pursuit of appeals which have no prospect of success. The other object of the scheme is to ensure that the level of Judge dealing with the application for permission to appeal, and the appeal if permission is given, is appropriate to the dispute. This is a sensible scheme which accords with the object of access to justice and the Woolf reforms. It has the merit of proportionality. To permit an applicant to by-pass the scheme by pursuing a claim for judicial review before a judge of the Administrative Court is to defeat the object of the exercise. We believe that this should not be permitted unless there are exceptional circumstances . . .[30]

The case concerned a refusal of permission, but the Court made clear that the same principles applied to an attempt to obtain judicial review of a grant of permission.[31]

### When the basic principle applies

6.22　Whether this basic principle applies depends on a combination of factors. They were set out by Court of Appeal in *R (Sinclair Investments (Kensington) Ltd) v Lands Tribunal*.[32] The Court was concerned with disputes over service charges. They were heard by a leasehold valuation tribunal. An appeal lay with the permission of either the tribunal or the Lands Tribunal. The landlord applied for permission to appeal, which was refused both by the tribunal and by a surveyor member of the Lands Tribunal. Neuberger LJ said:[33]

. . . the resolution of the question at issue must be resolved by reference to (a) the generic nature of the issues involved (in this case, residential service charge disputes), (b) the effect of the statutory procedures concerned, particularly those relating to appeals . . . (c) the nature and constitution of the tribunals involved in those procedures, and (d), in so far as it can be ascertained, the legislative intention . . . These factors must be assessed (a) against fundamental policy considerations, namely the desirability of finality, with the minimising of delay and cost, and the desirability of achieving the legally correct answer, and (b) against the practicalities, such as the burdens on the Administrative Court and, in this case, the pressures on the Lands Tribunal.

6.23　There is an undefined exception to the basic principle, of which there has been only one identified instance to date. This was permission decisions of the former Immigration Appeal Tribunal. In *R (Sivasubramaniam) v Wandsworth County Court*,[34] the Court of Appeal said that judicial review was allowed because of the nature of the issues involved and the risk of error:[35]

In asylum cases, and most cases are asylum cases, fundamental human rights are in play, often including the right to life and the right not to be subjected to torture. The number of applications for asylum is enormous,

---

30　[2003] 1 WLR 475 at [47]–[48].
31　[2003] 1 WLR 475 at [55].
32　[2006] 3 All ER 650.
33　[2006] 3 All ER 650 at [41].
34　[2003] 1 WLR 475.
35　[2003] 1 WLR 475 at [52].

the pressure on the tribunal immense and the consequences of error considerable.

6.24 This exception did not apply to the statutory review procedures for immigration and asylum appeals.[36] However, judicial review was permissible in such cases if necessary in order to prevent gross procedural unfairness.[37]

## The limited grounds for judicial review if the principle applies

6.25 Judicial review is allowed to disrupt a statutory scheme if there has been a jurisdictional error. In *R (Sivasubramaniam) v Wandsworth County Court*,[38] the Court of Appeal decided that the judges of the Administrative Court should dismiss such applications summarily[39] except:

> . . . on the ground of jurisdictional error in the narrow, pre-*Anisminic* sense, or procedural irregularity of such a kind as to constitute a denial of the applicant's right to a fair hearing.[40]

6.26 Jurisdictional error does not include mere errors of law. The Court of Appeal rejected an argument that it did in *Gregory v Turner*.[41] Nor does it include gross and obvious errors of law. Sullivan J rejected an argument that it did at first instance in *Sinclair Gardens Investments (Kensington) Ltd v The Lands Tribunal*:[42]

> Whether an error of law is 'gross and obvious' is very much a question of degree and judgment. Many perceived errors of law are 'gross and obvious' in the mind of the losing party. Since it will often be impossible to decide whether the error is 'gross and obvious' without hearing full legal argument, applying such a test when considering applications for permission to claim judicial review would subvert the statutory scheme just as effectively as removing the need to show exceptional circumstances.[43]

6.27 What does amount to a jurisdictional error in the pre-*Anisminic* sense was considered by the Court of Appeal in *Gregory v Turner*.[44] The Court approved[45] the summary in the argument of counsel for the Commission in *Anisminic Ltd v Foreign Compensation Commission*:[46]

> Category (1). Cases where the tribunal has no jurisdiction to embark on an inquiry and make a determination unless a condition precedent was

36 This applies to the original statutory review scheme (Collins J in *R (G) v Immigration Appeal Tribunal* [2004] 1 WLR 2953 confirmed by Court of Appeal in [2005] 1 WLR 1445) and to the scheme under the Asylum and Immigration (Treatment of Claimants, etc) Act 2004 (*R (F Mongolia) v Secretary of State for the Home Department* [2007] EWCA Civ 769; (2007) *Times* 28 August).

37 *R (AM (Cameroon)) v Asylum and Immigration Tribunal* [2007] EWCA Civ 131; (2007) *Times* 11 April.

38 [2003] 1 WLR 475.

39 [2003] 1 WLR 475 at [54].

40 [2003] 1 WLR 475 at [56].

41 [2003] 1 WLR 1149 at [39].

42 [2004] EWHC 1910 (Admin) at [50].

43 But contrast the view of Scott Baker J in *R (Anayet Begum) v Social Security Commissioners* [2002] EWHC 401 (Admin), discussed below, on the need for an error to be obvious.

44 [2003] 1 WLR 1149.

45 [2003] 1 WLR 1149 at [40].

46 [1969] 2 AC 163 at 161.

satisfied. If in the view of the court the condition was not satisfied, then the so-called determination is a nullity . . .

Category (2). Where the statute expressly forbids the tribunal to exercise jurisdiction over the subject-matter of the inquiry and determination . . .

Category (3). Where the tribunal has no jurisdiction to make the order it in fact made.

Category (4). Cases in which there have been different reasons for the decision and in which the distinction between nullity and error in law may not have been considered . . . These are difficult cases in that it is sometimes hard to see what the precise point was but it may be possible to build up from them a proposition of general validity that a tribunal has no jurisdiction to make a determination if it has acted in complete disregard of its duties.

6.28    The Court of Appeal in *Gregory v Turner* discussed this final category,[47] saying that:

What is required, at least, is some fundamental departure from the correct procedures.[48]

## Judicial review of decisions without reasons

6.29    The proper approach to judicial review of a decision in which reasons are not given was considered by the Court of Appeal in *R v Secretary of State for Social Services ex p Connolly*.[49] The Court of Appeal was concerned with a refusal of leave by a Commissioner. An appeal lay to the Commissioner on a question of law. The applicant had been refused judicial review of that refusal and had appealed against that decision to the Court of Appeal. Slade LJ said:

. . . the onus must, in my judgment, lie on the applicant to show either (a) that the reasons which in fact caused the commissioner to refuse leave were improper or insufficient, or (b) that there were no good grounds on which such leave could have been refused in the proper exercise of the commissioner's discretion. He may well discharge this onus by showing that the decision sought to be challenged was on the face of it clearly erroneous in law or, alternatively, gave rise to a substantially arguable point of law. However, if it can be seen that there are still good grounds upon which the commissioner would have been entitled to refuse leave in the proper exercise of his discretion, the court should, in my opinion, assume that he acted on those grounds unless the applicant can point to convincing reasons leading to a contrary conclusion.[50]

6.30    This approach has been applied to cases in which reasons have been given.

6.31    The approach has been qualified by later authority. Scott Baker J summarised the current law in *R (Begum) v Social Security Commissioners*:[51]

The position is that mere arguability is not the test, a higher hurdle must be surmounted. The point must be obvious; that is one which would have

---

47  [2003] 1 WLR 1149 at [40]–[43].
48  [2003] 1 WLR 1149 at [41].
49  [1986] 1 WLR 421.
50  [1986] 1 WLR 421 at 432.
51  [2002] EWHC 401 (Admin) at [20].

a strong prospect of success were leave to be granted. An obvious point, it seems to me, is one that stands out and not one that can only be gleaned by a paper chase through various documents which may underlie the decision-maker's decision.[52]

## Judicial review of specialist policy

6.32   If a specialist body's decision involves the balancing of policy issues, the courts are reluctant to find that it involved an abuse of power.[53]

## Costs against the tribunal

6.33   In *R (Davies) v Birmingham Deputy Coroner*,[54] the Court of Appeal set out the rules relating to costs against a tribunal whose decision is subject to an application for judicial review. The position is as follows.

- If the tribunal takes no part in the proceedings, it will not be liable for costs unless (i) there was a flagrant instance of improper behaviour or (ii) the tribunal unreasonably declined or neglected to sign a consent order disposing of the proceedings.
- If the tribunal takes an active part in the proceedings, it will be liable for costs unless its involvement was merely to assist in a neutral way. However, costs may be awarded against the tribunal if, for example, the successful party has no other source of funding.

6.34   In principle, a protective costs order can be made to protect the tribunal, although this is perhaps unlikely to be necessary for a public body.[55]

## Cross-border issues

6.35   Applications for judicial review arise under the law of England and Wales for the purposes of TCEA s15, even if the original decision was governed by the law of Scotland.[56]

6.36   A decision made in England or Wales may be subject to judicial review in Scotland if the claimant was resident in Scotland.[57]

## Representations by the Secretary of State

6.37   The Secretary of State responsible for a particular jurisdiction is entitled to make representations on judicial review. In *R (Cowling) v Child Support Commissioners' Office*,[58] a parent with care's solicitor argued that the Secretary of State responsible for child support should not be allowed to appear in judicial review proceedings as it was inconsistent with his duty

---

52   See also chapter 4.
53   *R (Legal Remedy UK Ltd) v Secretary of State for Health* (2007) *Times* 29 June.
54   [2004] 1 WLR 2739.
55   *R (Ministry of Defence) v Wiltshire and Swindon Coroner* [2005] 4 All ER 40.
56   *MB v First-tier Tribunal and CICA* [2012] UKUT 286 (AAC); *NF v First-tier Tribunal and CICA* [2012] UKUT 287 (AAC).
57   *Tehrani v Secretary of State for the Home Department* [2007] 1 AC 521.
58   [2009] 1 FLR 332.

to do only what is in the best interests of the child. Underhill J rejected that argument:[59]

> Mr Henshaw [counsel for the Secretary of State] made it clear in his skeleton argument that the Secretary of State saw his role as essentially that of amicus. Such a role is of assistance to the court and in the interests of justice. Mr Burrows [for the parent with care] was able to suggest no actual prejudice to the claimant, other than the obvious prejudice that she would prefer to have no argument in opposition to her submissions. Mr Burrows' objection was at the level of theory. Even at that level I do not believe that his point is well-founded. I do not accept that such responsibility as the Secretary of State may formally have for the operations of the Child Support Agency in pursuing proper claims for the benefit of children and resident parents is inconsistent with the role which he is undertaking in these proceedings.

## Alternative Dispute Resolution

6.38   Legal proceedings do not offer an ideal solution to every dispute. The outcome is win or lose, limited to legally relevant interests, often uncertain, and possibly slow and costly. Alternative dispute resolution (ADR) recognises that parties have interests beyond those that are legally relevant and that an appropriate outcome should try to identify common ground and reconcile those interests that are in conflict. It can also be cheaper and quicker, although this is not necessarily so for every type of procedure.

### Forms of alternative dispute resolution

6.39   The forms of procedure available may be classified by reference to different criteria. One form of classification uses the nature of third party involvement as the criterion. This produces four categories. First are procedures, such as arbitration, in which a third party makes a legally binding decision. Second is neutral evaluation, in which a third party gives an independent opinion on the likely outcome of the case.[60] Third are procedures, such as mediation, in which a third party helps the parties reach an agreement. Fourth is direct negotiation between the parties.

### Alternative dispute resolution under TCEA

6.40   Chapter 2 of the White Paper on *Transforming Public Services: Complaints, Redress and Tribunals*[61] set out a long-term aim of transforming the way that people deal with legal problems and disputes. TCEA s2(3)(d) is consistent with that approach:

> (3) A holder of the office of Senior President of Tribunals must, in carrying out the functions of that office, have regard to–
>
>    . . .

59   [2009] 1 FLR 332 at [24].
60   *Evaluation of Early Neutral Evaluation Alternative Dispute Resolution in Social Security and Child Support Tribunal*, Carolyn Hay, Katherine McKenna and Trevor Buck, Ministry of Justice Research Series 2/10, January 2010.
61   Cm 6243.

>    (d) the need to develop innovative methods of resolving disputes that
>    are of a type that may be brought before tribunals.

6.41    The law has not reached the point of requiring parties to attempt to resolve
their disputes through alternative dispute resolution before resorting to
law.[62] Accordingly, in furtherance of the duty under section 2(3)(d), the
rules of procedure provide that tribunals should merely inform the parties
about appropriate alternative methods for the resolution of their dispute
and, if the parties wish and it is compatible with the overriding objective,
facilitate their use.[63]

6.42    The rules are an exhortation; they do not impose a duty. However,
this does not mean that they are ineffective, as the research on mediation
shows that judicial encouragement has a significant impact on the willingness of parties to use the procedure.[64] A failure to use an alternative form
of dispute resolution may also be relevant to costs.[65]

6.43    If the rules of procedure provide for mediation, TCEA s24 applies.

## Appropriate procedures

6.44    Alternative dispute resolution is more appropriate to private law disputes
than public law ones. However, some forms may be appropriate to public law, neutral evaluation in particular. Moreover, some government
departments (such as Her Majesty's Revenue and Customs) are more
open to negotiation than others (such as the Department for Work and
Pensions).

## Alternative techniques in tribunal proceedings

6.45    A case before a tribunal is a legal proceeding. It is not an alternative form
of dispute resolution. As Pill LJ said in *Haringey London Borough Council v
Awaritefe*:[66]

>    ... the court must remind itself that it is the judge not of standards of
>    administration but of the law. It is to be expected, and indeed hoped, that
>    there is very considerable coincidence between what is required of a local
>    authority by way of good administration and what is required by law. There
>    may however be cases where conduct which may be categorised as poor
>    administration, or even maladministration, does not fall below the stand-
>    ard required by the law.[67]

6.46    However, even within tribunal proceedings, there may be more scope to
operate some of the techniques employed in alternative dispute resolution
than is possible in court proceedings.

---

62  But the availability of an alternative remedy is a factor in judicial review proceedings:
*Humphries v Secretary of State for Work and Pensions* [2008] 2 FLR 2116 at [109].

63  See: UTR r3; GRC Rules r3; HESC Rules r3; Lands Rules r3; PC Rules r4; SEC Rules
r3; Tax Rules r3; WPAFC Rules r3. The relevant CPR provisions are rr1.4(2)(e) and (f)
(case management) and 44.5(3)(a)(ii) (costs).

64  See Lord Justice Jackson's *Review of Civil Litigation Costs: Preliminary Report* 2009,
Chapter 43, paras 6.19 and 6.26.

65  *Halsey v Milton Keynes General NHS Trust* [2004] 1 WLR 3002 and chapter 7.

66  (1999) 32 HLR 517.

67  (1999) 32 HLR 517 at 531.

6.47     One technique from alternative dispute resolution is to agree on fair criteria by reference to which a dispute should be resolved. A tribunal has to apply the law. That leaves no scope for the parties to agree on the principles that the tribunal should apply. However, the tribunal can assist the party to understand that there are principles and what they are. The party may not be satisfied that other factors are irrelevant, but at least will understand the confines within which the tribunal has to operate and appreciate the significance of its inquiries and outcome.

6.48     Another technique from alternative dispute resolution is to focus on the party's underlying concerns and interests. A tribunal proceeding is more suited than that of a court to dealing with the issues that underlie a party's case. They are able to address the party's real interests and concerns rather than limit themselves to the legal issues that arise. For example: claimants in overpayment social security appeals may feel aggrieved that the overpayment decision brands them as liars and cheats. They may have been prompted to appeal on this account rather than by any disagreement with the facts of what happened or with the way the law has been applied. If the decision does not carry any implication of dishonesty, and it often does not, the tribunal can explain that and, perhaps, emphasis it in the decision.

## Ex gratia schemes

6.49     These are not usually classified as a form of alternative dispute resolution. They may provide a remedy where the law provides none, or they may provide an alternative to, or supplement, the remedy that the law offers.

6.50     A minister is entitled to withdraw a scheme. Its mere existence does not create a legitimate expectation of consultation before withdrawal.[68]

6.51     Someone aggrieved should attempt to use a scheme that can provide an appropriate remedy before applying for judicial review.[69]

---

68  *R (Bhatt Murphy (a Firm)) v Independent Assessor* [2008] EWCA Civ 755; (2008) *Times* 21 July.
69  *Humphries v Secretary of State for Work and Pensions* [2008] 2 FLR 2116 at [109].

## CHAPTER 7

# Proceedings

*continued*

# Case management

7.1    Case management is the process by which the tribunal controls the proceedings from the time when they are begun to the final disposal of the case.[1] That control must be exercised in the context of, and to further, the overriding objective[2] and the right to fairness in the proceedings.[3] Its purpose is to ensure that the proceedings are conducted in a way that is most effective in resolving the issues between the parties and most efficient in the use of the tribunal's time and resources.[4] Its aim is to ensure that the case is decided in the shortest possible time given the issues raised and the resources available.

## The nature of case management in practice

7.2    Case management involves five related features. First, it is proactive. It is not limited to being reactive to the applications of the parties. Second, it is not dictated by the wishes of any particular party or of all the parties. Third, it is not limited to a consideration of the particular case. It takes account of the functioning of the tribunal system as a whole and, through that system, of the impact that the management of one case has on others. Fourth, it applies throughout the whole of the proceedings to control progress. Fifth, it provides individualised and personalised control for particular cases or classes of case, not just general control through standard rules and procedures.

7.3    The ways in which these features manifest themselves vary according to the nature of the cases that come before the tribunal. In some tribunals, the routine cases may be sufficiently catered for by the rules of procedure so that little or no management is required. For other cases and in other tribunals, more detailed management may be needed. These are some of the approaches and practices that may be found in the case management procedures of a tribunal system:

- The tribunal controls the progress of the case. This may involve setting a timetable for the orderly progress of the case and for bringing the proceedings to a conclusion as quickly and efficiently as possible.
- The tribunal has a role in, or control of, the identification of the issues that will be considered. If permission to initiate proceedings is needed and the tribunal's jurisdiction is limited to issues of law, it may be appropriate to front load the judicial effort so that the issues are identified at the beginning of the proceedings.
- The tribunal gives directions that help the parties to understand the nature of the proceedings and what is required of them.

---

1   For an instance of the Administrative Court commending a case management approach to a tribunal, see *R (Camacho) v Law Society* [2004] 4 All ER 126 in the extracts in the Appendix, which are not included in the Weekly Law Report. For the rebuff from the tribunal, see [7] of the main judgment.
2   See chapter 3
3   Given by natural justice and article 6. See chapter 3.
4   *Ul-Haq v Shah* [2010] 1 WLR 616 at [39].

- The tribunal decides whether an oral hearing is required for particular issues or at all.
- Once a case is ready, it is decided as soon as resources allow.
- Time is allowed for preparing the case for hearing that is appropriate given the issues raised and the level of decision-making.
- No step is taken, by the tribunal or the parties, unless it adds value to the decision-making process.
- The tribunal may control the time spent by the parties on presenting evidence.[5]
- The tribunal informs the parties about, and facilitates the use of, alternative methods of resolving their dispute.[6]

## Directions

7.4　It would be too cumbersome to make specific provision governing every aspect of a tribunal's procedure or to cover every eventuality that might occur in individual cases. By express provision or necessary implication, there must be a residual power for a tribunal to control its procedure and the progress of proceedings.

7.5　This power must be exercised within the constraints imposed by law on the tribunal's freedom of action. It cannot, for example, dispense of its own initiative with the duty to provide reasons. However, it may displace default provisions and exercise the powers and discretions conferred on it.

7.6　Under TCEA, the rules of procedure: (i) stipulate that the tribunal has power to regulate its own procedure; (ii) supplement this by an express general power to give directions in relation to the conduct or disposal of proceedings; (iii) give a non-exhaustive list of the possible subject matter for a direction; and (iv) make specific provision for some of those matters.

7.7　Directions issued by the tribunal may assist the parties in understanding the nature of the proceedings and what is required of them in their case.[7]

### *General powers*

7.8　UTR r5 is illustrative of the general powers:[8]

**5 Case management powers**
(1) Subject to the provisions of the 2007 Act and any other enactment, the Upper Tribunal may regulate its own procedure.
(2) The Upper Tribunal may give a direction in relation to the conduct or disposal of proceedings at any time, including a direction amending, suspending or setting aside an earlier direction.
(3) In particular, and without restricting the general powers in paragraphs (1) and (2), the Upper Tribunal may–

---

5　*R v Jisl and Tenkin* (2004) *Times* 1 April.
6　See: UTR r3; GRC Rules r3; HESC Rules r3; Lands Rules r3; PC Rules r4; SEC Rules r3; Tax Rules r3; WPAFC Rules r3. There is no equivalent in the IAC Rules.
7　*RC v CMEC and WC* [2009] UKUT 62 (AAC) at [58].
8　See also: GRC Rules r5; HESC Rules r5; IAC Rules r4; Lands Rules r5; PC Rules r6; SEC Rules r5; Tax Rules r5; WPAFC Rules r5. The CPR equivalent is r3.1.

(a) extend or shorten the time for complying with any rule, practice direction or direction;

(b) consolidate or hear together two or more sets of proceedings or parts of proceedings raising common issues, or treat a case as a lead case;

(c) permit or require a party to amend a document;

(d) permit or require a party or another person to provide documents, information, evidence or submissions to the Upper Tribunal or a party;

(e) deal with an issue in the proceedings as a preliminary issue;

(f) hold a hearing to consider any matter, including a case management issue;

(g) decide the form of any hearing;

(h) adjourn or postpone a hearing;

(i) require a party to produce a bundle for a hearing;

(j) stay (or, in Scotland, sist) proceedings;

(k) transfer proceedings to another court or tribunal if that other court or tribunal has jurisdiction in relation to the proceedings and–

    (i) because of a change of circumstances since the proceedings were started, the Upper Tribunal no longer has jurisdiction in relation to the proceedings; or

    (ii) the Upper Tribunal considers that the other court or tribunal is a more appropriate forum for the determination of the case;

(l) suspend the effect of its own decision pending an appeal or review of that decision;

(m) in an appeal, or an application for permission to appeal, against the decision of another tribunal, suspend the effect of that decision pending the determination of the application for permission to appeal, and any appeal;

(n) require any person, body or other tribunal whose decision is the subject of proceedings before the Upper Tribunal to provide reasons for the decision, or other information or documents in relation to the decision or any proceedings before that person, body or tribunal.

7.9    Rule 5(1) codifies the power that all courts and tribunals have, subject only to any limitation imposed by legislation.[9] That power is necessary, because legislation cannot cover every possibility.[10] It allows a tribunal to adopt appropriate practice or procedures to fill the gaps in the rules of procedure.[11] The tribunal's procedure does not end when it begins to consider its decision.[12]

7.10    The tribunal only needs power (express or implied) to make legally binding decisions or to give directions that have may legal consequences.[13] It does not need statutory authority for actions that do not have direct legal

9  Lord Woolf in *R (Roberts) v Parole Board* [2005] 2 AC 738 at [44]. The source of this power is not clear. It is sometimes referred to as an inherent power. However, Lord Woolf denied this, saying that it existed because it was a characteristic of courts (at [44]) and tribunals and that it was an implied power (at [66]).

10  [2005] 2 AC 738 at [48].

11  For example: by allowing a party to be accompanied by an assistant in *R v Leicester City Justices ex p Barrow* [1991] 2 QB 260.

12  *Virdi v Law Society* [2010] 1 WLR 2840 at [33].

13  *Virdi v Law Society* [2010] 1 WLR 2840 at [28].

consequences, such as consulting a suitably qualified clerk.[14] The tribunal may do such things, provided that the proceedings are fair.[15]

7.11 The power must be exercised to further its purpose. A case management power deals with the order and conduct of the proceedings at a hearing.[16] As it applies to a hearing, its purpose is to regulate the course of the hearing in order to ensure that it is conducted efficiently and fairly. As a discretionary power, it must be exercised judicially.[17] It must be exercised in a way that allows all those entitled to be present to fulfil their appropriate roles, whether as members of the tribunal, parties, representatives, witnesses or assessors. But those persons must co-operate with the tribunal: see the discussion of UTR r2(4) and its equivalents in chapter 3.

7.12 This power is only subject to TCEA and other enactments. The rules of procedure are enactments, but practice directions and practice statements are not. Nor are directions given under the rules, such as UTR r5(2) and its equivalents.

7.13 The power cannot be used to subvert the purpose and provision of rules dealing with specific issues. It cannot be used to impose a lower standard for a particular purpose than that expressly set by a different rule. For example: it cannot be used to reduce the standard required for a case to be struck out.[18] Nor can it be used to circumvent the procedural protection that applies when the power to strike out a case is being considered.[19]

7.14 Although they are framed as powers, the elements of the overriding objective may operate to require the tribunal to give a direction on a particular matter and even a specific direction.

7.15 The proper use of the overriding objective should prevent unnecessary reliance on the particular form in which issues are presented. UTR r48 and its equivalents[20] give a tribunal power to treat some forms of application as another:

> The Tribunal may treat an application for a decision to be corrected, set aside or reviewed, or for permission to appeal against a decision, as an application for any other one of those things.

7.16 This is but an instance of, and does not restrict, a tribunal's general power to apply the appropriate procedure to the substance of any communication from a party or a witness.[21] The power must not be applied to override the express wishes of a competent representative.[22]

## Specific powers

7.17 In addition to these general powers, tribunals are given specific powers on particular matters. Tribunals have specific power to make orders or

14 *Virdi v Law Society* [2010] 1 WLR 2840 at [28].
15 *Virdi v Law Society* [2010] 1 WLR 2840 at [28].
16 *Care First Partnership Ltd v Roffey* [2001] ICR 87.
17 *Aberdeen Steak Houses Group plc v Ibrahim* [1988] ICR 550.
18 *Care First Partnership Ltd v Roffey* [2001] ICR 87.
19 *Kelly v Ingersoll-Rand Co Ltd* [1982] ICR 476.
20 GRC Rules r45; HESC Rules r50; IAC Rules r36; Lands Rules r58; PC Rules r56; SEC Rules r41; Tax Rules r42; WPAFC Rules r39.
21 See the discussion of the enabling approach in chapter 1.
22 *PS v Camden and Islington NHS Foundation Trust* [2011] UKUT 143 (AAC) at 20].

directions on disclosure of documents and information[23] and on evidence and submissions. UTR r15(1) is illustrative of the latter:[24]

> (1) Without restriction on the general powers in rule 5(1) and (2) (case management powers), the Upper Tribunal may give directions as to–
>   (a) issues on which it requires evidence or submissions;
>   (b) the nature of the evidence or submissions it requires;
>   (c) whether the parties are permitted or required to provide expert evidence, and if so whether the parties must jointly appoint a single expert to provide such evidence;
>   (d) any limit on the number of witnesses whose evidence a party may put forward, whether in relation to a particular issue or generally;
>   (e) the manner in which any evidence or submissions are to be provided, which may include a direction for them to be given–
>     (i)  orally at a hearing; or
>     (ii) by written submissions or witness statement; and
>   (f) the time at which any evidence or submissions are to be provided.

7.18   This power to control the evidence and issues is, perhaps, the single most valuable power in ensuring the effective and efficient use of the proceedings. It may be operated at the interlocutory stage or during a hearing. The extent to which it is applied at the interlocutory stage will depend on the tribunal's workload and the judicial resources available.

7.19   And the Upper Tribunal has power to make directions on the respondent's response to an appeal (r24(1)) and the appellant's reply (r25(1)).

## Checklists

7.20   Tribunals should not create judge-made checklists to supplement what is contained in the rules. This practice was deprecated by the Court of Appeal in respect of the CPR in *Sayers v Clarke Walker (a firm)*[25] and *Woodhouse v Consignia plc*.[26]

7.21   The cases discussed the relevance of CPR 3.9 when considering a sanction for failure to comply (in that case with a time limit). At the time, that rule provided:

> (1) On an application for relief from any sanction imposed for a failure to comply with any rule, practice direction or court order the court will consider all the circumstances including–
>   (a) the interests of the administration of justice;
>   (b) whether the application for relief has been made promptly;
>   (c) whether the failure to comply was intentional;
>   (d) whether there is a good explanation for the failure;
>   (e) the extent to which the party in default has complied with other rules, practice directions, court orders and any relevant preaction protocol;
>   (f) whether the failure to comply was caused by the party or his legal representative;

---

23  See chapter 10.
24  See also: GRC Rules r15(1); HESC Rules r15(1); IAC Rules r14(1); Lands Rules r16(1); PC Rules r18(1); SEC Rules r15(1); Tax Rules r15(1); WPAFC Rules r15(1). The CPR equivalent is r32.1.
25  [2002] 1 WLR 3095 at [18] and [23].
26  [2002] 1 WLR 2558 at [35].

(g) whether the trial date or the likely trial date can still be met if relief is granted;

(h) the effect which the failure to comply had on each party; and

(i) the effect which the granting of relief would have on each party.

(2) An application for relief must be supported by evidence.

7.22 In *R (Howes) v Child Support Commissioners*,[27] Black J held that it was inappropriate to create or import checklists. She was there concerned with the Child Support Commissioners (Procedure) Regulations 1999, which were not based on an overriding objective. Her comments are, though, of general application:

> Mr Burrows does not produce any authority for importing the CPR 3.9 approach or even simply the checklist in CPR 3.9(1) into the Child Support Commissioners (Procedure) Regulations 1999. I note that in the case of *Sayers v Clarke Walker (a firm)* [2002] EWCA Civ 645, [2002] 1 WLR 3095, upon which he relies as a useful explanation of the operation in practice of CPR 3.9, the Court of Appeal referred back to the earlier case of *Audergon v La Baguette* [2002] EWCA Civ 10, (2002) *The Times*, January 31, in which it had deplored the creation of judge-made check-lists which it considered an approach which carried the inherent 'danger that a body of satellite authority may be built up ... leading in effect to the rewriting of the relevant rule through the medium of judicial decision'. It seems to me that that danger potentially exists as much when one imports a checklist from one set of rules to another as when one invents one's own checklist. There was no reason why the Child Support Commissioner (Procedure) Regulations could not have contained an equivalent provision to CPR 3.9 or a checklist of some sort for the use of Commissioners considering the issue of special reasons if that had been thought appropriate. No doubt the sort of matters to which reference is made in CPR 3.9(1) may quite often also be relevant in cases considered by Commissioners under regulation 11(3) but I do not think it appropriate to impose upon Commissioners an obligation to refer to CPR 3.9(1). The concept of special reasons is a broad and flexible one and the factors that are relevant will be dependent upon the circumstances of the individual case.[28]

7.23 *Howes* was applied to the Administrative Appeals Chamber in *R (CD) v First-tier Tribunal (SEC)*.[29]

7.24 In *Neary v Governing Body of St Albans Girls' School*,[30] the Court of Appeal linked the relevance of the CPR to the adequacy of a tribunal's reasons. Smith LJ explained:

> ... the judge must consider all the relevant factors and must avoid considering any irrelevant ones. He might well find the list in CPR 3.9(1) to be a helpful checklist, although he would be well advised to remember that, in the instant case, that list might not cover everything relevant. But he is not under any duty expressly to set out his views on every one of those factors. His decision must comply with the basic requirements as set out in *English v Emery Reimbold & Strick* [2002] 1 WLR 2409. Litigants are entitled to know why they have won or lost and appellate courts must be able to see whether or not the judge has erred. In a case of this kind, it seems to me that the basic requirements are that the judge must make clear the facts that he has

27 [2008] 1 FLR 1691.

28 [2008] 1 FLR 1691 at [39].

29 [2010] UKUT 181 (AAC).

30 [2010] ICR 473.

regarded as relevant. He must say enough for the reason for his decision to be understood by a person who knows the background. In a case where the draconian sanction of strike-out has been imposed, it will be necessary for the judge to demonstrate that he has weighed the factors affecting proportionality and reached a tenable decision about it. That does not mean that he must use any particular form of words. Any requirement for a particular form of words leads readily to the adoption of them as a mantra. But it must be possible to see that the judge has asked himself whether in the circumstances the sanction had been just.[31]

It is, though, permissible for the Upper Tribunal to indicate factors that a tribunal should take into account without prescribing or giving guidelines on how the tribunal should exercise its discretion.[32]

## The powers in action

7.25   Many of these powers are discussed elsewhere.

7.26   One respect in which the courts have restricted the tribunal's case management powers is in relation to deciding that a party has no case to answer. A tribunal may use this power to decide not to hear the other side on the ground that the burden of proof has not been discharged.[33] However, this is exceptional. The power should only be exercised in this way if the party's case is hopeless. And a tribunal must hear one party's case before doing so.[34] Otherwise, the tribunal should hear argument and evidence from all parties, regardless of whether there is a burden on any particular party or not.[35]

7.27   In some types of case, it may be inappropriate to dispose of a case on this basis at all. This is especially so in split hearings involving the welfare of children.[36]

## Procedure in relation to directions

7.28   This is governed by the rules of procedure. UTR r6 is illustrative.[37]

7.29   The tribunal has power to give, amend, suspend and set aside directions. If a party finds it difficult or impossible to comply with a direction, the proper course is to apply under these powers. A party is not entitled to disregard a direction[38] or a witness summons.[39] In the case of an application for permission to appeal, it is primarily the duty of the appellant to comply with the directions, even if they are addressed generally to the parties.[40]

31  [2010] ICR 473 at [52].
32  *R (YT) First-tier Tribunal and Criminal Injuries Compensation Authority* [2013] UKUT 0201 (AAC) at [3.8]–[3.9] in Appendix 2.
33  *Hackney London Borough Council v Usher* [1997] ICR 705 at 713.
34  *R v N Ltd* (2008) *Times* 25 August.
35  *Logan v Customs and Excise Commissioners* [2004] ICR 1.
36  *Re R (Family Proceedings: No Case to Answer)* [2009] 2 FLR 83.
37  See: UTR r6; GRC Rules r6; HESC Rules r6; Lands Rules r6(1); PC Rules r7; SEC Rules r6; Tax Rules r6; WPAFC Rules r6.
38  Black J in *R (Davies) v Commissioners Office* [2008] 1 FLR 1651 at [14].
39  *CB v Suffolk County Council* [2010] UKUT 413 (AAC) at [28].
40  *Re M-W (Care proceedings: expert evidence)* [2010] 2 FLR 46 at [5].

7.30 Any party to the proceedings may apply for a direction, stating the reasons for the application. However, the value of the case management powers would be severely limited if the tribunal could only act on application by one of the parties. TCEA Sch 5 para 6 therefore authorises provision for the tribunal to act on its own initiative. This power has been exercised.[41]

7.31 The directions will not necessarily be given formally in writing. They may be given less formally in the course of the hearing (for example: by not allowing particular evidence to be given) or be implicit in the way that the hearing is conducted (for example: by the order in which parties are invited to present their case).

7.32 The Upper Tribunal may treat a decision of the First-tier Tribunal as made under its power to amend, suspend or set aside a direction, if that was the substance of the matter, even if that tribunal purported to act under a different authority.[42]

7.33 The tribunal's power to give and to change directions and to do so on its own initiative allows it correct mistakes. This is a useful and proper exercise of the power, but it must be used on principled grounds and not simply because of a change of mind.[43]

7.34 An application to amend, suspend or set aside a direction should only be made on good grounds.[44] The decision on the application must be made on the circumstances then obtaining, not on those obtaining at the time the direction was given.[45]

7.35 A party should not be allowed to repeat an application for a direction by relying on material that could have been used in support of the previous application. This ensures that the tribunal's limited resources are properly allocated and protects the other party in the interests of finality.[46]

## Reconsideration of interlocutory decisions

7.36 All courts and tribunals have power to reconsider their decisions. One power of reconsideration applies to interlocutory decisions made without a hearing.

7.37 If the decision has been made without notice to the other parties, it can be reconsidered. This power allows a tribunal to discharge the decision. The basis of this power is the fact that the other party was not heard. As Cotton LJ explained in *Boyle v Sacker*:[47]

> . . . discharging an order is not the same thing as reversing or varying an order, it does not go on the ground that there has been an erroneous decision, but on the ground that the opposing party has not had an opportunity to be heard.[48]

---

41 See: UTR r6(1); GRC Rules r6(1); HESC Rules r6(1); IAC Rules r5(1); Lands Rules r6(1); PC Rules r7(1); SEC Rules r6(1); Tax Rules r6(1); WPAFC Rules r6(1). The CPR equivalent is r3.3.

42 *HM/2772/2010* at [22]; *Ofsted v AF* [2011] UKUT 72 (AAC) at [21]; *Information Commissioner v PS* [2011] UKUT 94 (AAC) at [73]–[75].

43 *SCT Finance Ltd v Bolton* [2003] 3 All ER 434 at [58].

44 *Chanel Ltd v F W Woolworth & Co Ltd* [1982] 1 WLR 485 at 492.

45 *Tibbles v SIG plc* [2012] 1 WLR 2591 at [49].

46 *Woodhouse v Consignia plc* [2002] 1 WLR 2558 at [55].

47 (1888) 39 Ch D 249.

48 (1888) 39 Ch D 249 at 251.

7.38   This reasoning extends to decisions that have been made without a hearing for any of the parties.

7.39   It is only appropriate to apply for a reconsideration if there are strong reasons for doing so.[49]

7.40   Reconsideration is a power, not a duty. According to the Tribunal of Commissioners in *R(I) 7/94*, it can only arise if an application is made.[50]

7.41   The power to reconsider is not limited to judicial bodies. It applies also to decision-makers. In *R (C) v Lewisham London Borough Council*,[51] the issue was the local authority's duty to provide accommodation. Ward LJ said that the legislative scheme envisaged only one review, but went on:[52]

> That is not to say that a local authority may not choose as a matter of their discretion to entertain such a request for a further review or a further extension of time.

He went on to emphasise that, being discretionary, there was little chance of obtaining a judicial review of an authority's 'refusal to consider such a further indulgence'.[53]

7.42   It may be permissible, or even appropriate, for the reconsideration to be undertaken by the same tribunal. In *Khreino v Khreino*,[54] an application for permission to appeal to the Court of Appeal was refused on paper and renewed at an oral hearing. One of the Lords Justice at the oral hearing was the one who had refused the application on the papers. The Court held that this was permissible, as an oral hearing of an application would not simply be a reconsideration of the points made and rejected on paper. Thorpe LJ emphasised that a renewed application would only be appropriate in exceptional circumstances.[55] And Mummery LJ identified matters appropriate for consideration at an oral hearing which had not been dealt with on the papers – matters that had occurred since the application, new authorities that might apply, errors or omissions in the paper application.[56]

7.43   Some of this reasoning may not apply under TCEA. In particular, for those jurisdictions in which there is a right to renew an application at an oral hearing, the arguments raised will not necessarily be new ones.

## Failure to comply and enforcement

7.44   TCEA does not deal with the effect of either (i) a failure to comply with a requirement in a rule, a practice direction or a direction or (ii) the irregularity that may result from that failure. However, the rules of procedure deal with both.

---

49  Neuberger J in *Re Blenheim Leisure (Restaurants) Ltd (No 3)* (1999) *Times* 9 November; Lord Widgery CJ in *R v Kensington and Chelsea Rent Tribunal ex p MacFarlane* [1974] 1 WLR 1486 at 1493.
50  *R(I) 7/94* at [35].
51  [2003] 3 All ER 1277.
52  [2003] 3 All ER 1277 at [59].
53  [2003] 3 All ER 1277 at [59].
54  [2000] 1 FLR 578.
55  [2000] 1 FLR 578 at 580.
56  [2000] 1 FLR 578 at 581.

7.45 The rules do not deal with the effect of a failure to comply with a practice statement.

### Failure to comply

7.46 Failure to comply presumes a duty. It is inherent in the nature of the rules of procedure and practice directions that they are, where appropriately worded, mandatory. Directions may also be mandatory in their terms, but the rules do not state that there is a duty to comply with directions. However, this is implied by the provisions for amending, suspending and setting aside a direction. It is also implied by the nature of the provisions that apply in the event of a failure to comply with a direction.

7.47 It may not be possible or appropriate for a party to comply with a rule or a practice direction. In that case, the proper course is to apply for the tribunal to give a direction or for the time for compliance to be extended.[57]

7.48 The rules of procedure provide for the tribunal to take such action as it considers just following a failure to comply. UTR r7(2) is illustrative:[58]

> (2) If a party has failed to comply with a requirement in these Rules, a practice direction or a direction, the Upper Tribunal may take such action as it considers just, which may include–
> (a) waiving the requirement;
> (b) requiring the failure to be remedied;
> (c) exercising its power under rule 8 (striking out a party's case); or
> (d) except in mental health cases, restricting a party's participation in the proceedings.

This only applies to failures by a party. It does not apply to a failure by the tribunal. For example: it does not apply if the tribunal failed to give a party reasonable notice of an oral hearing. Restricting participation under subpara (d) must involve something less that striking out or barring, as they are covered by subpara (c) and r8.

7.49 Relief may be given subject to conditions,[59] provided that they are attainable.[60] The aim of conditions is to ensure that the case is dealt with fairly and justly rather than to punish or penalise.[61]

7.50 Failures that are attributable to a representative are discussed in chapter 3.

7.51 The First-tier Tribunal may also refer certain failures to the Upper Tribunal. These are set out in UTR r7(3):

> (3) Paragraph (4) applies where the First-tier Tribunal has referred to the Upper Tribunal a failure by a person to comply with a requirement imposed by the First-tier Tribunal–
> (a) to attend at any place for the purpose of giving evidence;
> (b) otherwise to make themselves available to give evidence;
> (c) to swear an oath in connection with the giving of evidence;

---

57 See chapter 6.
58 See also: GRC Rules r7(2); HESC Rules r7(2); IAC Rules r6(2); Lands Rules r7(2); PC Rules 8(2) and (3); SEC Rules r7(2); Tax Rules r7(2); WPAFC Rules r7(2).
59 *Price v Price (trading as Poppyland Headwear)* [2003] 3 All ER 911; *Days Healthcare U Ltd v Pihsiang Machinery Manufacturing Co Ltd* [2006] 4 All ER 233.
60 *M V Yorke Motors (a Firm) v Edwards* [1982] 1 WLR 444.
61 *Mubarak v Mubarik (Contempt in Failure to Pay Lump Sum: Standard of Proof)* [2007] 1 FLR 722 at [90].

  (d) to give evidence as a witness;

  (e) to produce a document; or

  (f) to facilitate the inspection of a document or any other thing (including any premises).[62]

7.52    The Upper Tribunal has powers under TCEA s25. It can use these powers
in respect of its own proceedings or, on a referral by the First-tier Tribunal,
in respect of certain failures to comply with requirements of that tribunal.[63] The Upper Tribunal may only exercise its powers if the failure was
material to the issues before the First-tier Tribunal.[64]

7.53    If the tribunal has power to order costs, the failure may be reflected in
the award.

## Irregularity

7.54    The rules provide that an irregularity resulting from a failure to comply
does not *of itself* render the proceedings, or any step in them, void. UTR
r7(1) is illustrative:[65]

  (1) An irregularity resulting from a failure to comply with any requirement in these Rules, a practice direction or a direction, does not of itself
  render void the proceedings or any step taken in the proceedings.[66]

7.55    The rules do not define 'irregularity'. It clearly means that something
has not been done regularly in accordance with the rules.[67] However, it
may not include every consequence of a failure to comply. In *In re Pritch-
ard deceased*[68], the Court of Appeal decided that, under the Rules of the
Supreme Court then in force, there were some defects that rendered proceedings a nullity rather than merely irregular. The Rules were amended
to remove this distinction.[69] However, it is still relevant under CPR. For
example: the court decided that a failure to serve proceedings was not an
error of procedure that could be remedied under the CPR equivalent to
rule 7(1).[70]

7.56    The words 'of itself' show that there may be something more than the
irregularity itself that may deprive the proceedings or a step taken in them

---

62  The power to refer is contained in: GRC Rules r7(3); HESC Rules r7(3); IAC Rules
r6(3); PC Rules r8(5); SEC Rules r7(3); Tax Rules r7(3); WPAFC Rules r7(3).

63  UTR r7(3) and (4).

64  *MR v CMEC and DM* [2009] UKUT 283 (AAC) at [3]. The Upper Tribunal's reasoning
was based on the extent of its own powers under TCEA s25. This is an irrelevant
consideration under UTR r7(3) and (4). However, the tribunal's conclusion is surely
correct as a matter of principle.

65  See also: GRC Rules r7(1); HESC Rules r7(1); IAC Rules r6(1); Lands Rules r7(1);
PC Rules 8(1); SEC Rules r7(1); Tax Rules r7(1); WPAFC Rules r7(1). CPR take a
different approach. They focus on the procedural error rather than on the irregularity
that results from it: r3.10.

66  In the absence of an express provision, the effect of a failure to comply is a matter of
interpretation: *District Court of Vilnius v Barcys* [2008] 1 All ER 733.

67  'Deficiency' is likewise interpreted broadly: *Hall v Wandsworth London Borough
Council* [2005] 2 All ER 192 at [29].

68  [1963] Ch 502.

69  The new rule was discussed by the Court of Appeal in *Harkness v Bell's Asbestos and
Engineering Ltd* [1967] 2 QB 729.

70  *Olafsson v Gissurarson* [2007] 2 All ER 88 and on appeal on a different issue [2008] 1
WLR 2016.

of any legal force or effect. Whether this is so will be determined under the basic principles that govern the effect of a failure to comply with a procedural provision. These are discussed at para 2.80 onwards above.

7.57    Irregularities arising from a failure to comply with a time limit are discussed at para 7.68 onwards below.

### Overall view

7.58    The appropriate response to the same failing by a party may arise in different contexts. For example: the appellant's conduct in the proceedings may lead to an application by the respondent that the proceedings be struck out and an application by the appellant for the requirements to be waived or both. The decision should not be affected by the context in which it is raised. It is important to take an overall view of the impact on the proceeding, as Sir Thomas Bingham MR explained in *Costellow v Somerset County Council*:[71]

> In the great mass of cases, it is appropriate for the court to hear the summonses together, since in considering what justice requires the court is concerned to do justice to both parties, the plaintiff as well as the defendant, and the case is best viewed in the round.[72]

### Failure to notify a decision

7.59    This is discussed in chapter 2.

## On appeal

7.60    A case management decision can be made appealable with appropriate wording.[73] Under TCEA, it is appealable as a decision that is not an excluded decision under *LS v London Borough of Lambeth*.[74] It may also be challenged through an appeal against the final decision.

7.61    If a tribunal exercises its case management powers reasonably, it will be supported on appeal.[75] Even before the days of case management, courts recognised that expedition was a legitimate consideration.[76]

## Delay

7.62    Significant delay is not generally a feature either of proceedings before tribunals or of their decisions.[77] The issue for delay is how to avoid it. This is

---

71  [1993] 1 WLR 256.

72  [1993] 1 WLR 256 at 264.

73  *R v Clark* (2007) *Times* 29 October.

74  [2010] UKUT 461 (AAC).

75  See Lord Templeman in *Ashmore v Corporation of Lloyd's* [1992] 1 WLR 446 at 454 and *R v Jisl and Tenkin* (2004) *Times* 1 April.

76  Lord Reid recognised the legitimacy of expedition in *Wiseman v Borneman* [1971] AC 297 at 308, while accepting that it had to be balanced against the need for the each party to have an opportunity to consider the other party's evidence.

77  See the comments of Mummery LJ in respect of employment tribunals in *Connex South Eastern Ltd v Bangs* [2005] ICR 763 at [13].

a case management issue. In *Connex South Eastern Ltd v Bangs*,[78] the Court of Appeal approved of the advice given by the Employment Appeal Tribunal below under the name *Kwamin v Abbey National plc*.[79] The issue was the effect of delay between the hearing and the making of the decision, but the Tribunal gave general advice on avoiding delay at all stages:[80]

- active case management to minimise delays before a case comes on for hearing;
- co-operation between the parties and the tribunal in fixing an appropriate estimate for the time needed for the hearing;
- adjournments for as short a period as possible and if possible to a fixed date;
- setting a time within the tribunal system for reaching decisions;
- allowance of time for the members to discuss the case and for the reasons to be written;
- reminders of the time that has elapsed since the hearing.

## Delegation

7.63   The exercise of a judicial power or duty cannot be delegated,[81] without statutory authority.

7.64   The power to delegate judicial functions to staff is governed by TCEA Sch 5 para 3. This power is exercised in the rules of procedure. UTR r4 is illustrative:[82]

(1) Staff appointed under section 40(1) of the 2007 Act (tribunal staff and services) may, with the approval of the Senior President of Tribunals, carry out functions of a judicial nature permitted or required to be done by the Upper Tribunal.

(2) The approval referred to at paragraph (1) may apply generally to the carrying out of specified functions by members of staff of a specified description in specified circumstances.

(3) Within 14 days after the date on which the Upper Tribunal sends notice of a decision made by a member of staff under paragraph (1) to a party, that party may apply in writing to the Upper Tribunal for that decision to be considered afresh by a judge.

7.65   The Senior President has issued practice statements on *Delegation Of Functions To Staff.*

7.66   A tribunal may have an express power to correct mistakes made by persons exercising one of its delegated functions. This power may also be implied as part of the tribunal's power over its own procedure.[83]

---

78  [2005] ICR 763 at [20].
79  [2004] ICR 841.
80  [2004] ICR 841 at [6]–[10] and [16].
81  *Barnard v National Dock Labour Board* [1953] 2 QB 18; Lord Parker CJ in *R v Governor of Brixton Prison ex p Enahoro* [1963] 2 QB 455 at 465–466;
82  See also: GRC Rules r4; HESC Rules r4; Land Rules r4; PC Rules r5; SEC Rules r4; Tax Rules r4; WPAFC Rules r4.
83  *Re Macro (Ipswich) Ltd* [1996] 1WLR 145 at 154–155. The discussion refers to inherent power or jurisdiction, but the context suggests that the power is implicit or implied.

## The limits to case management

7.67    A case management power has its limits. A general power to manage proceedings does not, for example, allow a tribunal to do something that is not within its power. For example: it does not allow a tribunal to reinstate proceedings that have been withdrawn,[84] unless there is power to do so. Nor can it authorise something that is expressly forbidden by the rules of procedure.[85]

# Vexatious litigants and others

## Vexatious litigants

7.68    In *IB v Information Commissioner*,[86] an information rights case that began in the General Regulatory Chamber of the First-tier Tribunal, the Upper Tribunal decided that a person who was subject to an order under Senior Courts Act 1981 s42 could not bring proceedings in either the First-tier Tribunal or the Upper Tribunal without the permission of the High Court. This was distinguished in respect of the social security jurisdiction of the Social Entitlement Chamber of the First-tier Tribunal by *AO and BO v Shepway District Council*.[87]

## Civil restraint orders

7.69    These orders apply only to the courts specified in the order, which cannot include the First-tier Tribunal or the Upper Tribunal.[88]

# Time limits

## The importance of time limits

7.70    A proper approach to time limits is important for the (actual or potential) parties to proceedings, to the efficient organisation of the tribunal system, and to the tribunal that deals with a case. For the parties, time limits can ensure certainty and finality. For the tribunal system, they assist the efficient disposal of cases in an appropriate time. And for the tribunal that hears a case, they raises issues of jurisdiction. As Burton J explained in *Clark v Midland Packaging Ltd*:[89]

> The question, then, is one wholly of principle, arising out of the importance which this appeal tribunal places, as do other courts, upon compliance with time limits. This is not simply a pernickety approach by the courts. Compliance with time limits may have very considerable importance in relation

---

84   Brooke LJ in *Khan v Heywood and Middleton Primary Care Trust* [2007] ICR 24 at [76].
85   May LJ in *Vinos v Marks and Spencer plc* [2001] 3 All ER 784 at [20].
86   [2011] UKUT 370 (AAC), [2012] AACR 26.
87   [2013] UKUT 009 (AAC)
88   *JW v Secretary of State for Work and Pensions* [2009] UKUT 198 (AAC).
89   [2005] 2 All ER 266 at [5].

to the bringing of appeals. If an appeal is out of time, then the question as to whether it can go forward becomes one of jurisdiction; albeit, of course, there is a discretion to be exercised, on the face of it there is no jurisdiction in an appeal court to hear an out of time appeal. Therefore the public is entitled to be protected from cases going forward which are out of time, and cluttering up the courts. There is still life in the old latin maxim, *sit finis litium*, and a successful party below is entitled to assume, once the time limit is up, that the decision below remains unchallenged and can be enforced and acted upon.[90]

7.71   It is permissible to have regard to the importance of certainty by preventing the continuance of litigation when deciding whether the power to extend time has been exercised properly.[91]

## Relevant issues

7.72   Time limits raise two issues: calculation and compliance.

7.73   For calculation, three questions arise. All depend on the interpretation of the legislation. When does time begin to run? When does it end? Which days, if any, are excluded in calculating the period in between? These matters are considered below.

7.74   For compliance, two factual questions arise. When was the document despatched? When did it arrive? These matters are considered at para 7.111 onwards.

## Calculating time

7.75   The rules of procedure make general provision about calculating time. UTR r12(1) and (2) is illustrative:[92]

> (1) An act required by these Rules, a practice direction or a direction to be done on or by a particular day must be done by 5pm on that day.
> (2) If the time specified by these Rules, a practice direction or a direction for doing any act ends on a day other than a working day, the act is done in time if it is done on the next working day.[93]

7.76   The rules define working day. UTR r1(3) is illustrative:[94]

> 'working day' means any day except a Saturday or Sunday, Christmas Day, Good Friday or a bank holiday under section 1 of the Banking and Financial Dealings Act 1971.

7.77   A tribunal office may be closed on a day that is a working day within the definition in the rules. That eventuality is not covered by rule 12. However,

---

90   See the same judge in *Woodward v Abbey National plc (No 2)* [2005] ICR 1702 at [3]–[4] and [30]. That decision disapproved of the decision in *Clark*, but not in respect of the passage cited. Also see Cotton LJ in *Esdaile v Payne* (1889) 40 Ch D 520 at 533.

91   See Ward LJ's reasoning in the case of an administrative discretion to extend time in *R (C) v Lewisham London Borough Council* [2003] 3 All ER 1277 at 46.

92   See also: GRC Rules r12; HESC Rules r12; IAC Rules r11; Lands Rules r12; PC Rules r15; SEC Rules r12; Tax Rules r12; WPAFC Rules r12.

93   This does not extend the time by or within which an act must be done; it merely deems it to be done in time: *Hodgson v Armstrong* [1967] 2 QB 299.

94   See also: GRC Rules r12(3); HESC Rules r1(3); IAC Rules r1(4); Lands Rules r12(3); PC Rules r15(3); SEC Rules r12(3); Tax Rules r12(3); WPAFC Rules r12(3).

in those circumstances the period is interpreted as expiring only on the next day when the office is open for business.[95] This is a general principle that operates independently of the rules of procedure.[96]

## The power to extend time

7.78 This is one of the tribunal's case management powers.[97] In *Petition of JM v Advocate General for Scotland*, Lord Boyd distinguished (in the context of the Criminal Injuries Compensation Scheme) between a power to waive a time limit and a power to extend the time, with only the latter being a case management function.[98]

7.79 Even if the power is not contained in the tribunal's rules of procedure, the tribunal can extend time in an exceptional case if the party would otherwise effectively be denied a right of access to the appeal process and is not personally at fault.[99]

7.80 The decision whether or not to extend time may be taken in advance or after the event.

7.81 The power is given to the tribunal, not to the parties. However, the views of the other parties may be relevant to the exercise of the tribunal's discretion. In practice under SEC Rules r23, a decision-maker may ensure that time is extended by not objecting.

7.82 In the absence of an express provision, it is a matter of interpretation whether failure to comply with the time limit renders a purported appeal invalid.[100]

## General principles

7.83 The tribunal has a discretion whether or not to extend time. It must be exercised, like any other discretion under the rules, judicially and in the light of the overriding objective. Otherwise, the Upper Tribunal has said that any guidance 'would either be so general as to be meaningless or would be likely to spark time-consuming and unnecessary satellite litigation.'[101] Nevertheless, some guidance can be gleaned from the cases.

7.84 A person who applies to proceed out of time must justify being allowed to do so.[102] This burden is not a triviality.[103] The mere fact of delay is not itself sufficient to justify extending time. There must be material on which

---

95 *Pritam Kaur v S Russell & Sons Ltd* [1973] QB 336.

96 *Mucelli v Government of Albania* [2009] 1 WLR 276; *R (Modaresi) v Secretary of State for Health* [2011] EWCA Civ 1359, upheld by the Supreme Court in [2013] UKSC 53.

97 See: UTR r5(3)(a); GRC Rules r5(3)(a); HESC Rules r5(3)(a); Lands Rules r5(3)(a); SEC Rules r5(3)(a); Tax Rules r5(3)(a); WPAFC Rules r5(3)(a).

98 [2013] CSOH 169 at [26].

99 *Pomiechowski v Poland* [2012] 1 WLR 1604; *R (Adesina) v Nursing and Midwifery Council* [2013] 1 WLR 3156.

100 *District Court of Vilnius v Barcys* [2008] 1 All ER 733. See chapter 2.

101 *Ofsted v AF* [2011] UKUT 72 (AAC) at [21].

102 Megarry V-C in *Re Salmon (dec'd)* [1981] Ch 167 at 175.

103 [1981] Ch 167 at 175.

the discretion can be exercised. Otherwise, the purpose of a time limit would be subverted.[104]

7.85    The power to allow an appeal against the public law decision of a tribunal to proceed out of time should not be exercised readily.[105]

7.86    Neither the parties nor the tribunal have power to allow proceedings to be initiated outside the period set by legislation without legislative authority.[106]

7.87    There may be a difference in the willingness with which a court will allow a case to proceed out of time according to whether the time limit is laid down by statute or in the rules of procedure. There is authority that time may be extended more readily in the latter.[107] However, the modern approach is to emphasise the importance of keeping to a timetable and not to allow a time limit to be used merely as a target to aim for.

7.88    The fact that the delay was attributable to the fault of a representative is not decisive either for or against the party who has applied for time to be extended, even if the party may have a claim against that representative.[108]

7.89    Factors relating to funding and obtaining advice will only be relevant if they explain the failure to initiate proceedings at any time within the period allowed.[109]

7.90    The fact that a party relied on case-law that has since been changed may be relevant.[110]

7.91    There is no general principle that governs how strictly a time limit is to be applied. As Sedley LJ explained in *Chief Constable of Lincolnshire Police v Caston*:[111]

> . . . there is no principle of law which dictates how generously or sparingly the power to enlarge time is to be exercised. In certain fields (the lodging of notices of appeal at the EAT is a well-known example), policy has led to a consistently sparing use of the power. That has not happened, and ought not to happen, in relation to the power to enlarge the time for bringing ET [employment tribunal] proceedings . . .

## Exercising the discretion in advance

7.92    Exercising the discretion in advance involves adjusting the default timetable for the proceedings in order to take account of the circumstances and needs of the particular case. The governing principle is that the timetable should allow the proceedings to be concluded in the shortest time possible given the issues raised and the resources available to the parties and to the tribunal.

---

104  Swinfed Eady MR in *Re J Wigfull & Sons' Trade Marks* [1919] 1 Ch 52 at 58; Lord Guest in *Ratnam v Cumarasamy* [1965] 1 WLR 8 at 12.
105  *Regalbourne Ltd v East Lindsey District Council* [1993] COD 297 at 298.
106  Holman J in *Gwynedd Council v Grunshaw* [2000] 1 WLR 494 at 498.
107  Megarry V-C in *Re Salmon (dec'd)* [1981] Ch 167 at 175.
108  *R (YT) v First-tier Tribunal and Criminal Injuries Compensation Authority* [2013] UKUT (AAC) 0201 (AAC) at [4.22] in Appendix 2.
109  *Woodward v Abbey National plc (No 2)* [2005] ICR 1702 at [33].
110  *Woodward v Abbey National plc (No 2)* [2005] ICR 1702 at [46].
111  [2009] EWCA Civ 1298 at [31].

## Exercising the discretion after the event

7.93    Exercising the discretion after the event involves remedying an irregularity as a result of failure to comply with the timetable for the proceedings.

7.94    The factors relevant to the exercise of the discretion after the event were listed by McCowan LJ in *Norwich and Peterborough Building Society v Steed*:[112]

> The matters which this court takes into account in deciding whether to grant an extension of time are first, the length of the delay; secondly, the reasons for the delay; thirdly, the chances of the appeal succeeding if the application is granted; and fourthly the degree of prejudice to the respondent if the application is granted.[113]

The Court was concerned with the factors relevant to an application for permission to appeal, but they are of general application. Other factors may also be relevant under the overriding objective, such as the impact on other users of the tribunal system.[114]

7.95    *C M Van Stillevoldt BV v E L Carriers Inc*[115] is an example of McCowan LJ's approach. Griffiths LJ took account of the following factors when extending time: (i) the delay was short; (ii) there were personal and professional reasons explaining the delay by the solicitor; (iii) there was an arguable case on appeal; (iv) apart from having to defend the appeal itself, the other party was not prejudiced.

7.96    The significance of each of these factors will depend on the stage of the proceedings. The case-law is concerned with the more significant delays and reflects the approach in those circumstances. That approach may need to be adjusted for different circumstances. For example: the reasons for delay are likely to be more significant in the case of a failure to initiate proceedings than in the case of a failure to respond to an appeal within the time allowed.

7.97    The principles governing the exercise of the discretion in the employment jurisdiction were summarised in *Muschett v Hounslow London Borough Council*:[116]

> The leading authorities are cited in each case by the Registrar and the legal principles emerge from them. They are *Kanapathiar v London Borough of Harrow* [2003] IRLR 571; *United Arab Emirates v Abdelghafar* [1995] ICR 65; *Aziz v Bethnal Green City Challenge Company Ltd* [2000] IRLR 111; *Woodward v Abbey National plc (No 2)* [2005] ICR 1702 and *Steeds v Peverel Management Services Ltd* [2001] EWCA Civ 419 at [38]–[40], as applied to an employment tribunal case in *Chohan v Derby Law Centre* [2004] IRLR 685.

> In short those principles are as follow and I accept in part the approach of Mr Moretto of counsel in his written skeleton argument. (i) The interests of the parties and the public are in certainty and finality of legal proceedings and thus make the court's response more strict about time limits on appeal than at first instance. (ii) An extension of time is an indulgence requested from the court. The Employment Appeal Tribunal must be satisfied that

112  [1991] 1 WLR 449.
113  [1991] 1 WLR 449 at 450.
114  *R (KS) v FTT and CICA* [2012] UKUT 281 (AAC) at [11].
115  [1983] 1 WLR 207 at 212–213.
116  [2009] ICR 424 at [4]–[5].

there is a full honest and acceptable explanation of the reasons for the delay (*United Arab Emirates v Abdelghafar* [1995] ICR 65, 70, 71). (iii) The 42-day time limit will only be relaxed in rare and exceptional cases for there is no excuse even in the case of an unrepresented party for ignorance of the time limits (*Abdelghafar*, at p 71). (iv) The Employment Appeal Tribunal will have regard to the length of delay and be astute to any evidence of procedural abuse or intentional default (*Abdelghafar*, at p 71). (v) It has often been emphasised that compliance with the time limit is of the essence (*Woodward v Abbey National plc (No 2)* [2005] ICR 1702, paras 3 and 4). (vi) An excuse may not be sufficient unless it explains why a notice of appeal was not lodged through the entirety of the period. This means that an analytic approach should be taken to different parts of the period. Since the test is not 'not reasonably practicable' as it is for many employment protection rights at first instance, it is not fatal to an appeal that the appellant was able during part of the period to comply. To take examples given in argument: a claimant receives the judgment and resolves to appeal in week 1 but suffers a stroke and is physically unable to lodge an appeal in time. A sympathetic approach would be forthcoming for the second segment, of course, but also for the first as it would not be just to debar someone for not acting immediately on receipt of a judgment. A less sympathetic approach to the first segment might be taken if the stroke occurred in week 6. All would depend on the facts adduced in explanation for not acting during that time. (vii) In short as Mummery LJ said in *Abdelghafar* [1995] ICR 65, 72, the three questions are:

(a) what is the explanation for the default? (b) does it provide a good excuse for the default? (c) are there circumstances which justify the tribunal taking the exceptional step . . .?

(viii) In tribunals at first instance, the fault of a legal adviser to enter proceedings in time should not be visited upon the claimant for otherwise there would be a windfall: see *Steeds v Peverel Management Services Ltd* [2001] EWCA Civ 419. While this rule does not apply directly in the Employment Appeal Tribunal, it is a factor which when combined with others might contribute to the exercise of discretion. (ix) The Practice Statement [2005] ICR 660 makes clear that all documents should be produced as required by the Rules and the Practice Direction and that this applies also to litigants in person. Pill LJ in *Dunham v Hull & East Riding Overseas Plastic Surgery* [2006] EWCA Civ 557 at [20]–[22] stated:

> . . . the duty of complying with time limits is upon the parties and their advisers. If a party chooses . . . to leave it very late, it is the responsibility of the party to ensure that the relevant document is served within the time limit It is not the duty of a member of staff of the Employment Appeal Tribunal to advise litigants as to procedures to be followed.

These principles have to applied with caution in other fields, taking account of the different provisions that apply and the different context.[117]

### The reason for the delay

7.98   The reason for the delay is a first, but not necessarily the conclusive, consideration. In *Jurkowska v Hlmad Ltd*,[118] Rimer LJ explained:

---

117  *R (YT) v First-tier Tribunal and Criminal Injuries Compensation Authority* [2013] UKUT 0201 (AAC) at [4.16]–[4.17] in Appendix 2.

118  [2008] ICR 841 at [19].

In the ordinary case a good explanation and excuse will have to be shown. But, even if the explanation does not amount to a good excuse, there may be exceptional circumstances which anyway justify an extension.[119]

7.99    There are different views about the party's decision to act only at the last minute. On the one hand, as Rimer LJ said in *Jurkowska v Hlmad Ltd*:[120]

> . . . an appellant is fully entitled to take the full 42 days for instituting his appeal. He of course runs a risk in doing so, because things can go wrong at the last minute.

But, on the other hand, as Sedley LJ said in that case:[121]

> The real question is whether, given the generous time limit, there was a good and acceptable excuse for missing it.

## The length of the delay

7.100   Even if there is an acceptable explanation for the delay, it is relevant to consider the length of the delay. A delay may be too long to justify time being extended.

## The merits of the case

7.101   The merits of the case may tell for or against time being extended.

7.102       They are always relevant, subject to the terms of the legislation.[122] This is so even if there is a good excuse for the whole of the period of delay. As Lord Donaldson MR explained in *Norwich and Peterborough Building Society v Steed*,[123] where the merits had already been decided:

> Once the time for appealing has elapsed, the respondent who was successful in the court below is entitled to regard the judgment in his favour as being final. If he is to be deprived of his entitlement, it can only be on the basis of a discretionary balancing exercise, however blameless may be the delay on the part of the would-be appellant.[124]

The merits are relevant even if the appeal lies as of right and without permission.[125] The significance of the merits will depend on the other factors. They may have little significance if the delay was short and excusable,[126] but greater significance if the delay was long and not wholly excusable.[127]

---

119  See also *Regalbourne Ltd v East Lindsey District Council* [1993] COD 297 at 298.

120  [2008] ICR 841 at [48].

121  [2008] ICR 841 at [69].

122  For example: in *Short v Birmingham City Council* [2005] HLR 6 at [19], Tugendhat J decided that the merits were not relevant as permission to appeal out of time could only be given if there was good reason for failing to bring the appeal in time.

123  [1991] 1 WLR 449.

124  [1991] 1 WLR 449 at 455.

125  *R (Birmingham City Council) v Crown Court at Birmingham* [2010] 1 WLR 1287 at [32].

126  *Palata Investments Ltd v Burt & Sinfield Ltd* [1985] 1 WLR 942 was limited to this proposition by Lord Donaldson MR in *Norwich and Peterborough Building Society v Steed* [1991] 1 WLR 449 at 455, despite the apparent breadth of the comments about the relevance of the merits. See also the similar reasoning by Ward LJ in the case of an administrative discretion to extend time in *R (C) v Lewisham London Borough Council* [2003] 3 All ER 1277 at [49].

127  *Norwich and Peterborough Building Society v Steed* [1991] 1 WLR 449 at 455.

7.103    According to *R v Secretary of State for the Home Department ex p Mehta*,[128] it is not appropriate to go into the merits in much detail.

7.104    In considering the merits, it is relevant to take into account the reluctance of an appellate body to interfere with procedural decisions.[129]

7.105    The narrower approach taken on striking out a case for lack of prosecution is not relevant to allowing a case to proceed out of time, because there the issue is whether a party should be deprived of an existing right to continue with the proceedings.[130]

### Prejudice – the effect of extending or refusing to extend time on the parties

7.106   Prejudice requires a consideration of the effect of extending or refusing time on the parties. It involves a judgment of the balance of prejudice that each party may suffer, depending on how the discretion is exercised.

### Special reasons or circumstances

7.107   Legislation may link the extension of time with special reasons or special or particular circumstances. These authorities may be relevant to the exercise of the general discretion under the rules of procedure.

7.108    In *R v Secretary of State for the Home Department ex p Mehta*,[131] Lord Denning MR said of a rule that an appeal that was out of time could be allowed 'to proceed if the authority is of the opinion that, by reason of special circumstances, it is just and right so to do':

> . . . the rule gives the tribunal a discretion to do what is just and right. It should be liberally interpreted by them so as not to let an appellant suffer unfairly.[132]

7.109   Expressions like this allow a wider consideration than whether compliance was practicable. That is a factor that may be taken into account, but it is not the only factor.[133]

7.110    Time is more likely to be extended on appeal if a point of general application is involved rather than a point of particular application.[134]

7.111    A retrospective change in the law on which a decision was based is not of itself a ground on which time should be extended for applying for leave

---

128  [1975] 1 WLR 1087 at 1091.

129  Lord Westbury in *Boston v Lelièvre* (1870) LR 3 PC 157 at 163; *Mayor, Aldermen and Citizens of the City of Montreal v Brown and Springle* (1876) 3 App Cas 168 at 184; Lord Guest in *Ratnam v Cumarasamy* [1965] 1 WLR 8 at 12. All these were cases involving decisions by courts in other countries, but the principle is a general one.

130  *Regalbourne Ltd v East Lindsey District Council* [1993] COD 297 at 298, citing Lord Guest in *Ratnam v Cumarasamy* [1965] 1 WLR 8 at 12.

131  [1975] 1 WLR 1087.

132  [1975] 1 WLR 1087 at 1091.

133  [1975] 1 WLR 1087 per Lord Denning MR and Browne LJ at 1090 and 1092.

134  [1975] 1 WLR 1087: Lord Denning MR at 1091, distinguishing the comments he made in *R v Preston Supplementary Benefits Appeal Tribunal ex p Moore* [1975] 1 WLR 624 at 632. Those comments, which relate to points of particular application, were made in the context of judicial review at a time when, as the comments show, there was no appeal from the tribunal to a court. Nonetheless, the distinction is still relevant.

to appeal.[135] The issue is whether it is just to extend time.[136] An extension has been granted on the ground that a party's future, as opposed to past, obligations had been determined wrongly on the law as it now stood.[137] By way of analogy, a retrospective change in the law has been held to be a special circumstance for the purposes of issue estoppel.[138]

### Reasons for delay or reasonably practicable to comply

7.112 Legislation may link the extension of time to the reasons for delay[139] or to whether it was reasonably practicable to comply with the time limit. These authorities may be relevant to the exercise of the general discretion under the rules of procedure.

7.113 The 'reasonably practicable to comply' test applies to employment tribunals. Under the authorities, a party is entitled to rely on the ordinary course of post.[140] If the internet is available, a party is entitled to rely on the website working properly.[141]

## The power to shorten time

7.114 Like extending time, the decision whether to shorten time is a discretion that must be exercised judicially in the light of the overriding objective. Unlike extending time, it can only be exercised in advance to adjust the default timetable for the proceedings.

## Notification and service

7.115 Service is a legal act.[142] It involves an action that is in law sufficient to amount to the formal communication of a legally significant decision or other document. That communication may be to the tribunal or to someone else.

7.116 The rules of procedure provide for service of documents. They provide for the forms in which service may be effected and with any time limits on service.

## The importance of consistency

7.117 It is at least desirable, if not actually essential, that there should be consistency in the application of principles to different forms of service. In

---

135 *Craig v Phillips* (1877) 7 Ch D 249.
136 *Re J Wigfull & Sons' Trade Marks* [1919] 1 Ch 52; *Re Berkeley* [1945] Ch 1.
137 *Property and Reversionary Investment Corporation Ltd v Templar* [1977] 1 WLR 223.
138 Browne-Wilkinson V-C in *Arnold v National Westminster Bank plc* [1989] Ch 63.
139 For example: the Housing Act 1996 s204(2A) allows an appeal to be brought after the end of the period allowed if 'there was a good reason for the applicant's failure to bring the appeal in time and for any delay in applying for permission'.
140 *Consignia plc (formerly the Post Office) v Sealy* [2002] ICR 1193.
141 *Tyne and Wear Autistic Society v Smith* [2005] ICR 663.
142 Notification is also used. For an unsuccessful attempt to distinguish service and notification see *Akram v Adam* [2005] 1 WLR 2762 at [37]–[43].

*Woodward v Abbey National plc (No 2)*,[143] Burton J took account of the importance of consistency between the rules that applied to communications by post, fax and email.

## Permitted methods of sending and delivery of documents

7.118 The rules of procedure provide for the sending and delivery of documents.[144] UTR r13(1) to (5) is illustrative:[145]

**13 Sending and delivery of documents**

(1) Any document to be provided to the Upper Tribunal under these Rules, a practice direction or a direction must be–

(a) sent by pre-paid post or by document exchange or delivered by hand to the address specified for the proceedings;

(b) sent by fax to the number specified for the proceedings; or

(c) sent or delivered by such other method as the Upper Tribunal may permit or direct.

(2) Subject to paragraph (3), if a party provides a fax number, email address or other details for the electronic transmission of documents to them, that party must accept delivery of documents by that method.

(3) If a party informs the Upper Tribunal and all other parties that a particular form of communication, other than pre-paid post or delivery by hand, should not be used to provide documents to that party, that form of communication must not be so used.

(4) If the Upper Tribunal or a party sends a document to a party or the Upper Tribunal by email or any other electronic means of communication, the recipient may request that the sender provide a hard copy of the document to the recipient. The recipient must make such a request as soon as reasonably practicable after receiving the document electronically.

(5) The Upper Tribunal and each party may assume that the address provided by a party or its representative is and remains the address to which documents should be sent or delivered until receiving written notification to the contrary.

## E-mail

7.119 If the tribunal agrees to accept a document by e-mail, service is effective as soon as a message is delivered to the website even if it is not forwarded to the tribunal by the website host at the time or even at all.[146]

## Straddling the time limit

7.120 The delivery of a document to a tribunal or a party may not be complete by the time of the deadline. For example: only some of the pages of a fax may have been transmitted. If the rules of procedure provide that the complete documentation for lodging a claim or appeal must be served by or within

---

143 [2005] ICR 1702 at [30].

144 In the absence of provision, 'any effective means of sending documents is permitted or authorised': Dyson LJ *Levy v Secretary of State for Work and Pensions* [2006] EWCA Civ 890 at [28].

145 See also: GRC Rules r13; HESC Rules r13; IAC Rules r12; Lands Rules r13; PC Rules r16; SEC Rules r13; Tax Rules r13; WPAFC Rules r13.

146 *Tyne and Wear Autistic Society v Smith* [2005] ICR 663.

the stated time, it will not be valid if any part is received late.[147] Otherwise, it is possible that the service may be effective.[148]

## Service by post

7.121 As the rules of procedure authorise service by post, the issue arises whether section 7 of the Interpretation Act 1978 applies. This Act applies to primary legislation and, within the terms of section 23, to secondary legislation. Section 7 provides:

> Where an Act authorises or requires any document to be served by post (whether the expression 'serve' or the expression 'give' or 'send' or any other expression is used) then, unless the contrary intention appears, the service is deemed to be effected by properly addressing, pre-paying and posting a letter containing the document and, unless the contrary is proved, to have been effected at the time at which the letter would be delivered in the ordinary course of post.

### The scope of section 7

7.122 Section 7 deals with service and when it is effected. It does not deal with the issue of when a document was actually despatched. This distinction was drawn by the Court of Appeal in *Gdynia American Shipping Lines (London) Ltd v Chelminski*.[149] The Court was concerned with a requirement in rule 3(3)(a) of the Employment Appeal Tribunal Rules 1993 that an appeal had to be instituted within '42 days from the date on which extended reasons for the decision . . . were sent to the Appellant'. Pill LJ explained:[150]

> In my judgment, the word 'sent' in rule 3(3) of the 1993 Rules is to be given its ordinary meaning and that is unaffected by section 7 of the 1978 Act. That section is concerned with the circumstances in which service is deemed to be effected and when, in such circumstances, it is effected. Section 7 is engaged to the extent that it is relevant if a decision were to be required as to when service is effected. That raises a different question from the question when the document was sent and the rules provide that it is the date of sending from which time begins to run. The deeming provisions of section 7 operate when service, or sending, by post is authorised but they operate to determine the date on which service is deemed to be effected and have no bearing on the issue in this case, which is when the documents were sent. The section does not bear upon the date of sending, which is the date provided by the Rules as the date from which time is calculated. It would have been relevant in the present case if rule 3(3)(a) had provided that time ran from the date when service was effected.

7.123 The distinction between despatch and service is not simply a matter of the language used. There is an issue of interpretation which must be decided

---

147  *Woodward v Abbey National plc (No 2)* [2005] ICR 1702. The Employment Appeal Tribunal there decided that for faxed documents the time of receipt was judged by the record of the Tribunal's fax log.

148  Burton J in *Clark v Midland Packaging Ltd* [2005] 2 All ER 266. That decision was disapproved in *Woodward v Abbey National plc (No 2)* [2005] ICR 1702 by the same judge, but that decision relied at least in part on the tribunal's rule that the complete documentation must be received.

149  [2004] ICR 1523.

150  [2004] ICR 1523 at [10].

in order to determine whether the issue is one of despatch or service. The issue is complicated by the fact that the same language may be used to refer both to despatch and service. In *Chelminski*, for example, the legislation used the word 'sent', which the Court of Appeal held referred to despatch. However, section 7 refers to 'send' as a synonym for 'service'. In *Chelminski*, the court interpreted the provision as dealing with the date from which the time for appealing ran and not with the service of the extended reasons.

7.124     Nor does section 7 deal with the issue of when a document is actually received. In *Levy v Secretary of State for Work and Pensions*,[151] the Court of Appeal was concerned with a claim for a social security benefit that had been posted but had not arrived. The Court held that under the legislation the key issue was when the claim was made and that the legislation fixed this date as the date that the claim was received. Accordingly, section 7 did not apply.[152]

## Analysis of section 7

7.125   This section contains two separate deeming provisions. One deals with whether service has been effected and the other with when. In *R v County of London Quarter Sessions Appeals Committee ex p Rossi*,[153] Parker LJ analysed it as follows:

> This section, it will be seen, is in two parts. The first part provides that the despatch of a notice or other document in the manner laid down, shall be deemed to be service thereof. The second part provides that unless the contrary is proved that service is effected on the day when in the ordinary course of post the document would be delivered. This second part, therefore, dealing as it does with delivery, comes into play, and only comes into play, in a case where under the legislation to which the section is being applied the document has to be received by a certain time. If in such a case 'the contrary is proved', that is, that the document was not received by that time or at all, then the position appears to be that, though under the first part of the section the document is deemed to have been served, it has been proved that it was not served in time.[154]

7.126   The significance of the date of receipt was emphasised by the Divisional Court of Queen's Bench in *R v Kensingston and Chelsea Rent Tribunal ex p MacFarlane*.[155] The tenant in that case had not received notice of the hearing. The Court decided that, although the tribunal was not at fault, the notice it had sent had not been effective. Lord Widgery CJ said:

> The authorities show that, notwithstanding the terms of section [7], if a notice required to be served is a notice of the kind where the date of service is important, it is always open to a person who has failed to receive a notice in the ordinary course of post to prove that it was not received by him at the relevant time, the time relevant to the particular matter with which the notice is concerned. It has further been decided that in notices of that

---

151 [2006] EWCA Civ 890.
152 [2006] EWCA Civ 890 at [29] (Dyson LJ) and [46] (Pill LJ).
153 [1956] 1 QB 682.
154 [1956] 1 QB 682 at 700.
155 [1974] 1 WLR 1486.

character it is possible to prove that the notice was not served in time by showing that it was not served at all.[156]

7.127 Although the first part of the section is subject to a contrary intention appearing in the legislation, it is not subject to proof to the contrary. This led Salmon LJ in *Thomas Bishop Ltd v Helmville Ltd*[157] to say:

> It is unnecessary to consider whether, in a case in which the date of service is irrelevant, it would be open to a defendant to rebut the presumption under the first part of section [7] that service had been effected. It seems strange should he not be entitled to do so, but the language of the statute may create difficulties which the present case does not, however, make it necessary for me to attempt to resolve.[158]

### Contrary intention

7.128 Whether this is shown, according to Parker LJ in *R v County of London Quarter Sessions Appeals Committee ex p Rossi*:[159]

> . . . must depend on the exact words used in the legislation in question, and on the object with which the document is sent.[160]

7.129 The word 'send' is often used. In its usual meaning, this refer only to the act of despatch. In *CA Webber (Transport) Ltd v Railtrack plc*,[161] the Court of Appeal was concerned with section 23 of the Landlord and Tenant Act 1927, which refers to service of a notice 'by sending it through the post'. Peter Gibson LJ said:

> 'Through' in the phrase 'sending . . . through' to my mind naturally connotes the method of sending. It says nothing of the onward transmission of the type contended for . . .[162]

7.130 However, the context may indicate that more is required. This was acknowledged in *Retail Dairy Company Ltd v Clarke*.[163] The court interpreted the word 'send' in the deeming provision in that case as requiring only despatch, but recognised that the context could indicate otherwise. Ridley J said:

> Sending in the ordinary sense is merely despatching. The word 'send' may, however, be used in connection with other words so as to imply that by 'sending' is meant such a sending as that the thing may by the time specified pass into the hands of the person to whom it was sent.[164]

7.131 A requirement that a document be 'presented' excludes the deeming provisions of section 7, as the document must actually reach the recipient. In *House v Emerson Electric Industrial Controls*,[165] the industrial tribunal

---

156 [1974] 1 WLR 1486 at 1492.
157 [1972] 1 QB 464.
158 [1972] 1 QB 464 at 470–471.
159 [1956] 1 QB 682.
160 [1956] 1 QB 682 at 701.
161 [2004] 1 WLR 320.
162 [2004] 1 WLR 320 at [43]. See also *Gdynia American Shipping Lines (London) Ltd v Chelminski* [2004] ICR 1523.
163 [1912] 2 KB 388.
164 [1912] 2 KB 388 at 393.
165 [1980] ICR 795.

legislation provided that a complaint must be presented to the tribunal before the end of a specific time. The Employment Appeal Tribunal held that this meant that it must actually be received. Talbot J said:

> Section 7 deals with the position where an Act authorises or requires any document to be served by post. What is required here . . . is that the complaint shall be *presented* to the tribunal. In our view – and there is previous authority to support it – one cannot equate 'present' with 'post.'[166]

7.132   Whether or not section 7 is excluded requires a consideration of the legislative context as a whole. For example: under TCEA, the rules of procedure allow a tribunal to set aside a decision made if service has not actually been effected.[167] This may suggest that section 7 does apply. If it did not, this provision would be unnecessary. (There was no such provision in *R v Kensingston and Chelsea Rent Tribunal ex p MacFarlane*.[168])

### Proof to the contrary

7.133   If section 7 applies, the deeming provision as to the time of service only applies unless the contrary is proved. There is no limit to the form of proof. In particular, it is not necessary to prove that the document was returned undelivered.[169] It is unlikely that the contrary will often be proved[170] and any evidence to that effect should be tested rigorously.[171]

## Deeming provisions

7.134   Section 7 is a deeming provision. The rules of procedure under TCEA have not used expressions such as 'deem' or 'treat as'. However, they do contain rules that operate in substance as deeming provisions. For example: UTR r38(a) provides that the tribunal may proceed in a party's absence if reasonable steps have been taken to notify the party of the hearing. Some of the authorities on deeming and denying access to a court may be relevant to such provisions.

---

166 [1980] ICR 795 at 801–802.
167 See chapter 15.
168 [1974] 1 WLR 1486.
169 *Thomas Bishop Ltd v Helmville Ltd* [1972] 1 QB 464. The issue of return is relevant as the authorities draw a distinction between a judgment regularly obtained and one which was irregularly obtained. If a judgment has been obtained against a party irregularly, that party has a right to have it set aside, whereas if it has been obtained regularly, the court has a discretion to set it aside and will consider the merits of the case before doing so. Judgment is regularly obtained if the court did not know of the non-delivery, but if it did know (for example, because it had been returned) the judgment is irregularly obtained. See Denning LJ in *R v County of London Quarter Sessions Appeals Committee ex p Rossi* [1956] 1 QB 682 at 693–694. This approach was endorsed as in compliance with article 6 by the Court of Appeal in *Akram v Adam* [2005] 1 WLR 2762 at [41]–[43].
170 Salmon LJ in *Thomas Bishop Ltd v Helmville Ltd* [1972] 1 QB 464 at 471.
171 Buckley LJ at 475. For an example of the contrary being shown, see *Levy v Secretary of State for Work and Pensions* [2006] EWCA Civ 890 at [30]–[32] (Dyson LJ) and [46] (Pill LJ).

### Interpretation of deeming provisions

7.135 These provisions are capable of producing unfair results. The courts recognise the dangers by limiting their scope. They are in principle permissible, but subject to controls.

7.136     In *DEG-Dettsche Investitions und Entwicklungsgesellschaft mbH v Koshy*,[172] the Court of Appeal approved of the statement on the proper approach to the interpretation of deeming provisions in Francis Bennion's *Statutory Interpretation*:[173]

> The intention of a deeming provision, in laying down an hypothesis, is that the hypothesis shall be carried as far as necessary to achieve the legislative purpose, but no further.

7.137 The use of the word 'deem' may mean 'treat as irrefutably'. But, according to its context, it is also capable of being rebutted. This was recognised by Mummery LJ in the Court of Appeal in *Anderton v Clwyd County Council (No 2)*,[174] where he said:

> ... the word 'deemed', as a matter of construction, is capable of meaning 'presumed until the contrary is proved . . .'[175]

7.138 In the case of article 6, the provision must be proportionate and legitimate.

### Denial of access to a court or tribunal

7.139 If a deeming provision operates to bar access to a court or tribunal, it is not effective for that purpose. *R v Secretary of State for the Home Department ex p Saleem*[176] was a domestic law case. Statute authorised rules 'regulating the exercise of the rights of appeal'. The rules provided that a document sent by post was deemed to be received two days later, 'regardless of when or whether it was received'. This rule could operate to deny access to the Immigration Appeal Tribunal. There were alternative remedies, but they were not as effective as an appeal. The Court of Appeal decided that access to a tribunal was a basic or fundamental right akin to access to a court. An infringement of this right was permissible, provided that it was authorised by statute. The authority might be conferred expressly or by necessary implication. In the latter case, it must also be reasonable. As Roch LJ explained:

> Even where the need for such a rule does arise by implication either because the purpose of Parliament cannot be achieved without it or the function of Parliament[177] has laid on a person or body cannot be discharged without it, the rule will be ultra vires[178] the rule-making power if the rule as framed is unreasonable: if it is wider than necessary; if it infringes the fundamental right to a greater extent than is required.[179]

---

172 [2001] 3 All ER 878 at [16] (setting out counsel's argument relying on this passage) and [20] (accepting that argument).
173 5th edn, Butterworths 2008 p950.
174 [2002] 1 WLR 3174.
175 [2002] 1 WLR 3174 at 30.
176 [2001] 1 WLR 443.
177 To make sense, this should read 'the function that Parliament'.
178 That is, 'outside the power of'.
179 [2001] 1 WLR 443 at 450.

The deeming rule in question was not valid, because it was unreasonable and operated to exclude rather than regulate the right of appeal. Having decided that the deeming rule did not apply, the Court decided that the gap thereby created in the legislation was filled by section 7 of the Interpretation Act 1978. The Court left open whether the deeming provision was valid in respect of notices other than an appeal to the Appeal Tribunal.

7.140    This does not mean that every restriction on access, however trivial, amounts to a denial of access. Access to a court is not denied merely because the effect of a deeming provision is to reduce minimally the time available in which to initiate proceedings: *Beanby Estates Ltd v Egg Stores (Stamford Hill) Ltd*.[180]

7.141    Even if the limitation is not minimal, a restriction on access may be permissible. Access to a court or tribunal as a Convention right is not absolute. In *Anderton v Clwyd County Council (No 2)*,[181] the Court of Appeal was concerned with a case in which a notice was served late under a deeming provision, but had actually arrived in time. Mummery LJ said:[182]

> . . . the right of access to the courts is not absolute and that it may be subject to implied limitations: *Golder v United Kingdom* (1975) 1 EHRR 524 at 537 (para 38)). Thus, procedural rules setting time limits that cannot be waived or extended and laying down timetables for the conduct of litigation can, and often will, be lawful limitations on the Article 6 right imposed in pursuit of the legitimate aim of the good administration of justice. The limitations are allowed by the margin of appreciation afforded to States in regulating the right of access to a court, provided, however, that the limitations (a) do not restrict or reduce the access in such a way or to such an extent that the very essence of the right is impaired; (b) pursue a legitimate aim; and (c) represent a reasonable relationship of proportionality between the means employed and the aim sought to be achieved: *Stubbings v United Kingdom* (1996) 23 EHRR 213 at 233, paragraphs 48 and 52; *Ashingdane v United Kingdom* (1985) 7 EHRR 528 at 546, paragraph 57.

The Court decided that certainty was a legitimate aim for the deeming provision to promote.

### Other cases

7.142    If the case does not involve a denial of access to a court or tribunal, an interpretative balancing exercise is undertaken.

7.143    *Beanby Estates Ltd v Egg Stores (Stamford Hill) Ltd*[183] was a Convention right case concerning a notice under the Landlord and Tenant Act 1954 which was subject to a deeming provision in section 23 of the Landlord and Tenant Act 1927. Neuberger J held that the deeming provision had to be interpreted by reference to its language, context and purpose.[184] This required the court:

> . . . to balance . . . certainty . . . allocation of risk, and the purpose behind s23 . . . against the fact that there will be occasional harsh or unfair results.[185]

180  [2003] 1 WLR 2064 at [76].
181  [2002] 1 WLR 3174.
182  [2002] 1 WLR 3174 at [31].
183  [2003] 1 WLR 2064.
184  [2003] 1 WLR 2064 at [60].
185  [2003] 1 WLR 2064 at [86].

7.144 This approach was confirmed by the Court of Appeal in *CA Webber (Transport) Ltd v Railtrack plc.*[186]

## Unilateral and transactional acts

7.145 The courts draw a distinction between acts that are unilateral and those that transactional. A unilateral act is one that is effective without any act on the part of the recipient. A transactional act is one that is only effective with collaboration or some reciprocal action by the recipient.

7.146 The rules of procedure under TCEA may specify whether it is sufficient for a document to be sent (for example: UTR r30(1)) or whether receipt is required (for example: UTR r21(3)). To that extent, the distinction between unilateral and transactional acts is not relevant. However, in some rules the language is not so clear. In those cases, the distinction is relevant.

7.147 Notice requires communication and involves more than the despatch of the relevant documents. In a contract case, Russell LJ said:

> But the requirement of 'notice . . . to', in my judgment, is language which should be taken expressly to assert the ordinary situation in law that acceptance requires to be communicated or notified to the offeror, and is inconsistent with the theory that acceptance can be constituted by the act of posting . . .[187]

But this may not require actual knowledge by the recipient:

> What if the letter had been delivered through the letter-box of the house in due time, but the defendant either deliberately or fortuitously not been there to receive it . . .? . . . The answer might well be that in the circumstances the defendant had impliedly invited communication by use of an orifice in his front door designed to receive communications.[188]

Lawton LJ agreed:

> A notice is a means of making something known . . . If a notice is to be of any value it must be an intimation to someone. A notice which cannot impinge on anyone's mind is not functioning as such.[189]

7.148 The same reasoning was applied to initiating legal proceedings by post[190] and by email.[191]

7.149 *Presenting a document to a tribunal* is effected by delivery and is a unilateral act. It does not involve any collaboration or reciprocal act by the recipient. A case is presented when delivered to the recipient office, even if there is no one present to receive it. The proceedings are commenced on receipt. In *Swainston v Hetton Victory Club Ltd,*[192] the Court of Appeal decided that a complaint to an industrial tribunal had been 'presented to the tribunal', as required by statute, when it was put through the letter box

---

186 [2004] 1 WLR 320.
187 *Holwell Securities Ltd v Hughes* [1974] 1 WLR 155 at 158. See also Browne-Wilkinson J in *Swainston v Hetton Victory Club Ltd* [1983] 1 All ER 1179 at 1182.
188 *Holwell Securities Ltd v Hughes* [1974] 1 WLR 155 at 158.
189 *Holwell Securities Ltd v Hughes* [1974] 1 WLR 155 at 160.
190 *Swainston v Hetton Victory Club Ltd* [1983] 1 All ER 1179 at 1184.
191 *Tyne and Wear Autistic Society v Smith* [2005] ICR 663 at [25]–[26].
192 [1983] 1 All ER 1179.

of the tribunal office, even though that was done on a Sunday when the office was shut. Waller LJ said:

> In my opinion it is difficult to say that presentation requires any action on the part of the body to which presentation is made. Delivery of a document to the proper quarter does not require action on the part of anybody at that quarter . . . [S]ubsequent registration . . . is not part of the presentation.[193]

7.150   *Filing* in the sense of *delivery to a place* is also a unilateral act. In *Van Aken v Camden London Borough Council*,[194] the Court of Appeal decided that a party had filed a document, as required by the Civil Procedure Rules, by 'delivering it . . . to the court office' when it was posted through the letter box of the relevant office. Ward LJ said:[195]

> . . . delivery seems to me to involve a unilateral, not a transactional, act. The ordinary meaning of the words, therefore, 'posting through the letterbox', as was done here, would be sufficient.

7.151   However, *delivery to a particular person* requires actual receipt by the person. In *Aadan v Brent London Borough Council*,[196] the Court of Appeal decided that a party had not filed a document, as required by the County Court Rules, by 'filing it in the court office by delivering it to the proper officer' until it was received by that officer. This could not be done when the office was closed. Chadwick LJ said that, in the context of the Rules:

> 'delivery' requires some element of reception. A document is not delivered to an individual unless the individual is there to receive it.[197]

## Abstract issues

7.152   Courts deal only with issues in the context of a dispute between the parties. They do not deal with points that are of only abstract interest to them, however important they may be. Tribunals take the same approach.

### Why?

7.153   There are at least four reasons for this approach.

7.154   First, it is the nature of judicial proceedings that they deal with issues in the context of the facts of a particular case. In *Ainsbury v Millington*,[198] Lord Bridge said:

> It has always been a fundamental feature of our judicial system that the courts decide disputes between the parties before them; they do not pronounce on abstract questions of law when there is no dispute to be resolved.[199]

---

193  [1983] 1 All ER 1179 at 1184.
194  [2003] 1 WLR 684.
195  [2003] 1 WLR 684 at [58].
196  (1999) 32 HLR 848.
197  (1999) 32 HLR 848 at 854.
198  [1987] 1 WLR 379.
199  [1987] 1 WLR 379 at 381.

7.155 Second, dealing with an issue in the abstract can cause problems for those it is intended to help. In *R (Burke) v General Medical Council*,[200] the Court of Appeal said:

> The court should not be used as a general advice centre. The danger is that the court will enunciate propositions of principle without full appreciation of the implications that these will have in practice, throwing into confusion those who feel obliged to attempt to apply those principles in practice.[201]

7.156 Third, it is the nature of some issues that they cannot be considered in the abstract. The fairness of a hearing is an example. It can only be determined in the context of the evidence and the case as a whole. It was for these reasons that the Court of Appeal decided in *Coles v Barracks*[202] that an issue of fairness (in that case, whether evidence should be disclosed) could not be determined as a preliminary, case management issue.

7.157 Fourth, by taking issues in a particular order, some may be rendered abstract. Taking such a course may, as Tuckey LJ explained in *Palfrey v Wilson*,[203] be 'in the interest of saving expense and dealing with cases proportionately and expeditiously'.

## What is not an abstract issue?

7.158 No abstract issues arises just because:

- it is no longer of general relevance or importance, so long as it affects the rights of the parties to the case;[204]
- the court deals with a case on agreed or even assumed facts;[205]
- an appellate court deals with an issue in principle, leaving the application of the principles to a lower-tier decision-maker.[206]

See below for abstract issues and matters of opinion.

7.159 It may be possible to generate a live issue for the purposes of an appeal by making an appropriately worded declaration. However, this was criticised by the Court of Appeal in *R (Weaver) v London and Quadrant Housing Trust*.[207]

## Non-binding and other matters of opinion

7.160 An issue that concerns an opinion that is non-binding is not abstract if the opinion is potentially of value to the parties.[208] And a decision whether the decision-maker was entitled to form that opinion is a live issue, not an abstract one.[209]

200 [2006] QB 273 at [21].
201 This reasoning would not apply to the Upper Tribunal giving guidance on matters that are regularly before the tribunal. See chapter 13 below.
202 [2007] ICR 60 at [71]–[72] and [81]–[83].
203 [2007] EWCA Civ 94 at [5]; (2007) *Times* 5 March.
204 *R (Bushell) v Newcastle upon Tyne Licensing Justices* [2006] 1 WLR 496.
205 The classic example is *Donoghue v Stevenson* [1932] AC 562, although that was not a tribunal case.
206 As explained by Lord Woolf in *R (Roberts) v Parole Board* [2005] 2 AC 738 at [35].
207 [2009] 4 All ER 865 at [86]–[91].
208 *Re DLP Ltd's Patent* [2008] 1 All ER 839 at [20].
209 [2008] 1 All ER 839 at [20].

## When may an abstract issue be pursued?

7.161   The principles applied by the courts give guidance on the circumstances in which tribunals should allow an abstract issue to be pursued. It depends on whether the issue is one of private law, public law or procedural law. An invitation from the First-tier Tribunal is not sufficient.[210]

## Private law issues

7.162   In *Ainsbury v Millington*,[211] the House of Lords reaffirmed the basic principle that the courts do not deal with points that are of only abstract interest to the parties, however important they may be. Lord Bridge gave three examples of circumstances in which it might be appropriate to decide an abstract issue: (i) friendly settlement cases; (ii) test cases; and (iii) cases pursued in order to resolve an issue on costs.[212] The fact that an issue is of interest to the legal and wider community is not sufficient.[213]

7.163       In *Rolls-Royce plc v Unite the Union*,[214] the Court of Appeal agreed to decide an issue on age discrimination. Wall LJ set out five reasons for doing so: (i) the issue was one of statutory construction, which was a matter of public importance and one of the court's proper functions; (ii) the parties were not agreed on the issue and it would arise again in future; (iii) the issue was important and would affect a large number of people, not only the company's employees; (iv) the propriety of proceeding had received different answers from different High Court judges; and (v) the parties wanted the issue decided and had argued it fully, and the court had spent a considerable time on it.[215] Arden LJ added that although there was no alleged victim before the court, there was a dispute between the parties on matters that affected individual contracts of employment.[216]

7.164       These principles are limited to 'disputes concerning private law rights between the parties to the case'.[217] In *Bowman v Fels*,[218] the Court of Appeal decided that they do not apply if a public law issues arises in the context of a private dispute.

7.165       Neuberger LJ set out the position in *Hutcheson v Popdog Ltd*:[219]

> Both the cases and general principle seem to suggest that, save in exceptional circumstances, three requirements have to be satisfied before an appeal, which is academic as between the parties, may (and I mean 'may') be allowed to proceed: (i) the court is satisfied that the appeal would raise a point of some general importance; (ii) the respondent to the appeal agrees to it proceeding, or is at least completely indemnified on costs and is not

---

210  *Vodafone Ltd v British Telecommunications plc* [2010] 3 All ER 1028 at [48].
211  [1987] 1 WLR 379.
212  [1987] 1 WLR 379 at 381.
213  Thorpe LJ in *Harb v King Fahd Bin Abdul Aziz* [2006] 1 WLR 578 at [29].
214  [2010] 1 WLR 318.
215  [2010] 1 WLR 318 at [54]–[57].
216  [2010] 1 WLR 318 at [151].
217  Lord Slynn in *R v Secretary of State for the Home Department ex p Salem* [1999] 1 AC 450 at 456.
218  [2005] 1 WLR 3083 at [6]–[7] and [13]–[14].
219  [2012] 1 WLR 782 at [15].

otherwise inappropriately prejudiced; (iii) the court is satisfied that both sides of the argument will be fully and properly ventilated.

## Public law issues

7.166 The power to decide issues in which at least one of the parties no longer has an interest is wider in the case of public law than private law. However, the House of Lords decided that there are limits to the power. In *R v Secretary of State for the Home Department ex p Salem*,[220] Lord Slynn said that the power must 'be exercised with caution' and only if 'there is a good reason in the public interest for doing so'.[221] He gave as an example:

> ... when a discrete point of statutory construction arises which does not involve detailed consideration of facts and where a large number of similar cases exist or are anticipated so that the issue will most likely need to be resolved in the near future.[222]

These conditions were not satisfied in that case, because there were few such cases and they all depended on their particular facts.

7.167 The courts have not tried to define more precise criteria than those set out by Lord Slynn. Rather, they have identified the particular facts and circumstances that justify considering the issue in a particular case.

- In *Attorney-General v BBC*,[223] Viscount Dilhorne explained that the House of Lords was dealing with an issue that no longer arose between the parties, because they wanted the House to deal with it and it would remove uncertainty as to the bodies to which the law of contempt applied.[224]
- In *R v Board of Visitors of Dartmoor Prison ex p Smith*,[225] the Court of Appeal heard an appeal on a public law issue, despite the fact that the applicant for judicial review no longer had an interest in the outcome. The Court gave as its only reason that the case raised 'questions of general public interest'.[226]
- In *Bowman v Fels*,[227] the Court of Appeal dealt with the interpretation of a statute in the context of private law litigation, despite the fact that the provision in question created a criminal offence.[228] The Court emphasised the importance and difficulty of the issue and the desire of the parties and the interveners in the litigation that it should be decided.[229]

---

220 [1999] 1 AC 450.
221 [1999] 1 AC 450 at 457.
222 [1999] 1 AC 450 at 457. These conditions do not have to be satisfied in every case: *Hampshire County Council v JP* [2009] UKUT 239 (AAC) at [17].
223 [1981] AC 303.
224 [1981] AC 303 at 336–337.
225 [1987] QB 106.
226 [1987] QB 106 at 115.
227 [2005] 1 WLR 3083.
228 [2005] 1 WLR 3083 at [18].
229 [2005] 1 WLR 3083 at [15]. This point is emphasised in *Harb v King Fahd Bin Abdul Aziz* [2006] 1 WLR 578 at [29] and [54].

- In *Floe Telecom Ltd v Office of Communications*,[230] the Court of Appeal dealt with an issue that did not arise on the appeal because it was important for future cases and appropriate to deal with it.
- In *R (W) v Commissioner of Police for the Metropolis*,[231] the Court of Appeal listed four factors that persuaded it to deal with the issue: (i) the issue was one of interpretation that was a matter of general importance; (ii) the parties were able to consider the issues in the context of particular facts and invited the court to do so; (iii) the authority of the decision of the Administrative Court that was under appeal would otherwise remain in limbo as a precedent; and (iv) the issues were clear cut.

## Procedural issues

7.168    These are akin to public law issues. In *Don Pasquale (a firm) v Customs and Excise Commissioners*,[232] the Court of Appeal agreed to hear an appeal on a procedural issue concerning the deposit that could be required of a taxpayer who was pursuing an appeal on his liability for VAT. The contentious issue between the parties had been settled. Lord Donaldson MR considered that this issue had some analogy with a public law issue and was influenced by the fact that it would otherwise be very difficult to bring the issue before the Court of Appeal again.[233] The Court imposed a condition that the Commissioners must not seek an order of costs against the taxpayer.

## Permission to appeal

7.169    Permission to appeal may be refused on the ground that the issue raised is an abstract one.[234]

## Preliminary issues

7.170    Tribunals have power to split one issue from the others in the case and deal with it separately as a preliminary issue. This is a case management power.[235]

7.171    The proper exercise of this power can avoid the time that would otherwise be spent on dealing with other issues that no longer arise given the decision on the preliminary issue. However, if used inappropriately, the practice can increase the time spent on, and the costs of, the case. As Lord Scarman said in *Tilling v Whiteman*:[236]

230  [2006] 4 All ER 688 at [6]–[7].
231  [2007] QB 399 at [17].
232  [1990] 1 WLR 1108.
233  [1990] 1 WLR 1108 at 1110.
234  Scott Baker J in *R (Begum) v Social Security Commissioners* [2002] EWHC 401 (Admin) at [22].
235  See: UTR r5(3)(e); GRC Rules r5(3)(e); HESC r5(3)(e); IAC Rules r4(3)(e); Lands Rules r5(3)(e); PC Rules r6(3)(g); SEC Rules r5(3)(e); Tax Rules r5(3)(e); WPAFC Rules r5(3)(e).
236  [1980] AC 1.

> Preliminary points of law are too often treacherous short cuts. Their price can be, as here, delay, anxiety, and expense.[237]

For these general reasons, as well as for others unique to a particular jurisdiction,[238] the courts regularly counsel against the use of preliminary issues.[239]

## When a preliminary issue is appropriate

7.172　David Steel J set out criteria for directing the hearing of a preliminary issue in the Court of Appeal in *McLoughlin v Jones*:[240]

> In my judgment, the right approach to preliminary issues should be as follows. (a) Only issues which are decisive or potentially decisive should be identified. (b) The questions should usually be questions of law. (c) They should be decided on the basis of a schedule of agreed or assumed facts. (d) They should be triable without significant delay, making full allowance for the implications of a possible appeal. (e) Any order should be made by the court following a case management conference.

The final requirement may be less appropriate in the tribunal context.

7.173　Neuberger J gave a fuller list in *Steele v Steele*.[241] (i) Could it dispose of the whole or one aspect of the case? (ii) Could it significantly cut the cost of preparation for the hearing and the hearing itself? (iii) If the issue was one of law, how much effort was required to identify the relevant facts? (iv) If it was one of law, could it be determined on agreed facts? (v) Would the determination of the issue unreasonably fetter the parties or the court in achieving a just result? (vi) Was there a risk that it would increase costs or delay the trial? (vii) How likely was it that the issue would have to be determined? (viii) Was it likely that the determination of the issue against one party would lead to that party presenting a different case in order to avoid the effect of the determination? (ix) Was it just and right to direct a preliminary issue?

7.174　Issues of jurisdiction may be decisive of the case[242] and suitable for decision as a preliminary issue.

## When a preliminary issue is not appropriate

7.175　An issue can only properly be severed if it is not dependent on any other issue. This difficulty is likely to arise if the issue is one involving both fact and law.[243]

---

237　[1980] AC 1 at 25.
238　For an example in the employment tribunals, see Morison J giving the judgment of the Employment Appeal Tribunal in *Sutcliffe v Big C's Marine Ltd* [1998] ICR 913 at 918–919.
239　For the views of the House of Lords, see *Boyle v SCA Packaging Ltd* [2009] ICR 1056.
240　[2002] QB 1312 at [66].
241　(2001) *Times* 5 June.
242　*Potts v IRC* (1982) 56 TC 25 at 35.
243　Waller LJ in *Dudarec v Andrews* [2006] 1 WLR 3002 at [15].

7.176    The admissibility of evidence is better dealt with at the substantive hearing rather than as a preliminary issue, because the judge at the hearing will be better informed about the case.[244]

7.177    An issue relating to the fairness of a particular course of action must be determined in the context of the evidence and of the case as a whole. It is, therefore, not suitable as a preliminary issue.[245]

## If the preliminary issue does not dispose of the case

7.178    Black J considered the status of a decision taken at split hearings in *North Yorkshire County Council v B*.[246] Her reasoning is applicable to the determination of preliminary issues if they do not dispose of the proceedings. The case concerned decisions on different issues by different judges in care proceedings.[247] Her analysis was:

> It cannot be argued, in my judgment, that the decisions in care proceedings only crystallise when the court is about to make a final order. I am not saying that decisions are not open to a later attempt to persuade the subsequent judge to change earlier conclusions and findings in the right circumstances. In the right circumstances they can be open to later challenge, and res judicata, or issue estoppel, in its traditional form has a limited place in family proceedings . . . It may be that the situation is better understood if one recognises that once the court embarks on part one of a split hearing it has, in fact, embarked on the final determination of the care proceedings. The process of determination in a split case is spread out over months, or maybe even more time than that in some cases, but it is still a single process,[248] albeit with different hearings, and even in some cases with different judges.[249]

7.179    If the decision on a preliminary issue is not decisive of the case, there may be an issue of how the tribunal should be constituted to deal with the remaining issues. This is discussed in chapter 8.

## On appeal

7.180    On appeal, a decision to try a preliminary issue should be upheld unless the decision to do so was plainly wrong.[250]

244  Mummery LJ in *Stroude v Beazer Homes Ltd* [2005] EWCA Civ 265 at [10], (2005) *Times* 28 April.
245  *Coles v Barracks* [2007] ICR 60.
246  [2008] 1 FLR 1645.
247  This practice was disapproved by the House of Lords in *Re B (Children) (Care Proceedings: Standard of Proof)* [2009] 1 AC 11 at [74]–[76].
248  See also the House of Lords in *Re B (Children) (Care Proceedings: Standard of Proof)* [2009] 1 AC 11 at [74]–[76].
249  [2008] 1 FLR 1645 at [17].
250  *Ashmore v Corporation of Lloyds* [1992] 1 WLR 446; *Grupo Torras SA v Al Sabah (No 2)* (1997) *Times* 17 April.

# Handling dependent cases

7.181　The outcome of one case may depend on the outcome of another. The circumstances may be unique to an individual case. For example: an appeal may be stayed to await the outcome of related judicial review proceedings. Or the circumstances may relate to a number of cases.

7.182　The rules of procedure provide two powers to deal with these possibilities. The case management power to stay is appropriate in all cases.[251] If a number of cases is involved, the case management power in respect of lead cases may also be appropriate.[252]

## Staying proceedings

7.183　If proceedings are stayed, no further action is taken in them until the stay is lifted. The proceedings are held in abeyance. This is an efficient way of dealing with cases whose disposal must await a decision in other proceedings.

7.184　Tribunals do not have inherent power to stay proceedings for abuse of process. This power must be conferred, either expressly or by implication.[253]

7.185　As a case management power, it is not appropriate to stay proceedings as a way of effectively disposing of them.

7.186　Staying is different from postponing and adjourning.[254] Those processes relate to the hearing of the case. They do not halt the proceedings. They are a step in the proceedings that depend on whether the case is ready for hearing or the tribunal is ready to decide it. However, in practice, the powers overlap. For example: a party who has a criminal case pending may apply for listing to be deferred, for a hearing to be postponed or for the proceedings to be stayed. The practical effect is the same.

## Lead cases

7.187　If the outcome of a number of cases may depend on the outcome of an individual case, it may be appropriate to await the outcome of that case. That case should be treated as a lead case and the related cases should be stayed. All tribunals have the case management power to treat a case as a lead case. Some rules of procedure make specific provision for the procedure to be followed in respect of lead cases;[255] others do not. Moreover, the express provision only applies if the lead case is before the same tribunal. It does not apply if the lead case is before a higher tribunal or court. If, for

---

251　See: UTR r5(3)(j); GRC Rules r5(3)(j); HESC Rules r5(3)(j); IAC Rules r4(3)(j); Lands Rules r5(3)(j); PC Rules rr6(3)(m) and 39; SEC Rules r5(3)(j); Tax Rules r5(3)(j); WPAFC Rules r5(3)(j).

252　See: UTR r5(3)(b); GRC Rules r5(3)(b); HESC Rules r5(3)(b); Lands Rules r5(3)(b); PC Rules r6(3)(b); SEC Rules r5(3)(b); Tax Rules r5(3)(b); WPAFC Rules r5(3)(b). There is no equivalent power in the IAC Rules.

253　*R (Harpers Leisure International Ltd) v Guildford Borough Council* (2009) *Times* 14 August.

254　See chapter 8.

255　See: GRC Rules r18; PC Rules r23; SEC Rules r18; Tax Rules r18; WPAFC Rules r18.

whatever reason, the lead case provisions do not apply, they nonetheless provide a model for directions under the tribunal's general powers.

7.188 The lead case procedure provides a convenient and efficient means of managing and then deciding the related cases. The related cases are stayed until the lead case has been decided. They are then decided in accordance with the lead case unless a party can persuade the tribunal that that decision does not apply.

## Other approaches

7.189 Staying is not the only approach that can be taken to blocks of related cases. In some cases, the decision-maker has power to direct the tribunal to decide the cases on a particular assumption of what the law is.[256] If that assumption turns out to be wrong, the decision-maker has power to correct the mistake. Another possibility is that the tribunal could decide the cases on the law as it is and, if necessary, set them aside under its review power[257] when the law is authoritatively established. This approach is only appropriate if it appears that the outcome of the lead case can be predicted with confidence.

# Abatement

7.190 Abatement is the suspension of proceedings pending the appointment of someone to represent a party who has died.[258] In theory, this is a case management power, as the proceedings are capable of being revived. However, for practical purposes they may often be regarded as closed.[259]

## Survival of proceedings

7.191 If a party dies, the first issue is: do the proceedings survive? The answer depends on: (i) the nature of the proceedings; (ii) the interpretation of the relevant legislation; and (iii) if appropriate, section 1(1) of the Law Reform (Miscellaneous Provisions) Act 1934. The authorities were analysed in *Barder v Caluori*.[260]

## Representation for the deceased

7.192 If the proceedings survive, the second issue is: who is to represent the deceased party? Legislation may make provision for this, as regulation 34 of the Social Security and Child Support (Decisions and Appeals) Regulations 1999 does. Otherwise an executor or administrator may act on behalf of the estate.

---

256 See chapter 15.
257 See chapter 15.
258 *Smith v Williams* [1922] 1 KB 158 at 164.
259 *R(I) 2/83*.
260 [1988] AC 20. See also *Harb v King Fahd Bin Abdul Aziz* [2006] 1 FLR 825.

## Options pending appointment

7.193 The third issue is: what happens to the proceedings pending the appointment, if any, of a representative? This was considered in a series of cases by the Commissioners. It may sometimes be possible to give a decision disposing of the appeal. A decision-maker who is the appellant may be willing to withdraw the appeal.[261] A decision-maker who is the respondent may undertake not to enforce the decision under appeal if the appeal is dismissed.[262] If the decision-maker has appealed in the party's favour, it may be appropriate to allow the appeal.[263] Otherwise, it is preferable to abate the case rather than dismiss it.[264] In *Bristol City Council v FV*,[265] the Upper Tribunal decided that abatement was not automatic, but depended on how the interests of justice would better be served.

## Costs

7.194 A tribunal has no power to award costs without authority.[266] Possible reforms of the rules have been suggested in a report by Warren J.

7.195 Under TCEA, costs of and incidental to all proceedings are in the discretion of the tribunal in which the proceedings take place (s29(1)) and the tribunal has full power to determine by whom and to what extent costs are to be paid (s29(2)).

7.196 This is subject to the rules of procedure (s29(3)). Under the rules of procedure, there are four costs regimes: no costs; wasted costs; unreasonable costs; and full costs. TCEA Sch 5 para 12 also authorises the rules to make provision regulating ancillary matters relating to costs.

7.197 According to *McPherson v BNP Paribas (London Branch)*,[267] the proper approach on an appeal against a costs order is that:

> Unless the discretion has been exercised contrary to principle, in disregard of the principle of relevance or is just plainly wrong, an appeal against a tribunal's costs order will fail.[268]

### No power to order costs

7.198 There is no power to order costs in these cases:

- mental health cases under HESC Rules (r10(2));
- any cases under SEC Rules (r10) and WPAFC Rules (r10).

261 As suggested by the Commissioner in *R(SB) 25/84* at [3].
262 As in *R(S) 7/56*.
263 As in *CS 13/48*, cited in *R(I) 7/62* at [6].
264 *R(I) 2/83* and *R(SB) 25/84*.
265 [2011] UKUT 494 (AAC) at [11].
266 *Jones v Department of Employment* [1989] QB 1 at 25; *R(FC) 2/90* in the Commissioner's supplementary reasons.
267 [2004] ICR 1398.
268 [2004] ICR 1398 at [26].

7.199   Even if costs are available, it is not the usual practice to award costs in cases involving children.[269]

## Order for wasted costs

7.200   There is power to make a wasted costs order in these cases:

- cases under GRC Rules (r10(1)(a));
- cases other than mental health cases under HESC Rules (r10(1)(a));
- cases under IAC Rules (r9(2)(a));
- any cases under PC Rules (r13(1)(a));
- any cases under Tax Rules (r10(1)(a)).

7.201   Wasted costs are costs order against a legal representative under TCEA s29(4):

> (4) In any proceedings mentioned in subsection (1), the relevant Tribunal may–
>     (a) disallow; or
>     (b) (as the case may be) order the legal or other representative concerned to meet, the whole of any wasted costs or such part of them as may be determined in accordance with Tribunal Procedure Rules.
> (5) In subsection (4) 'wasted costs' means any costs incurred by a party–
>     (a) as a result of any improper, unreasonable or negligent act or omission on the part of any legal or other representative or any employee of such a representative; or
>     (b) which, in the light of any such act or omission occurring after they were incurred, the relevant Tribunal considers it is unreasonable to expect that party to pay.
> (6) In this section 'legal or other representative', in relation to a party to proceedings, means any person exercising a right of audience or right to conduct the proceedings on his behalf.[270]

7.202   A wasted costs order is exceptional and tribunals should proceed with caution before making one.[271] A party may apply for an order against that party's own representative or the other party's.[272] Although the order may have a penal effect on the representative, it can only be made in respect of costs caused by the representative's conduct.[273]

7.203   The meaning of 'improper, unreasonable or negligent' was discussed by the Court of Appeal in *Ridehalgh v Horsefield*:[274]

> 'Improper' means what it has been understood to mean in this context for at least half a century. The adjective covers, but is not confined to, conduct which would ordinarily be held to justify disbarment, striking off, suspension from practice or other serious professional penalty. It covers any significant breach of a substantial duty imposed by a relevant code of professional conduct. But it is not in our judgment limited to that. Conduct which would be regarded as improper according to the consensus of

269   *R v R (Costs: Child Case)* [1997] 2 FLR 95 at 98, per Staughton LJ.
270   The equivalent for the courts is section 51(6)–(7) of the Senior Courts Act 1981.
271   Peter Gibson LJ in *Byrne v Sefton Health Authority* [2002] 1 WLR 775 at [39].
272   *Brown v Bennett (No 2)* [2002] 1 WLR 713.
273   *Ridehalgh v Horsefield* [1994] Ch 205 at 237.
274   [1994] Ch 205.

professional (including judicial) opinion can be fairly stigmatised as such whether or not it violates the letter of a professional code.

'Unreasonable' also means what it has been understood to mean in this context for at least half a century. The expression aptly describes conduct which is vexatious, designed to harass the other side rather than advance the resolution of the case, and it makes no difference that the conduct is the product of excessive zeal and not improper motive. But conduct cannot be described as unreasonable simply because it leads in the event to an unsuccessful result or because other more cautious legal representatives would have acted differently. The acid test is whether the conduct permits of a reasonable explanation. If so, the course adopted may be regarded as optimistic and as reflecting on a practitioner's judgment, but it is not unreasonable.

The term 'negligent' ... should be understood in an untechnical way to denote failure to act with the competence reasonably to be expected of ordinary members of the profession.[275]

7.204 The representative's defence may be hampered by an inability to produce material that is covered by privilege. This must be allowed for when deciding whether the conditions for a wasted costs order have been established.[276]

## Order for unreasonable costs

7.205 There is power to make an order for costs if a party or representative has acted unreasonably in bringing, defending or conducting proceedings in these cases, and if a decision, direction or order of the Charity Commission was unreasonable:

- cases under GRC Rules (r10(1)(b) and (c));
- cases other than mental health cases under HESC Rules (r10(1)(b));
- cases under IAC Rules (r9(2)(b);
- cases under PC Rules (r13(1)(b));
- any cases under Tax Rules (r10(1)(b)).

7.206 The Court of Appeal explained the proper approach to this power in *Yerrakalva v Barnsley Metropolitan Borough Council*.[277] The tribunal has to look at the whole picture of what happened in the case and to decide whether there has been unreasonable conduct in bringing, defending or conducting the case. In doing this, it has to identify the conduct, what was unreasonable about it and what effects it had. It can be dangerous to adopt an over-analytical approach. There need not be a precise causal link between the unreasonable conduct in question and the specific costs being claimed. The tribunal should focus on applying the language of the rules.[278]

275 [1994] Ch 205 at 232–233.
276 *Medcalf v Mardell* [2003] 1 AC 120.
277 [2012] ICR 420 at [39] and [41].
278 *Sud v London Borough of Ealing* [2013] EWCA Civ 949 at [75].

7.207    For the meaning of 'unreasonable', see the cases above on wasted costs.[279]

7.208    A claimant who withdraws a claim may have conducted proceedings unreasonably so as to be liable for costs. The issue in such a case is not whether the withdrawal was unreasonable, but whether the proceedings had been conducted unreasonably.[280]

7.209    There is no presumption that a regulator who acts reasonably in bringing or defending proceedings should pay the costs of a successful party, at least at first instance.[281]

7.210    The fact that a tribunal ultimately decides that it was perverse to pursue an argument does not necessarily mean that it was unreasonable to do so; the issue is not to be decided with the benefit of that hindsight.[282]

7.211    The Court of Appeal has held that: (i) a party's ability to pay is not a relevant factor; and (ii) an award should cover as a minimum the costs attributable to the unreasonable behaviour.[283]

7.212    If the tribunal makes a costs order under these rules, it should explain the reasons for, and the basis of, the award.[284] Their purpose is to compensate, not to punish.[285]

## Order for full costs and reimbursement of fee

7.213    There is power to order full costs under PC Rules r13(1)(c) in land registration cases and in cases under Tax Rules r10(1)(c) and (d). Rule 10(1)(c) deals with Complex cases in which the taxpayer has not requested protection from liability for costs; rule 10(1)(d) makes similar provision for MP expenses cases. There is power under IAC Rules for the tribunal, if it allows an appeal, to order the Secretary of State to pay costs in order to reimburse fees.

### Liability in the Upper Tribunal

7.214    Costs in the Upper Tribunal are governed by UTR r10.[286] In essence, the Upper Tribunal's powers reflect the power of the First-tier Tribunal in respect of the jurisdiction in question. However, the Upper Tribunal may always make an award of costs in these cases: judicial review proceedings; if the conditions for a wasted costs are satisfied; if the tribunal considers that a party or its representative has acted unreasonably in bringing, defending or conducting proceedings; and in a financial services case if the decision referred was unreasonable.

7.215    In judicial review proceedings that are within the exclusive jurisdiction of the Upper Tribunal, the tribunal should adopt the same approach to

279 The authorities are used interchangeably in *Buckinghamshire County Council v ST* [2013] UKUT 468 (AAC), quoted in *DK v NHS England* [2014] UKUT 0171 (AAC).
280 *McPherson v BNP Paribas (London Branch)* [2004] ICR 1398.
281 *R (Perinpanathan) v City of Westminster Magistrates' Court* [2010] 4 All ER 680.
282 *Buckinghamshire County Council v ST* [2013] UKUT 468 (AAC) at [26].
283 *Kovacs v Queen Mary and Westfield College* [2002] ICR 919.
284 *Lodwick v London Borough of Southwark* [2004] ICR 884 at [23]–[27].
285 *Davidson v John Calder (Publishers) Ltd* [1985] ICR 143 at 146.
286 See also Lands Rules r10.

costs as would be taken on an appeal from the tribunal that is the respondent to the proceedings.[287] The same approach has been applied to the Upper Tribunal's judicial review jurisdiction in criminal injuries compensation.[288] The Upper Tribunal has yet to decide on the principles governing costs on discretionary transfers from the High Court.

## Alternative dispute resolution

7.216 A failure to agree to participate in alternative dispute resolution can affect a successful party's award of costs. The principles were set out by the Court of Appeal in *Halsey v Milton Keynes General NHS Trust*.[289] An attempt to make alternative dispute resolution compulsory would impede a party's access to a court:

> It seems to us that to oblige truly unwilling parties to refer their disputes to mediation would be to impose an unacceptable obstruction on their right of access to the court. The court in Strasbourg has said in relation to article 6 of the European Convention on Human Rights that the right of access to a court may be waived, for example by means of an arbitration agreement, but such waiver should be subjected to 'particularly careful review' to ensure that the claimant is not subject to 'constraint': see *Deweer v Belgium* (1980) 2 EHHR 439, para 49. If that is the approach of the ECtHR to an *agreement* to arbitrate, it seems to us likely that *compulsion* of ADR would be regarded as an unacceptable constraint on the right of access to the court and, therefore, a violation of article 6. Even if (contrary to our view) the court does have jurisdiction to order unwilling parties to refer their disputes to mediation, we find it difficult to conceive of circumstances in which it would be appropriate to exercise it.

A refusal to agree to participate is only relevant to an award of costs if the party acted unreasonably in refusing to participate. The unsuccessful party has to show this.[290] Encouragement by the court is relevant – the stronger the encouragement, the more likely it is to be unreasonable to refuse.[291] Public bodies are in no different position from private ones.[292]

---

287  *R (LR) v First-tier Tribunal (HESC)* [2013] UKUT 0294 (AAC).
288  *H v First-tier Tribunal and CICA* [2014] UKUT 0338 (AAC).
289  [2004] 1 WLR 3002 at [9].
290  [2004] 1 WLR 3002 at [13].
291  [2004] 1 WLR 3002 at [29].
292  [2004] 1 WLR 3002 at [34]–[35].

# Hearing

*continued*

# Nature and types of hearing

## What is a hearing?

8.1 A hearing involves the members of the tribunal meeting as a body. In *R v Army Board of the Defence Council ex p Anderson*,[1] Taylor LJ said:

> There must be a proper hearing of the complaint in the sense that the board must consider, as a single adjudicating body, all the relevant evidence and contentions before reaching its conclusions. This means, in my view, that the members of the board must meet. It is unsatisfactory that the members should consider the papers and reach their individual conclusions in isolation and, perhaps as here, having received the concluded views of another member.[2]

8.2 This does not mean that the members must be physically present together in a particular location. Under TCEA, it is sufficient for them to communicate via modern technology. The definition in UTR r1(3) is illustrative:[3]

> ... 'hearing' means an oral hearing and includes a hearing conducted in whole or in part by video link, telephone or other means of instantaneous two-way electronic communication.

8.3 As well as a meeting, a hearing requires consideration of the case put by each party to the proceedings. This requires that each party must be given the opportunity to produce evidence and provide arguments to support the case put to the tribunal[4] and to rebut the other party's case.[5] It also requires that, apart from special considerations such as national security, each party must know the case put by the other.[6] These requirements are derived from the principles of natural justice and article 6.

8.4 It is not necessary for the parties to the proceedings to be present in order for there to be a hearing.[7]

## Oral hearings and paper hearings

8.5 A hearing may be an oral hearing or a paper hearing on the documents alone. An oral hearing is one that the parties to the proceedings are invited to attend. A paper hearing on the documents is one that the parties to the proceedings are not invited to attend. The word 'hearing' is appropriate

---

1 [1992] QB 169.

2 [1992] QB 169 at 187.

3 See also: GRC Rules r1(3); HESC Rules r1(3); IAC Rules r1(4); Lands Rules r1(3); PC Rules r1(3); SEC Rules r1(3); Tax Rules r1(3); WPAFC Rules r1(3).

4 Lord Reading CJ in *The King v Tribunal of Appeal under the Housing Act 1919* [1920] 3 KB 334 at 340–341; Taylor LJ in *R v Army Board of the Defence Council ex p Anderson* [1992] QB 169 at 188.

5 *Score Draw Ltd v Finch* (2007) *Times* 9 April.

6 Taylor LJ in *R v Army Board of the Defence Council ex p Anderson* [1992] QB 169 at 189.

7 Lord Wright MR in *R v Income Tax Special Commissioners ex p Elmhirst* [1936] 1 KB 487 at 500.

for both procedures.[8] However, the rules of procedure under TCEA use 'hearing' in the sense of an oral hearing.[9]

8.6    A hearing, though, is essential. If the rules of procedure allow a case to be determined without a hearing, this means without an oral hearing.[10]

8.7    The difference between an oral hearing and a paper hearing lies in whether the parties are entitled to attend, not whether they actually attend. This is significant in that one party may attend an oral hearing in the absence of the others, but no party may attend a paper hearing.

8.8    Under TCEA, a tribunal may proceed with an oral hearing in the absence of a party. Two conditions must always be satisfied:[11] (i) the party was notified of the hearing or reasonable steps were taken to do so;[12] and (ii) it is in the interests of justice to proceed with the hearing. Even if (i) is satisfied, it may still be a breach of natural justice to proceed in the party's absence.[13] In deciding whether (ii) is satisfied, it is relevant to take account of the powers to remedy the position if it is later established that the party did not actually receive the notice.[14]

8.9    There are additional conditions before a tribunal may proceed in the absence of the patient in a mental health case under HESC Rules (r39(2)): (iii) the medical examination requirement must be satisfied; and (iv) the patient must have decided not to attend or be unable to do so as a result of ill health.

## Should the tribunal hold an oral hearing?

8.10    Whether to hold an oral hearing and the form of any hearing are case management powers.[15]

### In the First-tier Tribunal

8.11    The basic approach is that the First-tier Tribunal is under a duty to hold an oral hearing before making a decision, unless two conditions are satisfied:[16] (i) each party must have consented to the matter being decided

---

8   Russell LJ in *R v Immigration Appeal Tribunal ex p Jones* [1988] 1 WLR 477 at 481.

9   See: UTR r1(3); GRC Rules r1(3); HESC Rules r1(3); Lands Rules r1(3); PC Rules r1(3); SEC Rules r1(3); Tax Rules r1(3); WPAFC Rules r1(3).

10  Lord Reading CJ in *The King v Tribunal of Appeal under the Housing Act 1919* [1920] 3 KB 334 at 340.

11  See: UTR r38; GRC Rules r36; HESC Rules rr27 (other than mental health cases) and 39(1) (mental health cases); IAC Rules r28; Lands Rules r49; PC Rules r34; SEC Rules r31; Tax Rules r33; WPAFC Rules r29.

12  If the party did not receive the notice, the tribunal has power to set its decision aside: see chapter 15.

13  *MH v Pembrokeshire County Council* [2010] UKUT (AAC) 28 (AAC).

14  *KH v CMEC* [2012] UKUT 329 (AAC) at [19] and [28]. The remedial powers mentioned by the judge were (i) the tribunal's power to set aside its own decision on the basis of the absence of a party from a hearing and (ii) the power to set aside on appeal for breach of natural justice.

15  See: UTR r5(3)(f) and (g); GRC Rules r5(3)(f) and (g); HESC Rules r5(3)(f) and (g); IAC Rules r4(3)(f) and (g); Lands Rules r5(3)(f) and (g); PC Rules r6(3)(h) and (i); SEC Rules r5(3)(f) and (g); Tax Rules r5(3)(f) and (g); WPAFC Rules r5(3)(f) and (g).

16  See: GRC Rules r32(1); HESC Rules r23(1) (other than mental health cases); PC Rules r34; SEC Rules r27(1); Tax Rules r29(1); WPAFC Rules r25(1).

without an oral hearing; and (ii) the tribunal must consider that it is able to decide the matter without one.

8.12 Condition (ii) may be applied in advance before a case is put to a tribunal for decision or at a paper hearing. Presumably the test is whether an oral hearing is reasonably required; otherwise the condition would never be satisfied.

8.13 There are three exceptions to the basic approach. First, for mental health cases under HESC Rules, the duty to hold an oral hearing is absolute (r35). Second, there are special rules under IAC Rules to take account of the special circumstances of immigration and asylum cases (r25(1) and Sch para 9). And for criminal injuries compensation cases under SEC Rules, the tribunal may decide the proceedings without an oral hearing, but must hold one to reconsider the decision on the application of any party (r 27(4)–(6)).

8.14 The duty applies to decisions that dispose of the proceedings, except for decisions:

- deciding post-decisions matters – correction, set aside, review and permission to appeal;[17]
- striking out or barring,[18] except in mental health cases under HESC Rules and under IAC Rules;
- implementation of a court order in a land registration case.[19]

### In the Upper Tribunal

8.15 In the Upper Tribunal, the holding of an oral hearing is in the discretion of the tribunal, but it must have regard to any view expressed by a party on the matter (UTR r34; Lands Rules r46). This implies that the parties must be given a chance to express a view.

8.16 The discretion to hold an oral hearing must be exercised in accordance with the overriding objective. The key consideration is likely to coincide with the common law test for requiring an oral hearing: what is necessary in order to ensure a fair hearing?[20]

8.17 If the Upper Tribunal sets aside a decision, it may re-make it. In doing so, it may make findings of fact. If this involves deciding disputed issues of fact, the tribunal must hold an oral hearing.[21]

---

17 See: GRC Rules r32(2); HESC Rules rr23(2) (other than mental health cases) and 35(2) (mental health cases); IAC Rules r25(3); SEC Rules r27(2); Tax Rules r29(2); WPAFC Rules r25(2).

18 See: GRC Rules r32(3); HESC Rules r23(3) (other than mental health cases); PC Rules r31(4); SEC Rules r27(3); Tax Rules r29(3); WPAFC Rules r25(3).

19 PC Rules r31(4).

20 Taylor LJ in *R v Army Board of the Defence Council ex p Anderson* [1992] QB 169 at 187–188.

21 *Jucius and Juciuvienè v Lithuania* [2009] 1 FLR 403. But see the discussion in the following paragraphs.

## The right to an oral hearing

8.18    The decision whether or not to hold an oral hearing where the rules of procedure do not so require will be informed by the principles that apply at common law or under article 6.

8.19    The form that the hearing takes is subject to the overriding requirement that it be a fair one. This is the position under both domestic law and article 6.[22] The test is whether fairness requires a hearing in the light of the facts of the case and the importance of what is at stake.[23] The purpose is to assist in decision-making and to allow participation.[24] It is never acceptable to decide against a hearing in order to save time, trouble or expense,[25] although the person must have something to say that is relevant to the decision to be taken.[26]

### At common law

8.20    There is no requirement that an oral hearing is required for all cases in all circumstances,[27] unless fairness so requires.[28] The duty to act fairly depends on the circumstances of the case.[29] In some circumstances, an oral hearing may be essential; in other circumstances, it may not.[30] In *R (Ewing) v Department for Constitutional Affairs*,[31] Sullivan J said that:

> I would accept, as a very broad generalisation, that fairness is more likely to require an oral hearing in proceedings before the High Court, as opposed to an administrative tribunal, bearing in mind the kinds of issues that are determined by the court, as opposed to administrative tribunals.

8.21    One relevant circumstance is whether it will be necessary to determine an issue of disputed fact. However, this is not the sole decisive factor. As Lord Bingham explained in *R (West) v Parole Board*:[32]

> While an oral hearing is most obviously necessary to achieve a just decision in a case where facts are in issue which may affect the outcome, there are other cases in which an oral hearing may well contribute to achieving a just decision. The possibility of a detainee being heard either in person or, where necessary, through some form of representation has been recognised by the European Court as, in some instances, a fundamental procedural guarantee in matters of deprivation of liberty . . .

---

22   The relationship between domestic law and the Convention right was explained in *Osborn v The Parole Board* [2013] UKSC 61 at [54]–[63].

23   *Osborn v The Parole Board* [2014] 1 All ER 369 at [2(i)].

24   *Osborn v The Parole Board* [2014] 1 All ER 369 at [2(iv)].

25   *Osborn v The Parole Board* [2014] 1 All ER 369 at [2(viii)] and [72].

26   *Osborn v The Parole Board* [2014] 1 All ER 369 at [2(iv)] and [68].

27   Taylor LJ in *R v Army Board of the Defence Council ex p Anderson* [1992] QB 169 at 187

28   Sullivan J in *R (Ewing) v Department for Constitutional Affairs* [2006] 2 All ER 993 at [27].

29   Clarke LJ in *R (Thompson) v Law Society* [2004] 1 WLR 2522 at 45.

30   [2004] 1 WLR 2522 at [45]–[46].

31   [2006] 2 All ER 993 at [32].

32   [2005] 1 WLR 350 at [31] and [35]. Although the quotations from Lord Bingham's speech relate to the position at common law, they are equally application to article 6: see [44]. See also *Osborn v The Parole Board* [2014] 1 All ER 369 at [73]–[79].

Even if important facts are not in dispute, they may be open to explanation or mitigation, or may lose some of their significance in the light of other new facts. While the Parole Board's task is certainly to assess risk, it may well be greatly assisted in discharging it (one way or the other) by exposure to the prisoner or the questioning of those who have dealt with him. It may often be very difficult to address effective representations without knowing the points that are troubling the decision-maker.

Lord Hope emphasised the disadvantages of a practice of not holding oral hearings. He referred to the Board's institutional reluctance to hold oral hearings and said:

It would not be surprising if a consequence of that reluctance was an approach, albeit unconscious and unintended, which undervalued the importance of issues of fact that the prisoner wished to dispute. If the system is such that oral hearings are hardly ever held, there is a risk that cases will be dealt with instead by making assumptions. Assumptions based on general knowledge and experience tend to favour the official version as against that which the prisoner wishes to put forward.[33]

8.22    However, efficient and proportionate case management often requires, or justifies, consideration on the papers alone.[34]

### Under article 6

8.23    An oral hearing is an instance of the fundamental principle of open justice[35] and maintenance of public confidence in the judicial system.[36] However, there are limits to that principle. And there are exceptions to it.[37]

8.24    The European Court of Human Rights has drawn a distinction between the right to an oral hearing and the need to hold one. There must be a right to a hearing, but the right may be waived or there may be exceptional circumstances that justify not holding an oral hearing. In *Lundevall v Sweden*,[38] the Court said:

The Court first finds that the entitlement to a 'public hearing' in Article 6 § 1 necessarily implies a right to an 'oral hearing'. However, the obligation under Article 6 § 1 to hold a public hearing is not an absolute one. Thus, a hearing may be dispensed with if a party unequivocally waives his or her right thereto and there are no questions of public interest making a hearing necessary. A waiver can be done explicitly or tacitly, in the latter case for example by refraining from submitting or maintaining a request for a hearing . . .

Furthermore, a hearing may not be necessary due to exceptional circumstances of the case, for example when it raises no questions of fact or law which cannot be adequately resolved on the basis of the case-file and the parties' written observations . . .[39]

---

33 [2005] 1 WLR 350 at [66].

34 *Collier v Williams* [2006] 1 WLR 1945 at [34].

35 *Re A* [2006] 1 WLR 1361 at [37].

36 *Moser v Austria* [2007] 1 FLR 702 at [93].

37 *Re A* [2006] 1 WLR 1361 at [37].

38 [2002] ECHR 733 at [34]; Application No 38629/97 Judgment on 12 November 2002.

39 *Salomonsson v Sweden* [2002] ECHR 736; Application No 38978/97 Judgment on 12 November 2002 was to the same effect.

There is not necessarily a right to an oral hearing at all stages of a case. The Court referred to oral hearings in a sequence of appeals:

> In this connection, the Court reiterates that in proceedings before a court of first and only instance there is normally a right to a hearing . . . However, the absence of a hearing before a second or third instance may be justified by the special features of the proceedings at issue, provided a hearing has been held at first instance . . . Accordingly, unless there are exceptional circumstances that justify dispensing with a hearing, the right to a public hearing under Article 6 § 1 implies a right to an oral hearing at least before one instance.[40]

According to the second sentence in this passage, the relevant factor is whether an oral hearing has been held below, not whether there was a right to one. In the case, the benefit claimant had a right to an oral hearing in the tribunal below, but had waived that right. But the Court held that he nonetheless should have been allowed an oral hearing on appeal, because his oral evidence was relevant to the issue that the tribunal had to determine.[41] However, an oral hearing is not necessary if the issue for determination does not need oral input, even if no oral hearing has been held below.[42]

8.25    One factor that may be taken into account in the case of an appellate body is the need for an expeditious handling of its case load.[43]

8.26    Lord Hope summarised the effect of the Strasbourg jurisprudence in *R (Dudson) v Secretary of State for the Home Department*:[44]

> What is at issue is the general right to a 'fair and public hearing' in article 6(1). There is no absolute right to a public hearing at every stage in the proceedings at which the applicant or his representatives are heard orally. The application of the article to proceedings other than at first instance depends on the special features of the proceedings in question. Account must be taken of the entirety of the proceedings of which they form part, including those at first instance. Account must also be taken of the role of the person or person conducting the proceedings that are in question, the nature of the system within which they are being conducted and the scope of the powers that are being exercised. The overriding question, which is essentially a practical one as it depends on the facts of each case, is whether the issues that had to be dealt with at the stage could properly, as a matter of fair trial, be determined without hearing the applicant orally.

8.27    In *Moser v Austria*,[45] the European Court of Human Rights decided that entire classes of case should not be excluded from public, and therefore oral, hearing without any discretion to hold one in an appropriate case[46] and that public scrutiny was more important in disputes between individuals and the State than in private disputes.[47]

---

40  [2002] ECHR 736 at [36].
41  [2002] ECHR 736 at [39]–[40].
42  *Döry v Sweden* [2002] ECHR 731; Application No 28394/95 Judgment on 12 November 2002 at [42]–[43], where the issue concerned the interpretation of medical evidence.
43  *Hoppe v Germany* (2002) 38 EHRR 285 at [63].
44  [2006] 1 AC 245 at [34].
45  [2007] 1 FLR 702.
46  [2007] 1 FLR 702 at [95]–[96].
47  [2007] 1 FLR 702 at [97].

8.28     The domestic cases emphasise that the procedures available to the parties must be considered as a whole. If they allow a court of full jurisdiction to deal with the issues raised, there is no violation of article 6. So, a failure to hold an oral hearing where one was required at one stage will not be a violation if the issue can be dealt with appropriately in later proceedings. In practice, the issue is whether an appeal or judicial review is sufficient to allow the issues to be determined appropriately. This will depend on the issues raised in the case and on the powers of the court or tribunal on appeal or judicial review. Judicial review is usually concerned with the legality of a decision and with the procedures followed. It does not usually allow a further investigation into the facts. However, this may be done exceptionally, as in *R (Wilkinson) v Broadmoor Special Hospital*,[48] in which even the cross-examination of expert witnesses was permitted.

8.29     A review by a body with full jurisdiction which extends to issues of fact need not resolve those issues by hearing oral evidence. In *R (N) v Doctor M*,[49] the Court of Appeal said:

> So far as we are aware, there is nothing in the Strasbourg jurisprudence to indicate that, even in a case where the question whether there has been a violation of a Convention right depends on disputed issues of fact or expert opinion, Art 6 requires those issues to be determined by oral evidence.[50]

8.30     The result is that it may not be necessary to hold an oral hearing at any stage of the proceedings.[51]

8.31     An oral hearing is not necessary if a tribunal is only concerned with permission to appeal and does not make a full examination of the case.[52]

## Public hearings and private hearings

8.32     If the tribunal holds an oral hearing, it may be in public or in private. The difference determines who may attend. This is discussed below.

8.33     The basic approach is that hearings are in public, unless the tribunal directs that all, or part, of it is to be held in private.[53] This is consistent with the principle of open justice;[54] it is permissible to depart from this if it is necessary in the interests of justice or for the protection of an individual.[55] Privacy in the case of hearings affecting children is generally compliant with article 6.[56]

---

48  [2002] 1 WLR 419.

49  [2003] 1 FLR 667.

50  [2003] 1 FLR 667 at [41].

51  As in *R (on the application of Thompson) v The Law Society* [2004] 2 All ER 113.

52  *Lundevall v Sweden* [2002] ECHR 733; Application No 38629/97 Judgment on 12 November 2002 at [35].

53  See: UTR r37(1)–(3); GRC Rules r35(1)–(3); HESC Rules r26(1)–(3) (other than mental health cases); IAC Rules r27(1)–(3); Lands Rules r48(1), (3), (4) and (5); PC Rules, r33(1)-(4); SEC Rules r30(1), (3) and (4); Tax Rules r32(1)–(3); WPAFC Rules r28(1)–(3).

54  This is a common law principle that also applies to a statutory body, subject to any statutory provisions and any countervailing reasons: *Kennedy v Charity Commission* [2014] 2 All ER 847 at [128].

55  *A v British Broadcasting Corporation* [2014] 2 All ER 1037.

56  *Pelling v Bruce-Williams* [2004] Fam 155.

8.34    There are three exceptions to the basic approach.

8.35    First, mental health cases under HESC Rules (but not under UT Rules) must be held in private unless it is in the interests of justice to hold the hearing in public (r38(1)). If the patient applies for a public hearing, the tribunal must consider: (i) the extent to which reporting could be controlled; (ii) the nature and extent of the patient's understanding of the request; (iii) the patient's safety at the hearing; and (iv) the impact on the patient's condition.[57]

8.36    In *AH v West London Mental Health Trust and the Secretary of State for Justice*,[58] the three-judge panel decided that this was compatible with the patient's Convention right under article 6. The panel identified the following factors as relevant when considering whether to direct a public hearing:

- Is it consistent with the subjective and informed wishes of the applicant (assuming he is competent to make an informed choice)?
- Will it have an adverse effect on his mental health in the short or long term, taking account of the views of those treating him and any other expert views?
- Are there any other special factors for or against a public hearing?
- Can practical arrangements be made for an open hearing without disproportionate burden on the authority?[59]

8.37    In *Independent News and Media v A*,[60] the Court of Appeal considered the right of access to proceedings in the Court of Protection. The Court decided that it was necessary to take account of a party's right to a private life under Article 8 and the media's right to freedom of expression under Article 10.

8.38    Second, criminal injuries compensation cases under SEC Rules (but not under UTR) must be held in private unless two conditions are satisfied: (i) the appellant has consented to the hearing being held in public; and (ii) it is in the interest of justice to do so (r30(2)).

8.39    Third, a case under Tax Rules may be held in private in five circumstances: (i) in the interests of public order or national security; (ii) to protect a person's right to respect for their private and family life; (iii) to maintain confidentiality of sensitive information; (iv) to avoid serious harm in the public interest; (v) to hold a public hearing would prejudice the interests of justice (r32(2)). Strictly, this is not an exception. It gives the tribunal a power in the circumstances specified. It is more in the nature of a list of factors that must be taken into account in exercising the power to direct a private hearing. However, given the nature of the factors, it is likely that the tribunal will direct a private hearing if one of them is satisfied.

---

57  *R (Mersey Care NHS Trust) v Mental Health Review Tribunal* [2005] 1 WLR 2469.

58  [2010] UKUT 264 (AAC).

59  *AH v West London Mental Health Trust and the Secretary of State for Justice* [2010] UKUT 264 (AAC) at [44].

60  [2010] 2 FLR 1290.

## Attendance

8.40 Whether a hearing is in public or in private determines who may attend. If it is in public, anyone may attend who has not been excluded. If it is in private, the tribunal may determine who is entitled to attend. Unless the press or general public are interested in attending, there is little practical significance between the two types of hearing.

8.41 For some people, the position is the same for both types of hearing: the parties, their representatives, others who attend to assist and support them, witnesses, and other persons concerned. These are all entitled to attend, subject to the general and special powers of exclusion.

8.42 The parties have a right to attend a hearing.[61] This is subject to special powers of exclusion:

- under HESC Rules, the power to exclude an applicant under section 166(5) of the Education Act 2002 (r24); and
- under Tax Rules, the power to hold proceedings without notice (r30).

8.43 Representatives who have been notified to the tribunal are entitled to attend under their power to do anything that the party may do.[62] Otherwise, representatives may only attend if they accompany the party.[63] There is no power for these representatives to attend without the party.

8.44 Obviously, those who accompany a party to the hearing, whether or not to assist in presenting the case, may only attend with the party.[64]

8.45 Witnesses must be allowed to attend to give evidence. However, there is a special power to exclude them from the hearing until they give evidence.[65] In some circumstances, it may be desirable, or even necessary, for a witness to hear other evidence. It may only be in this way that an expert can give an informed opinion on the basis of that other evidence. Otherwise, the basis for exclusion is the risk that the witnesses will adjust their evidence to fit evidence that has already been given. However, they may already know what that evidence is.

8.46 There are others who are concerned in the proceedings and also have the right to attend under HESC Rules:

- children in special educational needs cases and discrimination in schools cases (r24(b));
- anyone notified of proceedings in a mental health case (r36(2)).

---

61 See: UTR r35; GRC Rules r33(1); HESC Rules rr24(a) and 36; IAC Rules r27; Lands Rules r48(2); SEC Rules r28; Tax Rules r30; WPAFC Rules r26.

62 See: UTR r11(3); GRC Rules r11(3); HESC Rules r11(3); IAC Rules r10(4); Lands Rules r11(3); SEC Rules r11(5); Tax Rules r11(3); WPAFC Rules r11(4).

63 See: UTR r11(5); GRC Rules r11(5); HESC Rules r11(5); Lands Rules r11(5); PC Rules r14(3); SEC Rules r11(7); Tax Rules r11(5); WPAFC Rules r11(6). There is no equivalent power in IAC Rules.

64 See: UTR r11(5); GRC Rules r11(5); HESC Rules r11(5); Lands Rules r11(5); PC Rules r14(5); SEC Rules r11(7); Tax Rules r11(5); WPAFC Rules r11(6). There is no equivalent power in IAC Rules.

65 See: UTR r37(5); GRC Rules r35(5); HESC Rules rr26(6) and 38(5); IAC Rules r27(5); Lands Rules r48(7); PC Rules r33(6); SEC Rules r30(6); Tax Rules r32(5); WPAFC Rules r28(5).

## Exclusion from a hearing

8.47    In addition to the special powers already identified, the Upper Tribunal and First-tier Tribunal have a general power to exclude individuals from a hearing. It applies regardless of the capacity in which the person would be entitled to attend the hearing, but only in defined circumstances. UTR r37(4) is illustrative:[66]

> (4) The Upper Tribunal may give a direction excluding from any hearing, or part of it–
>
> (a) any person whose conduct the Upper Tribunal considers is disrupting or is likely to disrupt the hearing;
>
> (b) any person whose presence the Upper Tribunal considers is likely to prevent another person from giving evidence or making submissions freely;
>
> (c) any person who the Upper Tribunal considers should be excluded in order to give effect to a direction under rule 14(2) (withholding information likely to cause harm);
>
> (d) any person where the purpose of the hearing would be defeated by the attendance of that person; or
>
> (e) a person under the age of eighteen years.

8.48    In the context of the Freedom of Information Act 2000, the Court of Appeal has decided that rules equivalent to para(4)(d) are validly made and may properly apply to a legal representative, although the tribunal should aim to follow a procedure that best reconciles the divergent interests of the parties and minimises any disadvantages.[67]

# Notice of hearing

8.49    Notice is essential if there is to be a fair hearing.

## Notice of an oral hearing

8.50    Each party must have reasonable notice of the time and place of the hearing and of any change to the time or place.[68]

8.51    The basic approach is that reasonable notice means at least 14 days, although this may be shortened if the parties consent or the case is urgent or exceptional.[69] However, shorter notice than 14 days is fixed for the following cases:

---

66  See also: GRC Rules r35(4); HESC Rules rr26(5) (other than mental health cases) and 38(4) (mental health cases); IAC Rules r27(4); Lands Rules r48(6); PC Rules 33(5); SEC Rules r30(5); Tax Rules r32(4); WPAFC Rules r28(4).

67  *Browning v Information Commissioner and DBIS* [2014] EWCA Civ 1050 at [28], [33] and [35].

68  See: UTR r36(1); GRC Rules r34(1); (other than mental health cases) HESC Rules r25(1); IAC Rules r26; Lands Rules r47(1); PC Rules r32(1); SEC Rules r29(1); Tax Rules r31(1); WPAFC Rules r27(1). The requirement to give notice of any change would be implied: *R v County of London Quarter Sessions Appeals Committee ex p Rossi* [1956] 1 QB 682.

69  See: UTR r36(2)(b); GRC Rules r34(2); HESC Rules rr25(2)(c) (other than mental health cases) and 37(4)(b) (mental health cases); Lands Rules r47(2); PC Rules r32(2); SEC Rules r29(2)(b); Tax Rules r31(2); WPAFC Rules r27(2). There is no equivalent power in IAC Rules.

8.52    Under HESC Rules:

- at least three working days are required for suspension cases (r25(2)(a));
- at least seven days are required for orders under section 166(5) of the Education Act 2002 (r25(2)(b));
- at least three working days are required for proceedings under section 66(1)(a) of the Mental Health Act 1983 (r37(4)(a)).

8.53    Under SEC Rules, between one and five days are required for asylum support cases under (r29(2)(a));

8.54    Under UT Rules, at least two working days are required for judicial review proceedings under (r36(2)(a)).

8.55    In addition in some mental health cases, HESC Rules prescribe the period when the hearing must start:

- proceedings under section 66(1)(a) of the Mental Health Act 1983 must start within seven days of the application notice being received by the tribunal (r37(1));
- proceedings under section 75(1) of the Mental Health Act 1983 must start between five and eight weeks of the reference being received by the tribunal (r37(2)).

## Notice of a paper hearing

8.56    If the hearing is to be on the papers alone without any party present, the parties do not need to know the precise time and place of the hearing. However, they may wish to submit further evidence or to make written submissions. In order to do this, they need to know the deadline for providing these if they are to be put to the tribunal. This is essential if the proceedings are to be fair.

## Assessors

8.57    An assessor is a person appointed to provide independent assistance to the tribunal.

8.58    The role of assessor has a long history in the courts. There are general powers for the High Court[70] and the County Court[71] to sit with assessors. Specific provision is also made for assessors to be used in race relations cases.[72] The court decisions on the use of assessors mainly involve shipping and workmen's compensation[73] cases. Tribunals exercising a social security jurisdiction were authorised[74] or required[75] to sit with assessors. The Commissioners considered their use in reported decisions.

---

70  Senior Courts Act 1981 s70.
71  County Courts Act 1984 s63.
72  Race Relations Act 1976 s67(4).
73  Workmen's Compensation Act 1925 Sch 1 para 5, now repealed.
74  For example: Social Security Administration Act 1992 s56, now repealed.
75  Social Security (Incapacity for Work) (General) Regulations 1995 reg 21, now revoked.

8.59     The legislation may provide for the role of the assessor.[76] Otherwise, the principles laid down by the courts and the Commissioners are generally applicable to all cases involving assessors, subject to an assessment of their continuing validity in the context of the relevant procedural legislation, and of their compliance with modern standards of natural justice and article 6.

## Under TCEA

8.60    TCEA s28 gives the First-tier Tribunal and the Upper Tribunal power to direct that an assessor shall assist the tribunal.[77] The tribunal may exercise this power if 'a matter before it requires special expertise not otherwise available to it'. The person or persons appointed must appear to have the relevant knowledge or experience. The Lord Chancellor may establish panels of persons suitable to be assessors, but the tribunal need not select from them.

## The presence of the assessor

8.61    The assessor must have access to the evidence on which assistance is required. In *R v Deputy Industrial Injuries Commissioner ex p Jones*[78] the Division-al Court explained how this worked. In the case of a hearing on the papers, the assessor must be shown the relevant documents and advise accordingly.[79] In the case of an oral hearing, the assessor must be present either throughout the hearing or for those parts of the hearing to which the assessor's assistance will be relevant. It is not sufficient for the assessor to read notes of the oral evidence.[80]

## The functions of the assessor

8.62    The primary function of the assessor is to help the tribunal to understand the evidence. This was explained in the House of Lords by the Lord Chancellor, Viscount Simon, in *Richardson v Redpath Brown and Co Ltd*:[81]

> He is an expert available to the arbitrator to consult if the arbitrator requires assistance in understanding the effect and meaning of technical evidence. He may, in proper cases, suggest to the arbitrator questions which the arbitrator himself might put to an expert witness with a view to testing the witness's view or to making plain his meaning. The arbitrator may consult him in case of need as to the proper technical inferences to be drawn from

---

76  For example: National Insurance (Industrial Injuries) (Determination of Claims and Questions) Regulations 1948 reg 16(2) provided that 'An assessor sitting with a local tribunal as aforesaid shall not take any part in the determination or decision of that tribunal except in an advisory capacity'.

77  This provision is in accordance with the former Council on Tribunals' recommendation that there should be express statutory authority for the use of an assessor – *Guide to Drafting Tribunal Rules* (2003), p182.

78  [1962] 2 QB 677.

79  [1962] 2 QB 677 at 686–687.

80  [1962] 2 QB 677 at 687.

81  [1944] AC 62.

proved facts, or to the extent of the difference between apparently contra-dictory conclusions in the expert field.[82]

8.63 The assessor may also help by suggesting relevant issues of fact that should be investigated by the tribunal.

8.64 The assessor helps the tribunal to understand the evidence, but does not give evidence.[83] Nor may the assessor carry out a physical examination of the claimant in order to gather evidence for the tribunal.[84]

8.65 The tribunal has power to regulate its procedure at a hearing. The asses-sor must operate within the procedure adopted. But the tribunal must adopt a procedure that allows all those present, including the assessor, to fulfil the functions of their respective roles.

8.66 The matters on which the assessor gives advice may be suggested by any source. The members of the tribunal may have points which they wish to raise with the assessor. Any party to the proceedings, or any representa-tive, may suggest points on which the tribunal would benefit from the assessor's advice. These should be put to the assessor if they are consistent with the role of informing and advising on an issue relevant to the case.

8.67 The assessor's role is not a merely passive one of providing informa-tion on request. If there is a matter on which advice seems appropriate, the assessor should draw this to the tribunal's attention. The procedure at the hearing must allow this to be done.

8.68 The assessor may also suggest questions which might be put to a wit-ness. These may relate to otherwise unexplored but relevant issues. Or they may test the witness's evidence or make its meaning plain.[85]

8.69 In *R(I) 14/51*, the Commissioner said that questions suggested by an assessor should be put through the chairman.[86] His comments show that he was concerned that a technical exchange between an assessor and an expert witness might be incomprehensible to the tribunal and have the effect of prolonging the proceedings without enlightening the tribunal. Subject to this danger, the matter is one for the tribunal to determine as part of the regulation of its procedure at the hearing. The practice of asking the assessor to direct questions through the presiding judge has two advantages: it ensures that only relevant questions are asked and it maintains and emphasises the particular status and role of the assessor. It can, however, become tedious, cumbersome, time-consuming and incon-venient, all of which a tribunal would probably wish to avoid.

8.70 It is preferable that the assessor should not be asked directly to give an opinion on the issue that the tribunal has to decide, although in the circumstances of a particular case it may not be possible to frame a ques-tion in any other way.[87] Ideally the questions should be framed in more general terms so as to elicit information which will help the tribunal to determine that issue. This approach avoids any suggestion or suspicion that the assessor is making the decision rather than the tribunal.

82 [1944] AC 62 at 70.
83 *R v Deputy Industrial Injuries Commissioner ex p Jones* [1962] 2 QB 677 at 689.
84 *Richardson v Redpath Brown and Co Ltd* [1944] AC 62 at 69–70.
85 At 70.
86 At [7(1)(i)].
87 *R(I) 14/51* at [7(1)].

8.71    It is good practice for the presiding judge to record the assessor's contributions.

## Disclosure of advice

8.72    This issue was considered by the Court of Appeal in *Ahmed v Governing Body of the University of Oxford*[88] in the context of assessors assisting a judge in a racial discrimination case. Waller LJ set out the view of the Court:

> The next question is to what extent the judge should disclose during the case and before final submissions the advice that he is getting from the assessors? Mr Allen submitted that as a matter of natural justice the parties were entitled to know the advice that the judge was getting so that they could deal with it. He referred us to *Mahlikilil Dhalamini v R* [1942] AC 583; *Bharat v R* [1959] AC 533; *Nwabueze v General Medical Council* [2000] 1 WLR 1760; *Roylance v General Medical Council* [2000] 1 AC 311 and *R v Deputy Industrial Injuries Commissioner ex p Jones* [1962] 2 QB 677. Advice can of course cover a range of matters, and in our view as a general proposition Mr Allen's formulation is too wide. We suggest that the principles one gets from those authorities are these. (1) If a fact finding Tribunal or assessors involved in the findings of fact are to be directed on the law, that direction should normally be given in open court and the direction should be accurate; for the importance of open court see the *Mahlikilil* case; for the importance of the direction being accurate see *Bharat v R*. (2) If the advice is in the nature of expert evidence to which the parties should be entitled to respond, disclosure will normally be required; see the *Mahlikilil* case. (3) Where a corporate judicial decision has to be made the detail of the discussion and the manner in which the conclusion was reached should normally remain confidential; see *Roylance*'s case.[89]

8.73    The proper approach is determined by the requirements of natural justice and of article 6[90] in the context of the role played by the assessor in the type of proceedings involved.

8.74    In *Watson v General Medical Council*,[91] Stanley Burnton J considered the roles of an assessor and a legal adviser to the Council. An assessor advised on factual issues on which there was no appeal, while a legal adviser advised on questions of law on which an appeal lay to the High Court. He held that advice given by an assessor should be given openly to the parties so that they could comment on it before the tribunal made its decision. Likewise in the social security context, the courts and the Commissioners held that any advice received by the tribunal must be made known to the parties to the tribunal who are present and they should have an opportunity to comment on it.[92]

---

88  [2003] 1 WLR 995.
89  [2003] 1 WLR 995 at [33].
90  *Owners of the Ship Bow Spring v Owners of the Ship Manzanillo II* [2005] 1 WLR 144 at [57]–[61].
91  [2006] ICR 113.
92  *R v Deputy Industrial Injuries Commissioner ex p Jones* [1962] 2 QB 677 at 685–686; *R(I) 14/51* at [7(1)(ii)].

## Status of the assessor

8.75 An assessor is not a member of the tribunal and so has no judicial powers or duties and no automatic right to remain with the tribunal while it
arrives at its decision.[93] Equally, an assessor is not a party to the proceedings and is not subject to any provisions which apply to those parties. Nor
is an assessor a witness.[94] It follows that there is no *right* to question an
assessor.[95]

## Independence of assessor

8.76 The assessor must be in a position to give completely impartial and unbiased advice to a tribunal. This will not be possible if the assessor has
some professional or personal relationship with any of the parties.

## The tribunal's responsibility for decision-making

8.77 It follows from the advisory function of the assessor that the decision is
for the tribunal. The tribunal must make the decision itself and must not
abdicate to the assessor its responsibility for making that decision or for
deciding any issue that arises for decision. If necessary, it must refuse
to follow the assessor's advice. This was spelt out by Lord Sumner in the
House of Lords in *The Australia*:[96]

> Authority for the proposition that assessors only give advice and that judges
> need not take it, but must in any case settle the decision and bear the
> responsibility, is both copious and old. It is for them to believe or to disbe-
> lieve the witnesses, and to find the facts, which they give to their assessors
> and which must be accepted by them. If they entertain an opinion contrary
> to the advice given, they are entitled and even bound, though at the risk of
> seeming presumptuous, to give effect to their own view . . .[97]

This passage needs adjustment to reflect the fact that the role of assessors
in some contexts is to help the tribunal make the findings of fact in the
first place.

8.78 If a tribunal does disregard the advice of the assessor, the tribunal's
reasons should record that this was done and explain why.

# Postponement and adjournment

## Terminology

8.79 A hearing may be aborted before it has begun or it may be abandoned
before it is complete. Aborting a hearing is called a postponement and
abandoning a hearing is called an adjournment.

---

93 *R(I) 14/51* at [7].
94 *R(I) 14/51* at [7] and *R(I) 23/57* at [13].
95 *R(I) 14/51* at [7] and *R(I) 23/57* at [13].
96 [1927] AC 145.
97 [1927] AC 145 at 152.

8.80    The failure to define or otherwise distinguish between adjournment and postponement does not matter, as the difference is largely irrelevant to the principles that govern the exercise of the power. For convenience, therefore, this section refers only to adjournments, unless it is necessary to make the distinction.

## The power

8.81    Courts have inherent power to adjourn.[98] It is probable that tribunals have an inherent or implied power, as part of the power to regulate their own procedure. Under TCEA, the rules of procedure confer an express power to adjourn. It is a case management power. UTR r5(3)(h) is illustrative:[99]

> (3) In particular, and without restricting the general powers in paragraphs (1) and (2), the Upper Tribunal may–
>
> . . .
>
> (h) adjourn or postpone a hearing; . . .

8.82    The principles discussed in this section apply when a case is removed from one session to be included in a later session of the tribunal. They do not apply before a case is listed. Nor do they apply to short adjournments within a session; re-organising the list or taking a break in the proceedings are governed by the tribunal's power to regulate its own procedure.[100]

8.83    A proper understanding of the power to adjourn is relevant to:

- the parties and their representatives so that they may present their applications to the best advantage;
- the tribunal so that it may apply the principles appropriately;
- those who have to evaluate the efficiency of a tribunal system so that they can properly assess the significance of the decision and distinguish when the power has been exercised appropriately and necessarily and when it has not.

8.84    The power is conferred on the tribunal. It is not delegated: see chapter 7.

## The exercise of the discretion

8.85    The power is always discretionary and is governed broadly by the same principles that govern all discretions.

8.86    It must be exercised judicially. But that says no more than that it must be exercised in accordance with the following principles.

8.87    A power must always be exercised for the purpose for which it was conferred. The purpose of an adjournment is to ensure that the parties to the proceedings have a fair hearing in accordance with the principles of natural justice[101] and article 6. The discretion must be exercised to ensure

---

98  Farwell J in *Hinckley and South Leicestershire Permanent Benefit Building Society v Freeman* [1941] Ch 32 at 39.

99  See also: GRC Rules r5(3)(h); HESC Rules r5(3)(h); IAC Rules r4(3)(h) and Sch para 12; Lands Rules r 5(3)(h); PC Rules r6(3)(j); SEC Rules r5(3)(h); Tax Rules r5(3)(h); WPAFC Rules r5(3)(h).

100  See chapter 7.

101  Lord Parker CJ in *R v The Medical Appeal Tribunal (Midland Region) ex p Carrarini* [1966] 1 WLR 883 at 887.

that that purpose is attained. So, an adjournment of a property adjustment order for three years was not a proper exercise of the discretion.[102] Nor was an adjournment of a hearing before a mental health review tribunal in order to see if the patient would improve or could sustain an improvement.[103] Unreasonable delay attributable to the State may also violate article 6.[104]

8.88    The discretion must be exercised in relation to the facts of the individual case and not on the basis of authority or analogy with previous decisions.[105] Generally, authorities do not bind in exercises of discretion, because that would override the discretion. However, authorities are relevant for three reasons. First, they establish the principles on which a tribunal must exercise its discretion. Second, the exercise of this, like all, discretions will involve an error of law if there was a clear mistake. The authorities, therefore, show some of the limits within which the application must be decided. Third, they also contain some indications of the general approach that should be taken.

8.89    Older authorities are now subject to reconsideration to take account of the overriding objective. As Lightman J explained in *Albon (trading as NA Carriage Co) v Naza Motor Trading Sdn Bhd (No 5)*:[106] 'no doubt considerations held critical in the authorities cited are relevant, but not decisive'.

8.90    The tribunal dealing with the application must take account of all circumstances relevant to the application and must not take account of any circumstances that are irrelevant. It must be decided on the circumstances relevant to the time of the application, not those that pertained earlier.[107] But earlier events may set the context in which the application has to be decided. For example: they may show a pattern of delay.

8.91    As the power is discretionary, it is permissible to adjourn without condition or only on terms.[108] If the applicant will not accept the terms offered, it is permissible to refuse to adjourn.[109]

## Deciding whether to adjourn

8.92    There must always be a good reason for adjourning a hearing.[110] That requirement breaks down into three stages of enquiry for a tribunal when deciding whether to adjourn. First, it must identify the purpose that an adjournment would serve. Second, it must investigate why this was not anticipated and catered for. Third, it must consider the effect an adjournment would have on the parties and on the operation of the tribunal system. In practice, these stages may not be so distinct. For example: the

---

102  *Rodewald v Rodewald* [1977] Fam 192.
103  *R v Nottingham Mental Health Review Tribunal ex p Secretary of State of the Home Department* (1988) *Times* 12 October.
104  *Vernillo v France* (1991) 13 EHRR 880 and *Darnell v United Kingdom* (1993) 18 EHRR 205.
105  Lord Wright in *Evans v Bartlam* [1937] AC 473 at 488–489.
106  [2008] 1 WLR 2380 at [18].
107  Scott LJ in *Dick v Piller* [1943] 1 All ER 627 at 629 (not in the report at [1943] KB 497).
108  Scott LJ in *Dick v Piller* [1943] KB 497 at 500.
109  *Hickson v Hickson* [1953] 1 QB 420.
110  *Unilever Computer Services Ltd v Tiger Leasing SA* [1983] 1 WLR 856.

purpose that would be served by adjourning to await the outcome of related proceedings is determined by the impact it will have on the party concerned and vice versa.

## The purpose of the adjournment

8.93 The purpose of a delay will either be to allow a party to be ready to proceed or to allow the tribunal a chance to hear the case. A party may not be ready because: (i) the evidence is incomplete; (ii) the argument is not fully prepared; (iii) someone (such as a witness or a representative) is not available; or (iv) the decision in another case is awaited. The most likely reason why the tribunal may not have a chance to hear the case is that there was insufficient time, usually on account of time spent on other cases or of evidence and submissions provided at the last minute. It may also be waiting on the decision in another case.

### Obtaining evidence

8.94 This is a common reason for applying for an adjournment.

8.95 There is no special approach for requests for an adjournment in order to obtain expert evidence.[111]

### Preparing argument

8.96 This is less common as a reason for applying for an adjournment than wanting time to obtain more evidence. It will usually arise from delays in obtaining representation. However, it would be appropriate to adjourn if a significant new issue arose at the last minute, perhaps at the hearing, which could not reasonably have been anticipated and for which one of the parties was not prepared.

### Attendance by a party: understanding its importance

8.97 In *Hanson v Church Commissioners for England*,[112] it became clear in the final stages of proceedings before a rent assessment tribunal that the tenant, whose objection had led to the proceedings, had not understood the consequences of failing to attend the hearing. Roskill LJ said:

> I am very conscious of the irritation as well as the extra expense which last minute adjournments can cause, particularly with tribunals of this nature, and I recognise the desire of any tribunal to avoid such adjournments whenever possible. But sometimes, if justice is to be done, adjournments are essential.[113]

### Attendance: representative unavailable

8.98 In *Royal Bank of Scotland v Craig*,[114] the counsel who was due to represent the defendant was unavailable. The judge refused to allow time for new

---

111 *Winchester Cigarette Machinery Ltd v Payne* (1993) *Times* 19 October.
112 [1978] QB 823.
113 [1978] QB 823 at 838.
114 (1997) 94 (39) LS Gaz 39.

counsel to be instructed and to become familiar with the case. The Court of Appeal held that the judge had not asked the right question: would the defendant be prejudiced if the case proceeded? The Court decided that the claimant was entitled to an adjournment as he had been the innocent victim of mismanagement by his original counsel.

8.99    In *Priddle v Fisher & Sons*,[115] it was held wrong in law for a tribunal to proceed when it received a message shortly after the start of the hearing to say that the representative of one of the parties was too ill to attend and the party was prevented from reaching the venue by snow. This was so despite the fact that the party did not ask for an adjournment.

### Attendance: illness

8.100    It may be wrong in law to refuse to adjourn to allow a party who is ill to attend to give evidence that is important.[116] The requirements were summarised by Lightman J in *Albon (trading as NA Carriage Co) v Naza Motor Trading Sdn Bhd (No 5)*:[117]

> These authorities established that an adjournment should be granted if four conditions were satisfied. The first was that the witness was unable to attend on grounds of ill-health. The second was that the witness's evidence was reasonably necessary if the party's case was to be properly presented. The third was that there was a reasonable prospect that the witness would be able to attend an adjourned hearing at a specific and reasonable future date. The fourth was that the other party would suffer no injustice which cannot be remedied by an award of costs or otherwise.

8.101    In *Teinaz v Wandsworth London Borough Council*[118] the Court of Appeal considered how a court should deal with an application for an adjournment based on medical advice not to attend. Peter Gibson LJ gave this advice:[119]

> Where the consequences of the refusal of an adjournment are severe, such as where it will lead to the dismissal of the proceedings, the tribunal or court must be particularly careful not to cause an injustice to the litigant seeking an adjournment . . .

> A litigant whose presence is needed for the fair trial of a case, but who is unable to be present through no fault of his own, will usually have to be granted an adjournment, however inconvenient it may be to the tribunal or court and to the other parties. That litigant's right to a fair trial under Article 6 of the European Convention on Human Rights demands nothing less. But the tribunal or court is entitled to be satisfied that the inability of the litigant to be present is genuine, and the onus is on the applicant for an adjournment to prove the need for such an adjournment.

> If there is some evidence that a litigant is unfit to attend, in particular if there is evidence that on medical grounds the litigant has been advised by a qualified person not to attend, but the tribunal or court has doubts as to whether the evidence is genuine or sufficient, the tribunal or court has

115 [1968] 1 WLR 1478.
116 *Dick v Piller* [1943] KB 497 and *Rose v Humbles* [1970] 1 WLR 1061 and [1972] 1 WLR 33.
117 [2008] 1 WLR 2380 at [14].
118 [2002] ICR 1471.
119 [2002] ICR 1471 at [20]–[22].

a discretion whether or not to give a direction such as would enable the doubts to be resolved. Thus, one possibility is to direct that further evidence be provided promptly. Another is that the party seeking the adjournment should be invited to authorise the legal representatives for the other side to have access to the doctor giving the advice in question. The advocates on both sides can do their part in assisting the tribunal faced with such a problem to achieve a just result. I do not say that a tribunal or court necessarily makes any error of law in not taking such steps. All must depend on the particular circumstances of the case.

## Other proceedings

8.102    An adjournment may be sought to await the outcome of civil or criminal proceedings before another tribunal or a court. These may be proceedings that involve one of the parties or will give an authoritative ruling on a legal issue. If one of the cases involves the care of a child, the child's welfare is paramount.[120]

## Other civil proceedings

8.103    An adjournment is appropriate if the outcome of one proceeding is dependent on the outcome of the other. Whether this is so requires an analysis of the issues in each proceedings and the relevance of the findings in each case to the other. For example: in *BUPA Care Homes (CFC Homes) Ltd v Muscolino*,[121] an employment tribunal refused to adjourn to await the outcome of related proceedings before the Care Standards Tribunal. The Employment Appeal Tribunal dismissed the appeal against the refusal, deciding that each case raised different issues and that the findings in each would not be binding in the other. Elias J was sanguine about the possibility of inconsistent findings in the two proceedings:[122]

> If she wishes to pursue both her independent claims, then in so far as there is any conflict in the decisions, that is a matter which, if it causes her to feel aggrieved, is a consequence of her having determined to pursue proceedings down both channels.

## Criminal proceedings

8.104    If one of the cases is criminal, the issue arises whether there will be any prejudice to the party's defence in the criminal case in disclosing evidence before the trial or any impediment to the civil case in this evidence not being available. Given the limitations on the right to silence, this consideration may have less relevance than it once did. Richards LJ explained how the issue should be considered in *Mote v Secretary of State for Work and Pensions*:[123]

> I do not accept that the Human Rights Act 1998 requires any material change of approach in this area. In my judgment the court still enjoys a real discretion whether or not to adjourn. The authorities make clear that a relevant consideration is whether the continuation of the civil proceedings

---

120  *Re TB (Care Proceedings: Criminal Trial)* [1995] 2 FLR 801 at 805.
121  [2006] ICR 1329.
122  [2006] ICR 1329 at [19].
123  Reported as *R(IS)* 4/08 at [31].

will give rise to a real risk of prejudice to the defendant in the criminal proceedings. If there is a risk of prejudice, then I would expect it to weigh heavily in favour of an adjournment pending the conclusion of the criminal proceedings, but it will not necessarily be decisive. I accept, of course, that the court must not act in breach of the defendant's Convention rights; but it is difficult to see how the continuation of the civil proceedings could give rise in itself to a breach of those rights. As the tribunal chairman held in the present case, the civil proceedings can be conducted in such a way as to respect them. An additional and important safeguard lies in the powers of the judge in the criminal proceedings to stay those proceedings for abuse of process or to limit the evidence admitted at the trial if, in the circumstances then prevailing, it is necessary to do so in order to prevent a breach of Convention rights or to ensure a fair trial. The civil court or tribunal can take into account the existence of those powers when considering the exercise of its own discretion whether to adjourn.

8.105    In *R v Levey*,[124] the Court of Appeal emphasised the importance of co-ordinated listing of criminal and civil proceedings. This will not be so easily achieved if the civil case is before a tribunal.

### Authoritative decisions

8.106    Tribunals will usually adjourn or stay cases to await authoritative decisions in cases that are currently being considered by the Upper Tribunal or the courts. Ultimately, though, everything depends on the circumstances of the individual case. In *Re Yates' Settlement Trusts*,[125] the hearing of an application to approve a settlement had been adjourned to await the outcome of an appeal pending before the House of Lords, the principle in which would affect the outcome of the case. Sir Raymond Evershed MR said that in principle it was permissible to adjourn in order to await the outcome of a case before a higher court.[126] However, the Court of Appeal decided that the adjournment had been wrong in the circumstances of the case, because the settlor was old and ill. It was, no doubt, also relevant that the settlement was a compromise and that the adjournment had been of the judge's own motion. In other words, there were no opposing interests that might be prejudiced by the adjournment.

## The need for an adjournment

8.107    The parties and their advisers should prepare their cases in advance. Preparation involves anticipating problems that may arise and taking appropriate steps to avoid them so far as possible. The tribunal must always consider whether the circumstance that has given rise to the possible need for an adjournment could have been avoided by one of the parties. This is so in domestic law[127] and under article 6.[128] If it could have been avoided, that is a factor against an adjournment. However, it is not necessarily

124  [2007] 1 FLR 462.
125  [1954] 1 WLR 564.
126  [1954] 1 WLR 564 at 567.
127  *R v The Medical Appeal Tribunal (Midland Region) ex p Carrarini* [1966] 1 WLR 883 at 888.
128  *R (Lappin) v HM Customs and Excise* [2004] EWHC 953 (Admin).

decisive. For example: a party who is not represented and does not understand the nature of the proceedings may not realise what is required until the hearing.

## The impact on the parties and on the tribunal system

8.108    In *Albon (trading as NA Carriage Co) v Naza Motor Trading Sdn Bhd (No 5)*,[129] Lightman J decided that the overriding objective applies to the exercise of the discretion. This requires the tribunal to take account of the interests of the parties and the impact of the adjournment on other parties and on the system as a whole.

8.109    As regards the case for an adjournment, the tribunal will have to assess the reasons given and to evaluate their impact in the context of competing interests. The former requires the tribunal to make its own assessment of whether an adjournment would achieve its purpose and not just accept the argument put by the party. It cannot do this if the application is not sufficiently specific on that purpose. For example: on an application to adjourn for further evidence, the tribunal will have to consider the nature of the evidence sought, the chances that it will be obtained, and its likely significance for the party's case if it is.

8.110    In assessing the effect of a failure to adjourn, the tribunal may have to take account of the strength of the party's case as it stands. The merits are a potentially relevant consideration.[130] However, they may depend on whether or not the adjournment is granted. For example: it may determine whether more evidence will be available. And it may affect the chances of success. For example: the presence of a representative may have an impact on the likelihood of success.

8.111    It is tempting to consider that a case is clear and that further delay would serve no purpose. But it is wise to bear in mind the judicial experience recorded by Megarry J in *John v Rees*:[131]

> As everybody who has anything to do with the law well knows, the path of the law is strewn with examples of open and shut cases which, somehow, were not; of unanswerable charges which, in the event, were completely answered; of inexplicable conduct which was fully explained; of fixed and unalterable determinations that, by discussion, suffered a change. Nor are those with any knowledge of human nature who pause to think for a moment likely to underestimate the feelings of resentment of those who find that a decision against them has been made without their being afforded any opportunity to influence events.[132]

8.112    As regards the other party, the tribunal will have to consider whether an adjournment would cause any prejudice or detriment. Part of that assessment will involve a consideration of the motivation behind the application. An application inevitably means that one of the parties or a representative wishes to delay the progress of a case. That may be for legitimate reasons.

---

129  [2008] 1 WLR 2380.
130  *Albon (trading as NA Carriage Co) v Naza Motor Trading Sdn Bhd (No 5)* [2008] 1 WLR 2380 at [21].
131  [1970] Ch 345.
132  At 402.

For example: it may be in order to obtain more evidence. Or it may for be for an illegitimate tactical reason. For example: it may preserve a party's right to remain in the United Kingdom pending the final determination of a claim for asylum or it may delay the time when an overpayment of benefit has to be repaid. The tribunal has to decide whether the purpose identified, the explanation given or the alleged impact on the party is genuine or specious.

8.113     As regards the interests of other cases and of the tribunal system as a whole, an adjournment will result in delay for other cases as they make way in the listing for the adjourned case. Individually, this may not seem significant. However, cumulatively adjournments have a bigger impact on the progress of the tribunal's caseload.

8.114     It is also relevant to take into account whether the adjournment would allocate more than an appropriate share of the court's resources to the case and whether the parties and their representatives had behaved responsibly.[133]

8.115     It is wrong to adjourn indefinitely.[134] A lengthy delay will most likely be justified by the need to await for a lead case or for an authoritative ruling from a higher court. That is considered under the principles applicable to staying a case: see chapter 7.

## Applying for an adjournment

8.116   The way that a tribunal handles an application for adjournment and the factors it must take into account when doing so indicate how an application should be presented. Ideally, it should:

- say what purpose an adjournment will serve;
- explain why it has become necessary;
- provide evidence in support, such as a medical certificate, which should be as specific as possible;
- say why the difficulty could not have been avoided or anticipated;
- say why alternative steps could not be taken to avoid delay. (For example: if a representative is not available, why another representative could not be found);
- say what the effect will be for the party if the case proceeds;
- say how soon the case can be relisted. A delay for a specific time or to await a particular event is more likely to succeed that one for an indefinite and unspecified period.

8.117   It is a mistake to assume that an application will be granted. Parties and representatives often fail to attend the hearing on the assumption that it will not proceed. This is a mistake. The tribunal will consider the application on its merits. If the merits do not justify an adjournment, the hearing will proceed. This is the risk that a party runs. In some cases, such as illness, attendance may not be an option.

---

133 *Albon (trading as NA Carriage Co) v Naza Motor Trading Sdn Bhd (No 5)* [2008] 1 WLR 2380 at [19].

134 Farwell J in *Hinckley and South Leicestershire Permanent Benefit Building Society v Freeman* [1941] Ch 32 at 38.

## Directions on an adjournment

8.118 Whenever a case is adjourned, it is good practice for the tribunal to review the case and consider whether any directions are appropriate to ensure that the hearing is effective when the case is relisted.

## The decision and reasons

8.119 If there is doubt whether or not a hearing was adjourned, the issue is resolved by reference to the substance of what was done, not by the language used.[135]

8.120     In some circumstances, it may be necessary to give reasons for a decision regarding an adjournment. Failure to give reasons may make the decision wrong in law, unless the reason is obvious.[136]

## Challenging the exercise of the discretion: appeal and judicial review

8.121 A decision on an application to adjourn a hearing may be appealable. In *Re Yates' Settlement Trusts*,[137] Sir Raymond Evershed MR set out the principle:

> . . . if a judge adjourns or refuses to adjourn a case, he has performed a judicial act which can be reviewed by the Court of Appeal; although I need not say that an adjournment or a refusal of an adjournment is a matter which *prima facie* is entirely within the discretion of the judge. The Court of Appeal would, therefore, be very slow to interfere with any such order, but there is no doubt that the Court of Appeal has jurisdiction to entertain appeals in such matters.[138]

8.122 Whether or not a decision is appealable depends on the scope of the right of appeal. It is not an excluded decision from the right of appeal under section 11 TCEA and it is within the general meaning of 'decision' in section 11. A refusal to adjourn was held to be a decision under section 11(1) of the Tribunals and Inquiries Act 1992.[139]

8.123     The extent to which a decision may be challenged on appeal depends on whether the appeal lies on fact or law or both. If an appeal lies only on an issue of law, it will not necessarily be sufficient to show that the decision was based on a mistake of fact.[140]

8.124     In practice, the issue may not be of great importance. If a refusal to adjourn has affected the outcome of the case, it will show an error of law in the decision ultimately made. And in practice there may not be time to challenge a decision, especially a refusal, before the case is heard. Only long adjournments are likely to give rise to any injustice.

---

135 *Barnsley v Marsh* [1947] QB 672; *R v Sekhon* [2003] 1 WLR 1655 at [48].

136 See the reasoning of Lord Parker CJ in *R v The Medical Appeal Tribunal (Midland Region) ex p Carrarini* [1966] 1 WLR 883 at 888 and of Laws LJ in *Carpenter v Secretary of State for Work and Pensions* reported as *R(IB) 6/03* at [23]–[24].

137 [1954] 1 WLR 564.

138 [1954] 1 WLR 564 at 621.

139 *Priddle v Fisher & Sons* [1968] 1 WLR 1478.

140 Du Parcq LJ in his dissenting judgment in *Dick v Piller* [1943] KB 497, approved in principle but not on the facts of the case by Scott LJ.

## Showing an error of law

8.125   The basis on which the exercise of a discretion to adjourn will be wrong in law is governed by the same principles as any other discretion.[141]

8.126   In some cases, this has been expressed in terms of the process by which the discretion was exercised. So, courts refer to the exercise being wrong in principle, which includes taking account of irrelevant considerations and overlooking relevant ones[142] and deciding arbitrarily.[143]

8.127   In other cases, it has been expressed in terms of the effect on one of the parties. So, courts refer to the justice or injustice to the parties. In *Rose v Humbles*,[144] Buckley J said:

> . . . if the discretion has been exercised in such a way as to cause what can properly be regarded as an injustice to any of the parties affected, then the proper course for an appellate court to take is to ensure that the matter is further heard.[145]

And in *Maxwell v Keun*,[146] Lawrence LJ noted that the requested adjournment would not prejudice the other party.[147] In the same case, Atkin LJ referred to an exercise of the discretion that defeated and destroyed the rights of one of the parties, linking this to the justice of the case:

> . . . in the exercise of a proper judicial discretion no judge ought to make such an order as would defeat the rights of a party and destroy them altogether, unless he is satisfied that he has been guilty of such conduct that justice can only properly be done to the other party by coming to that conclusion.[148]

8.128   In practice, process and effect are often no more than different ways of stating the same defect, the one emphasising the cause and the other emphasising its consequence.

## Record of proceedings

8.129   An accurate record is essential to sound decision-making. It is unwise to rely on memory, which can be incomplete, inaccurate and even inventive.[149] If the proceedings are recorded, the Information Commissioner has decided that there is no right to a copy of the recording under the Freedom of Information Act 2000, as it is a document created for the purposes of the proceedings.

---

141  See chapter 4.
142  Croom-Johnson J in *Dick v Piller* [1943] KB 497 at 507.
143  Farwell J in *Hinckley and South Leicestershire Permanent Benefit Building Society v Freeman* [1941] Ch 32 at 39.
144  [1970] 1 WLR 1061.
145  [1970] 1 WLR 1061 at 1071.
146  *Maxwell v Keun* [1928] 1 KB 645.
147  [1928] 1 KB 645 at 659. See also *Royal Bank of Scotland v Craig* (1997) 39 LS Gaz 39.
148  [1928] 1 KB 645 at 657.
149  Scott Plous, *The Psychology of Judgment and Decision Making* (1993, McGraw Hill), chapter 3, 'Memory and Hindsight Biases', p37.

## The duty to make a record

8.130    The rules of procedure under TCEA make no provision for a record of proceedings. Nonetheless, a presiding judge is under a duty to take a note of the evidence.[150] The duty derives from the judge's judicial status. The record of evidence may be needed by the Upper Tribunal in order to investigate whether a finding of fact or decision was perverse.[151] The record is distinct from any personal notes that the members may make to assist them in making a decision. As the court explained in *R (McIntyre) v Parole Board*:[152]

> The notes constituting the record are quite distinct from notes taken by the chair for his or her own use or notes made by a judge or chair where there is an audio or visual recording of the proceedings. Such notes do not constitute the record. Nor do they constitute personal data. They are made by the judge or chair or panel member solely for the purpose of assisting in and in preparation for the reaching of the reasoned decision; they are not a record of the proceedings. Their absolute confidentiality is integral to the independent and impartial decision making function of a judge or tribunal or panel member and the proper administration of justice. They are in effect notes made for the preparation of the judgment. They are no different to a preliminary draft of a judgment. If such notes are held by an administrative officer or on a computer system operated by an administrative body for the judge, tribunal or panel member, they are held on behalf of the judge, tribunal or panel member and remain under the sole control of the judge, tribunal or panel member. No person has a right of access to them. They must never be disclosed or provided to any person.

## Under TCEA: the Senior President's Practice Statement

8.131    The Senior President has issued a practice statement on *Record of Proceedings in Social Security and Child Support Cases in the Social Entitlement Chamber*:

1.  In this Practice Statement 'social security and child support case' has the meaning given in rule 1(3) of the Tribunal Procedure (First-tier Tribunal) (Social Entitlement Chamber) Rules 2008.[153]
2.  A record of the proceedings at a hearing must be made by the presiding member, or in the case of a Tribunal composed of only one member, by that member.
3.  The record must be sufficient to indicate any evidence taken and submissions made and any procedural applications, and may be in such medium as the member may determine.
4.  The Tribunal must preserve–
    a.  the record of proceedings;
    b.  the decision notice; and
    c.  any written reasons for the Tribunal's decision for the period specified in paragraph 5.

---

150  *R(I) 81/51* at 23; *R(I) 42/59* at [35]; *Houston v Lightwater Farms Ltd* [1990] ICR 502; *R (McIntyre) v Parole Board* [2013] EWHC 1969 (Admin) at [18]–[20]. Nowadays, the record may take the form of a recording of the proceedings.

151  *Piggott Brothers & Co Ltd v Jackson* [1992] ICR 85.

152  [2013] EWHC 1969 (Admin) at [23].

153  The definition reads: '"social security and child support case" means any case allocated to the Social Entitlement Chamber except an asylum support case or a criminal injuries compensation case'.

5. The specified period is six months from the date of–
   a. the decision made by the Tribunal;
   b. any written reasons for the Tribunal's decision;
   c. any correction under Rule 36 of the above Rules;
   d. any refusal to set aside a decision under Rule 37; or
   e. any determination of an application for permission to appeal against the decision, or until the date on which those documents are sent to the Upper Tribunal in connection with an appeal against the decision or an application for permission to appeal, if that occurs within the six months.
6. Any party to the proceedings may within the time specified in paragraph 5 apply in writing for a copy of the record of proceedings and a copy must be supplied to him.

8.132   This repeats regulation 55 of the Social Security and Child Support (Decisions and Appeals) Regulations 1999 (now revoked). However, its status as a practice statement is unclear.[154]

## The contents of the record

8.133   This has to be considered at two stages: at the hearing and on appeal. At the hearing, the importance of the content lies primarily in the need to refer to the evidence when deliberating on the decision and writing the reasons. On appeal, the importance of the content depends on whether the tribunal is exercising a factual jurisdiction. If it is not, it needs sufficient to decide whether or not the tribunal made an error of law. If it is, it may need more detail. This may arise in two circumstances. First, if an appeal lies on any ground and is not limited to issues of law. Second, if an appeal may only be allowed on an error of law, but the tribunal may re-make the decision rather than remit the case for rehearing. If the tribunal is to exercise that jurisdiction, it will need a complete note of the relevant evidence.[155] In other circumstances, this may not be needed.[156]

8.134   Ideally, the presiding judge should keep a record of proceedings that contains everything that the tribunal needs in order to make its decision as well as everything that might be needed if the case goes on appeal. Every procedural step should be recorded. Every question asked should be set out along with who asked it and of whom. Every answer should be recorded and the witness identified. Every argument put should be set out and attributed. All additional documentary evidence presented at the hearing should be noted along with the person who presented it. Finally, any relevant observations made of the parties or witnesses during the hearing should be noted.

8.135   In practice, this is not attainable and may distract the judge from hearing the case. There is, however, a minimum that is required of any record of proceedings. It should record:

- all documentary evidence submitted at the hearing and by whom;
- the essence of the relevant parts of the oral evidence, identifying who gave it;[157]

154  See the discussion in chapter 3.
155  *R(I) 81/51* at [23]; *R(U) 16/60* at [5].
156  *CSSB/0212/1987* at [3]; *CIS/12032/1996* at [7].
157  *R(SB) 8/84* at [25].

- the essence of any arguments put to the tribunal,[158] identifying who made them;
- significant procedural events, such as an application for an adjournment;
- any relevant observations of, or conduct by, anyone present, such as the ability to walk without a stick.

8.136   There is less need for a record of proceedings at a paper hearing. However, it may be useful to record the evidence that was before the tribunal and whether any procedural issues were considered.

## Recording evidence

8.137   There is a technique that can be used to record evidence without taking a verbatim record. The essence is to eliminate irrelevancies, to select the essence of what is relevant, and to concatenate questions and answers. The result is a continuous narrative of the relevant evidence. If the precise terms of the evidence are crucial, it can be recorded verbatim using quotation marks and perhaps with the accompanying question. References to and repetition of documentary evidence can be recorded merely by reference to the page and paragraph of the relevant document.

8.138        Assume the following exchange:

1. Where was Mr W when you arrived in the office?
2. At his desk.
3. Did he remain at his desk?
4. No.
5. When did he leave it?
6. Let me see. It was in mid-afternoon, before the messenger came for the post. It couldn't have been as late as 4, but it was after 3. Probably about quarter to 4 or so. No, I remember, it was almost exactly 3.30, because I heard the Town Hall clock strike. Yes, 3.30.
7. What did he do then?
8. You mean straightaway?
9. Yes.
10. He stood up, stretched and looked around the office.
11. What he did do then?
12. He picked up a paper knife from his desk.
13. Did you have a clear view?
14. Yes.
15. Did anyone or anything obstruct your view?
16. No.
17. What did he do with the knife?
18. He walked over to Miss X and stabbed her with it.

8.139   One analysis of this exchange could be this. The answer at 10 can be omitted as irrelevant to the case. The answers at 14 and 16 can be omitted – they are either repetitious or confirmatory of the answer at 12. The exchange at 8 and 9 is also irrelevant – it is purely for clarification. The reasoning included in answer 6 can be omitted, leaving just the witness's conclusion

---

158  *R(DLA) 3/08* at [10].

as to the time. That leaves the other answers which can be recorded compendiously with their questions:

At 3.30, I saw W leave his desk, take a paper knife and stab X.

8.140 Of course, this is just one interpretation. According to the circumstances, a different summary might be required. For example: if the precise time was significant, the answer at 6 might be important and deserve to be recorded, perhaps verbatim. Or if the witness's view of the incident was in doubt, the answers at 14 and 16 would be relevant. But whatever the requirements of a particular case, the principle is the same. Eliminate irrelevancies and summarise the essence of the questions and answers together, leaving verbatim quotations of the evidence for evidence of which the precise wording is important.

## The form of the record

8.141 If the record is kept in the form of a recording of the hearing, judges will for practical purposes still need to make a written record sufficient for the purposes of the tribunal's deliberations and the writing of its reasons.

8.142 Whether the record is kept in writing or otherwise, it must be intelligible or be capable of being rendered intelligible to those who use it.[159]

## Production of the record

8.143 The First-tier Tribunal is under a duty to provide the record of proceedings on request by the Upper Tribunal.[160] If it does not do so, the Upper Tribunal may order production under UTR r5(3)(n).

8.144 The Court of Appeal only calls for a judge's notes if there is a conflict of fact about what happened or what was said before the judge.[161]

## Challenges to the record

8.145 The Employment Appeal Tribunal adopts the practice that any dispute about the accuracy or completeness of the record must be put to the presiding judge and thereafter that record will be accepted as correct unless the parties agree otherwise.[162] A similar procedure was suggested by the Commissioners for social security cases,[163] but this was not adopted.[164] The Commissioners did not operate a fixed procedure and were prepared to accept the claimant's recollection of the evidence given.[165] This was consistent with the approach taken by the Court of Appeal in *De Silva v Social*

---

159 *R(DLA) 3/08* at [13]–[14].
160 *Houston v Lightwater Farms Ltd* [1990] ICR 502.
161 Sedley LJ in *McKee v Secretary of State for Work and Pensions* [2004] EWCA Civ 334 at [12] (refusing an application for permission to appeal).
162 *Dexine Rubber Co Ltd v Alker* [1977] ICR 434; *Aberdeen Steak Houses Group plc v Ibrahim* [1988] ICR 550. And see the approach of the Court of Appeal in *Hayman v Rowlands* [1957] 1 WLR 317.
163 *R(SB) 10/82* at [15].
164 *CS/4537/1998* at [13].
165 *R(DLA) 3/08* at [24].

*Security Commissioner,*[166] in which there was a challenge to the accuracy of the record of the evidence.

## Personal comments

8.146    As evidence proceeds, a judge may wish to record impressions, comments, points to check or questions to ask later. As Lord Scott explained in the Privy Council in *Cobham v Frett:*[167]

> . . . every experienced judge . . . is likely to make notes as the trial progresses recording the impressions being made on him by the witnesses. Notes of this character would not, without the judge's permission or special request being made to him, form part of the record of an appeal. They might be couched in language quite unsuitable for public record. In the present case delay, with a consequent dimming of the judge's recollection of the evidence and of the witnesses demeanour, was not a ground of appeal.[168]

8.147    Such notes are not strictly part of the record of proceedings. If they are recorded, their provenance must be clear. Recording them on a separate piece of paper would ensure that they are kept apart from the record of proceedings and avoid any need for them to be disclosed to the parties or on appeal. However, this may be inconvenient in practice and runs the risk that they cannot later be related to the relevant witness or evidence. There are other ways in which they can be recorded but marked as separate from the evidence and the submissions of the parties. They may be recorded on the opposite of the page in the judge's notebook, they may be ruled off from the evidence and submissions, or they may be recorded within the narrative but in brackets.

## Deliberations

8.148    A record of proceedings need not contain the tribunal's deliberations that led to the decision.[169] However, it may be convenient to make a note of these at the end of the record to assist recollection when writing reasons.

# Resumed hearings and rehearings

8.149    A number of issues arise when a tribunal resumes a hearing after an adjournment or rehears a case after its decision has been set aside. How should the tribunal be constituted? What information should it have before it? What issues should it consider?

## Composition of the tribunal

8.150    This will depend on the terms of the legislation and the directions given by the tribunal that set the decision aside.

---

166 [2001] EWCA Civ 539.
167 [2001] 1 WLR 1775.
168 [2001] 1 WLR 1775 at 1783.
169 *R(DLA) 3/08* at [26].

8.151    If the hearing is resumed after an adjournment, the tribunal may be constituted in the same way as before or differently. If the tribunal is constituted by the same members, no difficulty arises. If it is constituted differently, ideally the members should all be different. As the Tribunal of Commissioners said in *R(U) 3/88*:[170]

> ... it seems to us undesirable for a member to have a residual knowledge of evidence given at the earlier hearing which is not shared by the other members – knowledge of what was said as distinct from what was written down.

8.152    If the decision is set aside by the tribunal itself, the set aside and review powers make no provision for the constitution of the tribunal at the rehearing. Natural justice and article 6 will almost always dictate that the tribunal be differently constituted for the rehearing.

8.153    If the decision is set aside by the Upper Tribunal, TCEA s12(3)(a) allows the Upper Tribunal to direct that the members of the First-tier Tribunal who are chosen to reconsider the case must not be the same as those who made the decision that has been set aside. This is a power not a duty, so the Upper Tribunal may direct that the case may, or even must, be reheard by the same members. Section 14(3)(a) makes equivalent provision if a decision of the Upper Tribunal is set aside by the Court of Appeal.

## Information before the tribunal

8.154    There are two categories of information that a party may not wish to be before the tribunal at the resumed hearing or rehearing.

### The evidence that was available at the previous hearing

8.155    In principle, the evidence that was before the tribunal at the previous hearing should be available on the rehearing. The evidence was available or taken at that hearing. The fact that the hearing was adjourned or the hearing set aside does not affect the relevance or admissibility of the evidence. This was considered by the Tribunal of Commissioners in *R(U) 3/88*. The Tribunal decided that the notes of evidence taken at a previous hearing should be available for the rehearing.[171]

8.156    There is a power to exclude evidence[172] and it may be appropriate to exercise that power to exclude some or all of the evidence previously taken. This is a general power and there are no potential limits to the circumstances in which it may be appropriate. There may be doubt about the accuracy or completeness of the record of the evidence taken. For example: if the proceedings were not recorded, a party may challenge the record of proceedings. Or there may be a doubt about the reliability of the evidence previously taken. For example: the way in which the evidence was elicited may cast doubt on its reliability. Or it may be impossible for the evidence to be assessed by the new tribunal. For example: an observation of a party's behaviour, recorded at the previous hearing, will be available to the

---

170  *R(U) 3/88* at [7].
171  *R(U) 3/88* at [7].
172  See chapter 10.

new tribunal only through the (probably contested) record. Or admitting the evidence could lead to further evidence and argument in relation to it that distracts from the key issues in the case. All of the previous examples would potentially give rise to such issues.

8.157    Even if factors such as these do not lead to the evidence being excluded, it may be appropriate to take them into account when assessing the reliability and probative worth of the evidence.

### The decision that was set aside

8.158    Should a tribunal that rehears a case see the decision that was set aside? This was considered by the Court of Appeal in *Swash v Secretary of State for the Home Department*.[173] If a decision is set aside, it should usually be available to the tribunal that rehears the case, as it may help to identify issues. This is so even if the findings of fact in the decision were rendered invalid by reason of law. However, the tribunal that rehears the case must take care not to be influenced by the discredited findings.

8.159    In exceptional cases, the decision should not be before the tribunal at a rehearing. For example: if the decision was set aside on the ground of actual bias, it might be appropriate that its discredited findings and reasoning should not be available to taint the rehearing. An application to this effect should be made to the tribunal that directs the rehearing.

## Issues for consideration

8.160    A decision may be set aside under its procedural error power (UTR r43 and its equivalents),[174] its review power or on appeal.

8.161    The scope of a rehearing consequent upon the exercise of the procedural error power is determined by what is set aside. The tribunal has power to set aside a decision or part of a decision. There is no power to limit the issues that must be considered afresh. If the whole decision is set aside, the decision must be re-made. If only part of a decision is set aside, only that part has to be re-made. As a matter of law, the issues raised will be identified as if the decision were being made for the first time.

8.162    The position is the same if the rehearing is consequent upon the exercise of the review power, except that there is no power to set aside only part of a decision on review.

8.163    The scope of a rehearing consequent upon a successful appeal is determined by the directions given by the Upper Tribunal. TCEA s12(2)(b)(i) gives the Upper Tribunal power to set aside a decision of the First-tier Tribunal and remit the case with directions for its reconsideration. Those directions may limit the issues that arise on the rehearing.[175] Otherwise, the issues raised will be identified as if the decision were being made for the first time.

---

173  [2007] 1 All ER 1033.

174  See: GRC Rules r41; HESC Rules r45; IAC Rules r32; Lands Rules r54; PC Rules r51; SEC Rules r37; Tax Rules r38; WPAFC Rules r35.

175  *Aparau v Iceland Frozen Foods plc* [2000] ICR 341; *Way v Poole Borough Council* [2007] EWCA Civ 1145; (2007) *Times* 25 October.

# Representatives

## Support for parties

9.1　A party may benefit from support in presenting a case to a tribunal in three ways: companionship, assistance and representation. Conceptually these are distinct functions, but in practice they are not so easily kept separate.

9.2　A companion is someone who comes with the party for companionship and moral support, but who plays no part in the hearing. Although companions make no direct contribution to proceedings, they can fulfil a valuable function by putting the party at ease and able to function better in an unfamiliar environment.

9.3　An assistant is someone who helps the party to present a case. For example: the assistant may help the party find relevant documents or jog the party's memory on points to make. In the courts, an assistant is known as a *McKenzie* friend.[1] This term is not employed under TCEA.

9.4　A representative puts the case for the party to the tribunal or advises or assists the party on doing so. There are usually no rules of limited audience for a tribunal. If there are not, a representative need not be legally qualified. There is, indeed, no requirement that a representative have any form of accreditation from anyone. The representative may attend and speak at the hearing, prepare a written submission for the tribunal, or advise the party on how to present the case.

9.5　These categories are not necessarily mutually exclusive. The roles may not be distinct or easy to distinguish: a companion may jog a party's memory and an assistant may also provide companionship and support. In *R(G) 1/93*, the same person acted as representative, interpreter and witness.

### The value of representatives

9.6　Tribunals should be accessible.[2] However, the nature of the issues that arise may be such that it is unrealistic to expect a lay party to manage without representation, even with the assistance of the tribunal. As Mummery LJ said of employment tribunals in *Connex South Eastern Ltd v Bangs*:[3] 'Tribunal cases have become more complex and difficult, both factually and legally.'

### Choice of representative

9.7　This is a generally a matter for the party,[4] not the tribunal or the other parties. As Carnwath LJ said in *Khan v Commissioners for Revenue and Customs*:[5]

> Unless the tribunal had some other reason to doubt [his representative's] competence, they would have had no business to inquire into the background of his choice of representative, or his knowledge of the availability of legal aid.

---

1　Despite the wishes of the Court of Appeal in *R v Leicester City Justices ex p Barrow* [1992] 2 QB 260.
2　TCEA ss2(3)(a) and 22(4)(b).
3　[2005] ICR 763 at 14.
4　Representatives in immigration and asylum cases are subject to control.
5　[2006] EWCA Civ 89 at [53]; (2006) *Times* 21 March.

## Under TCEA

9.8   TCEA Sch 5 para 9 provides:

> Rules may make provision conferring additional rights of audience before the First-tier Tribunal or the Upper Tribunal.

9.9   The rules of procedure allow a party to appoint a legal[6] or other representative. The representative's powers and rights depend on whether the appointment is notified to the tribunal or, in some cases, to the decision-maker.[7]

9.10   If the appointment has been notified to the tribunal, the representative may do anything on behalf of the party except sign a witness statement and has a right to all the documents that would otherwise be sent to the party, including (presumably) notice of an oral hearing. UTR r11(3) and (4) is illustrative:[8]

> (3) Anything permitted or required to be done by a party under these Rules, a practice direction or a direction may be done by the representative of that party, except signing a witness statement.
> (4) A person who receives due notice of the appointment of a representative–
>   (a) must provide to the representative any document which is required to be provided to the represented party, and need not provide that document to the represented party; and
>   (b) may assume that the representative is and remains authorised as such until they receive written notification that this is not so from the representative or the represented party.

9.11   If the appointment has not been notified to the tribunal, the representative has the power to attend a hearing and, with the tribunal's permission, may act as a representative or assist in presenting the party's case, but no other powers or rights.[9]

9.12   The rules of procedure allow a party to be accompanied and, with the tribunal's permission, assisted in presenting a case at a hearing. UTR r11(5) is illustrative:[10]

> (5) At a hearing a party may be accompanied by another person whose name and address has not been notified under paragraph (2) but who, subject to paragraph (8) and with the permission of the Upper Tribunal, may act as a representative or otherwise assist in presenting the party's case at the hearing.

It is not clear whether this provision applies only to representatives and assistants rather than to some who is merely and solely a companion.

6   As defined in: UTR r11(9); HESC Rules r1(3); Lands Rules r11(7); SEC Rules r1(3); Tax Rules r11(7); WPAFC Rules r1(3).
7   See: SEC Rules r11(3); WPAFC Rules r11(3).
8   See also: GRC Rules r11(3) and (4); HESC Rules r11(3) and (4); IAC Rules r10(4) and (5); Lands Rules r11(3) and (4); PC Rules r14(3) and (4); SEC Rules r11(3) and (4); Tax Rules r11(3) and (4); WPAFC Rules r11(3) and (4).
9   See: UTR r11(5) and (6); GRC Rules r11(5) and (6); HESC Rules r11(5) and (6); Lands Rules r11(5); PC Rules 14(5) and (6); SEC Rules r11(5) and (6); Tax Rules r11(5) and (6); WPAFC Rules r11(5) and (6). There is no equivalent power in IAC Rules.
10   See also: GRC Rules r11(5); HESC Rules r11(5); Lands Rules r11(5); PC Rules 14(5); SEC Rules r11(5); Tax Rules r11(5); WPAFC Rules r11(5). There is no equivalent power in IAC Rules.

9.13      Special rules apply in mental health cases. UTR r11(7) and (8) is illustrative:[11]

> (7) In a mental health case if the patient has not appointed a representative the Upper Tribunal may appoint a legal representative for the patient where–
>   (a) the patient has stated that they do not wish to conduct their own case or that they wish to be represented; or
>   (b) the patient lacks the capacity to appoint a representative but the Upper Tribunal believes that it is in the patient's best interests for the patient to be represented.
> (8) In a mental health case a party may not appoint as a representative, or be represented or assisted at a hearing by–
>   (a) a person liable to be detained or subject to guardianship or after-care under supervision, or who is a community patient, under the Mental Health Act 1983; or
>   (b) a person receiving treatment for mental disorder at the same hospital home as the patient.

## Control of representatives under TCEA

9.14      The courts have recognised that it may be necessary to control representatives, assistants and, if they are a separate class, companions.[12]

9.15      Under TCEA, the only express control of a representative is the power for at tribunal to make a wasted costs order (s29(4)). This creates a personal liability, but is limited to legal representatives as defined by section 29(6).

9.16      Otherwise, representatives are subject to the same duty as the parties to help the tribunal to further the overriding objective and to co-operate with the tribunal generally. If representatives fail to comply with the rules of procedure, practice directions or directions, the consequences may be visited on the party. These matters are discussed in chapter 3.

9.17      Representatives are also subject to the general powers of control given to the tribunal. It has power to regulate its own procedure, to control those who may attend a private hearing, to exclude persons from attending all or part of a hearing, and to exclude witnesses until they give evidence. If the tribunal is considering whether to exercise these powers, it will have to reconcile its need to regulate its procedure with the right to be represented, assisted and accompanied. One way is to use the discretionary element of the powers to impose conditions on the representative's conduct, with exclusion used as the last resort. These powers might have been used effectively to overcome the difficulties that the tribunals experienced in some of the cases below.

9.18      The tribunal has power to confine the representative to relevant matters and to control the way in which these matters are investigated and presented. As Mummery LJ explained in *Bache v Essex County Council*:[13]

---

11  See also: HESC Rules r11(7) and (8). The power was discussed by the Upper Tribunal in *AA v Cheshire and Wirral Partnership NHS Foundation Trust* [2009] UKUT 195 (AAC) at [10]–[25].

12  *R v Leicester City Justices ex p Barrow* [1992] 2 QB 260.

13  [2000] 2 All ER 847.

Just as the tribunal is under a duty to behave fairly, so are the parties and their representatives. The tribunal is accordingly entitled to require the parties and their representatives to act in a fair and reasonable way in the presentation of their evidence, in challenging the other side's evidence and in making submissions. The ruling of the tribunal on what is and is not relevant and on what is the fair and appropriate procedure ought to be respected even by a party and his representative who do not agree with a ruling.[14]

9.19   But if a representative does not behave as Mummery LJ envisaged, the tribunal generally has no power to prevent a representative from presenting a case. This issue was considered in *Bache v Essex County Council*.[15] The case concerned a hearing before an employment tribunal at which the employee had been represented by an unqualified and inexperienced representative. The tribunal decided that the representative was prolonging the proceedings and clouding the issues. It decided not to allow him to continue to act as representative, although it allowed him to assist the employee. The Court of Appeal decided that the tribunal had no power to do this. The limit of the tribunal's power in normal circumstances was set out by Peter Gibson LJ:

It is not in dispute that a tribunal has the power ... to control the way a party or his representative conducts his case before the tribunal. Thus, the tribunal can exclude irrelevant evidence and argument and stop lines of questioning and submissions which do not assist.[16]

For circumstances outside the normal:

I fully recognise that so to hold could leave tribunals with potentially very difficult situations ... when a representative may try to persist in doing what he has been told not to do. If the representative so acts with the knowledge and approval of the party, that may in an extreme case constitute an abuse of process such as may disentitle the party from relief or from being entitled to defend the proceedings. The conduct may in an extreme case constitute contempt, though the tribunal itself will not be able to punish for contempt but may have to cause contempt proceedings to be instigated ... It is perhaps unfortunate that the leave of the tribunal is no longer a requirement for representation by a representative ... But that is a matter for Parliament.[17]

9.20   The tribunal's scope for action if it is insulted by a representative is also limited. This issue was considered by the Court of Appeal in *Bennett v Southwark London Borough Council*.[18] The case concerned a hearing before an employment tribunal at which the employee's representative accused the tribunal of being racially prejudiced against him in refusing his application to adjourn. The tribunal recused itself, directing a rehearing before a differently constituted tribunal. That tribunal then struck out the proceedings. Ward LJ was of the view that the first tribunal was entitled to recuse itself on the ground that it could no longer act impartially. Sedley

---

14   [2000] 2 All ER 847 at 855.
15   [2000] 2 All ER 847.
16   [2000] 2 All ER 847 at 852.
17   [2000] 2 All ER 847 at 853.
18   [2002] ICR 881.

and Longmore LJJ disagreed. Sedley LJ explained how a tribunal should react if faced with insults:[19]

> Undoubtedly there are situations in which the emergence, for example, of an unanticipated financial interest means that the tribunal has already reached the point of no return whatever the parties say. But where the reason is an advocate's aberrant and offensive behaviour, as it was here, there are numerous reasons not to abort the hearing until a serious endeavour has been made to defuse the situation, and more than one way to do so.

> One way (and perhaps the best way in the case of a single outburst) is to ignore it. Another, if having retired the tribunal feel as this tribunal did, is to point out to the advocate the potential consequences of his behaviour and invite him, if he cannot justify his remarks, to withdraw them. If he withdraws them, there is no reason in the ordinary way why the case cannot go on.

> Even if he does not withdraw, and assuming of course that no proper justification is offered, the tribunal may still need to consider whether, given the potential injustice to the other side and the public expense which recusing themselves will bring, they cannot, perhaps after a break, continue with the hearing with unclouded minds. Courts and tribunals do need to have broad backs, especially in a time when some litigants and their representatives are well aware that to provoke actual or ostensible bias against themselves can achieve what an application for adjournment cannot. Courts and tribunals must be careful to resist such manipulation, not only where it is plainly intentional but equally where the effect of what is said to them, however blind the speaker is to its consequences, will be indistinguishable from the effect of manipulation . . .

> If the advocate persists in defying the tribunal without arguable justification, the tribunal can invite the Attorney General to consider proceeding against him for contempt of court . . .

The Court of Appeal also decided that the later tribunal had not been entitled to strike out the proceedings, as the overall conduct of the proceedings was neither scandalous nor an abuse of process.

## Court control over legal representatives

9.21   The courts have asserted power to prevent barristers and solicitors from acting in court proceedings. It is not clear whether the relevant distinction is between courts and tribunals or between cases of competence and others.

9.22       In *In re L (Minors) (Care Proceedings: Solicitors)*,[20] the High Court was concerned with care proceedings brought by a local authority. The solicitor for the local authority was cohabiting with the solicitor for one of the parents. Wilson J ordered that the local authority's solicitor be removed from the record. It was not in dispute that the court had power to make this type of order:[21]

> An elemental component of the jurisdiction of the Supreme Court is power to control its own process and indeed its own officers. It is not disputed that the court has power to determine whether a particular firm of solicitors

19  [2002] ICR 881 at [17]–[20].
20  [2001] 1 WLR 100.
21  [2001] 1 WLR 100 at [18].

should play a role in the forensic exercise of which it is the director. The court has an analogous power to refuse to hear a particular advocate: see now section 27(4) of the Courts and Legal Services Act 1990.

The issue for the court was the basis on which the power should be exercised. Wilson J emphasised the nature of the proceedings and the importance of the local authority being seen to act impartially in them.[22]

9.23    In *Geveran Trading Co Ltd v Skjevesland*,[23] the Court of Appeal was concerned with a bankruptcy petition. The barrister for one of the creditors had had a personal relationship some years before with the debtor's wife. The Court held that he was entitled to represent the creditor. Arden LJ set out the Court's analysis of the basis on which there was power to prevent an advocate appearing:[24]

> We, therefore, reject the submission . . . that the only circumstances in which the court can act to prevent an advocate from acting is where he has confidential information. The case law demonstrates that in exceptional circumstances an advocate can be prevented from acting even where he does not have such information.

> Where a party objects to an advocate representing his opponent, that party has no right to prevent the advocate from acting based on the Code of Conduct as the content and enforcement of that Code are not a matter for the court. However, the court is concerned with the duty of the advocate to the court and the integrity of the proceedings before it. The court has an inherent power to prevent abuse of its procedure and accordingly has the power to restrain an advocate from representing a party if it is satisfied that there is a real risk of his continued participation leading to a situation where the order made at trial would have to be set aside on appeal. The judge has to consider the facts of the particular case with care . . . However, it is not necessary for a party objecting to an advocate to show that unfairness will actually result. We accept Mr Jones' submission that it may be difficult for the party objecting so to do. In many cases it will be sufficient that there is a reasonable lay apprehension that this is the case because as Lord Hewart CJ memorably said in *R v Sussex Justices ex parte McCarthy* [1923] 1 KB 256, it is important that justice should not only be done, but seen to be done. Accordingly, if the judge considers that the basis of objection is such as to lead to any order of the trial being set aside on an appeal . . . he should accede to an order restraining an advocate from acting. But we stress that the judge must consider all the circumstances carefully. A connection, for instance, between counsel for one party and a witness on the other side may be an important factor where the evidence is of fact but, depending on the nature of the connection, it may be less important where the evidence is of an expert nature and the cross-examination is likely to be on questions of technical expertise. The judge should also take into account the type of case and the length of the hearing, and any special factor affecting the role of the advocate, for instance, if he is prosecuting counsel, counsel for a local authority in care proceedings or as a friend of the court.

9.24    The Court also considered the practicalities of raising an objection to a representative. Arden LJ set out the proper approach:[25]

---

22  [2001] 1 WLR 100 at [34]–[38].
23  [2003] 1 WLR 912.
24  [2003] 1 WLR 912 at [41]–[42].
25  [2003] 1 WLR 912 at [47].

If a party objects to the advocate for the other party, he should make that clear to the other party without delay. If it is necessary for the court to rule on the objection, the party taking the objection should make an application at the latest at the start of the hearing or (if later) as soon as the circumstances giving rise to the objection are known to him. If there is an interim hearing in the case, and the circumstances are known, the court should be informed of the objection at the interim hearing and invited to give directions as to when the objection should be heard. If there is no interim hearing it may in some cases be sensible for the party wishing to make the objection to make a separate application as soon as the circumstances become known to him in order to avoid the risk of an adjournment of the substantive hearing if the objection is sustained. In the same way, it may be sensible for the advocate to whom the objection relates to inform the court of the matters disclosed to the other side earlier than the start of the substantive hearing at which he proposes to act so that the court can consider the matter for itself at an early stage.

## Public funding for representation

9.25   The circumstances in which article 6 requires public funding for representation are discussed in chapter 3.

9.26   If a representative receives funding from the Legal Services Commission (or legal aid in Scotland) in respect of proceedings before the Upper Tribunal, a copy of the funding certificate must be sent to the tribunal and notice of the funding to all the parties.[26]

9.27   Parties who are not represented may benefit from the services of the Pro Bono Units or Free Representation Units.

## If the representative is not available

9.28   This raises the issue whether to postpone or adjourn, which is discussed in chapter 8. In *R v Social Security Commissioner ex p Bibi*,[27] Collins J said: 'I appreciate that there is no absolute right to representation, but there is an absolute right to be dealt with fairly . . .'

## The duty to co-operate

9.29   This is discussed in chapter 3. Representatives are not entitled to watch a tribunal make a remediable error and then use that as a ground of appeal against the tribunal's decision. The representative should draw these matters to its attention.

## Tribunal advocacy

9.30   The techniques of good advocacy apply whatever the context. There are no rules or techniques that are unique to tribunals. However, there are some aspects that deserve emphasis in a tribunal context.

26  UTR r18.
27  Unreported 23 May 2000 at [18].

## Variation

9.31    The greatest difficulty in giving general advice about advocacy in tribunals is variation. There is variation from jurisdiction to jurisdiction. Representatives who appear in a particular jurisdiction will learn the approach taken. Others will have to enquire. There is also variation within a jurisdiction according to the preferences of the presiding judge and the nature and quality of the representation on each side. Again, experience and enquiry are the best guides of what to expect.

## The tribunal's expertise and preparation

9.32    Two features should be common to all tribunals. First, the members of the tribunal should be knowledgeable of, and probably expert in, the subject matter. Second, the tribunal will have prepared the case by reading the papers and previewing the issues that arise from them.[28] Representatives should assume that the tribunal is familiar with the law and the documents (evidence and submissions) in their presentation of the case.

## Time

9.33    Many, but not all, tribunals operate under tight time constraints. With time at a premium, representatives should prepare and present their cases accordingly. Time does not allow for the more elaborate development of a case that may be appropriate in proceedings that are conducted under less pressure.

9.34    Representatives can assist tribunals in good time management by: presenting material to the tribunal in advance; doing so in a way that assists the tribunal; relying on the tribunal's knowledge of the case and the law; and avoiding unnecessary repetition.

## Preparation

9.35    A representative must be fully prepared for a case. This involves three distinct but related aspects: marshalling the evidence and arguments in support of the client's case; planning how to respond to the strongest case that the other party could present; and anticipating the concerns that the tribunal might have. In the nature of things, the representative will not need to use all, or even much, of what has been prepared. But it is better to be prepared than unable to respond at the hearing.

## Planning the case

9.36    The purpose of advocacy is to be achieve a particular outcome. In order to be effective, it is essential to identify the objective (outcome) required. This will dictate the content, which will in turn suggest a structure. It is then necessary to consider presentation.

28  Preparation is an important factor in ensuring good quality decision-making: Transforming Justice with Knowledge, Lawrence W Sherman, High Sheriff of London's Talk on 10 March 2014 at Fishmongers' Hall.

## Objectives

9.37   In the most general sense, the objective will always be the same: to achieve the best outcome reasonably obtainable for the client. In order to be useful, this will have to find expression by reference to the issues in the particular case. It may be possible to identify the objectives at the outset. In practice, it is more likely that they will emerge by a reciprocal process with the content: the working out of the content for an objective will lead to the identification of further objectives that in turn will affect the content of the argument.

## Content

9.38   A tribunal is almost by definition knowledgeable of the case and of the law. A representative can assume, unless told otherwise, that the tribunal knows the law and has read the papers. The representative need not, and should not, set out the evidence that the tribunal already has in the papers. Formal proof of written evidence is not usually required. It is sufficient to refer to points that the representative wants to emphasise. Usually, the representative need not, and should not, expound the law; it is sufficient to highlight important points and or something that the tribunal may not be familiar with. Exceptionally, it may be appropriate to argue a novel or difficult point.

9.39   No tribunal has a limitless amount of time to devote to a case. Representatives have to accept this and adjust their advocacy accordingly. They do so by focusing on the issues that are in dispute.

9.40   Representatives must be realistic. A representative must put the case that the client wants, but all representatives have a duty to advise their clients realistically on what can be obtained. A good case for partial success can be lost in the exaggeration needed to seek more.

## Structure

9.41   It is unlikely that there will only be one structure appropriate to a case. It will, therefore, be a matter of choice. But structure there must be. A randomly assembled case is unlikely to be effective. If it is, it will be despite rather than because of the structure.

## Oral presentation

9.42   It is always appropriate to be polite. There is never any justification for rudeness and it will not be effective.

9.43   Overblown oratory and high-flown rhetoric are not appropriate. It will not be effective and will be unnecessarily time consuming.

9.44   A confrontational and aggressive style will not help. It will antagonise the tribunal to no purpose, take time and divert attention from the substance of an argument. An aggressive cross-examination style is not appropriate in many tribunals.

9.45   A conversational style appropriate to a business meeting is best suited to most tribunals.

9.46   A presentation that is crisp and clear will be appreciated.

9.47     A co-operative approach with the tribunal and the other parties is the ideal. Representatives should co-operate with the tribunal by complying with any timetable for written submissions or documentary evidence and with the procedural directions of the tribunal at the hearing. These are there for a purpose: to make the proceedings as efficient as possible for all users of the tribunal. Representatives should co-operate with the other party by making appropriate concessions on the facts and the law. They should assist the tribunal to follow the case, for example by referring to relevant page numbers in the evidence. Ideally, they should provide written evidence and submissions in good time for the tribunal to read them before the hearing and preferably before the day of the hearing. This will allow the representative and the tribunal to make the best use of the time available.

## Interruptions

9.48     Representatives must expect interruptions. Judges question a representative in order to check they have understood the case, to test its accuracy, coherence and relevance, and to ensure that nothing is overlooked.[29] These interruptions are valuable as they give an indication of the factors that are troubling the judge about the case and allow the representative to deal with them.

9.49     Most judges do not interrupt of the sake of it. They do not aim to be unpleasant or to prevent representatives from putting their arguments. If they do interrupt frequently, the representative should consider whether that reflects a problem with the case being presented rather than with the judge hearing the case.

9.50     If a judge's interruptions are inappropriate, the representative has three options.

9.51     One option is to object on the ground that the judge is descending into the arena or preventing the advocate from presenting the case.

9.52     If the judge has created the appearance of bias, another option is to ask the judge to stand down and transfer the case to another judge for decision.

9.53     The third option is to appeal on the ground that the judge deprived the party of a fair hearing[30] or was guilty of apparent bias. The courts have taken a realistic attitude to the difficulties in confronting a tribunal.[31] However, even after making appropriate allowances, there is a risk with this option, as the representative may have to explain why these concerns were not raised at the time. Representatives are not allowed to use such complaints as a convenient excuse to obtain a rehearing.

## Supporting the work of the tribunal

9.54     Representatives are not entitled to watch a tribunal fail to investigate a matter and then use that as a ground of appeal against the tribunal's

---

29 Denning LJ in *Jones v National Coal Board* [1957] 2 QB 55 at 63.
30 As happened in *Jones v National Coal Board* [1957] 2 QB 55.
31 See chapter 3.

decision. They are under a duty to co-operate with the tribunal[32] and must draw these matters to its attention.

## Written submissions

9.55    In practice, tribunals that operate under particular time constraints are likely to welcome full written submissions provided in advance. The submission should present the party's case clearly and succinctly. It should stand instead of oral presentation; it should not be read out. It will save time during the hearing, which can focus on taking evidence and discussing any matters that concern the tribunal.

9.56    The basic rules for a written submission vary according to whether the focus is on the facts, as is typical of the First-tier Tribunal, or on the law, as is typical of the Upper Tribunal.

9.57    A submission that focuses on the facts should follow these rules:

- identify the submission by reference to the case and party;
- use numbered paragraphs and headings;
- present the submission in a structured and orderly way;
- say at the beginning the outcome sought;
- say what is and is not in dispute;
- deal with the law only in so far as necessary. Usually a passing reference is the most that is needed, unless the interpretation is controversial or a particular provision is crucial;
- say what the evidence proves. There is no need to repeat the evidence. It may, though, be appropriate to quote a particularly supportive passage. If so, use quotation marks;
- deal with difficulties.[33] For example: the evidence may be incomplete or there may be conflicting evidence;
- guide the tribunal to the relevant pages in the papers.

9.58    Here is a simple example of a written submission in a personal independence payment appeal, supporting an argument for an award of points for the activity of moving around:

> Mrs Jones asks you to increase her score by adding 10 points for her mobility difficulties. She has severe osteoarthritis in her wrists and both knees – see the Consultant's letter at page 53. She takes strong pain killers for this – see prescription list at page 48. Her pain severely limits her walking in distance and time – see her claim pack at pages 7–8. Her GP knows her well, confirms that her mobility is significantly restricted by pain, and reports difficulties using a stick or frame – see the report at page 43. The decision-maker's findings are based on medical advice (pages 90–92) that is inconsistent with the opinion of the Consultant which is confirmed by x-ray.

This simple submission tells the tribunal what the claimant seeks and the evidence that supports it. It refers to the law only in passing by referring to the use of a stick. It explains why the conflicting evidence is not reliable.

---

32  See chapter 3.

33  Research as shown that admitting to difficulties before the other party draws attention to them reduces the impact that they have on the outcome: David Hardman, *Judgment and Decision Making*, British Psychological Society and Blackwell, 2009, p45.

And it helps the tribunal by setting out the case clearly and succinctly with references to the relevant pages in the papers.

9.59     A submission that focuses on the law should follow these rules:

- identify the submission by reference to the case and party;
- use numbered paragraphs and headings;
- present the submission in a structured and orderly way;
- say how the tribunal went wrong in law;
- say what outcome is sought. (For example: should the Upper Tribunal re-make the decision or remit the case for rehearing?);
- say what is and is not in dispute;
- deal with the law only in so far as necessary. In a straightforward case, this may be assumed. However, if the appeal raises an issue of interpretation, the law must be dealt with in detail. Make the submission as self-contained as possible;
- set out the relevant terms of the legislation;
- identify relevant authorities with their references. State the proposition for which they are cited. Refer to, and quote, any passages that are important. Limit citation to the most authoritative or the most pertinent;
- provide copies of the authorities if the tribunal will not have them to hand;
- deal with difficulties. For example: there may be a previous decision that supports the tribunal's interpretation of the law;
- guide the tribunal to the relevant pages in the papers.

## Skeleton arguments

9.60     In some tribunals, skeleton arguments may be used. They are different from written submissions. They provide a framework for the presentation of oral argument rather than a substitute for it.

9.61     The Court of Appeal commented on skeleton arguments in *Tombstone Ltd v Raja*.[34] The comments were made in the context of practice direction under CPR, but the points are of general application:[35]

> We end this judgment with a criticism of the excessive length and complexity of Tombstone's skeleton argument. It has 110 pages of text plus 64 pages of Appendices. Although its authors set out to assist the court, as well as the client, by a very thorough presentation of Tombstone's case, it is sensible to set reasonable limits to its length.

> Mr Onslow described it 'as an extremely long document' for a case that, while unusual, was not unduly complex. The appeal was from a judgment of modest length (27 pages). It was very hard, he said, to see what justified such voluminous arguments. Most of the legal issues have been settled by existing authority. No primary findings of fact are challenged on the appeal. He added that, from Healys' perspective, this had added to the length of their skeleton argument (56 pages), which they had tried to keep as short as possible. It had also added considerably to the cost and length of the appeal.

> The length of Tombstone's skeleton did not assist the court. In fact, it tended to detract from Tombstone's case, which was accurately and far more succinctly stated by Mr Onslow in his written and oral responses to

34  [2009] 1 WLR 1143.
35  [2009] 1 WLR 1143 at [122]–[128].

it. His team adopted the technique of briefly stating the points taken by Tombstone and then concisely commenting on them.

Practitioners who ignore practice directions on skeleton arguments (see CPR 52PD paras 5.10 'Each point should be stated as concisely as the nature of the case allows') and do so without the imposition of any formal penalty are well advised to note the risk of the court's negative reaction to unnecessarily long written submissions. The skeleton argument procedure was introduced to assist the court, as well as the parties, by improving preparations for, and the efficiency of, adversarial oral hearings, which remain central to this court's public role.

We remind practitioners that skeleton arguments should not be prepared as verbatim scripts to be read out in public or as footnoted theses to be read in private. Good skeleton arguments are tools with practical uses: an agenda for the hearing, a summary of the main points, propositions and arguments to be developed orally, a useful way of noting citations and references, a convenient place for making cross references, a time-saving means of avoiding unnecessary dictation to the court and laborious and pointless note-taking by the court.

Skeleton arguments are aids to oral advocacy. They are not written briefs which are used in some jurisdictions as substitutes for oral advocacy. An unintended and unfortunate side effect of the growth in written advocacy (written opening and closing submissions and 'speaking notes', as well as skeleton arguments) has been that too many practitioners, at increased cost to their clients and diminishing assistance to the court, burden their oppon-ents and the court with written briefs. They are anything but brief. The result is that there is no real saving of legal costs, or of precious hearing, reading and writing time. As has happened in this case, the opponent's skeleton argument becomes longer and the judgment reflecting the lengthy written submissions tends to be longer than is really necessary to explain to the parties why they have won or lost an appeal.

The skeletal nature of written advocacy is in danger of being overlooked. In some cases we are weighed down by the skeleton arguments and when we dare to complain about the time they take up, we are sometimes told that we can read them 'in our own time' after the hearing. In our judgment, this is not what appellate advocacy is about, or ought to be about, in this court.

## Attendance

9.62   Research published in 1989 showed that representatives significantly increased a party's chance of success.[36] Research published in 2009 showed that representatives were more effective when they assisted parties before the hearing than when they attended.[37]

## Representing non-contentious parties

9.63   Representatives of non-contentious parties should adopt an approach that it consistent with the nature of that party's involvement in the proceedings. This is discussed in chapter 1.

36  Hazel Genn and Yvette Genn, *The Effectiveness of Representation in Tribunals.*
37  Michael Adler, 'Tribunals Ain't What They Used To Be' (2009) March *Adjust* (the Administrative Justice and Tribunals Council newsletter).

# CHAPTER 10

# Evidence

*continued*

# Types and sources of evidence

## Evidence

10.1   Evidence is apparently factual information or material. 'Apparently', because it may not be reliable. 'Factual', to distinguish it from legal material or argument on the facts. 'Material', because it may involve inspecting a physical object. According to the context and usage, it can mean information or material that:

- a party wishes to present in support of a case or to qualify or refute that of another party; or
- the tribunal allows the party to present; or
- is admitted into consideration by the tribunal; or
- is accepted as probative by the tribunal.

10.2   Here, the usage depends on, and should be clear from, the context.

## Types of evidence

10.3   Evidence may be classified in a number of ways.

### Direct and circumstantial

10.4   Evidence may be given directly of facts in issue or it may be given on other matters from which those facts can be ascertained.[1] The former is known as direct evidence, the latter as circumstantial evidence. Circumstantial evidence is used as a basis for drawing inferences.[2] It is the evidence that is circumstantial, not the fact proved by the evidence.

10.5   The same evidence may be both direct and circumstantial. Assume that a witness gives evidence of fact A, which is a fact in issue. The evidence is direct evidence of fact A. But it may also be used as a basis for inferring fact B. In that respect, it is circumstantial evidence.

10.6   It may be necessary to use both direct and circumstantial evidence in relation to the same fact. The most obvious instances are anything that can only be known by the person concerned, such as the person's mental state or experience of pain. The person concerned can give direct evidence of, say, pain. But that evidence can only be confirmed or refuted by circumstantial evidence.

### Ancillary evidence

10.7   Some evidence may be directed not at the facts in issue, but at other evidence. It may be presented to undermine that evidence. For example: it may be used to show that a witness is a poor judge of distance. Or it may be presented to support that other evidence. For example: it may be used to show that the witness has good powers of observation.

---

1  Gray J in *Al Amoudi v Brisard* [2007] 1 WLR 113 at [33].
2  See chapter 11.

## Corroboration

10.8   Evidence is corroborative of other evidence if it supports that evidence by increasing its probative worth. It may do so directly or indirectly. It may be necessary as a matter of law, but for tribunals it will usually be necessary or desirable for evidential reasons.[3]

10.9   Corroboration is necessary as a matter of law only if the evidence is not sufficient in law if it is given by a particular witness. For example: the witness's capacity may be disabled by age or mental in capacity.

10.10   Otherwise, mere repetition does not necessarily increase the probative worth of evidence. For example: evidence from a number of witnesses who were equally badly placed is of no greater value than the evidence of each one. The probative worth of evidence is only increased by corroboration if the other evidence is not affected by the same factors that potentially reduce the worth of the evidence being corroborated.

10.11   In some circumstances, it may seem that corroborative evidence is purely cumulative in its effect. Assume that five equally placed witnesses give the same evidence. This may seem merely cumulative. But even here, the value of the cumulative evidence is that it removes possible concerns about perception, recollection, powers or description and all other factors that might affect the probative worth of the evidence of each witness considered individually.

### Fresh evidence

10.12   This refers to evidence that was not previously available. The classification is relevant in two circumstances. First, in some types of appeal evidence is only admissible if it is fresh evidence. Second, it may be a condition of a review by a decision-maker that it be based on fresh evidence. The meaning is the same in both cases.

10.13   It was defined in the context of the admissibility of evidence on appeal by Denning LJ in *Ladd v Marshall*:[4]

> To justify the reception of fresh evidence . . . three conditions must be fulfilled: first, it must be shown that the evidence could not have been obtained with reasonable diligence for use at the trial; secondly, the evidence must be such that, if given, it would probably have an important influence on the result of the case, though it need not be decisive; thirdly, the evidence must be such as is presumably to be believed, or in other words, it must be apparently credible, though it need not be incontrovertible.[5]

10.14   In the context of a review of a decision, it was defined to similar effect by the Court of Appeal in *R v Medical Appeal Tribunal (North Midland Region) ex p Hubble*.[6]

10.15   The principles were laid down in the context of civil appeals, in which evidence had been adduced before the court below. They must be applied

---

3   If tribunal relies on corroboration for evidential reasons, it is good practice to make this clear in its reasons for decision, as representatives may otherwise argue that the tribunal has required corroboration as a matter of law.

4   [1954] 1 WLR 1489.

5   [1954] 1 WLR 1489 at 1491.

6   [1959] 2 QB 408.

flexibly in the context of an appeal from a decision-maker. In such appeals, fresh evidence should be admitted if it is in the interests of justice to do so.[7]

10.16 As Hale LJ noted in *Hertfordshire Investments Ltd v Bubb*:[8] 'The *Ladd v Marshall* criteria are principles rather than rules ...'. They may be relaxed in children's cases, but only to take account of unusual circumstances.[9]

10.17 In addition to the listed conditions, it is relevant to consider delay. As Ward LJ explained in *Lifely v Lifely*:[10]

> Delay was not a relevant matter in *Ladd v Marshall* but there is no reason why delay should not be brought into account in exercising the court's discretion whether or not to admit fresh evidence. It is plainly a material factor.

The Court also balanced the rights of the parties under Articles 8 and 10 of the European Convention, as the evidence adduced was private.

10.18 If a tribunal reopens a case after a hearing but before its decision is promulgated, these conditions are applied more flexibly, although the threshold for allowing in the new evidence remains a high one.[11]

## Where the evidence comes from

10.19 The material on which the tribunal makes its findings of fact may be put to it by the parties, their representatives and their witnesses or come of the tribunal's own knowledge or expertise.

10.20 The parties may present material orally or in writing. It need not be corroborated, although this may affect the probative worth of the material. It may be given of the witness's personal knowledge or it may be hearsay – that is, something the witness heard from someone else. Occasionally, an object may be produced as evidence, but this is likely to be rare in tribunals.

10.21 The evidence may be received by the tribunal's own observation. For example: a tribunal may observe a claimant's ability to walk during a hearing in a disability case or the location of particular landmarks on a site visit in a boundary dispute.

10.22 Evidence recorded in a decision in one case may be relied on in later cases, provided the parties are aware of it and able to comment on it.[12]

## Evidence given by representatives

10.23 As regards evidence given by a representative with personal knowledge, this is admissible as any other evidence, especially if the representative has a particular expertise.

---

7 *British Telecommunications plc v Office of Communications* [2011] 4 All ER 372 at [68]–[74].

8 [2000] 1 WLR 2318 at 2325.

9 Waite LJ in *Re S (Discharge of Care Order)* [1995] 2 FLR 639 at 646. See also *K v K (Abduction) (No 2)* [2010] 1 FLR 1310.

10 [2008] EWCA Civ 904 at [38]; (2008) *Times* 27 August.

11 *Fisher v Cadman* (2005) *Times* 23 June.

12 *R v Deputy Industrial Injuries Commissioner ex p Moore* [1965] 2 QB 456. *R(I) 5/61* is an instance of a decision being reported solely for the evidence recorded it in.

10.24    As regards evidence given by a representative without personal know-ledge on a *contested* matter, the Commissioners said that tribunals were not entitled to rely on such evidence.[13] However, this may overstate the position. A tribunal has power to direct the manner in which evidence may be provided.[14] As part of its enabling role, it may allow a representa-tive to set out the evidence of a party who is nervous, inarticulate or other-wise unable to present the evidence. Whether it does so will depend on the circumstances, including: (i) whether the party is able to confirm that the representative has correctly stated the evidence; and (ii) whether it will be possible to question the party on the evidence given by the representative.

## The tribunal's own knowledge

10.25    This may be general, local, specific or specialist.

### General knowledge

10.26    This is the information of which courts and tribunals take judicial notice. It covers information that is generally known or can be easily found from a source of reference. Examples are the day of the week on which a particu-lar date fell in a particular year and the meaning of words.

### Local knowledge

10.27    This is information that is known to those who live or work in a particular locality, such as the location of a particular building, the distance between locations and the provision of a public transport service. If the tribunal is a local one, it may be entitled to rely on its members' knowledge of local conditions.[15]

### Specific knowledge

10.28    This relates uniquely to the case and comes of the tribunal's observations of the parties or of some relevant location. The evidence can only be taken into account if it is relevant and reliable; it must then be given its proper significance.[16]

### Specialist knowledge

10.29    This is likely to come from panel members who were appointed for that knowledge. It may be used in a number of ways.

10.30    First, a member's expertise may help in obtaining evidence during a hearing. The tribunal may, for example, have power for a medically

13  *R(I) 36/61* at [18]; *R(I) 13/74* at [9]; *R(SB) 10/86* at [5].
14  See: UTR r15(1)(e); GRC Rules r15(1)(g); HESC Rules r15(1)(e); IAC Rules r14(1)(e); Lands Rules r16(1)(e); PC Rules r18(1)(g); SEC Rules r15(1)(e); Tax Rules r15(1)(e); WPAFC Rules r15(1)(e).
15  Lord Reading CJ in *The King v Tribunal of Appeal under the Housing Act 1919* [1920] 3 KB 334 at 341.
16  *R(DLA) 8/06*.

qualified member to carry out a medical examination. Or a member's accounting knowledge may be used to identify relevant questions.

10.31    Second, the member's knowledge may be used to help the tribunal in assessing the evidence.

10.32    Third, the member's knowledge may be used to explain, complement or even contradict other evidence.[17] This is permitted in order to redress the imbalance that may exist between the knowledge of the parties and their access to advice and evidence.[18] However, this knowledge must be disclosed if one of the parties would be taken by surprise or would have no knowledge of it,[19] especially if it would be detrimental to that party.[20] The tribunal should explain in its reasons how and why it has used this knowledge.[21]

10.33    The distinction between the specialist knowledge of the members of a tribunal and expert evidence on the issues must be maintained. It is not permissible for members to obtain expert advice on the issues in a case and then take that into account as their own specialist knowledge. In *R v City of Westminster Assessment Committee ex p Grosvenor House (Park Lane) Ltd*,[22] the Court of Appeal was concerned with the valuation of property for rating purposes. The Committee made use of an expert report on the effect of the war on valuation. The majority of the Court of Appeal decided that the report should have been disclosed to the parties, whether it was obtained before or after the proceedings began and whether it was general or specific in character. du Parcq LJ explained why:

> It is said that as the committee is entitled to use its own knowledge and experience, and is not obliged to state the result of those to the contestants, it must follow that it can enlarge its knowledge by calling in an independent expert without coming under the necessity of revealing his evidence. One answer to this contention and we think a sufficient answer, is that the experience of an expert tribunal, such as this, is part of its equipment for determining the case. Litigants must take that experience as they find it: and because the tribunal is assumed to be impartial they have no grievance if they cannot test it by cross-examination. An expert witness or adviser, however eminent, is in a very different position. He must not be substituted for the tribunal. Those whose claim is being considered have a right to question and to test every statement he makes, and any opinion he expresses. If that opportunity is denied them, justice is not done.[23]

10.34    Nor may the tribunal undertake its own research without allowing the parties a chance to deal with it. *Busmer v Secretary of State for Defence*[24]

---

17  Lord Parker CJ in *Crofton Investment Trust Ltd v Greater London Rent Assessment Committee* [1967] 2 QB 955 at 967.

18  Lord Goddard CJ in *R v Brighton and Area Rent Tribunal ex p Marine Parade Estates (1936) Ltd* [1950] 2 KB 410 at 420.

19  Lord Parker CJ in *Crofton Investment Trust Ltd v Greater London Rent Assessment Committee* [1967] 2 QB 955 at 968.

20  Willmer LJ in *R v Deputy Industrial Injuries Commissioner ex p Moore* [1965] 1 QB 456 at 476.

21  Lord Denning MR in *Metropolitan Properties Co (FGC) Ltd v Lannon* [1969] 1 QB 577 at 597.

22  [1941] 1 KB 53.

23  [1941] 1 KB 53 at 69.

24  [2004] EWHC 29 (Admin).

was an appeal against the decision of a Pensions Appeal Tribunal. After the hearing the medical member of the tribunal undertook some further research into the source documents on which some of the evidence was based. Newman J held that the tribunal should have adjourned the hearing with notice that the research would be conducted and reconvened to allow the parties to comment on it.[25]

10.35    The use of specialist knowledge may involve some fine distinctions in the way that the knowledge is deployed. They were analysed by Phillips J giving the judgment of the Employment Appeal Tribunal in *Dugdale v Kraft Foods Ltd*:[26]

> The members of industrial tribunals are appointed because of their special knowledge and experience, and we have no doubt that they are entitled to draw upon it in playing their part in assisting the tribunal as a whole to reach a decision. The main use which they will make of this knowledge and experience is for the purpose of explaining and understanding the evidence which they hear. Certainly, they are entitled to use their knowledge and experience to fill gaps in the evidence about matters which will be obvious to them but which might be obscure to a layman. More difficult is the case where evidence is given which is contrary to their knowledge and experience. If such an occasion arises, we think that they ought to draw to the attention of the witnesses the experience which seems to them to suggest that the evidence given is wrong, and ought not to prefer their own knowledge or experience without giving the witnesses an opportunity to deal with it. Provided that this opportunity is given there seems to us to be no reason why they should not draw on their own knowledge and experience in this way also. But it is highly desirable that in any case where particular use is made by an industrial tribunal of the knowledge or experience of one or more of their members in reaching their decision this fact should be stated, and that particulars of the matter taken into account should be fully disclosed.[27]

## Questions and answers

10.36    Most, but not all, evidence will be given as an answer to a question. Even a written statement is likely to have been compiled from the answers to a series of questions. The terms of the questions are part of the context in which the answers must be interpreted.

10.37    If the evidence was given at the hearing, the tribunal will have heard both the questions and the answers. Its understanding of the latter will be informed by the context of the former. However, it is possible that the question may have been interpreted differently by the tribunal and the witness. This is not always apparent. The witness may have information or a perception that affects the interpretation of the question and affects the information that is selected as the answer.

---

25  [2004] EWHC 29 (Admin) at [31].

26  [1977] ICR 48.

27  [1977] ICR 48 at 54–55. For a similar analysis applied to advice obtained by a local government officer reviewing a decision on priority need for accommodation, see the judgment of Carnwath LJ in *Hall v Wandsworth London Borough Council* [2005] 2 All ER 192.

10.38    If the evidence is recorded in a statement without the questions, it is much more difficult for the tribunal to take the questions into account. It will take the statement at face value unless the issue of interpretation is raised by a party. If a party challenges the apparent meaning of the statement on the ground that it has to be understood in the context of the questions asked, the tribunal must assess the argument. It cannot avoid the task on the ground that it is impossible. Nor can it rely on the statement as binding regardless of how it came to be compiled.

10.39    A statement is not necessarily to be taken as conclusive of a person's evidence just because it is signed.[28]

## Issues covered by an inquiry

10.40    The report of an inquiry is admissible on the findings of fact and on the conclusions reached, for example on a person's suitability for particular work. A tribunal is not bound by the findings or conclusions, but if it differs, it should explain why.[29]

# Law of evidence

## Evidence and procedure

10.41    The distinction between evidence and procedure is a result of history, not of principle. As Adrian Zuckerman explained in *Civil Procedure*:[30]

> By a quirk of history, however, rules of evidence came to be seen as representing substantive law rather than procedural law. It came to be accepted that procedural rule-making powers did not apply to rules of evidence. Matters of procedure were regulated by rules of court while questions of evidence were regulated by statute and common law. The manner of obtaining and presenting evidence was a matter of practice and procedure, and therefore governed by rules of court. But the admissibility of evidence was a matter for the 'substantive law of evidence', over which the rule-making bodies had no authority . . .[31]

10.42    This is subject to contrary provision. TCEA Sch 5 para 10(2) provides:

> (2) Rules may modify any rules of evidence provided for elsewhere, so far as they would apply to proceedings before the First-tier Tribunal or Upper Tribunal.[32]

---

28  *Barclays Bank plc v Schwartz* (1995) *Times* 2 August, has sometimes been wrongly used to the contrary. The court was concerned with the validity and enforceability of a guarantee. It decided that illiteracy was not to be equated with intoxication or mental incapacity and that, even if the bank was aware of the illiteracy, the transaction was not on this account harsh and unconscionable so as to found relief in equity.

29  Leveson J in *Secretary of State for Education and Skills v Mairs* [2005] ICR 1714.

30  2nd edn, Thomson Sweet & Maxwell, 2006.

31  2nd edn, Thomson Sweet & Maxwell, 2006, para 1.45.

32  See para 10.150 below.

## The law of evidence

10.43    The law of evidence as applied in the courts may be summarised as a basic principle of relevance, which is subject to a series of exclusions based on a variety of considerations. The exclusions each have their own exceptions.

10.44    In strict theory, the principle of relevance may not be part of the law of evidence, but merely presupposed by it, leaving to the *law* of evidence only the exclusions and their exceptions. This is not purely of theoretical interest. If it is correct and the 'rules' of evidence do not apply in a tribunal, it is only the exclusions that do not apply. It does not mean that the requirement of relevance is abandoned.

10.45    The trend is towards admitting evidence rather than excluding it. Factors that once would have led to evidence being excluded are now relevant to the probative worth of the evidence. This is not a recent trend; it was noted as long ago as 1861[33] and is now seen as the conceptually appropriate analysis.

10.46    The issue for tribunals is whether particular exclusions apply as they do in the courts. There may be an express provision to this effect.[34] The existence of a power to prescribe the evidence required, even if not exercised, may indicate that the strict rules do not apply.[35]

10.47    There may be an express provision that the 'strict' or 'technical' rules do not apply or need not be applied. Even if there is no relevant provision, there may be authority that these rules do not apply,[36] subject to the overriding obligation to ensure a fair hearing.[37] An example is the decision of the Employment Appeal Tribunal in *Leighton v Construction Industry Training Board*.[38] The tribunal below had devoted time to considering the extent to which extrinsic evidence was admissible to help interpret a contract. The Appeal Tribunal deprecated this and said:

> ... the primary function of industrial tribunals is to do justice between employer and employee and not to raise barriers to a search for a fair and common sense answer by recourse to rules of evidence which in this field of litigation may be archaic and arcane.[39]

10.48    The precise scope of these strict or technical rules has not been precisely delineated. It may be that they vary according to the nature of the tribunal, the proceedings or the issue. It is important to know what they are for two reasons: each tribunal needs to know what rules apply to it and

33  By Cockburn CJ in *R v Birmingham Overseers* (1861) 1 B & S 763 at 767.

34  For example: Social Security Act 1998 s16(5).

35  This was the view of Willmer LJ in *R v Deputy Industrial Injuries Commissioner ex p Moore* [1965] 1 QB 456 at 474. However, he may have misinterpreted the enabling power. It may have referred to the nature and content of the evidence to be produced rather than to the rules of evidence that applied. There is such an enabling power in the Social Security Act 1998 Sch 5 para 3.

36  *R v Deputy Industrial Injuries Commissioner ex p Moore* [1965] 1 QB 456 at 488; *Wednesbury Corporation v Ministry of Housing and Local Government (No 2)* [1966] 2 QB 275 at 303; *T A Miller Ltd v Minister of Housing and Local Government* [1968] 1 WLR 992 at 995.

37  Geoffrey Lane LJ in *R v Board of Visitors of Hull Prison ex p St Germain (No 2)* [1979] 1 WLR 1401 at 1409.

38  [1978] ICR 577.

39  [1978] ICR 577 at 580.

legislation may make its application depend on whether or not the strict rules apply.[40]

10.49    Legal professional privilege and litigation privilege[41] are good examples of the difficulties that arise over the scope of the strict rules of evidence.[42] These privileges provide some protection for correspondence between a lawyer and a client and for material in respect of litigation. The client need not allow disclosure of the correspondence, material or their contents, although they may be proved by other evidence. This is a rule of evidence and a fundamental condition on which the administration of justice as a whole rests,[43] as well as a human right.[44] The privilege is that of the client, not the lawyer. The client may waive the privilege. Whether there has been a waiver depends on fairness and therefore on reliance, and should not be too readily found from casual references to that advice in negotiations.[45]

10.50    These privileges apply to tribunals. The Court of Appeal said they did in *Three Rivers District Council v Governor and Company of the Bank of England (No 6)*,[46] although the Court was there concerned with inquiries rather than the sort of tribunals covered by this book. And the Upper Tribunal decided that they did in *LM v London Borough of Lewisham*.[47] As it is not just a rule of evidence but a human right, it is likely that it still applies even in those tribunals to which the strict rules of evidence do not apply.

10.51    Even if the exclusory court rules of evidence do not apply, it is relevant to bear them in mind. They may exclude evidence for a good reason and that reason may be a relevant factor in the assessment of the evidence that is received.

10.52    One basis for distinguishing the exclusions that apply to tribunals from those that do not is whether they are fundamental to the process of judicial inquiry. This was considered by the House of Lords in *Official Solicitor to the Supreme Court v K*.[48] The House was concerned with whether the mother of a ward of court was entitled to see all the evidence available to the Official Solicitor. Lord Devlin said:

> All justice flows from the prerogative. Save in so far as their powers are limited by statute, all judges do as they think fit. But what 'they think fit' is not determined by each individually and ad hoc; it is determined by their collective wisdom and embodied in judge-made rules. In the field of procedure these rules are those which Upjohn LJ in the Court of Appeal rightly

---

40  For example: the Civil Evidence Act 1995 s11 provides that the Act applies to 'any tribunal, in relation to which the strict rules of evidence apply'. As the Act deals with hearsay, this provision suggests that that rule is part of the strict rules of evidence.

41  Legal professional privilege, but not litigation privilege, applies in non-adversarial jurisdictions: *Re L (Police Investigation: Privilege)* [1996] 1 FLR 731. Legal professional privilege does not apply to anyone other than a qualified lawyer: *R (Prudential plc) v Special Commissioner of Income Tax* [2011] All ER 316.

42  Self-incrimination is another example.

43  Lord Taylor in *R v Derby Magistrates' Court ex p B* [1996] AC 487 at 507; Toulson J in *General Mediterranean Holdings SA v Patel* [2000] 1 WLR 272 at 280– 288.

44  *R (Morgan Grenfell & Co Ltd) v Special Commissioner of Income Tax* [2003] 1 AC 563 at [7]–[8].

45  *Bennett v Sunderland City Council* [2009] ICR 479.

46  [2004] QB 916 at [32].

47  [2009] UKUT 204 (AAC).

48  [1965] AC 201.

called 'the ordinary principles of judicial inquiry'. They include the rules that all justice shall be done openly and that it shall be done only after a fair hearing; and also the rule that is in point here, namely, that judgment shall be given only upon evidence that is made known to all parties. Some of these principles are so fundamental that they must be observed by everyone who is acting judicially, whether he is sitting in a court of law or not; and these are called the principles of natural justice. The rule in point here is undoubtedly one of those. There are also rules of less importance designed to aid in the administration of justice and to regulate procedure. They are rules of convenience rather than of principle; and the rule against hearsay . . . is among them. No one would suggest that it is contrary to natural justice to act upon hearsay.

But a principle of judicial inquiry, whether fundamental or not, is only a means to an end. If it can be shown in any particular class of case that the observance of a principle of this sort does not serve the ends of justice, it must be dismissed; otherwise it would become the master instead of the servant of justice.[49]

The House decided that the mother did not have a right to see all the evidence in view of the nature of the proceedings and the issue.

10.53    On Lord Devlin's analysis, exclusions would apply if they are fundamental to the process of judicial inquiry in a particular tribunal.

10.54    In *Mahon v Air New Zealand Ltd*,[50] Lord Diplock also relied on natural justice as the key to the approach to evidence in a tribunal:

The rules of natural justice that are germane to this appeal can, in their Lordships' view, be reduced to those two that were referred to by the English Court of Appeal in *R v Deputy Industrial Injuries Commissioner ex p Moore* [1965] 1 QB 456 at 488–490, which was dealing with the exercise of an investigative jurisdiction . . . The first rule is that the person making a finding in the exercise of such a jurisdiction must base his decision on evidence that has some probative value in the sense described below . . .

The technical rules of evidence applicable to civil or criminal litigation form no part of the rules of natural justice. What is required by the first rule is that the decision to make the finding must be based on *some* material that tends logically to show the existence of facts consistent with the finding and that the reasoning supportive of the finding, if it be disclosed, is not logically self-contradictory.[51]

10.55    This goes too far. If it were right, no exclusions would apply. However, there is authority that some do, at least in some circumstances and for some tribunals: see above.

## Relevance

10.56    In *R v Greater Birmingham Supplementary Benefit Appeal Tribunal ex p Khan*,[52] Lord Widgery CJ emphasised the probative worth of the material before the tribunal:

. . . it [the tribunal] should not regard itself as being bound strictly to the rules of evidence as they are applied in a court of law. It is open to the

49  [1965] AC 201 at 237–238.
50  [1984] AC 808.
51  [1984] AC 808 at 820–821.
52  [1979] 3 All ER 759.

tribunal in this particular type of case to take into account all the circumstances, so far as they are probative, so far as they help to conclude proof of the truth in the individual case.[53]

10.57 In other words, in making findings of fact, a tribunal must rely on material that is relevant in indicating the likelihood of those facts.[54]

10.58 Evidence is relevant if it satisfies two requirements. First, it must directly or indirectly[55] be probative of a fact. Second, that fact must be material to an issue that the tribunal has to decide. Materiality is determined by reference to the legislation and case-law that governs the issue. In other words, evidence is relevant if it consists of factual information or material that assists the tribunal in making findings of fact material to the issues in dispute.

10.59 The fact that evidence is relevant does not mean that it is necessarily admissible. It is a condition precedent to admissibility.[56]

## Receivability and admissibility

10.60 Logically these issues may seem prior to the issue of relevance. However, they are of less practical significance and the possible relevance of the evidence will be a factor that has to be taken into account when deciding them.

10.61 Receivability and admissibility are separate in theory but related in practice. Evidence is receivable if the tribunal may hear, read or see the evidence. Evidence is admissible if the tribunal is allowed to take it into account making its findings of fact.

### Receivability

10.62 Generally, a tribunal should receive evidence from all parties rather than decide the case on the burden of proof or strike it out.

10.63 In *George A Palmer v Beeby*,[57] an industrial tribunal had found that employees had been unfairly dismissed. It had heard evidence from the employer, but had made a decision without hearing evidence from the employees. The Employment Appeal Tribunal directed a rehearing. Kilner Brown J set out the principle that the tribunal should have followed:

> The point of principle which arises in this case, which we consider to be of importance, is that where there is an arguable case and it is not a hopeless case, it is never satisfactory for an industrial tribunal to take a short cut and say that the employer has failed to shoulder the burden of proving that he had acted reasonably.[58]

---

53  [1979] 3 All ER 759 at 763.

54  Lord Simon in *Director of Public Prosecutions v Kilbourne* [1973] AC 729 at 756.

55  Accepting that evidence may be indirectly probative overcomes the point made by Lord Simon in *Director of Public Prosecutions v Kilbourne* [1973] AC 729 at 756 that sometimes irrelevant evidence is admissible.

56  *R v Turner* [1975] QB 834 at 841.

57  [1978] ICR 196.

58  [1978] ICR 196 at 198. See further in chapter 14.

10.64   In *Merelie v Newcastle Primary Care Trust*,[59] the issue was when it was appropriate to strike out a case if a party is not represented. The court decided that if a party is not represented it may be appropriate to allow the case to be presented, however implausible it may seem on paper.

10.65   A tribunal may refuse to receive evidence even though it is admissible, because it is merely repetitious.[60] It may also be appropriate to refuse to receive evidence that might impede rather than assist, the tribunal in making its decision. This was acknowledged by the Employment Appeal Tribunal in *Coral Squash Clubs Ltd v Matthews*.[61] Slynn J said that evidence should be received and assessed:

> ... unless it feels that the evidence which it is proposed to tender is such that its admission could in some way adversely affect the reaching of a proper decision in the case.[62]

10.66   A tribunal may refuse to receive evidence that is not admissible, for example because it is irrelevant.[63] However, it may be necessary to receive the evidence in order to decide whether it is admissible. Even if it is clear that the evidence is not admissible, the tribunal may prefer to receive the evidence as it is given and to deal with this issue when deliberating and giving its reasons for decision. This is likely to be the more efficient approach if the evidence is given by an unrepresented party who does not understand what is and is not relevant and who is not used to presenting information coherently and concisely. It is 'well within a judge's capability' to avoid being influenced by irrelevant matters.[64]

### Admissibility

10.67   There is some authority that a tribunal should refuse to admit evidence that is unfair or prejudicial. In *Snowball v Gardner Merchant Ltd*,[65] the Employment Appeal Tribunal commented that:

> It [a tribunal] may on the other hand decide not to admit evidence which would be admissible under the strict rules of evidence, if, for example it considered it unfair to do so, or as in the field of criminal law, its prejudicial effect outweighed its probative value.[66]

10.68   However, article 6 does not allow a judge to exclude evidence that has substantial probative value.[67]

---

59  (2004) *Times* 1 December.
60  *Jones v National Coal Board* [1957] 2 QB 55 at 64; *Wednesbury Corporation v Ministry of Housing and Local Government (No 2)* [1966] 2 QB 275 at 302.
61  [1979] ICR 607.
62  [1979] ICR 607 at 611.
63  *Jones v National Coal Board* [1957] 2 QB 55 at 64; *Wednesbury Corporation v Ministry of Housing and Local Government (No 2)* [1966] 2 QB 275 at 302; *Bache v Essex County Council* [2000] ICR 313 at 319 (Peter Gibson LJ) and 324 (Ferris J).
64  Lord Phillips CJ in *Swash v Secretary of State for the Home Department* [2007] 1 WLR 1264 at [20]. See also the comments of, and passages quoted by, Buxton and Sedley LJJ at [29] and [32].
65  [1987] ICR 719.
66  [1987] ICR 719 at 722.
67  *R v Musone* [2007] 1 WLR 2467.

## Opinion evidence

10.69  Section 3 of the Civil Evidence Act 1972 deals with opinion evidence. It applies to 'civil proceedings', which includes proceedings 'before any tribunal, in relation to which the strict rules of evidence apply'.[68] Section 3 provides:

(1) Subject to any rules of court made in pursuance of . . . this Act, where a person is called as a witness in any civil proceedings, his opinion on any relevant matter on which he is qualified to give expert evidence shall be admissible in evidence.

(2) It is hereby declared that where a person is called as a witness in any civil proceedings, a statement of opinion by him on any relevant matter on which he is not qualified to give expert evidence, if made as a way of conveying relevant facts personally perceived by him, is admissible as evidence of what he perceived.

(3) In this section, 'relevant matter' includes an issue in the proceedings in question.

10.70  These provisions distinguish between expert witnesses and others.

10.71  Expert witnesses may give evidence on any matter within their expertise, but not on matters within ordinary human experience.[69]

10.72  Reading subsection (1) together with the definition in subsection (3) produces the result that an expert may even give evidence on a matter that is the ultimate issue to be decided. This was confirmed by Butler-Sloss LJ in *Re M and R (Sexual Abuse: Expert Evidence)*.[70] The correct approach is this.[71] The issue goes to the probative worth, not the admissibility, of the evidence. If expert evidence on the ultimate issue is irrelevant, it should be excluded on that ground. If it is potentially relevant, it should be admitted and given appropriate significance. However, the decision of the ultimate issue is for the tribunal, not the expert.

10.73  Evidence from an expert who has a close relationship with the party may not be admissible under subsection (1). The test was set out by Evans-Lombe J in *Liverpool Roman Catholic Archdiocesan Trustees Inc v Goldberg (No 3)*:[72]

I accept that neither section 3 nor the authorities under it expressly exclude the expert evidence of a friend of one or the parties. However, in my judgment, where it is demonstrated that there exists a relationship between the proposed expert and the party calling him which a reasonable observer might think was capable of affecting the views of the expert so as to make them unduly favourable to that party, his evidence should not be admitted however unbiased the conclusions of the expert might probably be. The question is one of fact, namely, the extent and nature of the relationship between the proposed witness and the party.[73]

---

68  Civil Evidence Act 1972 s5(1).

69  *R v Turner* [1975] QB 834 at 841.

70  [1996] 2 FLR 195.

71  [1996] 2 FLR 195 at 211.

72  [2001] 1 WLR 2337 at [13].

73  The law is more tolerant of a relationship between counsel and an expert witness: see the comments of Arden LJ in *Geveran v Skjevesland Trading Co Ltd* [2003] 1 WLR 912 at [42].

10.74   An expert who is asked to give an opinion on the basis of facts found by the tribunal must accept those facts.[74]

10.75   Expert evidence must be independent. It may be admissible despite a conflict of interests, but this must be disclosed so that the court or tribunal can decide if the evidence could be relied on.[75]

10.76   An expert witness has immunity from civil proceedings in respect of evidence given in court and statements made for the purpose of giving evidence, but may be subject to discipline by a professional body.[76]

10.77   Those who are not expert may only give their opinions in the way allowed by subsection (2). This covers opinions which are a compendious way of stating the cumulative effect of a number of observations that may not have registered in the witness's mind individually. For example: a lay witness may give evidence that someone was depressed or anxious. That is not a medical opinion given as an expert diagnosis. Rather, it is merely a convenient way of expressing the numerous features of appearance and behaviour which led the witness to form that opinion.

10.78   A finding of fact made in one proceedings is not admissible as evidence on the same matter in later proceedings.[77] The reason is that the finding of fact represented the opinion of the fact-finder on the probabilities shown by the evidence.

10.79   As the issue with opinion is relevance, all tribunals should logically apply the same rules as the courts, regardless of whether or not the strict rules of evidence apply. However, in practice there are two differences if the strict rules do not apply. First, it may be impractical in a tribunal hearing to exclude opinion evidence. The parties and their representatives may not understand the distinction and trying to limit the evidence may disrupt, and even inhibit, the flow of evidence. Second, evidence may be submitted from a wider range of 'experts' than would be accepted by a court. The same considerations that exclude and control expert evidence apply to all judicial proceedings. But, for both these reasons, freedom from the strict rules of evidence may change the point of impact of these considerations from admissibility to the assessment of their probative worth.[78] Tribunals should not reject expert evidence just because the expert is not available for cross-examination.[79] More caution is required if the opinion is given by a member of the executive of the State, such as a police officer.[80]

## Evidence that has been destroyed

10.80   Evidence that would have been relevant to the proceedings may have been destroyed. This may have been done by a party to the proceedings, by the tribunal itself or by someone else. It may have been done routinely or

---

74   *Re J (Contact)* (2007) *Times* 17 August.
75   *Toth v Jarman* [2006] 4 All ER 1276.
76   *Meadow v General Medical Council* [2007] QB 462.
77   *Secretary of State for Trade and Industry v Bairstow* [2004] Ch 1 at [15]–[27]; *Conlon v Simms* [2008] 1 WLR 484.
78   For example: *Hampshire County Council v JP* [2009] UKUT 239 (AAC) at [34]; *Secretary of State for the Home Department v MN and KY* [2014] UKSC 30 at [35]–[36].
79   *Secretary of State for the Home Department v MN and KY* [2014] UKSC 30 at [36].
80   *RS v CICA* [2014] 1 WLR 1313 at [7]–[8].

exceptionally. And it may have been done with the intention of preventing its use as evidence.

10.81   The loss of evidence by destruction may potentially operate to the benefit or the detriment of the party who destroyed it. If the evidence was destroyed by a party to the proceedings with the intention of preventing its use as evidence, it is likely that it would have been to that party's detriment. It is permissible to draw an inference that its contents were adverse to that party.[81] However, the destruction of the document might deprive the party who destroyed it of any benefit that it might have been, for example as corroboration.[82] In practice, the effects of destruction are reduced by the possibility of proving the contents of the documents by other evidence.[83]

10.82   If the destruction deprives one party of the chance to meet an issue in the proceedings, it may be impossible for there to be a fair hearing on that issue.[84]

10.83   If the evidence was deliberately destroyed before the proceedings were begun, the issue is whether they were destroyed in an attempt to pervert the course of justice. If they were, it is possible in the court system to strike out the proceedings.[85] However, this is not possible under TCEA, as the rules of procedure do not allow proceedings to be struck out for conduct before the proceedings have begun.[86] If the evidence was destroyed after the proceedings began, the issue is whether a fair hearing is possible and, if not, what action can be taken.[87]

## Obtaining evidence

10.84   This section deals mainly with the techniques to use when constructing and asking questions. It also deals with the related matters of summoning witnesses and ordering the production of documents.

### Questioning

10.85   The subject matter of the questions depends on the nature of the proceedings and is dealt with elsewhere.[88] The techniques of questioning are inextricably linked with those of listening.

10.86   For convenience, this section will refer only to judges, but its contents apply to all members, whether judges or not. They are also relevant for representatives.

10.87   It is likely that at some time all judges in every tribunal will have to question a party or a witness. In some tribunals, the judge will have to ask

---

81  *The Ophelia* [1915] P 129 and [1916] 2 AC 206, discussed in *R(IS) 11/92*.

82  *R(IS) 11/92* at [30].

83  *R(IS) 11/92* at [38].

84  *Post Office Counters Ltd v Mahida* [2003] EWCA Civ 1583; (2003) *Times* 31 October. Unfortunately, the Court of Appeal did not distinguish between unfairness for the Civil Procedure Rules and unfairness for article 6.

85  *Douglas v Hello! Ltd* [2003] 1 All ER 1087 at [86].

86  See chapter 12.

87  *Douglas v Hello! Ltd* [2003] 1 All ER 1087 at [90].

88  See chapter 11 for guidance on the sort of question to ask in particular circumstances.

most, if not all, of the questions. In other tribunals, the judge will only need to ask supplementary questions. The extent to which this is necessary will depend on the nature of the proceedings, the issues that arise, the experience of those parties to the proceedings who are not represented, and the skill of any representative who attends. The judge may have to elicit a coherent statement of evidence from a party who is not represented. It is also likely that a judge will have to ask questions to amplify, clarify or even challenge evidence that has been given.

10.88    Questioning must always aim to be effective. When it is undertaken by a judge, it must also aim to be appropriate to the nature of the proceedings and the judge's role in them.

10.89    Questioning by a judge is almost always different from questioning by one of the parties, whether personally or through a representative. A party who calls a witness knows what the witness has to say. Ideally, the questioning will be based on a statement of that evidence. At the least, it will be based on prior knowledge of that evidence. Either way, the purpose of the questioning is to elicit the evidence from the witness in a clear and structured way. This form of questioning to elicit an account is likely to be unnecessary or impossible for judges. Either they will know what the witness is going to say, in which case there is no need for it to be elicited. Or they will not, in which case their questioning cannot be based on knowledge of what the witness has to say.

10.90    A party who questions a witness called by the other party has two concerns. One is to discredit any unfavourable evidence given; the other is to extract favourable evidence. Some of the techniques employed in doing so are never appropriate for judges. Their aim must be to elicit evidence that is as complete and as accurate as they can obtain. And they must do so in a way that strives to retain the confidence of the parties, which limits the manner of questioning that is appropriate.

10.91    In short, the techniques used by a judge are more likely to resemble those used by an adviser in an initial interview than those used by lawyers in court.

## General principles of questioning

10.92    The courts recognise the danger that a judge who questions too much may appear to favour one side or the other.[89] Tribunal judges do not always have the luxury of competent representatives to elicit the evidence for them. They regularly have to do it for themselves. They may have to take the lead in questioning or supplement the questions asked by representatives.

10.93    But whatever the reason for questions from the tribunal, they must be asked in a way that is consistent with the tribunal's status as an independent, judicial decision-maker. Judges must not ask questions in a partisan way. Nor should they create the impression that they are doing so. This does not mean that their questions may not challenge the evidence being given; that may be necessary in order to allow the witness to deal with concerns that the judge has about the evidence given. However, the manner in which that is done is important.

89  Denning LJ in *Jones v National Coal Board* [1957] 2 QB 55 at 64.

10.94 As part of the enabling approach to proceedings, the tribunal should try to establish an atmosphere in which the witness will feel responsive and co-operative. This can be done by body language. Adopt an open posture. Maintain eye contact with the witness. But do not stare; that is intimidating. Continuous eye contact is not natural and so is not comfortable. Be attentive to what the witness is saying. Avoid distractions. This approach will be enhanced by the judge taking a neutral approach to questions with a view to obtaining as clear a statement as possible of the party's case. The use of appropriate techniques of questioning and listening will emphasise that this is what the tribunal is doing. For example: the judge can show that the evidence has been understood by incorporating it into future questions. So, if the tribunal has just heard evidence that the employer was critical of the party's work, the next question might be: when your employer criticised your work, how did you react?

10.95 Style is a personal matter, but a conversational style can be appropriate, provided that it is to a point and not casual or rambling.

10.96 Aggression and hostility are not appropriate for a judge. The impression they create is not consistent with impartiality. And they are probably not particularly effective; they may even be counterproductive.

10.97 The judge should anticipate how parties may interpret or react to particular questions. They may be offended, embarrassed or just puzzled. They may interpret questions that are challenging as impugning their honesty or integrity. They may interpret the questions as showing that the tribunal has prejudged the case or is biased or predisposed against them. The judge should prevent these problems as far as possible. This can, to some extent at least, be prevented by explaining why the questions have to be asked. It would be tedious and unacceptable to have to justify every question. But sometimes a witness who is reluctant to answer a personal and intimate question, for example, may be willing if the reason for it is explained. And it may help to maintain a good rapport.

10.98 Do not ask questions that the witness will have to interpret. This makes it difficult for the witness to answer. It also makes it difficult to assess the answer without knowing how the witness interpreted the question and applied that interpretation. Take as an example this question: 'How soon after you start walking do you experience severe discomfort?' This leave the witness to interpret 'severe discomfort'. And the answer will not disclose what that interpretation was or how the standard set was applied to how the witness felt when walking. It is better to obtain the evidence in a different way, by asking questions that leave no scope for interpretation. For example: 'How do you feel when you are walking?'

10.99 Questions are asked for three reasons and there is a logical order to those reasons. Ask first for information, then to clarify, and finally to probe or test the evidence.

## Basic rules of questioning

10.100 With those principles in mind, there are some basic rules that can be followed.

10.101    Aim to obtain an account of matters relevant to the issues that is as complete and accurate as possible in the circumstances. The purpose of questioning by a judge is not motivated by the self-interest that may affect questioning by the parties.

10.102    Know what evidence has to be obtained. Questions can only be framed appropriately if they reflect a clear understanding of the evidence that the tribunal needs.

10.103    Ask, do not tell. The purpose of questioning is to obtain from a witness information that is relevant to the proceedings, not to provide information to a witness. It may be necessary to provide some information in order to make a question clear. If so, it should be kept to a minimum.

10.104    Ask, do not argue. A question should not be argumentative. It may be appropriate to discuss the evidence with a party or a representative. But this should be kept separate from the task of obtaining the evidence. Get the evidence first, then discuss it.

10.105    Stick to what is relevant. Asking irrelevant questions wastes time and may create the impression that the judge does not understand what the proceedings are about.

10.106    Ask questions politely and calmly. Avoid emotion. Take a business-like approach. This will help encourage the witness to respond accordingly and help to defuse potential conflict with a witness.

10.107    Make the questions clear and precise. Keep questions as short as possible. Use language that the witness will understand and a sentence structure that the witness can follow. In this way, the questioning is likely to be more effective, because the witness will know what information is required.

10.108    Ask one thing at a time. Ask a question that combines two or more points, and the chances are that the witness will probably only answer the final point. The other points are likely to go unanswered and the tribunal may form the impression, wrongly, that the witness has evaded answering.

10.109    Allow the witness time to answer completely before moving on.

10.110    Listen to the answer. This will help to frame the next question.

10.111    Give the witness a chance to counter views that the tribunal may be forming from the evidence. Do this by structuring questions in a way that allows, or even encourages, the witness to contradict those views.[90]

## Eliciting an account

10.112  By a process of asking a question, listening to the answer and the framing another question based on the answer, the witness's evidence will be obtained in an efficient, clear and structured way.

10.113    There is likely to be some indication of what a witness is to say. If not, the only approach is to begin with an open question.

10.114    Ask an open question to help a witness give a general account. An open question is one that does not narrowly restrict the answer. An example is: what happened at the interview? This leaves the witness to decide what to

---

90  Scott Plous, *The Psychology of Judgment and Decision Making*, McGraw Hill, 1993, Chapter 20, 'Self-fulfilling Prophecies', pp239–240.

include and what to leave out. An open question may be relatively wide or narrow in its scope. That has the advantage that it may elicit information that was not previously known and open up new lines of enquiry. But it also has dangers. The witness may leave out relevant material, through not knowing what is relevant. Or the witness may know that something is relevant, but find it easy to leave it out to create a false impression. So, this type of question is more effective if combined with other types, particularly closed questions.

10.115    Ask a closed question to elicit information on a specific point. A closed question is one that indicates narrowly what sort of information is required. Sometimes it can be answered with yes or no. Like: did you tell your supervisor about the accident? Sometimes not. Like: how long did you stay away from work? A closed question indicates the sort of information that the answer should contain. Like an open question, it may be relatively wide or narrow in its scope. It does not indicate what the answer should be. This is in contrast to a leading question.

10.116    Generally, it is better to avoid asking leading questions on matters that are in dispute. A leading question is one that indicates the answer that is required. Like: you did report that you had started work, didn't you? Having told the witness what to say, the answer may command less respect, even if it is correct, than if it were elicited differently. This advice is subject to two caveats. First, there may be circumstances in which a relevant question can only be asked in a leading way. If used, leading questions should only be put when other forms of question have been used. Second, it is possible to make too much of the danger of leading questions, as most witnesses are likely to know what evidence is required of them. Strictly, it is only appropriate to classify a question as leading when asked by a representative.[91] However, the danger is the same whether the question is asked by a representative or by a judge. There are, though, some circumstances in which it is appropriate for a judge to ask a question in a form that leaves the witness in no doubt about the judge's thinking. This will be appropriate when the judge is putting a provisional view on the evidence to the witness for comment, provided that the parties are given sufficient opportunity to deal with the point raised.[92]

10.117    Deal with one point at a time. Only move on when the evidence is complete. Do not ramble randomly from one point to another next. Obtain the evidence in a structured sequence. All this will help the witness to give all relevant evidence and the tribunal to follow the evidence and ensure that something is not overlooked.

## Amplification, clarification and challenging

10.118   These may be necessary as part of eliciting an account or as a follow-up to evidence given without the tribunal's assistance.

10.119    Ask for elaboration if the evidence appears to be incomplete on its face or the judge suspects that there is more to be said. Like: tell me more about . . .

---

91  Buxton LJ in *Currey v Currey* [2005] 1 FLR 952 at [33].
92  [2005] 1 FLR 952: Thorpe and Buxton LJJ at [18], [20] and [33].

10.120    Ask for clarification if the evidence is not clear. Attempting a para-phrase of the evidence given may help identify whether or not it has been understood correctly. Like: have I understood you correctly that . . .?

10.121    Challenge evidence if it is inconsistent with, or contradicted by, other evidence or if it seems improbable. The challenge draws attention to the point of concern and provides a chance to deal with it. It is consistent with a neutral approach to the evidence. To emphasise this, the questioning should not be aggressive or hostile. An explanation of the reason for the question can emphasise its relevance and why the witness should have a chance to deal with it.

## Particular types of witness or evidence

10.122    *The verbose witness: concentrate on relatively closed questions.* If open questions are necessary or appropriate, limit the scope for freedom of answer. Interrupt the witness in order to focus the answer.

10.123    *The terse witness: concentrate on relatively open questions.* Avoid closed questions that can be answered with only yes or no. Use questions that require fuller or more detailed answers.

10.124    *The witness who appears to be evasive or avoids answering: persist in requiring an answer to the question.* This may show that it was a false impression; the witness may have not understood the question. Use relatively narrow questions, whether open or closed, in order to limit the opportunity to evade or avoid. Persist only as long as necessary to show that the witness will say nothing more specific. It may be appropriate to point out to the witness that the evidence is not clear and allow another chance to be more specific.

10.125    *The suspected liar.*[93] A judge who suspects or believes that a witness is deliberately lying must give the witness a chance to deal with that concern. The judge must already have a basis for suspicion or belief. It may be appropriate to test this further. One way of doing this is to ask more and more detailed questions. This will make it difficult for the witness to invent a story. Another way, which can be used independently of or in conjunction with detailed questions, is to ask the witness to repeat evidence that has been given, preferably in a different order.[94] This may show discrepancies. Do not, though, expect word perfect repetition. This is itself suspicious. If after this testing the judge remains of the view that the witness may be deliberately lying, this should be put to the witness with reasons. There may be a satisfactory explanation.

10.126    *The witness who has a mental disability: the tribunal must use language that the witness can understand and avoid certain types of question.*[95] Some forms of questioning can produce inaccurate answers from someone with a mental disability. First, some people with a mental disability are likely to answer

93    On the problems with identifying someone who is deliberately lying, see chapter 11.

94    'How to tell a suspect is lying – see if he knows it backwards' (2007) *Times* 7 June.

95    Rebecca Milne and Ray Bull, *Investigative Interviewing: Psychology and Practice*, Wiley, 1999, chapter 7.

'yes' to every question. This danger can be avoided by not asking questions that invite a yes or no answer. The better approach is to ask questions in the alternative. So do not ask: do you dress yourself? Instead ask: do you dress yourself or does someone help you? And do not always put the answer first that is more likely or more favourable (or unfavourable); vary between putting it first or second. If the alternative form of question is asked, the alternatives put must be comprehensive of the possibilities. Second, repetition of the same question can suggest that the answer previously given was wrong and lead to the witness giving a different answer. Third, comments to encourage the witness to say more must not limit the information to be given. Saying 'right' as a way of encouraging further disclosure seems innocuous, but can suggest that the information given so far is the only type of information that is required. Fourth, avoid the use of personal pronouns. Fifth, make clear when moving from one topic to the next so that the witness is not confused. See further below.

10.127 *Children.* This is unlikely to be necessary in a tribunal, but requires special consideration.[96] See further below.

10.128 *Wearing the veil.* If the witness is prepared to remove the veil, arrangements should be made for the case to be heard by a female panel and to allow the judges to see the witness's expression and demeanour while ensuring that her face cannot be seen by any males present.[97]

## Cross-examination

10.129 The cross-examination of witnesses may be inappropriate in the context of a particular tribunal. It may be discouraged or even prohibited under the tribunal's power to regulate its own procedure.[98] This is so for a number of reasons.

10.130 First, the aggressive tone and manner that may, but need not, be associated with cross-examination may be inconsistent with the atmosphere in which a tribunal seeks to make the parties and their witnesses feel comfortable and able to give of their best.[99]

10.131 Second, despite judicial support for the value of cross-examination,[100] there is an argument that the traditional approach to cross-examination is not an effective method of getting to the truth.[101]

10.132 Third, it may be inconsistent with the essentially inquisitorial nature and philosophy of the tribunal.[102]

96 Rebecca Milne and Ray Bull, *Investigative Interviewing: Psychology and Practice*, Wiley, 1999, chapter 8.

97 *Re S (Practice: Muslim Women Giving Evidence)* [2007] 2 FLR 461 at [15]–[17].

98 The manner in which evidence is obtained and presented is part of the procedure: see para 10.40.

99 The so-called enabling approach: see chapter 1.

100 Lord Bridge in *R v Blastland* [1986] AC 41 at 54; Pill LJ in *Dyason v Secretary of State for the Environment* (1998) 75 P&CR 506 at 512.

101 Jill Hunter, 'Battling a Good Story: Cross-examining the Failure of the Law of Evdence' in Paul Roberts and Mike Redmayne (eds), *Innovations in Evidence and Proof,* Hart Publishing, 2008.

102 See chapter 1.

10.133   If there is no cross-examination, the tribunal must compensate for this through its inquisitorial approach. As Pill LJ explained in *Dyason v Secretary of State for the Environment*[103] in the context of a planning appeal:

> If cross-examination disappears, the need to examine propositions in that way does not disappear with it . . . The absence of an accusatorial procedure places an inquisitorial burden upon an Inspector.[104]

10.134   As already explained, the traditional style of cross-examination is not appropriate for judges to undertake. In the absence of express pro-vision, it is for the tribunal to decide whether the parties should be allowed to employ it. The tribunal may, through its power to regulate its own proced-ure, direct the parties on the style of questioning that is acceptable.

## Children, vulnerable adults and sensitive witnesses

10.135   The Upper Tribunal has decided that, in dealing with potential child wit-nesses, the tribunal must give appropriate significance to a child's right to be heard under article 12 of the United Nations Convention on the Rights of the Child 1989 and to have a fair hearing and a family life under articles 6 and 8 of the European Convention on Human Rights.[105] The judge said that the same principles should govern participation by a child in all juris-dictions, but recognised that their application might vary according to the jurisdiction being exercised.[106] The Senior President's practice direction on 'First Tier and Upper Tribunal – Child, Vulnerable Adult and Sensi-tive Witnesses' is to be revised to take account of the modern authorities discussed in that decision.

## Witness summons

10.136   In order to obtain evidence, it may be necessary to direct a person to attend, to give evidence and to produce documents. These rules do not have specific statutory authority; they are within the traditional meaning of practice and procedure.[107] There is a general case management power. UTR r5(3)(d) is illustrative:[108]

> (3) In particular, and without restricting the general powers in paragraphs (1) and (2), the Upper Tribunal may–
>
>   . . .
>
>   (d) permit or require a party or another person to provide documents, information, evidence or submissions to the Upper Tribunal or a party; . . .'

There is also more specific provision. UTR r16 is illustrative:[109]

---

103  (1998) 75 P&CR 506.
104  (1998) 75 P&CR 506 at 512.
105  *JP v Secretary of State for Work and Pensions* [2014] UKUT 0275 (AAC).
106  *JP v Secretary of State for Work and Pensions* [2014] UKUT 0275 (AAC) at [19].
107  See chapter 10.
108  See also: GRC Rules r5(3)(d); HESC Rules r5(3)(d); IAC Rules r4(3)(d); Lands Rules r5(3)(d); PC Rules r6(3)(d); SEC Rules r5(3)(d); Tax Rules r5(3)(d); WPAFC Rules r5(3)(d).
109  See also: GRC Rules r16; HESC Rules r16; IAC Rules r15; Lands Rules r18; PC Rules r20; SEC Rules r16; Tax Rules r16; WPAFC Rules r16.

**16 Summoning or citation of witnesses and orders to answer questions or produce documents**

  (1) On the application of a party or on its own initiative, the Upper Tribunal may–

    (a) by summons (or, in Scotland, citation) require any person to attend as a witness at a hearing at the time and place specified in the summons or citation; or

    (b) order any person to answer any questions or produce any documents in that person's possession or control which relate to any issue in the proceedings.

  (2) A summons or citation under paragraph (1)(a) must–

    (a) give the person required to attend 14 days' notice of the hearing or such shorter period as the Upper Tribunal may direct; and

    (b) where the person is not a party, make provision for the person's necessary expenses of attendance to be paid, and state who is to pay them.

  (3) No person may be compelled to give any evidence or produce any document that the person could not be compelled to give or produce on a trial of an action in a court of law in the part of the United Kingdom where the proceedings are due to be determined.

  (4) A person who receives a summons, citation or order may apply to the Upper Tribunal for it to be varied or set aside if they did not have an opportunity to object to it before it was made or issued.

  (5) A person making an application under paragraph (4) must do so as soon as reasonably practicable after receiving notice of the summons, citation or order.

  (6) A summons, citation or order under this rule must–

    (a) state that the person on whom the requirement is imposed may apply to the Upper Tribunal to vary or set aside the summons, citation or order, if they did not have an opportunity to object to it before it was made or issued; and

    (b) state the consequences of failure to comply with the summons, citation or order.

10.137 The application of these powers should reflect the inquisitorial nature of the proceedings.[110]

10.138 In *MR v CMEC and DM*,[111] the Upper Tribunal distinguished between rule 5(3)(d), which was 'concerned with case management powers and in particular with the provision of documents, information, evidence or submissions in order to allow the tribunal to regulate its procedure', and rule 16, which was 'concerned with the scope of the evidence which can be before the tribunal in order to decide the issues before it'. This seems a fine distinction.

## Summoning witnesses

10.139 The power to issue a summons may be exercised against a party to the proceedings[112] as well as others. It must not be used oppressively.[113] In

---

110 *Inner West London Assistant Deputy Coroner v Channel 4 Television Corporation* (2007) *Times* 11 December.

111 [2009] UKUT 283 (AAC) at [8].

112 *R v B County Council ex p P* [1991] 1 WLR 221 at 226.

113 [1991] 1 WLR 221 at 227.

deciding whether to issue a summons, the tribunal should take account of any expenses that a witness would incur in attending.[114]

10.140    There is no absolute bar on children giving evidence.[115] These principles apply:

- it must be exercised with caution;[116]
- the age of the child will be relevant;[117]
- the relevant time for judging whether a summons should be issued is when the evidence will be given;[118]
- a summons should normally only be used if the child is over the age of 12.[119]

10.141    A summons requires a person to attend at a hearing. The definition of 'hearing' in UTR r1(3) and its equivalents[120] allows a person to attend without being physically present:

> 'hearing' means an oral hearing and includes a hearing conducted in whole or in part by video link, telephone or other means of instantaneous two-way electronic communication.

A person does not attend by giving pre-recorded evidence. However, the tribunal has power to direct how the evidence is to be provided,[121] which could include pre-recording.

10.142    In the case of an expert or other professional, it is relevant for the tribunal to consider whether attending to give evidence would disrupt or impede other important work which the expert or other professional has to do.[122] In such a case, the tribunal should also consider whether there are other ways alternatives to personal attendance.[123]

10.143    A person who does not wish to be summonsed is not entitled to ignore it.[124] The proper course is apply for the summons to be set aside and the tribunal should be prepared to treat any letter from the person summonsed as an application for this.[125] A witness who is not a party cannot appeal against the decision to issue the summons; the appropriate remedy is judicial review.[126]

---

114  *CB v Suffok County Council* [2010] UKUT 413 (AAC) at [24].

115  *Re W (children) (care proceedings: evidence)* [2010] 1 WLR 701.

116  [1991] 1 WLR 221 at 228 and 232–233.

117  *Re P (Witness Summons)* [1997] 2 FLR 447 at 454.

118  *R v Highbury Corner Magistrates' Court ex p D* [1997] 1 FLR 683.

119  *Re P (Witness Summons)* [1997] 2 FLR 447 at 454. But in *R v Highbury Corner Magistrates' Court ex p D* [1997] 1 FLR 683 a summons was issued to a child of nine, subject to the condition that his suitability as a witness would be decided at the time he was due to give evidence.

120  See also: GRC Rules r1(3); HESC Rules r1(3); IAC Rules r1(4); Lands Rules r18; PC Rules 1(3); SEC Rules r1(3); Tax Rules r1(3); WPAFC Rules r1(3).

121  See: UTR r15(1)(e); GRC Rules r15(1)(g); HESC Rules r15(1)(e); IAC Rules r14(1)(e); Lands Rules r16(1)(e); PC Rules r18(1)(g); SEC Rules r15(1)(e); Tax Rules r15(1)(e); WPAFC Rules r15(1)(e).

122  *Society of Lloyd's v Clementson (No 2)* (1996) *Times* 29 February; *CB v Suffok County Council* [2010] UKUT 413 (AAC) at [24].

123  *CB v Suffok County Council* [2010] UKUT 413 (AAC) at [29].

124  *CB v Suffok County Council* [2010] UKUT 413 (AAC) at [28].

125  *CB v Suffok County Council* [2010] UKUT 413 (AAC) at [25] and [28].

126  *CB v Suffok County Council* [2010] UKUT 413 (AAC) at [26].

*Ordering the production of documents*

10.144 Production of documents may be required on the date of hearing or before.[127]

10.145 An order may only be made against someone who is not a party to the proceedings if production of the document is necessary for disposing of the case or for saving costs.[128]

10.146 Documents are not limited to paper documents. UTR r1(3) provides:[129]

> ... 'document' means anything in which information is recorded in any form, and an obligation under these Rules to provide or allow access to a document or a copy of a document for any purpose means, unless the Tribunal directs otherwise, an obligation to provide or allow access to such document or copy in a legible form or in a form which can be readily made into a legible form; ...

This covers all media that can record evidence or information, such as tape recordings[130] and film.[131]

10.147 Tax documents are protected from disclosure by a public interest immunity, regardless of whether or not this immunity is claimed by the tax authorities. However, this immunity may be overridden by public interest in the administration of justice. The burden of justifying disclosure is on the person seeking disclosure. In making the decision, the tribunal should have regard to the relevance of the documents and to the necessity of disposing fairly of the case.[132]

10.148 The Bankers' Books Evidence Act 1879 applies to production of evidence by a bank. Production of a bank statement is not a breach of the bank's duty of confidentiality to its customer.[133] But it is an offence to disclose information relating to the business or other affairs of any person that has only been acquired for the purposes of the Banking Act 1987,[134] unless the person concerned consents or the information is already public.[135]

## Admission and exclusion of evidence

10.149 This section is concerned with the evidence that the tribunal may or may not take into account. It also deals with the related issues of the evidence that the tribunal will allow to be presented and the manner in which it will receive it.

127 *Khanna v Lovell White Durrant (a firm)* [1995] 1 WLR 121.
128 *Macmillan Inc v Bishopsgate Investment Management plc (No 1)* [1993] 1 WLR 837 and 1372.
129 See also: GRC Rules r1(3); HESC Rules r1(3); PC Rules 1(3); SEC Rules r1(3); Tax Rules r1(3); WPAFC Rules r1(3).
130 *Grant v Southwestern and County Properties Ltd* [1975] Ch 185.
131 *Senior v Holdsworth ex p Independent Television News Ltd* [1975] QB 23.
132 See *Lonrho plc v Fayed (No 4)* [1994] QB 775.
133 *Robertson v Canadian Imperial Bank of Commerce* [1994] 1 WLR 1393.
134 Banking Act 1987 s82 and *Bank of Credit and Commerce International (Overseas) Ltd (in liquidation) v Price Waterhouse (No 2)* [1998] Ch 84.
135 There are other exceptions, but they are unlikely to be relevant to a tribunal.

10.150    These matters are distinct from the issue whether evidence that is taken into account may be withheld from one of the parties. That issue is dealt with separately.[136] The issues may, though, be connected, as it may be appropriate to exclude evidence that cannot be disclosed to a party.

## The powers

10.151    The tribunal's control over the evidence that it may admit or exclude from its consideration is governed by paragraph 10 of Schedule 5 TCEA:

(1) Rules may make provision about evidence (including evidence on oath and the administration of oaths).

(2) Rules may modify any rules of evidence provided for elsewhere, so far as they would apply to proceedings before the First-tier Tribunal or Upper Tribunal.

10.152    UTR r15(2) is illustrative of the rules made under that authority: [137]

(2) The Upper Tribunal may–

(a) admit evidence whether or not–

(i) the evidence would be admissible in a civil trial in the United Kingdom; or

(ii) the evidence was available to a previous decision-maker; or

(b) exclude evidence that would otherwise be admissible where–

(i) the evidence was not provided within the time allowed by a direction or a practice direction;

(ii) the evidence was otherwise provided in a manner that did not comply with a direction or a practice direction; or

(iii) it would otherwise be unfair to admit the evidence.

## Evidence

10.153    The enabling power, and the rules made under it, apply only to evidence. They do not apply to material that is not part of the law of evidence. As explained above, the rules of procedure included the rules relating to disclosure of evidence, the attendance of witnesses and the manner of giving evidence are, but not the admissibility of evidence. That is subject to statutory authority to the contrary. Paragraph 10(1) of Schedule 5 to TCEA authorises rules to be made about evidence and paragraph 10(2) authorises the rules of evidence to be modified. Evidence is not defined; its scope is assumed. However, there is no bright-line that distinguishes evidence from other rules.[138] Authority may assist. For example: rules of policy, such as issue estoppel, are not evidence.[139]

---

136  In para 10.173 onwards.

137  See also: GRC Rules r15(2); HESC Rules r15(2); IAC Rules r14(2); Lands Rules r16(2);PC Rules r18(6); SEC Rules r15(2); Tax Rules r15(2); WPAFC Rules r15(2). CPR 32.1(2) deals with excluding otherwise admissible evidence.

138  For an academic discussion, see William Twining, 'What is the Law of Evidence?' in *Rethinking Evidence*, Northwestern, 1994.

139  Diplock LJ in *Mills v Cooper* [1967] 2 QB 459 at 469. On which, see chapter 2.

## Receiving evidence

10.154 Admitting and excluding evidence is concerned with the evidence that a tribunal may take into account in making its decision. It is different from receiving evidence, which it may have to do in order to decide if it is admissible.[140]

## Admitting evidence

10.155 The power to admit evidence that would not otherwise be admissible will only be relevant in practice to those tribunals in which the strict rules of evidence apply. If those rules do not apply, there is little scope for admitting other evidence. For example: if the key factor that determines admissibility is the relevance of the evidence, it is unlikely that a tribunal would wish to admit evidence that was not relevant.

10.156　If the tribunal admits evidence that it would not otherwise be allowed to take into account, it will be necessary to justify doing so, including by reference to the overriding objective.

10.157　The right to withhold evidence may be a constitutional or human right. In *R (Morgan Grenfell & Co Ltd) v Special Commissioner of Income Tax*,[141] the House of Lords recognised that legal professional privilege was such a right and that, as such, it could can only be overridden expressly or by necessary implication.

## Excluding evidence

10.158 The power to exclude evidence that would otherwise be admissible will be relevant whether or not the strict rules of evidence apply. If those rules do not apply, there will be greater scope for excluding evidence.

10.159　The power under r16(2) and its equivalents is additional to the power to exclude evidence that is clearly irrelevant, immaterial or repetitive.[142]

10.160　Expert evidence to support the reliability of evidence given on oath is also usually excluded.[143] One exception relates to the reliability of a child's evidence, although the evaluation of that evidence remains a matter for the tribunal.[144]

10.161　If the tribunal excludes evidence that it would otherwise be allowed to take into account, it will be necessary to justify doing so, including by reference to the overriding objective.

10.162　In deciding whether or not to exclude evidence, it is always relevant to consider the effect. For example:

---

140　The distinction is discussed at para 10.59 onwards.

141　[2003] 1 AC 563 at [7]–[8]. In *R v Derby Megistrates' Court ex p B* [1996] AC 487 at 507, Lord Taylor described legal professional privilege as 'a fundamental condition on which the administration of justice as a whole rests'.

142　*Wednesbury Corporation v Ministry of Housing and Local Government (No 2)* [1966] 2 QB 275 at 302 and *R(SB)* 6/82 at [5].

143　*R v Robinson (Raymond)* [1994] 3 All ER 346.

144　*Re N (a Minor) (Child abuse: Evidence)* (1996) *Times* 25 March, and *Re M and R (Child Abuse: Evidence)* [1996] 2 FLR 195.

- if the effect is likely to have a significant impact on the outcome of the proceedings, it may be disproportionate to exclude it on the ground that it was submitted late;
- the decision-maker may be required to take the evidence into account and may have power to supersede the tribunal's decision on the ground that it was wrong in fact, thereby rendering the tribunal's decision irrelevant.

10.163   Other relevant factors include: (i) the extent to which the evidence is controversial; (ii) its value in reaching correct conclusions on the facts; (iii) whether the evidence will focus disproportionately on collateral matters; (iv) any potential unfairness of taking the evidence into account; (v) the burden on the parties and the tribunal of producing and assessing the evidence. This last point is of particular relevance in a tribunal where the time available for a hearing is more curtailed than in court proceedings.

10.164       In *O'Brien v Chief Constable of South Wales Police*,[145] Lord Bingham discussed the competing factors that would be relevant in a case involving similar fact evidence:

> The second stage of the enquiry requires the case management judge or the trial judge to make what will often be a very difficult and sometimes a finely balanced judgment: whether evidence or some of it (and if so which parts of it), which *ex hypothesi* is legally admissible, should be admitted. For the party seeking admission, the argument will always be that justice requires the evidence to be admitted; if it is excluded, a wrong result may be reached. In some cases, as in the present, the argument will be fortified by reference to wider considerations: the public interest in exposing official misfeasance and protecting the integrity of the criminal trial process; vindication of reputation; the public righting of public wrongs. These are important considerations to which weight must be given. But even without them, the importance of doing justice in the particular case is a factor the judge will always respect. The strength of the argument for admitting the evidence will always depend primarily on the judge's assessment of the potential significance of the evidence, assuming it to be true, in the context of the case as a whole.
>
> While the argument against admitting evidence found to be legally admissible will necessarily depend on the particular case, some objections are likely to recur. First, it is likely to be said that admission of the evidence will distort the trial and distract the attention of the decision-maker by focus-ing attention on issues collateral to the issue to be decided. This is an argument which has long exercised the courts (see *Metropolitan Asylum District Managers v Hill* (1882) 47 LT 29, 31 per Lord O'Hagan) and it is often a potent argument, particularly where trial is by jury. Secondly, and again particularly when the trial is by jury, it will be necessary to weigh the potential probative value of the evidence against its potential for causing unfair prejudice: unless the former is judged to outweigh the latter by a considerable margin, the evidence is likely to be excluded. Thirdly, stress will be laid on the burden which admission would lay on the resisting party: the burden in time, cost and personnel resources, very considerable in a case such as this, of giving disclosure; the lengthening of the trial, with the increased cost and stress inevitably involved; the potential prejudice to witnesses called upon to recall matters long closed, or thought to be closed;

145  [2005] 2 AC 534 at [5]–[6].

the loss of documentation; the fading of recollections . . . But the present case vividly illustrates how real these burdens may be. In deciding whether evidence in a given case should be admitted the judge's overriding purpose will be to promote the ends of justice. But the judge must always bear in mind that justice requires not only that the right answer be given but also that it be achieved by a trial process which is fair to all parties.

## Applying rule 15(2)

10.165    Lord Carnwath commented on the effect of rule 15(2) in *Secretary of State for the Home Department v MN and KY*:[146]

Generally, therefore, the area of legitimate debate is about relevance and weight, not admissibility.[147]

The issue for the tribunal is not whether evidence can be admitted, it is whether it should be admitted.[148] Relevance is the key consideration, but it is also necessary to take account of the probative worth of the evidence if it were admitted [149] and fairness.[150] It is not permissible to use rule 15(2) to compel the production of privileged material.[151]

## Evidence that cannot be compelled

10.166    The power to admit or exclude evidence that is not otherwise admissible will only be relevant if the evidence is available. A party or witness may be protected from disclosing evidence by the rules of procedure. UTR r16(3) is illustrative:[152]

(3) No person may be compelled to give any evidence or produce any document that the person could not be compelled to give or produce on a trial of an action in a court of law in the part of the United Kingdom where the proceedings are due to be determined.

If the evidence of, or the document containing, the legal advice is not given, there is no scope for the tribunal to admit it.

10.167    Judges are competent, but not compellable, witnesses in relation to their judicial function, although a judge would be expected to give evidence if it was vital.[153]

---

146 [2014] UKSC 30 at [24].
147 For examples of an attempt at reasoning from first principles in respect of previous guilty pleas, although not framed in terms of rule 15(2), see *AM v Secretary of State* [2013] UKUT 094 (AAC) and *Newcastle City Council v LW* [2013] UKUT 0123 (AAC).
148 *LN v Surrey NHS Primary Care Trust* [2011] UKUT 76 (AAC) at [22].
149 *LN v Surrey NHS Primary Care Trust* [2011] UKUT 76 (AAC) at [23]–[24].
150 *Hoyle v Rogers* [2014] 3 All ER 550.
151 *LM v London Borough of Lewisham* [2009] UKUT 204 (AAC).
152 See also: GRC Rules r16(3); HESC Rules r16(3); IAC Rules r15(3); Lands Rules r18(3); PC Rules r20(3); SEC Rules r16(3); Tax Rules r16(3); WPAFC Rules r16(3).
153 *Warren v Warren* [1997] QB 488.

## Controlling the evidence presented

10.168   In addition to the tribunal's control over the admission of evidence, it has power to control the evidence that that it will allow to be presented to it and the manner in which it is presented. UTR r15(1) is illustrative:[154]

> (1) Without restriction on the general powers in rule 5(1) and (2) (case management powers), the Upper Tribunal may give directions as to–
>
> (a) issues on which it requires evidence or submissions;
>
> (b) the nature of the evidence or submissions it requires;
>
> (c) whether the parties are permitted or required to provide expert evidence, and if so whether the parties must jointly appoint a single expert to provide such evidence;
>
> (d) any limit on the number of witnesses whose evidence a party may put forward, whether in relation to a particular issue or generally;
>
> (e) the manner in which any evidence or submissions are to be provided, which may include a direction for them to be given–
>
> (i)  orally at a hearing; or
>
> (ii) by written submissions or witness statement; and
>
> (f) the time at which any evidence or submissions are to be provided.

## Limiting the number of witnesses

10.169   Under UTR r15(1)(d) and its equivalents, the tribunal may limit the number of witness to be called. The circumstances in which that power might be used were discussed by Geoffrey Lane LJ in *R v Board of Visitors of Hull Prison ex p St Germain (No 2)*:[155]

> Clearly in the proper exercise of his discretion a chairman may limit the number of witnesses, either on the basis that he has good reason for considering that the total number sought to be called is an attempt by the prisoner to render the hearing of the charge virtually impracticable or where quite simply it would be quite unnecessary to call so many witnesses to establish the point at issue. But mere administrative difficulties, simpliciter, are not in our view enough. Convenience and justice are often not on speaking terms: see *per* Lord Atkin in *General Medical Council v Spackman* [1943] AC 627, 638.[156]

## Control of questioning

10.170   In addition to its powers under UTR r15(1), the tribunal must ensure that their time is used efficiently for the benefit of their users as a whole. This entitles it to prevent repetition, prolixity, discursiveness, irrelevance and the oppression of witnesses.[157]

---

154  See also: GRC Rules r15(1); HESC Rules r15(1); IAC Rules r14(1); Lands Rules r16(1); PC Rules r18(1); SEC Rules r15(1); Tax Rules r15(1); WPAFC Rules r15(1). CPR 32.1(1) deals with excluding otherwise admissible evidence.

155  [1979] 1 WLR 1401.

156  [1979] 1 WLR 1401 at 1406.

157  *R v Whybrow* (1994) *Times* 14 February.

## Evidence on oath or affirmation

10.171   The rules of procedure under TCEA authorise the tribunal to allow or require evidence to be given on oath. UTR r15(3) is illustrative.[158]

> (3) The Upper Tribunal may consent to a witness giving, or require any witness to give, evidence on oath, and may administer an oath for that purpose.

10.172   The rules of procedure make no mention of an affirmation. However, section 5 of, and Schedule 1 to, the Interpretation Act 1978 provide that references to oath include affirmation.

10.173   Even without an express provision, Lord Atkin considered that tribunals may have power to administer an oath under section 16 of the Evidence Act 1851:[159]

> Every court, judge, justice, officer, commissioner, arbitrator, or other person, now or hereafter having by law or by consent of parties authority to hear, receive, and examine evidence, is hereby empowered to administer an oath to all such witnesses as are legally called before them respectively.

10.174   If a witness refuses to take an oath before the First-tier Tribunal, the matter may be referred to the Upper Tribunal.[160]

10.175   Whether or not evidence was given on oath or affirmation is relevant to its probative worth.[161]

## Disclosure and non-disclosure of documents and information

10.176   This section is concerned with the disclosure or non-disclosure of documents and information. They will principally consist of evidence that the tribunal may take into account. In CPR, disclosure means telling the other parties that a document exists or has existed. This is not a term that is used in the rules of procedure under TCEA and disclosure is here used to cover both disclosure of the existence of a document and its production for use by the tribunal.

10.177   The issue of the evidence that the tribunal may admit or exclude from its consideration is dealt with separately.[162] The issue of disclosure to the parties may have to be decided first, as the document or information may have to be received by the tribunal before its admission or exclusion can be decided.

---

158  See also: GRC Rules r15(3); HESC Rules r15(3); IAC Rules r14(3); PC Rules r18(7); SEC Rules r15(3); Tax Rules r15(3); WPAFC Rules r15(3).

159  *General Medical Council v Spackman* [1943] AC 627 at 638.

160  See: GRC Rules r7(3)(c); HESC Rules r7(3)(c); PC Rules r8(5)(c); SEC Rules r7(3)(c); Tax Rules r7(3)(c); WPAFC Rules r7(3)(c).

161  Viscount Simon LC in *General Medical Council v Spackman* [1953] AC 627 at 636–637.

162  At para 10.146 onwards.

## The basic principle of disclosure to the parties

10.178 The basic principle is that evidence on which the tribunal relies must be disclosed to all the parties to the proceedings. This was set out by Lord Hodson in *Official Solicitor to the Supreme Court v K*.[163]

> It is said with force . . . that it is contrary to natural justice that the contentions of a party in a judicial proceeding may be overruled by considerations in the judicial mind which the party has no opportunity of criticising or controverting because he or she does not know what they are; moreover, the judge may (without the inestimable benefit of critical argument) arrive at a wrong conclusion on the undisclosed material. Even worse, the undisclosed evidence may, if subjected to criticism, prove to be misconceived or based on false premises.[164]

## Exceptions to the basic principle

10.179 There are exceptions to this basic principle.

10.180 The first source of exceptions is the common law. There is a requirement that regard be had to the welfare of the child. This is exemplified by *Re B (A Minor) (Disclosure of Evidence)*.[165] According to Balcombe LJ, this requirement only applies 'in any case which is directly concerned with the welfare of a child'.[166] And according to Glidewell LJ, it only operates if 'the disclosure of the evidence would be so detrimental to the welfare of the child or children under consideration as to outweigh the normal requirements for a fair trial that all evidence must be disclosed, so that all parties can consider it and if necessary seek to rebut it'.[167]

10.181 There is also a common law duty of confidentiality that may apply to documents held, for example, by a health authority about a mental patient. The fact that a document was given to a party in confidence does not of itself prevent its disclosure under this rule. Two issues arise for the tribunal. The first issue is whether the confidentiality is relevant to another ground on which disclosure may be refused. As Lord Cross explained in *Alfred Crompton Amusement Machines Ltd v Customs and Excise Commissioners (No 2)*:[168]

> 'Confidentiality' is not a separate head of privilege, but it may be a very material consideration to bear in mind when privilege is claimed on the ground of public interest. What the court has to do is to weigh on the one hand the considerations which suggest that it is in the public interest that the documents in question should be disclosed and on the other hand those which suggest that it is in the public interest that they should not be disclosed and to balance one against the other.[169]

The second issue is whether, in the exercise of its discretion, the tribunal should direct disclosure. The fact that a document is confidential is

---

163 [1965] AC 201.
164 [1965] AC 201 at 234.
165 [1993] 1 FLR 191.
166 [1993] 1 FLR 191 at 203.
167 [1993] 1 FLR 191 at 201. For the approach in adoption, see *Re K (Adoption: Disclosure of Information)* [1997] 2 FLR 74.
168 [1974] AC 405.
169 [1974] AC 405 at 433–434.

relevant to the exercise of this discretion.[170] The impact on a party's physical or mental health is a factor that might justify refusing to direct disclosure. This is, in principle, consistent with Article 8 of the European Convention on Human Rights.[171]

10.182 The issue of confidentiality was approached rather differently by the three-judge panel of the Upper Tribunal in *Dorset Healthcare NHS Trust v MH*:[172]

> Sometimes such documents are submitted to the responsible authority holding the medical records with an express requirement that they be kept confidential from the patient (and sometimes also from even the patient's solicitors). In any event, that authority often considers, rightly, that it owes a duty of confidence to the relevant third-parties and is unwilling to disclose documents to the patient (and occasionally even to the patient's solicitors) without an order.

It is not clear whether the tribunal considered that all such records were subject to disclosure on order or only those that were not subject to an express duty.

10.183 The second source of exceptions is statute.[173] The major instance is section 97(3) of the Nationality, Immigration and Asylum Act 2002.[174]

10.184 The third source of exceptions is the tribunal's rules of procedure. Apart from specific provision, tribunals under TCEA may prohibit disclosure under its power to regulate its own procedure.[175] The tribunal may have power to direct that evidence is not disclosed as part of an express unqualified power to give directions or as a power implied as a matter of necessity in order to enable the tribunal to perform its function.[176]

## Non-disclosure under TCEA

10.185 The TCEA Sch 5 para 11(1) authorises rules that provide for information or evidence to be withheld from one of the parties or generally:

(1) Rules may make provision for the disclosure or non-disclosure of information during the course of proceedings before the First-tier Tribunal or Upper Tribunal.

(2) Rules may make provision for imposing reporting restrictions in circumstances described in Rules.

10.186 The rules or procedure made under that authority apply to documents and information rather than evidence. The documents are likely to contain evidence and the information to amount to evidence. However, there may be material that is not strictly evidence, but which nonetheless falls within the rule. For example: disclosing a representative's identity might put that person at risk of serious harm.

---

170 *Science Research Council v Nassé* [1980] AC 1028.
171 *Gaskin v United Kingdom* (1989) 12 EHRR 36.
172 [2009] UKUT 4 (AAC) at [23].
173 *Al Rawi v Security Service* [2010] 4 All ER 562.
174 Discussed in *MT (Algeria) v Secretary of State for the Home Department* [2008] QB 533.
175 Lord Woolf in *Roberts v Parole Board* [2005] 2 AC 738 at [44]. At [66], Lord Woolf described this as an implied power.
176 [2005] 2 AC 738 per Lord Woolf at [56] and [65].

10.187    These powers are exercised in the rules of procedure by general and specific provision. The general power distinguishes between non-disclosure to the public and non-disclosure to the parties.

## Non-disclosure to the public

10.188    There may be circumstances in which it would not be appropriate for evidence to be disclosed to the public. UTR r14(1) and (7) is illustrative:

> (1) The Upper Tribunal may make an order prohibiting the disclosure or publication of–
>    (a) specified documents or information relating to the proceedings; or
>    (b) any matter likely to lead members of the public to identify any person whom the Upper Tribunal considers should not be identified.
>
> (7) Unless the Upper Tribunal gives a direction to the contrary, information about mental health cases and the names of any persons concerned in such cases must not be made public.

10.189    The default position is that information about mental health cases and the names of any persons concerned in them may only be disclosed if the tribunal directs. Otherwise, all information may be disclosed unless the tribunal directs.

10.190    Rule 14(1) contains broad powers to withhold disclosure. However, it only identifies the potential subject matter of the power. It says nothing of the circumstances in which the power should be exercised.

### The subject matter of the power

10.191    Under (a), the only condition is that the document or information must be capable of being specified.

10.192    Under (b), the matter must relate to the discovery of the person's identity. The test is likelihood. 'Likely' takes it meaning from its context. In the context of a jurisdictional threshold to a discretionary power, a modest threshold may be appropriate, such as 'may well'.[177] It is lower in the scale of probability than 'more probable than not' (the balance of probabilities test).[178] It has also been equated with a 'real possibility' – a possibility that cannot sensibly be ignored[179] – and with something that could well happen.[180]

### The exercise of the power

10.193    These will have to be considered in the light of the overriding objective and of the factors relevant to non-disclosure .

10.194    There must be a reason why the documents, information or the person's identity should be protected. This may be for its own sake, but usually it will be for the consequences that may follow from disclosure. Under

---

177  *Three Rivers District Council v Governor and Company of the Bank of England (No 4)* [2003] 1 WLR 210 at [32]; *Black v Sumitomo Corporation* [2002] 1 WLR 1562 at [72].
178  *Three Rivers District Council v Governor and Company of the Bank of England (No 4)* [2003] 1 WLR 210 at [33] and *Cream Holdings Ltd v Banerjee* [2003] Ch 650 at [12].
179  *Re O (Minors) (Care: Preliminary Hearing)* [2004] 1 AC 523 at [16].
180  *Boyle v SCA Packaging Ltd* (2009) *Times* 6 July.

(b), the test of likelihood relates only to the chances of identification, not to the chances that the consequences will follow. But the latter will be relevant to whether the power should be exercised.

10.195 In practice, this power may be exercised by making the decision anonymous. Under r32(6) Tax Rules, this is compulsory if the tribunal publishes a report of a decision resulting from a hearing that was held, wholly or partly, in private.

## Non-disclosure to a person

10.196 There may be circumstances in which it would not be appropriate for evidence to be disclosed to a person. Usually, that person will be one of the parties. UTR r14(2)–(6) is illustrative:[181]

> (2) The Upper Tribunal may give a direction prohibiting the disclosure of a document or information to a person if–
>   (a) the Upper Tribunal is satisfied that such disclosure would be likely to cause that person or some other person serious harm; and
>   (b) the Upper Tribunal is satisfied, having regard to the interests of justice, that it is proportionate to give such a direction.
> (3) If a party ('the first party') considers that the Upper Tribunal should give a direction under paragraph (2) prohibiting the disclosure of a document or information to another party ('the second party'), the first party must–
>   (a) exclude the relevant document or information from any documents that will be provided to the second party; and
>   (b) provide to the Upper Tribunal the excluded document or information, and the reason for its exclusion, so that the Upper Tribunal may decide whether the document or information should be disclosed to the second party or should be the subject of a direction under paragraph (2).
>
> . . .
>
> (5) If the Upper Tribunal gives a direction under paragraph (2) which prevents disclosure to a party who has appointed a representative, the Upper Tribunal may give a direction that the documents or information be disclosed to that representative if the Upper Tribunal is satisfied that–
>   (a) disclosure to the representative would be in the interests of the party; and
>   (b) the representative will act in accordance with paragraph (6).
> (6) Documents or information disclosed to a representative in accordance with a direction under paragraph (5) must not be disclosed either directly or indirectly to any other person without the Upper Tribunal's consent.

10.197 These provisions require a two stage consideration.

10.198 The first stage is an assessment of the likelihood of serious harm to the person affected. The chance must be higher than a mere possibility, but not necessarily as great as a probability. The meaning of 'likely' has been discussed above. There is no limit on the form of harm. It may be physical or mental. It also includes harm to a person's reputation or business.

---

181 See also: GRC Rules r14; HESC Rules r14; IAC Rules r13; Lands Rules r15; PC Rules r17; SEC Rules r14; WPAFC Rules r14.

10.199     The second stage is to make a judgment whether giving the direction would be proportionate, taking the interests of justice into account.

10.200     If a tribunal makes an order for non-disclosure, it must also order that neither the order itself nor information about it be disclosed. Otherwise, it would be self-defeating.

10.201     The tribunal must not exercise its power to make a non-disclosure order in respect of information about one party's case, unless it is still possible for the other party to give proper instructions to a representative and to respond to that case.[182]

## Specific powers of non-disclosure

10.202 These are in addition to the general powers. Some rules make specific provision for particular classes of case.[183] Their specific provision removes the need for an individual decision to be made in each case.

10.203     The Upper Tribunal rule only applies to appeals. It does not apply on a reference by the First-tier Tribunal under its review power in TCEA s9(5)(b) or for the Upper Tribunal to use its enforcement powers under TCEA s25.[184] The Upper Tribunal gives specific directions for the management of those references.[185]

## Fairness and balance

10.204 The decision whether or not to allow disclosure requires a balance between the right to a fair hearing and any other relevant Convention rights.[186]

10.205     Non-disclosure is not necessarily incompatible with fairness. As Lord Woolf said in *Roberts v Parole Board*:[187]

> An experienced judge is able to make some appropriate allowance for the fact that evidence or information is not tested as well as would normally be the case in an adversarial hearing. In addition there are usually steps which the judge can take which will minimise the scale of non-disclosure and its effect . . .

> There can be an infinite variety of circumstances as to the degree of information that is withheld completely or partially without any significant unfairness being caused.

10.206 One possibility is that the information withheld from a party may be disclosed to the party's representative on condition that it is not disclosed to the party. This is permissible under r14(5)–(6). However, this only applies to non-disclosure under r14. It does not apply to confidential information under r19.

---

182  *RM v St Andrew's Hospital* [2010] UKUT 119 (AAC); *Secretary of State for the Home Department v AF (No 3)* [2010] 2 AC 269; *Tariq v Home Office* [2010] ICR 1034 at [43]–[44]; *Bank Mellat v Her Majesty's Treasury* [2012] QB 91 at [18] and [21]; *R v R(L)* [2011] 1 WLR 359.

183  SEC Rules r19; UTR r19,

184  GRC Rules r7(3); HESC Rules r7(3); IAC Rules r6(3); PC Rules r8(5); SEC Rules r7(3); Tax Rules r7(3); WPAFC Rules r7(3).

185  Lands Rules r45; UTR r26A.

186  For example: *A Local Authority v A* [2010] 2 FLR 1757.

187  [2005] 2 AC 738 at [70] and [76].

10.207 If the fairness of the hearing will be impaired, the tribunal will have to consider whether that evidence should be excluded.[188] If it would not be proper to exclude the evidence, fairness must give way and the tribunal must conduct the proceedings as appropriate to give effect to the direction for non-disclosure under r14(11). This rule does not apply to confidentiality under r19, but that limits the right to fairness by necessary implication.

## Data protection

10.208 Section 35 of the Data Protection Act 1998 provides:

**35 Disclosures required by law or made in connection with legal proceedings etc**

(1) Personal data are exempt from the non-disclosure provisions where the disclosure is required by or under any enactment, by any rule of law or by the order of a court.

(2) Personal data are exempt from the non-disclosure provisions where the disclosure is necessary–

(a) for the purpose of, or in connection with, any legal proceedings (including prospective legal proceedings); or

(b) for the purpose of obtaining legal advice;

or is otherwise necessary for the purposes of establishing, exercising or defending legal rights.

10.209 If a tribunal directs disclosure, section 35(1) applies and the Act cannot be relied on to justify non-disclosure.[189]

---

188 For this power, see para 10.157 onwards.

189 *R (Davies) v Commissioners Office* [2008] 1 FLR 1651 at [11] and [14]. Ward LJ refused permission to appeal to the Court of Appeal: [2008] EWCA Civ 1031.

# Findings

*continued*

# Nature of a fact

11.1   The nature of a fact is not just of theoretical interest. It assists in both the gathering of evidence and its assessment by providing a framework, albeit only partial, within which the reliability of evidence can be tested.[1]

## The purpose of an inquiry into the facts

11.2   Judges are under a duty to find the facts on any contested issue.[2]

11.3   One view of the aim of an inquiry into the facts is that it is to discover the true facts. Judges sometimes make remarks that appear to support this. In *Jones v National Coal Board*,[3] the Court of Appeal said of the judge's duty: 'His object, above all, is to find out the truth . . .'[4] And twice in *O'Brien v Chief Constable of South Wales Police*[5] Lord Bingham referred to the 'right answer' on the facts. But such statements beg the question of what is meant by 'truth' and 'right'.

11.4   There is a limit to which the true facts can be ascertained. As Lord Brandon recognised in *Barder v Caluori*,[6] 'justice requires cases to be decided, *as far as practicable*, on the true facts relating to them'.[7] And what is practicable is limited by the evidence available, as Lord Denning MR recognised in *Harmony Shipping Co SA v Saudi Europe Line Ltd*.[8] And by who bears the burden of proof, as Lord Denning recognised in *Air Canada v Secretary of State for Trade*:[9] 'The due administration of justice does not always depend on eliciting the truth. It often depends on the burden of proof'.[10]

11.5   In practice, the best that can be achieved is to come as close to the true facts as possible. The extent to which this can be achieved is severely limited by a number of factors. The result of the combination of these factors is that the facts found by the tribunal may be significantly different from the 'true facts' of the case.[11]

11.6   These factors are considered below. They can be interpreted as leading to a different analysis of the aim of an inquiry into the facts. On this analysis, the discovery of the true facts is at best an aspiration; the possibility of the facts found coinciding with the true facts is only a matter of chance. Viewed in this way, a fact is no more than the outcome of applying a process of reasoning to the evidence.

---

1   For further elements of a framework for testing evidence see paras 11.69 onwards.

2   Viscount Simonds in *Benmax v Austin Motor Co Ltd* [1955] AC 370 at 373.

3   [1957] 2 QB 55.

4   [1957] 2 QB 55 at 63. See also: Lord Dunedin in *Thompson v The King* [1918] AC 221 at 226.

5   [2005] 2 AC 534 at [4] and [6].

6   [1988] AC 20.

7   [1988] AC 20 at 41 emphasis added.

8   [1979] 1 WLR 1380 at 1385. See also: Lord Wilberforce in *Air Canada v Secretary of State for Trade* [1983] 2 AC 394 at 438.

9   [1983] 2 AC 394.

10   [1983] 2 AC 394 at 411.

11   The way in which we form beliefs is important to an understanding of evidence and the factors that can influence it. For simple and complex models of how beliefs are formed, see 'A cognitive neuroscience of belief' in Halligan and Aylward, *The Power of Belief*, Oxford, 2006, especially pp12–17.

## Availability of evidence

11.7   Tribunals have to decide cases on the evidence available. This may be more limited that the evidence that exists or could be obtained. There are many reasons why evidence may not be available. A party may withhold it, not know that it exists or how it can be obtained, not have access to it or not be able to afford the cost of obtaining it.

## Value of evidence

11.8   Even if evidence is available, its value as indicating the 'true' facts can be limited in a number of ways. The discussion assumes that all the witnesses are trying to give honest accounts of what happened.

## Perception and interpretation

11.9   Perception includes, but is not limited to, observation. It covers the full range of senses. It also conveys the element of subjectivity in the exercise in contrast to the objectivity that can be suggested by 'observation'.

11.10      The event[12] was experienced by those involved and witnessed by others. They each have a perception of what happened. This perception may be physically partial. For example: a witness may not have been well placed to see all that occurred. And the perception, whether physically partial or complete, may be affected by the intellectual, cultural, mental or emotional characteristics of the witness. For example: the witness may be opposed to any violence or dislike one of those involved.

11.11      A witness's perception and interpretation of an event may be distinct processes. For example: the witness may see the employee approaching the supervisor at a particular speed. A witness who is always cautious when moving around the work place may interpret this as the employee rushing towards the supervisor, whereas a less cautious witness may interpret it as the employee approaching the supervisor at normal speed. Alternatively, interpretation and perception may be inextricably connected. For example: a witness affected by colour prejudice may see a black employee strike a white supervisor, whereas another witness may see only a black employee trying to prevent a white supervisor from slipping.

11.12      The witness's evidence will be affected by interpretation and perception. The tribunal has to attempt to penetrate through to the real event.

## Recollection

11.13   The tribunal will only hear of the event to the extent that the witness can recall it. This will be limited by the extent and accuracy of the witness's recollection. A further process of selection and interpretation may occur at this stage. The result may be that some elements of what the witness saw are lost while other parts of it are embellished.

---

12   This is a deliberately vague word. According to the issue, it may be something that has happened, or something that was seen or heard, or the value of something, or a state of affairs, such as a person's health.

11.14    The nature of memory is explained in the key points from the report of the British Psychological Society Research Board on *Guidelines on Memory and the Law* (2008), which are set out below at paragraph 11.115.

## Communication

11.15   Communication involves at least two parties: the person who reports and the person who hears. There is scope for inaccuracy on the part of both.

11.16    The witness's recollection must be expressed. The accuracy with which the event as recalled by the witness is correctly reported depends in part on the witness's command of language. This is partly a matter of the range of vocabulary, partly a matter of choice of vocabulary, and partly a matter of the fluency with which it can be deployed.

11.17    However clearly a witness may give evidence, it is possible for the tribunal to misinterpret it. It may do so for a variety of reasons. The evidence as given may depend on information that is not known to the tribunal. Or its meaning may be affected by the terms of the questions asked to elicit it, in ways which are not known to the tribunal. Or the tribunal may have preconceptions about the case which affect its interpretation. And so on.

## Admissibility

11.18   Before recollection is accepted as evidence, it must be admissible. The extent to which the rules of admissibility impose a significant limitation on the evidence that a tribunal may consider depends on whether the strict rules of evidence apply.[13] Excluding evidence will limit the evidence available to the tribunal. This may deprive it of relevant material, thereby hampering its ability to identify the true facts. But it may also assist in finding the true facts by excluding evidence that is unreliable or would otherwise hamper the fact-finding.

## Analysing the evidence

11.19   The tribunal has to assess the evidence. The criteria used may allocate greater probative worth to evidence that is not as accurate as other evidence. For example: a tribunal may find that a contemporaneous account is more likely to be accurate than a witness's later recollection, although the reverse is in fact the case.

## Evaluating the evidence

11.20   When the probative worth of the evidence has been analysed, the tribunal has to evaluate it by reference to the standard of proof.[14] In doing this, it may be allowed or required to apply presumptions. They may be based on probability, but do not guarantee accuracy.

---

13  See chapter 10.
14  See chapter 14.

## What is a fact?

11.21   For the purposes of the tribunal's decision, a fact is what is found by a tribunal. It may or may not be the 'true' fact. It is the end result of the filtering, and potentially distorting, processes of observation, perception, interpretation, recollection, communication, assessment and evaluation.

# Facts and inferences

## Primary facts and inferences

11.22   The primary facts are the findings of fact that the tribunal makes directly from the evidence.

11.23   A tribunal may have to make findings of fact on matters that are not directly covered by the evidence.[15] It does this by drawing inferences. Inferences are also called secondary facts. Drawing an inference is a process of reasoning that reaches a conclusion of fact from another fact or from a party's conduct in relation to the proceedings. Anything else is mere speculation.[16] The conclusion reached may be a fact in issue or an intermediate fact on which further reasoning can be based. Inference is used both to describe the process of finding the fact and the fact so found.

11.24   In this book, an inference drawn from another fact is called an evidential inference and an inference drawn from a party's conduct in relation to the proceedings is called a forensic inference. They are dealt with at paragraphs 11.29 onwards below.

11.25   Denning LJ explained the difference between primary facts and inferences in *British Launderers' Research Association v Central Middlesex Assessment Committee and Hendon Rating Authority*:[17]

> Primary facts are facts which are observed by witnesses and proved by oral testimony, or facts proved by the production of a thing itself, such as an original document . . . The conclusions from primary facts are, however, inferences deduced by a process of reasoning from them.[18]

## Compound fact

11.26   'Compound fact' is an expression that was used by Jessel MR in *Erichsen v Last*.[19] It is one that conveys the overall effect of a series of component facts, each of which has to be analysed in the context of all the other facts.[20]

---

15   A person's mental state can rarely be found by direct evidence: *McGreevy v Director of Public Prosecutions* [1973] 1 WLR 276 at 285.

16   Ryder J in *A Local Authority v A (No 1)* [2011] 2 FLR 137 at [18].

17   [1949] 1 KB 462.

18   [1949] 1 KB 462 at 471.

19   (1881) 8 QBD 414 at 416.

20   See chapter 4.

## Inferences of perception and evaluation of facts

11.27   The courts have distinguished between inferences of perception and evaluation.[21] Perception is concerned with finding facts. Evaluation is concerned with whether the facts found satisfy a legal test or standard. These are also known as issues of mixed law and fact or of fact and degree. In this book, references to inferences are generally to inferences of perception. Inferences of evaluation are treated as one form of judgment.

## Inference upon inference

11.28   Is it possible to draw an inference wholly or partly from another inference? The comments of Lord Hodson in *Rubber Investment Ltd v Daily Telegraph Ltd*[22] suggest that it is not. The case concerned an alleged libel contained in a newspaper article that the affairs of a company were being investigated by the police. Lord Hodson said:

> Suspicion, no doubt, can be inferred from the fact of the inquiry being held if such was the case, but to take the further step and infer guilt is, in my view, wholly unreasonable. This is to draw an inference from an inference and to take two substantial steps at the same time.[23]

This is an isolated comment and seems to go too far. It is right to bear in mind that a further inference is being based wholly or partly on a fact that is itself established by inference. It is right to be more cautious the further the fact-finding departs from the direct evidence. But in principle there should be no objection to a rational process of reasoning that moves from one inference to another.

# Evidential inferences

## Types of evidential inference

11.29   Inferences may be conclusive or persuasive.

11.30   A conclusive inference can only be based on certainty. It applies in circumstances where if A and B are both true, then C must also be true. Given the nature of legal proceedings and the standard of proof, it is seldom possible to be confident in a legal setting that certain facts are true. Without sound premises, this method of reasoning is not possible. That leaves persuasion.

11.31   A persuasive inference is based on probability. In the legal context, it begins with a search for further findings of fact that are consistent and coherent with the primary facts. For example: A goes for a walk in the park every Tuesday evening. Last Tuesday, A left at the normal time wearing walking shoes and took the bus that goes past the park. It is possible to infer that A did go to the park, although that is not certain.

11.32   By its nature, this approach can generate many possible and inconsistent inferences. The tribunal must decide whether to draw any inferences

21   Viscount Simonds in *Benmax v Austin Motor Co Ltd* [1955] AC 370 at 373.
22   [1964] AC 234.
23   [1964] AC 234 at 274.

and, if so, to select from those available. The choice has to be made in two contexts: (i) the findings relevant to the issue in question; and (ii) the burden of proof applicable to that issue.

11.33    Within that framework, a number of factors may be relevant. Their significance will depend on the circumstances of the case.

11.34    How much confidence does the tribunal have in the soundness of its findings of primary facts? The greater that confidence, the sounder the foundation for drawing inferences. The less that confidence, the more cautious it should be in drawing any further conclusions.

11.35    How well does a particular inference account for those primary findings? The better that account, the sounder the case for that inference.

11.36    How plausible is a particular inference? An inference may account for the primary findings, but it may not be plausible in the context of a particular case. This will be assessed by reference to the tribunal's understanding and experience of life, including experience of similar cases.

11.37    Does the inference identify a cause for the primary facts? This will not always be relevant. In some cases, it may be. For example: it may be possible to infer that the behaviour exhibited by a child is caused by the child having a particular medical condition.

11.38    The choice may be reduced, and the ultimate selection of an inference therefore assisted, by the nature of the process of inference adopted by the tribunal.

## Closed, open, comparative and own initiative processes

11.39   The process of inference is closed if the only issue is whether a particular inference can be drawn. For example: given the claimant's knowledge of the benefit system and disposal of capital, can it be inferred that this was done in order to secure entitlement to benefit?

11.40    The process is open if the issue is which of a number of permissible inferences should be drawn. For example: given the party's proven life-style, what level of income can be inferred?

11.41    In practice, both closed and open processes are likely to have a comparative element. The parties will probably argue for different inferences, presenting the tribunal with a choice and a chance to compare the arguments for the competing inferences. Is the disposal of capital better explained by a concern to secure entitlement to benefit or a desire to repay debts? Is the party's life-style more likely to be supported from income or from credit?

11.42    The tribunal will not necessarily be bound to accept any of the inferences suggested by the parties. It may of its own initiative identify an inference that has not been suggested by either party. In some cases, it may have no interest in, or basis for, doing this. Take the example of the disposal of capital before claiming benefit. The Secretary of State may argue that it was motivated by the desire to secure benefit while the claimant may argue that it was justified in order to pay off existing debts. It is unlikely that the tribunal will have any reason to substitute an inference favourable to the claimant, but different from the case actually put by the claimant. In other cases, a different inference may be appropriate. Take the inferring of income from life-style. The evidence will probably justify a range of inferences. Each parent will have an interest in arguing for a figure at either end of the range, whereas the tribunal may consider that a more realistic figure is somewhere nearer the centre.

11.43 The process may involve a comparative element even if it is not presented as such to the tribunal. The tribunal may nonetheless find it helpful to consider a range of possibilities when deciding which inference to draw. This may form part of a structured consideration as part of an objective, open-minded decision-making process.[24]

## The efficient use of inferences

11.44 The Court of Appeal in *Crewe Services and Investment Corporation v Silk*[25] encouraged county court judges to rely on common sense inferences rather than require expensive expert evidence. Robert Walker LJ referred to:

> . . . the practicalities of the disposal of business in the County Court. County Court judges constantly have to deal with cases that are inadequately prepared and presented, either as to the facts or as to the law (or both), and they must not be discouraged from doing their best to reach a fair and sensible result on inadequate materials. Moreover there is a strong public interest in encouraging litigants not to incur the expense of a proliferation of expert witnesses (in this case, actuaries and valuers have been mentioned) unless the additional expense of time and money can be justified.[26]

He then went on to explain how the county court judge could have obtained relevant evidence from witnesses already called, without the need for expert witnesses, and drawn sensible conclusions as to valuation from general experience. This reasoning is equally applicable to tribunals.

# Forensic inferences

## Nature

11.45 A forensic inference[27] may be drawn if a party or a witness refuses to co-operate with the tribunal. The inference is that co-operation would be detrimental to the party concerned. Once drawn, it is then taken into account in assessing the probative worth of the evidence as a whole. The effect may well be a decision that is less favourable than it would have been if the party had been co-operative.[28] A forensic inference may have a statutory basis.[29]

---

24  See chapter 14.
25  (2000) 79 P&CR 500.
26  (2000) 79 P&CR 500 at 509.
27  These are generally referred to as adverse inferences, but this is not a distinctive classifying feature as evidential inferences may also be adverse. The term forensic emphasises the basis on which the inference is drawn rather than its impact.
28  *Fairclough Homes Ltd v Summers* [2012] 1 WLR 2004 at [52].
29  HESC Rules r15(4)–(5).

## When a forensic inference is necessary

11.46   It is not always necessary to consider whether to draw a forensic inference from lack of co-operation. There are two circumstances in which it is not necessary.

11.47   First, a party who fails to provide evidence that could lead to some advantage is deprived of the chance of securing that advantage. There is no need to achieve this by drawing a forensic inference. So, if a claimant before an employment tribunal fails to provide evidence in support of an alleged incident, that issue is decided against that party for failing to discharge the burden of proof.

11.48   Second, the law may provide for the consequences of failure to co-operate. So under the child support scheme, a non-resident parent who fails to provide the necessary information for a maintenance calculation may be subject to a default maintenance decision.[30]

## Lack of co-operation that may permit a forensic inference

11.49   There is no limit to the circumstances in which a forensic inference may be appropriate. They cover almost every lack of co-operation with the tribunal, including the following.

### Refusing to answer questions

11.50   *Re O (Care proceedings: Evidence)*[31] concerned an allegation of violence by a mother towards her children. The mother refused to give evidence and Johnson J held that it was possible to infer from this that the allegations of violence were true.[32]

### Destroying documents or other property with the intention of preventing their use as evidence

11.51   This is the basis of the rule in *The Ophelia*.[33] It does not apply to routine destruction of documents.[34] As the contents of destroyed documents may be proved by other evidence,[35] it may not be necessary to draw an inference.

### Withholding written information in the possession of or available to the party

11.52   *Al-Khatib v Masry*[36] concerned ancillary relief on divorce. The wife alleged that the husband had assets in excess of £200,000,000. The husband failed to make anything like an accurate and complete disclosure. Munby J held that the evidence was not sufficient to allow him to find that the husband

---

30  Child Support Act 1991 s12(1).
31  [2004] 1 FLR 161 at [13] and [16].
32  [2004] 1 FLR 161 at [13] and ]16].
33  [1915] P 129 and [1916] 2 AC 206.
34  *R(IS) 11/92* at [36].
35  *R(IS) 11/92* at [38(f)].
36  [2002] 1 FLR 1053.

had the amount alleged, but that it was sufficient to infer that he had sufficient assets to allow the court to make a settlement at the level that the wife was claiming.[37] This was based on the analysis put by counsel for the wife that it was permissible to infer that the husband had calculated that he would obtain a more favourable settlement on this basis than if he made full disclosure. The judge used as a cross-check on this inference the evidence of the scale of the husband's business activities over 20 years and the commission he had been capable of earning.

### Failing to agree to undertake a test like a blood test or DNA testing for paternity

11.53 *Secretary of State for Work and Pensions v Jones*[38] concerned paternity. The mother alleged that a man was the father of her child, but he refused to take part in DNA testing. The Court of Appeal held that this refusal allowed the court to accept the mother's evidence of paternity.[39]

### Failing to co-operate in a procedure relevant to the court proceedings like family therapy

11.54 *Re S (Unco-operative mother)*[40] concerned a mother's willingness to participate in family therapy in order to help her children establish a relationship with their father. Thorpe LJ said that the weak reasons given by the mother could be used as the basis for an inference that she lacked commitment to this process.[41]

### Failing to attend the hearing of an appeal or to arrange for witnesses to attend

11.55 *Secretary of State for Health v C (Tribunal: Failure to draw inference)*[42] concerned a man's suitability to work with children. A woman alleged that he had raped her. On medical advice, she did not give oral evidence. The man did not attend to give evidence. The Court of Appeal held that, in those circumstances, the tribunal was entitled to conclude that the man had decided that his account could not withstand oral examination.

## Criminal matters

11.56 A party has no right to silence, even if this means disclosing matters relevant to criminal proceedings. As Megaw LJ explained in *Jefferson Ltd v Bhetcha*:[43]

---

37 [2002] 1 FLR 1053 at [96]. An appeal against Munby J's decision was allowed by the Court of Appeal on consent terms following mediation. The background is reported at [2005] 1 WLR 381. It does not affect the principles underlying the judge's reasoning for which the decision is cited here and elsewhere in this chapter.

38 [2004] 1 FLR 282.

39 [2004] 1 FLR 282 at [11]–[15].

40 [2004] 2 FLR 710.

41 [2004] 2 FLR 710 at [21]–[22].

42 (2003) *Times* 30 January.

43 [1979] 1 WLR 898.

The protection which is at present given to one facing a criminal charge – the so-called 'right of silence' – does not extend to give the defendant as a matter of right the same protection in contemporaneous civil proceedings.[44]

11.57   It may, though, be appropriate to adjourn to allow the criminal proceedings to be heard before the case before the tribunal. But in some cases, it is logical for the issue before the tribunal to be decided before the criminal case. See chapter 8.

## Lack of co-operation that does not permit a forensic inference

11.58   However, a forensic inference may not be drawn from a party's refusal to disclose information that is privileged.[45]

## Attitude to proceedings

11.59   By drawing a forensic inference, a tribunal uses lack of co-operation to identify one party's attitude to the other party's case. It is, therefore, always relevant to consider whether there is another explanation for the lack of co-operation. In *Re A (A minor) (Paternity: Refusal of blood test)*,[46] Waite LJ said of an alleged father who, within his rights, refused to provide blood samples for testing:

> . . . the inference that he is the father of the child should be virtually inescapable. He would certainly have to advance very clear and cogent reasons for this refusal to be tested – reasons which it would be just and fair and reasonable for him to be allowed to maintain.[47]

And in *Secretary of State for Health v C (Tribunal: Failure to draw inference)*,[48] Latham LJ said that the tribunal could have drawn the inference as a result of the man's failure to give evidence 'without any reason'.

11.60   If the reasons given are not sufficient to prevent an inference being drawn, they may nonetheless affect the significance of the inference in the circumstances of the case. As Lord Lowry explained in *R v Inland Revenue Commissioners ex p T C Coombs & Co*:[49]

> In our legal system generally, the silence of one party in face of the other party's evidence may convert that evidence into proof in relation to matters which are, or are likely to be, within the knowledge of the silent party and about which that party could be expected to give evidence. Thus, depending on the circumstances, a *prima facie* case may become a strong or even an overwhelming case. But, if the silent party's failure to give evidence (or to give the necessary evidence) can be credibly explained, even if not entirely justified, the effect of his silence in favour of the other party may be either reduced or nullified.[50]

---

44   [1979] 1 WLR 898 at 905.
45   Lord Chelmsford in *Wentworth v Lloyd* (1864) 11 ER 1154 at 1155; Aldous LJ in *Oxford Gene Technology Ltd v Affymetrix Inc (No 2)* [2001] RPC 18 (p310 at [317]).
46   [1994] 2 FLR 463.
47   [1994] 2 FLR 463 at 473.
48   (2003) *Times* 30 January.
49   [1991] 2 AC 283.
50   [1991] 2 AC 283 at 300.

11.61 A relevant factor in deciding the significance of a failure to co-operate is whether the party understood the risk involved in this stance. In some circumstances, the party must have realised the risk; for example, if the party is a lawyer. However, in other cases it may be relevant whether the tribunal warned the party of the possible consequence of failing to co-operate. In *Al-Khatib v Masry*,[51] Munby J emphasised that the husband had been given warning at an earlier hearing.[52] The mere recitation of a formula is, though, not sufficient. What the tribunal must take into account, when deciding what inference if any to draw, is the reality of whether the party concerned would have understood the significance of the risk that the warning conveyed.

11.62 Another relevant factor, related to understanding the risk of failure to co-operate, is whether the party knew the details of the other party's case. A forensic inference can only relate to information that the party knew was before the tribunal or might be put to the tribunal. One party will know the general terms of the other party's case from the documents. If the party fails to attend the hearing, the tribunal may conclude that the party has no answer to that case as presented. However, if the other party presents further allegations at the hearing, the tribunal is not entitled to infer that the party could not have answered the new allegations, because the party had no warning that these might be made.

## If a forensic inference cannot be drawn

11.63 If a party fails to co-operate but the circumstances do not allow the tribunal to draw a forensic inference, the effect is that the tribunal has to deal with the case on the basis of the evidence that is available. For example: a parent in a child support case may refuse to co-operate because of the effect that the proceedings are having on a new relationship. In those circumstances, the tribunal cannot draw a forensic inference against that party. It has to deal with the case on the evidence available. That evidence is likely to come from the other parent and may be out-of-date or not directly relevant to the issue. In the absence of evidence from the parent concerned, the tribunal may have to draw inferences from the evidence available in order to bring it up-to-date or to relate it to the issue. But these are evidential inferences. The reasoning process does not involve a forensic inference, because the party's lack of co-operation is not indicative of the strength of the case that could be put to the tribunal.

## Effect of a forensic inference

11.64 If a tribunal concludes that the lack of co-operation by one party to the proceedings indicates that party's view of the weakness of the case that could be presented, it may take this into account in assessing the evidence as a whole. It may form part of the tribunal's assessment that leads it to accept the other party's evidence on a particular point, as in *Re A (A minor)*

51 [2002] 1 FLR 1053.
52 [2002] 1 FLR 1053 at [93].

*(Paternity: Refusal of blood test)*,[53] where the refusal to co-operate was used to show acceptance of the allegation of paternity. Or it may form part of the tribunal's reasoning that leads it to draw an inference from the evidence available to it, as in *Al-Khatib v Masry*,[54] where the failure to co-operate was used to show that the husband had sufficient assets to allow a particular order to be made.

11.65    A forensic inference cannot operate in isolation from the evidence as a whole. As Abbott CJ explained in *R v Burdett*:[55]

> In drawing an inference or conclusion from facts proved, regard must always be had to the nature of the particular case, and the facility that appears to be afforded either of explanation or contradiction. No person is to be required to explain or contradict, until enough has been proved to warrant a reasonable and just conclusion against him, in the absence of explanation or contradiction; but when such proof has been given, and the nature of the case is such as to admit of explanation or contradiction, if the conclusion to which the proof tends be untrue, and the accused offers no explanation or contradiction; can human reason do otherwise than adopt the conclusion to which the proof tends?[56]

11.66   The forensic inference must operate as part of a process of reasoning. The point was made succinctly by Otton LJ in *Baker v Baker*:[57]

> Such inferences must be properly drawn and reasonable. On appeal it may be possible for either party to show that the inferences or the award [of ancillary relief in divorce proceedings] were unreasonable in the sense that no judge faced with the information before him could have drawn the inferences or awarded the figures that he did.[58]

11.67   A forensic inference cannot be used as a justification for guessing at the evidence that the party might or could have given.[59] Nor can it be used simply to impose a penalty on a party who does not co-operate. The key distinction was drawn by Ewbank J in *E v E (Financial Provision)*:[60]

> I have to say that the failures on the part of the husband would justify any inferences which were proper which could be drawn against him. At the same time it would be wrong to draw inferences that that husband had assets which, on an assessment of the evidence, I am satisfied he had not got.[61]

11.68   The terms of the inference drawn may, of course, operate as a penalty for a party who could have produced evidence that allowed findings more favourable than the inference.[62] But that effect is a matter of chance. It may be the effect of an inference, but it must not be the purpose, motivation or basis for the inference.

---

53  [1994] 2 FLR 463.
54  [2002] 1 FLR 1053.
55  (1820) 106 ER 873.
56  (1820) 106 ER 873 at 898.
57  [1995] 2 FLR 829.
58  [1995] 2 FLR 829 at 837.
59  *Prest v Petrodel Resources Ltd* [2013] 2 AC 415 at [45].
60  [1990] 2 FLR 233.
61  [1990] 2 FLR 233 at 242.
62  See Otton LJ in *Baker v Baker* [1995] 2 FLR 829 at 837.

# Analysing the evidence[63]

11.69 The relevant law determines the facts that are material and the standard of proof determines the degree of probability that has to be applied. The burden of proof determines who bears the consequences of the facts material to an issue not being proved to the required standard. Within that framework, the finding of facts is for the tribunal.[64]

11.70 In order to find the facts, the evidence always has to be assessed. It is the nature of evidence that it is always incomplete, commonly inconclusive, often ambiguous, with some favouring one party some another, and from sources of varying degrees of credibility and reliability.[65] Assessment involves analysing the factors that affect the probative worth of the evidence as a whole and evaluating the evidence as assessed by reference to the standard of proof.[66] The assessment must be the tribunal's own; it is not limited to choosing between the analyses put to it by the parties.[67] Coleridge J explained the position in *Re A (Removal Outside Jurisdiction: Habitual Residence)*:[68]

> In my judgment, a fact-finding judge is always entitled to consider version A put forward by one side and also version B put forward by the other and reach version C which represents a selection from or a mix or hybrid of the two competing versions. Such a course is always open to him providing the judge explains, by reference to the evidence, how and why he reaches a conclusion different from that contended for by either side.[69]

But as Ouseley J noted in *R (CJ) v Cardiff County Council*,[70] 'that may not always be appropriate where serious issues arise, as here, of credibility and false documentation concerning a large and crucial gap.'

11.71 The decisions of courts and tribunals given on appeals on points of law set the limits within which they will interfere with the fact-finding process. They set the limits within which the fact-finder must operate. Beyond this, they disclaim the responsibility of teaching the First-tier Tribunal how to

---

63 See Terence Anderson, David Schum and William Twining, *Analysis of Evidence*, 2nd edn, Cambridge, 2005, especially chapters 8 and 9; Richard Eggleston, *Evidence, Proof and Probability*, Butterworths, 1983; Lord Bingham, 'The Judge as Juror: The Judicial Determination of Factual Issues' (1985) 38 *Current Legal Problems* 1, reprinted in Lord Bingham, *The Business of Judging*, Oxford, 2000, p3; and Andrew Goodman, *How Judges Decide Cases: Reading, Writing and Analysing Judgments*, Universal, 2007, Parts 1 and 5.9. See also articles in *Tribunals* in appendix C.

64 This includes an appellate body if an appeal lies to the body on issues of fact or the body has jurisdiction over the facts once an error of law has been identified.

65 This analysis comes from Terence Anderson, David Schum and William Twining, *Analysis of Evidence*, 2nd edn, Cambridge, 2005, p246.

66 This is how assessing, analysing and evaluating are used here. They are not terms of art and may be used differently by judges and writers. For evaluating by reference to the standard of proof, see chapter 14.

67 *Woodhouse School v Webster* [2009] ICR 818.

68 [2011] 1 FLR 2025.

69 [2011] 1 FLR 2025 at [54].

70 [2011] 2 FLR 90 at [81].

assess evidence.[71] Nevertheless, on occasions they have offered general guidance or have commented on the judge's analysis of the evidence.[72]

11.72   The language of assessment and fact-finding is beset by metaphors. It is traditional to refer to balance and weight. This adds a spurious precision to the exercise, which involves judgment rather than precise calculation. In this chapter, this language is avoided in favour of references to the probative worth of evidence. As the standard of proof is concerned with certainty and confidence, the probative worth of evidence is determined by factors affecting the certainty and confidence with which findings may be made from it.

## Some general principles

### Common sense

11.73   In *Lord Advocate v Lord Blantyre*,[73] Lord Blackburn said that the probative worth of evidence was determined by 'the rules of common sense'.[74] That recognises that there is no specifically legal process of reasoning that differs from that used outside the law. However, as applied to tribunals it has three deficiencies.[75] First, common sense has not always proved sound when subjected to scientific scrutiny.[76] Second, even if it is valid, a common sense approach may not be sufficiently rigorous for legal purposes. Third, it does not acknowledge the possibility that the tribunal may have, and be allowed to use, special knowledge, experience or expertise that is not commonly available.

11.74   Nevertheless, the courts continue to insist that issues of causation must be determined by reference to common sense.[77]

### Rationality

11.75   In *R v Deputy Industrial Injuries Commissioner ex p Moore*,[78] Lord Diplock described the decision-making process in terms of logic rather than common sense:

> The requirement that a person exercising quasi-judicial functions must base his decision on evidence means no more than that it must be based on material which tends logically to show the existence or non-existence

---

71  Rix LJ in *Fryer-Kelsey v Secretary of State for Work and Pensions* reported as *R(IB) 6/05* at [25].

72  As in *Re W-P (Fact-finding Hearing)* [2009] 2 FLR 200 at [13].

73  (1879) 4 App Cas 770.

74  (1879) 4 App Cas 770 at 792. See also: Lord Diplock in *Walters v R* [1969] 2 AC 26 at 30; *O'Brien v Chief Constable of South Wales Police* [2005] 2 AC 534, discussed below.

75  It has a fourth deficiency as applied to courts. The rules of evidence may exclude material that would be relevant on a common sense view. See Lord Diplock in *R v Deputy Industrial Injuries Commissioner ex p Moore* [1965] 1 QB 456 at 488. This possibility remains, although the rules on admissibility have to a considerable extent been changed into factors relevant to the probative worth of the evidence.

76  For example: many people believe that it is common sense not to trust someone who looks away when speaking, but this has been proved unreliable as an indicator of honesty.

77  Lord Reid in *Stapley v Gypsum Mines Ltd* [1953] AC 663 at 681.

78  [1965] 1 QB 456.

of facts relevant to the issue to be determined, or to show the likelihood or unlikelihood of the occurrence of some future event the occurrence of which would be relevant. It means that he must not spin a coin or consult an astrologer; but he may take into account any material which, as a matter of reason, has some probative value in the sense mentioned above.[79]

And in *Mahon v Air New Zealand*,[80] he said:

What is required . . . is that the decision to make the finding must be based on *some* material that tends logically to show the existence of facts consistent with the finding and that the reasoning supportive of the finding . . . is not logically self-contradictory.[81]

Perhaps 'rationally' would be a better word than 'logically', as it avoids the technical rigours of modern logic.[82] This apart, these passages go some way to redress the first of the deficiencies in Lord Blackburn's remark. Although they do not expressly address the second deficiency, they leave open the possibility that the reasoning may be guided by sense that is special to the decision-maker as well as by sense that is common.

11.76    A rational approach is merely an instance of the right to fairness in the proceedings, whether under the principles of natural justice at common law or under article 6.

### What does rationality involve?

11.77    A rational approach requires a scrutiny of the evidence.[83] The evidence must be assessed. It is not sufficient to act on instinct or gut-reaction. The assessment must be undertaken by reference to criteria. Those criteria must be identified, else they cannot be subjected to scrutiny, and they must be relevant to the probative worth of the evidence. There is no scope for a formulaic approach. The criteria must be applied consistently to all the evidence. Different sorts of evidence may require different criteria, but there is no scope for applying the same criteria differentially.

11.78    It is the assessment of the evidence that must be rational. The criteria used must be rational. This does not mean that the evidence must be assessed on the basis that those concerned have acted rationally.[84]

11.79    A rational assessment of evidence takes account only of criteria that are relevant by generally accepted standards. As Lord Bingham explained in *O'Brien v Chief Constable of South Wales Police*:[85]

. . . it is on the whole undesirable that the process of judicial decision-making on issues of fact should diverge more than it need from the process followed by rational, objective and fair-minded people called upon to

79  [1965] 1 QB 456 at 94.
80  *Mahon v Air New Zealand* [1984] AC 808.
81  [1984] AC 808 at 821. See also Lord Simon in *DPP v Kilbourne* [1973] AC 729 at 756.
82  Having said this, logical fallacies are useful as identifying issues on which further questioning is appropriate.
83  Lord Hope in *R v Mirza* [2004] AC 1118 at [123].
84  There is a danger that decision-makers may interpret facts so as to make them understandable to themselves rather than as they were understood by the actors involved: Peter Halligan, 'Beliefs: shaping experience and understanding illness', in Halligan and Aylward, *The Power of Belief*, Oxford, 2006, pxv.
85  [2005] 2 AC 534 at 4. See also: *R v Chancler* [1976] 1 WLR 585 at 590; *R v Kearley* [1992] 2 AC 228 at 236.

decide questions of fact in other contexts where reaching the right decision matters.

11.80   Some potentially relevant criteria are considered below. They do not provide a formula for determining the probative worth of the evidence. They are merely factors to be taken into account in doing so.

## The significance of the burden and standard of proof

11.81   The factors must be applied sensibly and realistically to the evidence with appropriate regard to the incidence of the legal burden of proof. In *Rhesa Shipping Co SA v Edmunds*,[86] the House of Lords was concerned with an insurance claim following the loss of a ship at sea. The trial judge had accepted the owners' explanation for the loss, although he considered that it was extremely improbable. The House of Lords allowed the appeal and decided that the owners had not proved that the loss was covered by the insurance. Lord Brandon explained:

> . . . the legal concept of proof of a case on a balance of probabilities must be applied with common sense. It requires a judge of first instance, before he finds that a particular event occurred, to be satisfied on the evidence that it is more likely to have occurred than not. If such a judge concludes, on a whole series of cogent grounds, that the occurrence of an event is extremely improbable, a finding by him that it is nevertheless more likely to have occurred than not, does not accord with common sense.[87]

## The evidence as a whole

11.82   The evidence may be considered piece by piece. But it must be assessed as a whole.[88] This applies to the evidence of a witness as a whole[89] and to the evidence in the proceedings as a whole. The process was explained by Sedley LJ in *Karanakaran v Secretary of State for the Home Department*:[90]

> . . . a civil judge will not make a discrete assessment of the probable veracity of each item of the evidence: he or she will reach a conclusion on the probable factuality of an alleged event by evaluating *all* the evidence about it *for what it is worth*. Some will be so unreliable as to be worthless; some will amount to no more than straws in the wind; some will be indicative but not, by itself, probative; some may be compelling but contra-indicated by other evidence. It is only at the end point that, for want of a better yardstick, a probabilistic test is applied.[91]

11.83   *Re T (Abuse: Standard of Proof)*[92] illustrates the danger of not following this approach. The issue for the judge had been whether a child was being sexually abused. He analysed the medical evidence on its own and rejected it on the ground that it did not show abuse. In doing so, he did not take into account other evidence relevant to abuse. He then considered this

86  [1985] 1 WLR 948.
87  [1985] 1 WLR 948 at 956.
88  *Re W-P (Fact-finding Hearing)* [2009] 2 FLR 200 at [12].
89  *EPI Environmental Technologies Inc v Symphony Plastic Technologies plc* [2005] 1 WLR 3456 at [74].
90  [2000] 3 All ER 449 at 477.
91  [2000] 3 All ER 449 at 477.
92  [2004] 2 FLR 838.

other evidence and rejected it on the ground that it did not show abuse either. The Court of Appeal held that this was wrong in law. Butler-Sloss P explained why:

> It seems to me that the judge, having rejected the medical evidence in isolation from the non-medical evidence, found himself in the difficulty that evidence cannot be evaluated and assessed in different compartments. A judge in these difficult cases has to have regard to the relevance of each piece of evidence to other evidence and to exercise an overview of the totality of the evidence in order to come to the conclusion whether the case put forward by the local authority has been made out to the appropriate standard of proof.[93]

In other words, the judge should have assessed the evidence as a whole. Each part of the evidence may have supported or remedied the limitations of, or deficiencies in, the other evidence.

11.84　　It is wrong for a judge to form a provisional view of some of the evidence and make preliminary findings of fact based on that evidence before considering the effect of the expert evidence. In *Hall v Jakto Transport Ltd*,[94] the judge had taken this approach to the non-expert evidence. The Court of Appeal held that the judge should have considered the expert evidence at the same time, as it might have been relevant to the credibility of the other evidence. *Mibanga v Secretary of State for the Home Department*[95] is another example of a 'flawed fact-finding exercise' which led the tribunal 'to reach a conclusion by reference only to the appellant's evidence and then, if it be negative, to ask whether the conclusion should be shifted by the expert evidence'.[96]

### Coherence

11.85　　One approach to an overall assessment of the evidence is to seek the most coherent account that the evidence supports.[97] However, depending on the nature of the issue, this can be misleading. People may act or take decisions on incomplete information and on limited considerations. They may act impulsively without regard to all the possible consequences. Their conduct, viewed as a whole, may be inconsistent, irrational and contradictory. If these considerations may apply, it is safer not to seek coherence but to use it as a check on provisional conclusions on the facts.

## Assessing the probative worth of evidence

11.86　　The assessment of evidence is not generally governed by legislation. Section 8 of the Asylum and Immigration (Treatment of Claimants, etc) Act 2004 is an exception.[98]

---

93　[2004] 2 FLR 838 at [33]. See also [15] for counsel's successful argument.

94　(2005) *Times* 30 November.

95　[2005] INLR 377.

96　[2005] INLR 377: Wilson J at [23] and [24].

97　Neil MacCormick, *Legal Reasoning and Legal Theory*, Oxford, 1978, pp90–93.

98　Discussed in *JT (Cameroon) v Secretary of State for the Home Department* [2009] 1 WLR 1411.

11.87     A tribunal is entitled to reject any evidence, regardless of whether it is contested, consistent or agreed.[99] But it must always have a reason for disbelieving it.[100] If the evidence conflicts, the tribunal must decide which it prefers. If evidence is not challenged and there is no fact or circumstance to displace it or to cast doubt on it, the tribunal must accept it.[101]

11.88     The first task in considering evidence is to decide whether it is relevant to a fact in dispute. If it is not, it cannot be taken into account. If it is relevant, the tribunal must assess its probative worth. This is done by assessing its credibility, its reliability and its significance. In this chapter, credibility refers to the honesty and integrity of the witness and reliability refers to the evidence given.[102] In practice, it is not possible to keep these two concepts totally distinct. But they are useful in suggesting a structured, although not rigid, approach to assessing the probative worth of evidence.

## Credibility[103]

11.89  Credibility refers to the witness rather than to the evidence. Specifically, it refers to the honesty and integrity of the witness. To what extent is the witness trying to tell the truth? It is a matter of degree, because a witness may lack credibility on some but not all parts of the evidence.

11.90     The credibility of a witness may be assessed by reference to: (i) the way that the witness gave evidence; (ii) the character and health of the witness; (iii) the reliability of the evidence given by the witness.

### The way the witness gave evidence

11.91  The courts have recognised the benefit of seeing and hearing a witness giving evidence.[104] This is in the context of limiting the extent to which an appellate court will interfere, even in an appeal on the facts, with a conclusion reached by a judge who took the oral evidence. The significance of these factors reflects the fact that a bare transcript of the evidence and the judge's judgment setting out the findings of fact cannot convey every nuance of the evidence as given in court.

11.92     The demeanour of the witness is sometimes considered relevant when assessing honesty.[105] This reflects the common belief that some features of demeanour indicate dishonesty. But all these features may all be accounted for in other ways.[106] Avoidance of eye contact may be cultural. Hesitation may allow an answer to be framed accurately. Reluctance to answer may be a result of embarrassment at the personal nature of the evidence.

99  *R v City of Westminster Assessment Committee ex p Grosvenor House (Park Lane) Ltd* [1941] 1 KB 53 at 61 and 70–71.
100  Collins J in *R v Social Security Commissioner ex p Bibi* unreported 23 May 2000.
101  *R v Matheson* [1958] 1 WLR 474 at 479.
102  The expressions are not terms of art and they may be used differently.
103  See Lord Pearce in *Onassis v Vergottis* [1968] 2 Lloyd's Rep 403 at 431.
104  *Powell and Wife v Streatham Manor Nursing Home* [1935] AC 243.
105  *Powell v Streatham Manor Nursing Home* [1935] AC 243.
106  Serjeant Sullivan explained the difficulties he encountered in giving honest evidence in *The Last Serjeant*, MacDonald, 1952, pp41–42.

11.93    The academic psychology literature classifies the phenomena that may indicate dishonesty into three categories.[107] They are: (i) physiological signs; (ii) the language used; and (iii) behaviour.

11.94    The physiological signs are the witness's rate of breathing, sweating, heart rate and brain activity. As they can only be measured by instruments, there is no scope of the use of these signs in a tribunal room. In any event, the signs indicate stress, not the cause of the stress, which may be unconnected with the honesty and integrity of the witness.

11.95    The language used involves an analysis of the way that evidence is expressed. It largely ignores the substance of what is said. The difficulty with this is that it requires material to compare how the witness normally speaks with the evidence given to the tribunal.

11.96    The person's behaviour refers to visual and oral signs that reflect the emotions of the witness. Research has shown how complex it can be to use emotions to distinguish between honesty and dishonesty. A leading researcher has provided a list of 38 factors that have to be taken into account in assessing the honesty of what someone says.[108] His whole book presents a sustained argument that correctly interpreting the signs that may indicate dishonesty is complex and that those signs have to be considered in combination and in their context.

11.97    The practical difficulties involved in a hearing room make the task even more complex. A witness will not have the tribunal's undiverted attention, as the judge will have to read documents or take a note of evidence. The layout of the room and background noise may hamper visual and aural observation. The matter is further complicated by the fact that the unfamiliar circumstances of a hearing may themselves lead an honest witness to exhibit signs that could in other circumstances be indicative of dishonesty.

11.98    Worryingly, research shows that people misunderstand the significance of cues to dishonesty and overrate their ability to detect them.[109]

11.99    Whatever the relevance of these supposed clues to honesty,[110] and whether they are derived from common experience or academic research, they have a limited relevance, because honesty is only one aspect of a tribunal's assessment of the evidence. At best, they help to identify a witness who is convinced that the evidence is truthful. This will sometimes be relevant, but it is more likely that the tribunal will be concerned with the reliability of the evidence rather than the honesty or integrity of the witness.

11.100    In practice, it is rare for a conflict of evidence to be resolved solely or primarily by reference to the demeanour of the witness.[111] It is safer in all cases to concentrate on assessing the evidence that is given rather than the

---

107  Aldert Vrij, *Detecting Lies and Deceit*, Wiley, 2000.

108  Paul Ekman, *Telling Lies*, Norton, 2001, Appendix Table 4.

109  Aldert Vrij, *Detecting Lies and Deceit*, Wiley, 2000, chapter 3.

110  The Law Commission was not convinced that a witness's demeanour was particularly significant as a factor in assessing the evidence. See the Commission's 1997 Report No 245 on *Hearsay in Criminal Proceedings: Hearsay and Related Topics* (Cm 3670).

111  *R (G) v Governors of X School* [2011] 4 All ER 625 at [80].

honesty of the witness who gave it. As Atkin LJ said in *Société d'Avances Commerciales v Merchants' Marine Insurance Co*:[112]

> ... the existence of a lynx-eyed Judge who is capable at a glance of ascertaining whether a witness is telling the truth or not is more common in fiction than in fact on the Bench, and, for my part, I think that an ounce of intrinsic merit or demerit in the evidence, that is to say, the value of the comparison of evidence with known facts, is worth pounds of demeanour.[113]

11.101   A former Chief Justice of the High Court of Australia made the same point, saying:

> I am sure that where inferences can be drawn from established facts, one is on much stronger ground in reaching the truth than by reliance on the demeanour of the witnesses.[114]

11.102   The manner in which evidence is given can, though, be a useful indication of how certain the witness is. There are non-controversial features that qualify what is being said. They are part of everyday experience, covering the tone of voice and the accompanying gestures and facial expressions. For example: a firm tone of voice may convey certainty, but an accompanying shrug of the shoulders or facial expression may indicate that the witness is less than certain about the accuracy of a piece of evidence. But these signs must be treated with caution. Depending on the circumstances, a witness may have an interest in creating an impression of either certainty or uncertainty.

### The character and health of the witness

11.103   In most tribunals, there is unlikely to be evidence directly on the character of the witness or party. It is more likely to emerge from an analysis of the reliability of the evidence. One relevant consideration is the extent to which the witness appears to be objective, dispassionate and disinterested.

11.104     In those tribunals that deal with disability issues, the mental health of a party may be relevant to that person's credibility.

### The reliability of the evidence given by the witness

11.105   If one piece of evidence is found to be unreliable, that may affect the credibility of the witness. However, it is important to assess this carefully. For example: the tribunal may decide that a witness is an unreliable judge of time or distance. But that does not mean that the witness is dishonest or unable to recall specific events in detail. Even if the tribunal decides that the witness is dishonest on one matter, that need not indicate general dishonesty. It may be no more than an attempt to support evidence that is otherwise honest. The Privy Council commented on the relevance of lies in the context of criminal law in *Broadhurst v The Queen*.[115] Lord Devlin said:

---

112  (1924) 20 Ll L Rep 140.
113  (1924) 20 Ll L Rep 140 at 152.
114  Sir Harry Gibbs, 'Judgment Writing' (1993) 67 ALJ 494 at 497.
115  [1964] AC 441.

There is a natural tendency for a jury to think that if an accused is lying, it must be because he is guilty, and accordingly to convict him without more ado. It is the duty of the judge to make it clear to them that this is not so. Save in one respect, a case in which an accused gives untruthful evidence is no different from one in which he gives no evidence at all. In either case the burden remains on the prosecution to prove the guilt of the accused. But if upon the proved facts two inferences may be drawn about the accused's conduct or state of mind, his untruthfulness is a factor which the jury can properly take into account as strengthening the inference of guilt. What strength it adds depends, of course, on all the circumstances and especially on whether there are reasons other than guilt that might account for untruthfulness.[116]

And in *EPI Environmental Technologies Inc v Symphony Plastic Technologies plc*,[117] Peter Smith J cautioned against assuming general dishonesty from what might have been a stupid lie told by a witness in order to bolster a good case.

11.106 The same approach applies to other misconduct in relation to the proceedings. As Mostyn J said in *AA v NA (Appeal: Fact-finding)*: 'It does not follow at all that litigation misconduct inevitably demonstrates intrinsic mendacity on the primary issues for adjudication.'[118]

11.107 The issue for the tribunal is whether a lie or other misconduct is indicative of general dishonesty. If (and only if) it is, the lie is relevant to the assessment of the witness's evidence generally. The same holds for any other inaccuracy in evidence. It is only relevant to the assessment of the witness's evidence as a whole if the circumstances are such that the inaccuracy infects other evidence as well.

11.108 Witnesses may also be willing to lie discriminately,[119] for example according to the importance of the point. Sir Richard Eggleston's opinion was:

> ... whether a witness will lie about a particular matter depends on his attitude to that matter – on the one hand, his motive for lying, and on the other, the relevance of the matter to the issues in the case.[120]

In other words, a witness may be prepared to lie about matters regarded as peripheral to the case but not about matters that are perceived to be important.[121] The witness's likely motivation is a key factor in assessing the significance of a lie.

## Reliability[122]

11.109 Credibility is not the same as reliability. As Sedley LJ said in *Anya v University of Oxford*:[123]

---

116 At 457.
117 [2005] 1 WLR 3456 at [74].
118 [2010] 2 FLR 1173 at [46].
119 Charles J in *A County Council v K, D and L* [2005] 1 FLR 851 at [28].
120 *Evidence, Proof and Probability*, 2nd edn, Butterworths, 1983, p196.
121 Serjeant Sullivan in *The Last Serjeant*, MacDonald, 1952, p98.
122 See paras 11.70ff above.
123 [2001] ICR 847 at [25].

> Credibility . . . is not necessarily the end of the road: a witness may be credible, honest and mistaken, and never more so than when his evidence concerns things of which he himself may not be conscious.

11.110 Judges have given guidance on some of the factors that should be used to assess the reliability of oral evidence. In *Armagas Ltd v Mundogas SA*,[124] Goff LJ said:

> I have found it essential in cases of fraud, when considering the credibility of witnesses, always to test their veracity by reference to the objective facts proved independently of their testimony, in particular by reference to the documents in the case, and also to pay particular regard to their motives and to the overall probabilities.[125]

11.111 In *Heffer v Tiffin Green (a firm)*,[126] Henry LJ applied this reasoning to an allegation that an accountant had submitted false accounts. He criticised the trial judge's acceptance of the evidence of a witness:

> But it was crucial to test his evidence against the objective facts, the contemporaneous documents, the motives of those involved or the lack of them and the overall probabilities.

These factors are always relevant, regardless of the nature or seriousness of the issue.

11.112 And in *Secretary of State for Work and Pensions v Roach*,[127] Leveson LJ explained:

> . . . it is trite to say that the credibility of a witness depends upon an assessment by the fact finder of a number of features. Without being exhaustive these include what is said, the way it is said, its internal consistency and the extent to which it corresponds with known facts or human experience; all this must be considered in the context of the perceptions of the witness.

11.113 In *Re F (A Minor) (Child Abduction)*,[128] Butler-Sloss LJ gave advice on assessing conflicting affidavit evidence and the use of the burden of proof:

> If the issue has to be faced on disputed non-oral evidence, the judge has to look to see if there is independent extraneous evidence in support of one side. That evidence has, in my judgment, to be compelling before the judge is entitled to reject the sworn evidence of a deponent. Alternatively, the evidence contained within the affidavit may in itself be inherently improbable and therefore so unreliable that the judge is entitled to reject it. If, however, there are no grounds for rejecting the written evidence on either side, the applicant will have failed to establish his case.[129]

This advice and in particular the need for compelling extraneous evidence, may reflect the nature of the proceedings, child abduction, in which oral evidence is discouraged.

11.114 There is no limit to the factors that are relevant to the reliability of evidence. The following is a useful checklist of factors that are likely to be

---

124 [1985] 1 Ll L Rep 1.
125 [1985] 1 Ll L Rep 1 at 57.
126 (1998) *Times* 28 December at [3.2].
127 Reported as R(CS) 4/07, at [31].
128 [1992] 1 FLR 548.
129 [1992] 1 FLR 548 at 553–554.

relevant. They also provide a partial framework for testing through questioning the reliability of the evidence presented.[130]

## Factors relating to the witness

- To the extent that it is relevant, is the witness credible?
- Is there a reason why the witness might have formed a false perception of the evidence?
- How accurate and reliable is the witness's memory? Are there any factors, such as illness, the passage of time or intervening events, that might affect this?
- Does the witness have a reason, conscious or not, to misrepresent or conceal the truth?
- How good a communicator is the witness?

## Factors relating to the witness's evidence

- Was the evidence given on oath[131] or in a sworn statement?[132]
- Is the evidence within the personal knowledge of the witness? Evidence that is not given of personal knowledge is hearsay. It is admissible,[133] but it is relevant to know how the witness learnt of it.
- How contemporaneous is the evidence to the time of the events in question? Time can affect the accuracy of recollection.
- Is the evidence to be taken literally? It may be clear that an expression has been used colloquially rather than literally. For example: 'It was miles' or 'It took me hours'. But even if the language is intended to be accurate, it may not be reliable. For example: time and distance are notoriously difficult to judge. And if it cannot be taken literally, it may not be inconsistent with, or contradictory of, other evidence.
- How clear, precise and detailed is the evidence? Clear, precise and detailed evidence is likely to be more useful to the tribunal than vague generalities. But, depending on the circumstances, too great a recall may not be plausible. And lack of clarity may also reflect the witness's capacity for self-expression.
- Is the evidence of the witness internally consistent?
- How plausible is the evidence? There is a danger in placing too much emphasis on this factor if the events took place in a context that is outside the tribunal's experience. This has been noted in asylum cases,[134] but may also be true for domestic cases involving, for example, ethnic minority cultures.
- Was the evidence obtained by leading questions? This evidence is admissible, but it is possible that the question suggested the answer

---

130 For further elements of a framework for testing evidence see paras 11.69 onwards.
131 Viscount Simon LC in *General Medical Council v Spackman* [1943] AC 627 at 636–637.
132 Butler-Sloss LJ in *Re F (A Minor) (Child Abduction)* [1992] 1 FLR 548 at 553.
133 The rationale for limiting the use of hearsay is that it is not appropriate evidence for a jury to assess. This rationale does not apply in tribunals, which do not involve juries: Parke B in *Wright v Doe* (1837) 112 ER 488 at 517.
134 Neuberger and Chadwick LJJ in *HK v Secretary of State for the Home Department* [2006] EWCA Civ 1037 at [29]–[30] and [70].

that was required. This may reduce the reliance that can be placed on it.[135] However, too much can be made of this. It is likely that a witness will have a good idea of what evidence is relevant and what will and will not be advantageous. A witness is likely to know the answer required, however the question is framed. And it is permissible for a tribunal member to put a question in a form that would be leading if asked by a representative, especially if this is done to put the member's provisional view of the evidence to a witness.[136]

- If the evidence is of belief or opinion, is it reasonable? The more unreasonable, the less likely it is to be found to be genuine.[137] But some people do genuinely hold bizarre opinions.

### Factors relating to other evidence and circumstances

- Other evidence must be assessed by the above criteria as well as being considered comparatively by the following criteria.
- Is the evidence of the witness consistent with or contradicted by other evidence?
- Is it corroborated? Evidence usually need not be corroborated as a matter of law, but corroboration can increase its probative worth.[138] Lack of corroboration can also be relevant to the probative worth of evidence. If it could be corroborated, has the party failed to produce that evidence (for example, by not calling a particular witness) without a plausible explanation.[139] In *TK (Burundi) v Secretary of State for the Home Department*,[140] Thomas LJ emphasised the importance of the evidence being available to the party:

  > The circumstances of this case in my view demonstrate that independent supporting evidence which is available from persons subject to this jurisdiction be provided wherever possible and the need for an Immigration Judge to adopt a cautious approach to the evidence of an appellant where independent supporting evidence, as it was in this case, is readily available within this jurisdiction, but not provided.

- Is the evidence contested? If it is not, the tribunal does not necessarily have to accept it;[141] it may not be plausible or it may conflict with specialist knowledge of the tribunal.
- If there is a factual dispute about the evidence, to what extent has it been tested by questioning.[142]
- To what extent was it within the power of the party to produce evidence on a particular matter?[143] This must be applied realistically in a tribunal,

---

135   *Moor v Moor* [1954] 1 WLR 927 may state the point too strongly for the way that many tribunals operate.
136   Thorpe and Buxton LJJ in *Currey v Currey* [2005] 1 FLR 952 at 20 and 33.
137   Lord Bingham in *R v K* [2002] 1 AC 462 at 23(2), citing Lord Lane CJ in *R v Williams* [1987] 3 All ER 411 at 415.
138   Lord Simon in *Director of Public Prosecutions v Kilbourne* [1973] AC 729 at 758.
139   *Fairchild v Glenhaven Funeral Services Ltd* [2002] ICR 798 at 13.
140   [2009] EWCA Civ 40 at 21.
141   *R(IS)* 14/93 at 7.
142   *Kataria v Essex Strategic Health Authority* [2004] 3 All ER 572 at 63.
143   Lord Bingham in *Fairchild v Glenhaven Funeral Services* [2002] ICR 798 at [13].

as the party may not be aware of how best to present a case or able to afford the costs involved in obtaining the evidence.

### Factors relating to the nature and effect of memory

11.115   The report of the British Psychological Society Research Board on *Guidelines on Memory and the Law* (2008) summarised its key points as follows:

i.   Memories are records of people's experiences of events and are not a record of the events themselves. In this respect, they are unlike other recording media such as videos or audio recordings, to which they should not be compared.

ii.   Memory is not only of experienced events but it is also of the knowledge of a person's life, i.e. schools, occupations, holidays, friends, homes, achievements, failures, etc. As a general rule memory is more likely to be accurate when it is of the knowledge of a person's life than when it is of specific experienced events.

iii.   Remembering is a constructive process. Memories are mental constructions that bring together different types of knowledge in an act of remembering. As a consequence, memory is prone to error and is easily influenced by the recall environment, including police interviews and cross-examination in court.

iv.   Memories for experienced events are always incomplete. Memories are time compressed fragmentary records of experience. Any account of a memory will feature forgotten details and gaps, and this must not be taken as any sort of indicator of accuracy. Accounts of memories that do not feature forgetting and gaps are highly unusual.

v.   Memories typically contain only a few highly specific details. Detailed recollection of the specific time and date of experiences is normally poor, as is highly specific information such as the precise recall of spoken conversations. As a general rule, a high degree of very specific detail in a long-term memory is unusual.

vi.   Recall of a single or several highly specific details does not guarantee that a memory is accurate or even that it actually occurred. In general, the only way to establish the truth of a memory is with independent corroborating evidence.

vii.   The content of memories arises from an individual's comprehension of an experience, both conscious and non-conscious. This content can be further modified and changed by subsequent recall.

viii.   People can remember events that they have not in reality experienced. This does not necessarily entail deliberate deception. For example, an event that was imagined, was a blend of a number of different events, or that makes personal sense for some other reason, can come to be genuinely experienced as a memory, (these are often referred to as 'confabulations').

ix.   Memories for traumatic experiences, childhood events, interview and identification practices, memory in younger children and older adults and other vulnerable groups all have special features. These are features that are unlikely to be commonly known by a non-expert, but about which an appropriate memory expert will be able to advise a court.

x.   A memory expert is a person who is recognised by the memory research community to be a memory researcher. It is recommended that, in addition to current requirements, those acting as memory expert witnesses be required to submit their full curriculum vitae to the court as evidence of their expertise.

## Significance

11.116 The significance of a piece of evidence can only be determined in relation
to a specific issue and in the context of the evidence as a whole.

11.117    As to the issue, the closer and more directly related to the issue for
decision, the greater the significance of the evidence. For example: evidence that a claimant has been seen sawing wood on a building site is
more significant to the issue whether he has been working than evidence
that he has been seen walking towards the site carrying a bag of tools.
The same evidence may be more significant to one issue than to another.
For example: evidence that a claimant was seen walking along a street in
the direction of a building site is not particularly significant to the issue
whether he was working at the site, but it may be highly significant to the
issue of his ability to walk a particular distance.

11.118    As to the context, the other evidence can affect the significance of a
particular piece of evidence. For example: evidence of a claimant walking
along a street near a building site becomes more significant if he is seen
regularly and at times when work is starting and finishing.

## Familiarity

11.119 It is essential to guard against the risk of familiarity. Psychological research
has shown that people judge those possibilities with which they are familiar to be more likely than those with which they are not.[144]

## Expert evidence[145]

11.120 It can be difficult for a tribunal that is not expert in an area to know how to
analyse or question expert evidence. The tribunal should assess the expert,
the area of expertise and the evidence.[146]

11.121    As regards the expert, the tribunal should consider the expert's qualifications and experience relevant to the issue before the tribunal.

11.122    As regards the area of expertise, the tribunal should consider the limits
within which the area of expertise can provide answers to issues relevant
to the case.

11.123    As regards the evidence, the tribunal should consider the factual basis
and the soundness of the expert's reasoned opinion.

11.124    So far as facts are concerned, the tribunal should identify the facts on
which the expert's opinion was based. It should then decide whether it
accepts those facts.

11.125    So far as the expert's reasoning is concerned, the tribunal should consider the extent to which it is transparent or opaque? Transparent reasoning sets out the expert's opinion together with the factual and other bases

---

144  Philip Johnson-Laird, *How We Reason*, Oxford, 2006, p198.

145  For an overall examination of the authorities on medical evidence, see Charles J in
*A County Council v K, D and L* [2005] 1 FLR 851 at [39]–[49].

146  For a slightly different analysis see Douglas Walton, *Fundamentals of Critical
Argumentation*, Cambridge, 2006, chapter 3, 'Argumentation Schemes'. The chapter
contains a valuable analysis of the structure of different forms of argument together
with schemes for challenging and evaluating them.

on which it is made. Opaque reasoning merely records the expert's opinion. Transparent and opaque reasoning are not distinct separate categories. They are extremes of a spectrum. The more transparent the reasoning the better, because it allows the tribunal to make its own assessment of the expert's reasoning.[147] It is also relevant to consider whether the expert's evidence is consistent with the views of the profession. The panel members may be aware of this from their background or it may be apparent from other evidence. However, if the area of expertise is outside that normally seen by the tribunal, it may not know whether the views expressed are representative of general opinion, a recognised minority view, or maverick.

11.126     A tribunal does not have to accept expert evidence.[148] The proper approach was set out by Evans LJ in *Dover District Council v Sherred and Tarling*:[149]

> ... issues of fact are for the judge to decide in accordance with the evidence given before him. Where expert evidence is admissible in order to enable the judge to reach a properly informed decision on a technical matter, then he cannot set his own 'lay' opinion against the expert evidence which he has heard. But he is not bound to accept the evidence even of an expert witness, if there is a proper basis for rejecting it in the evidence which he has heard, or the expert evidence is such that he does not believe it or for whatever reason is not convinced by it.[150]

11.127   The approach set out in *Dover* is illustrated by *Re B (Care: Expert Witness)*.[151] The Court of Appeal was concerned with medical evidence relevant to the care of a child. In such cases, the courts take a multi-disciplinary approach involving all disciplines relevant to the case. The judge had rejected the opinion of the only expert who gave evidence, preferring evidence from other witnesses. The Court of Appeal held that he was entitled to do this. Ward LJ explained the way in which expert medical evidence should be treated:

> The expert advises, but the judge decides. The judge decides on the evidence. If there is nothing before the court, no facts or no circumstances shown to the court which throw doubt on the expert evidence, then, if that is all with which the court is left, the court must accept it. There is, however, no rule that the judge suspends judicial belief simply because the evidence is given by an expert.[152]

Butler-Sloss LJ added the need to give reasons when differing from expert evidence:

> An expert is not in any special position and there is no presumption or belief in a doctor however distinguished he or she may be. It is, however, necessary for a judge to give reasons for disagreeing with experts' conclusions or recommendations. That, this judge did. A judge cannot substitute

147 This appears to be the distinction being drawn by Peter Smith J in *EPI Environmental Technologies Inc v Symphony Plastic Technologies plc* [2005] 1 WLR 3456 at [76].
148 *Hackney London Borough Council v Rottenberg* (2007) *Times* 9 February.
149 (1997) 29 HLR 864.
150 (1997) 29 HLR 864 at 867. See also *Armstrong v First York Ltd* [2005] 1 WLR 2751.
151 [1996] 1 FLR 667.
152 [1996] 1 FLR 667 at 670.

his views for the views of the experts without some evidence to support what it is he concludes.[153]

11.128    A tribunal should not develop its own theory against the evidence of the expert,[154] especially if the experts are agreed and have relied on a recognised source for their opinions.[155] However, if the tribunal contains a member with particular expertise, the member may use that expertise as a basis for assessing, and if need be differing from, the expert evidence.[156]

11.129    Megarry V-C said that an expert's opinion should always be provided in full and should be accompanied by the instructions to the expert.[157] However, they cannot be required if they are covered by privilege.[158]

11.130    Expert evidence should not be used to assist the tribunal in deciding on credibility.[159]

11.131    In *A Local Authority v A (No 2)*,[160] Ryder J approved of a practice of 'hot tubbing' whereby all expert witnesses were sworn and questioned together.

## A realistic approach to fact-finding

11.132    Tribunals should not, and do not, invent facts. However, their findings may be influenced by their perception of the justice or merits of the case. This perception operates through their approach to the evidence, including the application of the standard of proof. The members of the tribunal may not be conscious of its influence. It can lead a tribunal to give less significance to evidence or not pursue questions that might elicit unhelpful answers. A tribunal that considers that the merits favour one party may also be more easily persuaded that particular evidence is sufficient to prove a fact in favour of that party than if the evidence had been considered in a purely neutral way.

11.133    Quintilian understood the psychology at work in this:

> Proofs, it is true, may induce the judges to regard our case as superior to that of our opponent, but the appeal to the emotions will do more, for it will make them wish our case to be better. And what they wish, they will also believe.[161]

So did Pascal: 'All men whatsoever are almost always led into belief not because a thing is proved but because it is pleasing'.[162]

---

153 [1996] 1 FLR 667 at 674.
154 Charles J in *A County Council v K, D and L* [2005] 1 FLR 851 at [60].
155 *Re B (Fact-finding Hearing: Evidence)* [2009] 2 FLR 14 at [18].
156 *Dugdale v Kraft Foods Ltd* [1977] ICR 48 at 54–55.
157 *Gleeson v J Wippell & Co* [1977] 1 WLR 510 at 519.
158 *LM v London Borough of Lewisham* [2009] UKUT 204 (AAC).
159 Ward and Scott Baker LJJ in *Re S (Care: Parenting Skills: Personality Tests)* [2005] 2 FLR 658 at [57] and [71] respectively.
160 [2011] 2 FLR 162 at [22]–[23].
161 Quoted in Edward Corbett and Robert Connors, *Classical Rhetoric for the Modern Student*, 4th edn, Oxford, 1999, p290.
162 Quoted in Chaïm Perelman and Lucie Olbrechts-Tyteca, *The New Rhetoric: A Treatise on Argumentation*, Notre Dame, 2008, p61.

# CHAPTER 12

# Disposal

*continued*

# Forms of disposal

12.1 Proceedings before a tribunal may be concluded by an act of the party who initiated them, by the joint act of all the parties, by an act of the tribunal or by operation of law.

## Unilaterally

12.2 The party who initiated the proceedings may withdraw them. In some circumstances, this may require the consent of the other parties or of the tribunal.

## By agreement

12.3 The parties may compromise the proceedings by agreeing on the outcome. This may lead the party who initiated the proceedings to withdraw them. Or it may lead to the parties inviting the tribunal to make a decision by consent. That decision might be to dismiss the appeal.

## By the tribunal

12.4 The tribunal may conclude the proceedings by striking them out or by deciding them. Proceedings may be struck out on three grounds: (a) lack of jurisdiction; (b) failure to comply with procedural requirements; and (c) lack of merit. Proceedings are decided on the merits of the case.

## By operation of law

12.5 The proceedings may lapse if the subject matter ceases to exist.

12.6 The legislation may also use other concepts, such as abandonment used in immigration.[1]

# Lapse

12.7 Proceedings lapse when their subject matter ceases to exist. The only decision that the tribunal can give is that it no longer has jurisdiction.[2]

12.8 So, for example:

- an appeal may lapse if the decision against which the appeal is brought is changed;
- an application may lapse if it is brought to challenge a patient's detention in a mental hospital and the patient is discharged or made the subject of a community treatment order.[3]

---

1 *Shirazi v Secretary of State for the Home Department* [2004] 2 All ER 602.
2 In *Dorset Healthcare NHS Trust v MH* [2009] UKUT 4 (AAC), the Upper Tribunal gave as its decision: 'There be no decision on the appeal'.
3 As in *Dorset Healthcare NHS Trust v MH* [2009] UKUT 4 (AAC).

12.9   This is subject to provision to the contrary. Legislation may provide that the proceedings survive. For example: regulation 30 of the Social Security and Child Support (Decisions and Appeals) Regulations 1999 provides that an appeal against specified decisions shall not lapse if they are replaced or revised in a way that is not advantageous to the appellant. The appeal continues against the decision as replaced or revised. WPAFC Rules r22 makes equivalent provision for the war pension and armed forces compensation schemes.

12.10   Death will not necessarily cause the proceedings to lapse.[4] However, it will be necessary for someone with authority to represent the party in order for the proceedings to continue. This may be a personal representative or someone appointed under specific legislation, such as regulation 34 of the Social Security and Child Support (Decisions and Appeals) Regulations 1999.

12.11   However, proceedings may lapse on death if they are entirely personal to the person who has died.

12.12   Lapsing only occurs if the subject matter of the proceedings ceases to exist. This must be distinguished from other processes. So, for example:

- proceedings do not lapse just because the issue has become of abstract interest to the parties;
- nor do they lapse just because the other party concedes an issue or even the whole case.

In those examples, the tribunal retains jurisdiction to decide the issue.

12.13   In principle, the referral of an application could lapse if the application is withdrawn. However, there is authority that it survives until the referral is withdrawn. This was the view of the Court of Appeal in *Milton v Secretary of State for Work and Pensions*.[5] The Court refused permission to appeal against the decision of a Commissioner on this ground.

## Striking out and barring

12.14   Striking out is both a case management power and a method of summary disposal of proceedings. These two functions are linked by the need to ensure that proceedings are used for their proper purposes. It is not the function of a tribunal to spend time on cases that are destined to fail, whether for lack of jurisdiction or merit. Nor is it the function of a tribunal to spend unnecessary time on cases when a party is not properly pursuing the proceedings.

12.15   The power to strike out is not sufficient to ensure the proper use of proceedings. This may depend on the co-operation of the respondent, especially if it is a public body. For respondents, the only effective equivalent is to bar that party from further participation in the proceedings.

12.16   Respondents may also raise issues in the course of proceedings. As there are no separate cross proceedings in tribunals, those issues are raised in the same proceedings. In those circumstances, barring the respondent

---

4   They may merely abate: see chapter 7.
5   *R(CS) 1/07.*

from further participation in the proceedings effectively operates as the equivalent to striking out.

12.17     The same provisions and principles apply to both striking out and barring. For convenience, hereafter in this section only striking out is mentioned.

12.18     As there is no decision in proceedings that are struck out, the case has not been dismissed.

12.19     If striking out or barring is not a proportionate response, the tribunal may exercise its lesser power to restrict a party's participation in the proceedings.[6] In contrast to striking out and barring, this does not require notice to the party or an opportunity to make observations.

## Rationale

12.20     The justification for striking out is that the proceedings are abusing the tribunal's process.

12.21     In *Hunter v Chief Constable of the West Midlands Police*,[7] Lord Diplock explained the rationale for striking out as being:

> . . . to prevent misuse of its procedure in a way which, although not inconsistent with the literal application of its rules of procedure, would nevertheless be manifestly unfair to a party to litigation before it, or would otherwise bring the administration of justice into disrepute among right-thinking people.[8]

12.22     This explanation is now out-of-date for not covering the impact that a case may have on the operation of the system as a whole, and thereby on other users. Lord Woolf MR set the power in this context in *Swain v Hillman*:[9]

> It saves expense; it achieves expedition; it avoids the court's resources being used up on cases where this serves no purpose; and I would add, generally, that it is in the interests of justice. If a claimant has a case which is bound to fail, then it is in the claimant's interests to know as soon as possible that that is the position.[10]

## Under TCEA

12.23     The power to strike out must be conferred by the rules of procedure. Tribunals, unlike the courts,[11] have no inherent power to strike out.[12] However, a tribunal could achieve the same effect by adjourning a case indefinitely.[13] This is unnecessary under TCEA.

---

6  Under UTR r7(2)(d) and its equivalents.

7  [1982] AC 529.

8  [1982] AC 529 at 536.

9  [2001] 1 All ER 91.

10  [2001] 1 All ER 91 at 94.

11  *Hunter v Chief Constable of the West Midlands Police* [1982] AC 529 at 536.

12  *Kelly v Ingersoll-Rand Co Ltd* [1982] ICR 476 at 480. See also: *R (Harpers Leisure International Ltd ) v Guildford Borough Council* (2009) *Times* 14 August, in which Charles J decided that a tribunal had no inherent power to stay proceedings for an abuse of process; *Foulser v Commissioners for Her Majesty's Revenue and Customs* [2011] UKFTT 642 (TC), in which the First-tier Tribunal decided that it had no inherent jurisdiction to strike out in order to prevent abuse.

13  *O'Keefe v Southampton City Council* [1988] ICR 419 at 422.

12.24    There is no express power authorising rules of procedure in respect of striking out under TCEA. It is either embraced by 'practice and procedure' within section 22(1) or is an ancillary power under paragraph 16 of Schedule 5. UTR r8 is illustrative under TCEA:[14]

(1A) Except for paragraph (2), this rule does not apply to an asylum case or an immigration case.

(1) The proceedings, or the appropriate part of them, will automatically be struck out-
  (a) if the appellant or applicant has failed to comply with a direction that stated that failure by the appellant or applicant to comply with the direction would lead to the striking out of the proceedings or that part of them; or
  (b) in immigration judicial review proceedings, when a fee has not been paid, as required, in respect of an application under rule 30(4) or upon the grant of permission.

(2) The Upper Tribunal must strike out the whole or a part of the proceedings if the Upper Tribunal–
  (a) does not have jurisdiction in relation to the proceedings or that part of them; and
  (b) does not exercise its power under rule 5(3)(k)(i) (transfer to another court or tribunal) in relation to the proceedings or that part of them.

(3) The Upper Tribunal may strike out the whole or a part of the proceedings if–
  (a) the appellant or applicant has failed to comply with a direction which stated that failure by the appellant or applicant to comply with the direction could lead to the striking out of the proceedings or part of them;
  (b) the appellant or applicant has failed to co-operate with the Upper Tribunal to such an extent that the Upper Tribunal cannot deal with the proceedings fairly and justly; or
  (c) in proceedings which are not an appeal from the decision of another tribunal or judicial review proceedings, the Upper Tribunal considers there is no reasonable prospect of the appellant's or the applicant's case, or part of it, succeeding.

(4) The Upper Tribunal may not strike out the whole or a part of the proceedings under paragraph (2) or (3)(b) or (c) without first giving the appellant or applicant an opportunity to make representations in relation to the proposed striking out.

(5) If the proceedings have been struck out under paragraph (1) or (3)(a), the appellant or applicant may apply for the proceedings, or part of them, to be reinstated.

(6) An application under paragraph (5) must be made in writing and received by the Upper Tribunal within 1 month after the date on which the Upper Tribunal sent notification of the striking out to the appellant or applicant.

(7) This rule applies to a respondent or an interested party as it applies to an appellant or applicant except that–
  (a) a reference to the striking out of the proceedings is to be read as a reference to the barring of the respondent or interested party from taking further part in the proceedings; and

14  See also: GRC Rules r8; HESC Rules r8; Lands Rules r8; PC Rules r9; SEC Rules r8; Tax Rules r8; WPAFC Rules r8. The power under IAC Rules r7 is limited to non-payment of fees. The CPR equivalent is CPR 3.4.

(b) a reference to an application for the reinstatement of proceedings which have been struck out is to be read as a reference to an application for the lifting of the bar on the respondent or interested party from taking further part in the proceedings.

(8) If a respondent or interested party has been barred from taking further part in proceedings under this rule and that bar has not been lifted, the Upper Tribunal need not consider any response or other submission made by that respondent or interested party.

## General principles

12.25 In *Hunter v Chief Constable of the West Midlands Police*,[15] Lord Diplock implied that there was a duty to strike out proceedings that were an abuse of process. This is now out-of-date. In the context of article 6, the decision to strike out proceedings must be a proportionate response to the conduct that has prompted it. This emphasises the judgment that is involved, which the courts usually refer to as a discretion.

12.26 Striking out should be used as a last resort. As Lord Woolf MR explained in *Biguzzi v Rank Leisure plc*:[16]

> There are alternative powers which the courts have which they can exercise to make it clear that the courts will not tolerate delays other than striking out cases. In a great many situations those other powers will be the appropriate ones to adopt because they produce a more just result. In considering whether a result is just, the courts are not confined to considering the relative positions of the parties. They have to take into account the effect of what has happened on the administration of justice generally. That involves taking into account the effect of the court's ability to hear other cases if such defaults are allowed to occur. It will also involve taking into account the need for the courts to show by their conduct that they will not tolerate the parties not complying with dates for the reasons I have indicated.[17]

12.27 The courts have declined to set out a comprehensive list of categories of conduct that involve abuse of process. In *Ashmore v British Coal Corporation*,[18] Stuart-Smith LJ said:

> What may constitute such conduct must depend on all the circumstances of the case; the categories are not closed and considerations of public policy and the interests of justice may be very material.[19]

12.28 Striking out should only be used in the clearest cases of abuse. It is not an appropriate means of summary disposal for a difficult or important issue.[20] In *Dyson v Attorney-General*,[21] Fletcher Moulton LJ said:

> Differences of law, just as differences of fact, are normally to be decided by trial after hearing in court, and not to be refused a hearing in court by an order of the judge in chambers.[22]

15  [1982] AC 529 at 536.
16  [1999] 1 WLR 1926.
17  [1999] 1 WLR 1926 at 1933.
18  [1990] 2 QB 338.
19  [1990] 2 QB 338 at 348.
20  *Attorney-General of the Duchy of Lancaster v London and North Western Railway Co* [1892] 3 Ch 274.
21  [1911] 1 KB 410.
22  [1911] 1 KB 410 at 419.

It may be appropriate to strike out a party's case if it is exaggerated or is based in part on fraud. There will usually be other ways to handle the problem,[23] but the extent of the fraud or forgery may be so serious that it would affront the tribunal to allow the case to proceed.[24] There are also practical steps that can be taken to cope with parties who are persistent in correspondence that contains wild allegations that are expressed in an intemperate or aggressive tone.[25]

12.29    The decision whether or not to strike out involves a balancing of competing considerations; it must not be taken dogmatically. In *Johnson v Gore Wood & Co (a firm),*[26] Lord Bingham said that the decision involved:

> . . . a broad, merits-based judgment which takes account of the public and private interests involved and also takes account of all the facts of the case, focusing attention on the crucial question whether, in all the circumstances, a party is misusing or abusing the process of the court . . .[27]

If a party has forfeited the right to pursue a case, the other party's conduct is not relevant.[28]

12.30    Before CPR, the general rule in the courts was that striking out was only appropriate in the case of prejudice to another party, except where there was procedural abuse, questionable tactics or contumelious and intentional, or repeated and persistent, default.[29] This issue will now be subsumed by the balancing exercise required to apply the overriding objective.

12.31    Caution is required if the striking out will affect someone's ability to secure employment.[30] It will rarely be appropriate to strike out a case at the end of proceedings.[31] Once the hearing is complete, it will only be appropriate to use the strike out power in exceptional circumstances and, as a judgment is a possession under Article 1, Protocol 1 to the European Convention, it would have to be proportionate to do so.[32]

## Grounds for striking out and barring

12.32  Striking out is appropriate on three grounds: (i) lack of jurisdiction; (ii) likely outcome; and (iii) manner of conduct in the proceedings.

### Lack of jurisdiction

12.33  Striking out may be appropriate for cases over which the tribunal clearly has no jurisdiction. Proceedings are of no benefit to the party who presents

---

23  *Ul-Haq v Shah* [2010] 1 WLR 616 and *Fairclough Homes Ltd v Summers* [2012] 1 WLR 2004 at [50]–[51.

24  *Masood v Zahoor* [2010] 1 WLR 746 at [71].

25  *Dransfield v the Information Commissioner and Devon County Council* [2013] UKUT 0550 (AAC) at [16]–[19].

26  [2002] 2 AC 1.

27  [2002] 2 AC 1 at 31.

28  *Masood v Zahoor* [2010] 1 All ER 888 at [75].

29  *Costellow v Somerset County Council* [1993] 1 WLR 256 at 264.

30  *Welsh Ministers v Care Standards Tribunal* [2008] 1 WLR 2097.

31  *Masood v Zahoor* [2010] 1 All ER 888 at [72].

32  *Fairclough Homes Ltd v Summers* [2012] 1 WLR 2004 at [36] and [46]–[48].

such a case and detrimental to the other parties and to other users of the tribunal system. Similarly when the case can only, or more appropriately, be dealt with by another tribunal.

12.34    However, striking out is not appropriate if the tribunal's jurisdiction is a serious issue in the proceedings. Under UTR r8(2), the tribunal is under a duty to strike out a case over which it has no jurisdiction unless it transfers the case to another court or tribunal. This duty arises even if the lack of jurisdiction only becomes apparent after detailed analysis at an oral hearing. It therefore operates to prevent the tribunal deciding the issue of jurisdiction and allowing that issue to be tested on appeal. This may effectively deprive the party to that case of a right of appeal and others of the right of access to the tribunal in the future. As such, it may be outside the permissible scope of a procedural provision. There is no specific enabling power authorising this duty. It can only be authorised by the general power to make rules governing practice and procedure (TCEA s22(1)) or by the power to confer ancillary powers as are necessary for the proper discharge of the tribunal's function (TCEA Sch 5 para 16). It cannot be the latter, as it is not a necessary power. And the former cannot be used to remove jurisdiction: see chapter 3.

12.35    Under UTR r8(4), the party whose case would be struck out or who would be barred must be given the chance to make representations on the proposed order.

### Likely outcome

12.36    Striking out may be appropriate for cases that cannot succeed. Proceedings are of no benefit to the party who presents the case and detrimental to the other parties and to the other users of the tribunal system. It applies whether the claimant is asserting a positive case or merely putting the other party to proof.[33]

12.37    This is only appropriate if the outcome for the case is, realistically and for practical purposes, clear and incontestable. It may be appropriate if the opposing case is vague, evasive, incoherent or obviously ill-founded, although this may be overcome by amending the case.[34] The tribunal should avoid conducting a mini-hearing when deciding the issue.[35] Striking out is not usually appropriate if facts relevant to the ultimate outcome of the case are disputed.[36] And if a party is not represented, it may be appropriate to allow the case to be presented, however implausible it may seem on paper.[37]

12.38    The power of strike out on this ground should not be used without an oral hearing if the case involves unresolved issues of fact that require a

---

33  *Commissioners for Her Majesty's Revenue and Customs v Fairford Group plc* [2014] UKUT 0329 (TCC) at [30].
34  *Commissioners for Her Majesty's Revenue and Customs v Fairford Group plc* [2014] UKUT 0329 (TCC) at [30].
35  *Commissioners for Her Majesty's Revenue and Customs v Fairford Group plc* [2014] UKUT 0329 (TCC) at [41].
36  *Ezsias v North Glamorgan NHS Trust* [2007] ICR 1126 at [25]–[32].
37  *Merelie v Newcastle Primary Care Trust* (2004) *Times* 1 December.

hearing or the application of discretion on which oral evidence or argument might be appropriate.[38]

12.39   Under TCEA, the threshold is whether the case has no reasonable prospect of succeeding. This is similar or equivalent to 'no real prospect of succeeding'. In *Swain v Hillman*,[39] Lord Woolf MR said of this phrase:

> The words 'no real prospect of succeeding' do not need any amplification, they speak for themselves. The word 'real' distinguishes fanciful prospects of success or . . . they direct the court to the need to see whether there is a 'realistic' as opposed to 'fanciful' prospect.[40]

This will include a case that is manifestly misconceived.[41]

12.40   Under UTR r8(4), the party whose case would be struck out must be given the chance to make representations on the proposed order.

## Conduct in the proceedings

12.41   Striking out may be appropriate as a response to the way that a party is conducting the proceedings. The behaviour may be detrimental to the other parties and, by wasting time, to the other users of the tribunal system. Striking out on account of a party's conduct is a draconian step of last resort.[42] The tribunal should consider other ways of dealing with the case: (i) drawing adverse inferences; (ii) through its power to award costs, if it has one; (iii) by referring the case to the Upper Tribunal for punishment for contempt under TCEA s25.[43]

12.42   Under UTR r8(2) and (3)(a) and (b), the conduct that leads to striking out may take two forms: (i) failure to comply with a direction in which the party was warned of the risk; (ii) failure to co-operate to such an extent that the tribunal cannot deal with the proceedings fairly and justly.

12.43   Under UTR r8(4), the party whose case would be struck out under (ii) must be given the chance to make representations on the proposed order. No chance has to be given under (i).

12.44   In the courts, it may be an abuse of process to bring proceedings again on the same issue without fresh supporting evidence,[44] although this power must be exercised flexibly if the tribunal has an inquisitorial function.[45] Under TCEA, the same result can be obtained by directing the party to produce further evidence.

12.45   In the courts, it may also be an abuse of process to attempt to bring proceedings on an issue that could and should have been raised in earlier proceedings.[46] Under TCEA, the tribunal might decide that it could not

---

38  *R (AM) v First-tier Tribunal* [2013] UKUT 333 (AAC).

39  [2001] 1 All ER 91.

40  [2001] 1 All ER 91 at 92.

41  *E T Marler Ltd v Robertson* [1974] ICR 72, where the phrase 'frivolous or vexatious' was used in relation to the power to award costs; Stuart-Smith LJ in *Ashmore v British Coal Corporation* [1990] 2 QB 338 at 347.

42  *Fairclough Homes Ltd v Summers* [2012] 1 WLR 2004 at [49].

43  *Fairclough Homes Ltd v Summers* [2012] 1 WLR 2004 at [51].

44  *White v Aldridge QC and London Borough of Ealing* [1999] ELR 150.

45  [1999] ELR 150 at 157.

46  *Johnson v Gore Wood & Co (a firm)* [2002] 2 AC 1 at 31.

deal with the proceedings fairly and justly in such circumstances if the other party has relied on the issue not being raised in later proceedings.

12.46    It is not possible to strike out or bar in respect of conduct before the proceedings began.[47]

## The nature and effect of barring

12.47  The Upper Tribunal considered these issues in *SL v Secretary fo State for Work and Pensions and KL-D*.[48] (a) A decision to bar had to be made consistently with the overriding objective, which encouraged effective participation. (b) If the tribunal gave a direction with a view to barring a party who did not comply, it should ensure that this result did not follow from any breach, however minor. (c) Barring is only effective prospectively. It does not have retrospective effect. (d) The tribunal may summarily determine issues against the party, but this must not be used as a penal provision. The tribunal must act in accordance with the overriding objective when deciding whether to exercise this power and act fairly if it does so. This requires the tribunal to take proper account of evidence and arguments already submitted. (e) The person barred remains a party. (f) This means that the party retains the right to appeal and to ask for written reasons.[49] (g) An application for permission to appeal is a separate proceedings to which the barring does not extend. (h) If a case is remitted to the tribunal for rehearing, this gives rise to new proceedings to which the barring does not extend.

12.48    In *ZB v Secretary of State for Work and Pensions*,[50] the Upper Tribunal decided that the fact that a party had been barred might affect what was required by way of reasons for the tribunal's decision and how the Upper Tribunal exercised its power to refuse to set aside a decision despite an error of law.

## Overall view

12.49  The appropriate response to the same failing by a party may arise in different contexts. For example: the appellant's failure to comply with directions may lead to an application by the respondent that the proceedings be struck out or by the appellant for the irregularities be waived or both. The decision should not be affected by the context in which it is raised. It is important to take an overall view of the impact on the proceeding, as Sir Thomas Bingham MR explained in *Costellow v Somerset County Council*:[51]

> In the great mass of cases, it is appropriate for the court to hear the summonses together, since in considering what justice requires the court is concerned to do justice to both parties, the plaintiff as well as the defendant, and the case is best viewed in the round.[52]

47  For example: on account of the destruction of evidence. See chapter 10.
48  [2014] UKUT 0128 (AAC).
49  *ZB v Secretary of State for Work and Pensions* [2013] UKUT 0367 (AAC) at [11] and [14]
50  [2013] UKUT 0367 (AAC) at [15]. See also *CW v Secretary of State for Work and Pensions and another* [2014] UKUT 0290 (AAC).
51  [1993] 1 WLR 256.
52  [1993] 1 WLR 256 at 264.

## Reinstatement

12.50   In *Gaydamak v UBS Bahamas Ltd*,[53] the Privy Council provided a framework for factors to consider when considering reinstatement. The case concerned a party who failed to appear, but the principles have a general application. Applying *Grimshaw v Dunbar*,[54] the Privy Council identified three relevant factors:[55] (i) the reason for the failure that led to the striking out of the case; (ii) whether there was undue delay in applying for reinstatement; and (iii) whether the other party would be prejudiced by the reinstatement. As to the merits of the case, the Privy Council held that they were generally irrelevant:

> ... it would be a rare case in which an application by a blameless absent litigant for re-instatement of proceedings which had been struck out as a result of his absence were refused on account of the hopelessness of his case. And it is also, in their Lordships' opinion, apparent that it would be for the person resisting re-instatement of the proceedings on that ground to satisfy the court that the proceedings were indeed hopeless.[56]

12.51   In *Synergy Child Services Ltd v Ofsted*,[57] the Upper Tribunal added two more factors:

> When considering whether an appeal should be reinstated under rule 8(6) [HESC Rules], a Tribunal should have regard to the broad justice of the case, in the light of all the circumstances obtaining at the time the application for reinstatement is being considered.

The broad justice of the case is required by the overriding objective and taking account of changes of circumstances is necessary in order to apply factor (iii) in *Grimshaw*.

## Tactics

12.52   The threat of striking out the proceedings may persuade a party to cooperate and the power to reinstate the proceedings, if there is one, may be exercised to impose conditions as to the future conduct of the proceedings.

# Withdrawal

## The nature of withdrawal

12.53   Most proceedings are begun by the voluntary act of a party. As such, in principle that party should be able to withdraw them. However, this may be subject to the interests of the other parties and the public interest generally. This is likely to be controlled by giving the tribunal a discretion. This discretion may or may not involve a consideration of the merits of the

53  [2006] 1 WLR 1097.
54  [1953] 1 QB 408.
55  [1953] 1 QB 408 at [14]–[16].
56  [1953] 1 QB 408 at [18].
57  [2009] UKUT 125 (AAC) at [13].

case. These general principles require modification under TCEA and for some types of referral.

12.54 The rules of procedure under TCEA assume rather than define withdrawal. They do not stipulate its effect. It is necessary to find its effect and, therefore, the scope of the rule, in the nature of the concept. In CPR, the effect of withdrawal (there called discontinuance) is to discontinue proceedings or a part of proceedings. However, tribunal proceedings are less formal. Different parties may challenge different aspects of a decision before the tribunal without bringing separate proceedings or cross proceedings. Withdrawal cannot, therefore, be confined to the party who initiated the proceedings or cross proceedings. Nor can it be confined in its effect to the continuance of the proceedings. Instead, the rules allow any party to withdraw a case, without defining what that means.

12.55 'Case' must have a meaning akin to proceedings. It must be distinguished from an argument on a case or a concession. Withdrawing an argument or making a concession of law or fact is not withdrawal and does not require the consent of the tribunal.

## Under TCEA

12.56 There is no express power authorising rules of procedure in respect of withdrawal. It is either embraced by 'practice and procedure' within section 22(1) or an ancillary power under paragraph 16 of Schedule 5. UTR r17 is illustrative under TCEA:[58]

(1) Subject to paragraph (2), a party may give notice of the withdrawal of its case, or any part of it–
   (a) by sending or delivering to the Upper Tribunal a written notice of withdrawal; or
   (b) orally at a hearing.
(2) Notice of withdrawal will not take effect unless the Upper Tribunal consents to the withdrawal except in relation to an application for permission to appeal.
(3) A party which has withdrawn its case may apply to the Upper Tribunal for the case to be reinstated.
(4) An application under paragraph (3) must be made in writing and be received by the Upper Tribunal within 1 month after–
   (a) the date on which the Upper Tribunal received the notice under paragraph (1)(a); or
   (b) the date of the hearing at which the case was withdrawn orally under paragraph (1)(b).
(5) The Upper Tribunal must notify each party in writing that a withdrawal has taken effect under this rule.

## Withdrawal by applicants and appellants

12.57 Under UTR r17, any party may withdraw all or part of a case. The most likely party to withdraw will be the applicant or appellant who initiated the proceedings. For convenience, this section generally assumes that it is

58 See also: GRC Rules r17; HESC Rules r17; IAC Rules r17; Land Rules r20; PC Rules r22; SEC Rules r17; Tax Rules r17; WPAFC Rules r17. The CPR equivalent is CPR Part 38.

the appellant who wishes to withdraw an application for permission or an appeal.

## Withdrawal as of right

12.58   Withdrawal may be allowed as of right. This is the position for applications for permission to appeal under UTR r17(2). This reflects the fact that, at this stage, neither any other party nor the public generally are likely to have an interest in the proceedings continuing against the wish of the appellant. Any party who wishes the appeal to proceed may apply for permission and, if necessary, an extension of time in which to do so.

## Withdrawal with consent

12.59   Withdrawal may be allowed only with the consent of the tribunal. This is the position for appeals under UTR r17(2).

12.60   If consent is required, the tribunal will have to consider the interests of the appellant, the other parties and the public interest generally. This may also require a tribunal to take account of the nature of its function. These matters have been considered by the courts in cases in which the rules of procedure did not make provision for withdrawal.

12.61   In *Hanson v Church Commissioners for England*,[59] the case had come before the rent assessment committee on a reference from a rent officer following an objection from the tenant to the rent fixed by the rent officer. The court held that there was a public interest in the fixing of fair rents, so that an attempt at a unilateral withdrawal was not effective.

12.62   Lord Denning MR drew a distinction between private disputes, in which unilateral withdrawal was permissible, and those that involved a public interest, in which the wishes of other parties and the public interest had to be taken into account:

> The legal position as shown by the cases is that in the ordinary way where there is a dispute before a tribunal in a civil matter, either party has a right to withdraw his application or objection, as the case may be, at any time before the decision is given. That is shown by *Boal Quay Wharfingers Ltd v King's Lynn Conservancy Board* [1971] 1 WLR 1558, 1559, 1566.
>
> But when the dispute is one in which there is a public interest involved, it may not be permissible for one of the parties to withdraw on his own without the assent of the other; and, even if they both agree, he may not be able to withdraw unless the tribunal consents. It all depends on the construction which the courts place on the statute setting up the tribunal. That seems to me to be the correct interpretation of *Rex v Hampstead and St Pancras Rent Tribunal ex p Goodman* [1951] 1 KB 541 where *both* parties consented to the withdrawal of an application to pay the standard rent, and of the later case of *R v West London Rent Tribunal ex p Napper* [1967] 1 QB 169 where there was an attempted withdrawal that was not upheld.[60]

On this analysis, a purely private dispute could be terminated unilaterally. But a dispute with a public interest could only be terminated with the agreement of the other parties and the permission of the tribunal.

59  [1978] QB 823.
60  [1978] QB 823 at 832–833.

12.63    Lawton LJ spelt out the relationship between these interests:

> In my judgment, in the absence of a specific statutory prohibition, if the proceedings can be brought to an end without prejudicing any interest whether private or public, then they can be. Any other approach would lead to a waste of a tribunal's time and to the waste of both public and private money . . . If that sort of expenditure can be saved by agreement between the parties, it is in the public interest that it should. It is for the tribunal, before which the proceedings are, to decide whether prejudice may arise from the withdrawal of an objection. The simplest way of finding out whether there is any prejudice is to ask the parties. The best evidence of the absence of prejudice to the other party is for that party to give his consent. The tribunal, however, is the guardian of the public interest and must decide for itself whether withdrawal will prejudice that interest. In general I should have thought that the public interest would best be served by letting the parties decide for themselves what they want; but there may be circumstances known to the tribunal or brought to its attention which indicate otherwise.[61]

The examples of the public interest given by Lawton LJ show that the public interest included factors indicating that the parties' decisions may not have been freely given or fully informed.[62]

12.64    The terms of a tribunal's duty, once a case is before it, are also relevant. In *R v Income Tax Special Commissioners ex p Elmhirst*,[63] the Court of Appeal decided that an appeal against an assessment could not be withdrawn by the taxpayer, because the Commissioners were required by statute to consider not only the terms of the appeal, seeking a reduced assessment, but also whether an increased assessment was required. This is linked to the public interest that underlay the tribunal's duty. In the Divisional Court, Lord Hewart CJ had emphasised both the statutory duty and the public interest through that duty which was 'owed by the Commissioners to the hidden parties to the appeal – namely, the general body of the taxpayers'.[64]

## When may a withdrawal be made

12.65    In principle, a party should be able to withdraw a case at any time before the tribunal had made and promulgated its decision or otherwise disposed of the case. This is subject to the tribunal's consent, if required. A tribunal is likely to be astute to a tactical decision to withdraw a case that may go against the party. It is also subject to any issue as to costs.

12.66    The position in principle may be varied by legislation.[65]

---

61  [1978] QB 823 at 839.
62  [1978] QB 823 at 839.
63  [1936] 1 KB 487.
64  [1936] 1 KB 487 at 488–489.
65  In *R v Tottenham Districts Rent Tribunal ex p Fryer Bros. (Properties) Ltd* [1971] 2 QB 681, statute allowed withdrawal before the tribunal had 'entered upon consideration' of the case. The Court of Appeal held that a notice of withdrawal that arrived after the members had read the papers was too late.

## The effect of withdrawal on the issues

12.67   Withdrawal disposes of the party's case and, perhaps, of the whole of the proceedings. It does not finally determine the issues in the case.[66] As the House of Lords explained in *The Ardandhu*,[67] discontinuance (withdrawal) terminates the proceedings, but leaves the parties 'at large as to reassert their rights if they please'[68] and 'does not of itself operate as a release or an extinguishment of the claims, or in any other way bar further proceedings'.[69]

12.68   Accordingly, it may be possible for a party who has withdrawn a case to apply for it to be reinstated, as under UTR r17(3). Reinstatement requires the permission of the tribunal, which may be given or refused in the tribunal's discretion. The rules of procedure under TCEA do not expressly provide that permission is required, but it seems inherent in the need for the party to apply for reinstatement rather than merely giving notice.

12.69   It may also be possible for the party, or another party, to commence new proceedings raising the same issue, subject to complying with any time limits and obtaining any necessary permission.[70]

12.70   Some rules of procedure allow for withdrawal to take effect through dismissal.[71] Another possibility is that dismissal may be available as an additional step following withdrawal.[72] This disposes both of the proceedings and the issues raised in them.[73] If the withdrawal takes effect through a dismissal and has significance for other proceedings, the tribunal must make a formal order dismissing the claim or part of the claim that is withdrawn.[74]

12.71   The significance of the contrast between withdrawal and dismissal was considered by the Court of Appeal in *Khan v Heywood and Middleton Primary Care Trust*.[75] The rules of procedure allowed withdrawal and, in addition, provided that the proceedings could be dismissed. The claimant withdrew the proceedings before the employment tribunal, but they were not dismissed. He sought an order from the tribunal reinstating the proceedings under its case management powers. The Court of Appeal held that the rules did not contain a power to reinstate, but that as they had not been dismissed, the claimant could bring fresh proceedings. Wall LJ referred to:

> . . . the well-established distinction between a claim which has been withdrawn, but on which there is no judicial determination, and a claim which

---

66   *LO (Jordan) v Secretary of State for the Home Department* [2011] EWCA Civ 164.
67   (1887) 12 App Cas 256.
68   (1887) 12 App Cas 256 per Lord Halsbury LC at 260.
69   (1887) 12 App Cas 256 per Lord Herschell at 262.
70   *Buckbod Investments v Nana-Otchere* [1985] 1 WLR 342.
71   As in the Employment Tribunals (Constitution and Rules of Procedure) Regulations 2001 Sch 1 para15(2)(a).
72   As in the Employment Tribunals (Constitution and Rules of Procedure) Regulations 2004 r25.
73   *Staffordshire County Council v Barber* [1996] ICR 379 at 397.
74   Wall LJ in *Sivanandan v Enfield London Borough Council* [2005] EWCA Civ 10 at [122]; (2005) *Times* 20 January.
75   [2007] ICR 24.

has been dismissed by a judicial act. The first does not, of itself, create either issue or cause of action estoppel; the latter does.[76]

12.72 Exceptionally, it is permissible to raise an issue in later proceedings that could have been raised in the proceedings that were dismissed, provided that this is necessary in order to avoid an abuse of process.[77] This is likely to be allowed if the rules of procedure permit a withdrawal only by way of a dismissal and the dismissal of the particular case was in substance merely a discontinuance of the proceedings only and not of the underlying claim.[78]

12.73 There is no power for withdrawal through dismissal in the rules of procedure under TCEA. However, the parties may agree to a consent decision, which would have the same effect.

## The reinstatement process

12.74 There is no specific provision for the process to be followed when a party applies for a case to be reinstated or for notification of the outcome.

12.75 In practice, the views of the other parties will have to be taken into account when deciding whether or not to reinstate a case. And if it is, directions for the further conduct of the case will provide notice to the other parties.

## Withdrawal by respondents

12.76 Respondents may not simply oppose the case put by the applicant or appellant. They may present their own cases in proceedings brought by an applicant or appellant. For example: if both parents in a child support case wish to challenge different aspects of the First-tier Tribunal's decision, this will be allowed on the appeal of one parent only.

12.77 If a respondent withdraws a case, the proceedings continue, but that case no longer forms part of those proceedings.

## Withdrawal of a referral

12.78 The different types of referral are set out in chapter 5.

12.79 The rules of procedure under TCEA do not seem to have taken account of all the issues that may arise in respect of referrals. To some extent, the difficulties are bypassed by the definition of 'party'.

12.80 It is necessary to consider the separate position of the person who makes the reference and the parties to the case referred. The latter may include the person who makes the reference. However, this will not necessarily be so. For example: if the First-tier Tribunal refers a case to the Upper Tribunal under TCEA s9(5)(b) it is not a party to the case before that tribunal.

---

76 [2007] ICR 24 at [10].
77 *Staffordshire County Council v Barber* [1996] ICR 379 at 398.
78 *Ako v Rothschild Asset Management Ltd* [2002] ICR 899.

*If there was a duty to refer*

12.81    If the person who referred the case to the tribunal had no choice but to do so, the case cannot be withdrawn by that person. If the case is withdrawn, the duty would merely arise again. The rules may expressly prohibit withdrawal in such circumstances, as does HESC Rules r17(3).

12.82    If the circumstances change so that a reference is no longer required, the case in effect lapses. There is, though, no provision for proceedings to lapse in these circumstances under the rules of procedure under TCEA. However, the change of circumstances may allow one of the parties to withdraw. This may include the person who made the reference (see the definition of 'party' in UTR), unless the rules prohibit withdrawal. Otherwise the person who is the main subject of the reference may be able to withdraw.

*If there was no duty to refer*

12.83    If the person who referred the case had the choice whether or not to do so, the person may be a party and, therefore, entitled to withdraw. Under UTR, this will depend on whether what was referred was a 'question or matter' (see the definition of 'party' in rule 1(3)). Otherwise the person who is the main subject of the reference may be able to withdraw.

## Costs

12.84    A claimant who withdraws a claim may have conducted proceedings unreasonably so as to be liable for costs. The issue in such a case is not whether the withdrawal was unreasonable, but whether the proceedings had been conducted unreasonably.[79]

# Compromise

12.85    A compromise is an agreement between the parties to proceedings that settles a matter in dispute in those proceedings. Some form of formal decision by the tribunal may be necessary in order to bring the proceedings to an end so far as that issue is concerned.

## The categories of compromise

12.86    The cases on compromise and consent orders fall into three categories.

12.87    One category consists of cases in which it is not permissible for the parties to compromise proceedings.

12.88    The second category consists of cases in which a compromise cannot be imposed on the tribunal, but can be taken into account by the tribunal in deciding what order to make.

12.89    The third category consists of cases in which it is permissible to compromise without the consent of the tribunal.

---

79  *McPherson v BNP Paribas (London Branch)* [2004] ICR 1398.

12.90 The proper classification is determined by the nature of the issue that is involved. It is not determined by the nature of the parties or of the proceedings. Take the example of a public body. It cannot compromise a case to pay a social security benefit or grant planning permission in terms that conflict with the governing law. But it can compromise a case on an issue of interpretation of legislation, which then governs the case, or on a procedural issue.

## Cases in which it is not permissible to compromise

12.91 In order to understand concession in the context of government expenditure decisions, it is necessary to understand the authority under which public money is spent. This was explained by the Court of Appeal in *R (Hooper) v Secretary of State for Work and Pensions.*[80]

12.92 In order to be lawful, public expenditure involves a two-stage process: appropriation and authority.[81] First, funds must be allocated to particular purposes by the annual Appropriate Act. Second, the expenditure of the funds must be authorised by prerogative, common law or statute.

12.93 If legislation covers an area of expenditure comprehensively, any additional prerogative or common law that would otherwise exist is excluded.[82]

12.94 The power of expenditure may be extended, subject to two provisos.[83] First, it must not be inconsistent with legislation. Second, as a matter of constitutional practice, legislation is required if the expenditure will continue from year to year.

12.95 In deciding whether legislation is comprehensive and whether a prerogative or the common law is inconsistent with it, section 3 of the Human Rights Act 1998 requires that legislation be interpreted so as not to infringe a Convention right.

12.96 A statutory power of expenditure may be interpreted purposively in order to avoid anomalies and injustices that are not compatible with the general scheme of the legislation.[84] This can have the effect of authorising expenditure that is outside the literal wording.

12.97 In addition to the powers of public expenditure, there are powers not to collect money due to the State. For example: the Commissioners of Her Majesty's Revenue and Customs have the power of care and management of collection given to the Commissioners by section 1(1) of the Taxes Management Act 1970. This power can be exercised pragmatically in order to facilitate collection,[85] with the effect that some sums properly due might not be collected.

---

80  [2003] 1 WLR 2623; this is not affected by the appeal to the House of Lords [2005] 1 WLR 1681.
81  [2003] 1 WLR 2623 at [131].
82  [2003] 1 WLR 2623 at [127].
83  [2003] 1 WLR 2623 at [132].
84  *R (Wilkinson) v Inland Revenue Commissioners* [2003] 1 WLR 2683 at [46]; this is not affected by the appeal to the House of Lords [2005] 1 WLR 1718.
85  [2003] 1 WLR 2683 at [45].

12.98      Likewise the discretion on recovery of social security benefits[86] allows the Secretary of State and local authorities to refrain from collecting money that is properly recoverable.

12.99      Although there may be no power to make general payments or to refrain generally from collecting payments,[87] it remains possible to compromise proceedings in individual cases.[88] Obviously, this must be consistent generally with the authority's general power.

12.100     If a public party has no power to make a formal compromise, it may also be possible to achieve the same effect by other means.

12.101     First, if the public party does not challenge the facts put to the tribunal, the outcome will be determined by those facts.

12.102     Second, the public party may be able to agree with the other parties on how a particular judgment should be exercised, such as the suitability of a particular school for a child with special educational needs.

12.103     Third, the public party may exercise alternative powers to achieve the same effect. So, the Secretary of State for the Home Department may decline to compromise proceedings relating to asylum, but may grant instead exceptional leave to remain. And the Secretary of State for Work and Pensions may decline to compromise proceedings relating to a social security benefit, but may make an extra-statutory payment.

## Cases in which compromise is a factor taken into account by the tribunal

12.104  The authorities on this category concern consent orders in divorce proceedings. In *Jenkins v Livesey*,[89] the House of Lords decided that an agreement between the parties in ancillary relief proceedings could only be given effect in the discretion of the court if it was a proper one to make under the legislation.[90] This imposed on each party a duty to make full and frank disclosure to the other party and to the court so that the court's discretion could be exercised.[91]

12.105     The court takes account of an agreement reached by the parties as one of the circumstances of the case.[92] The agreement may be made subject to the approval of the court. If it is, the parties cannot resile from it.[93] When the matter comes before the court, it will be able to consider any issue whether an agreement was reached.[94]

---

86  Social Security Administration Act 1992 ss71 and 75.

87  But should there not be published guidelines on the circumstances in which overpayments will be recovered in order to comply with article 6(1)?

88  *R (Wilkinson) v Inland Revenue Commissioners* [2003] 1 WLR 2683 at [56]; this is not affected by the appeal to the House of Lords [2005] 1 WLR 1718. There may be statutory authority to compromise: see the Taxes Management Act 1970 s1(1) and, for appeals, s54.

89  [1985] AC 424.

90  [1985] AC 424 per Lord Brandon at 435–437.

91  [1985] AC 424 per Lord Brandon at 436–438.

92  *Edgar v Edgar* [1980] 1 WLR 1410.

93  *Soulsbury v Soulsbury* [2008] Fam 1 at [44]–[45], disapproving of *Xydhias v Xydhias* [1999] 2 All ER 386.

94  Thorpe LJ in *Xydhias v Xydhias* [1999] 2 All ER 386 at 395.

## Cases in which compromise is permissible

12.106 This category contains all cases that do not fall within the other categories. Employment cases are an example.

12.107    The terms of the agreement of the parties may be incorporated into a decision given by the tribunal with the consent of the parties. Alternatively, the agreement may operate as a freestanding contract with the proceedings brought to an end by withdrawal or dismissed by consent.

## Confidentiality

12.108 Negotiations towards a compromise may be made open or without prejudice. If they are without prejudice, they cannot be referred to in later proceedings, although they may lead to an offer that can be referred to for the purposes of any costs that the tribunal may have power to award.[95]

---

95  Thorpe LJ in *Xydhias v Xydhias* [1999] 2 All ER 386 at 397.

# Precedent

13.1   Precedent is used with different meanings. It may refer to the principles that determine a decision's authority and relevance in a later case, to the proposition for which a decision is authority, or to the decision itself. It is sometimes described as a doctrine, but that adds nothing. It is often referred to as stare decisis.

## The scope of precedent

13.2   Precedent may apply to issues of law, to issues of fact or guidance, or to issues of judgment. Each requires separate treatment.

## The functions of precedent

13.3   Precedent is concerned with efficiency, consistency and discipline in decision-making, which together enhance certainty in the application, and coherence in the development, of the law.

13.4   If every case had to be decided afresh without reference to previous decisions and the analysis in those decisions, the burden on the time and intellect of the judges would be intolerable. But precedent is concerned with more than efficiency and ease of decision-making. It determines the circumstances in which and the extent to which a tribunal is bound by its own decisions or those of another tribunal or a court. It is a means by which consistency of, and discipline in, decision-making is enhanced. It contributes to discipline in the development of the law, equality between parties in the application of the law, and to certainty and predictability for those to whom it applies. Precedent is not an essential factor that produces these benefits, nor is it the only one, but it does enhance them.

13.5   There are a number of ways in which authorities are used that do not fit easily or at all into the traditional statement and analysis of precedent. They are considered below. What unites them and, perhaps, provides the key to their reconciliation with tradition is the fact that they share in fulfilling the same functions.

## Decisions on issues of law

### The authority of a decision

13.6   Under standard legal theory, the courts distinguish between the legal principle on which a case is decided (the ratio) and other comments that were not essential to the decision (obiter comments). The ratio must be applied in later cases for so long as it retains its authority, unless it can be distinguished. A ratio may lose its authority if the decision creating it is set aside on review or appeal or if it is overruled in a later decision.

13.7   The true effect of the rules of precedent in a jurisdiction can only be understood by considering the combined operation of the rules of precedent and the rules that determine the scope of decisions.[1] However, this book will not explain how standard theory identifies the scope of an authority and the circumstances in which it may be distinguished. It will,

---

1  For a detailed analysis of this point see Neil MacCormick, *Rhetoric and the Rule of Law*, Oxford, 2005, Chapter 8, especially Part 3.

though, identify some respects in which that theory is inadequate to deal with the nature of some of the decisions made by the Upper Tribunal.

13.8 There is no single, definitive theory on how the ratio of a case is identified and distinguished from obiter comments. However, the ratio is usually defined by reference to the facts of the case, the outcome and the reasoning that links the two. There are different theories about how these factors should be combined to identify the ratio, which are capable of producing different results. But whatever theory is used, the ratio can only be identified if the facts of the case are known.

13.9 This analysis can be applied to some decisions made by the Upper Tribunal. The Tribunal may make a decision based either on the facts found by the First Tier-tribunal or on its own findings. That decision may be that the decision below was correct on the tribunal's reasoning or it may be made in substitution for the decision below. In these circumstances, it is possible to apply the analysis of ratio and obiter.

13.10 In other circumstances, this analysis cannot be applied, because neither the facts nor the ultimate outcome are known. The Upper Tribunal may give a decision that the First Tier-tribunal made an error on a point of law and direct a rehearing. As the facts are not yet known, the directions given for the rehearing will have to take account of the possible findings that may be made or be sufficiently general not to depend on the facts. Either way, it is impossible to identify a ratio in the absence of either the facts found or an outcome on those facts. It follows, as a general proposition, that the obiter comments cannot be identified simply on the basis that they are anything that is not a ratio. It may, though, be possible to identify some comments that were not essential on any analysis.

13.11 It would, perhaps, be preferable to refer to the authority of decisions of the Upper Tribunal as being based on propositions of law rather than on a ratio. The basis on which those propositions are identified must await judicial analysis or academic theory.

13.12 The inappropriateness of the ratio-obiter analysis is not unique to tribunals. The appellate courts may deal with an issue in principle, leaving the principles to be applied below. This is what the House of Lords did in *R (Roberts) v Parole Board*,[2] as Lord Woolf explained.[3] It is significant that Lord Woolf thought it worth mentioning as something out of the ordinary. This explains the Court of Appeal's discomfort in *Secretary of State for Work and Pensions v Slavin*[4] at having to deal with an issue in the absence of all relevant facts.

## The degrees of authority

13.13 Every decision that decides or discusses an issue of law relevant to a case has a value as a precedent. As a precedent, it may be binding, presumptive, persuasive or indicative.

13.14 Precedent is binding if it has to be followed. For example: all tribunals are bound by decisions of the Court of Appeal. Binding precedent emphasises the hierarchy of the courts and tribunals. Even the most binding

2 [2005] 2 AC 738.
3 [2005] 2 AC 738 at [35].
4 [2011] EWCA Civ 1515 at [37], [64] and [71].

precedent has to allow for the possibility of conflicting decisions. One approach is to allow a free choice between the conflicting decisions; the other is to provide a rule to determine which must be followed.

13.15 Precedent is presumptive if it will be followed except in certain circumstances. For example: the Commissioners professed to follow the decisions of other Commissioners unless this would lead to the perpetuation of error.[5] Presumptive precedent emphasises the comity among judges at the same level in the hierarchy. The circumstances in which presumptive precedent need not be followed may be defined or applied in a variety of ways that merge into either binding or persuasive precedent. The difference between the categories may depend more on how the rules of precedent are expressed than on substance.

13.16 Precedent is persuasive if it is neither binding nor presumptive, but is potentially relevant. Persuasive precedents are those from a court or tribunal lower in the hierarchy or from another jurisdiction. That jurisdiction may be from (a) another country, (b) a different area of law or (c) another court or tribunal. Obiter comments from a higher or equivalent body may also be persuasive. Persuasive precedent emphasises the quality of reasoning.

13.17 Precedent is indicative if it is illustrative of the way that a court or tribunal exercises a particular jurisdiction.

13.18 These are not rigid categories. Rather they are stages on a spectrum.

13.19 Hierarchy is central to binding precedent. And it has a role in presumptive precedent in that comity is there important because the judges involved are equivalent in the hierarchy. But it is largely irrelevant in persuasive precedent.

13.20 Comity can be seen as underlying or supporting respect for the hierarchy of the courts. And it has an independent role in presumptive precedent. But in persuasive precedent, it is of little significance, although it may be important if obiter comments of an equivalent or higher body are involved.

13.21 Quality of reasoning is central in persuasive precedent. And it has a role in presumptive precedent as a factor relevant to whether the precedent should be followed. But it has little significance in binding precedent, except perhaps in determining how broadly the precedent is interpreted.

13.22 Value to later tribunals is essential to all forms of precedent.

13.23 Precedent is more likely to be binding between tiers and more likely to be presumptive within a tier. But there are no rules that dictate this and no factors identifying the circumstances in which either form of precedent applies. Decisions given in other jurisdictions are more likely to be persuasive than decisions given within a jurisdiction.

## Decisions on issues of fact and guidance

13.24 In general, the courts do not approve of giving guidance.

13.25 In part, this reflects their desire not to gloss statutory language. As Lawrence Collins LJ said in *R (Assura Pharmacy Ltd) v NHS Litigation*

---

5 *R(I) 12/75* at [21].

*Authority*[6] of a judgment that laid down guidelines for the application of a particular regulation, it can be 'unwise to put a judicial gloss on the approach which decision-makers are bound or permitted by legislation to take'.[7]

13.26    It also partly reflects their reluctance to deal with abstract issues.[8] The danger was explained by the Court of Appeal in *R (Burke) v General Medical Council*:[9]

> The court should not be used as a general advice centre. The danger is that the court will enunciate propositions of principle without full appreciation of the implications that these will have in practice, throwing into confusion those who feel obliged to attempt to apply those principles in practice.

13.27    It further reflects the fact that tribunals exercise an appellate function and not a general regulatory or supervisory function over decision-makers.[10]

13.28    And in part it reflects the need to allow proper scope for the exercise of a discretion. As Hodson LJ said in *Moor v Moor*:[11] 'The court will not lay down rules of an exhaustive character as to the exercise of discretion'.[12]

13.29    In *Office of Communications v Floe Telecom Ltd (in liquidation)*,[13] Mummery LJ set out in some detail the objections to the practice:

> It is the unnecessary nature of the Tribunal's legal rulings in its judgment that is most troubling. The court itself drew the attention of the parties at the hearing to *R (Burke) v GMC* [2006] QB 273. There are sound reasons why courts and tribunals at all levels generally confine themselves to deciding what is necessary for the adjudication of the actual disputes between the parties. Deciding no more than is necessary may be described as an unimaginative, unadventurous, inactive, conservative or restrictive approach to the judicial function, but the lessons of practical experience are that unnecessary opinions and findings of courts are fraught with danger.

> Specialist tribunals seem to be more prone than ordinary courts to yield to the temptation of generous general advice and guidance. The wish to be helpful to users is understandable. It may even be commendable. But bodies established to adjudicate on disputes are not in the business of giving advisory opinions to litigants or potential litigants. They should take care not to be, or to feel, pressured by the parties or by interveners or by critics to do things which they are not intended, qualified or equipped to do. In general, more harm than good is likely to be done by deciding more than is necessary for the adjudication of the actual dispute.

> One of the dangers of unnecessary rulings is that, with only the assistance of the parties and without the benefit of wider consultation on relevant aspects of the public interest, the court's opinions, though meant to be helpful, may turn out to be damaging in practice and wrong in law. The

---

6   [2008] EWCA Civ 1356.

7   [2008] EWCA Civ 1356 at [69].

8   See chapter 7.

9   [2006] QB 273 at [21].

10   As explained by Lloyd LJ in *Floe Telecom Ltd v Office of Communications* [2006] 4 All ER 688 at [34].

11   [1954] 1 WLR 927.

12   [1954] 1 WLR 927 at 932. By implication, the court might lay down rules of a less than exhaustive character.

13   [2009] EWCA Civ 47 at [20]–[22]; (2009) *Times* 23 February.

court may be unaware of all the available arguments or ignorant of the practical implications of what it says. Those who rely on its advisory opinions when applying the law in practice may be misled or confused. A judgment aimed at giving authoritative advice and guidance may be misused by selective citation in different and unforeseen disputes and circumstances.

13.30    However, the Commissioners, the Employment Appeal Tribunal, the Immigration Appeal Tribunal, the Court of Appeal and the House of Lords have all emphasised the importance of consistency and certainty in decision-making. In accordance with this, they have given guidance on the law,[14] on procedure[15] and on the assessment of evidence.[16]

13.31    In *Shirazi v Secretary of State for the Home Department*,[17] the Court of Appeal recognised the scope for a judicial policy to apply in order to ensure consistency in the factual analysis of information that is common to a class of case. It endorsed the practice of the former Immigration Appeal Tribunal, which was designed to achieve consistency between cases and to save the need for the same issue to be analysed in every relevant case. Sedley LJ said:[18]

> I accept readily that it is not a ground of appeal that a different conclusion was open to the tribunal below on the same facts, nor therefore that another tribunal *has* reached a different conclusion on very similar facts. But it has to be a matter of concern that the same political and legal situation, attested by much the same in-country data from case to case, is being evaluated differently by different tribunals. The latter seems to me to be the case in relation to religious apostasy in Iran. The differentials we have seen are related less to the differences between individual asylum-seekers than to differences in the Tribunal's reading of the situation on the ground in Iran. This is understandable, but it is not satisfactory. In a system which is as much inquisitorial as it is adversarial, inconsistency on such questions

---

14  In *R(I) 2/06*, the Commissioners gave guidance on the assessment of disablement arising from a prescribed disease. In *Grundy (Teddington) Ltd v Plummer* [1983] ICR 367 at 375–376, the Employment Appeal Tribunal gave guidance on the general approach to what constitutes reasonable conduct by an employer. In *Flemming v Secretary of State for Work and Pensions*, reported as *R(G) 2/02*, at [24], the Court of Appeal gave general guidance on the interpretation of particular legislation, following the advice given by the Court of Appeal in Northern Ireland in *Bronwyn Wright-Turner v Department for Social Development*, reported as *R1/02 (ICA)*. In *Shirazi v Secretary of State for the Home Department* [2004] 2 All ER 602 at [29], the Court of Appeal approved the practice of giving guidance on the situation in particular countries. This was in turn approved by the House of Lords in *Januzi v Secretary of State for the Home Department* [2006] 2 AC 426 at [50]. And in the House of Lords in *R (Roberts) v Parole Board* [2005] 2 AC 738 at [35], Lord Woolf acknowledged that the issue of law was being dealt with on principle and that the effect on the appellant's rights would not be known until the facts had been found.

15  In *R(IS) 11/99* at [33], the Commissioner indicated that it would be preferable for an application for leave to appeal, which required a full statement of the tribunal's decision, to be interpreted in all cases as a request for a statement, if one had not already been provided.

16  In *Flemming v Secretary of State for Work and Pensions*, reported as *R(G) 2/02*, at [22] and [38], Pill and Chadwick LJJ gave advice on the assessment of evidence given by claimants on their hours of study. And in *EPI Environmental Technologies Inc v Symphony Plastic Technologies plc* [2005] 1 WLR 3456 at [74], Peter Smith J warned of the danger of assuming general dishonesty from what might have been a stupid lie told by a witness in order to bolster a good case.

17  [2004] 2 All ER 602.

18  [2004] 2 All ER 602 at [29].

works against legal certainty. That does not mean that the situation cannot change, or that an individual's relationship to it does not have to be distinctly gauged in each case. It means that in any one period a judicial policy (with the flexibility that the word implies) needs to be adopted on the effect of the in-country data in recurrent classes of case.

The practice was endorsed by Lord Hope in *Januzi v Secretary of State for the Home Department*[19] 'in the interests of fairness and consistency. But in the end of the day each case, whether or not such guidance is available, must depend on an objective and fair assessment of its own facts'.

13.32      In *Cadogan v Sportelli*,[20] the Court of Appeal took a similar approach in relation to valuation issues in the Lands Tribunal. That Tribunal had given guidance on the principles to be applied in valuing lease extensions. After considering the immigration authorities, Carnwath LJ said:[21]

> Although the present context is very different, there is an equal public interest in avoiding wasted expenditure, and the risk of inconsistent results, in successive LVT appeals on an issue such as that of deferment rates. The Tribunal could hardly have done more to ensure that the issues were fully ventilated and exhaustively examined. They had already been discussed in detail in *Arbib*. I have already referred to the steps taken by the Tribunal to bring together the present group of cases. Furthermore it is difficult to envisage a better qualified panel of experts for the purpose than those called in this case, or of specialist counsel on both sides of the argument.

> I agree with the Tribunal that an important part of its role is to promote consistent practice in land valuation matters. It was entirely appropriate for the Tribunal to offer guidance as they have done in this case, and, unless and until the legislature intervenes, to expect leasehold valuation tribunals to follow generally that lead.

13.33   Standard theory does not take account of this role for precedent. However, the benefits of guidance and consistency are shared by all forms of precedent. What precedent as guidance lacks is formal recognition as a form of precedent, which is traditionally confined to the ratio of a case and does not take account of other ways in which the underlying functions of precedent are achieved.

13.34      The juridical nature and function of such guidance was explained by Lord Diplock in *Wright v British Railways Board*:[22]

> A guideline as to quantum of conventional damages or conventional interest thereon is not a rule of law nor is it a rule of practice. It sets no binding precedent; it can be varied as circumstances change or experience shows that it does not assist in the achievement of even-handed justice or makes trials more lengthy or expensive or settlements more difficult to reach. But though guidelines change, too frequent alteration deprives them of their usefulness in providing a degree of predictability in the litigious process and to facilitating settlement of claims without going to trial.[23]

---

19  [2006] 2 AC 426 at [50].
20  [2008] 1 WLR 2142.
21  [2008] 1 WLR 2142 at [98]–[99].
22  [1983] 2 AC 773.
23  [1983] 2 AC 773 at 785. See also Lord Carnwath in *Secretary of State for the Home Department v MN and KY* [2014] UKSC 30 at [26]–[28].

13.35   Perhaps, the theoretical basis of the effect of these cases lies in two considerations.

13.36   First, there is the proper function of a court or tribunal that hears appeals from a tribunal. The traditional analysis of precedent presupposes a tribunal that is reactive, giving a decision on the issues that arise in the case and no more. The fact and guidance cases show that it is proper to be more proactive, assisting tribunals to avoid errors rather than correcting them when they occur. In this sense, its effect is no different from giving directions on the law for a rehearing before the facts are found.

13.37   Second, guidance does not intrude improperly into issues of judgment. It does not direct, but guide. It assists the fact-finding tribunal in avoiding error and, within the 'bounds of reasonable judgment',[24] it helps to improve the quality of the decision-making.

## Decisions on issues of judgment

13.38   As issues of judgment depend so much on the combination of facts in any particular case, it is not appropriate to reason by analogy from the facts of an earlier case with similar facts. In *R (Williams) v Horsham District Council*,[25] the Court of Appeal was concerned with the issue of whether a couple had their sole or main residence at a particular property. The tribunal had relied on earlier authority in attaching particular significance to the couple's security of tenure in the property in question. Lord Phillips MR explained why this was wrong:[26]

> ... because in a particular case one individual factor has been treated as of particular significance, it does not follow that it carries the same significance in a different factual scenario.

As the Court of Appeal remarked in *Nancollas v Insurance Officer*,[27] 'such is the rich variety of real life that truly identical situations are comparatively rare'.[28]

13.39   In the case of a discretion, there is a further consideration: a tribunal must not fetter the exercise of that discretion. In *Merchandise Transport Ltd v British Transport Commission*,[29] the Court of Appeal was concerned with an appeal against a decision of the Transport Tribunal that involved the exercise of a discretion. Danckwerts LJ said:

> But in the exercise of a discretionary power of this kind, an applicant is entitled to have his application considered on the merits and in the circumstances of his particular case. If the tribunal makes a practice of relying on previous decisions in respect of other applications that have come before the tribunal, there is, in my opinion, danger that the discretion of the tribunal may not be applied in an unfettered and proper manner having regard to the merits of the particular case, and, of course, having regard to

---

24  *Moyna v Secretary of State for Work and Pensions* [2003] 1 WLR 1929 at [25].
25  [2004] 1 WLR 1137.
26  [2004] 1 WLR 1137 at [22].
27  [1985] 1 All ER 833.
28  [1985] 1 All ER 833 at 835.
29  [1962] 2 QB 173.

the principles which are regarded as being incorporated in the provisions of the Act.[30]

13.40 However, decisions on discretions and other matters of judgment may have a precedent value as an authority for the legal proposition that particular factors are or are not relevant. As Lord Phillips MR explained in *R (Williams) v Horsham District Council*:[31] 'Reference to decided cases may be of assistance in identifying factors relevant to the question of which is a person's main residence.'

13.41 Decisions on discretions and other matters of judgment may also be useful as indicative precedents of how the tribunal typically exercises its jurisdiction. Their function is to make the tribunal's decision-making transparent, thereby providing guidance to parties in future cases and helping the tribunal to achieve consistency. The Court of Appeal recognised this in *Merchandise Transport Ltd v British Transport Commission*,[32] which concerned the discretionary decisions of the Transport Tribunal. Devlin LJ said:

> In my opinion a series of reasoned judgments such as the tribunal gives is bound to disclose the general principles upon which it proceeds. I think that that is not only inevitable but also desirable. It makes for uniformity of treatment and it is helpful to the industry and to its advisers to know in a general way how particular classes of applications are likely to be treated.[33]

13.42 However, the scope for guidance in cases that depend on judgment is limited. This was recognised by the Court of Appeal in *Nancollas v Insurance Officer*:[34]

> As to guidelines, it would be possible to point to material factors . . . But any such list would mislead, if, as is almost inevitable, it was once thought to be comprehensive. We could list factors which are irrelevant, but again any examples would have to be so extreme as to be unhelpful, because otherwise we might be dismissing a factor which, in exceptional circumstances which we have not envisaged, might nevertheless have some weight.[35]

13.43 Once again, standard theory does not take account of this role for precedent. However, the benefits of guidance and consistency are shared by all forms of precedent. What indicative precedent lacks is formal recognition as a form of precedent, which is traditionally confined to the ratio of a case and does not take account of other ways in which the underlying functions of precedent are achieved. This approach ignores its practical importance. As the judge remarked in *Re Taylor (a bankrupt)*:[36] '. . . It is in the exercise of discretion, not rulings on "black-letter law" that consistency at first instance has a particular inherent value'.

---

30  [1962] 2 QB 173 at 208.
31  [2004] 1 WLR 1137 at [22].
32  [1962] 2 QB 173.
33  [1962] 2 QB 173 at 193.
34  [1985] 1 All ER 833.
35  [1985] 1 All ER 833 at 840.
36  [2007] Ch 150 at [46].

## Decisions on matters of practice and procedure

13.44   As Brooke LJ said of pre-CPR case-law in *Woodhouse v Consignia plc*:[37] 'One of the great demerits of the former procedural regimes was that simple rules got barnacled with authority'. Decisions under TCEA, as with CPR, are now concerned with the balance of considerations in the individual circumstances of the particular case. As such, they will not generate precedents. This lack of precedent on issues of procedure and practice will make the rules of procedure under TCEA, as with CPR, more accessible to those who are not familiar with, or do not have access to, the case-law. Precedent will, though, be relevant as an indication of the general approach to be taken under the rules.

## Decisions and lines of authority

13.45   In the United Kingdom, precedent is usually stated in terms of the status of individual decisions. An alternative approach is to accord precedent value not to individual decisions as such but only when they form part of a consistent line of authority.[38] A consistent line of authority is already relevant within the traditional statement of precedent as a factor to take into account when deciding whether to follow a decision whose status as a precedent is only presumptive.[39] However, consistency of authorities can be advanced as an alternative theory, in place of the traditional statement. And in some jurisdictions at least, it may be advanced as a more accurate description of how the law operates.

13.46      An emphasis on lines of authority rather than on individual decisions more accurately reflects the way in which the scope and interpretation of a decision is determined by later authorities than the traditional statement. There is a spectrum. At one end, a decision of a higher court that is binding may be distinguished so frequently and readily that it becomes a decision binding only in respect of its own unique facts. In plainer terms, it is disregarded for all practical purposes, despite the theory that it retains the status of precedent as defined. At the other end, the scope of a decision may be expanded so that it bears little resemblance to the original basis on which it was made. In between, there are probably the majority of decisions whose present authority can only be understood accurately in the context of later decisions which have discussed and then distinguished or applied them. Even silence in later decisions may reflect acquiescence in a decision.

13.47      On this analysis, the legal proposition for which a case is an authority is decided by later cases. They may accept the case on its original basis, they may qualify it or they may expand it. The legal proposition is never fixed.

---

37   [2002] 1 WLR 2558 at [32].

38   There are two possible formulations. One is to recognise that later authorities determine, or perhaps alter, the proposition for which a decision is an authority. This retains the theory of British law that authority derives from individual decisions. The other is to recognise authority as deriving from a sequence of authorities. This is more in keeping with some Continental approaches to precedent.

39   *R(AF) 1/07* at [21] refers to a consistent line of authority as relevant to the willingness with which a Commissioner would depart from the authority of decisions of the High Court in its former co-ordinate jurisdiction.

Even if it never changes, its ongoing authority results from the fact that it is accepted without qualification. There is always the potential for change. Later decisions may overrule it, distinguish it (to limit its scope, perhaps to its own facts) or use it to create a wider proposition of law. The scope of an authority and its value as precedent is an ongoing process, being reinforced or undermined each time it is considered.

13.48    A statement in terms of a line of authority is more appropriate to precedent as indicative of how a tribunal will exercise its judgment. It also allows the law to be presented more accurately when it is initially developing or is in a state of transition. The case-law may be developing so that it may be more accurately stated in terms of a developing trend than in terms of the status of existing authority. A statement of the status of individual decisions would not take account of trends that are not yet firmly established, although these may be of greater significance than the decisions that are currently of binding status.

13.49    An emphasis on lines of authority may also more accurately reflect the practice in particular tribunals. For example: the willingness of individual Commissioners to depart from earlier, even (or perhaps especially) recent, decisions allowed the law to develop more efficiently at their level with less recourse to the Court of Appeal than the stated rules would allow. The operation of precedent between the Commissioners in areas of current controversy would have been most accurately stated in terms of the line of authority that was generally accepted by them. This may also have more accurately reflected the practice of the tribunals below, which disregarded Commissioners' decisions that were inconsistent with the prevailing line of authority. They did not generally allow themselves the freedom of choosing to follow either line, as the Commissioners' rules of precedent strictly allowed.

13.50    In part, disagreement between judges reflects their different views of what the law is or of how it should develop. But it is also a factor of organisation. If cases on a new issue are dealt with as and when they arise, later cases with different combinations of facts and circumstances may show that a completely different decision or a different formulation of the law is appropriate. New arguments may have the same effect. This can lead to a series of cases that state the law in different terms. However, if a series of cases with different factual combinations can be anticipated, it may be appropriate to wait until a decision can be taken based on the experience of a number of cases and full argument. This is likely to produce a more appropriate formulation that will command more respect in later cases.

## Precedent and reports

13.51   There may or may not be a link between precedent and the reports of the tribunal's decisions. The reporting of a decision may have no relevance to the precedent value of that decision, as is the case for the Employment Appeal Tribunal. Or reporting (and highlighting) may determine those decisions which are of precedent value, as in the Asylum and Immigration Tribunal. Or reporting may confer a special status on a decision, as was the case of decisions of the Commissioners. In this final case, reporting is only significant for precedent if there is a conflict in the decisions that have been given, in which case the reported decision must be preferred.

13.52     Reporting can only confer a special status for precedent if the selection is under the control of the judges. This was the approach of the Commissioners and of the Asylum and Immigration Tribunal. The former only reported a decision if it commanded the support of the majority of Commissioners at the time.[40]

13.53     There has been limited analysis of how reporting affects the status of a decision as a precedent. In the earliest cases, the Commissioners linked the purpose of reporting decisions (for the guidance of tribunals and decision-makers) with the duty to follow them.[41] It was then but a short step to say that reported decisions, having been issued for guidance, took priority over those that have not been reported. (The reporting of decisions was also recommended by the Franks Committee as proof of consistency and as a guide to the parties and their advisers.)[42] Leggatt[43] recommended that only selected decisions of the Upper Tribunal should be binding. In this, he was adopting the approach in immigration. He wrongly equated this with the approach of the Commissioners, which selected for reporting but did not limit citation.[44]

13.54     Whether or not precedent and reports are formally linked, the courts or tribunals may try to limit citation to decisions that have been reported.

## Precedent and practice directions

13.55   The Asylum and Immigration Tribunal achieves the same result as precedent by the use of practice directions under section 107(3) of the Nationality, Immigration and Asylum Act 2002:

> (3) A practice direction may, in particular, require the Tribunal to treat a specified decision as authoritative in respect of a particular matter.

13.56   As with the link between precedent and reporting, there has been no analysis of how this fits into a theory of precedent based on judicial decision-making. Perhaps, being statutory, it does not need to be. If it is to fit, perhaps the solution lies in two factors. First, the selection is made judicially, albeit not within the context of a particular decision. The same is true of the precedent based on reporting. Second, the types of cases to which this applies may show a repetition of facts and circumstances that differs from that usually met in litigation. This may justify a special rule.

13.57     TCEA s23 authorises the Senior President of Tribunals and a Chamber President to give directions as to practice and procedure. Section 23(6) assumes that those directions may include 'guidance about . . . the application or interpretation of the law'. This is not consistent with the usual meaning of practice and procedure as relating to the methods to be used

---

40  *R(I) 12/75* at [17(c)].

41  *CSG 9/49 (KL)* at [3] and *CS 414/50 (KL)* at [2].

42  *The Report of the Committee on Administrative Tribunals and Enquiries* Cmnd. 218 (1957), para 102.

43  *Tribunals for Users – One System, One Service* (2001), paras 6.20–6.26.

44  It is said that the approach in immigration was based on Leggatt's misunderstanding of the Commissioners' approach.

by a court or tribunal in deciding cases rather than to the substantive law that the tribunal has to apply.[45]

## Precedent of tribunal decisions

13.58   According to Carnwath LJ in *Cadogan v Sportelli*:[46] '. . . It will be principally for the new [upper] tribunal to lay down guidelines as to the precedent effect of its decisions for different purposes'.

### Within the Upper Tribunal

13.59   The correct approach to precedent between courts of coordinate jurisdiction was set out in *Re Taylor (a bankrupt)*.[47] The judge must:

> . . . make his decision on the merits of the submissions put before him, giving appropriate weight but no more to authorities which may be persuasive but which, by law, are not binding. The point is of particular importance where the issue of law is one of jurisdiction . . . It is in the exercise of discretion, not rulings on 'black-letter law' that consistency at first instance has a particular inherent value.[48]

The court rejected[49] as impractical the approach taken in *Colchester Estates (Cardiff) v Carlton Industries plc*,[50] under which the later of two conflicting decisions of equal status was to be followed if the earlier decision was fully considered in the later decision.

13.60   Tribunals equivalent in status to the Upper Tribunal have taken the approach set out in *Re Taylor (a bankrupt)*[51] in respect of their own decisions, albeit with different emphases.

13.61   The Commissioners set out their system of precedent in *R(I) 12/75*:[52]

> In so far as the Commissioners are concerned, on questions of legal principle, a single Commissioner follows a decision of a Tribunal of Commissioners[53] unless there are compelling reasons why he should not, as, for instance, a decision of superior Courts affecting the legal principles involved. A single Commissioner in the interests of comity and to secure certainty and avoid confusion on questions of legal principle normally follows the decisions of other single Commissioners . . . It is recognised however that a slavish adherence to this could lead to the perpetuation of error and he is not bound to do so.

---

45  See chapter 3.
46  [2008] 1 WLR 2142 at [99].
47  [2007] Ch 150.
48  [2007] Ch 150 at [46].
49  [2007] Ch 150 at [43].
50  [1986] Ch 80. The Commissioners followed this approach in *R(IS) 13/01* at [4] and *R1/00(FC)* at [7]–[8], but abandoned it following *Taylor*: *R(IS) 9/08*. The Employment Appeal Tribunal had already taken the *Taylor* approach in *Digital Equipment Co Ltd v Clements (No 2)* [1997] ICR 237.
51  [2007] Ch 150.
52  *R(I) 12/75* at [21].
53  Three Commissioners sitting together. The equivalent is now a three-judge panel of the Upper Tribunal.

13.62   Two three-judge panels of the Upper Tribunal have confirmed that these principles apply to the Administrative Appeals Chamber of the Upper Tribunal, pending further guidance by case-law or practice direction.[54]

13.63   The National Industrial Relations Court followed the practice of the House of Lords in its 1966 Practice Statement.[55] In *Chapman v Goonvean and Rostowrack China Clay Co Ltd*,[56] the Court decided:

> Accordingly we wish to say that this court regards the use of precedent as an indispensable foundation upon which to decide what is the law and its application to individual cases. It provides at least some degree of certainty upon which individuals can rely in the conduct of their affairs, as well as a basis for orderly development of legal rules in the field of industrial relations. The court nevertheless recognises that too rigid adherence to precedent may lead to injustice in a particular case and also unduly restrict the proper development of industrial law. The court, therefore, while treating its own former decisions as normally binding, will consider itself free to depart from them when it appears right to do so. In this connection the court will bear in mind the danger of disturbing retrospectively decisions which have formed the general basis of industrial relations agreements and practices.[57]

13.64   The practice for the successor to that Court, the Employment Appeal Tribunal, was stated with different ordering but to the same effect by Morison J in *Secretary of State for Trade and Industry v Cook*:[58]

> The appeal tribunal is not bound by its previous decisions, although they will only be departed from in exceptional circumstances, or where there are previous inconsistent decisions.[59]

13.65   The House of Lords' Practice Statement was also adopted by the Commissioners in respect of decisions of Tribunals of Commissioners. In *R(U) 4/88*, a Tribunal of Commissioners gave an indication of some of the factors relevant to whether a decision of a previous Tribunal should be followed:

> As to previous decisions of Tribunals of Commissioners, we would not think it right to endeavour to spell out comprehensively the risks from disturbance which should be borne in mind. However, they clearly include disturbing the basis for decisions which may reasonably be taken to have affected many thousands of citizens and have been acted upon by adjudication officers and tribunals over many years, and also decisions which may be taken to have passed the scrutiny of Parliament without adverse comment.[60]

---

54  *Dorset Healthcare NHS Trust v MH* [2009] UKUT 4 (AAC) at [37] and *SoSD v AD and MM* [2009] UKUT 10 (AAC) at [132].
55  [1966] 1 WLR 1234.
56  [1973] ICR 50.
57  [1973] ICR 50 at 58.
58  [1997] ICR 288.
59  [1997] ICR 288 at 292.
60  *R(U)* 4/88 at [17].

## Between the Upper Tribunal and First-tier Tribunal

13.66 As a superior court of record, the Upper Tribunal's decisions are binding on the First-tier Tribunal.[61] Previously it was not clear whether precedent formally applied so that a First-tier Tribunal was bound by decisions of the Upper Tribunal that hears appeals from it. In *Chief Adjudication Officer v Woods*,[62] Evans LJ said that the decisions of the Commissioners would be acted upon in future cases 'even if not strictly binding'. However, legislation has assumed that precedent applies[63] and in *Secretary of State for Work and Pensions v Menary-Smith*,[64] May LJ treated precedent as applying and the distinction between binding principle and obiter discussion as being relevant. In practice, it may not matter whether or not there is a formal rule of precedent. If the Upper Tribunal will set aside a decision that differs in law from one of its decisions, that is precedent in all but name. Of course, if there is a conflict between decisions made by the Upper Tribunal, the First Tier-tribunal has to decide which to follow.

13.67 The Commissioners set out their system of precedent in *R(I) 12/75*:

Commissioners speak with equal authority. All their decisions ... may be cited to Commissioners, local tribunals and insurance officers. Where they decide questions of legal principle they must be followed by insurance officers and local tribunals in cases involving the application of that principle, unless they can be distinguished. It should be borne in mind that similarity in underlying facts does not automatically give rise to similarity in the principle to be applied and questions of fact should not be elevated into questions of legal principle.

If confronted with decisions which conflict, insurance officers and local tribunals must prefer the decision of a Tribunal of Commissioners (whether a unanimous or majority decision) to that of a single Commissioner. A reported decision ... should *prima facie* be given more weight than an unreported decision. Subject to the foregoing insurance officers and local tribunals must choose between conflicting decisions and there is no obligation on them to prefer the earlier to the later or *vice versa*.[65]

## Within the First-tier Tribunal

13.68 The First-tier Tribunal is not bound by its own decisions,[66] which are persuasive only.

13.69 This approach reflects the practical difficulties that precedent would encounter if applied to most of the First-tier Tribunal's jurisdictions. As Leggatt[67] noted:

There are obvious practical difficulties in expecting many tribunals sitting across the country, with wide differences in experience and constitution, and a remit to consider each individual case on its merits, to develop a consistent view of the law.

---

61  *R (Cart) v Upper Tribunal* [2010] 1 All ER 908 at [75].
62  *R(DLA) 5/98.*
63  Social Security Act 1998 s27 and Child Support Act 1991 s28ZC.
64  [2006] EWCA Civ 1751 at [24] and [28].
65  *R(I) 12/75* at [19]–[20].
66  *Hampshire County Council v JP* [2009] UKUT 239 (AAC) at [15].
67  *Tribunals for Users – One System, One Service* (2001), para 6.19.

13.70   It also prevents the perpetuation of error. In *West Midland Baptist (Trust) Association (Inc) v Birmingham Corporation*,[68] the Court of Appeal disapproved the Lands Tribunal's practice of following its previous decisions. Salmon LJ drew attention to the disadvantage of precedent on issues of general application:

> No doubt previous decisions of the tribunal on points of law should be treated by the tribunal with great respect and considered as persuasive authority, even when made by a layman. But they should never be treated as binding. It is important that such decisions should be most carefully scrutinised and if necessary rejected, particularly in cases such as the present which raise points of law of outstanding importance with far-reaching consequences.[69]

And Sachs LJ pointed out the anomaly that would otherwise arise between the Tribunal and the High Court:

> I find it difficult to see why all the individual members of that tribunal should invariably and for ever unquestioningly bow the knee to the decisions of any single one of their colleagues, however distinguished, when even High Court judges are not bound blindly to follow each other's judgments. Such a practice can produce unfortunate results.[70]

## Predecessor tribunals

13.71   If a tribunal is not bound by its own decisions, neither is it bound by those made by its predecessor tribunal that was not so bound.

13.72   Nor is a tribunal necessarily bound by a predecessor tribunal that did regard itself as bound by its own decisions. In *Portec (UK) Ltd v Mogensen*,[71] the Employment Appeal Tribunal decided that it was not bound by decisions of its predecessor, the National Industrial Relations Court, although its decisions were 'of great persuasive authority and we would not lightly different from the principles which are there to be found'.[72]

13.73   However, the decisions of the National Insurance Commissioners were followed by the Social Security Commissioners. The latter were the direct successors of the former under a new name to reflect a widened jurisdiction. This was in contrast to the Employment Appeal Tribunal, which was new and wholly distinct from the National Industrial Relations Court.

## For other purposes

13.74   Most decisions made by tribunals are only binding between the parties. Their decisions are only binding generally (judgments in rem) in those rare cases where legislation confers jurisdiction on the tribunal to make such decisions.[73] It is not an abuse of process to argue against a tribunal's

---

68  [1967] 2 QB 188.
69  [1967] 2 QB 188 at 210.
70  [1967] 2 QB 188 at 225.
71  [1976] ICR 396.
72  [1976] ICR 396 at 568.
73  *R (PM) v Hertfordshire County Council* [2010] EWHC 2056 (Admin) at [40]–[47].

decision for other purposes.[74] It would, though, be highly undesirable to allow contradictory findings on issues of precedent fact.[75]

## Precedent of court decisions

### Decisions of the Court of Appeal and the Supreme Court

13.75    Both the Upper Tribunal and the First-tier Tribunal are bound by decisions of these courts.

### Decisions of the High Court on statutory appeal

13.76    If an appeal lies from a tribunal to the High Court, the tribunal is bound by decisions of that Court.[76]

13.77        If the appellate jurisdiction is transferred to a tribunal, the decisions formerly made by the court are not binding on that tribunal. Originally the authority of a decision in these circumstances depended on the status of the judges involved.[77] It now depends on the nature of the jurisdiction, the body over which it was exercised and the status of the Upper Tribunal as a superior court of record. This was the approach taken by the Upper Tribunal in *Secretary of State for Justice v RB*,[78] following the analysis of the Court of Appeal in *Chief Supplementary Benefit Officer v Leary*[79] in the context of supplementary benefits. Initially the decisions of the supplementary benefit appeal tribunal were subject to judicial review before the Divisional Court. In 1978 an appeal was created to the High Court under the Tribunals and Inquiries Act 1971. This was revoked in 1980 in favour of an appeal to the Commissioner under the social security legislation. The issue for the court was whether the Commissioner was bound by decisions of the High Court on appeal under the 1971 Act. The Court held that decisions given by the latter were not binding, as the jurisdiction was narrow and transferred for convenience.[80]

13.78        A decision of the High Court will be followed by the Upper Tribunal as a matter of comity. Normally, it would be followed unless the tribunal was convinced that the judgment was wrong. However, within its specialist jurisdictions, the Upper Tribunal 'may in a proper case feel less inhibited in revisiting issues decided even at High Court level, if there is good reason to do so'.[81]

### Decisions of the High Court on judicial review

13.79    The Upper Tribunal is bound by decisions of the High Court on judicial review of its own decisions. In *Secretary of State for Justice v RB*,[82] the Upper

74  *R (PM) v Hertfordshire County Council* [2010] EWHC 2056 (Admin) at [70]–[72].
75  *R (CJ) v Cardiff City Council* [2012] 2 All ER 836 at [22].
76  *Minister of Pensions v Higham* [1948] 2 KB 153 at 155 per Denning J.
77  Brett MR in *The Vera Cruz (No 2)* (1884) 9 PD 96 at 98.
78  [2010] UKUT 454 (AAC) at [39]–[43].
79  [1985] 1 WLR 84.
80  [1985] 1 WLR 84 at 89–90.
81  *Secretary of State for Justice v RB* [2010] UKUT 454 (AAC) at [41].
82  [2010] UKUT 454 (AAC).

Tribunal decided that decisions of the High Court on judicial review of other tribunals were equivalent to decisions in coordinate jurisdiction.[83] The Tribunal decided that the assumption to the contrary by the Court of Appeal in *Chief Supplementary Benefit Officer v Leary*[84] was based on a concession.[85] That approach had been confirmed by Purchas LJ in *Commock v Chief Adjudication Officer*.[86] However, those comments were not necessary to the decisions and were made without argument.[87] The Tribunal's approach is consistent with the view of Hodgson J in *R v Social Security Commissioner ex p Akbar*.[88] The judge quashed a Commissioner's refusal of leave, but said that his reasoning on a substantive point of law was not binding on the Commissioner who would decide the appeal.

13.80    The National Industrial Relations Court first doubted whether it was bound by decisions of the Divisional Court[89] and then decided it was not.[90] However, as its reasoning was based on the lack of judicial review in Scotland, it no longer applies.[91]

13.81    Its successor, the Employment Appeal Tribunal, is not bound by decisions below the Court of Appeal. In *Portec (UK) Ltd v Mogensen*,[92] the Tribunal decided that it was not bound by any decisions of the High Court. Bristow J set out the Tribunal's opinion that decisions of those courts were not binding, but: 'must be of great persuasive authority and we would not lightly differ from the principles which are there to be found'.[93] The Tribunal gave no reasons for this view.

13.82    There is no court authority on whether the same principles apply to other tribunals from which appeal lies to the Court of Appeal.

## Decisions of the High Court in a shared jurisdiction

13.83    If the High Court and a tribunal share a jurisdiction so that it may be exercised by either, the decisions of the High Court are binding on the tribunal, even if the decisions are made by a deputy High Court judge.[94] The lower court's jurisdiction in these circumstances is not coordinate. This only applies where the tribunal is an inferior court. That is not so in the case of the Upper Tribunal, which is a superior court of record.[95]

## Decisions of High Court judges sitting in the Upper Tribunal

13.84    There is no authority relevant to the precedent value of a decision of the Upper Tribunal that is made by a High Court judge sitting in that Tribunal.

83  [2010] UKUT 454 (AAC) at [45]–[46].
84  [1985] 1 WLR 84 at 89.
85  [2010] UKUT 454 (AAC) at [45].
86  Reported as an Appendix to *R(SB) 6/90*.
87  *R(IS) 15/99* at [14].
88  Unreported 28 October 1991.
89  *Secretary of State for Employment v Atkins Auto Laundries Ltd* [1972] 1 WLR 507 at 512.
90  *Chapman v Goonvean and Rostowrack China Clay Co Ltd* [1973] ICR 50 at 57.
91  *R(IS) 15/99* at [19].
92  [1976] ICR 396.
93  [1976] ICR 396 at 400.
94  *Howard de Walden Estates Ltd v Aggio* [2008] Ch 26 at [86]–[95].
95  *Secretary of State for Justice v RB* [2010] UKUT 454 (AAC) at [44].

It is not clear whether the relevant criterion is the status of the judge or the body in which that judge exercises a particular jurisdiction.

### England and Wales and Scotland

13.85 Special problems arise if a tribunal has jurisdiction for the whole of Great Britain. They arise, because the courts of Scotland below the House of Lords are separate from those of England and Wales. In *Marshalls Clay Products Ltd v Caulfield, Clarke v Frank Staddon Ltd*,[96] Laws LJ explained that the rules of precedent are laid down by the courts and are limited to the jurisdiction of those courts:

> The rules of precedent or *stare decisis* cognisable here are given by the common law ... The essence is that precedent confines the very power of the courts subject to it. It is not a rule of discretion or comity or anything of the kind. It is therefore of necessity a doctrine whose reach is limited to the jurisdiction in which the courts in question operate. The House of Lords is no exception; by statute its writ runs to three jurisdictions, and accordingly it binds the lower courts within each of those jurisdictions. Statute might also extend the scope of precedent, as was done by the European Communities Act 1972 ... Now, statutory provisions which give dominion to courts in one jurisdiction (international or otherwise) over courts in another are apt, here at least, to father constitutional tensions. But it is at least clear, and here is the point on this part of the case, that it would be a constitutional solecism of some magnitude to suggest that by force of the common law of precedent any court of England and Wales is in the strict sense bound by decisions of any court whose jurisdiction runs in Scotland only or – most assuredly – *vice versa*. Comity and practicality are another thing altogether. They exert a wholly legitimate pressure.[97]

13.86 There have been decisions that tribunals in one part of Great Britain are bound by decisions of appropriate courts in another. In *Minister of Pensions v Higham*,[98] Denning J said that the Pensions Appeal Tribunal was bound by decisions of the Court of Session in Scotland (equivalent to the High Court). And in *Portec (UK) Ltd v Mogensen*,[99] the Employment Appeal Tribunal decided that it was bound by decisions of the Inner House of the Court of Session in Scotland (equivalent to the Court of Appeal). In view of Laws LJ's analysis, those decisions are no longer binding.

### Consent orders

13.87 A Commissioner dealt with consent orders in *R(FC) 1/97*. Referring to a direction made to a social security appeal tribunal by the Court of Appeal, the Commissioner said:

> I do not accept that this direction, which was made to the tribunal to whom the case was remitted, establishes any principle or binds any other tribunal. The direction was made by consent, without argument and is unsupported by any reasons at all. A Consent Order of this description does not bind

---

96 [2004] ICR 1502.
97 [2004] ICR 1502 at [32].
98 [1948] 2 KB 153 at 155.
99 [1976] ICR 396 at 400.

anyone other than the parties to the Order and the tribunal to whom the direction was given.[100]

## Reasons in cases of no precedent value

13.88   Lord Woolf CJ issued a *Practice Direction (Citation of Authorities)*[101] on 8 April 2001 limiting the citation of certain classes of authorities. These are:

> 6.2 . . . the following categories of judgment
> Applications attended by one party only
> Applications for permission to appeal
> Decisions on applications that only decide that the application is
>      arguable
> County court cases . . .

An authority in any of these categories may only be cited if:

> 6.1 . . . it clearly indicates that it purports to establish a new principle or to extend the present law. In respect of judgments delivered after the date of this direction, that indication must take the form of an express statement to that effect. In respect of judgments delivered before the date of this direction that indication must be present in or clearly deducible from the language used in the judgment.

This reflects the pre-existing rule that judgments given on applications for permission to appeal were not regarded as binding authorities.[102]

## European Court of Human Rights authorities

13.89   Section 2(1) of the Human Rights Act 1998 requires courts and tribunal to take into account the Strasbourg jurisprudence. The courts have decided that precedent overrides or confines the scope of this duty.

13.90   In *Kay v Lambeth London Borough Council*,[103] the House of Lords decided that the status of a decision of the House under domestic precedent was not affected by later and conflicting decisions of the European Court of Human Rights. In the event of a conflict between a Strasbourg and a decision of the House, the proper course was to follow the latter and give permission to appeal so that the conflict could be resolved by the House.

13.91   The House recognised a limited exception that applied only in extreme circumstances. The example given was *D v East Berkshire Community Health NHS Trust*,[104] in which the Court of Appeal declined to follow a decision of the House of Lords on the ground that the policy consideration on which it was based no longer applied in view of later Strasbourg jurisprudence. Lord Bingham emphasised the special facts of that case, which if not unique were most unlikely to recur.

13.92   In *R (RJM) v Secretary of State for Work and Pensions*,[105] the House of Lords decided that the same approach applied to decisions of the Court

---

100  *R(FC) 1/97* at [28].
101  [2001] 1 WLR 1001.
102  Lord Woolf MR in *Clark v University of Lincolnshire and Humberside* [2000] 1 WLR 1988 at [43].
103  [2006] 2 AC 465.
104  [2004] QB 558.
105  [2009] 1 AC 311.

of Appeal, although that Court should be free (but not obliged) to depart from its previous decisions if they were inconsistent with a subsequent decision of the European Court of Human Rights.[106] No doubt, this overtakes the decision of the Court of Appeal in that case,[107] which recognised that the Court could accept a concession by the Secretary of State that, following a development in the Strasbourg jurisprudence, a previous domestic authority no longer applied.

### European Court of Justice authorities

13.93 The Court of Appeal has taken the same approach to EC law. In *Armstrong v Newcastle upon Tyne Hospital Trust*,[108] Buxton LJ said that once the House of Lords had determined the scope of EC law, domestic courts were not entitled to resort to the decisions of the European Court of Justice for a different or wider meaning.[109] It may, though, be possible to refer a question to that Court (see below).

## Preliminary rulings

13.94 A ruling that is made to govern the future conduct of proceedings is not binding if it is inconsistent with a later decision, whether or not it is binding.[110]

## References to the European Court of Justice

13.95 The normal principles of precedent do not govern whether a reference may be made to the European Court of Justice. The Court of Appeal has decided that it is permissible to refer a question even if it is covered by the authority of a decision of that Court.[111] However, the decision to refer may be open to challenge on appeal.

## Retrospective and prospective effect

13.96 Usually a decision of a tribunal, like a decision of a court, is retrospective in its effect. However, statute may provide that in specified circumstances it is only prospective.[112] There is nothing inherently unjust in this.[113] Exceptionally the House of Lords may make one of its decisions prospective in

---

106 [2009] 1 AC 311 at [66].
107 [2007] 1 WLR 3067 at [21]–[24].
108 [2006] IRLR 124.
109 [2006] IRLR 124 at [101].
110 *R v M* (2007) *Times* 17 May.
111 *Trent Taverns Ltd v Sykes* (1999) *Times* 3 March.
112 Social Security Act 1998 s27 and Child Support Act 1991 s28ZC provide for a degree of prospective judicial decision-making.
113 Evans LJ in *Chief Adjudication Officer v Woods* reported as *R(DLA)* 5/98.

effect,[114] as may the European Court of Justice[115] and the European Court of Human Rights.[116]

## Suspension of precedential effect of decision

13.97   Under TCEA, tribunals have power to suspend the effect of a decision. This does not extend to the value of the decision as a precedent. See chapter 15.

---

114   *Re Spectrum Plus Ltd* [2005] 2 AC 680.
115   See the discussion in *R (Bidar) v Ealing London Borough Council* [2005] QB 812 at [64]–[71].
116   As in *Goodwin v United Kingdom* (2002) 35 EHRR 16.

# CHAPTER 14

# The decision

*continued*

14.1   Tribunals must act within their statutory jurisdiction, because that defines the limits of their power. They must act judicially, because that is their nature. They must decided the issues that arise for resolution, because that is their function. And they must make decisions that are clear, sufficiently complete and capable of being implemented, because the discharge of their duty to decide the issues judicially must be effective.

14.2   The decision itself should be stated clearly and precisely. It is good practice to state the decision in the terms of the legislation and to cite that legislation. The subject of the decision will determine what has to be included. But depending on the circumstances, the following are likely to be important: the effective date of the decision; the period for which it applies; the amount of any money involved. It is essential to state the decision in a form that can be understood and implemented.

## Decisions on particular issues

14.3   A tribunal may limit its decision to the issues that have been decided on the appeal.[1] This is, of course, subject to the terms of the governing legislation.

## Calculations

14.4   Tribunals must not abdicate the details of a decision to the decision-maker. However, the tribunal may properly refer matters of calculation to the decision-maker.[2] This is provided that: (i) the basis for the calculation is clear from the tribunal's decision; (ii) the tribunal gives power to refer any dispute over the calculation back to the tribunal. This is, of course, subject to the terms of the governing legislation.

## Standard notices and precedents

14.5   The tribunal may provide standard notices for completion or standard forms of words to assist judges to record the decision correctly. Alternatively, judges may devise their own. Whatever their provenance, standard notices and precedents should help to ensure that all relevant matters are recorded. Uniformity should help to avoid any doubt that might arise from different formulations by different judges.

## Public document

14.6   A decision is a public document.[3]

---

1   *R(IS) 2/08.*

2   *R(SB) 16/83* at [21].

3   *Solihull Metropolitan Borough Council Housing Benefit Review Board v Simpson* (1994) 27 HLR 41 at 47. The case concerned the decision of the Board, but the legislation in question was in equivalent terms to those used in the rules of procedure under TCEA. And see *Hodgson v Imperial Tobacco Ltd* [1998] 1 WLR 1056 at 1070.

# Public judgment under article 6

14.7   Article 6(1) provides:

> ... Judgment shall be pronounced publicly but the press and public may be excluded from all or part of the trial in the interest of morals, public order or national security in a democratic society, where the interests of juveniles or the protection of the private life of the parties so require, or to the extent strictly necessary in the opinion of the court in special circumstances where publicity would prejudice the interests of justice.

14.8   The European Court of Human Rights has not given a literal interpretation to the requirement that judgment *shall* be pronounced publicly. In *Pretto v Italy*,[4] it took account of the variation in practice among States, as shown in the preparatory documents for the Convention. It decided:[5]

> The Court therefore does not feel bound to adopt a literal interpretation. It considers that in each case the form of publicity to be given to the 'judgment' under the domestic law of the respondent State must be assessed in the light of the special features of the proceedings in question and by reference to the object and purpose of Article 6(1).

Later, it set out the object of the provision as being:[6]

> . . . to ensure scrutiny of the judiciary by the public with a view to safeguarding the right to a fair trial . . .

It took account of the nature of the proceedings in deciding that article 6(1) was satisfied if the judgment was publicly available:[7]

> . . . at any rate in cassation proceedings [which are limited to issues of law], no less achieved by a deposit in the court registry, making the full text available to everyone, than by a reading in open court of a decision dismissing an appeal or quashing a previous judgment, such reading sometimes being limited to the operative provisions.

14.9   *Axen v Germany*[8] also concerned cassation-style proceedings.[9] An appeal had been rejected as ill-founded without an oral hearing and in a decision that was served only on the parties. The Court held that this was sufficient in view of 'the course of the proceedings taken as a whole'.[10] One feature of those proceedings was that the decision under appeal had been pronounced publicly.[11]

14.10   Publicity given to a judgment must not frustrate the legitimate purpose of holding some proceedings, or parts of proceedings, in private. In order to prevent this, it may be permissible for no publicity to be given or for the terms of the judgment to be anonymised.[12]

---

4   (1983) 6 EHRR 182.
5   (1983) 6 EHRR 182 at [26].
6   (1983) 6 EHRR 182 at [27].
7   (1983) 6 EHRR 182 at [27].
8   (1983) 6 EHRR 195.
9   But see the concurring opinion: (1983) 6 EHRR 195 at 203.
10   (1983) 6 EHRR 195 at [32].
11   (1983) 6 EHRR 195 at [28]. *Moser v Austria* [2007] 1 FLR 702 at [99]–[104] is an example of a case in which the European Court on Human Rights held that judgment had not been publicly pronounced.
12   See *P v BW* [2004] Fam 22 at [60] and the decision of the European Court of Human Rights in *B v United Kingdom* cited at [54]–[57].

# Forms of decision

14.11   The TCEA only provides for the forms of decision that may be given on an appeal to the Upper Tribunal under section 11. Otherwise, the forms of decision are governed by the legislation under which the appeal is heard.

## Appeals under TCEA ss11 and 12

14.12   The forms of decision by the Upper Tribunal on an appeal under section 11 are partly governed by section 12. They depend on whether the tribunal finds that the decision under appeal involved the making of an error on a point of law.

14.13      An error of law was originally seen as a mistake. If the tribunal had made a mistake, the issue then arose of disposal. If the mistake had not affected the outcome, it might be possible to dispose of the case without a rehearing. This depended on the powers available on appeal. It might be possible to set the decision aside and substitute one to the same effect or to short-circuit the process and simply dismiss the appeal.

14.14      In time, the issue of materiality moved from being a disposal issue to part of the jurisdictional criteria of an appeal. It became incorporated into the definition of error of law. This reached its highest in the judgment of Brooke LJ in *R (Iran) v Secretary of State for the Home Department*.[13] He incorporated materiality into his statement of each of the common errors of law and added it as an overarching requirement for all errors of law.

14.15      This presents a difficulty for drafting. Which view of error of law should the drafting assume? TCEA s12(2)(a) takes the safe course by conferring an express power not to set aside a decision despite an error of law.

14.16      If the Upper Tribunal finds that the decision did involve the making of an error on a point of law, it has the powers given by section 12. It may refuse to set aside the decision, set aside the decision and remit the case for reconsideration, or set aside the decision and re-make it.

14.17      The Upper Tribunal has power under section 12(2)(a) not to set aside the First-tier Tribunal's decision aside despite the fact that it involved an error of law. However, if it exercises that power, it cannot make findings of fact. The power to do that (s12(4)(b)) only arises if the decision under appeal is set aside.

14.18      The possible forms of decision are not comprehensively stated. TCEA does not use the concept of dismissing an appeal or stipulate when it is appropriate to do so. However, this is the only form of decision available if the tribunal does not find that the decision under appeal involved the making of an error on a point of law. It is also the only form available if the tribunal does not have jurisdiction to hear the appeal.

14.19      The Upper Tribunal has no power on an appeal to give a declaration.[14] However, the legal position can be made clear in the tribunal's reasons, in

---

13   [2005] EWCA Civ 982.
14   *London Borough of Camden v FG* [2010] UKUT 249 (AAC) at [81].

effect providing a declaration in narrative form. This approach has been taken by the courts[15] and the Upper Tribunal.[16]

14.20　It is not necessary to deal with every ground of appeal in order to set aside a decision.[17]

## Evidence

14.21　In *VH v Suffolk County Council*,[18] the judge explained when additional evidence would be relevant on an appeal before the Upper Tribunal:

> The first question for the Upper Tribunal under this section is: did the making of the First-tier Tribunal's decision involve the making of an error on a point of law? The Upper Tribunal must answer this question on the evidence that was before the First-tier Tribunal. A tribunal cannot go wrong in law by failing to take account of evidence that was not before it. See the decisions of the Social Security Commissioner in *R(S) 1/88* at [3] and of Underhill J in *R (S) v Hertfordshire County Council* [2006] EWHC 328 (Admin) at [25]. If the answer to this question is 'no', the Upper Tribunal's only power is to dismiss the appeal. If the answer is 'yes', a second question arises.
>
> The second question is: how should the tribunal dispose of the case? There are three options: (a) leave the First-tier Tribunal's decision in place; (b) remit the case to the First-tier Tribunal; (c) re-make the decision. The tribunal may take account of additional evidence in order to decide which form of disposal is appropriate. If it decides to re-make the decision, evidence will also be needed of current circumstances.
>
> In practice, it can be difficult for parties to know when additional may be relevant. For example, an oral hearing of an application may also consider the appeal and disposal. The Upper Tribunal, and representatives for other parties, need to be flexible in receiving evidence whose ultimate relevance will depend on how the case proceeds. Forcing a party to produce the additional evidence only if and when it is required could lead to inefficiency and delay.[19]

## Set aside or not set aside?

14.22　If the Upper Tribunal finds that the decision under appeal involved the making of an error on a point of law, it may set it aside (s12(1) and (2)(a)). This is a power, not a duty. The tribunal may, but need not, set the decision aside.

14.23　　The scope of the discretion not to set aside will depend on how the tribunal interprets 'making of an error on a point of law'.[20] If it decides that this covers all errors of law, regardless of their possible impact on the outcome of the case below, this power will allow it to dismiss an appeal if the error could not have affected the outcome. However, if it decides that it

---

15　*R (Kay) v Commissioner of Police of the Metropolis* [2008] 1 WLR 2723 (despite the preference of Baroness Hale at [54]) and *Rolls-Royce plc v Unite the Union* [2010] 1 WLR 318 at [41]–[42].

16　*BB v South London and Maudsley NHS Foundation Trust* [2010] UKUT 32 (AAC) and *KF, MO and FF v Birmingham and Solihull NHS Mental Health Foundation Trust* [2010] UKUT 185 (AAC).

17　*Floe Telecom Ltd v Office of Communications* [2006] 4 All ER 688 at [28].

18　[2010] UKUT 203 (AAC).

19　[2010] UKUT 203 (AAC) at [7]–[9].

20　See chapter 4.

only covers errors that are material in the sense that they affected, or may have affected, the outcome, the scope of the discretion will be limited.

14.24    Whatever the interpretation, the discretion may be used if the decision on that issue is no longer of practical significance to the parties.

## Remit or re-make?

14.25   If the Upper Tribunal sets a decision aside on an appeal, it has two options: it has power either to remit for reconsideration or to re-make the decision under appeal (s12(1) and (2)(b)).

### Remitting

14.26   An appellate tribunal may only exercise its own powers. It cannot, having allowed an appeal, exercise powers that are conferred on the tribunal below.[21]

14.27    The Upper Tribunal may direct a complete rehearing or remit specific or limited issues.[22]

### Constitution

14.28   Section 12(3)(a) allows the Upper Tribunal to remit a case to a differently-constituted tribunal. However, the circumstances may allow the case to be remitted to a tribunal constituted in the same way.[23] This is compatible with article 6[24] and there is no objection in principle to the case being reheard by a judge who refused permission to appeal to the Upper Tribunal.[25]

14.29    The Employment Appeal Tribunal analysed the factors relevant to the exercise of this discretion in *Sinclair Roche & Temperley v Heard and Fellows*.[26] (i) What constitution would be the more proportional? (ii) Has the passage of time affected the ability of the same panel to hear the case? (iii) Is there a risk of bias, pre-judgment or partiality? (iv) If the decision under appeal was totally flawed, could the same panel could get it right this time? (v) Could the same panel put its previous decision and views to one side? (vi) Can the same panel be professional in its approach to a rehearing?

14.30    If the Upper Tribunal remits the case to the same tribunal, it is good practice to give alternative directions in case that tribunal cannot be re-assembled within a reasonable time.

21  *Floe Telecom Ltd v Office of Communications* [2006] 4 All ER 688.
22  *Aparau v Iceland Frozen Foods plc* [2000] ICR 341; *Jones (t/a Shamrock Coaches) v Department of Transport Welsh Traffic Area* (2005) *Times* 24 January; *Way v Poole Borough Council* (2007) *Times* 25 October; *Burrell v Micheldever Tyre Services Ltd* [2014[ EWCA Civ 716 at [20]. For an instance in which legislation permits a limited remittal to the Secretary of State, see *R (Perrett) v Secretary of State for Communities and Local Government* [2010] 2 All ER 578.
23  *Secretary of State for the Home Department v AF (No 2)* [2008] 2 All ER 67; *Burrell v Micheldever Tyre Services Ltd* [2014[ EWCA Civ 716 at [20].
24  *Jones (t/a Shamrock Coaches) v Department of Transport Welsh Traffic Area* (2005) *Times* 24 January.
25  *Mahomed v Morris* (200) *Times* 3 February.
26  [2004] IRLR 763.

## Directions[27]

14.31   Section 12(2)(b)(i) requires the Upper Tribunal to give directions for the reconsideration of the case. These directions will be ones relating to the substantive law. Section 12(3)(b) allows the Upper Tribunal to give procedural directions in connection with the reconsideration of the case. This power is in addition to directions given under section 12(2)(b)(i). The procedural directions that are appropriate may vary from time to time and depend on such factors as the constitution of the tribunal for the rehearing and the nature of the parties' representation. By their nature, they will not be comprehensive and will only apply unless the First-tier Tribunal directs otherwise.

## Re-making

14.32   If the Upper Tribunal re-makes the decision, it has power only to make the decision that the First-tier Tribunal could make if it were re-making the decision, but it may make such findings of fact as it considers appropriate (s12(2)(b)(ii) and (4)).

14.33   The Upper Tribunal can only make the decision that the First-tier Tribunal could make if it were re-making the decision.[28] This affects the scope of the decision that the Upper Tribunal may make in two ways. First, it limits the Upper Tribunal to the powers that would be available to the First-tier Tribunal. But second, it allows the Upper Tribunal to take account of any change of circumstances, if that power would be available to the First-tier Tribunal.[29]

14.34   The Upper Tribunal may re-make the decision on the basis of the findings made by the First-tier Tribunal. The default position is that an appellate body should accept the findings made below unless they were not supported by the evidence or were clearly wrong.[30] However, the Upper Tribunal may make its own findings. These may be in addition to, or substitution for, those of the First-tier Tribunal. The Upper Tribunal is more likely to differ from the First-tier Tribunal in respect of inferences than findings of primary fact.[31]

14.35   In some jurisdictions, it is the general policy to direct a rehearing rather than make findings of fact and re-make a decision.[32] Under TCEA, the wide powers given to the Upper Tribunal suggest that a general policy is inappropriate.

---

27 On the different powers to give directions, see *Dransfield v the Information Commissioner and Devon County Council* [2013] UKUT 0550 (AAC) at [10].

28 This includes the power to vary the sanction imposed: *R (Chief Constable of Avon and Somerset Constabulary) v Police Appeals Tribunal* (2004) *Times* 11 February.

29 See chapter 4.

30 *P v Secretary of State for the Home Department* (2004) *Times* 14 December.

31 Viscount Simonds and Lord Morton in *Benmax v Austin Motor Co Ltd* [1955] AC 370 at 373–374 and 374.

32 This is the practice in employment: *Dobie v Burns International Security Services (UK) Ltd* [1984] ICR 812 at 818; *Elmbridge Housing Trust v O'Donoghue* [2004] EWCA Civ 939; (2004) *Times* 24 June. And in immigration: *P v Secretary of State for the Home Department* [2005] Imm AR 84.

14.36     The decision whether to remit a case or re-make a decision is discretionary.[33] Among the relevant factors are those listed below.

### Evidence

14.37   The Upper Tribunal cannot substitute a decision unless it has the necessary evidence. If it is to rely on the evidence recorded by the First-tier Tribunal, it must be sure that the record is complete and that all relevant evidence was obtained. If not, it must obtain the evidence for itself in order to re-make the decision. As the Upper Tribunal is likely to be located more centrally than the First-tier Tribunal, it may be more convenient for this evidence to be obtained at a rehearing.

### Change of circumstances

14.38   If the tribunal at the rehearing is able to take account of up-to-date circumstances, changes in those circumstances will be relevant to the disposal of the appeal.[34]

### Knowledge and experience

14.39   The panel members of the First-tier Tribunal may[35] have knowledge, experience or expertise that is not available, or so readily available, to the Upper Tribunal. If the evidence is not complete, this factor may indicate a rehearing. Even if the evidence is complete, the panel members of the First-tier Tribunal may be better able to assess it. If local knowledge is required or helpful, a rehearing is the better course.

### Clear direction on the law

14.40   The ease with which the Upper Tribunal can direct the First-tier Tribunal on the law to be applied is a further factor. If the law is clear or can be stated clearly, a rehearing is possible. However, the law may be particularly difficult to state clearly, perhaps without having specific findings on which to base the statement. If so, it may be better to re-make the decision rather remit the case to the First-tier Tribunal with inadequate directions for reconsideration.

### Precedent status

14.41   There can be a danger in the Upper Tribunal giving a decision on the facts. The status of that tribunal and the publication of its decisions may create the impression that the decision on the facts has value as a precedent. This false impression can cause problems for the First-tier Tribunal and decision-makers, especially if the decision is relied on by representatives.

---

33  This was conceded to the House of Lords in *Saber v Secretary of State for the Home Department* [2008] 3 All ER 97 at [10].
34  *Saber v Secretary of State for the Home Department* [2008] 3 All ER 97.
35  *Burrell v Micheldever Tyre Services Ltd* [2014[ EWCA Civ 716 at [17].

*Time considerations*

14.42   The possibility of a further appeal may suggest re-making a decision in order to bring the proceedings to an end. Also, the size of the respective workloads of the First-tier and Upper Tribunals may indicate whether directing a rehearing or re-making a decision is more appropriate.

*Inadequacy of reasons and materiality*

14.43   According to Lord Nicholls in *Shamoon v Chief Constable of the Royal Ulster Constabulary*:[36]

> Insufficiency of reasons ordinarily leads to the case being remitted for a rehearing ... Such a direction is not appropriate if there was no evidence on which a properly directed tribunal could have upheld the claimant's application.

*Procedural errors*

14.44   Procedural errors that amount to an error of law but have not affected the outcome should not usually justify a rehearing.

## Appeals to the Court of Appeal under TCEA

14.45   The powers of the Court of Appeal under section 14 on appeal against a decision of the Upper Tribunal are the same as for the Upper Tribunal under section 12.

## Appeals under other legislation

14.46   The legislation providing for an appeal may take various forms.

14.47   The legislation may provide merely for an appeal without specifying any form that the decision may take. This suggests, depending on the context, that the decision on appeal may take any form that the decision-maker could have given. In *R(IB) 2/04*, a Tribunal of Commissioners said of such a provision:[37]

> It is accepted by both Counsel – and, indeed, it is universally accepted, that appeal tribunals have some powers of decision, such as to substitute the proper decision on a claim in allowing an appeal against an initial decision on a claim. Since these powers must be found by a process of implication, in our view the absence of express statutory powers for an appeal tribunal in any particular instance can have little, if any, significance.

Another power that must always be implied is to dismiss the appeal.

14.48   The legislation, having provided for an appeal, may specify the forms that a decision may take and the grounds on which or circumstances in which each may be made. For example: section 100B(2) of the Taxes Management Act 1970 sets out the circumstances in which various forms of decision must be given. Depending on the context, these different forms of legislation may or may not be narrower than merely providing for an

---

36   [2003] ICR 337 at [15].
37   *R(IB) 2/04* at [18].

appeal. At the least, they provide a framework of language for expressing the tribunal's decision.

## Referrals

14.49   The forms of decision that may be made on a referral depend on the nature of the referral.

14.50     If no decision has yet been taken, the tribunal takes the decision as for the first time.

14.51     If a decision has been taken and referred, the legislation may specify the forms that the decision may take. For example: section 109(3) of the Social Security Act 1975 provided that a medical appeal tribunal 'may confirm, reverse or vary the decision in whole or in part as on an appeal'.[38]

## Consent orders

14.52   A tribunal may have power to make a consent order incorporating the agreement of the parties. This may be given by statute or by the rules of procedure.

### The power to make a consent order

14.53   There is no specific enabling power that authorises the making of consent orders. However, the rules of procedure provide for this. The First-tier Tribunal and the Upper Tribunal have power to make a consent order if they consider it appropriate to do so and need not give reasons if they do so. UTR r39 is illustrative:[39]

> (1) The Upper Tribunal may, at the request of the parties but only if it considers it appropriate, make a consent order disposing of the proceedings and making such other appropriate provision as the parties have agreed.
> (2) Notwithstanding any other provision of these Rules, the Upper Tribunal need not hold a hearing before making an order under paragraph (1), or provide reasons for the order.

14.54   The power can only be exercised in order to dispose of the proceedings. It does not authorise a Tomlin order, which merely stays the proceedings on terms set out in the Schedule.[40]

14.55     The designation as an order rather than a decision may be significant, because other provisions of UTR refer only to decisions. It is not clear if a consent order is a decision for other purposes, either at all or in respect of those matters that the tribunal has no jurisdiction to decide. For example: is it a decision for the purposes of an appeal under TCEA ss11 or 13?

---

38  Re-enacted as Social Security Administration Act 1992 s46(3) and now repealed by Social Security Act 1998 s86(2) and Sch 8. This provision dealt with references, but by implication also set out the possible forms of decision on an appeal.

39  See also: GRC Rules r37; HESC Rules r29 (other than mental health cases); PC Rules r35; SEC Rules r32; Tax Rules r34; WPAFC Rules r30. There is no equivalent power in IAC Rules.

40  *Community Care North East v Durham County Council* [2010] 4 All ER 733 at [25].

## Jurisdiction to make a particular order

14.56 The power to make a consent order is conferred on the First-tier Tribunal and the Upper Tribunal by the rules of procedure. The rules may not create a jurisdiction which does not otherwise exist.[41]

14.57 Accordingly, a tribunal has no jurisdiction to make a consent order that is, in its terms, outside its jurisdiction. For example: a consent order by a tribunal making a declaration of incompatibility under the Human Rights Act 1998 would be outside its jurisdiction.

14.58 Likewise, a tribunal should not make a consent order that it would not be authorised to make on the facts and circumstances of the case. This is subject to provision to the contrary, as legislation may allow a tribunal to make an order even if it would not otherwise do so. It may even require it to do so: section 13(3) of the Social Security Act 1998 and section 23A(3) of the Child Support Act 1991 require a First-tier Tribunal to set aside its decision if the parties express the view that it was erroneous in law, even if it does not agree.

14.59 In theory, a tribunal should not make an order that the facts and circumstances do not allow. In practice, however, without the knowledge of the facts or assumptions on which the parties have reached their agreement, the tribunal may not know whether the decision was one that it was permissible to make.

14.60 Otherwise, there are two justifications for a consent order containing matters that the tribunal has no jurisdiction to decide. First, the matters may be included as undertakings. Second, they may record a concession that a decision-maker may make outside the context of the proceedings, such as agreeing to undertake a reconsideration. However, the First-tier Tribunal does not have power to enforce the undertaking or punish a party for failing to comply. It is not clear whether the Upper Tribunal may do so under TCEA s25.

14.61 If the consent order is to be effective, it must provide for the disposal or future conduct of the proceedings. If it contains a decision that is within the tribunal's jurisdiction that disposes of the proceedings, that will be sufficient. Otherwise, the parties must agree to the proceedings being stayed, withdrawn or dismissed.

## Consent orders based on contract

14.62 An order may be described as made 'by consent'. Those words are ambiguous. The two meanings and their significance were explained by Lord Denning MR in *Siebe Gorman and Co Ltd v Pneupac Ltd*:[42]

> There are two meanings to the words 'by consent' . . . One meaning is this: the words 'by consent' may evidence a real contract between the parties. In such a case the court will only interfere with such an order on the same grounds as it would with any other contract. The other meaning is this: the words 'by consent' may mean 'the parties hereto not objecting'. In such a case there is no real contract between the parties. The order can be altered

41 Diplock LJ in *Garthwaite v Garthwaite* [1964] P 356 at 395.
42 [1982] 1 WLR 185.

or varied by the court in the same circumstances as any other order that is made by the court without the consent of the parties.[43]

The former is the technical meaning.[44]

14.63　Until a contractual compromise is given effect to in a consent order, its enforcement is a matter of contract. Thereafter, the contract is replaced by the consent order. It is that order that must be enforced or challenged, not the contract that it embodied. In *de Lasala v de Lasala*,[45] the Privy Council set out the following principles:

- once a court order has been made, it determines the legal effect of the parties' agreement;[46]
- if the order is not complied with, the proper course is to seek to enforce that order.[47] The order may be enforceable by the tribunal itself. This is rare; most tribunals do not have power to enforce their own orders. Or the order may be enforceable as if it were a court order. This is the position under TCEA. Section 27 provides that sums payable pursuant to a decision are recoverable as if they were payable under a court order. Or the order may have a liberty to apply provision. This will allow the case to be brought back before the tribunal, although this cannot give the tribunal jurisdiction to enforce the order;
- the proper ways to challenge an order are by appeal or by an action to set it aside.[48]

14.64　Once made, a consent order is binding between the parties and is of no effect on anyone else.[49]

## Consent orders not based on contract

14.65　If the parties are not able to make their agreement the subject of an enforceable contract, it may nonetheless have effect, for example under the law of legitimate expectation.

## Undertakings

14.66　These are appropriate for matters over which the court or tribunal has no jurisdiction.[50] They do not usually form part of the order, but they are binding as if they were, even if they are outside the tribunal's jurisdiction[51] Their enforcement is a matter of punishment, not compensation. As Buckley J explained in *Re Hudson*:[52]

43　[1982] 1 WLR 185 at 189.
44　Lord Greene MR in *Chandless-Chandless v Nicholson* [1942] 2 KB 321 at 324.
45　[1980] AC 546.
46　[1980] AC 546 at 560.
47　[1980] AC 546 at 560.
48　[1980] AC 546 at 561. On the practicalities, see Ormrod LJ in *Robinson v Robinson* [1982] 1 WLR 786.
49　*R(FC) 1/97* at [28].
50　Lord Brandon in *Jenkins v Livesey* [1985] AC 424 at 444.
51　*B v Home Office* [2012] 4 All ER 276 at [133] and [136].
52　[1966] Ch 209.

An undertaking, however, is not an order. It is true that an undertaking to do or to abstain from doing something other than payment of money may have the same effect as a mandatory or a restrictive injunction; for a breach of such an undertaking, like a breach of an injunction, exposes the culprit to the risk of imprisonment or possibly of sequestration or a fine. These are penal sanctions aimed at enforcing compliance with either a promise made to the court or an order of the court, as the case may be. They are not remedies the purpose of which is to compensate some other party for damage he has suffered as the result of the breach or for recovering any property or enforcing any right of his.[53]

14.67 This is so even if the undertaking is a condition precedent to the operation of the consent order.[54] However, the undertaking may form part of a contract between the parties, collateral to the terms of the order.[55] And for some limited purposes it may be equivalent to an order.[56]

14.68 Like a court, the Upper Tribunal has residual discretion in exceptional circumstances to release a party from an undertaking.[57]

## Appropriate

14.69 It is the making of the order, rather than the order itself, that has to be appropriate. However, the contents of the order will be relevant to whether it is appropriate to make it.

14.70 'Appropriate' is not defined. What is appropriate must depend on the circumstances of the particular case.

14.71 One relevant factor is the distinction drawn by the Bowman Committee in its *Review of the Court of Appeal (Civil Division)* of September 1997, between the public and private purposes of an appeal:

> There is a private and a public purpose of appeals in civil cases.
>
> The private purpose is to correct an error, unfairness or wrong exercise of discretion which has led to an unjust result.
>
> The public purpose is to ensure public confidence in the administration of justice and, in appropriate cases, to:
> - clarify and develop the law, practice and procedure; and
> - help maintain the standards of first instance courts and tribunals.[58]

The making of a consent order is a private purpose and is not appropriate as a means of fulfilling the public purpose. The features of the case will determine whether there is a public element in the case or in the order that the parties have agreed. If there is, that is an indication that it may not be appropriate to make the order.

53 [1966] Ch 209 at 213–214.
54 *Thwaite v Thwaite* [1982] Fam 1.
55 Buckley J in *Re Hudson* [1966] Ch 209 at 213–214; *Independiente Ltd v Music Trading On-Line (HK) Ltd* [2007] 4 All ER 736.
56 *Gandolfo v Gandolfo* [1981] QB 359; *Symmons v Symmons* [1993] 1 FLR 317.
57 *B v Home Office* [2012] 4 All ER 276 at [133] n67.
58 In chapter 1.

## Challenging a consent order

14.72   The rules of procedure contain powers to correct, set aside, review and give permission to appeal against a 'decision'. These apply to the extent that the consent order is, or embodies, a decision.

14.73   Apart from these provisions, the courts have laid down some general principles on the circumstances in which a consent order may be challenged.

14.74   A consent order may be challenged on the grounds of fraud or mistake.[59] If the order could only be made upon enquiry by the tribunal into all the circumstances, it can be set aside for lack of full and frank disclosure by the parties,[60] provided that a substantially different order would have made if the full circumstances had been known.[61]

14.75   It is theoretically possible for a consent order to be void for uncertainty. However, in practice the courts will overcome difficulties of interpretation in working out or clarifying an order.[62]

14.76   In *Eden v Humphries & Glasgow Ltd*,[63] the Employment Appeal Tribunal held that a consent order based on a contract could only be set aside if the underlying contract were also set aside. As the Tribunal had no power over the parties' contract, it could not set aside the order withdrawing the appeal. This is difficult to reconcile with the principle that the consent order replaces the contract.[64]

## Authority to agree to a consent order

14.77   A representative may have actual or apparent authority to agree to a consent order. Solicitors have apparent authority. Accordingly, if a representative with apparent authority agrees to a consent order, it will bind the party even if the representative had no actual authority to do so.[65]

## Costs

14.78   If the consent order is made in a jurisdiction in which costs may be awarded, the usual approach would be an order that no costs be paid.[66]

## Contempt

14.79   If a consent order is made on the basis of false statements by one of the parties, that party may be guilty of contempt.[67]

---

59   *de Lasala v de Lasala* [1980] AC 546 at 561.
60   Lord Brandon in *Jenkins v Livesey* [1985] AC 424 at 438, 440 and 442.
61   [1985] AC 424 per Lord Brandon at 445.
62   *Scammell v Dicker* [2005] 3 All ER 838.
63   [1981] ICR 183.
64   *de Lasala v de Lasala* [1980] AC 546.
65   *Times Newspapers Ltd v Fitt* [1981] ICR 637.
66   *Re F (Family Proceedings: Costs)* [2008] 2 FLR 1662 at [12].
67   *Kirk v Walton* [2009] 1 All ER 257.

# Standard and burden of proof

## The burdens and standard of proof

14.80   There are two burdens of proof: the legal burden and the evidential burden. The incidence of a burden identifies the party who bears that burden. The incidence of the legal burden identifies the party who takes the consequence that an issue cannot be established. The standard of proof determines the degree of certainty or confidence with which the facts, and perhaps any related matters of judgment,[68] relevant to an issue have to be established. The incidence of the evidential burden identifies the party who, on the evidence available at any particular stage of the proceedings, will fail on an issue in the absence of further evidence.

## Statutory interpretation

14.81   In the case of a statutory provision, the incidence of the burdens of proof and the requisite standard of proof are determined by statutory interpretation. The language of the legislation will be important. However, some expressions do not indicate a standard of proof. Rather they indicate the nature and quality of the evidence necessary to satisfy that standard. So the word 'convincingly' does not indicate a standard.[69] The rule in *Pepper v Hart*[70] can be used to allow reliance on Parliamentary statements on the issue.[71]

## The legal burden

14.82   This burden determines the person who bears the risk if a case is not proved to the requisite standard.[72] It is applied at the end of the case[73] and does not vary from one party to another during the hearing.

14.83   There is only one burden on an issue. The tribunal has to decide whether that burden has been discharged. If it is not discharged, the case is not proven on that issue and the party who bears the burden loses on that issue. The tribunal's only duty is to decide whether the party has discharged the burden on the issue. It is not under a duty to come to a definite conclusion on the truth of the matter. It is not even under a duty to chose between the rival contentions of the parties, although the case is likely to have been presented as a contest between rival accounts. In *Rhesa Shipping Co SA v Edmunds*,[74] the House of Lords was concerned with an insurance claim following the loss of a ship at sea. The parties put forward different explanations for the loss. The trial judge found the owners' explanation to be extremely improbable and that of the insurer to be virtually impossible. He decided in favour of the owners. The House of Lords

---

68   *R (N) v Mental Health Review Tribunal (Northern Region)* [2006] QB 468 at [99]–[104].
69   *R (P) v West London Youth Court* [2006] 1 WLR 1219 at [23].
70   [1993] AC 593.
71   *Chief Constable of Merseyside Police v Harrison* [2007] QB 79.
72   For the standard, see below at para 14.105 onwards.
73   If the case is heard in stages, at the end of the stage in which the issue is determined.
74   [1985] 1 WLR 948.

decided that the judge had overlooked the significance of the burden. Lord Brandon emphasised the significance of the burden of proof:

> ... the burden of proving, on a balance of probabilities, that the ship was lost by perils of the seas is and remains throughout on the ship owners. Although it is open to the underwriters to suggest and seek to prove some other cause of loss, against which the ship was not insured, there is no obligation on them to do so. Moreover, if they chose to do so, there is no obligation on them to prove, even on the balance of probabilities, the truth of their alternative case.[75]

The judge should have found against the owners, because they had not discharged the legal burden of showing that the loss of their ship was covered by their policy of insurance.

## The relevance of the burden

14.84  The legal burden on an issue is only relevant if the tribunal is unable to make findings of fact relevant to that issue on the requisite standard.[76] As Viscount Dunedin explained in *Robins v National Trust Co Ltd*:[77]

> But onus as a determining factor of the whole case can only arise if the tribunal finds the evidence pro and con so evenly balanced that it can come to no such conclusion. Then the onus will determine the matter.[78]

14.85  Once the facts have been found, the role of the burden ceases. As Holman J explained in *Pabari v Secretary of State for Work and Pensions*:[79]

> Once the facts have been established, it is not in my view helpful or appropriate to speak of a burden of proof. The task of the decision-maker is simply to make a correct legal analysis, and then correctly to apply the law to, and make a judgment about, the facts so established.

14.86  There is no burden in judicial review proceedings on an issue of precedent fact. The court must decide this in its inquisitorial role.[80]

## The incidence of the burden

14.87  This is ultimately a matter of policy, either of the common law or as expressed in legislation. However, some principles are discernible.

14.88     A basic principle is that the legal burden is on the party who seeks to disturb the status quo at the time of the case. If a claim is made for a right, the burden is on the claimant. If a right has been conferred or a penalty has been imposed, that is the status quo and the burden is on the person seeking to change it. In *Kataria v Essex Strategic Health Authority*,[81] the issue was whether a disqualification should be removed from a medical practitioner. Stanley Burnton J set out the responsibility of the parties:[82]

---

75  [1985] 1 WLR 948 at 951.
76  On the standard, see below at para 14.102 onwards.
77  [1927] AC 515.
78  [1927] AC 515 at 520. See also Lord Thankerton in *Watt v Thomas* [1947] AC 484 at 487.
79  [2005] 1 All ER 287 at [27].
80  *R (CJ) v Cardiff City Council* [2012] 2 All ER 836.
81  [2004] 3 All ER 572.
82  [2004] 3 All ER 572 at [41].

The practitioner makes a request for a review under section 49N of a national disqualification, which but for that request would continue to have effect. If he puts no evidence or material before the FHSAA, his request must be rejected, i.e. the tribunal must confirm the disqualification. It follows that he bears the onus of establishing that the disqualification should be revoked.[83] However, the respondent to his request will bear the onus of proving any facts it asserts, such as any alleged misconduct of the practitioner since the date of his disqualification. Once the tribunal has determined the facts relevant to its decision, the question for the tribunal in an efficiency case (see section 49F(2)) is whether the revocation of the disqualification would be prejudicial to the efficiency of the services in question. Once the facts have been found, the answer to that question will rarely depend on the onus one way or the other.

14.89 However, the burden of proving an exception is on the party who seeks to rely on that exception. In *Kerr v Department for Social Development*,[84] Lord Hope said:

> It is also a general rule that he who desires to take advantage of an exception must bring himself within the provisions of the exception.

14.90 In deciding whether a provision constitutes an exception, it is permissible to take account of the wording of the provision and its legislative history.[85]

14.91 If a case is heard completely afresh on appeal, the legal burden on the appeal is as it was below. This was explained by Lord Goddard CJ in *Drover v Rugman*,[86] when explaining the procedure on appeal from petty sessions to quarter sessions:

> When a case goes to quarter sessions it is reheard; the person seeking an order proves his case over again.[87]

14.92 The courts are reluctant to require a party to prove a negative. In *Joseph Constantine Steamship Line Ltd v Imperial Smelting Corporation Ltd*,[88] Viscount Maugham said that the proposition:

> . . . was founded on considerations of good sense and it should not be departed from without strong reasons.[89]

Lord Russell said that:

> . . . the proving of a negative, a task always difficult and often impossible, would be a most exceptional burden to impose on a litigant.[90]

And Lord Wright described the imposition of a burden to prove a negative as unusual and said that the exceptions were so few and of such a nature as to emphasise the general rule.[91]

---

83 The Chief Commissioner took the same approach in relation to review decisions in *R(I) 1/71* at [16].
84 [2004] 1 WLR 1372 at [16].
85 [2004] 1 WLR 1372 per Baroness Hale at [68].
86 [1951] 1 KB 380.
87 [1951] 1 KB 380 at 382.
88 [1942] AC 154.
89 [1942] AC 154 at 174.
90 [1942] AC 154 at 177.
91 [1942] AC 154 at 194.

14.93 It is also sometimes said that the burden lies on the person who has exclusive knowledge of the facts. The House of Lords' analysis in *Kerr v Department for Social Development*[92] provides some support for this. But so far as the traditional analysis of the burden of proof is concerned, it is not correct. The correct position was explained by Lawton LJ in *R v Edwards*:[93]

> There is not, and never has been, a general rule of law that the mere fact that a matter lies within the knowledge of the defendant is sufficient to cast the onus on him. If there was any such rule, anyone charged with doing an unlawful act with a specified intent would find himself having to prove his innocence because if there ever was a matter which could be said to be peculiarly within a person's knowledge it is the state of his own mind. Such rule as there is relating to negative averments in informations and indictments developed from the rules for pleading provisos and exceptions in statutes and is limited in its application.[94]

The Court of Appeal decided that if an offence was subject to an exception, it was for the defendant to show that the exception applied, not for the prosecution to prove that it did not.[95]

14.94 In *R v Hunt*,[96] the House of Lords decided that the ease of discharging the burden was a relevant factor in interpreting a legislative provision, especially in a criminal case. Lord Griffiths referred to:

> ... practical considerations affecting the burden of proof and, in particular, the ease or difficulty that the respective parties would encounter in discharging the burden. I regard this last consideration as one of great importance for surely Parliament can never lightly be taken to have intended to impose an onerous duty on a defendant to prove his innocence in a criminal case, and a court should be very slow to draw any such inference from the language of a statute.[97]

14.95 The incidence of the burden may depend on the other issues in the case. In *Marshall v Commission for Social Care Inspection*,[98] two issues arose: (i) the person's fitness to carry on a care home; and (ii) whether the registration of her home should be cancelled. If the issues arise separately, the burden on (i) is on the individual and the burden on (ii) is on the Commission. In *Marshall*, both issues arose and the judge held that the burden was on the individual on both issues, because the facts relevant to each issue were potentially inextricably linked.

## Legislation

14.96 Legislation may allocate the burden expressly[99] or by implication.[100] It is sometimes said that statute may also provide that there is no burden on an issue.[101] However, in so far as a provision requires proof of facts, one

92 [2004] 1 WLR 1372.
93 [1975] QB 27.
94 [1975] QB 27 at 35.
95 [1975] QB 27 at 40.
96 [1987] AC 352.
97 [1987] AC 352 at 374.
98 [2009] EWHC 1286 (Admin).
99 Equality Act 2010 s136 is an example.
100 Lord Griffiths in *R v Hunt* [1987] AC 352 at 374.
101 Employment Rights Act 1996 s98(4)(b) is said to be an example.

party will always bear the risk that the relevant facts cannot be established on the evidence available.

### The order of proceedings

14.97   The incidence of the burden does not necessarily determine the order in which the parties are heard. That is a matter of procedure for the tribunal to determine. The order in which the parties are heard may or may not reflect the legal burden of proof, depending on the extent to which the tribunal follows the court model of procedure.

## The evidential burden

14.98   This burden determines who has to produce (further) evidence in order to succeed on a particular issue. Its incidence may vary from party to party during the hearing, depending on the state of the evidence at any particular time. It follows that it may or may not be on the same person who has the legal burden.

14.99   The incidence of this burden may also be determined by legislation.[102] That interpretation may be required in order to avoid a violation of a Convention right.[103]

14.100   Otherwise, the incidence is determined by asking which party would succeed if no further evidence were produced. The operation of this burden and the danger involved in its use were explained by Browne-Wilkinson V-C in *Brady v Group Lotus Cars Cos plc*:[104]

> That [legal] burden of proof in technical terms stays throughout where it starts. If, on the other hand, evidence is given which in the absence of other evidence or other factors would be sufficient to discharge the burden, then as a matter of ordinary common sense and judicial method the tribunal will decide that the burden of proof has been discharged. That is all that is meant by a shift in the evidential burden. In my experience, every time the phrase 'evidential burden' is used it leads to error, particularly when the tribunal in question consists of laymen; for myself I think it could well be done without.[105]

14.101   In theory, the burden is determined by the state of the evidence as a whole. However, one part of the evidence may be sufficiently probative that in practice the other party must produce evidence to counter it. An example of this occurred in *Pant v Secretary of State for the Home Department*.[106] The Secretary of State alleged that a document produced by an asylum seeker was not genuine. The document was apparently genuine. Scott Baker LJ said that although the evidence had to be assessed as a whole, a party who

---

102   See the distribution of burdens in discrimination cases analysed by the Court of Appeal in *Igen Ltd (formerly Leeds Careers Guidance) v Wong* [2005] ICR 931 at 18.

103   See the House of Lords' analysis in *R v Lambert* [2002] 2 AC 545.

104   [1987] 2 All ER 674.

105   [1987] 2 All ER 674 at 686–687. See also Mustill LJ in the same case in the Court of Appeal: [1987] 3 All ER 1050 at 1059.

106   [2003] EWCA Civ 1964; (2003) *Times* 26 November.

alleged that an apparently genuine document was not had in practice a burden of producing evidence to support the allegation.[107]

## The role of the burden

14.102   The incidence of this burden tracks the state of each party's case as the hearing proceeds. It is relevant for two purposes.

14.103   Its first purpose is to identify that further evidence is needed on a particular point. This is useful for parties who are not professionally represented. They may not realise the full import of the evidence against them until this becomes clearer during the hearing. If the tribunal takes account of the incidence of this burden, it will (in applying the enabling and inquisitorial approaches) be able to ensure that the party has understood the significance of the evidence produced so far and investigate whether there is other relevant evidence available.

14.104   The second purpose of this burden is to identify the stage of the proceedings at which particular evidence should be produced. This is useful in courts or tribunals in which proceedings follow a rigid order, if it is relevant to know when particular evidence should be produced. The burden will determine what questions need to be asked in cross-examination or re-examination of witnesses. It will also determine for the party whose case is presented first the evidence that must be available in order to avoid the case being determined without hearing from the other party.[108] But in most tribunals, the order of presentation of evidence is likely to be flexible and the incidence of this burden less relevant for this purpose.

## The standard of proof

14.105   The standard of proof[109] is the degree of likelihood with which an issue must be established. It is seldom possible to establish facts with certainty. In practice, the law usually has to be applied to facts established on the basis of probability rather than certainty.[110] Probability is the measure of confidence that a tribunal has in making its findings of fact.

14.106   British common law recognises only two standards: the civil standard and the criminal standard.[111] The legislative context may exceptionally require a different standard.[112]

---

107  [2003] EWCA Civ 1964 at [23].

108  This is discouraged. See below and in chapter 12.

109  The courts sometimes speak of persuasion rather than proof: *R (N) v Mental Health Review Tribunal (Northern Region)* [2006] QB 468 at [100] and *Re B (Children) (Care Proceedings: Standard of Proof)* [2009] 1 AC 11 at [4].

110  See Lord Nicholls in *Re H (Minors) (Sexual Abuse: Standard of Proof)* [1996] AC 563 at 587.

111  *Re Doherty* [2008] 1 WLR 1499 at [23]; *Re B (Children) (Care Proceedings: Standard of Proof)* [2009] 1 AC 11 at [13].

112  So in the case of asylum, the claimant is required only to show a reasonable degree of likelihood of persecution: *R v Secretary of State for the Home Department ex p Sivakumaran* [1988] AC 958.

14.107　Tribunals will usually have to apply the civil standard.[113] This was described by Denning J in *Miller v Minister of Pensions*:[114]

> If the evidence is such that the tribunal can say: 'We think it more probable than not', the burden is discharged . . .[115]

14.108　The civil standard requires facts to be proved on the balance of probabilities. The evidence must do more than show that the facts are possible. It must also show that they are more than probable. It must show that they are more likely than not.

14.109　The civil standard also applies to civil penalties for dishonest or negligent tax returns.[116] It even applies if the issue arising in civil proceedings is whether an offence has been committed.[117] The difference between the standards has been reaffirmed in cases involving child protection and welfare. In *Re U and B (Serious Injury: Standard of Proof)*,[118] Butler-Sloss P said:

> There would appear to be no good reason to leap across a division, on the one hand, between crime and preventative measures taken to restrain defendants for the benefit of the community and, on the other hand, wholly different considerations of child protection and child welfare . . .

The difference also has a significance in assessing conflicting Convention rights. The civil standard is more suited to this exercise than the criminal standard.[119]

14.110　Exceptionally, a tribunal may have to apply the criminal standard, which requires proof beyond reasonable doubt.

### Facts founding inferences

14.111　Facts from which inferences are drawn have to be proved to the balance of probabilities, not a lesser standard.[120]

### Facts and judgment

14.112　The standard only applies to facts. It does not apply to matters of judgment. This distinction was drawn in *Secretary of State for the Home Department v Rehman*.[121] The House of Lords was concerned with whether there was a threat to national security. Lord Hoffmann said:

> In any case, I agree with the Court of Appeal that the whole concept of standard of proof is not particularly helpful in a case such as the present.

---

113　For exceptions see articles 40(3) and 41(5) of the Naval, Military and Air Forces Etc. (Disablement and Death) Service Pensions Order 2006.

114　[1947] 2 All ER 372.

115　[1947] 2 All ER 372 at 374.

116　*Revenue and Customs Commissioners v Khawaja* [2009] 1 WLR 398.

117　*Hornal v Neuberger Products Ltd* [1957] 1 QB 247 (fraud) and *Re Dellow's Will Trusts* [1964] 1 WLR 451 (felonious killing).

118　[2004] 2 FLR 263 at [13].

119　Tugendhat J in *Hipgrave v Jones* [2005] 2 FLR 174 at [53].

120　This was the majority view of the House of Lords in *Re H (Minors) (Sexual Abuse: Standard of Proof)* [1996] AC 563.

121　[2003] 1 AC 153. See also Lord Cooke in *Higgs v Minister of National Security* [2000] 2 AC 228 at 260; Lord Bingham in *R v Lichniak* [2003] 1 AC 903 at [16]; Munby J in *R (DJ) v Mental Health Review Tribunal* (2005) *Times* 18 April.

In a criminal or civil trial in which the issue is whether a given event happened, it is sensible to say that one is sure that it did, or that one thinks it
more likely than not that it did. But the question in the present case is not
whether a given event happened but the extent of future risk, this depends
upon an evaluation of the evidence of the appellant's conduct against a
broad range of facts with which they may interact.[122]

14.113   However, the standard of proof may be relevant in relation to some aspects
of judgment. It will be relevant if an issue involves both a determination of
facts and an exercise of judgment. In *R (N) v Mental Health Review Tribunal (Northern Region)*,[123] the Court of Appeal decided[124] that there could be
gradations of persuasion on issues of judgment and that it was artificial to
distinguish between fact and judgment on issues that are mixed ones of
fact and evaluation. The Court concluded:[125]

We also think it likely that the tribunal's task will be made easier if, instead
of dividing up the issues into matters that are susceptible to proof to a
defined standard and those that are not, it approaches the entire range of
issues by reference to the standard of proof on the balance of probabilities,
whilst recognising that in practice the standard of proof will have a much
more important part to play in the determination of disputed issues of fact
than it will generally have in matters of judgment as to appropriateness and
necessity.

14.114   However, the distinction between fact and judgment was maintained, without reference to that case, by the Court of Appeal in *Thompstone v Tameside
& Glossop Acute Services NHS Trust*,[126] the Court was there concerned with
the duty to consider whether to make a periodical payments order in a personal injuries case. It decided that the legal burden and standard of proof
were not appropriate to the exercise, although an evidential burden did
apply to any party asserting a matter of fact to prove that fact to the normal
standard.[127]

14.115      The standard may also be applied to the likelihood of facts occurring in
the future and in making that assessment the tribunal may be entitled, or
required, to take account of past facts that have been established to a lower
standard than the civil burden. Lord Nicholls explained the basic approach
in *Re O (Minors) (Care: Preliminary Hearing)*.[128] The issue concerned the
assessment of the risk of future harm to a child. Lord Nicholls said:[129]

The same broad principle is applicable when courts or tribunals peer into
the future and assess the likelihood that a particular event will occur. This
is an inherently imprecise exercise, so far as human conduct is concerned.
In theory it is a different exercise from deciding whether somebody did or
did not do something in the past. Whether or not an alleged event occurred
in the past raises a question of proof. In truth, the event either happened or
not. That is not so with a future forecast. The future has not happened, and

122 [2003] 1 AC 153 at [56].
123 [2006] QB 468.
124 [2006] QB 468 at [99]–[104].
125 [2006] QB 468.
126 [2008] 1 WLR 2207.
127 [2008] 1 WLR 2207 at [55] and [66]–[68].
128 [2004] 1 AC 523.
129 [2004] 1 AC 523 at [12]–[13].

future human conduct is never certain. But in practice, the past is often as uncertain as the future. The judge cannot know for certain what happened and can only assess the degree of likelihood that something happened. The same is true of the future. The decision maker has to assess the degree of likelihood that an inherently uncertain event will occur. The degree of likelihood – beyond reasonable doubt, more probable than not, real possibility and so on – required in any particular legal context raises a question of legal policy.

Here again, the policy decision on the requisite degree of likelihood is a separate question from the policy decision on the matters the court or tribunal may take into account. As to the latter, the matters a decision-maker may take into account are normally bounded only by the need for them to be relevant, that is, they must be such that, to greater or lesser extent, they will assist the decision-maker in reaching a rational conclusion. The context may, indeed, require that this principle should apply in its full width. ... The legal context may permit, or require, the decision-maker to take into account a real possibility that a past event occurred, or even a mere possibility. Rationality does not require that only past events established on a balance of probabilities can be taken into account. Or the context may require otherwise. The range of matters the decision-maker may take into account when carrying out this exercise depends upon the context. This, again, is a question of legal policy, not logic.

### Applied to the issue as a whole

14.116 The standard of proof must be applied to the evidence on an issue as a whole, not to individual pieces of evidence. This was explained by Sedley LJ in *Karanakaran v Secretary of State for the Home Department:*[130]

The civil standard of proof, which treats anything which probably happened as having definitely happened, is part of a pragmatic legal fiction. It has no logical bearing on the assessment of the likelihood of future events or (by parity of reasoning) the quality of past ones. It is true that in general legal process partitions its material so as to segregate past events and apply the civil standard of proof to them: so that liability for negligence will depend on a probabilistic conclusion as to what happened. But this is by no means the whole process of reasoning. In a negligence case, for example, the question will arise whether what happened was reasonably foreseeable. There is no rational means of determining this on a balance of probabilities: the court will consider the evidence, including its findings as to past facts, and answer the question as posed. More importantly, and more relevantly, a civil judge will not make a discrete assessment of the probable veracity of each item of the evidence: he or she will reach a conclusion on the probable factuality of an alleged event by evaluating *all* the evidence about it *for what it is worth.* Some will be so unreliable as to be worthless; some will amount to no more than straws in the wind; some will be indicative but not, by itself, probative; some may be compelling but contra-indicated by other evidence. It is only at the end-point that, for want of a better yardstick, a probabilistic test is applied. Similarly a jury trying a criminal case may be told by the trial judge that in deciding whether they are sure of the defendant's guilt they do not have to discard every piece of evidence which they are not individually sure is true: they should of course discard anything they think suspect and anything which in law must be disregarded, but for the rest each element of the evidence should be given the weight and prominence they think right and the final question answered in the light of all of it. So it is fallacious to think of probability (or certainty) as a uniform criterion of fact-finding in our courts: it is no more than the final touchstone, appropriate to the nature of the issue, for testing a body of evidence of often diverse cogency.[131]

### Not a flexible standard

14.117   It has been said that the balance of proof is a flexible standard that varies according to the nature and seriousness of the issues as well as the inherent probability of the allegations. That is wrong. Those factors apply, if at all, in applying a single standard, the balance of probabilities.[132]

### Factors relevant to the balance

14.118   The persuasiveness required to satisfy the standard varies according to the circumstances of the case.

14.119   One factor that is relevant to satisfying the standard is the likelihood, or inherent probability, of the fact in issue. The more likely the fact, the less persuasive need be the case to satisfy it. The less likely the fact, the more persuasive must be the case. This is a matter of ordinary experience and common sense, not law.[133] Lord Hoffmann gave a clear, if not very likely, example of this flexibility in *Secretary of State for the Home Department v Rehman*:[134]

> . . . some things are inherently more likely than others. It would need more cogent evidence to satisfy one that the creature seen walking in Regent's Park was more likely than not to have been a lioness than to be satisfied to the same standard of probability that it was an Alsatian.

However, the probabilities must be determined in the context of the case. In *Re B (Children) (Care Proceedings: Standard of Proof)*,[135] Baroness Hale took up Lord Hoffmann's example to make the point:

> . . . Consider the famous example of the animal seen in Regent's Park. If it is seen outside the zoo on a stretch of greensward regularly used for walking dogs, then of course it is more likely to be a dog than a lion. If it is seen in the zoo next to the lions' enclosure when the door is open, then it may well be more likely to be lion than a dog.

14.120   Lord Nicholls explained how seriousness could be related to probability in *Re H (Minors) (Sexual Abuse: Standard of Proof)*:[136]

> When assessing the probabilities the court will have in mind as a factor, to whatever extent is appropriate in the particular case, that the more serious the allegation the less likely it is that the event occurred and, hence, the stronger should be the evidence before the court concludes that the allegation is established on the balance of probability. Fraud is less likely than negligence. Deliberate physical harm is usually less likely than accidental physical injury. A stepfather is usually less likely to have repeatedly raped

---

131   [2000] 3 All ER 449 at 477.

132   *Re B (Children) (Care Proceedings: Standard of Proof)* [2009] 1 AC 11 at [70].

133   Lord Carswell in *Re Doherty* [2008] 1 WLR 1499 at [28]; Lord Hoffmann in *Re B (Children) (Care Proceedings: Standard of Proof)* [2009] 1 AC 11 at [15].

134   [2003] 1 AC 153 at [141].

135   [2009] 1 AC 11 at [72].

136   [1996] AC 563.

and had non-consensual oral sex with his underage stepdaughter than on some occasion to have lost his temper and slapped her. Built into the preponderance of probability standard is a generous degree of flexibility in respect of the seriousness of the allegation.[137]

14.121 However, as with any other factor relevant to the inherent probability, this will depend on the circumstances and can only be determined in the context of a particular case. In *Re B (Children) (Care Proceedings: Standard of Proof)*,[138] Baroness Hale explained that they were not relevant in the context of a child's allegations of abuse in care proceedings. The consequences were serious for the family whether proved or not and there was no logical or necessary connection between the seriousness of the allegation and its likelihood.[139] Whereas in *Re Doherty*,[140] Lord Carswell explained that both factors were relevant.[141] The case involved allegations of buggery against a niece, but the examples he used were not related particularly to that type of case. Lord Brown emphasised that the seriousness of the consequences were relevant in so far as they indicated the probabilities of what happened, but otherwise went to the standard to be applied.[142]

14.122 Allegations of fraud are always regarded as serious. But a mere failure to make full disclosure of assets to a court or tribunal is not equated with fraud for this purpose.[143]

14.123 The extent to which the degree of persuasiveness varies cannot be determined precisely. As Waite LJ said in *Re A (A Minor) (Paternity: Refusal of Blood Test)*:[144]

> The weighing process involved ... must not be over-elaborate. The court should not attempt, in a precise – almost mathematical – way to determine precisely what degree of probability is appropriate to the gravity of the issue. There is ample scope for the influence of common sense and the insight gained by first impression.[145]

14.124 The extent to which persuasive evidence is required can effectively change the fact in issue or, at least, the focus on the facts. In *Flemming v Secretary of State for Work and Pensions*,[146] the issue was the number of hours for which a student attended a course of study. The Court of Appeal decided that this was a question of fact, but emphasised the importance of the college's estimate of the hours needed for the course over the student's own evidence. Chadwick LJ said:

> Second, ascertainment of the hours for which a person attends a course of education is a question of fact, to be determined by the Secretary of State or a tribunal. Third, the tribunal of fact should have particular regard to the amount of time which those who conduct a course expect a student to devote to contact hours and supervised study in order satisfactorily to

137 [1996] AC 563 at 586.
138 [2009] 1 AC 11.
139 [2009] 1 AC 11 at [71]–[72].
140 [2008] 1 WLR 1499.
141 [2008] 1 WLR 1499 at [28].
142 [2008] 1 WLR 1499 at [45]–[48].
143 Butler-Sloss LJ in *Baker v Baker* [1995] 2 FLR 829 at 834.
144 [1994] 2 FLR 463.
145 [1994] 2 FLR 463 at 470.
146 *R(G) 2/02.*

complete the course. I recognise that the 'average' student is an elusive concept, that the less able but diligent student will take longer than the time expected, and that the more able (or less diligent) student will take (or devote) less than the time expected . . . A tribunal of fact should, I think, be very slow to accept that a person expects or intends to devote – or does, in fact, devote – significantly less time to the course than those who have conduct of the course expect of him; and very slow to hold that a person who is attending a course considered by the educational establishment to be a part time course is to be treated as receiving full-time education because he devotes significantly more time than that which is expected of him.

This comes close to changing the fact in issue from the number of hours of actual attendance to the number of hours of expected attendance.

## The relevance of article 6

14.125   The standard of proof operates in the context of the requirement for fairness in the proceedings. This additional protection may remove the need for the standard to be close or equivalent to the criminal standard.[147]

## Alternative formulations

14.126   Some judges have suggested different formulations of the civil standard in order to take account of its gradations. In *Re J S (A Minor)*,[148] Ormrod LJ suggested:

> Perhaps we should recognise that our time-honoured phrase is not a happy one to express a concept which, though we all understand it, is very elusive when it comes to definition. . . . The civil burden might be formulated . . . 'the plaintiff (or the party on whom the burden rests) must satisfy the court that it is reasonably safe in all the circumstances of the case to act on the evidence before the court, bearing in mind the consequences which will follow'.[149]

14.127   And in *Thomas Bates & Son Ltd v Wyndham's (Lingerie) Ltd*,[150] Buckley LJ suggested:

> The requisite degree of cogency of proof will vary with the nature of the facts to be established and the circumstances of the case. I would say that in civil proceedings a fact must be proved with that degree of certainty which justice requires in the circumstances of the particular case. In every case the balance of probability must be discharged, but in some cases that balance may be more easily tipped than in others.[151]

14.128   However, although these reformulations recognise the gradations that may apply within the standard, they provide no clearer guidance than the traditional statements on its application. These suggestions are, in any event, now redundant given the emphasis of the House of Lords on the

---

147   *Mubarak v Mubarak* [2007] 1 FLR 722 at [73].
148   [1981] Fam 22.
149   [1981] Fam 22 at 29.
150   [1981] 1 WLR 505.
151   [1981] 1 WLR 505 at 514.

existence of two clearly distinct standards of proof in *Re Doherty*[152] and *Re B (Children) (Care Proceedings: Standard of Proof)*.[153]

## Mathematics and probabilities

14.129 The balance of probabilities is not determined mathematically or statistically. The isolated remarks in support of a more mathematical approach have been guarded. In *Davies v Taylor*,[154] Lord Simon of Glaisdale said that:

> Beneath the legal concept of probability lies the mathematical theory of probability. Only occasionally does this break surface – apart from the concept of proof on a balance of probabilities, which can be restated as the burden of showing odds of at least 51 to 49 that such-and-such has taken place or will do so.[155]

But he then qualified this by saying:

> But much proof depends on credibility, as to which probability is (at least, as yet) only one factor to be weighed.[156]

14.130 Ormrod LJ expressed the generally accepted view in *Re J S (A Minor)*:[157]

> The concept of 'probability' in the legal sense is certainly different from the mathematical concept . . .[158]

14.131 And in *R v Adams (No 2)*,[159] the Court of Appeal, in a criminal case, disapproved the presentation of statistical analyses of probabilities. Lord Bingham CJ described their use as:

> . . . a recipe for confusion, misunderstanding and misjudgment, possibly even among counsel, but very probably among judges and, as we conclude, almost certainly among jurors . . . We are very clearly of opinion that in cases such as this, lacking special features absent here, expert evidence should not be admitted to induce juries to attach mathematical values to probabilities arising from non-scientific evidence adduced at the trial.[160]

## If it is not possible to make findings of fact

14.132 Usually, the evidence will be such that it is possible to make findings of fact on the balance of probabilities. As Lord Hope said in *Pickford v Imperial Chemical Industries plc*:[161]

> There is no doubt that in most cases the question of onus ceases to be of any importance once all the evidence is out and before the court.[162]

152 [2008] 1 WLR 1499.
153 [2009] 1 AC 11.
154 [1974] AC 207.
155 [1974] AC 207 at 219.
156 [1974] AC 207 at 219.
157 [1981] Fam 22.
158 [1981] Fam 22 at 29. Ho Hock Lai deals with the distinction in detail in *A Philosophy of Evidence Law*, 2009, Oxford, pp110–143, distinguishing between logical or epistemic probability and physical or objective probability. Probability in law is of the former type.
159 [1998] 1 Cr App R 377.
160 [1998] 1 Cr App R 377 at 384.
161 [1998] 1 WLR 1189.
162 [1998] 1 WLR 1189 at 1200.

And as Baroness Hale said in *Re B (Children) (Care Proceedings: Standard of Proof)*[163] of a judge who found himself unable to decide on the balance of probabilities:

> My Lords, if the judiciary in this country regularly found themselves in this state of mind, our civil and family justice systems would rapidly grind to a halt . . .

Judges should not recuse themselves on account of such difficulties.[164]

14.133   This is so even if the evidence as a whole is inadequate in content and had been poorly presented. This was recognised by the Court of Appeal in *Crewe Services and Investment Corporation v Silk*.[165] Robert Walker LJ referred to:

> . . . the practicalities of the disposal of business in the County Court. County Court judges constantly have to deal with cases that are inadequately prepared and presented, either as to the facts or as to the law (or both), and they must not be discouraged from doing their best to reach a fair and sensible result on inadequate materials.[166]

14.134   When it is possible to make findings of fact, the burden becomes irrelevant, because the case can be decided on the evidence.

14.135   If possible, a tribunal should make findings of fact relevant to the matters in issue rather than decide that the evidence is not sufficient to show that the burden has been discharged. It should only decide the case on the burden without hearing the other parties in exceptional or frivolous cases.[167] This will only be appropriate if there is no evidence on which findings can be made or the probabilities are evenly balanced. Cases in which a judge may rely on the burden rather than on an analysis of the evidence are rare.[168]

14.136   In *Rhesa Shipping Co SA v Edmunds*,[169] Lord Brandon referred to the preference of judges to decide cases on the facts rather than on the burden of proof:

> No judge likes to decide cases on the burden of proof if he can legitimately avoid having to do so. There are cases, however, in which, owing to the unsatisfactory state of the evidence or otherwise, deciding on the burden of proof is the only just course for him to take.[170]

14.137   However, this is not just a matter of judicial preference. It is a matter of duty. The tribunal is under a duty to make findings if that is possible. This was explained by the Court of Appeal in *Morris v London Iron and Steel Co Ltd*.[171] May LJ explained the basic duty on judges of fact:

> Judges should, so far as is practicable and so far as it is in accordance with their conscientious duty, make findings of fact. But it is in the exceptional

163  [2009] 1 AC 11 at [31].
164  [2009] 1 AC 11 at [81].
165  (2000) 79 P&CR 500.
166  (2000) 79 P&CR 500 at 509.
167  *Logan v Customs and Excise Commissioners* [2004] ICR 1.
168  *Cooper v Floor Cleaning Machines Ltd* [2004] RTR 254.
169  [1985] 1 WLR 948.
170  [1985] 1 WLR 948 at 955–956.
171  [1988] QB 493.

case that they may be forced to reach a conclusion that they do not know on which side of the line the decision ought to be.[172]

And Buckley LJ set out the consequence of an inability to make findings of fact:

> In such a case, in the absence of any recognised presumptions which arise under the law ... which may provide a means of solving the problem in a case of that nature, where a tribunal is unable to form a conclusion, it has no alternative to falling back upon the burden of proof as the means of resolving the dispute between the parties.[173]

## Other analyses

14.138  The courts have suggested two other analyses in preference to burden of proof.

14.139  One analysis is that either there is no burden of proof in tribunals which operate an inquisitorial approach or the burden operates differently in those tribunals. This was suggested by Lord Denning MR in *R v National Insurance Commissioner ex p Viscusi*.[174] Lord Denning said of an appeal relating to a claim for disablement benefit that:

> The proceedings are not to be regarded as if they were a law suit between opposing parties. The injured person is not a plaintiff under a burden of proof.[175]

Buckley LJ agreed, but recognised that:

> ... the fact remains that the medical board or the medical appeal tribunal, as the case may be, must be satisfied that the claimant is entitled to benefit; and so, in a sense, and subject to such statutory assumptions as are prescribed by the Act itself, it does rest with the claimant in the end to make out his claim.[176]

14.140  In *Prest v Petrodel Resources Ltd*,[177] Lord Sumption did not go as far as Lord Denning, but said in the context of family proceedings:

> The concept of the burden of proof, which has always been one of the main factors inhibiting the drawing of adverse inferences from the absence of evidence or disclosure, cannot be applied in the same way to proceedings of this kind as it is in ordinary litigation.[178]

14.141  The other analysis is the co-operative model, suggested by the House of Lords in *Kerr v Department for Social Development*[179] Baroness Hale said:

> What emerges from all this is a co-operative process of investigation in which both the claimant and the department play their part. The department is the one which knows what questions it needs to ask and what information it needs to have in order to determine whether the conditions of entitlement have been met. The claimant is the one who generally speaking

---

172  [1988] QB 493 at 504.
173  [1988] QB 493 at 507.
174  [1974] 1 WLR 646.
175  [1988] QB 493 at 651.
176  [1988] QB 493 at 654.
177  [2013] 2 AC 415.
178  [2013] 2 AC 415 at [45].
179  [2004] 1 WLR 1372 at [62]–[63].

can and must supply that information. But where the information is available to the department rather than the claimant, then the department must take the necessary steps to enable it to be traced.

If that sensible approach is taken, it will rarely be necessary to resort to concepts taken from adversarial litigation such as the burden of proof . . .

Lord Hope set out the basic principles that apply:[180]

In this situation there is no formal burden of proof on either side. The process is essentially a fact-gathering exercise, conducted largely if not entirely on paper, to which both the claimant and the department must contribute. The claimant must answer such questions as the department may choose to put to him honestly and to the best of his ability. The department must then make such inquiries as it can to supplement the information which the claimant has given to it. The matter is then in the hands of the adjudicator. All being well, the issue of entitlement will be resolved without difficulty.

But there some basic principles which may be used to guide the decision where the information falls short of what is needed for a clear decision to be made one way or the other: (1) Facts which may reasonably be supposed to be within the claimant's own knowledge are for the claimant to supply at each stage in the inquiry. (2) But the claimant must be given a reasonable opportunity to supply them.

Knowledge as to the information that is needed to deal with his claim lies with the department, not with him. (3) So it is for the department to ask the relevant questions. The claimant is not to be faulted if the relevant questions to show whether or not the claim is excluded by the Regulations were not asked. (4) The general rule is that it is for the party who alleges an affirmative to make good his allegation. It is also a general rule that he who desires to take advantage of an exception must bring himself within the provisions of the exception. As Lord Wilberforce observed, exceptions are to be set up by those who rely on them: *Nimmo v Alexander Cowan & Sons Ltd* [1968] AC 107, 130.

14.142    This co-operative approach could be seen as merely a different way of stating and explaining the operation of the burden of proof. However, it goes further than either the legal or the evidential burden. It goes further than the legal burden by imposing the equivalent of a duty of disclosure on the decision-maker. And it goes further than the evidential burden in that it applies despite the fact that the claim would not succeed on the evidence presented by the claimant. The evidential burden reflects the persuasiveness of the evidence presently available; the duty to co-operate remedies the deficiencies in that evidence.

14.143    The approach has not yet been developed. In particular, it remains to be seen how it will be applied to impose responsibilities on claimants to disclose information that is potentially contrary to their interests.

14.144    Whether or not there is a burden of proof in particular types of case, the decision-maker is still under a duty to decide the issue that arises in terms of the legislation.[181]

---

180  [2004] 1 WLR 1372 at [15]–[16].
181  Lord Woolf in *R (Roberts) v Parole Board* [2005] 2 AC 738 at [47].

## Contempt

14.145 In the case of contempt, the standard varies according to the nature of the relief sought. On an application for committal to prison, the criminal standard applies; otherwise, the civil standard applies.[182]

# Making the decision

14.146 This section deals with the process of decision-making rather than its content.

## The nature of decision-making

14.147 Decision-making involves identifying issues relevant to the outcome of the proceedings and deciding them in a rational manner. The three elements of a decision are the facts, the law and the application of the law to the facts and circumstances of the case. For each of these elements, the issues must be identified and analysed in order to reach a conclusion. Those conclusions must then be explained.

14.148 In *Scott v Scott*,[183] Lord Shaw described the ideal of judicial decision-making:

> The judgment of the Court is then pronounced upon the law and facts of the case, and in discharging this very responsible duty, the judge publicly, in open court, assigns the reasons for his decision, stating the principles and authorities on which he decides the matters of law, and reciting or adverting to the various parts of the evidence from which he deduces his conclusions of fact; and thus the matter in controversy between the parties becomes adjudged.[184]

14.149 In *Heffer v Tiffin Green (a Firm)*,[185] Henry LJ described the process of fact-finding in the course of explaining how the trial judge had gone wrong:

> What was needed was clear identification and treatment of the issues.
>
> The judge's decision was shown by his judgment to have been arrived at without sufficient regard being paid to the building blocks of the reasoned judicial process, where the evidence on each issue is marshalled, the weight of the evidence analysed, all tested against the probabilities based on the evidence as a whole, with clear findings of fact and all reasons given.[186]

14.150 Unspoken, but permeating both these descriptions, is the rational nature of the process.

---

182  *Mubarak v Mubarak* [2007] 1 FLR 722 at [71]–[72].
183  [1913] AC 417.
184  [1913] AC 417 at 473, quoting from the Report of the Committee on Ecclesiastical Courts of 1832.
185  (1998) *Times* 28 December at [2.3].
186  (1998) *Times* 28 December at [2.3] and [6.2].

## An evolving process

14.151   Decision-making is not a separate process that is undertaken once the evidence has been obtained and the arguments have been presented. The assessment of the evidence and the evaluation of the arguments begins with the preview of the case and continues during the hearing. This is not to say that issues are prejudged. Only that questions arise, and may be resolved, as the hearing progresses. For example: doubts about the reliability of evidence may be resolved by further questioning or by the evidence of a later witness. And concerns about a legal issue of interpretation or application may be addressed in argument.

14.152   This evolving process during the hearing may appear to determine the case. For example: evidence may be considered unreliable, which once rejected makes the outcome of the proceedings inevitable. But even in this case, it is worth pausing before deciding in order to consider the issue in a structured way that is best undertaken, and perhaps only possible, in the calm and quiet after the hearing.

14.153   There is a danger of forming a provisional view and then evaluating later evidence in conformity with that view. It is sometimes suggested that any consideration of the case should be suspended while evidence is being given and argument presented. But this is neither possible nor desirable. It is not possible, because the mind is inevitably assessing evidence and argument, even if that process is not conscious. And even if it were possible, it would not be desirable, because it would prevent relevant questions being asked of witnesses and pertinent points being raised in argument.

## Maintaining an open mind

14.154   There are realistic and effective ways of maintaining an open mind. They can, at least, reduce the chance of self-justifying reasoning.

14.155   One approach is to focus with precision on the factors relevant to the assessment of the evidence and the application of the law to the facts found, avoiding generality of reasoning. Take as an example the assessment of evidence of a person's disability. General comments such as 'I wasn't really persuaded by his evidence' or 'Her GP did not take matters any further' may be correct, but they are capable of concealing preconceptions or prejudices. Focusing on relevant factors such as whether clinical findings or dosage of medication are consistent with the asserted disability limits the scope for other influences to intrude into the decision-making.

14.156   Another approach is to adopt a structured reconsideration at the end of the hearing. Research has shown that this is especially effective if it involves constructing the strongest arguments that can be made for and against a particular point of view.[187] This process is improved if it is informed by an understanding of how beliefs are formed.[188]

---

187   Scott Plous, *The Psychology of Judgment and Decision Making*, McGraw-Hill, 1993, chapter 19, 'Overconfidence', p228.

188   For simple and complex models of how beliefs are formed, see of *The Power of Belief*, Oxford, 2006, chapter 1, 'A cognitive neuroscience of belief', especially pp12–17.

14.157    A further approach is to emphasise the logical process involved in the decision-making. Research has shown that this can help to overcome inbuilt biases.[189] As Christine Boyle wrote, citing Canadian authorities in support of the advice:

> While a fact-finder will not necessarily be able to bring her whole reasoning process to a conscious level of articulation, some explicit attention to possible counter-assumptions and recognition of the steps involved in a chain of inferences would increase the legitimacy of fact-finding as a process governed by law.[190]

## The dynamics of decision-making

14.158    Once the hearing is complete, the process will differ depending on whether the tribunal consisted of a single judge or involved other members.

14.159    If the tribunal consists of a single judge, there can be a seamless transition from the continuing assessment and evaluation that took place during the hearing. But even here a conscious and systematic consideration of the issues helps to ensure that all the relevant issues are identified and thought through. This can be helped by the use of a checklist of issues to be considered and by making a structured note of the reasons, unless they are being written immediately.

14.160    If the tribunal consists of more than one member, there will still be a continuity from the ongoing process during the hearing. But with this difference: the thoughts of the individual members during the hearing must be pooled for decision-making. A structured approach must be taken to ensure that no issues of fact or law are overlooked. Usually, that approach will be led by the presiding judge. The approach must also be collegiate to ensure that the decision reached is that of the tribunal as a whole.

## Structured decision-making

14.161    For the purpose of exposition, it is possible to divide the process of decision-making into a series of structured steps.

14.162    The first step is to hear the evidence.

14.163    The second step is to identify the law that may be relevant. This will depend on the evidence that has been given. That evidence will determine the law that is *potentially* relevant. This law must be identified before or during the hearing in order to ensure that all the relevant evidence is obtained. When the tribunal has made its findings of fact, some of this potentially relevant law may become irrelevant.

14.164    The third step is to resolve any issues of interpretation in the law. The relevant law, once identified and interpreted, will determine the facts that have to be found.

14.165    The fourth step is to assess the evidence.

189  J A Fugelsang and K N Dunbar, *Law and the Brain*, chapter 8, 'A cognitive neuroscience framework for understanding causal reasoning and the law', p163.

190  Paul Roberts and Mike Redmayne (eds), *Innovations in Evidence and Proof*, Hart Publishing, 2008, chapter 3, 'A Principles Approach to Relevance: the Cheshire Cat in Canada', pp115–116.

14.166    Once this has been done, the fifth step is to make the findings of fact and, if necessary, to draw inferences from them.[191]

14.167    When the facts have been found, the sixth step is to apply the law to the facts found. This will determine the outcome of the case.

14.168    The seventh step is to record the reasons that have been articulated during the decision-making. If the reasons are to be written later, this may take the form of notes for later reference.

14.169    However, in practice, there is an element of circularity. For example: it is necessary to identify the relevant law, but that depends on the facts, and the facts cannot be found unless they are relevant, but they can only be identified from the relevant law. So, the steps cannot be tackled in a rigid sequence; it may be necessary to move back and forth between them.

## Issues of judgment

14.170    The process of decision-making that involves assessing the combined effect of a number of separate factors is discussed in chapter 4.

## Time

14.171    A tribunal should take as much time as is necessary to make its decision, adjourning if need be.[192]

## Consistency

14.172    There is a tension within the application of law between the desire for consistency (whether between the same or different parties) and the individual freedom for decision-makers. The latter freedom is enhanced by the limited scope of an appeal on a point of law in respect of matters of judgment.[193]

14.173    In *Matadeen v Pointu*,[194] Lord Hoffmann set consistency in the context of the rule of law:

> . . . such a principle is one of the building blocks of democracy and necessarily permeates any democratic constitution. Indeed, their Lordships would go further and say that treating like cases alike and unlike cases differently is a general axiom of rational behaviour. It is, for example, frequently involved by the courts in proceedings for judicial review as a ground for holding some administrative act to have been irrational . . .[195]

14.174    In *ZH (Bangladesh) v Secretary of State for the Home Department*,[196] Sedley LJ referred, in the context of the exercise of a Government policy, to:

---

191  See chapter 11.

192  Ward LJ in *Re G (a Child) (Care proceedings: Placement for adoption)* (2005) *Times* 1 August.

193  See chapter 4.

194  [1999] 1 AC 98.

195  [1999] 1 AC 98 at 109.

196  [2009] EWCA Civ 8 at [33], reported as *Hussain (Zakir) v Secretary of State for the Home Department* (2009) *Times* 9 April.

> . . . the legal obligation of government not to act inconsistently with its own policy unless there is some good reason for doing so: see *British Oxygen v Board of Trade* [1971] AC 610. More than this would be to give internal guidance the force of law; less would be to tolerate double standards in public administration.

14.175 There is a variety of devices through which the law seeks to reconcile the competing policies of consistency between cases and freedom for decision-makers in exercising matters of judgment.[197] These principles apply with greater flexibility in public law cases.

## Consistency in the exercise of a discretion

14.176 In *Jurkowska v Hlmad Ltd*,[198] Sedley LJ explained how a judicial policy could ensure consistency in the exercise of a discretion. The context was the power of the Employment Appeal Tribunal to extend time within an appeal could be lodged:[199]

> Every discretionary power, both administrative and judicial, carries an inbuilt problem. To ensure a reasonable degree of consistency – an elementary requirement both of adjudication and of public administration – a policy is frequently helpful and sometimes indispensable. It means that people have some idea where they stand and that arbitrary distinctions are not made between similar cases. In public administration a policy of this kind is commonly found in unitary written form. In the judicial sphere it is ordinarily found either in appellate decisions designed to give guidance or in a series of first-instance decisions from which a policy or practice emerges. Less often it may be found in a practice statement of some kind. But, if the discretion is to continue to be real, decision-makers must not let a policy ossify into a rule: they must always be prepared to deviate from it if the facts warrant it.
>
> In this way, a discretion which starts life at the centre of a statutory power, trammelled only by broad principles of law, shifts to the periphery of the power as its exercise comes, more or less rapidly, to be policy-guided. This is the natural and proper process which, as Lord Justice Rimer recounts in his judgment, has taken place in relation to the statutory discretion to enlarge time for appealing from an employment tribunal to the EAT. It is a process which in its nature seeks to ensure something that is now spelt out in Rule 2A(2)(a) – that the parties are on an equal footing, not only as between themselves but in relation to other parties in other cases.

## Consistency in respect of evidence common to a class of case

14.177 In *Shirazi v Secretary of State for the Home Department*,[200] Sedley LJ took a similar approach to judicial policy in the interests of consistency, in that case on country guidance decisions in asylum appeals.[201]

197  This issue is linked with precedent and finality. See chapters 2 and 13.
198  [2008] ICR 841.
199  [2008] ICR 841 at [63]–[64].
200  [2004] 2 All ER 602.
201  See chapter 13.

## Consistency between parties

14.178   Lord Hobhouse commented on this in *Uratemp Ventures Ltd v Collins*.[202] The issue for the House of Lords was whether the lack of cooking facilities prevented the claimant's home being a dwelling. Lord Hobhouse emphasised that consistency was achieved by focusing on the language of the legislation rather than on its application to the particular facts in earlier cases:[203]

> I will only add the further observation that the complications in the present case, as in some earlier cases, have arisen from treating factual decisions as if they involved the formulation of propositions of law. Consistency of approach is required from case to case. But that should not lead to the elaboration of a simple factual description with a supposed legal overlay preventing the language of the statute from being given effect to in each individual case in accordance with its ordinary meaning.

And as the Tribunal of Commissioners said in *R(I) 12/75*: 'questions of fact should not be elevated into questions of legal principle'.[204]

## Consistency in respect of the same party

14.179   This has been particularly considered in the context of asylum and immigration cases. In *Devaseelan*,[205] the Immigration Appeal Tribunal set out guidelines for achieving consistency in fact-finding in cases involving the same parties by treating the first decision as a starting point on matters of fact but subject to due allowance for any difference in the issues and the evidence between the two cases.

14.180   In *Ocampo v Secretary of State for the Home Department*,[206] the Court of Appeal applied this, in Auld LJ's words, to 'cases like the present where the parties involved are not the same but there is a material overlap of evidence'.[207] This approach was approved in *AA (Somalia) and AH (Iran) v Secretary of State for the Home Department*,[208] subject to two qualifications set out by Carnwath LJ:

> First, ... 'material' requires some elaboration. It recognises I think that exceptions to the ordinary principle that factual decisions do not set precedents ... should be closely defined. To extend the principle to cases where there is no more than an 'overlap of evidence' would be too wide, and could introduce undesirable uncertainty, in all the cases to which the principle has been applied so far, including *Ocampo*, the claims have not merely involved overlapping evidence, but have arisen out the same factual matrix such as the same relationship or the same event or series of events. I would respectfully read Auld LJ's reference to 'cases such as the present' as limiting the principle to such cases.

202   [2002] 1 AC 301.
203   [2002] 1 AC 301 at [20].
204   [2002] 1 AC 301 at [19].
205   [2002] UKIAT 00282.
206   [2006] EWCA Civ 1276, reported as *GO (Colombia) v Secretary of State for the Home Department* (2006) *Times* 27 October.
207   [2006] EWCA Civ 1276 at [25].
208   [2007] EWCA Civ 1040 at [69]–[70].

Secondly, in applying the guidelines to cases involving different claimants, there may be a valid distinction depending on whether the previous decision was in favour or against the Secretary of State. The difference is that the Secretary of State was a direct party to the first decision, whereas the claimant was not. It is one thing to restrict a party from relitigating the same issue, but another to impose the same restriction on someone who, although involved in the previous case, perhaps as a witness, was not formally a party.

14.181 Consistency between a tribunal and a decision-maker was considered by Bennett J as a preliminary issue in judicial review proceedings in *R (M) v Lambeth London Borough Council*.[209] A tribunal hearing an asylum appeal decided that the claimant was under 18. It did so in ignorance of an assessment by the local authority that he was 18 or over. The judge made cautious reference to the importance of consistency:

> What I do decide is that, *if* there is a principle of consistency which can be applied where a judicial body makes a decision to which the administrative body was not a party and with which the administrative body differs, then in the instant case the administrative body considered the judicial decision and had good and sound reasons for differing from it. It would be extraordinary if Lambeth were, in some way bound to follow such a decision where the very person (i.e. M) who in effect is seeking to enforce it on Lambeth, failed to bring to the attention of the AIT pertinent facts which might have had the result of the AIT deciding the case adversely to him and thus consistently with Lambeth's decision of December 2006. Further, Mr Straker provided no argument that Lambeth could have somehow had the decision of the AIT set aside.[210]

14.182 Consistency in respect of the same party was discussed in *R (PM) v Hertforshire County Council*.[211] The case also concerned an age determination. A tribunal had found that an asylum-seeker had reached 18 and the local authority decided that it was bound by that conclusion. The court held that it was not. On consistency, the judge emphasised that: (i) the local authority had not been party to the tribunal's decision; (ii) the tribunal's decision was only binding between the parties; (iii) the authority would have different evidence available; and (iv) the issues were different for the tribunal and the authority.[212]

## Consistency between successive claims by the same party

14.183 In principle, there should be consistency between successive claims for the same benefit. In practice, there are likely to be differences in the terms in which the claims are expressed and in the supporting evidence. Even if there are not, the decision on each claim is a separate decision in respect of a distinct period and is not binding in respect of other claims and periods.[213] Nevertheless, the Commissioners emphasised the importance of consistency between successive claims for a social security benefit,

209 [2008] 1 FLR 1026.
210 [2008] 1 FLR 1026 at [163].
211 [2010] EWHC 2056 (Admin).
212 [2010] EWHC 2056 (Admin) at [74]–[87].
213 *R v National Insurance Commissioner ex p Viscusi* [1974] 1 WLR 646.

relying on the need for an adequate explanation of the difference as the control mechanism in those cases in which the reason for the change in entitlement was not self-evident.[214] This approach to consistency through the requirement of an explanation has also been adopted by the European Court of Human Rights.[215]

## Consistency on reconsideration

14.184   In immigration and asylum, reconsideration may be directed on specific issues. If that is done, the tribunal must accept the findings previously made on other issues.[216]

## Legislation

14.185   Legislation may limit the extent to which consistency can be achieved. For example: section 46A of the Child Support Act 1991 and section 17 of the Social Security Act 1998 both provide that findings of fact and determinations embodied in or necessary to decisions are not conclusive unless regulations so provide.

# Majority or unanimity

14.186   The relevant Act or the rules of procedure may expressly provide for decision-making to be unanimous or by a majority. If the latter, they may also expressly provide whether the member who chairs the tribunal has a casting vote.

14.187     In the absence of express provisions, the issue is governed by the decision of the Court of Appeal in *Picea Holdings Ltd v London Rent Assessment Panel*.[217] Lord Parker CJ set out the correct approach:

- if the issue is purely of private interest, the decision must be unanimous;
- if the issue is of public interest, the decision may be taken by a majority;
- however, even if the issue is one of public interest, majority decision-making must be consistent with the governing legislation as a whole.

14.188   There are two first instance decisions that held that decision-making in respect of a war pension had to be unanimous, whether that result was to the claimant's advantage[218] or disadvantage.[219] The Court of Appeal in *Picea Holdings Ltd v London Rent Assessment Panel*[220] did not overrule those

---

214   *R(M) 1/96.* This was despite the comments of Roskill LJ in *R v National Insurance Commissioner ex p Viscusi* [1974] 1 WLR 646 at 658–659.
215   *Higgins v France* (1998) 27 EHRR 703 at [43].
216   *MY (Turkey) v Secretary of State for the Home Department* [2008] EWCA Civ 477; (2008) *Times* 21 April.
217   [1971] 2 QB 216.
218   *Brain v Minister of Pensions* [1947] KB 625.
219   *Minister of Pensions v Horsey* [1949] 2 KB 526.
220   [1971] 2 QB 216.

decisions, but it did not accept that they laid down a general principle.[221] They apply only in England and Wales. The position in Scotland was first left open;[222] then it was decided that majority decisions were permissible.[223] The Pensions Appeal Tribunal in Northern Ireland followed the Scottish approach.

## Under TCEA

14.189 Regulation 8 of the First-tier Tribunal and Upper Tribunal (Composition of Tribunal) Order 2008 provides:

> If the decision of the tribunal is not unanimous, the decision of the majority is the decision of the tribunal; and the presiding member has a casting vote if the votes are equally divided.

## Good practice

14.190 Even if the rules of procedure allow the decision to be made by a majority, every effort should be made to reach a unanimous decision. One approach is to delay making a decision for the minority to consider the written reasons of the majority.[224] If the difference of opinion is between the presiding judge and the lay members and it relates to whether the burden of proof is discharged, the members should generally concede that there must be a reasonable doubt on the issue. In *Brown v Minister of Pensions*,[225] the Scottish court was concerned with the burden of proof in war pension cases, which was more favourable than usual to the claimant. The court said:

> ... when the question is the sufficiency of the evidence to discharge such an onus, and when an express injunction has been laid upon the tribunal to give the claimant the benefit of any reasonable doubt, only the most powerful considerations can justify the medical and service members in outvoting the legal chairman. Such a decision necessarily imports that in the view of the majority the chairman's dissent is not reasonable. We should have thought that the bare fact that the chairman was in favour of a certificate of entitlement and held his views sufficiently strongly to enter an express dissent would itself have convinced the tribunal as a whole that there must be a reasonable doubt to which it was their simplest duty to concede effect.[226]

---

221 [1971] 2 QB 216 at 224–225.

222 *Brown v Minister of Pensions* [1946] SC 471.

223 *Secretary of State for Social Security v KM* [1998] ScotCS 67.

224 *Anglia Home Improvements Ltd v Kelly* (2004) *Times* 30 June.

225 [1946] SC 471.

226 [1946] SC 471 at 476, cited with approval in *Secretary of State for Social Security v KM* [1998] ScotCS 67.

## Reasons for decision

### Courts and tribunals

14.191   Courts make orders and judges deliver judgments explaining those orders. Tribunals are more likely to make decisions and give reasons for them. The difference is not just one of terminology.[227]

14.192   A tribunal's reasons differ in a number of respects from judgments delivered in court. It is much less likely that a tribunal will give its reasons orally at the end of the hearing. It is more efficient to spend its time hearing cases and to provide its reasons later.

14.193   In some tribunals, there is no duty to give reasons unless they are requested by one of the parties. In these cases, the lack of an oral judgment allows the parties time to consider whether to apply for reasons to be provided.

14.194   As a result of this separation of the reasons from the making of the decision, the process of writing cannot assist in clarifying the tribunal's reasoning and, perhaps, the outcome. This can be offset to some extent if the tribunal makes it a habit to record the steps in its reasoning at the time it makes the decision for later use.

### Reasons under TCEA

14.195   A tribunal may be under a duty to provide reasons for particular decisions and has a power to provide reasons for decisions in respect of which the duty does not arise.

#### The duty

14.196   The terms of the duty vary.[228]

14.197   These duties distinguish between decisions that finally dispose of all issues in the proceedings and decisions that dispose of proceedings. UTR 1(3) defines 'dispose of proceedings':

> . . . 'dispose of proceedings' includes, unless indicated otherwise, disposing of a part of the proceedings.

References to disposal of all issues may indicate that disposal of part of the proceedings is not included. However, it may not: the rule may require reasons if it disposes of all issues in a part of the proceedings. For example: the decision may deal with a preliminary issue affecting part but not all of the appellant's case. The interpretation of the rules is complicated by the fact that some use both expressions.

---

227   Maurice Kay LJ in *Secretary of State for Work and Pensions v Morina* [2007] 1 WLR 3033 at [7].

228   UTR r40; GRC Rules r38; HESC Rules rr30, 42 and 43; IAC Rules r29 and Sch para 10; Lands Rules r51; PC Rules r36; SEC Rules r34; Tax Rules r35; WPAFC Rules r32.

14.198    There is no duty to provide reasons for consent orders[229] or for decisions dealing with correction, set aside, review or permission to appeal.[230]

### The power

14.199  A tribunal may not be under a duty to provide reasons, because: (i) the decision does not dispose of the proceedings; (ii) the decision does dispose of the proceedings, but is excluded from the duty (decisions dealing with correction, set aside, review or permission to appeal); or (iii) the decision does dispose of the proceedings, but no application has been made in time for reasons to be provided.

14.200    In all of these cases, the tribunal has power to provide reasons. In some cases, it is allowed by the rules.[231] In other cases, there is an extra-statutory common law power to give reasons.[232]

### Non-disclosure and confidentiality

14.201  Reasons given by a tribunal must take account of the need to withhold information from individuals[233] and, although the rules do not so provide, confidential information.[234]

## The reasons for decision

14.202  The law sets the minimum standard that a decision and its reasons must attain. This is dealt with in chapter 4. This section is concerned with the practice of drafting. Good practice deals with matters that are not covered by the legal standard and sets a higher level of attainment than the law. *R (TS) v Angela Bowen (Chair of SENDIST) and Solihull Metropolitan Borough Council*[235] illustrates the distinction. The judge complained that the tribunal's reasons did not neatly fit into the structure of a statement of special educational needs, but nonetheless found that the reasons were adequate in law.

14.203    This is not a handbook on drafting.[236] However, some advice is appropriate. It is directed primarily at the First-tier Tribunal.

---

229  See: UTR r39(2); GRC Rules r37(2); HESC Rules r29(2) (other than mental health cases); Lands Rules r51(3); PC Rules r35(2); SEC Rules r32(2); Tax Rules r34(2); WPAFC Rules r30(2). There is no equivalent power in IAC Rules.

230  See: UTR r40(2); HESC Rules rr30(2) (other than mental health cases) and 41(2) (mental health cases); IAC Rules r29(2); Lands Rules r51(2); PC Rules r36(2); SEC Rules r34(2); Tax Rules r35(2); WPAFC Rules r32(1).

231  See: UTR r40(4); GRC Rules r38(3); HESC Rules rr30(4) (other than mental health cases) and 41(4) (mental health cases); IAC Rules r29(3)(b); Lands Rules r51(4); PC Rules r36(3); SEC Rules r34(2); WPAFC Rules r32(1).

232  *CH 2553/05* at 24.

233  See: UTR r40(2), although strictly the duty is confined to the decision notice; GRC Rules r38(2); HESC Rules rr30(2) (other than mental health cases) and 41(2) (mental health cases); IAC Rules r29(2); PC Rules r36(2); SEC Rules r34(5); WPAFC Rules r32(4). Tax Rules contain only a power to withhold information from the public: r14.

234  Under UTR r19; SEC Rules r19.

235  [2009] EWHC 5 (Admin).

236  See Louise Mailhot and James D Carnwath *Decisions, Decisions*, Les Éditions, 1998; and Andrew Goodman, *How Judges Decide Cases: Reading, Writing and Analysing Judgments*, Universal, 2007, part 7. See also articles in *Tribunals* in appendix C.

14.204    There are three criteria for drafting reasons. In descending order of importance they are: content, clarity and style. These are not separate matters; they are connected. Style can affect clarity, and lack of clarity can affect content.

## Who are the reasons for?

14.205   A key issue is: who is the audience for the reasons? The answer will affect how they are written.

14.206    A decision will always be addressed to an unsuccessful party.[237] A successful party may also be interested in knowing the tribunal's reasoning, as it may be useful for the future, either in later stages of the case in question or in other cases. The tribunal may also address remarks to the representative of one or more of the parties or to representatives in general. If the decision is given on appeal, the tribunal may say something that is relevant to the tribunal or decision-maker whose decision is under appeal or to the tribunal or decision-maker to which the case is remitted for reconsideration. If there is the possibility of an appeal, the decision may be written in part with the appellate body in mind. If the decision is of precedent value, it may be written for decision-makers, lower tribunals and tribunals of the same level. It may also be relevant to possible changes in legislation and may be addressed to the policy makers or those who draft the legislation.

14.207    Even if reasons are not drafted for a particular user or class of user, they have to take into account the way that that user or class may use, or misuse, them. For example: a decision may be principally addressed to the unrepresented claimant who lost, but the way that it is worded should take account of the possibility that loose statements could be taken out of context by representatives in later cases.

14.208    In some cases, it will be sufficient to draft the reasons for one audience, possibly with some adjustment to address others as well. In other cases, one part of the reasons may be written for one audience and other parts for another. In yet other cases, one part of the reasons may have to be expressed in alternative ways for the benefit of all those who may be interested. For example: a detailed analysis of the law may have to be set out if an appeal is anticipated, but may also be summarised in simple terms for an unrepresented party.

14.209    Although each case is individual, it is possible to identify the general form that reasons at a particular level are likely to take.

14.210    A decision by the First-tier Tribunal will be primarily written for the benefit of the parties. It will concentrate on the facts and must provide sufficient information to allow an unsuccessful party to decide whether to appeal against the decision.

14.211   A decision by the Upper Tribunal on an issue of law will also be addressed to the parties. But it fulfils a different function. It will concentrate on the law rather than the facts and may be directed to the decision-maker or

---

237  There may not be a winner and a loser, as each party may obtain some benefit from the decision. For example: if the issue was the party's income, some expenses may be allowed for tax purposes and other not.

tribunal who must reconsider the case or to future tribunals or decision-makers as a precedent.

## What should the reasons contain?

14.212 Once the audience has been identified, the content and the amount of detail that the reasons contain will depend on the issues involved in the decision, the time available and the ethos of the tribunal. To take two contrasting examples. A parking adjudicator typically has to deal with limited issues quickly after a hearing that lasts only a few minutes and is likely to produce short reasons. An employment tribunal may deal with complex issues involving conflicting evidence heard over days or weeks and its reasons are likely to run to many pages of detailed analysis.

14.213 Whatever their length, the reasons should show that the tribunal identified the issues that arose, analysed the evidence rationally, made the necessary findings of fact, interpreted the law correctly, and came to a permissible decision on the findings of fact.

14.214 This does not mean that each of those matters has to be set out separately or at great length. What matters is that the reasons should show that they have been done.

14.215 There are a number of devices that can be used to reduce the length of the reasons. In most cases before the First-tier Tribunal, the only audience will be the parties and their representatives. They will be an informed audience as to the evidence before the tribunal; it will be available in the papers or in the record of proceedings. They may also be informed on the law; it will either be in the papers or known to the representatives. The judge can either take those matters as read or refer to them only as necessary in explaining the tribunal's decision.

14.216 Incorporating information by reference is a convenient, time-saving device. But it must be used properly. In *Givaudan & Co Ltd v Minister of Housing and Local Government*,[238] Megaw J allowed for this possibility and set out the conditions for its proper use:

> There can be no objection to the inclusion, by reference, in the Minister's statement of reasons, of the inspector's conclusions, provided that those conclusions are, in themselves, sufficiently clearly and unambiguously expressed.[239]

The danger in this approach is that any inadequacy in the material incorporated will render the tribunal's decision itself inadequate. If it does, the tribunal must ensure that it does not appear to have abdicated its duty to think matters through for itself.[240]

14.217 Those matters that do have to be set out or emphasised can be dealt with succinctly. Take as an example the reason for rejecting an argument in an employment and support allowance appeal. The judge may write: 'The claimant told us that she had difficulties getting up her stairs as she did not have a banister. That is not relevant, because the test concerns only

---

238 [1967] 1 WLR 250.
239 [1967] 1 WLR 250 at 259.
240 *Newcastle upon Tyne Hospitals NHS Foundation Trust v Armstrong* [2010] ICR 674 at [46].

two steps with the benefit of a handrail.' Those two sentences record the tribunal correctly identified the issue, understood the law and applied it correctly.

14.218    In dealing with evidence, the reasons should show how the tribunal dealt with the evidence produced by an unsuccessful party. If the evidence is not mentioned, the party may believe that it has not been considered and that this failure caused the tribunal to make the wrong decision. Even if the evidence is not relevant to the legal issues, the party may not see it that way and an explanation will make that clear. What is obvious to a judge is not necessarily clear to a claimant before a tribunal.

14.219    It is good practice for a tribunal to give a complete statement of its reasoning. As a matter of adequacy, it is not essential to express what can be seen by inference.[241] However, it is more helpful for the tribunal to give its reasons rather than leave the readers to deduce them.

14.220    If the rules of procedure contain a checklist,[242] the tribunal should show that it has considered all the items on the list so that the Upper Tribunal may know that it has taken all relevant factors into account.[243]

## Anonymity

14.221    Rule 32(6) Tax Rules provides for anonymity in published reports of decisions of the Tax Chamber of the First-tier Tribunal:

> (6) If the Tribunal publishes a report of a decision resulting from a hearing which was held wholly or partly in private, the Tribunal must, so far as practicable, ensure that the report does not disclose information which was referred to only in a part of the hearing that was held in private (including such information which enables the identification of any person whose affairs were dealt with in the part of the hearing that was held in private) if to do so would undermine the purpose of holding the hearing in private.

14.222    Otherwise the Senior President has issued a practice statement on Form of Decisions and Neutral Citation which states:

> 8. Where anonymity was previously given to a party in a tribunal case, that practice will continue pending further review.[244]

## How can the reasons be made clear?

14.223    A tribunal's reasons must be clear, whatever their contents. In a sense, everything that is not content is style. However, it is important to distinguish clarity from other aspects of style. Reasons should always be clear; all other aspects of style are a matter of preference.

241  See Lord Lane CJ in *R v Immigration Appeal Tribunal ex p Khan (Mahmud)* [1983] QB 790 at 794.

242  See chapter 7.

243  *Woodhouse v Consignia plc* [2002] 1 WLR 2558 at [33].

244  For an analysis of the competing interests in a particular case, see the judgment of Henderson J in *Commissioners for Her Majesty's Revenue and Customs v Banerjee (No 2)* [2009] 3 All ER 930.

14.224   Writing reasons for decision is an exercise in communication. In order to be effective, they must be clear. And to be clear they must be clear to the parties and to others who may have to read them.

14.225   Reasons cannot be clear if the judge does not know what to say and how to say it. Planning is essential for most judges; few are able to produce a good set of reasons without thought.

14.226   There are three aspects to clarity: contents, expression and arrangement.

14.227   The contents must be clear before they can be expressed in clear language and with a clear arrangement. No amount of clarity of expression or elegance of arrangement can compensate for confused or inadequate reasoning. They only serve to expose it. Findings of fact should be clearly identified and distinguished from a statement of the evidence. Reasons should be distinguished from arguments and conclusions.

14.228   Expression covers the use of language and the length and structure of sentences and paragraphs. The language used should be clear and understandable to the principal audience(s). Some jargon and terms of art are necessary, but many are not. The judge should explain those that are necessary and find a clear substitute for those that are not. Abbreviations and acronyms should always be explained at their first use. Euphemisms are best avoided. It may appear kinder to say 'we had difficulty reconciling the claimant's evidence with the medical evidence' than 'we rejected the claimant's evidence because it was incompatible with the objective medical evidence'. But the latter is clear while the former is not. Is the tribunal saying that it did manage to reconcile the evidence, although it found it difficult to do so, or is it saying that it did not accept the claimant's evidence because of the conflict?

14.229   The reasons should be split into paragraphs that contain a single topic or idea. Those paragraphs should not be so long as to hamper the reader in absorbing what the reasons say and navigating around them. Sentences should not be too long and punctuation should be used to used to help make the meaning clear at first reading.

14.230   Arrangement involves the order in which the contents are presented and the manner of their presentation. Headings are useful for the reader and the writer, especially if the reasons are of any length. For the reader, they help to show the structure of the reasons and to find a way around them easily. For the writer, they impose a structure, which assists in ensuring that the reasons are comprehensive of matters to be included and contributes to their clarity.

14.231   In *Jasim v Secretary of State for the Home Department*,[245] Sedley LJ emphasised that form should follow from purpose:

> It is important, since the purpose of these documents is to be able to be understood and analysed, that reasons should be set out – as indeed they commonly are – in manageable paragraphs and sub-paragraphs, with cross-headings where appropriate.

Pill LJ agreed, adding that a structured form could also assist the writer of the reasons.[246]

---

245 [2006] EWCA Civ 342 at [4]; (2006) *Times* 17 May.
246 [2006] EWCA Civ 342 at [47].

14.232    But too much structure can obstruct understanding. In *Williams v J Walter Thompson Group Ltd*,[247] the Court of Appeal found extensive numbering in roman numerals inconvenient.

## What style should be adopted?

14.233   Ideally, the style should be dictated by the content and contribute to the clarity of the reasons. However, it is a personal matter and inevitably there is considerable variation between judges.

14.234   *The structure of the decision.* Some judges set out the procedural history of the case, summarise the evidence, make findings of fact, identify the relevant law and then apply the law to the facts to produce the conclusion. Others set out the issues and deal with each in turn.

14.235   *The language used.* Some judges prefer more formal language, while others use more colloquial expressions. This may vary according to the audience.

14.236   *The length.* Some judges are more verbose in their expression, others more concise. However, decisions should not be unduly long, even in the most complex cases.[248]

14.237   *The layout of the decision.* Some judges use headings; others do not. All judges are required to use numbered paragraphs. The Senior President has issued a practice statement on Form of Decisions and Neutral Citation which states:

> 2.   First-tier Tribunal and Upper Tribunal decisions must be prepared for delivery, or issued as approved decisions, with paragraph numbering.

14.238   *The use of evidence, arguments and law.* Some judges set out evidence, some summarise it, some merely refer to it, and others incorporate it by reference to a particular document or to the record of proceedings. The same options apply to the arguments of the parties and the statement of the law.

14.239    Whatever the style adopted, the reasons should always be expressed politely and dispassionately. This is appropriate even, or especially, when expressing criticism of a person, conduct or evidence.

14.240    Criticism should be avoided unless it is necessary to the decision.

## When is humour appropriate?

14.241   Humour is seldom appropriate, if ever. And it is not easy to identify when it is appropriate. It is best avoided. Even the mildest remark can be misunderstood. In *Secretary of State for Work and Pensions v Chiltern District Council*,[249] the author had commented that, in view of the number of issues raised, the case was one to take to a desert island. In the Court of Appeal, Arden LJ seemed to miss the humour but felt able to deduce from that

---

247  [2005] IRLR 376.
248  *Albion Water Ltd v Dŵr Cymru Cyf* [2009] 2 All ER 279 at [131].
249  Reported in the Court of Appeal as *R(H) 2/03*.

statement a tinge of regret on the author's part at the outcome of the appeal.

## Standard form and content

14.242   Reasons may be standardised in their form or their content.

14.243   A standard form can help ensure that the decision is given in a structured form.[250] The tribunal may provide a standard form for use or recommend one through training. Judges may also develop their own standard forms.

14.244   The Court of Appeal in *Solihull Metropolitan Borough Council Housing Benefits Review Board v Simpson*[251] approved this sort of approach to providing structured reasons. It is possible to spell out a list of headings from the courts' decisions. In *Evans and others v Secretary of State for Social Security*,[252] the Court of Appeal was concerned with four appeals from medical appeal tribunals. It suggests a framework for a decision:

- identify the issues before the tribunal;
- show that the tribunal dealt with them;
- identify the evidence that the tribunal relied on; and
- show that the tribunal acted lawfully.

A checklist would do just as well.

14.245   Standard content is more dangerous than a standard form, as it may not be sufficiently related to the issues, evidence and argument in the particular case. However, it is particularly useful for recording matters that have to be repeated regularly and whose accuracy or relevance does not depend on the particular case.

14.246   Whatever the standard practice followed, the reasons must be appropriate or adapted to the facts and circumstances of the case. In *Mansur v Turkey*,[253] the European Court of Human Rights has taken account of the facts that reasons given by a Turkish court were in stereotyped terms in holding that there had been a violation of article 5(3).

## Signature

14.247   Under TCEA, a signature is not required. However, it is good practice to sign a master copy of the final version in order to avoid error and dispute.[254]

---

250   Kennedy and Mann LJJ in *Solihull Metropolitan Borough Council Housing Benefit Review Board v Simpson* (1994) 27 HLR 41 at 48 and 50.

251   (1994) 27 HLR 41 at 48.

252   *R(I) 5/94.* This case is usually known as *Kitchen* after one of the parties. In *R (W) v SENDIST and London Borough of Hillingdon* [2005] ELR 599 at [26], Stanley Burnton J commended the practice of identifying issues as a structure for a tribunal's reasons.

253   (1995) Series A No 319-B.

254   Kennedy and Mann LJJ in *Solihull Metropolitan Borough Council Housing Benefit Review Board v Simpson* (1994) 27 HLR 41 at 48 and 50.

## Draft decisions

14.248   A tribunal may issue a decision in draft in order to allow the parties, or more likely their representatives, to draw attention to minor errors in the facts, the arguments or its citations of legislation and case-law. It provides a party or representative with a chance to identify matters that have not been covered in the reasons. Exceptionally, it may also allow them to make submissions on the substance of the decision.[255] However, this is discouraged.[256]

## Oral and written decisions

14.249   The rules of procedure may specify the form in which the decision may be given – oral or written – or permit either. If a choice is allowed, expressly or by implication, it is a matter for interpretation which constitutes the promulgation of the decision[257] after which the tribunal's function is discharged.

## Conflict between oral and written decisions

14.250   If there is, by mistake, a conflict between the oral and written decision, it may be possible to correct one to bring it into accord with what the tribunal intended.[258]

14.251       If, however, it appears that the tribunal has changed its mind, it may involve an error of law.[259]

## Decisions as precedents

14.252   A decision of the Upper Tribunal is more likely to deal with issues of law and less likely to deal with issues of fact than a decision of the First-tier Tribunal. If it is likely to have value as a precedent, there are considerations that do not apply to other decisions. But, like all decisions, their form and content need to take account of users. And users will be concerned with the use to which the decision will be put. That identifies the focus on the decision, the reasons that support it, and the practical implications for the future. The process by which the tribunal came to its conclusion on the law is of less, or even no, importance to anyone except the judge who made it.

14.253       On that approach, it is possible to identify the matters that may be included in decreasing order of importance. Importance determines two

---

255 *R (Mohamed) v Secretary of State for Foreign and Commonwealth Affairs* [2010] EWCA Civ 158.

256 *Egan v Motor Services (Bath) Ltd* [2008] 1 WLR 1589 and *R (Edwards) v Environment Agency* [2008] 1 WLR 1587.

257 *SK (Sri Lanka) v Secretary of State for the Home Department* [2008] EWCA Civ 495 at [21]; (2008) *Times* 27 May.

258 *Preston Banking Co v Williams Allsup and Sons Ltd* [1895] 1 Ch 141. See further chapter 15.

259 *Gutzmore v J Wardley (Holdings) Ltd* [1993] ICR 581; *SK (Sri Lanka) v Secretary of State for the Home Department* [2008] EWCA Civ 495 at [24]; (2004) *Times* 27 May.

considerations: whether the particular matter should be included and, if it is, the detail and prominence that is appropriate.

- A short statement of the issue to assist the reader in following the reasoning.
- The decision made.
- An introduction explaining something of the history and how the litigation developed.[260]
- The tribunal's reasons for that decision. Lord Macmillan's advice in *The Writing of Judgments*[261] was:

  The strength of a judgment lies in its reasoning and it should therefore be convincing.

- The relevant legislation, identified and set out, as it may not be readily accessible later.
- The arguments presented by the parties and the tribunal's conclusion on those arguments, which also serve to indicate arguments that the tribunal did not consider.
- The stages of reasoning by which the judge came to the ultimate conclusion. Lord Macmillan's advice in *The Writing of Judgments*[262] was:

  It is undesirable to cumber a judgment with all the apparatus of research which Bench and Bar have utilised in ascertaining the principle of law to be applied.

- The procedural steps by which the party's arguments were elicited.

## Reasons as justification

14.254 A tribunal's decisions may be influenced, consciously or otherwise, by factors that are not relevant in law. If so, the tribunal's reasons must justify its decision by reference to legally relevant criteria. As Chaïm Perelman and Lucie Olbrechts-Tyteca wrote:

It is a common, and not necessarily regrettable, occurrence even for a magistrate who knows the law to formulate his judgment in two steps: the conclusions are first inspired by what conforms most closely with his sense of justice, the technical motivation being added on later . . . Strictly legal reasons are adduced only for the purpose of justifying the decision to another audience.[263]

14.255 This process is distinct from a decision that is made on the basis of instinct or intuition, which has to be dissected by the conscious mind in order to reveal the reasons behind it.

---

260 *Re S and others (Residence)* [2008] 2 FLR 1377 at [7].
261 (1948) 26 Can BR 491 at 491.
262 (1948) 26 Can BR 491 at 498.
263 Chaïm Perelman and Lucie Olbrechts-Tyteca, *The New Rhetoric: A Treatise on Argumentation*, Notre Dame, 2008, p43.

# Promulgation and control over decisions and reasons

14.256 In civil law, a tribunal retains jurisdiction to decide a case until it has given a decision and that decision has been formally issued.[264] That process is called perfection or promulgation; the terms are interchangeable. It is only at that point that the tribunal's jurisdiction over the dispute comes to an end.[265] This affects the power to change a tribunal's decision or the reasons for that decision. Before then, the tribunal retains power to change its decision. Afterwards, there is power to correct it or set it aside only in limited circumstances.

## Promulgated

14.257 A tribunal retains jurisdiction to decide a case until its decision has been promulgated. That means until it has been communicated to the parties in the form provided for in the governing legislation. The legislation may stipulate what has to be promulgated for this purpose. In *Baxendale-Walker v Law Society*,[266] for example, section 48(1) of the Solicitors Act 1974 made clear that it was the decision itself that had to be promulgated; the reasons could be issued separately and later. Under TCEA, promulgation occurs when the decision has been put into writing and sent to the parties.[267]

## Changes before promulgation

14.258 Until promulgation, a tribunal may make any change it wishes in the decision. This includes coming to a completely different conclusion.[268] In *Stewart v Engel*,[269] Sir Christopher Slade described this as 'not merely consistent with, but also a proper application of the overriding objective'.[270]

14.259    The decision may be changed on the tribunal's own initiative or on the application of one of the parties.[271] It is irrelevant whether the decision recalled was given orally or in writing. The tribunal may act because new evidence has been produced or a new argument put to it. Or it may

---

264 In criminal matters, a court loses its jurisdiction as soon as it has announced its decision orally: *R v Essex Justices ex p Final* [1963] 2 QB 816; *R v Coates* [2004] 1 WLR 3043. The position is now more flexible than it once was in order to take account of the giving of reasons: Maurice Kay J in *Steward v Director of Public Prosecutions* [2004] 1 WLR 592 at [11]. On the effect of the release of a draft judgment see: *R v Steele* (2006) *Times* 5 September. And in *Birmingham City Council v Yardley* [2004] EWCA Civ 1756 at [18]; (2004) *Times* 13 December, the Court of Appeal spoke as if a judgment was final for enforcement purposes, despite being subject to the judge's final approval and although no order had been drawn up.

265 This is so even if the time for appealing runs from an earlier date: *Paulin v Paulin* [2009] 3 All ER 88.

266 [2006] 3 All ER 675.

267 [2000] 1 WLR 2268.

268 *In re L and another (Children) (Preliminary Findings: Power to Reverse)* [2013] 1 WLR 634.

269 *R (Anufrijeva) v Secretary of State for the Home Department* [2004] 1 AC 604 at [26]. Lord Millett said at [39] that although a decision did not have legal effect until it was communicated, an uncommunicated decision could be effective for some purposes.

270 [2000] 1 WLR 2268 at 2276.

271 *Re Harrison's Share under a Settlement* [1955] Ch 260.

act simply because it has changed its mind about the evidence and arguments that were before it. The courts have said that this power to reconsider should be exercised only 'in the most exceptional circumstances'[272] or for 'strong reasons'.[273] Every case depends on its own circumstancs, but the overriding objective is always to deal with the case justly.[274] The power is best exercised when the tribunal itself identifies a mistake and should not be used in a way that subverts the appeal process.[275]

14.260    However, the tribunal may go wrong in law if it has previously announced its apparently final decision to the parties and then substitutes a different, written one.[276]

## Draft decisions

14.261 These principles apply also to a draft decision that has been issued for the parties to identify typing and other obvious mistakes.[277] The representatives may be allowed the chance to make oral submissions on the change in the decision, but this is a matter for the tribunal's discretion.[278] The purpose of issuing a decision in draft is to identify mistakes, but the courts discourage invitations to a judge to reconsider the conclusions expressed in a draft judgment.[279]

## Fairness

14.262 Any change must be consistent with the overriding objective and the normal principle of fairness. This does not necessarily mean that the tribunal must allow further submissions or another hearing, as the parties have already had the chance to put forward their evidence and arguments. However, this may be necessary if the change occurs because of new evidence or argument.

## Changes after promulgation

14.263 For the tribunal's powers over its decision after promulgation, see chapter 15: Post decision.

---

272  *Re Barrell Enterprises* [1973] 1 WLR 19; *Taylor v Lawrence* [2003] QB 528 at [13].
273  *Compagnie Noga D'Importation et D'Exportation SA v Abacha* [2001] 3 All ER 513 at [43].
274  *In re L and another (Children) (Preliminary Findings: Power to Reverse)* [2013] 1 WLR 634 at [27].
275  *Compagnie Noga D'Importation et D'Exportation SA v Abacha* [2001] 3 All ER 513 at [47]. Compare the comment of Arden J quoted at [44].
276  *Gutzmore v J Wardley (Holdings) Ltd* [1993] ICR 581. However, this will not be wrong in law if it was clear that the decision as announced orally was inadvertently not what was intended. See *Adam and Harvey Ltd v. International Maritime Supplies Co Ltd* [1967] 1 WLR 445. This case involved a correction after promulgation, but the reasoning is applicable.
277  *Robinson v Bird* [2003] EWCA Civ 1820; (2004) *Times* 20 January.
278  [2003] EWCA Civ 1820 at [98].
279  *Egan v Motor Services (Bath) Ltd* [2008] 1 WLR 1589 and *R (Edwards) v Environment Agency* [2008] 1 WLR 1587.

# Post decision

*continued*

# Control after promulgation of final decision

15.1 Once a decision has been promulgated, a tribunal loses jurisdiction to decide the case. However, it retains limited powers in respect of the decision. There is a potential tension between these powers and the right of appeal.

15.2 This tension was considered in the courts by Rix LJ in *Compagnie Noga D'Importation et D'Exportation SA v Abacha*.[1] He quoted Arden J to the effect that it is preferable for a tribunal to correct its own errors if it can rather than leave the parties to an appeal.[2] But he said that it was wrong for a court to use its own powers to subvert the appeal process.[3] Rix LJ described what was involved in that process:

> ... it is the nature of the legal process that, once judgment has been rendered, analysis thereafter becomes clarified and refined, and citation of authority is applied to the findings made at first instance so as to illuminate that clarification and refinement of analysis of which I speak. But that is the function of the appeal process.

15.3 The tension may not be so easily resolved in the tribunals, as the tribunals' powers of review may extend into the area of appeal as defined by Rix LJ. In this context, it may be better to consider the functions of an appeal in order to decide if the issues raised are suitable ones for an appeal to the Upper Tribunal.

## The range of powers

15.4 The scope of the courts' jurisdiction once a decision has been promulgated was set out under five heads by Robert Walker LJ in *DEG-Dettsche Investitions und Entwicklungsgesellschaft mbH v Koshy*:[4]

> It is common ground that there is no general power for the court to vary an order after it has been passed and entered. Rimer J identified four real or apparent exceptions: first, the correction of obvious errors under the slip rule; second, supplementing (rather than varying) an order; third, cases where the order itself provides for its variation; and fourth, where there is a statutory right of review by a court of co-ordinate jurisdiction (for instance under s 375 of the Insolvency Act 1986). The judge did not suggest that his list was exhaustive and there appears to be a further exception where an order requires to be worked out, and a material change of circumstances occurs before it has been worked out (see *Jordan v Norfolk County Council* [1994] 1 WLR 1353 at 1358–1359).[5]

15.5 There are equivalent powers for tribunals under TCEA. They are dealt with in this chapter, except for the third class identified by Robert Walker LJ.

---

1 [2001] 3 All ER 513.

2 [2001] 3 All ER 513 at [44]. See also the Employment Appeal Tribunal in *Trimble v Supertravel Ltd* [1982] ICR 440 at 442. Arden J had overlooked a concession made during the hearing. However, if the legislation confers an express power to vary a decision, it should only be exercised in exceptional circumstances: *Papanicola (as trustee in bankruptcy for Mak) v Humphreys* [2005] 2 All ER 418 at [25].

3 [2001] 3 All ER 513 at [47].

4 [2001] 3 All ER 878.

5 [2001] 3 All ER 878 at [21].

# The tribunal's powers apart from legislation

### Review

15.6    In *Akewushola v Secretary of State for the Home Department*,[6] Court of Appeal held that a tribunal has no inherent power of review. Sedley LJ said:

> I do not think that, slips apart, a statutory tribunal – in contrast to a superior court – ordinarily possesses any inherent power to rescind or review its own decisions. Except where the High Court's jurisdiction is unequivocally excluded by privative legislation, it is there that the power of correction resides.[7]

15.7    This applies even if the practice of review has been accepted by the public body affected.[8]

15.8    As the Upper Tribunal is a superior court of record, it may have more inherent powers by virtue of TCEA s25.[9]

### Fraud

15.9    A decision may be set aside if it was obtained by fraud of, or procured by, a party to the proceedings.[10]

### Reconsideration of final decisions[11]

15.10    There is an exceptional power for an appellate body to reopen a case. It first came to prominence in the Court of Appeal's decision in *Taylor v Lawrence*[12] and has been extended to the High Court in both its original[13] and appellate jurisdiction.[14] The power is not appropriate to decisions that are subject to correction on appeal.[15] It is primarily concerned with cases where the litigation process has been critically undermine.[16] The mere fact that a mistake has occurred is not exceptional or sufficient to invoke this power.[17]

### The social security jurisdiction

15.11    The Commissioners claimed a jurisdiction to set aside decisions that were made in procedural error. The authorities were analysed by Mr Commissioner Hallett in the Appendix to *R(U) 3/89*. He called the power an inher-

---

6   [2000] 1 WLR 2295.

7   [2000] 1 WLR 2295 at 2301.

8   *R (Secretary of State for Defence) v President of the Pensions Appeal Tribunal (England and Wales)* [2004] 2 All ER 159.

9   See chapter 3.

10   *Taylor v Lawrence* [2003] QB 528 at [26]; *Cinpres Gas Injection Ltd v Melea Ltd* (2008) *Times* 29 February.

11   For reconsideration of interlocutory decisions, see chapter 7.

12   [2003] QB 528.

13   *R (AM (Cameroon)) v Asylum and Immigration Tribunal* [2008] 1 WLR 2062.

14   *Seray-Wurie v Hackney London Borough Council* [2003] 1 WLR 257 at [17].

15   *R (AM (Cameroon)) v Asylum and Immigration Tribunal* [2008] 1 WLR 2062.

16   *In re Uddin (A Child)* [2005] 1 WLR 2398 at [18].

17   *R (Nicholas) v Upper Tribunal and Secretary of State for Work and Pensions* [2013] EWCA Civ 799 at [20].

ent one and identified its source in the Commissioners' power to control their own procedure.[18] The instances he cited covered failure to deal with requests for an oral hearing, proceedings on the erroneous assumption that the claimant was not going to submit further evidence, and breaches of natural justice like deciding a case on a point not put to the parties.[19]

15.12　　In *R(I) 7/94*, a Tribunal of Commissioners said that, if a tribunal had power to reconsider a decision, it only arose on application.[20]

## Correction of accidental mistakes

15.13　A tribunal loses its jurisdiction to decide a case once its decision has been promulgated. The purpose of promulgation is to give effect to the decision made by the tribunal. In order to give full effect to this purpose, there must be a power to correct accidental mistakes in the decision as promulgated and in the reasons given for it.

### Under TCEA

15.14　Under TCEA, this power is authorised by paragraph 15 of Schedule 5. Paragraph 15(1) authorises the rules of procedure to allow for the correction of accidental errors in a decision or record of a decision. Rules of procedure have been made under that authority. UTR r42 is illustrative:[21]

> The Upper Tribunal may at any time correct any clerical mistake or other accidental slip or omission in a decision or record of a decision by–
> (a) sending notification of the amended decision, or a copy of the amended record, to all parties; and
> (b) making any necessary amendment to any information published in relation to the decision or record.

### When correction is allowed

15.15　The power allows a decision to be corrected. It does not allow a decision to be changed from the one that the tribunal intended to make.[22] The court rule was used to allow the correction of oversights, but this result is now achieved using the power to vary an order.[23]

15.16　　The decision as promulgated may be corrected so as to accord with the decision that was announced orally. In this case, the difference between the oral and written decision shows that a mistake has been made, although it does not show which is the correct version.

---

18　*R(U) 3/88* at [5(1)].
19　*R(U) 3/88* at [5(2)] and [6].
20　*R(I) 7/94* at [35].
21　See also: GRC Rules r40; HESC Rules r44; IAC Rules r31; PC Rules r50; SEC Rules r36; Tax Rules r37; WPAFC Rules r34. The CPR equivalent is CPR 40.12.
22　Lord Halsbury in *Preston Banking Co v Williams Allsup and Sons Ltd* [1895] 1 Ch 141 at 143; *Wordingham v Royal Exchange Trust Co Ltd* [1992] Ch 412; *R&V Versicherung AG v Risk Insurance and Reinsurance Solutions SA* (2007) *Times* 26 February; *AS v Secretary of State for Work and Pensions* [2011] UKUT 159 (AAC) at [16].
23　*Tibbles v SIG plc* [2012] 1 WLR 2591 at [53].

15.17    Even if the two versions of the decision are in accord, the decision as promulgated may still be corrected so as to accord with the decision as the tribunal intended to announce it. In this case, the mistake is not apparent from the difference between the two versions of the decision. The circumstances of the case may make it clear that a mistake has occurred. For example: the interlocutory discussion may show the true intention,[24] as may the nature and extent of the changes.[25] Ultimately, however, it is necessary to trust the honesty and integrity of the judge who made the decision.

15.18    In *Munks v Munks*,[26] the Court of Appeal decided that a decision that was made without jurisdiction could not be corrected and had to be set aside. However, that must be read in its context: the judge there intended to make the order at a time when he had no jurisdiction. The Court did not decide that a correction, properly made to reflect the intention of the judge, could not have brought the decision within jurisdiction.

## A power, not a duty

15.19    The rule only confers power to correct a decision as promulgated. There is no duty to do so. Usually, it is appropriate to exercise the power. But in some cases, it may not be appropriate. The test is whether something has happened since the decision was promulgated that makes it inexpedient or inequitable to correct it.[27] The mere fact of delay is not enough.[28]

## Who may exercise the power

15.20    The power is conferred on the tribunal. The constitution of the tribunal will be governed by the First-tier Tribunal and Upper Tribunal (Composition of Tribunal) Order 2008 and practice statements issued thereunder. The power has not been confined to a tribunal of the same constitution as made the decision. There is no objection in principle to the power being conferred on administrative staff.[29] However, correction is not within the Senior President's practice statements on delegation to staff.[30]

## Inherent power

15.21    According to Sedley LJ in *Akewushola v Secretary of State for the Home Department*, the power to correct slips is the only inherent power of a statutory tribunal.[31] This follows from the tribunal's duty to make a decision and the function of promulgation to issue that decision.

24  As in *Adam & Harvey Ltd v International Maritime Supplies Co Ltd* [1967] 1 WLR 445.
25  *AS v Secretary of State for Work and Pensions* [2011] UKUT 159 (AAC) at [16].
26  [1985] FLR 576.
27  *Moore v Buchanan* [1967] 1 WLR 1341.
28  *Tak Ming Co Ltd v Yee Sang Metal Supplies Co* [1973] 1 WLR 300 at 307–307.
29  For example: the power was conferred on a clerk by Social Security and Child Support (Decisions and Appeals) Regulations 1999 reg 56(1) (revoked). Compare the inherent power, discussed below.
30  See chapter 7.
31  [2000] 1 WLR 2295 at 2301.

15.22    The TCEA Sch 5 para 15(3) preserves any power to correct errors that is otherwise exercisable.

15.23    The power is inherent in the tribunal.[32] So, it may be exercised by any appropriately constituted tribunal with jurisdiction, whether or not the same as the one that is alleged to have made the mistake. But it cannot be exercised by an administrative official.[33]

## Powers to amend reasons for decision

15.24    The power to correct is limited to accidental errors in order that the decision as promulgated reflects the decision made by the tribunal. It does not allow the tribunal to amend the reasons for its decision or to add reasons that it did not intend to include. However, there are powers that allow for a tribunal to amend or supplement its reasons. First, the courts have also recognised that a tribunal may be allowed, or invited, to supplement its reasons.[34] Second, the Upper Tribunal has power under UTR r5(3)(n) to:

> (n) require any person, body or other tribunal whose decision is the subject of proceedings before the Upper Tribunal to provide reasons for the decision, or other information or documents in relation to the decision or any proceedings before that person, body or tribunal.

Third, there is the tribunal's power on review.[35]

## Directions

15.25    The rules of procedure allow a tribunal to amend a direction, on application by a party or on its own initiative.[36] As the tribunal also has power to set aside a direction and issue another in different terms, it will probably never be necessary to determine the precise scope of the power to amend.

# Setting aside

## Terminology

15.26    Setting aside may refer to the result of a procedure that has the effect of cancelling a decision or it may refer to a particular procedure. In this section, it refers to the procedure by which a tribunal's decision may be set aside for procedural deficiencies. A consent order is a decision for this purpose.[37]

---

32  Sedley LJ in *Akewushola v Secretary of State for the Home Department* [2000] 1 WLR 2295 at 2301.

33  *Memminger-IRO GmbH v Trip-Lite Ltd* (1992) *Times* 9 July.

34  See chapter 4.

35  See para 15.39 onwards.

36  See chapter 7.

37  *R (LR by ER) v FfT (HESC) and Hertfordshire CC* [2012] UKUT 213 (AAC) at [21]–[31].

## Authority

15.27   Tribunals do not have an inherent power to set aside their decisions.[38] This must be authorised by statute. The TCEA Sch 5 para 15 authorises rules of procedure for correcting accidental errors and setting aside decisions:

> (1) Rules may make provision for the correction of accidental errors in a decision or record of a decision.
> (2) Rules may make provision for the setting aside of a decision in proceedings before the First-tier Tribunal or Upper Tribunal–
>> (a) where a document relating to the proceedings was not sent to, or was not received at an appropriate time by, a party to the proceedings or a party's representative;
>> (b) where a document relating to the proceedings was not sent to the First-tier Tribunal or Upper Tribunal at an appropriate time;
>> (c) where a party to the proceedings, or a party's representative, was not present at a hearing related to the proceedings; or
>> (d) where there has been any other procedural irregularity in the proceedings.
> (3) Sub-paragraphs (1) and (2) shall not be taken to prejudice, or to be preju-diced by, any power to correct errors or set aside decisions that is exercisable apart from rules made by virtue of those sub-paragraphs.

15.28   UTR r43(1) to (3) is illustrative:[39]

> (1) The Upper Tribunal may set aside a decision which disposes of proceedings, or part of such a decision, and re-make the decision or the relevant part of it, if–
>> (a) the Upper Tribunal considers that it is in the interests of justice to do so; and
>> (b) one or more of the conditions in paragraph (2) are satisfied.
> (2) The conditions are–
>> (a) a document relating to the proceedings was not sent to, or was not received at an appropriate time by, a party or a party's representative;
>> (b) a document relating to the proceedings was not sent to the Upper Tribunal at an appropriate time;
>> (c) a party, or a party's representative, was not present at a hearing related to the proceedings; or
>> (d) there has been some other procedural irregularity in the proceedings.
> (3) Except where paragraph (4) applies, a party applying for a decision, or part of a decision, to be set aside under paragraph (1) must make a written application to the Upper Tribunal so that it is received no later than 1 month after the date on which the Upper Tribunal sent notice of the decision to the party.

## Initiating the process

15.29   The process may be initiated by an application from a party under rule 43(3). There is no express authority for, or prohibition on, the tribunal

---

38  Sedley LJ in *Akewushola v Secretary of State for the Home Department* [2000] 1 WLR 2295 at 2301.
39  See also: GRC Rules r41; HESC Rules r45; IAC Rules r32; Lands Rules r54; PC Rules r51; SEC Rules r37; Tax Rules r38; WPAFC Rules r35.

acting of its own initiative. This power may be implied, as it would be consistent with the enabling power in that respect under TCEA Sch 5 para 6.

## Who may exercise the power

15.30 The power is conferred on the tribunal. The constitution of the tribunal will be governed by the First-tier Tribunal and Upper Tribunal (Composition of Tribunal) Order 2008 and practice statements issued thereunder. The power has not been confined to a tribunal of the same constitution as made the decision. It is not within the Senior President's practice statements on the delegation.[40]

## The scope of the power

15.31 The power is limited to the procedural deficiencies set out in paragraph (2). In addition, the power can only be exercised if the tribunal considers it is in the interests of justice to do so under paragraph (1)(a). The power must also be interpreted and applied in the context of the overriding objective.

15.32 The default position is that a party who has been deprived of an oral hearing by some mishap is entitled to have the decision set aside so that a hearing can be held.[41] It is relevant to consider: (i) why the party did not attend the hearing; (ii) the length of, and the reasons for, any delay in applying for the decision to be set aside; and (iii) whether the other party would be prejudiced if the decision were set aside and the case reheard.

15.33 The power is limited to procedural errors; it does not allow a decision to be set aside for matters that relate to the substance of the decision.[42] The Employment Appeal Tribunal came to this conclusion on the basis of the respective roles of the industrial tribunal's power of review (set aside) and an appeal.[43] The Commissioners also limited set aside powers to procedural matters by reasoning from the scope of the enabling power.[44]

## Other powers of set aside

15.34 The TCEA Sch 5 para15(3) preserves other powers to set aside a decision. Those powers are as follows.

15.35 A decision may be set aside if obtained by fraud of, or procured by, a party to the proceedings.[45]

15.36 The Upper Tribunal has the same powers, rights, privileges and authority as the High Court in respect of the attendance and examination of witnesses, the production and inspection of documents, and all other matters incidental to the Upper Tribunal's functions (s25(1)). These may include more extensive powers to set aside decisions.

---

40 See chapter 7.
41 *Grimshaw v Dunbar* [1953] 1 QB 408.
42 *R (LR by ER) v FfT (HESC) and Hertfordshire CC* [2012] UKUT 213 (AAC) at [47].
43 *Trimble v Supertravel Ltd* [1982] ICR 440 at 442.
44 *R(U) 3/89* at [24] of the Appendix to the decision.
45 *Taylor v Lawrence* [2003] QB 528 at [26]; *Cinpres Gas Injection Ltd v Melea Ltd* (2008) *Times* 29 February.

15.37    The review procedure under TCEA provides for setting aside a decision, including for procedural deficiencies. However, the scope of this
power is limited by the rules of procedure.[46]

15.38    All these set aside powers are additional to the power to set aside a
decision on appeal for error of law.[47] So, the Upper Tribunal may set aside
a decision on that ground even if the First-tier Tribunal has refused to
exercise its set aside powers on the same facts.

## Review

15.39  Review is a process under TCEA by which the First-tier Tribunal or Upper
Tribunal considers whether it has made a mistake 'on a matter in a case'.
The powers are contained in TCEA ss9 and 10; the rules of procedure pre-
scribe the circumstances in which those powers may be exercised.

### The scope of the process

15.40  The process applies to a decision on any matter in a case, except for those
matters excluded from the right of appeal (ss9(1) and 10(1)).

15.41    There is no definition of 'a matter in a case'. It is wide enough to cover
matters both of substance and procedure.

15.42    Each decision may only be considered for review, or reviewed, once. If
a tribunal has reviewed a decision, it cannot do so again. If it has decided
'that an earlier decision should not be reviewed', it cannot later decide to
review it. (ss9(10) and 10(8)) A decision 'that an earlier decision should not
be reviewed' must refer to a refusal to review rather than a decision to take
no action on a review. This follows from the nature of a review as a process
rather than an outcome. It also follows from the statutory language, since
otherwise the reference to not reviewing a decision more than once would
be redundant.

15.43    Decisions made under the review powers are excluded from the right
of appeal (ss11(5)(d) and 13(8)(d)). However, when a matter is re-decided,
that creates a new decision, which itself is subject to the power of review
and the right of appeal (ss9(11) and 10(9)).

### Outcomes

15.44  Under TCEA, a tribunal has a menu of powers on review; they are discretionary (ss9(1) and 10(1)). It may refuse to review. If it does review, it may:
(a) correct accidental errors in the decision or the record of the decision;
(b) amend the reasons given for the decision; (c) set the decision aside; or
(d) not take action on the review. (ss9(4) and 10(4))

15.45    However, TCEA authorises these powers to be restricted by the rules
of procedure (ss9(3) and 10(3)). The rules have severely restricted the powers of review. They may only be exercised in limited circumstances and,
for the most part, only on an application for permission to appeal. This

46  See above.
47  *R(SB) 23/83* at [3].

effectively overrides the power for the tribunal to act on its own initiative under sections 9(2)(a) and 10(2)(a). [48]

15.46   In *JS v Secretary of State for Work and Pensions*,[49] a three-judge panel of the Upper Tribunal decided how the power to amend reasons should be applied. The judge dealing with the review should identify the error of law that justifies the review. If the judge considers that it might be appropriate to amend the reasons, the parties should be given the chance to make representations. The presiding judge should be asked to provide reasons and the judge dealing with the review should then decide if they would constitute amendments for the purpose of the review power. It is only appropriate to amend reasons if it would not be appropriate to set the decision aside. The power must not be used to subvert the appeal process. There must be some objective guarantee that the changes are not merely justifications. A presiding judge who is dealing with a review should approach it in the same spirit. On appeal, the Upper Tribunal has jurisdiction to decide whether the changes to the reasons were amendments for that purpose.

## Effect of setting aside a decision

15.47   Once a decision has been set aside on review, it is no longer subject to the right of appeal. This may occur before or during the appeal process (ss11(5)(e) and 13(8)(e)).[50] In the latter case, the appeal will lapse.

15.48      The decision to set aside a decision under review may itself be the subject of a review, but only to allow accidental errors to be corrected in the decision or the record of the decision (ss9(9) and 10(7)).

## Review under the rules of procedure

15.49   The First-tier Tribunal may review for errors of law identified on an application for permission to appeal to the Upper Tribunal.[51] Under HESC Rules, a decision in a special educational needs case may also be reviewed for a change of circumstances since it was made (r48(2)). Under PC Rules, the test is whether a ground of appeal is likely to be successful (r55(1)). This reflects the fact that an appeal may lie from this Chamber otherwise than for error of law.

15.50      The Upper Tribunal may review on an application for permission to appeal to the Court of Appeal in two circumstances. Rule 45(1) provides:[52]

    (a) when making the decision the Upper Tribunal overlooked a legislative provision or binding authority which could have had a material effect on the decision; or

    (b) since the Upper Tribunal's decision, a court has made a decision which is binding on the Upper Tribunal and which, had it been made before

---

48   *JS v Kingston upon Hull City Council* [2014] UKUT 0043 (AAC).

49   [2013] UKUT 100 (AAC).

50   This is in accordance with general principle: *R(SB) 1/82* at [12].

51   See: GRC Rules r44(1)(a); HESC Rules r49(1)(a); IAC Rules r35(1)(a); SEC Rules r40(2)(b); Tax Rules r41(1)(b); WPAFC Rules r38(1)(b).

52   See also Lands Rules r56(1).

the Upper Tribunal's decision, could have had a material effect on the decision.

These restrict the scope of the Upper Tribunal's review power. The circumstances specified would both be errors of law under the First-tier Tribunal's review powers.

15.51 And for references to the Upper Tribunal under the Forfeiture Act 1982, the Upper Tribunal may review in three circumstances. Rule 47(2) provides:

> ...
>
> (b) the decision was made in ignorance of, or was based on a mistake as to, some material fact; or
>
> (c) there has been a relevant change in circumstances since the decision was made.

15.52 A tribunal cannot protect itself from the power of review by deciding for itself that it is not in error of law.[53]

## Who may exercise the power

15.53 The power is conferred on the tribunal. The constitution of the tribunal will be governed by the First-tier Tribunal and Upper Tribunal (Composition of Tribunal) Order 2008 and practice statements issued thereunder. The power has not been confined to a tribunal of the same constitution as made the decision. It is not within the Senior President's practice statements on the delegation.[54] There is, though, no reason in principle why the former presiding judge should not undertake the review.[55]

15.54 If the First-tier Tribunal sets a decision aside, it may re-decide it or refer the matter to the Upper Tribunal (s9(5)); the Upper Tribunal must re-decide a matter that is referred to it (s9(6)).[56] If the Upper Tribunal sets a decision aside, it must re-decide the matter (s10(5)). Only the matter that was the subject of the decision may be re-decided or referred. If a Tribunal re-decides a matter, it may make appropriate findings of fact (ss9(8) and 10(6)). If the Upper Tribunal decides a matter on referral, it may make any decision that the First-tier Tribunal could have made (s9(7)).

## The tribunal's approach to review

15.55 The fact that a tribunal is undertaking a review of its own decision is significant. In *DK (Serbia) v Secretary of State for the Home Department*,[57] the Court of Appeal emphasised the importance of this feature in the context of the reconsideration powers of the Asylum and Immigration Tribunal. Latham LJ explained:[58]

---

53  *LM v Secretary of State for Work and Pensions* [2009] UKUT 185 (AAC) at [5]–[6].

54  See chapter 7.

55  *AA v Cheshire and Wirral Partnership NHS Foundation Trust* [2009] UKUT 195 (AAC) at [26]–[27]; *DL v London Borough of Redbridge* [2010] UKUT 293 (AAC) at [15]–[19].

56  The procedure before the Upper Tribunal is governed by Lands Rules r45 and UTR r26A.

57  [2007] 2 All ER 483.

58  [2007] 2 All ER 483 at 20 and 22.

The jurisdiction is one which is being exercised by the same tribunal, conceptually, both at the first hearing of the appeal, and then at any reconsideration. That seems to me to be the key to the way in which reconsiderations should be managed in procedural terms.

As far as what has been called the second stage of a reconsideration is concerned, the fact that it is, as I have said, conceptually a reconsideration by the same body which made the original decision, carries with it a number of consequences. The most important is that any body asked to reconsider a decision on the grounds of an identified error of law will approach its reconsideration on the basis that any factual findings and conclusions or judgments arising from those findings which are unaffected by the error of law need not be revisited. It is not a rehearing: Parliament chose not to use that concept, presumably for good reasons. And the fact that the reconsideration may be carried out by a differently constituted tribunal or a different Immigration Judge does not affect the general principle of the 2004 Act, which is that the process of reconsideration is carried out by the same body as made the original decision. The right approach, in my view, to the directions which should be considered by the immigration judge ordering reconsideration or the Tribunal carrying out the reconsideration is to assume, notionally, that the reconsideration will be, or is being, carried out by the original decision-maker.

## Content and tone of review decisions

15.56   The reasons given in a review decision may be quite short and assume that the parties understand the background. They need not be of the length, or in the style, appropriate for a self-contained decision of the Upper Tribunal that has to be understood without the parties' knowledge of the case.[59]

15.57   In *R v Lancashire County Council ex p Huddleston*,[60] Sir John Donaldson MR said: 'judges of the inferior courts when challenged on the exercise of their jurisdiction traditionally explain fully what they have done and why they have done it, but are not partisan in their own defence'.[61] The same tone is appropriate for review decisions.

## Applications for permission to appeal

15.58   For the most part, the review powers may only be exercised on an application for permission. On the face of it, this allows any party to initiate the review process by submitting a document in the form of an application for permission against any decision and at any stage of the proceedings. However, even if this would be sufficient to initiate the review process, the tribunal would probably exercise its discretion to refuse to review. The need for an application for permission prevents the tribunal from exercising the power of review on its own initiative.[62]

59   *R (RB) v First-tier Tribunal* (Review) [2010] UKUT 160 (AAC) at [32].
60   [1986] 2 All ER 941.
61   [1986] 2 All ER 941 at 945.
62   *JS v Kingston upon Hull City Council* [2014] UKUT 0043 (AAC).

## Review and appeal

15.59   There is a tension between the scope of a review and an appeal in the case of errors of law. Two issues arise. First, when is the review power available? It is only available if the tribunal is satisfied that there is an error of law. In contrast, permission to appeal may be given if it is merely arguable that there is an error. Second, when should the review power be used? It is discretionary, so permission may be given if the case is an appropriate one for the Upper Tribunal even if review is available. In *Compagnie Noga D'Importation et D'Exportation SA v Abacha*, Rix LJ said although courts could correct their own mistakes, they should not subvert the appeal process.[63] In *R (RB) v First-tier Tribunal* (Review),[64] the Upper Tribunal took the same approach.

## Similar powers

15.60   The TCEA makes it clear that the review procedure is not a comprehensive code. It also provides separately for correcting accidental slips and for setting aside a decision on procedural grounds.[65]

15.61   Legislation may also make specific provision for decisions to be set aside on procedural or substantive grounds.[66]

15.62   It is not clear if reconsideration[67] of an interlocutory decision continues to operate outside the review process or is subsumed within the review process. If it is subsumed, a decision not to reconsider will bar any further review.

# Suspending the effect of a decision

## The power

15.63   Under TCEA, the First-tier Tribunal has power to suspend the effect of its decisions and the Upper Tribunal has power to suspend the effect of both its decisions and those of the First-tier Tribunal, pending an appeal or review. This is a case management power. UTR r5(3)(l) and (m) is illustrative:[68]

>   (3) In particular, and without restricting the general powers in paragraphs (1) and (2), the Upper Tribunal may–

---

63   [2001] 3 All ER 513 at [47].
64   [2010] UKUT 160 (AAC).
65   See paras 15.26 onwards.
66   Social Security Act 1998 s13(3) requires a tribunal to set aside a decision if each of the principal parties expresses the view that it was erroneous in point of law. Child Support Act 1991 s23A(3) makes equivalent provision for child support. In practice, the other parties are only asked if they agree with an application for permission to appeal if it is made by the Secretary of State.
67   See chapter 7.
68   See also: GRC Rules r5(3)(l); HESC Rules r5(3)(l); IAC Rules r4(3)(l); Lands Rules r5(3)(l) and (m); PC Rules r6(3)(o); SEC Rules r5(3)(l); Tax Rules r5(3)(l); WPAFC Rules r5(3)(l). The CPR equivalent is CPR 52.7 (where the process is called 'stay'), but this applies to orders and decisions, not to their effects.

. . .

(l)  suspend the effect of its own decision pending an appeal or review of that decision;

(m) in an appeal, or an application for permission to appeal, against the decision of another tribunal, suspend the effect of that decision pending the determination of the application for permission to appeal, and any appeal; . . .

15.64   There is no express enabling power for these rules. They must be authorised by paragraph 16 of Schedule 5 TCEA as ancillary powers that are necessary to the proper exercise of the tribunal's functions.

## The scope of the power

15.65   The power may be used in at least two different circumstances.

15.66   First, the power allows suspension in order to preserve the status quo and to render the appeal or review process effective.[69] For example: if the successful party is allowed to enforce the decision pending appeal, it may be impossible to restore the position if the appeal is successful.

15.67   Second, the power allows suspension in order to relieve the hardship that one party may suffer if the decision is enforced but then reversed on appeal.

15.68   The power applies to the effect of a decision, not just the decision itself. This allows the Upper Tribunal to suspend not only the decision of the First-tier Tribunal but the decision of the decision-maker that was under appeal. Otherwise, the power to suspend could be ineffective.

15.69   The power does not allow a suspension in order to relieve a party of having to apply the decision to other cases unless and until it has been confirmed on appeal.[70] For example: a decision-maker may have to apply the reasoning in the decision to numerous other cases, all of which will have to be redecided if the decision is reversed on appeal.

15.70   Nor does the power allow a suspension of the effect of a decision that a provision was made without statutory authority. The effect of a such a decision is merely declaratory that the provision was made without authority and was of no effect in law. It would be incompatible with the nature of such a decision to suspend its effect.[71]

## Deciding whether to exercise the power

15.71   The power is discretionary. It must be exercised judicially and in the light of the overriding objective. Sullivan LJ explained the process in *Department for Environment, Food and Rural Affairs v Downs:*[72]

> A stay is the exception rather than the rule, solid grounds have to be put forward by the party seeking the stay, and, if such grounds are established, a balancing exercise weighing the risks of injustice to each side if a stay is or is not granted. It is fair to say that those reasons are normally of some form

69  *R (H) v Ashworth Special Hospital Authority* [2003] 1 WLR 127 at [42].

70  *Secretary of State for the Home Department v AD and MM (No 2)* [2009] UKUT 69 (AAC).

71  *Ahmed v HM Treasury* [2010] 4 All ER 829.

72  [2009] EWCA Civ 257 at [8]–[9].

of irremediable harm if no stay is granted . . . It is unusual to grant a stay to prevent the kind of temporary inconvenience that any appellant is bound to face because he has to live, at least temporarily, with the consequences of an unfavourable judgment which he wishes to challenge to the Court of Appeal.

15.72   One relevant factor is whether there are other powers that allow the party's position to be protected. For example: the social security legislation contains powers that prescribe the handling of cases that depend on test cases[73] and that authorise the Secretary of State to suspend payment of benefit.[74]

15.73   The Upper Tribunal considered the exercise of the power in *Carmarthenshire County Council v MW & JW*.[75] The judge took a flexible approach, refusing to treat any particular likelihood of a successful appeal as a threshold criterion.[76] He also declined to treat the existence of a solid ground for exercising the power as a separate requirement from the balancing exercise of discretion.[77]

## Procedure

15.74   The procedure for applying to the Upper Tribunal for a suspension is contained in UTR r20A.

## Urgent applications

15.75   Ideally, the person affected should be allowed a chance to make representations on the suspension. However, the circumstances may justify the tribunal in ordering suspension urgently. The breach of fairness in this procedure can be remedied by allowing the person a chance to apply for the suspension to be removed. Alternatively, the tribunal could order a suspension for a short period only, so that the person would have a chance to make representations before the issue is reconsidered.

## Emergency applications

15.76   If the First-tier Tribunal refuses to suspend its decision, the Upper Tribunal has power to do so. It will have that power in two circumstances: (i) on an application for permission to appeal; and (ii) if the First-tier Tribunal gave permission, on an appeal. The matter may be so urgent that there is no time to lodge the application or appeal in accordance with the rules of procedure at the tribunal's office. In that case, an application may be made to the duty High Court judge taking out-of-hours work. That judge will sit as a Judge of the Upper Tribunal and will have to decide: (i) whether to waive the failure to comply with the requirements of the rules on the

---

73  Social Security Act 1998 ss25–26; Child Support Act 1991 ss28ZA–28ZB.
74  See: Social Security Act 1998 s21(2)(c) and (d); Child Support, Pensions and Social Security Act 2000 Sch 7 para 13(2)(c) and (d).
75  [2010] UKUT 348 (AAC); [2011] AACR 17.
76  [2010] UKUT 348 (AAC); [2011] AACR 17 at [20]–[21].
77  [2010] UKUT 348 (AAC); [2011] AACR 17 at [25].

making of an application for permission or the providing notice of an appeal; and (ii) whether to suspend the decision of the First-tier Tribunal.

## Detention of a patient

15.77   The power to order the continued detention of a patient in a mental health case must be used sparingly.[78]

## Judicial review

15.78   In *R (JW through DW) v The Learning Trust*,[79] the Upper Tribunal considered an application for a judicial review of a decision-maker's decision. In effect, the applicant sought suspension of the decision pending an appeal to the First-tier Tribunal. The tribunal decided that it had jurisdiction, but that it had to be exercised sparingly if the tribunal's rules of procedure do not allow for interim relief and the decision-maker's rules contain no power of suspension.

---

78   *R (H) v Ashworth Special Hospital Authority* [2003] 1 WLR 127 at [48].
79   [2009] UKUT 197 (AAC).

# APPENDICES

# Tribunals, Courts and Enforcement Act 2007[1]

## PART 1: TRIBUNALS AND INQUIRIES

### CHAPTER 1: TRIBUNAL JUDICIARY – INDEPENDENCE AND SENIOR PRESIDENT

#### Independence of tribunal judiciary

1   In section 3 of the Constitutional Reform Act 2005 (guarantee of continued judicial independence), after subsection (7) insert–

'(7A) In this section 'the judiciary' also includes every person who–
  (a) holds an office listed in Schedule 14 or holds an office listed in subsection (7B), and
  (b) but for this subsection would not be a member of the judiciary for the purposes of this section.

(7B) The offices are those of–
  (a) Senior President of Tribunals;
  (b) President of Employment Tribunals (Scotland);
  (c) Vice President of Employment Tribunals (Scotland);
  (d) member of a panel of chairmen of Employment Tribunals (Scotland);
  (e) member of a panel of members of employment tribunals that is not a panel of chairmen;
  (f) adjudicator appointed under section 5 of the Criminal Injuries Compensation Act 1995.'

#### Senior President of Tribunals

2 (1) Her Majesty may, on the recommendation of the Lord Chancellor, appoint a person to the office of Senior President of Tribunals.

(2) Schedule 1 makes further provision about the Senior President of Tribunals and about recommendations for appointment under subsection (1).

(3) A holder of the office of Senior President of Tribunals must, in carrying out the functions of that office, have regard to–
  (a) the need for tribunals to be accessible,
  (b) the need for proceedings before tribunals–
    (i) to be fair, and
    (ii) to be handled quickly and efficiently,
  (c) the need for members of tribunals to be experts in the subject-matter of, or the law to be applied in, cases in which they decide matters, and
  (d) the need to develop innovative methods of resolving disputes that are of a type that may be brought before tribunals.

(4) In subsection (3) 'tribunals' means–
  (a) the First-tier Tribunal,
  (b) the Upper Tribunal,
  (c) employment tribunals, and
  (d) the Employment Appeal Tribunal.

### CHAPTER 2: FIRST-TIER TRIBUNAL AND UPPER TRIBUNAL

#### *Establishment*

#### The First-tier Tribunal and the Upper Tribunal

3 (1) There is to be a tribunal, known as the First-tier Tribunal, for the purpose of exercising the functions conferred on it under or by virtue of this Act or any other Act.

(2) There is to be a tribunal, known as the Upper Tribunal, for the purpose of exercising the functions conferred on it under or by virtue of this Act or any other Act.

(3) Each of the First-tier Tribunal, and the Upper Tribunal, is to consist of its judges and other members.

(4) The Senior President of Tribunals is to preside over both of the First-tier Tribunal and the Upper Tribunal.

(5) The Upper Tribunal is to be a superior court of record.

## Members and composition of tribunals

### Judges and other members of the First-tier Tribunal

4 (1) A person is a judge of the First-tier Tribunal if the person–

   (a) is a judge of the First-tier Tribunal by virtue of appointment under paragraph 1(1) of Schedule 2,

   (b) is a transferred-in judge of the First-tier Tribunal (see section 31(2)),

   (c) is a judge of the Upper Tribunal,

   (ca) is within section 6A, or

   (e) is a member of a panel of Employment Judges.

  (2) A person is also a judge of the First-tier Tribunal, but only as regards functions of the tribunal in relation to appeals such as are mentioned in subsection (1) of section 5 of the Criminal Injuries Compensation Act 1995, if the person is an adjudicator appointed under that section by the Scottish Ministers.

  (3) A person is one of the other members of the First-tier Tribunal if the person–

   (a) is a member of the First-tier Tribunal by virtue of appointment under paragraph 2(1) of Schedule 2,

   (b) is a transferred-in other member of the First-tier Tribunal (see section 31(2)),

   (c) is one of the other members of the Upper Tribunal, or

   (d) is a member of a panel of members of employment tribunals that is not a panel of Employment Judges.

  (4) Schedule 2–

   contains provision for the appointment of persons to be judges or other members of the First-tier Tribunal, and

   makes further provision in connection with judges and other members of the First-tier Tribunal.

### Judges and other members of the Upper Tribunal

5 (1) A person is a judge of the Upper Tribunal if the person–

   (a) is the Senior President of Tribunals,

   (b) is a judge of the Upper Tribunal by virtue of appointment under paragraph 1(1) of Schedule 3,

   (c) is a transferred-in judge of the Upper Tribunal (see section 31(2)),

   (e) is the Chief Social Security Commissioner, or any other Social Security Commissioner, appointed under section 50(1) of the Social Security Administration (Northern Ireland) Act 1992,

   (f) is a Social Security Commissioner appointed under section 50(2) of that Act (deputy Commissioners),

   (g) is within section 6(1),

   (h) is a deputy judge of the Upper Tribunal (whether under paragraph 7 of Schedule 3 or under section 31(2)), or

   (i) is a Chamber President or a Deputy Chamber President, whether of a chamber of the Upper Tribunal or of a chamber of the First-tier Tribunal, and does not fall within any of paragraphs (a) to (h).

  (2) A person is one of the other members of the Upper Tribunal if the person–

   (a) is a member of the Upper Tribunal by virtue of appointment under paragraph 2(1) of Schedule 3,

   (b) is a transferred-in other member of the Upper Tribunal (see section 31(2)), or

   (c) is a member of the Employment Appeal Tribunal appointed under section 22(1)(c) of the Employment Tribunals Act 1996.

  (3) Schedule 3–

   contains provision for the appointment of persons to be judges (including deputy judges), or other members, of the Upper Tribunal, and

   makes further provision in connection with judges and other members of the Upper Tribunal.

### Certain judges who are also judges of First-tier Tribunal and Upper Tribunal

6 (1) A person is within this subsection (and so, by virtue of sections 4(1)(c) and 5(1)(g), is a judge of the First-tier Tribunal and of the Upper Tribunal) if the person–

(za) is the Lord Chief Justice of England and Wales,

(zb) is the Master of the Rolls,

(zc) is the President of the Queen's Bench Division of the High Court in England and Wales,

(zd) is the President of the Family Division of the High Court in England and Wales,

(ze) is the Chancellor of the High Court in England and Wales,

(a)  is an ordinary judge of the Court of Appeal in England and Wales (including the vice-president, if any, of either division of that Court),

(b)  is a Lord Justice of Appeal in Northern Ireland,

(c)  is a judge of the Court of Session,

(d)  is a puisne judge of the High Court in England and Wales or Northern Ireland,

(da) is a deputy judge of the High Court in England and Wales,

(db) is the Judge Advocate General,

(e)  is a circuit judge,

(f)  is a sheriff in Scotland,

(g)  is a county court judge in Northern Ireland,

(h)  is a district judge in England and Wales or Northern Ireland, or

(i)  is a District Judge (Magistrates' Courts).

(2) References in subsection (1)(c) to (i) to office-holders do not include deputies or temporary office-holders.

### Certain judges who are also judges of the First-tier Tribunal

6A    A person is within this section (and so, by virtue of section 4(1)(ca), is a judge of the First-tier Tribunal) if the person–

(a)  is a deputy Circuit judge,

(b)  is a Recorder,

(c)  is a person who holds an office listed–

   (i)  in the first column of the table in section 89(3C) of the Senior Courts Act 1981 (senior High Court Masters etc), or

   (ii) in column 1 of Part 2 of Schedule 2 to that Act (High Court Masters etc),

(d)  is a deputy district judge appointed under section 102 of that Act or section 8 of the County Courts Act 1984,

(e)  is a Deputy District Judge (Magistrates' Courts), or

(f)  is a person appointed under section 30(1)(a) or (b) of the Courts-Martial (Appeals) Act 1951 (assistants to the Judge Advocate General).

### Chambers: jurisdiction and Presidents

7 (1) The Lord Chancellor may, with the concurrence of the Senior President of Tribunals, by order make provision for the organisation of each of the First-tier Tribunal and the Upper Tribunal into a number of chambers.

(2) There is–

(a)  for each chamber of the First-tier Tribunal, and

(b)  for each chamber of the Upper Tribunal,

to be a person, or two persons, to preside over that chamber.

(3) A person may not at any particular time preside over more than one chamber of the First-tier Tribunal and may not at any particular time preside over more than one chamber of the Upper Tribunal (but may at the same time preside over one chamber of the First-tier Tribunal and over one chamber of the Upper Tribunal).

(4) A person appointed under this section to preside over a chamber is to be known as a Chamber President.

(5) Where two persons are appointed under this section to preside over the same chamber, any reference in an enactment to the Chamber President of the chamber is a reference to a person appointed under this section to preside over the chamber.

(6) The Senior President of Tribunals may (consistently with subsections (2) and (3)) appoint a person who is the Chamber President of a chamber to preside instead, or to preside also, over another chamber.

(7) The Senior President of Tribunals may (consistently with subsections (2) and (3)) appoint a person who is not a Chamber President to preside over a chamber.

(8) Schedule 4 (eligibility for appointment under subsection (7), appointment of Deputy Chamber Presidents and Acting Chamber Presidents, assignment of judges and other members of the First-tier Tribunal and Upper Tribunal, and further provision about Chamber Presidents and chambers) has effect.

(9) Each of the Lord Chancellor and the Senior President of Tribunals may, with the concurrence of the other, by order–
  (a) make provision for the allocation of the First-tier Tribunal's functions between its chambers;
  (b) make provision for the allocation of the Upper Tribunal's functions between its chambers;
  (c) amend or revoke any order made under this subsection.

### Senior President of Tribunals: power to delegate

8 (1) The Senior President of Tribunals may delegate any function he has in his capacity as Senior President of Tribunals–
  (a) to any judge, or other member, of the Upper Tribunal or First-tier Tribunal;
  (b) to staff appointed under section 40(1).

(1A) A function under paragraph 1(1) or 2(1) of Schedule 2 may be delegated under subsection (1) only to a Chamber President of a chamber of the Upper Tribunal.

(2) Subsection (1) does not apply to functions of the Senior President of Tribunals under under any of the following–
  section 7(7);
  section 7(9);
  paragraph 2(1) of Schedule 3;
  paragraph 7(1) of Schedule 3;
  paragraph 2 of Schedule 4;
  paragraph 5(1) and (3) of Schedule 4;
  paragraph 5(5) to (8) of Schedule 4;
  paragraph 5A(2)(a) of Schedule 4;
  paragraph 5A(3)(a) of Schedule 4.

(3) A delegation under subsection (1) is not revoked by the delegator's becoming incapacitated.

(4) Any delegation under subsection (1) that is in force immediately before a person ceases to be Senior President of Tribunals continues in force until varied or revoked by a subsequent holder of the office of Senior President of Tribunals.

(5) The delegation under this section of a function shall not prevent the exercise of the function by the Senior President of Tribunals.

### Review of decisions and appeals

### Review of decision of First-tier Tribunal

9 (1) The First-tier Tribunal may review a decision made by it on a matter in a case, other than a decision that is an excluded decision for the purposes of section 11(1) (but see subsection (9)).

(2) The First-tier Tribunal's power under subsection (1) in relation to a decision is exercisable–
  (a) of its own initiative, or
  (b) on application by a person who for the purposes of section 11(2) has a right of appeal in respect of the decision.

(3) Tribunal Procedure Rules may–
  (a) provide that the First-tier Tribunal may not under subsection (1) review (whether of its own initiative or on application under subsection (2)(b)) a decision of a description specified for the purposes of this paragraph in Tribunal Procedure Rules;
  (b) provide that the First-tier Tribunal's power under subsection (1) to review a decision of a description specified for the purposes of this paragraph in Tribunal Procedure Rules is exercisable only of the tribunal's own initiative;
  (c) provide that an application under subsection (2)(b) that is of a description specified for the purposes of this paragraph in Tribunal Procedure Rules may be

made only on grounds specified for the purposes of this paragraph in Tribunal Procedure Rules;

(d) provide, in relation to a decision of a description specified for the purposes of this paragraph in Tribunal Procedure Rules, that the First-tier Tribunal's power under subsection (1) to review the decision of its own initiative is exercisable only on grounds specified for the purposes of this paragraph in Tribunal Procedure Rules.

(4) Where the First-tier Tribunal has under subsection (1) reviewed a decision, the First-tier Tribunal may in the light of the review do any of the following–
  (a) correct accidental errors in the decision or in a record of the decision;
  (b) amend reasons given for the decision;
  (c) set the decision aside.

(5) Where under subsection (4)(c) the First-tier Tribunal sets a decision aside, the First-tier Tribunal must either–
  (a) re-decide the matter concerned, or
  (b) refer that matter to the Upper Tribunal.

(6) Where a matter is referred to the Upper Tribunal under subsection (5)(b), the Upper Tribunal must re-decide the matter.

(7) Where the Upper Tribunal is under subsection (6) re-deciding a matter, it may make any decision which the First-tier Tribunal could make if the First-tier Tribunal were re-deciding the matter.

(8) Where a tribunal is acting under subsection (5)(a) or (6), it may make such findings of fact as it considers appropriate.

(9) This section has effect as if a decision under subsection (4)(c) to set aside an earlier decision were not an excluded decision for the purposes of section 11(1), but the First-tier Tribunal's only power in the light of a review under subsection (1) of a decision under subsection (4)(c) is the power under subsection (4)(a).

(10) A decision of the First-tier Tribunal may not be reviewed under subsection (1) more than once, and once the First-tier Tribunal has decided that an earlier decision should not be reviewed under subsection (1) it may not then decide to review that earlier decision under that subsection.

(11) Where under this section a decision is set aside and the matter concerned is then re-decided, the decision set aside and the decision made in re-deciding the matter are for the purposes of subsection (10) to be taken to be different decisions.

## Review of decision of Upper Tribunal

10 (1) The Upper Tribunal may review a decision made by it on a matter in a case, other than a decision that is an excluded decision for the purposes of section 13(1) (but see subsection (7)).

(2) The Upper Tribunal's power under subsection (1) in relation to a decision is exercisable–
  (a) of its own initiative, or
  (b) on application by a person who for the purposes of section 13(2) has a right of appeal in respect of the decision.

(3) Tribunal Procedure Rules may–
  (a) provide that the Upper Tribunal may not under subsection (1) review (whether of its own initiative or on application under subsection (2)(b)) a decision of a description specified for the purposes of this paragraph in Tribunal Procedure Rules;
  (b) provide that the Upper Tribunal's power under subsection (1) to review a decision of a description specified for the purposes of this paragraph in Tribunal Procedure Rules is exercisable only of the tribunal's own initiative;
  (c) provide that an application under subsection (2)(b) that is of a description specified for the purposes of this paragraph in Tribunal Procedure Rules may be made only on grounds specified for the purposes of this paragraph in Tribunal Procedure Rules;
  (d) provide, in relation to a decision of a description specified for the purposes of this paragraph in Tribunal Procedure Rules, that the Upper Tribunal's power

under subsection (1) to review the decision of its own initiative is exercisable only on grounds specified for the purposes of this paragraph in Tribunal Procedure Rules.

(4) Where the Upper Tribunal has under subsection (1) reviewed a decision, the Upper Tribunal may in the light of the review do any of the following–

    (a) correct accidental errors in the decision or in a record of the decision;

    (b) amend reasons given for the decision;

    (c) set the decision aside.

(5) Where under subsection (4)(c) the Upper Tribunal sets a decision aside, the Upper Tribunal must re-decide the matter concerned.

(6) Where the Upper Tribunal is acting under subsection (5), it may make such findings of fact as it considers appropriate.

(7) This section has effect as if a decision under subsection (4)(c) to set aside an earlier decision were not an excluded decision for the purposes of section 13(1), but the Upper Tribunal's only power in the light of a review under subsection (1) of a decision under subsection (4)(c) is the power under subsection (4)(a).

(8) A decision of the Upper Tribunal may not be reviewed under subsection (1) more than once, and once the Upper Tribunal has decided that an earlier decision should not be reviewed under subsection (1) it may not then decide to review that earlier decision under that subsection.

(9) Where under this section a decision is set aside and the matter concerned is then re-decided, the decision set aside and the decision made in re-deciding the matter are for the purposes of subsection (8) to be taken to be different decisions.

### Right to appeal to Upper Tribunal

**11** (1) For the purposes of subsection (2), the reference to a right of appeal is to a right to appeal to the Upper Tribunal on any point of law arising from a decision made by the First-tier Tribunal other than an excluded decision.

(2) Any party to a case has a right of appeal, subject to subsection (8).

(3) That right may be exercised only with permission (or, in Northern Ireland, leave).

(4) Permission (or leave) may be given by–

    (a) the First-tier Tribunal, or

    (b) the Upper Tribunal,

on an application by the party.

(5) For the purposes of subsection (1), an 'excluded decision' is–

    (a) any decision of the First-tier Tribunal on an appeal made in exercise of a right conferred by the Criminal Injuries Compensation Scheme in compliance with section 5(1)(a) of the Criminal Injuries Compensation Act 1995 (appeals against decisions on reviews),

    (aa) any decision of the First-tier Tribunal on an appeal made in exercise of a right conferred by the Victims of Overseas Terrorism Compensation Scheme in compliance with section 52(3) of the Crime and Security Act 2010,

    (b) any decision of the First-tier Tribunal on an appeal under section 28(4) or (6) of the Data Protection Act 1998 (appeals against national security certificate),

    (c) any decision of the First-tier Tribunal on an appeal under section 60(1) or (4) of the Freedom of Information Act 2000 (appeals against national security certificate),

    (d) a decision of the First-tier Tribunal under section 9–

        (i) to review, or not to review, an earlier decision of the tribunal,

        (ii) to take no action, or not to take any particular action, in the light of a review of an earlier decision of the tribunal,

        (iii) to set aside an earlier decision of the tribunal, or

        (iv) to refer, or not to refer, a matter to the Upper Tribunal,

    (e) a decision of the First-tier Tribunal that is set aside under section 9 (including a decision set aside after proceedings on an appeal under this section have been begun), or

    (f) any decision of the First-tier Tribunal that is of a description specified in an order made by the Lord Chancellor.

(6) A description may be specified under subsection (5)(f) only if–
  (a) in the case of a decision of that description, there is a right to appeal to a court, the Upper Tribunal or any other tribunal from the decision and that right is, or includes, something other than a right (however expressed) to appeal on any point of law arising from the decision, or
  (b) decisions of that description are made in carrying out a function transferred under section 30 and prior to the transfer of the function under section 30(1) there was no right to appeal from decisions of that description.
(7) Where–
  (a) an order under subsection (5)(f) specifies a description of decisions, and
  (b) decisions of that description are made in carrying out a function transferred under section 30,
  the order must be framed so as to come into force no later than the time when the transfer under section 30 of the function takes effect (but power to revoke the order continues to be exercisable after that time, and power to amend the order continues to be exercisable after that time for the purpose of narrowing the description for the time being specified).
(8) The Lord Chancellor may by order make provision for a person to be treated as being, or to be treated as not being, a party to a case for the purposes of subsection (2).

### Proceedings on appeal to Upper Tribunal
12 (1) Subsection (2) applies if the Upper Tribunal, in deciding an appeal under section 11, finds that the making of the decision concerned involved the making of an error on a point of law.
(2) The Upper Tribunal–
  (a) may (but need not) set aside the decision of the First-tier Tribunal, and
  (b) if it does, must either–
    (i) remit the case to the First-tier Tribunal with directions for its reconsideration, or
    (ii) re-make the decision.
(3) In acting under subsection (2)(b)(i), the Upper Tribunal may also–
  (a) direct that the members of the First-tier Tribunal who are chosen to reconsider the case are not to be the same as those who made the decision that has been set aside;
  (b) give procedural directions in connection with the reconsideration of the case by the First-tier Tribunal.
(4) In acting under subsection (2)(b)(ii), the Upper Tribunal–
  (a) may make any decision which the First-tier Tribunal could make if the First-tier Tribunal were re-making the decision, and
  (b) may make such findings of fact as it considers appropriate.

### Right to appeal to Court of Appeal etc.
13 (1) For the purposes of subsection (2), the reference to a right of appeal is to a right to appeal to the relevant appellate court on any point of law arising from a decision made by the Upper Tribunal other than an excluded decision.
(2) Any party to a case has a right of appeal, subject to subsection (14).
(3) That right may be exercised only with permission (or, in Northern Ireland, leave).
(4) Permission (or leave) may be given by–
  (a) the Upper Tribunal, or
  (b) the relevant appellate court,
  on an application by the party.
(5) An application may be made under subsection (4) to the relevant appellate court only if permission (or leave) has been refused by the Upper Tribunal.
(6) The Lord Chancellor may, as respects an application under subsection (4) that falls within subsection (7) and for which the relevant appellate court is the Court of Appeal in England and Wales or the Court of Appeal in Northern Ireland, by order make provision for permission (or leave) not to be granted on the application unless the Upper Tribunal or (as the case may be) the relevant appellate court considers–

- (a) that the proposed appeal would raise some important point of principle or practice, or
- (b) that there is some other compelling reason for the relevant appellate court to hear the appeal.

(6A) Rules of court may make provision for permission not to be granted on an application under subsection (4) to the Court of Session that falls within subsection (7) unless the court considers–
- (a) that the proposed appeal would raise some important point of principle, or
- (b) that there is some other compelling reason for the court to hear the appeal.

(7) An application falls within this subsection if the application is for permission (or leave) to appeal from any decision of the Upper Tribunal on an appeal under section 11.

(8) For the purposes of subsection (1), an 'excluded decision' is–
- (a) any decision of the Upper Tribunal on an appeal under section 28(4) or (6) of the Data Protection Act 1998 (appeals against national security certificate),
- (b) any decision of the Upper Tribunal on an appeal under section 60(1) or (4) of the Freedom of Information Act 2000 (appeals against national security certificate),
- (c) any decision of the Upper Tribunal on an application under section 11(4)(b) (application for permission or leave to appeal),
- (d) a decision of the Upper Tribunal under section 10–
  - (i) to review, or not to review, an earlier decision of the tribunal,
  - (ii) to take no action, or not to take any particular action, in the light of a review of an earlier decision of the tribunal, or
  - (iii) to set aside an earlier decision of the tribunal,
- (e) a decision of the Upper Tribunal that is set aside under section 10 (including a decision set aside after proceedings on an appeal under this section have been begun), or
- (f) any decision of the Upper Tribunal that is of a description specified in an order made by the Lord Chancellor.

(9) A description may be specified under subsection (8)(f) only if–
- (a) in the case of a decision of that description, there is a right to appeal to a court from the decision and that right is, or includes, something other than a right (however expressed) to appeal on any point of law arising from the decision, or
- (b) decisions of that description are made in carrying out a function transferred under section 30 and prior to the transfer of the function under section 30(1) there was no right to appeal from decisions of that description.

(10) Where–
- (a) an order under subsection (8)(f) specifies a description of decisions, and
- (b) decisions of that description are made in carrying out a function transferred under section 30,

the order must be framed so as to come into force no later than the time when the transfer under section 30 of the function takes effect (but power to revoke the order continues to be exercisable after that time, and power to amend the order continues to be exercisable after that time for the purpose of narrowing the description for the time being specified).

(11) Before the Upper Tribunal decides an application made to it under subsection (4), the Upper Tribunal must specify the court that is to be the relevant appellate court as respects the proposed appeal.

(12) The court to be specified under subsection (11) in relation to a proposed appeal is whichever of the following courts appears to the Upper Tribunal to be the most appropriate–
- (a) the Court of Appeal in England and Wales;
- (b) the Court of Session;
- (c) the Court of Appeal in Northern Ireland.

(13) In this section except subsection (11), 'the relevant appellate court', as respects an

appeal, means the court specified as respects that appeal by the Upper Tribunal under subsection (11).

(14) The Lord Chancellor may by order make provision for a person to be treated as being, or to be treated as not being, a party to a case for the purposes of subsection (2).

(15) Rules of court may make provision as to the time within which an application under subsection (4) to the relevant appellate court must be made.

## Proceedings on appeal to Court of Appeal etc.

**14** (1) Subsection (2) applies if the relevant appellate court, in deciding an appeal under section 13, finds that the making of the decision concerned involved the making of an error on a point of law.

(2) The relevant appellate court–
   (a) may (but need not) set aside the decision of the Upper Tribunal, and
   (b) if it does, must either–
      (i) remit the case to the Upper Tribunal or, where the decision of the Upper Tribunal was on an appeal or reference from another tribunal or some other person, to the Upper Tribunal or that other tribunal or person, with directions for its reconsideration, or
      (ii) re-make the decision.

(3) In acting under subsection (2)(b)(i), the relevant appellate court may also–
   (a) direct that the persons who are chosen to reconsider the case are not to be the same as those who–
      (i) where the case is remitted to the Upper Tribunal, made the decision of the Upper Tribunal that has been set aside, or
      (ii) where the case is remitted to another tribunal or person, made the decision in respect of which the appeal or reference to the Upper Tribunal was made;
   (b) give procedural directions in connection with the reconsideration of the case by the Upper Tribunal or other tribunal or person.

(4) In acting under subsection (2)(b)(ii), the relevant appellate court–
   (a) may make any decision which the Upper Tribunal could make if the Upper Tribunal were re-making the decision or (as the case may be) which the other tribunal or person could make if that other tribunal or person were re-making the decision, and
   (b) may make such findings of fact as it considers appropriate.

(5) Where–
   (a) under subsection (2)(b)(i) the relevant appellate court remits a case to the Upper Tribunal, and
   (b) the decision set aside under subsection (2)(a) was made by the Upper Tribunal on an appeal or reference from another tribunal or some other person, the Upper Tribunal may (instead of reconsidering the case itself) remit the case to that other tribunal or person, with the directions given by the relevant appellate court for its reconsideration.

(6) In acting under subsection (5), the Upper Tribunal may also–
   (a) direct that the persons who are chosen to reconsider the case are not to be the same as those who made the decision in respect of which the appeal or reference to the Upper Tribunal was made;
   (b) give procedural directions in connection with the reconsideration of the case by the other tribunal or person.

(7) In this section 'the relevant appellate court', as respects an appeal under section 13, means the court specified as respects that appeal by the Upper Tribunal under section 13(11).

## 'Judicial review'

## Upper Tribunal's 'judicial review' jurisdiction

**15** (1) The Upper Tribunal has power, in cases arising under the law of England and Wales or under the law of Northern Ireland, to grant the following kinds of relief–
   (a) a mandatory order;

   (b) a prohibiting order;
   (c) a quashing order;
   (d) a declaration;
   (e) an injunction.

(2) The power under subsection (1) may be exercised by the Upper Tribunal if–
   (a) certain conditions are met (see section 18), or
   (b) the tribunal is authorised to proceed even though not all of those conditions are met (see section 19(3) and (4)).

(3) Relief under subsection (1) granted by the Upper Tribunal–
   (a) has the same effect as the corresponding relief granted by the High Court on an application for judicial review, and
   (b) is enforceable as if it were relief granted by the High Court on an application for judicial review.

(4) In deciding whether to grant relief under subsection (1)(a), (b) or (c), the Upper Tribunal must apply the principles that the High Court would apply in deciding whether to grant that relief on an application for judicial review.

(5) In deciding whether to grant relief under subsection (1)(d) or (e), the Upper Tribunal must–
   (a) in cases arising under the law of England and Wales apply the principles that the High Court would apply in deciding whether to grant that relief under section 31(2) of the Senior Courts Act 1981 on an application for judicial review, and
   (b) in cases arising under the law of Northern Ireland apply the principles that the High Court would apply in deciding whether to grant that relief on an application for judicial review.

(6) For the purposes of the application of subsection (3)(a) in relation to cases arising under the law of Northern Ireland–
   (a) a mandatory order under subsection (1)(a) shall be taken to correspond to an order of mandamus,
   (b) a prohibiting order under subsection (1)(b) shall be taken to correspond to an order of prohibition, and
   (c) a quashing order under subsection (1)(c) shall be taken to correspond to an order of certiorari.

### Application for relief under section 15(1)

**16** (1) This section applies in relation to an application to the Upper Tribunal for relief under section 15(1).

(2) The application may be made only if permission (or, in a case arising under the law of Northern Ireland, leave) to make it has been obtained from the tribunal.

(3) The tribunal may not grant permission (or leave) to make the application unless it considers that the applicant has a sufficient interest in the matter to which the application relates.

(4) Subsection (5) applies where the tribunal considers–
   (a) that there has been undue delay in making the application, and
   (b) that granting the relief sought on the application would be likely to cause substantial hardship to, or substantially prejudice the rights of, any person or would be detrimental to good administration.

(5) The tribunal may–
   (a) refuse to grant permission (or leave) for the making of the application;
   (b) refuse to grant any relief sought on the application.

(6) The tribunal may award to the applicant damages, restitution or the recovery of a sum due if–
   (a) the application includes a claim for such an award arising from any matter to which the application relates, and
   (b) the tribunal is satisfied that such an award would have been made by the High Court if the claim had been made in an action begun in the High Court by the applicant at the time of making the application.

(7) An award under subsection (6) may be enforced as if it were an award of the High Court.

(8) Where–
- (a) the tribunal refuses to grant permission (or leave) to apply for relief under section 15(1),
- (b) the applicant appeals against that refusal, and
- (c) the Court of Appeal grants the permission (or leave), the Court of Appeal may go on to decide the application for relief under section 15(1).

(9) Subsections (4) and (5) do not prevent Tribunal Procedure Rules from limiting the time within which applications may be made.

### Quashing orders under section 15(1): supplementary provision

**17** (1) If the Upper Tribunal makes a quashing order under section 15(1)(c) in respect of a decision, it may in addition–
- (a) remit the matter concerned to the court, tribunal or authority that made the decision, with a direction to reconsider the matter and reach a decision in accordance with the findings of the Upper Tribunal, or
- (b) substitute its own decision for the decision in question.

(2) The power conferred by subsection (1)(b) is exercisable only if–
- (a) the decision in question was made by a court or tribunal,
- (b) the decision is quashed on the ground that there has been an error of law, and
- (c) without the error, there would have been only one decision that the court or tribunal could have reached.

(3) Unless the Upper Tribunal otherwise directs, a decision substituted by it under subsection (1)(b) has effect as if it were a decision of the relevant court or tribunal.

### Limits of jurisdiction under section 15(1)

**18** (1) This section applies where an application made to the Upper Tribunal seeks (whether or not alone)–
- (a) relief under section 15(1), or
- (b) permission (or, in a case arising under the law of Northern Ireland, leave) to apply for relief under section 15(1).

(2) If Conditions 1 to 4 are met, the tribunal has the function of deciding the application.

(3) If the tribunal does not have the function of deciding the application, it must by order transfer the application to the High Court.

(4) Condition 1 is that the application does not seek anything other than–
- (a) relief under section 15(1);
- (b) permission (or, in a case arising under the law of Northern Ireland, leave) to apply for relief under section 15(1);
- (c) an award under section 16(6);
- (d) interest;
- (e) costs.

(5) Condition 2 is that the application does not call into question anything done by the Crown Court.

(6) Condition 3 is that the application falls within a class specified for the purposes of this subsection in a direction given in accordance with Part 1 of Schedule 2 to the Constitutional Reform Act 2005.

(7) The power to give directions under subsection (6) includes–
- (a) power to vary or revoke directions made in exercise of the power, and
- (b) power to make different provision for different purposes.

(8) Condition 4 is that the judge presiding at the hearing of the application is either–
- (a) a judge of the High Court or the Court of Appeal in England and Wales or Northern Ireland, or a judge of the Court of Session, or
- (b) such other persons as may be agreed from time to time between the Lord Chief Justice, the Lord President, or the Lord Chief Justice of Northern Ireland, as the case may be, and the Senior President of Tribunals.

(9) Where the application is transferred to the High Court under subsection (3)–

(a) the application is to be treated for all purposes as if it–
    (i) had been made to the High Court, and
    (ii) sought things corresponding to those sought from the tribunal, and
(b) any steps taken, permission (or leave) given or orders made by the tribunal in relation to the application are to be treated as taken, given or made by the High Court.

(10) Rules of court may make provision for the purpose of supplementing subsection (9).

(11) The provision that may be made by Tribunal Procedure Rules about amendment of an application for relief under section 15(1) includes, in particular, provision about amendments that would cause the application to become transferrable under subsection (3).

(12) For the purposes of subsection (9)(a)(ii), in relation to an application transferred to the High Court in Northern Ireland–
(a) an order of mandamus shall be taken to correspond to a mandatory order under section 15(1)(a),
(b) an order of prohibition shall be taken to correspond to a prohibiting order under section 15(1)(b), and
(c) an order of certiorari shall be taken to correspond to a quashing order under section 15(1)(c).

### Transfer of judicial review applications from High Court

19 (1) In the Senior Courts Act 1981, after section 31 insert–

### '31A Transfer of judicial review applications to Upper Tribunal

(1) This section applies where an application is made to the High Court–
(a) for judicial review, or
(b) for permission to apply for judicial review.

(2) If Conditions 1, 2, 3 and 4 are met, the High Court must by order transfer the application to the Upper Tribunal.

(3) If Conditions 1, 2 and 4 are met, but Condition 3 is not, the High Court may by order transfer the application to the Upper Tribunal if it appears to the High Court to be just and convenient to do so.

(4) Condition 1 is that the application does not seek anything other than–
(a) relief under section 31(1)(a) and (b);
(b) permission to apply for relief under section 31(1)(a) and (b);
(c) an award under section 31(4);
(d) interest;
(e) costs.

(5) Condition 2 is that the application does not call into question anything done by the Crown Court.

(6) Condition 3 is that the application falls within a class specified under section 18(6) of the Tribunals, Courts and Enforcement Act 2007.

(7) Condition 4 is that the application does not call into question any decision made under–
(a) the Immigration Acts,
(b) the British Nationality Act 1981,
(c) any instrument having effect under an enactment within paragraph (a) or (b), or
(d) any other provision of law for the time being in force which determines British citizenship, British overseas territories citizenship, the status of a British National (Overseas) or British Overseas citizenship.'

(2) In the Judicature (Northern Ireland) Act 1978, after section 25 insert–

### '25A Transfer of judicial review applications to Upper Tribunal

(1) This section applies where an application is made to the High Court–
(a) for judicial review, or
(b) for leave to apply for judicial review.

    (2) If Conditions 1, 2, 3 and 4 are met, the High Court must by order transfer the application to the Upper Tribunal.

    (3) If Conditions 1, 2 and 4 are met, but Condition 3 is not, the High Court may by order transfer the application to the Upper Tribunal if it appears to the High Court to be just and convenient to do so.

    (4) Condition 1 is that the application does not seek anything other than–

       (a) relief under section 18(1)(a) to (e);

       (b) leave to apply for relief under section 18(1)(a) to (e);

       (c) an award under section 20;

       (d) interest;

       (e) costs.

    (5) Condition 2 is that the application does not call into question anything done by the Crown Court.

    (6) Condition 3 is that the application falls within a class specified under section 18(6) of the Tribunals, Courts and Enforcement Act 2007.

    (7) Condition 4 is that the application does not call into question any decision made under–

       (a) the Immigration Acts,

       (b) the British Nationality Act 1981,

       (c) any instrument having effect under an enactment within paragraph (a) or (b) , or

       (d) any other provision of law for the time being in force which determines British citizenship, British overseas territories citizenship, the status of a British National (Overseas) or British Overseas citizenship.'

(3) Where an application is transferred to the Upper Tribunal under 31A of the Senior Courts Act 1981 or section 25A of the Judicature (Northern Ireland) Act 1978 (transfer from the High Court of judicial review applications)–

  (a) the application is to be treated for all purposes as if it–

    (i) had been made to the tribunal, and

    (ii) sought things corresponding to those sought from the High Court,

  (b) the tribunal has the function of deciding the application, even if it does not fall within a class specified under section 18(6), and

  (c) any steps taken, permission given, leave given or orders made by the High Court in relation to the application are to be treated as taken, given or made by the tribunal.

(4) Where–

  (a) an application for permission is transferred to the Upper Tribunal under section 31A of the Senior Courts Act 1981 and the tribunal grants permission, or

  (b) an application for leave is transferred to the Upper Tribunal under section 25A of the Judicature (Northern Ireland) Act 1978 and the tribunal grants leave,

the tribunal has the function of deciding any subsequent application brought under the permission or leave, even if the subsequent application does not fall within a class specified under section 18(6).

(5) Tribunal Procedure Rules may make further provision for the purposes of supplementing subsections (3) and (4).

(6) For the purposes of subsection (3)(a)(ii), in relation to an application transferred to the Upper Tribunal under section 25A of the Judicature (Northern Ireland) Act 1978–

  (a) a mandatory order under section 15(1)(a) shall be taken to correspond to an order of mandamus,

  (b) a prohibiting order under section 15(1)(b) shall be taken to correspond to an order of prohibition, and

  (c) a quashing order under section 15(1)(c) shall be taken to correspond to an order of certiorari.

### Transfer of judicial review applications from the Court of Session

20 (1) Where an application is made to the supervisory jurisdiction of the Court of Session, the Court–

(a)  must, if Conditions 1 and 2 are met, and

(b)  may, if Conditions 1 and 3 are met, but Condition 2 is not,

by order transfer the application to the Upper Tribunal.

(2)  Condition 1 is that the application does not seek anything other than an exercise of the supervisory jurisdiction of the Court of Session.

(3)  Condition 2 is that the application falls within a class specified for the purposes of this subsection by act of sederunt made with the consent of the Lord Chancellor.

(4)  Condition 3 is that the subject matter of the application is not a devolved Scottish matter.

(6)  There may not be specified under subsection (3) any class of application which includes an application the subject matter of which is a devolved Scottish matter.

(7)  For the purposes of this section, the subject matter of an application is a devolved Scottish matter if it–

(a)  concerns the exercise of functions in or as regards Scotland, and

(b)  does not relate to a reserved matter within the meaning of the Scotland Act 1998.

(8)  In subsection (2), the reference to the exercise of the supervisory jurisdiction of the Court of Session includes a reference to the making of any order in connection with or in consequence of the exercise of that jurisdiction.

### Upper Tribunal's 'judicial review' jurisdiction: Scotland

21 (1)  The Upper Tribunal has the function of deciding applications transferred to it from the Court of Session under section 20(1).

(2)  The powers of review of the Upper Tribunal in relation to such applications are the same as the powers of review of the Court of Session in an application to the supervisory jurisdiction of that Court.

(3)  In deciding an application by virtue of subsection (1), the Upper Tribunal must apply principles that the Court of Session would apply in deciding an application to the supervisory jurisdiction of that Court.

(4)  An order of the Upper Tribunal by virtue of subsection (1)–

(a)  has the same effect as the corresponding order granted by the Court of Session on an application to the supervisory jurisdiction of that Court, and

(b)  is enforceable as if it were an order so granted by that Court.

(5)  Where an application is transferred to the Upper Tribunal by virtue of section 20(1), any steps taken or orders made by the Court of Session in relation to the application (other than the order to transfer the application under section 20(1)) are to be treated as taken or made by the tribunal.

(6)  Tribunal Procedure Rules may make further provision for the purposes of supplementing subsection (5).

### Miscellaneous

### Tribunal Procedure Rules

22 (1)  There are to be rules, to be called 'Tribunal Procedure Rules', governing–

(a)  the practice and procedure to be followed in the First-tier Tribunal, and

(b)  the practice and procedure to be followed in the Upper Tribunal.

(2)  Tribunal Procedure Rules are to be made by the Tribunal Procedure Committee.

(3)  In Schedule 5–

Part 1 makes further provision about the content of Tribunal Procedure Rules,

Part 2 makes provision about the membership of the Tribunal Procedure Committee,

Part 3 makes provision about the making of Tribunal Procedure Rules by the Committee, and

Part 4 confers power to amend legislation in connection with Tribunal Procedure Rules.

(4)  Power to make Tribunal Procedure Rules is to be exercised with a view to securing–

(a)  that, in proceedings before the First-tier Tribunal and Upper Tribunal, justice is done,

(b) that the tribunal system is accessible and fair,

(c) that proceedings before the First-tier Tribunal or Upper Tribunal are handled quickly and efficiently,

(d) that the rules are both simple and simply expressed, and

(e) that the rules where appropriate confer on members of the First-tier Tribunal, or Upper Tribunal, responsibility for ensuring that proceedings before the tribunal are handled quickly and efficiently.

(5) In subsection (4)(b) 'the tribunal system' means the system for deciding matters within the jurisdiction of the First-tier Tribunal or the Upper Tribunal.

## Practice directions

**23** (1) The Senior President of Tribunals may give directions–

(a) as to the practice and procedure of the First-tier Tribunal;

(b) as to the practice and procedure of the Upper Tribunal.

(2) A Chamber President may give directions as to the practice and procedure of the chamber over which he presides.

(3) A power under this section to give directions includes–

(a) power to vary or revoke directions made in exercise of the power, and

(b) power to make different provision for different purposes (including different provision for different areas).

(4) Directions under subsection (1) may not be given without the approval of the Lord Chancellor.

(5) Directions under subsection (2) may not be given without the approval of–

(a) the Senior President of Tribunals, and

(b) the Lord Chancellor.

(6) Subsections (4) and (5)(b) do not apply to directions to the extent that they consist of guidance about any of the following–

(a) the application or interpretation of the law;

(b) the making of decisions by members of the First-tier Tribunal or Upper Tribunal.

(7) Subsections (4) and (5)(b) do not apply to directions to the extent that they consist of criteria for determining which members of the First-tier Tribunal or Upper Tribunal may be chosen to decide particular categories of matter; but the directions may, to that extent, be given only after consulting the Lord Chancellor.

## Mediation

**24** (1) A person exercising power to make Tribunal Procedure Rules or give practice directions must, when making provision in relation to mediation, have regard to the following principles–

(a) mediation of matters in dispute between parties to proceedings is to take place only by agreement between those parties;

(b) where parties to proceedings fail to mediate, or where mediation between parties to proceedings fails to resolve disputed matters, the failure is not to affect the outcome of the proceedings.

(2) Practice directions may provide for members to act as mediators in relation to disputed matters in a case that is the subject of proceedings.

(3) The provision that may be made by virtue of subsection (2) includes provision for a member to act as a mediator in relation to disputed matters in a case even though the member has been chosen to decide matters in the case.

(4) Once a member has begun to act as a mediator in relation to a disputed matter in a case that is the subject of proceedings, the member may decide matters in the case only with the consent of the parties.

(5) Staff appointed under section 40(1) may, subject to their terms of appointment, act as mediators in relation to disputed matters in a case that is the subject of proceedings.

(6) In this section–

'member' means a judge or other member of the First-tier Tribunal or a judge or other member of the Upper Tribunal;

'practice direction' means a direction under section 23(1) or (2); 'proceedings' means proceedings before the First-tier Tribunal or proceedings before the Upper Tribunal.

### Supplementary powers of Upper Tribunal

25 (1) In relation to the matters mentioned in subsection (2), the Upper Tribunal–

(a) has, in England and Wales or in Northern Ireland, the same powers, rights, privileges and authority as the High Court, and

(b) has, in Scotland, the same powers, rights, privileges and authority as the Court of Session.

(2) The matters are–

(a) the attendance and examination of witnesses,

(b) the production and inspection of documents, and

(c) all other matters incidental to the Upper Tribunal's functions.

(3) Subsection (1) shall not be taken–

(a) to limit any power to make Tribunal Procedure Rules;

(b) to be limited by anything in Tribunal Procedure Rules other than an express limitation.

(4) A power, right, privilege or authority conferred in a territory by subsection (1) is available for purposes of proceedings in the Upper Tribunal that take place outside that territory (as well as for purposes of proceedings in the tribunal that take place within that territory).

### First-tier Tribunal and Upper Tribunal: sitting places

26　Each of the First-tier Tribunal and the Upper Tribunal may decide a case–

(a) in England and Wales,

(b) in Scotland, or

(c) in Northern Ireland,

even though the case arises under the law of a territory other than the one in which the case is decided.

### Enforcement

27 (1) A sum payable in pursuance of a decision of the First-tier Tribunal or Upper Tribunal made in England and Wales–

(a) shall be recoverable as if it were payable under an order of a county court in England and Wales;

(b) shall be recoverable as if it were payable under an order of the High Court in England and Wales.

(2) An order for the payment of a sum payable in pursuance of a decision of the First-tier Tribunal or Upper Tribunal made in Scotland (or a copy of such an order certified in accordance with Tribunal Procedure Rules) may be enforced as if it were an extract registered decree arbitral bearing a warrant for execution issued by the sheriff court of any sheriffdom in Scotland.

(3) A sum payable in pursuance of a decision of the First-tier Tribunal or Upper Tribunal made in Northern Ireland–

(a) shall be recoverable as if it were payable under an order of a county court in Northern Ireland;

(b) shall be recoverable as if it were payable under an order of the High Court in Northern Ireland.

(4) This section does not apply to a sum payable in pursuance of–

(a) an award under section 16(6), or

(b) an order by virtue of section 21(1).

(5) The Lord Chancellor may by order make provision for subsection (1) or (3) to apply in relation to a sum of a description specified in the order with the omission of one (but not both) of paragraphs (a) and (b).

(6) Tribunal Procedure Rules–

(a) may make provision as to where, for purposes of this section, a decision is to be taken to be made;

(b) may provide for all or any of subsections (1) to (3) to apply only, or not to apply except, in relation to sums of a description specified in Tribunal Procedure Rules.

### Assessors

**28** (1) If it appears to the First-tier Tribunal or the Upper Tribunal that a matter before it requires special expertise not otherwise available to it, it may direct that in dealing with that matter it shall have the assistance of a person or persons appearing to it to have relevant knowledge or experience.

(2) The remuneration of a person who gives assistance to either tribunal as mentioned in subsection (1) shall be determined and paid by the Lord Chancellor.

(3) The Lord Chancellor may–
    (a) establish panels of persons from which either tribunal may (but need not) select persons to give it assistance as mentioned in subsection (1);
    (b) under paragraph (a) establish different panels for different purposes;
    (c) after carrying out such consultation as he considers appropriate, appoint persons to a panel established under paragraph (a);
    (d) remove a person from such a panel.

### Costs or expenses

**29** (1) The costs of and incidental to–
    (a) all proceedings in the First-tier Tribunal, and
    (b) all proceedings in the Upper Tribunal,
shall be in the discretion of the Tribunal in which the proceedings take place.

(2) The relevant Tribunal shall have full power to determine by whom and to what extent the costs are to be paid.

(3) Subsections (1) and (2) have effect subject to Tribunal Procedure Rules.

(4) In any proceedings mentioned in subsection (1), the relevant Tribunal may–
    (a) disallow, or
    (b) (as the case may be) order the legal or other representative concerned to meet,
the whole of any wasted costs or such part of them as may be determined in accordance with Tribunal Procedure Rules.

(5) In subsection (4) 'wasted costs' means any costs incurred by a party–
    (a) as a result of any improper, unreasonable or negligent act or omission on the part of any legal or other representative or any employee of such a representative, or
    (b) which, in the light of any such act or omission occurring after they were incurred, the relevant Tribunal considers it is unreasonable to expect that party to pay.

(6) In this section 'legal or other representative', in relation to a party to proceedings, means any person exercising a right of audience or right to conduct the proceedings on his behalf.

(7) In the application of this section in relation to Scotland, any reference in this section to costs is to be read as a reference to expenses.

## CHAPTER 3: TRANSFER OF TRIBUNAL FUNCTIONS

### Transfer of functions of certain tribunals

**30** (1) The Lord Chancellor may by order provide for a function of a scheduled tribunal to be transferred–
    (a) to the First-tier Tribunal,
    (b) to the Upper Tribunal,
    (c) to the First-tier Tribunal and the Upper Tribunal with the question as to which of them is to exercise the function in a particular case being determined by a person under provisions of the order,
    (d) to the First-tier Tribunal to the extent specified in the order and to the Upper Tribunal to the extent so specified,
    (e) to the First-tier Tribunal and the Upper Tribunal with the question as to which of them is to exercise the function in a particular case being determined by, or under, Tribunal Procedure Rules,
    (f) to an employment tribunal,
    (g) to the Employment Appeal Tribunal,

(h) to an employment tribunal and the Employment Appeal Tribunal with the question as to which of them is to exercise the function in a particular case being determined by a person under provisions of the order, or

(i) to an employment tribunal to the extent specified in the order and to the Employment Appeal Tribunal to the extent so specified.

(2) In subsection (1) 'scheduled tribunal' means a tribunal in a list in Schedule 6 that has effect for the purposes of this section.

(3) The Lord Chancellor may, as respects a function transferred under subsection (1) or this subsection, by order provide for the function to be further transferred as mentioned in any of paragraphs (a) to (i) of subsection (1).

(4) An order under subsection (1) or (3) may include provision for the purposes of or in consequence of, or for giving full effect to, a transfer under that subsection.

(5) A function of a tribunal may not be transferred under subsection (1) or (3) if, or to the extent that, the provision conferring the function–

(a) would be within the legislative competence of the Scottish Parliament if it were included in an Act of that Parliament, or

(b) would be within the legislative competence of the Northern Ireland Assembly if it were included in an Act of that Assembly.

(6) Subsection (5) does not apply to–

(a) the Secretary of State's function of deciding appeals under section 41 of the Consumer Credit Act 1974,

(b) functions of the Consumer Credit Appeals Tribunal,

(c) the Secretary of State's function of deciding appeals under section 7(1) of the Estate Agents Act 1979, or

(d) functions of an adjudicator under section 5 of the Criminal Injuries Compensation Act 1995 (but see subsection (7)).

(7) Functions of an adjudicator under section 5 of the Criminal Injuries Compensation Act 1995, so far as they relate to Scotland, may be transferred under subsection (1) or (3) only with the consent of the Scottish Ministers.

(8) A function of a tribunal may be transferred under subsection (1) or (3) only with the consent of the Welsh Ministers if any relevant function is exercisable in relation to the tribunal by the Welsh Ministers (whether by the Welsh Ministers alone, or by the Welsh Ministers jointly or concurrently with any other person).

(9) In subsection (8) 'relevant function', in relation to a tribunal, means a function which relates–

(a) to the operation of the tribunal (including, in particular, its membership, administration, staff, accommodation and funding, and payments to its members or staff), or

(b) to the provision of expenses and allowances to persons attending the tribunal or attending elsewhere in connection with proceedings before the tribunal.

### Transfers under section 30: supplementary powers

31 (1) The Lord Chancellor may by order make provision for abolishing the tribunal by whom a function transferred under section 30(1) is exercisable immediately before its transfer.

(2) The Lord Chancellor may by order make provision, where functions of a tribunal are transferred under section 30(1), for a person–

(a) who is the tribunal (but is not the Secretary of State), or

(b) who is a member of the tribunal, or

(c) who is an authorised decision-maker for the tribunal,

to (instead or in addition) be the holder of an office specified in subsection (3).

(3) Those offices are–

(a) transferred-in judge of the First-tier Tribunal,

(b) transferred-in other member of the First-tier Tribunal,

(c) transferred-in judge of the Upper Tribunal,

(d) transferred-in other member of the Upper Tribunal, and

(e) deputy judge of the Upper Tribunal.

(4) Where functions of a tribunal are transferred under section 30(1), the Lord Chancellor must exercise the power under subsection (2) so as to secure that each person who immediately before the end of the tribunal's life–
(a)  is the tribunal,
(b)  is a member of the tribunal, or
(c)  is an authorised decision-maker for the tribunal,
becomes the holder of an office specified in subsection (3) with effect from the end of the tribunal's life (if the person is not then already the holder of such an office).

(5) Subsection (4) does not apply in relation to a person–
(a)  by virtue of the person's being the Secretary of State, or
(b)  by virtue of the person's being a Commissioner for the general purposes of the income tax;
and a reference in subsection (4) to the end of a tribunal's life is to when the tribunal is abolished or (without being abolished) comes to have no functions.

(6) For the purposes of this section, a person is an 'authorised decision-maker' for a tribunal if–
(a)  the tribunal is listed in column 1 of an entry in the following Table, and
(b)  the person is of the description specified in column 2 of that entry.

| *(1)*<br>*Tribunal* | *(2)*<br>*Authorised decision-maker* |
|---|---|
| Adjudicator to Her Majesty's Land Registry | Member of the Adjudicator's staff who is authorised by the Adjudicator to carry out functions of the Adjudicator which are not of an administrative character |
| The Secretary of State as respects his function of deciding appeals under section 41 of the Consumer Credit Act 1974 | Person who is a member of a panel under regulation 24 of the Consumer Credit Licensing (Appeals) Regulations 1998 (SI 1998/1203) |
| The Secretary of State as respects his function of deciding appeals under section 7(1) of the Estate Agents Act 1979 | Person appointed, at any time after 2005, under regulation 19(1) of the Estate Agents (Appeals) Regulations 1981 (SI 1981/1518) to hear an appeal on behalf of the Secretary of State |

(7) Where a function of a tribunal is transferred under section 30(1), the Lord Chancellor may by order provide for procedural rules in force immediately before the transfer to have effect, or to have effect with appropriate modifications, after the transfer (and, accordingly, to be capable of being varied or revoked) as if they were–
(a)  Tribunal Procedure Rules, or
(b)  employment tribunal procedure regulations, or Appeal Tribunal procedure rules, within the meaning given by section 42(1) of the Employment Tribunals Act 1996.

(8) In subsection (7)–
'procedural rules' means provision (whether called rules or not)–
(a)  regulating practice or procedure before the tribunal, and
(b)  applying for purposes connected with the exercise of the function;
'appropriate modifications' means modifications (including additions and omissions) that appear to the Lord Chancellor to be necessary to secure, or expedient in connection with securing, that the procedural rules apply in relation to the exercise of the function after the transfer.

(9) The Lord Chancellor may, in connection with provision made by order under section 30 or the preceding provisions of this section, make by order such incidental, supplemental, transitional or consequential provision, or provision for savings,

as the Lord Chancellor thinks fit, including provision applying only in relation to cases selected by a member–

(a) of the First-tier Tribunal,

(b) of the Upper Tribunal,

(c) of the Employment Appeal Tribunal, or

(d) of a panel of members of employment tribunals.

(10) Subsections (1), (2) and (7) are not to be taken as prejudicing the generality of subsection (9).

### Power to provide for appeal to Upper Tribunal from tribunals in Wales

32 (1) Subsection (2) applies if–

(a) a function is transferred under section 30(1)(a), (c), (d) or (e) in relation to England but is not transferred under section 30(1) in relation to Wales, or

(b) a function that is not exercisable in relation to Wales is transferred under section 30(1)(a), (c), (d) or (e) in relation to England and, although there is a corresponding function that is exercisable in relation to Wales, that corresponding function is not transferred under section 30(1) in relation to Wales.

(2) The Lord Chancellor may by order–

(a) provide for an appeal against a decision to be made to the Upper Tribunal instead of to the court to which an appeal would otherwise fall to be made where the decision is made in exercising, in relation to Wales, the function mentioned in subsection (1)(a) or (as the case may be) the corresponding function mentioned in subsection (1)(b);

(b) provide for a reference of any matter to be made to the Upper Tribunal instead of to the court to which a reference would otherwise fall to be made where the matter arises in exercising, in relation to Wales, the function mentioned in subsection (1)(a) or (as the case may be) the corresponding function mentioned in subsection (1)(b).

(3) The Lord Chancellor may by order provide for an appeal against a decision of a scheduled tribunal to be made to the Upper Tribunal, instead of to the court to which an appeal would otherwise fall to be made, where the decision is made by the tribunal in exercising a function in relation to Wales.

(4) In subsection (3) 'scheduled tribunal' means a tribunal in a list in Schedule 6 that has effect for the purposes of that subsection.

(5) An order under subsection (2) or (3)–

(a) may include provision for the purposes of or in consequence of, or for giving full effect to, provision made by the order;

(b) may include such incidental, supplemental, transitional or consequential provision or savings as the Lord Chancellor thinks fit.

### Power to provide for appeal to Upper Tribunal from tribunals in Scotland

33 (1) Subsection (2) applies if–

(a) a function is transferred under section 30(1)(a), (c), (d) or (e) in relation to England (whether or not also in relation to Wales) but is not transferred under section 30(1) in relation to Scotland,

(b) an appeal may be made to the Upper Tribunal against any decision, or any decision of a particular description, made in exercising the transferred function in relation to England, and

(c) no appeal may be made against a corresponding decision made in exercising the function in relation to Scotland.

(2) The Lord Chancellor may by order provide for an appeal against any such corresponding decision to be made to the Upper Tribunal.

(3) An order under subsection (2)–

(a) may include provision for the purposes of or in consequence of, or for giving full effect to, provision made by the order;

(b) may include such incidental, supplemental, transitional or consequential provision or savings as the Lord Chancellor thinks fit.

(4) An order under subsection (2) does not cease to have effect, and power to vary or

revoke the order does not cease to be exercisable, just because either or each of the conditions in subsection (1)(b) and (c) ceases to be satisfied in relation to the function and decisions concerned.

### Power to provide for appeal to Upper Tribunal from tribunals in Northern Ireland

34 (1) Subsection (2) applies if–

(a) a function is transferred under section 30(1)(a), (c), (d) or (e) in relation to England (whether or not also in relation to Wales) but is not transferred under section 30(1) in relation to Northern Ireland,

(b) an appeal may be made to the Upper Tribunal against any decision, or any decision of a particular description, made in exercising the transferred function in relation to England, and

(c) no appeal may be made against a corresponding decision made in exercising the function in relation to Northern Ireland.

(2) The Lord Chancellor may by order provide for an appeal against any such corresponding decision to be made to the Upper Tribunal.

(3) An order under subsection (2)–

(a) may include provision for the purposes of or in consequence of, or for giving full effect to, provision made by the order;

(b) may include such incidental, supplemental, transitional or consequential provision or savings as the Lord Chancellor thinks fit.

(4) An order under subsection (2) does not cease to have effect, and power to vary or revoke the order does not cease to be exercisable, just because either or each of the conditions in subsection (1)(b) and (c) ceases to be satisfied in relation to the function and decisions concerned.

### Transfer of Ministerial responsibilities for certain tribunals

35 (1) The Lord Chancellor may by order–

(a) transfer any relevant function, so far as that function is exercisable by a Minister of the Crown–

(i) to the Lord Chancellor, or

(ii) to two (or more) Ministers of the Crown of whom one is the Lord Chancellor;

(b) provide for any relevant function that is exercisable by a Minister of the Crown other than the Lord Chancellor to be exercisable by the other Minister of the Crown concurrently with the Lord Chancellor;

(c) provide for any relevant function that is exercisable by the Lord Chancellor concurrently with another Minister of the Crown to cease to be exercisable by the other Minister of the Crown.

(2) In this section 'relevant function' means a function, in relation to a scheduled tribunal, which relates–

(a) to the operation of the tribunal (including, in particular, its membership, administration, staff, accommodation and funding, and payments to its members or staff), or

(b) to the provision of expenses and allowances to persons attending the tribunal or attending elsewhere in connection with proceedings before the tribunal.

(3) In subsection (2) 'scheduled tribunal' means a tribunal in a list in Schedule 6 that has effect for the purposes of this section.

(4) A relevant function may not be transferred under subsection (1) if, or to the extent that, the provision conferring the function–

(a) would be within the legislative competence of the Scottish Parliament if it were included in an Act of that Parliament, or

(b) would be within the legislative competence of the Northern Ireland Assembly if it were included in an Act of that Assembly.

(5) Subsection (4) does not apply to any relevant function of the Secretary of State–

(a) under section 41 of the Consumer Credit Act 1974 (appeals), or

(b) under section 7 of the Estate Agents Act 1979 (appeals).

(6) Any reference in subsection (1) to a Minister of the Crown includes a reference to a Minister of the Crown acting jointly.

(7) An order under subsection (1)–

(a) may relate to a function either wholly or in cases (including cases framed by reference to areas) specified in the order;

(b) may include provision for the purposes of, or in consequence of, or for giving full effect to, the transfer or (as the case may be) other change as regards exercise;

(c) may include such incidental, supplementary, transitional or consequential provision or savings as the Lord Chancellor thinks fit;

(d) may include provision for the transfer of any property, rights or liabilities of the person who loses functions or whose functions become shared with the Lord Chancellor.

(8) An order under subsection (1), so far as it–

(a) provides under paragraph (a) for the transfer of a function, or

(b) provides under paragraph (b) for a function to become exercisable by the Lord Chancellor, or

(c) provides under paragraph (c) for a function to cease to be exercisable by a Minister of the Crown other than the Lord Chancellor,

may not, after that transfer or other change has taken place, be revoked by another order under that subsection.

(9) Section 1 of the 1975 Act (power to transfer Ministerial functions) does not apply to a function of the Lord Chancellor–

(a) so far as it is a function transferred to the Lord Chancellor under subsection (1)(a),

(b) so far as it is a function exercisable by the Lord Chancellor as a result of provision under subsection (1)(b), or

(c) so far as it is a function that has become exercisable by the Lord Chancellor alone as a result of provision under subsection (1)(c).

(10) In this section–

'Minister of the Crown' has the meaning given by section 8(1) of the 1975 Act but includes the Commissioners for Her Majesty's Revenue and Customs;

'the 1975 Act' means the Ministers of the Crown Act 1975.

### Transfer of powers to make procedural rules for certain tribunals

36 (1) The Lord Chancellor may by order transfer any power to make procedural rules for a scheduled tribunal to–

(a) himself, or

(b) the Tribunal Procedure Committee.

(2) A power may not be transferred under subsection (1) if, or to the extent that, the provision conferring the power–

(a) would be within the legislative competence of the Scottish Parliament if it were included in an Act of that Parliament, or

(b) would be within the legislative competence of the Northern Ireland Assembly if it were included in an Act of that Assembly.

(3) Subsection (2) does not apply to–

(a) power conferred by section 40A(3) of the Consumer Credit Act 1974 (power to make provision with respect to appeals), or

(b) power conferred by section 7(3) of the Estate Agents Act 1979 (duty of Secretary of State to make regulations with respect to appeals under section 7(1) of that Act).

(4) An order under subsection (1)(b)–

(a) may not alter any parliamentary procedure relating to the making of the procedural rules concerned, but

(b) may otherwise include provision for the purpose of assimilating the procedure for making them to the procedure for making Tribunal Procedure Rules.

(5) An order under subsection (1)(b) may include provision requiring the Tribunal

Procedure Committee to make procedural rules for purposes notified to it by the Lord Chancellor.

(6) An order under this section–

    (a) may relate to a power either wholly or in cases (including cases framed by reference to areas) specified in the order;

    (b) may include provision for the purposes of or in consequence of, or for giving full effect to, the transfer;

    (c) may include such incidental, supplementary, transitional or consequential provision or savings as the Lord Chancellor thinks fit.

(7) A power to make procedural rules for a tribunal that is exercisable by the Tribunal Procedure Committee by virtue of an order under this section must be exercised by the committee with a view to securing–

    (a) that the system for deciding matters within the jurisdiction of that tribunal is accessible and fair,

    (b) that proceedings before that tribunal are handled quickly and efficiently,

    (c) that the rules are both simple and simply expressed, and

    (d) that the rules where appropriate confer on persons who are, or who are members of, that tribunal responsibility for ensuring that proceedings before that tribunal are handled quickly and efficiently.

(8) In this section–

    'procedural rules', in relation to a tribunal, means provision (whether called rules or not) regulating practice or procedure before the tribunal;

    'scheduled tribunal' means a tribunal in a list in Schedule 6 that has effect for the purposes of this section.

## Power to amend lists of tribunals in Schedule 6

37 (1) The Lord Chancellor may by order amend Schedule 6–

    (a) for the purpose of adding a tribunal to a list in the Schedule;

    (b) for the purpose of removing a tribunal from a list in the Schedule;

    (c) for the purpose of removing a list from the Schedule;

    (d) for the purpose of adding to the Schedule a list of tribunals that has effect for the purposes of any one or more of sections 30, 32(3), 35 and 36.

(2) The following rules apply to the exercise of power under subsection (1)–

    (a) a tribunal may not be added to a list, or be in an added list, if the tribunal is established otherwise than by or under an enactment;

    (b) a tribunal established by an enactment passed or made after the last day of the Session in which this Act is passed must not be added to a list, or be in an added list, that has effect for the purposes of section 30;

    (c) if any relevant function is exercisable in relation to a tribunal by the Welsh Ministers (whether by the Welsh Ministers alone, or by the Welsh Ministers jointly or concurrently with any other person), the tribunal may be added to a list, or be in an added list, only with the consent of the Welsh Ministers;

    (d) a tribunal may be in more than one list.

(3) In subsection (2)(c) 'relevant function', in relation to a tribunal, means a function which relates–

    (a) to the operation of the tribunal (including, in particular, its membership, administration, staff, accommodation and funding, and payments to its members or staff), or

    (b) to the provision of expenses and allowances to persons attending the tribunal or attending elsewhere in connection with proceedings before the tribunal.

(4) In subsection (1) 'tribunal' does not include an ordinary court of law.

(5) In this section 'enactment' means any enactment whenever passed or made, including an enactment comprised in subordinate legislation (within the meaning of the Interpretation Act 1978).

## Orders under sections 30 to 36: supplementary

38 (1) Provision in an order under any of sections 30 to 36 may take the form of amendments, repeals or revocations of enactments.

(2) In this section 'enactment' means any enactment whenever passed or made,

including an enactment comprised in subordinate legislation (within the meaning of the Interpretation Act 1978).

(3) Any power to extend enactments to a territory outside the United Kingdom shall have effect as if it included–

   (a) power to extend those enactments as they have effect with any amendments and repeals made in them by orders under any of sections 30 to 36, and

   (b) power to extend those enactments as if any amendments and repeals made in them under those sections had not been made.

## CHAPTER 4: ADMINISTRATIVE MATTERS IN RESPECT OF CERTAIN TRIBUNALS

### The general duty

39 (1) The Lord Chancellor is under a duty to ensure that there is an efficient and effective system to support the carrying on of the business of–

   (a) the First-tier Tribunal,

   (b) the Upper Tribunal,

   (c) employment tribunals, and

   (d) the Employment Appeal Tribunal

   and that appropriate services are provided for those tribunals (referred to in this section and in sections 40 and 41 as 'the tribunals').

(2) Any reference in this section, or in section 40 or 41, to the Lord Chancellor's general duty in relation to the tribunals is to his duty under subsection (1).

(3) The Lord Chancellor must annually prepare and lay before each House of Parliament a report as to the way in which he has discharged his general duty in relation to the tribunals.

### Tribunal staff and services

40 (1) The Lord Chancellor may appoint such staff as appear to him appropriate for the purpose of discharging his general duty in relation to the tribunals.

(2) Subject to subsections (3) and (4), the Lord Chancellor may enter into such contracts with other persons for the provision, by them or their subcontractors, of staff or services as appear to him appropriate for the purpose of discharging his general duty in relation to the tribunals.

(3) The Lord Chancellor may not enter into contracts for the provision of staff to discharge functions which involve making judicial decisions or exercising any judicial discretion.

(4) The Lord Chancellor may not enter into contracts for the provision of staff to carry out the administrative work of the tribunals unless an order made by the Lord Chancellor authorises him to do so.

(5) Before making an order under subsection (4) the Lord Chancellor must consult the Senior President of Tribunals as to what effect (if any) the order might have on the proper and efficient administration of justice.

(6) An order under subsection (4) may authorise the Lord Chancellor to enter into contracts for the provision of staff to discharge functions–

   (a) wholly or to the extent specified in the order,

   (b) generally or in cases or areas specified in the order, and

   (c) unconditionally or subject to the fulfilment of conditions specified in the order.

### Provision of accommodation

41 (1) The Lord Chancellor may provide, equip, maintain and manage such tribunal buildings, offices and other accommodation as appear to him appropriate for the purpose of discharging his general duty in relation to the tribunals.

(2) The Lord Chancellor may enter into such arrangements for the provision, equipment, maintenance or management of tribunal buildings, offices or other accommodation as appear to him appropriate for the purpose of discharging his general duty in relation to the tribunals.

(3) The powers under–

(a) section 2 of the Commissioners of Works Act 1852 (acquisition by agreement), and

(b) section 228(1) of the Town and Country Planning Act 1990 (compulsory acquisition),

to acquire land necessary for the public service are to be treated as including power to acquire land for the purpose of its provision under arrangements entered into under subsection (2).

(4) In this section 'tribunal building' means any place where any of the tribunals sits, including the precincts of any building in which it sits.

### Fees

42 (1) The Lord Chancellor may by order prescribe fees payable in respect of–
    (a) anything dealt with by the First-tier Tribunal,
    (b) anything dealt with by the Upper Tribunal,
    (d) anything dealt with by an added tribunal, and
    (e) mediation conducted by staff appointed under section 40(1).

(2) An order under subsection (1) may, in particular, contain provision as to–
    (a) scales or rates of fees;
    (b) exemptions from or reductions in fees;
    (c) remission of fees in whole or in part.

(3) In subsection (1)(d) 'added tribunal' means a tribunal specified in an order made by the Lord Chancellor.

(4) A tribunal may be specified in an order under subsection (3) only if–
    (a) it is established by or under an enactment, whenever passed or made, and
    (b) is not an ordinary court of law.

(5) Before making an order under this section, the Lord Chancellor must consult–
    (a) the Senior President of Tribunals.

(6) The making of an order under subsection (1) requires the consent of the Treasury except where the order contains provision only for the purpose of altering amounts payable by way of fees already prescribed under that subsection.

(7) The Lord Chancellor must take such steps as are reasonably practicable to bring information about fees under subsection (1) to the attention of persons likely to have to pay them.

(8) Fees payable under subsection (1) are recoverable summarily as a civil debt.

(9) Subsection (8) does not apply to the recovery in Scotland of fees payable under this section.

### Report by Senior President of Tribunals

43 (1) Each year the Senior President of Tribunals must give the Lord Chancellor a report covering, in relation to relevant tribunal cases–
    (a) matters that the Senior President of Tribunals wishes to bring to the attention of the Lord Chancellor, and
    (b) matters that the Lord Chancellor has asked the Senior President of Tribunals to cover in the report.

(2) The Lord Chancellor must publish each report given to him under subsection (1).

(3) In this section 'relevant tribunal cases' means–
    (a) cases coming before the First-tier Tribunal,
    (b) cases coming before the Upper Tribunal,
    (c) cases coming before the Employment Appeal Tribunal, and
    (d) cases coming before employment tribunals.

## CHAPTER 6: SUPPLEMENTARY

### Delegation of functions by Lord Chief Justice etc.

46 (1) The Lord Chief Justice of England and Wales may nominate a judicial office holder (as defined in section 109(4) of the Constitutional Reform Act 2005) to exercise any of his functions under the provisions listed in subsection (2).

(2) The provisions are–
paragraphs 3(4) and 6(3)(a) of Schedule 2;

paragraphs 3(4) and 6(3)(a) of Schedule 3;
paragraphs 2(2) and 5(5) of Schedule 4;
paragraphs 21(2), 22, 24 and 25(2)(a) of Schedule 5.

(3) The Lord President of the Court of Session may nominate any of the following to exercise any of his functions under the provisions listed in subsection (4)–
   (a) a judge who is a member of the First or Second Division of the Inner House of the Court of Session;
   (b) the Senior President of Tribunals.

(4) The provisions are–
paragraphs 3(2) and 6(3)(b) of Schedule 2;
paragraphs 3(2) and 6(3)(b) of Schedule 3;
paragraphs 2(3) and 5(6) of Schedule 4;
paragraphs 23, 24, 25(2)(b) and (c) and 28(1)(b) of Schedule 5.

(5) The Lord Chief Justice of Northern Ireland may nominate any of the following to exercise any of his functions under the provisions listed in subsection (6)–
   (a) the holder of one of the offices listed in Schedule 1 to the Justice (Northern Ireland) Act 2002;
   (b) a Lord Justice of Appeal (as defined in section 88 of that Act);
   (c) the Senior President of Tribunals.

(6) The provisions are–
paragraphs 3(3) and 6(3)(c) of Schedule 2;
paragraphs 3(3) and 6(3)(c) of Schedule 3;
paragraphs 2(4) and 5(7) of Schedule 4;
paragraphs 24 and 25(2)(c) of Schedule 5.

(7) In Schedules 2 to 4 'senior judge' means–
   (a) the Lord Chief Justice of England and Wales,
   (b) the Lord President of the Court of Session,
   (c) the Lord Chief Justice of Northern Ireland, or
   (d) the Senior President of Tribunals.

### Co-operation in relation to judicial training, guidance and welfare

47 (1) Persons with responsibilities in connection with a courts-related activity, and persons with responsibilities in connection with the corresponding tribunals activity, must co-operate with each other in relation to the carrying-on of those activities.

(2) In this section 'courts-related activity' and 'corresponding tribunals activity' are to be read as follows–
   (a) making arrangements for training of judiciary of a territory is a courts-related activity, and the corresponding tribunals activity is making arrangements for training of tribunal members;
   (b) making arrangements for guidance of judiciary of a territory is a courts-related activity, and the corresponding tribunals activity is making arrangements for guidance of tribunal members;
   (c) making arrangements for the welfare of judiciary of a territory is a courts-related activity, and the corresponding tribunals activity is making arrangements for the welfare of tribunal members.

(3) Subsection (1) applies to a person who has responsibilities in connection with a courts-related activity only if–
   (a) the person is the chief justice of the territory concerned, or
   (b) what the person does in discharging those responsibilities is done (directly or indirectly) on behalf of the chief justice of that territory.

(4) Subsection (1) applies to a person who has responsibilities in connection with a corresponding tribunals activity only if–
   (a) the person is the Senior President of Tribunals, or
   (b) what the person does in discharging those responsibilities is done (directly or indirectly) on behalf of the Senior President of Tribunals.

(5) For the purposes of this section–
   (a) 'territory' means–
      (i) England and Wales,

(ii)  Scotland, or

(iii) Northern Ireland;

(b) the 'chief justice'–

(i)  of England and Wales is the Lord Chief Justice of England and Wales,

(ii)  of Scotland is the Lord President of the Court of Session, and

(iii) of Northern Ireland is the Lord Chief Justice of Northern Ireland;

(c) a person is a 'tribunal member' if the person is–

(i)  a judge, or other member, of the First-tier Tribunal or Upper Tribunal,

(ii)  a judge, or other member, of the Employment Appeal Tribunal, or

(iii) a member of a panel of members of employment tribunals (whether or not a panel of Employment Judges).

## Consequential and other amendments, and transitional provisions

48 (1) Schedule 8, which makes–

amendments consequential on provisions of this Part, and

other amendments in connection with tribunals and inquiries,

has effect.

(2) Schedule 9, which contains transitional provisions, has effect.

## Orders and regulations under Part 1: supplemental and procedural provisions

49 (1) Power–

(a) of the Lord Chancellor to make an order, or regulations, under this Part,

(b) of the Senior President of Tribunals to make an order under section 7(9), or

(c) of the Scottish Ministers, or the Welsh Ministers, to make an order under paragraph 25(2) of Schedule 7,

is exercisable by statutory instrument.

(2) The Statutory Instruments Act 1946 shall apply in relation to the power to make orders conferred on the Senior President of Tribunals by section 7(9) as if the Senior President of Tribunals were a Minister of the Crown.

(3) Any power mentioned in subsection (1) includes power to make different provision for different purposes.

(4) Without prejudice to the generality of subsection (3), power to make an order under section 30 or 31 includes power to make different provision in relation to England, Scotland, Wales and Northern Ireland respectively.

(5) No order mentioned in subsection (6) is to be made unless a draft of the statutory instrument containing it (whether alone or with other provision) has been laid before, and approved by a resolution of, each House of Parliament.

(6) Those orders are–

(a) an order under section 11(8), 13(6) or (14), 30, 31(1), 32, 33, 34, 35, 36, 37 or 42(3);

(b) an order under paragraph 15 of Schedule 4;

(c) an order under section 42(1)(a) to (d) that provides for fees to be payable in respect of things for which fees have never been payable;

(d) an order under section 31(2), (7) or (9), or paragraph 30(1) of Schedule 5, that contains provision taking the form of an amendment or repeal of an enactment comprised in an Act.

(7) A statutory instrument that–

(a) contains–

(i)  an order mentioned in subsection (8), or

(ii) regulations under Part 3 of Schedule 9, and

(b) is not subject to any requirement that a draft of the instrument be laid before, and approved by a resolution of, each House of Parliament,

is subject to annulment in pursuance of a resolution of either House of Parliament.

(8) Those orders are–

(a) an order made by the Lord Chancellor under this Part;

(b) an order made by the Senior President of Tribunals under section 7(9).

(9) A statutory instrument that contains an order made by the Scottish Ministers under

paragraph 25(2) of Schedule 7 is subject to annulment in pursuance of a resolution of the Scottish Parliament.

(10) A statutory instrument that contains an order made by the Welsh Ministers under paragraph 25(2) of Schedule 7 is subject to annulment in pursuance of a resolution of the National Assembly for Wales.

## PART 8: GENERAL

### Power to make supplementary or other provision

145 (1) The Lord Chancellor (or, in relation to Chapter 3 of Part 5 only, the Secretary of State) may by order make any supplementary, incidental, consequential, transitory, transitional or saving provision which he considers necessary or expedient for the purposes of, in consequence of, or for giving full effect to, any provision of this Act.

(2) An order under this section may in particular–

(a) provide for any provision of this Act which comes into force before another to have effect, until that other provision has come into force, with modifications specified in the order;

(b) amend, repeal or revoke any enactment other than one contained in an Act or instrument passed or made after the Session in which this Act is passed.

(3) The amendments that may be made by an order under this section are in addition to those made by or under any other provision of this Act.

(4) An order under this section may make different provision for different purposes.

(5) The power to make an order under this section is exercisable by statutory instrument.

(6) A statutory instrument containing an order under this section, unless it is an order to which subsection (7) applies, is subject to annulment in pursuance of a resolution of either House of Parliament.

(7) No order amending or repealing an enactment contained in an Act may be made under this section unless a draft of the order has been laid before and approved by a resolution of each House of Parliament.

### Repeals

146 Schedule 23 contains repeals.

### Extent

147 (1) Parts 1, 2 and 6 and this Part extend to England and Wales, Scotland and Northern Ireland.

(2) The other provisions of this Act extend only to England and Wales.

(3) Subsections (1) and (2) are subject to subsections (4) and (5).

(4) Unless provided otherwise, amendments, repeals and revocations in this Act extend to any part of the United Kingdom to which the provisions amended, repealed or revoked extend.

(5) The following extend also to the Isle of Man–

(a) section 143(1) and (2),

(b) the repeal by this Act of any provision specified in Part 6 of Schedule 23 that extends to the Isle of Man,

(c) sections 145 and 148(5) to (7) so far as relating to–

(i) section 143(1) and (2), and

(ii) the provisions of this Act by which the repeals mentioned in paragraph (b) are effected, and

(d) this section and section 149.

### Commencement

148 (1) Section 60 comes into force at the end of the period of two months beginning with the day on which this Act is passed.

(2) The provisions of Chapter 3 of Part 5 come into force in accordance with provision made by the Lord Chancellor or the Secretary of State by order.

(3) The provisions of Part 6 come into force, except as provided by subsection (4), in accordance with provision made by the Secretary of State by order.

(4) The provisions of Part 6 come into force, in so far as they extend to Scotland, in accordance with provision made by the Scottish Ministers by order.

(5) The remaining provisions of this Act, except sections 53, 55, 56, 57, 145, 147, 49, this section and Schedule 11, come into force in accordance with provision made by the Lord Chancellor by order.

(6) An order under this section may make different provision for different purposes.

(7) The power to make an order under this section is exercisable by statutory instrument.

## SCHEDULES

## SCHEDULE 1: SENIOR PRESIDENT OF TRIBUNALS

### PART 1: RECOMMENDATIONS FOR APPOINTMENT

*Duty to fill vacancies*

1 (1) If there is a vacancy in the office of Senior President of Tribunals, the Lord Chancellor must recommend a person for appointment to that office.

(2) Sub-paragraph (1) does not apply to a vacancy while the Lord Chief Justice of England and Wales agrees that it may remain unfilled.

*The two routes to a recommendation: agreement under this paragraph or selection under Part 2*

2 (1) Before the Lord Chancellor may recommend a person for appointment to the office of Senior President of Tribunals, the Lord Chancellor must consult–
   (a) the Lord Chief Justice of England and Wales,
   (b) the Lord President of the Court of Session, and
   (c) the Lord Chief Justice of Northern Ireland.

(2) Sub-paragraphs (3) and (4) apply if–
   (a) the outcome of consultation under sub-paragraph (1) is agreement between–
      (i)   the Lord Chancellor,
      (ii)  the Lord Chief Justice of England and Wales,
      (iii) the Lord President of the Court of Session, and
      (iv)  the Lord Chief Justice of Northern Ireland,
      as to the person to be recommended, and
   (b) the person is–
      (i)   an ordinary judge of the Court of Appeal in England and Wales,
      (ii)  a judge of the Court of Session who is a member of the First or Second Division of the Inner House of that Court, or
      (iii) a Lord Justice of Appeal in Northern Ireland.

(3) The Lord Chancellor must recommend the person for appointment to the office of Senior President of Tribunals, subject to sub-paragraph (4).

(4) Where the person–
   (a) declines to be recommended, or does not agree within a time specified to him for that purpose, or
   (b) is otherwise not available within a reasonable time to be recommended, the Lord Chancellor must, instead of recommending the person for appointment, consult afresh under sub-paragraph (1).

(5) If the Lord Chancellor has consulted under sub-paragraph (1) but subparagraphs (3) and (4) do not apply following that consultation, the Lord Chancellor must make a request to the Judicial Appointments Commission for a person to be selected for recommendation for appointment to the office of Senior President of Tribunals.

### PART 2: SELECTION BY THE JUDICIAL APPOINTMENTS COMMISSION

*Eligibility for selection*

3    A person is eligible for selection in pursuance of a request under paragraph 2(5) only if–
   (a) he satisfies the judicial-appointment eligibility condition on a 7-year basis,
   (b) he is an advocate or solicitor in Scotland of at least seven years' standing, or

(c) he is a barrister or solicitor in Northern Ireland of at least seven years' standing.

*The selection process*

4   In Chapter 2 of Part 4 of the Constitutional Reform Act 2005 (appointments), after section 75 insert–

'*Senior President of Tribunals*

**75A   Sections 75B to 75G apply where request made for selection**

(1) Sections 75B to 75G apply where the Lord Chancellor makes a request to the Commission under paragraph 2(5) of Schedule 1 to the Tribunals, Courts and Enforcement Act 2007 (request for person to be selected for recommendation for appointment to the office of Senior President of Tribunals).

(2) Those sections are subject to section 95 (withdrawal and modification of requests).

**75B   Selection process**

(1) On receiving a request the Commission must appoint a selection panel.

(2) The panel must–

(a) determine the selection process to be applied,

(b) apply the selection process, and

(c) make a selection accordingly.

(3) As part of the selection process the panel must consult–

(a) the Lord Chief Justice, if not a member of the panel,

(b) the Lord President of the Court of Session, if not a member of the panel, and

(c) the Lord Chief Justice of Northern Ireland, if not a member of the panel.

(4) One person only must be selected for the recommendation to which a request relates.

(5) Subsection (4) applies to selection under this section and to selection under section 75G.

(6) A selection panel is a committee of the Commission.

**75C   Selection panel**

(1) The selection panel must consist of four members.

(2) The first member is the Lord Chief Justice, or his nominee.

(3) The second member is a person designated by the Lord Chief Justice.

(4) Unless subsection (7) applies, the third member is the chairman of the Commission or his nominee.

(5) The fourth member is a lay member of the Commission designated by the third member.

(6) Subsection (7) applies if–

(a) there is no chairman of the Commission, or

(b) the chairman of the Commission is unavailable and has not nominated a person under subsection (4).

(7) In those cases the third member is a lay member of the Commission selected by the lay members of the Commission other than the chairman.

(8) A nominee of the Lord Chief Justice must be a Head of Division or a Lord Justice of Appeal.

(9) The person designated under subsection (3) must be–

(a) a person who holds, or has held, the office of Senior President of Tribunals,

(b) a person who holds, or has held, office as a Chamber President of a chamber of the First-tier Tribunal or of a chamber of the Upper Tribunal, or

(c) a person who holds, or has held, an office that, in the opinion of the Lord Chief Justice, is such that a holder of it would acquire knowledge or experience of tribunals broadly similar to that which would be acquired by–

       (i)   a person who holds the office of Senior President of Tribunals, or

      (ii)   a person who holds office as a Chamber President of a chamber of the First-tier Tribunal, or

    (iii)   a person who holds office as a Chamber President of a chamber of the Upper Tribunal.

(10) Before designating a person under subsection (3), the Lord Chief Justice must consult–

   (a) the Lord President of the Court of Session, and

   (b) the Lord Chief Justice of Northern Ireland.

(11) A person may not be appointed to the panel if he is willing to be considered for selection.

(12) A person may not be appointed to the panel as the nominee of more than one person.

(13) A person appointed to the panel otherwise than as a nominee may not be a nominee.

(14) The first member is the chairman of the panel.

(15) On any vote by the panel the chairman of the panel has an additional, casting vote in the event of a tie.

## 75D  Report

(1) After complying with section 75B(2) the selection panel must submit a report to the Lord Chancellor.

(2) The report must–

   (a) state who has been selected;

   (b) contain any other information required by the Lord Chancellor.

(3) The report must be in a form approved by the Lord Chancellor.

(4) After submitting the report the panel must provide any further information the Lord Chancellor may require.

## 75E  The Lord Chancellor's options

(1) This section refers to the following stages–

   *Stage 1* where a person has been selected under section 75B

   *Stage 2:* where a person has been selected following a rejection or reconsideration at stage 1

   *Stage 3:* where a person has been selected following a rejection or reconsideration at stage 2

(2) At stage 1 the Lord Chancellor must do one of the following–

   (a) accept the selection;

   (b) reject the selection;

   (c) require the selection panel to reconsider the selection.

(3) At stage 2 the Lord Chancellor must do one of the following–

   (a) accept the selection;

   (b) reject the selection, but only if it was made following a reconsideration at stage 1;

   (c) require the selection panel to reconsider the selection, but only if it was made following a rejection at stage 1.

(4) At stage 3 the Lord Chancellor must accept the selection, unless subsection(5) applies and he accepts a selection under it.

(5) If a person whose selection the Lord Chancellor required to be reconsidered at stage 1 or 2 was not selected again at the next stage, the Lord Chancellor may, at stage 3, accept the selection made at that earlier stage.

## 75F  Exercise of powers to reject or require reconsideration

(1) The power of the Lord Chancellor under section 75E to reject a selection at stage 1 or 2 is exercisable only on the grounds that, in the Lord Chancellor's opinion, the person selected is not suitable for the office of Senior President of Tribunals.

(2) The power of the Lord Chancellor under section 75E to require the selection panel to reconsider a selection at stage 1 or 2 is exercisable only on the grounds that, in the Lord Chancellor's opinion–

    (a) there is not enough evidence that the person is suitable for the office of Senior President of Tribunals, or

    (b) there is evidence that the person is not the best candidate on merit.

(3) The Lord Chancellor must give the selection panel reasons in writing for rejecting or requiring reconsideration of a selection.

### 75G Selection following rejection or requirement to reconsider

(1) If under section 75F the Lord Chancellor rejects or requires reconsideration of a selection at stage 1 or 2, the selection panel must select a person in accordance with this section.

(2) If the Lord Chancellor rejects a selection, the selection panel–

    (a) may not select the person rejected, and

    (b) where the rejection is following reconsideration of a selection, may not select the person (if different) whose selection it reconsidered.

(3) If the Lord Chancellor requires a selection to be reconsidered, the selection panel–

    (a) may select the same person or a different person, but

    (b) where the requirement is following a rejection, may not select the person rejected.

(4) The selection panel must inform the Lord Chancellor of the person selected following a rejection or a requirement to reconsider.

(5) Subsections (2) and (3) do not prevent a person being selected on a subsequent request under paragraph 2(5) of Schedule 1 to the Tribunals, Courts and Enforcement Act 2007.'

*Withdrawal and modification of requests under paragraph 2(5)*

**5** (1) Section 95 of the Constitutional Reform Act 2005 (withdrawal and modification of requests) is amended as follows.

(2) In subsection (1) (application of section), after '87' insert 'or paragraph 2(5) of Schedule 1 to the Tribunals, Courts and Enforcement Act 2007'.

(3) In subsection (4) (limitation on withdrawal of request under subsection (2)(c)), after '73(2),' insert '75E(2),'.

### PART 3: TERMS OF OFFICE

*Tenure, removal, resignation etc.*

**6** (1) If–

    (a) a person appointed to the office of Senior President of Tribunals is appointed on terms that provide for him to retire from the office at a particular time specified in those terms ('the end of the fixed-term'), and

    (b) the end of the fixed-term is earlier than the time at which the person is required by the 1993 Act to retire from the office,

the person shall, if still holding the office at the end of the fixed-term, vacate the office at the end of the fixed-term.

(2) Subject to sub-paragraph (1) (and to the 1993 Act), a person appointed to the office of Senior President of Tribunals shall hold that office during good behaviour, subject to a power of removal by Her Majesty on an address presented to Her by both Houses of Parliament.

(3) It is for the Lord Chancellor to recommend to Her Majesty the exercise of the power of removal under sub-paragraph (2).

(4) In this paragraph 'the 1993 Act' means the Judicial Pensions and Retirement Act 1993.

**7** (1) Sub-paragraph (2) applies to a person appointed to the office of Senior President of Tribunals on a recommendation made under paragraph 2(3).

(2) The person ceases to be Senior President of Tribunals if he ceases to fall within paragraph 2(2)(b).

**8**   A person who holds the office of Senior President of Tribunals may at anytime resign that office by giving the Lord Chancellor notice in writing to that effect.

**9** (1) The Lord Chancellor, if satisfied by means of a medical certificate that a person holding the office of Senior President of Tribunals–

(a) is disabled by permanent infirmity from the performance of the duties of the office, and

(b) is for the time being incapacitated from resigning the office, may, subject to sub-paragraph (2), by instrument under his hand declare the person to have vacated the office; and the instrument shall have the like effect for all purposes as if the person had on the date of the instrument resigned the office.

(2) A declaration under sub-paragraph (1) with respect to a person shall be of no effect unless it is made with the concurrence of–

(a) the Lord Chief Justice of England and Wales,

(b) the Lord President of the Court of Session, and

(c) the Lord Chief Justice of Northern Ireland.

### Remuneration, allowances and expenses

10    The Lord Chancellor may pay to the Senior President of Tribunals such amounts (if any) as the Lord Chancellor may determine by way of–

(a) remuneration;

(b) allowances;

(c) expenses.

### Oaths

11 (1) A person appointed to the office of Senior President of Tribunals must take the required oaths in the presence of–

(a) the Lord Chief Justice of England and Wales, or

(b) another holder of high judicial office (as defined in section 60(2) of the Constitutional Reform Act 2005) who is nominated by the Lord Chief Justice of England and Wales for the purpose of taking the oaths from the person.

(2) Sub-paragraph (1) applies whether or not the person has previously taken the required oaths after accepting another office.

(3) In this paragraph 'the required oaths' means–

(a) the oath of allegiance, and

(b) the judicial oath,

as set out in the Promissory Oaths Act 1868.

## PART 4: CERTAIN FUNCTIONS OF THE SENIOR PRESIDENT

### Meaning of 'tribunal member'

12 (1) For the purposes of this Part of this Schedule, each of the following is a 'tribunal member'–

(a) a judge, or other member, of the First-tier Tribunal or Upper Tribunal,

(c) a member of a panel of members of employment tribunals (whether or not a panel of Employment Judges),

(d) a judge, or other member, of the Employment Appeal Tribunal, and

(e) a person who is, or is a member of, a tribunal in a list in Schedule 6 that has effect for the purposes of section 30.

(2) In this Part of this Schedule 'tribunals' means–

(a) the First-tier Tribunal,

(b) the Upper Tribunal,

(d) employment tribunals,

(e) the Employment Appeal Tribunal, and

(f) any tribunal in a list in Schedule 6 that has effect for the purposes of section 30.

### Representations to Parliament

13    The Senior President of Tribunals may lay before Parliament written representations on matters that appear to him to be matters of importance relating–

(a) to tribunal members, or

(b) otherwise to the administration of justice by tribunals.

### Representation of views of tribunal members

14    The Senior President of Tribunals is responsible for representing the views of

tribunal members to Parliament, to the Lord Chancellor and to Ministers of the Crown generally.

## SCHEDULE 2: JUDGES AND OTHER MEMBERS OF THE FIRST-TIER TRIBUNAL

*Power to appoint judges of First-tier Tribunal*

1 (1) The Senior President of Tribunals may appoint a person to be one of the judges of the First-tier Tribunal.

(2) A person is eligible for appointment under sub-paragraph (1) only if the person–
   (a) satisfies the judicial-appointment eligibility condition on a 5-year basis,
   (b) is an advocate or solicitor in Scotland of at least five years' standing,
   (c) is a barrister or solicitor in Northern Ireland of at least five years' standing, or
   (d) in the opinion of the Senior President of Tribunals, has gained experience in law which makes the person as suitable for appointment as if the person satisfied any of paragraphs (a) to (c).

(3) Section 52(2) to (5) (meaning of 'gain experience in law') apply for the purposes of sub-paragraph (2)(d), but as if section 52(4)(i) referred to the Senior President of Tribunals instead of to the relevant decision-maker.

*Power to appoint other members of First-tier Tribunal*

2 (1) The Senior President of Tribunals may appoint a person to be one of the members of the First-tier Tribunal who are not judges of the tribunal.

(2) A person is eligible for appointment under sub-paragraph (1) only if the person has qualifications prescribed in an order made by the Lord Chancellor with the concurrence of the Senior President of Tribunals.

*Appointed and transferred-in judges and other members: removal from office*

3 (1) This paragraph applies to any power by which–
   (a) a person appointed under paragraph 1(1) or 2(1),
   (b) a transferred-in judge of the First-tier Tribunal,
   (ba) a person who is a deputy judge of the Upper Tribunal (whether by appointment under paragraph 7(1) or as a result of provision under section 31(2)), or
   (c) a transferred-in other member of the First-tier Tribunal,
   may be removed from office.

(2) If the person exercises functions wholly or mainly in Scotland, the power may be exercised only with the concurrence of the Lord President of the Court of Session.

(3) If the person exercises functions wholly or mainly in Northern Ireland, the power may be exercised only with the concurrence of the Lord Chief Justice of Northern Ireland.

(4) If neither of sub-paragraphs (2) and (3) applies, the power may be exercised only with the concurrence of the Lord Chief Justice of England and Wales.

*Terms of appointment*

4 (1) This paragraph applies–
   (a) to a person appointed under paragraph 1(1) or 2(1),
   (b) to a transferred-in judge of the First-tier Tribunal, and
   (c) to a transferred-in other member of the First-tier Tribunal.

(2) If the terms of the person's appointment provide that he is appointed on a salaried (as opposed to fee-paid) basis, the person may be removed from office–
   (a) only by the Lord Chancellor (and in accordance with paragraph 3), and
   (b) only on the ground of inability or misbehaviour.

(2A) If the terms of the person's appointment provide that the person is appointed on a fee-paid basis, the person may be removed from office–
   (a) only by the Lord Chancellor (and in accordance with paragraph 3), and
   (b) only on–
      (i) the ground of inability or misbehaviour, or
      (ii) a ground specified in the person's terms of appointment.

(2B) If the period (or extended period) for which the person is appointed ends before–

(a) the day on which the person attains the age of 70, or

(b) if different, the day that for the purposes of section 26 of the Judicial Pensions and Retirement Act 1993 is the compulsory retirement date for the office concerned in the person's case,

then, subject to sub-paragraph (2C), the Lord Chancellor must extend the period of the person's appointment (including a period already extended under this sub-paragraph) before it ends.

(2C) Extension under sub-paragraph (2B)–

(a) requires the person's agreement,

(b) is to be for such period as the Lord Chancellor considers appropriate, and

(c) may be refused on–

(i)  the ground of inability or misbehaviour, or

(ii) a ground specified in the person's terms of appointment,

but only with any agreement of a senior judge (see section 46(7)), or a nominee of a senior judge, that may be required by those terms.

(3) Subject to the preceding provisions of this paragraph (but subject in the first place to the Judicial Pensions and Retirement Act 1993 (c. 8) ), the person is to hold and vacate office as a judge, or other member, of the Upper Tribunal in accordance with the terms of his appointment, which are to be such as the Lord Chancellor may determine.

*Remuneration, allowances and expenses*

5 (1) Sub-paragraph (2) applies–

(a) to a person appointed under paragraph 1(1) or 2(1),

(b) to a transferred-in judge of the First-tier Tribunal, and

(c) to a transferred-in other member of the First-tier Tribunal.

(2) The Lord Chancellor may pay to a person to whom this sub-paragraph applies such amounts (if any) as the Lord Chancellor may determine by way of–

(a) remuneration;

(b) allowances;

(c) expenses.

*Certain judges neither appointed under paragraph 1(1) nor transferred in*

6 (1) In this paragraph 'judge by request of the First-tier Tribunal' means a person who is a judge of the First-tier Tribunal but who–

(a) is not the Senior President of Tribunals,

(b) is not a judge of the First-tier Tribunal appointed under paragraph 1(1),

(c) is not a transferred-in judge of the First-tier Tribunal,

(d) is not a Chamber President, or Acting Chamber President or Deputy Chamber President, of a chamber of the First-tier Tribunal,

(e) is not a judge of the First-tier Tribunal by virtue of section 4(1)(e) (chairman of employment tribunal), and

(g) is not a judge of the First-tier tribunal by virtue of section 4(2) (criminal injuries compensation adjudicator appointed by the Scottish Ministers).

(2) A judge by request of the First-tier Tribunal may act as a judge of the First-tier Tribunal only if requested to do so by the Senior President of Tribunals.

(3) Such a request made to a person who is a judge of the First-tier Tribunal by virtue of the combination of sections 4(1)(c) and 5(1)(g) may be made only with–

(a) the concurrence of the Lord Chief Justice of England and Wales where the person is–

(i)    an ordinary judge of the Court of Appeal in England and Wales,

(ii)   a puisne judge of the High Court in England and Wales,

(iii)  a circuit judge,

(iv)   a district judge in England and Wales,

(v)    a District Judge (Magistrates' Courts),

(vi)   the Master of the Rolls,

(vii)  the President of the Queen's Bench Division of the High Court of England and Wales,

        (viii)  the President of the Family Division of that court,

        (ix)    the Chancellor of that court,

        (x)     a deputy judge of that court, or

        (xi)   the Judge Advocate General;

   (b) the concurrence of the Lord President of the Court of Session where the person is–

        (i)   a judge of the Court of Session, or

        (ii)  a sheriff;

   (c) the concurrence of the Lord Chief Justice of Northern Ireland where the person is–

        (i)   a Lord Justice of Appeal in Northern Ireland,

        (ii)  a puisne judge of the High Court in Northern Ireland,

        (iii) a county court judge in Northern Ireland, or

        (iv) a district judge in Northern Ireland.

(3A) A request made under sub-paragraph (2) to a person who is a judge of the First-tier Tribunal by virtue of section 4(1)(ca) may be made only with the concurrence of the Lord Chief Justice of England and Wales.

  (4) Sub-paragraph (5) applies–

   (a) to a judge by request of the First-tier Tribunal, and

   (b) to a person who is a judge of the First-tier Tribunal by virtue of section 4(1)(e) (chairman of employment tribunal).

  (5) The Lord Chancellor may pay to a person to whom this sub-paragraph applies such amounts (if any) as the Lord Chancellor may determine by way of–

   (a) remuneration;

   (b) allowances;

   (c) expenses.

*Other members neither appointed under paragraph 2(1) nor transferred in*

7 (1) In this paragraph 'ex officio member of the First-tier Tribunal' means a person who is a member of the First-tier Tribunal by virtue of–

   (a) section 4(3)(d) (members of employment tribunals who are not Employment Judges), or

   (b) the combination of sections 4(3)(c) and 5(2)(c) (members of Employment Appeal Tribunal appointed under section 22(1)(c) of the Employment Tribunals Act 1996).

  (2) The Lord Chancellor may pay to an ex officio member of the First-tier Tribunal such amounts (if any) as the Lord Chancellor may determine by way of–

   (a) remuneration;

   (b) allowances;

   (c) expenses.

*Training etc.*

8     The Senior President of Tribunals is responsible, within the resources made available by the Lord Chancellor, for the maintenance of appropriate arrangements for the training, guidance and welfare of judges and other members of the First-tier Tribunal (in their capacities as such judges and other members).

*Oaths*

9 (1) Sub-paragraph (2) applies to a person ('J')–

   (a) who is appointed under paragraph 1(1) or 2(1), or

   (b) who becomes a transferred-in judge, or a transferred-in other member, of the First-tier Tribunal and has not previously taken the required oaths after accepting another office.

  (2) J must take the required oaths before–

   (a) the Senior President of Tribunals, or

   (b) an eligible person who is nominated by the Senior President of Tribunals for the purpose of taking the oaths from J.

  (3) A person is eligible for the purposes of sub-paragraph (2)(b) if any one or more of the following paragraphs applies to him–

(a) he holds high judicial office (as defined in section 60(2) of the Constitutional Reform Act 2005);

(b) he holds judicial office (as defined in section 109(4) of that Act);

(c) he holds (in Scotland) the office of sheriff.

(4) In this paragraph 'the required oaths' means (subject to sub-paragraph (5))–

(a) the oath of allegiance, and

(b) the judicial oath,

as set out in the Promissory Oaths Act 1868.

(5) Where it appears to the Lord Chancellor that J will carry out functions as a judge or other member of the First-tier Tribunal wholly or mainly in Northern Ireland, the Lord Chancellor may direct that in relation to J 'the required oaths' means–

(a) the oath as set out in section 19(2) of the Justice (Northern Ireland) Act 2002, or

(b) the affirmation and declaration as set out in section 19(3) of that Act.

## SCHEDULE 3: JUDGES AND OTHER MEMBERS OF THE UPPER TRIBUNAL

*Power to appoint judges of Upper Tribunal*

1 (1) Her Majesty, on the recommendation of the Lord Chancellor, may appoint a person to be one of the judges of the Upper Tribunal.

(2) A person is eligible for appointment under sub-paragraph (1) only if the person–

(a) satisfies the judicial-appointment eligibility condition on a 7-year basis,

(b) is an advocate or solicitor in Scotland of at least seven years' standing,

(c) is a barrister or solicitor in Northern Ireland of at least seven years' standing, or

(d) in the opinion of the Senior President of Tribunals, has gained experience in law which makes the person as suitable for appointment as if the person satisfied any of paragraphs (a) to (c).

(3) Section 52(2) to (5) (meaning of 'gain experience in law') apply for the purposes of sub-paragraph (2)(d), but as if section 52(4)(i) referred to the Senior President of Tribunals instead of to the relevant decision-maker.

*Power to appoint other members of Upper Tribunal*

2 (1) The Senior President of Tribunals may appoint a person to be one of the members of the Upper Tribunal who are not judges of the tribunal.

(2) A person is eligible for appointment under sub-paragraph (1) only if the person has qualifications prescribed in an order made by the Lord Chancellor with the concurrence of the Senior President of Tribunals.

*Appointed and transferred-in judges and other members: removal from office*

3 (1) This paragraph applies to any power by which–

(a) a person appointed under paragraph 1(1) or 2(1),

(b) a transferred-in judge of the Upper Tribunal,

(ba) a person who is a deputy judge of the Upper Tribunal (whether by appointment under paragraph 7(1) or as a result of provision under section 31(2)), or

(c) a transferred-in other member of the Upper Tribunal,

may be removed from office.

(2) If the person exercises functions wholly or mainly in Scotland, the power may be exercised only with the concurrence of the Lord President of the Court of Session.

(3) If the person exercises functions wholly or mainly in Northern Ireland, the power may be exercised only with the concurrence of the Lord Chief Justice of Northern Ireland.

(4) If neither of sub-paragraphs (2) and (3) applies, the power may be exercised only with the concurrence of the Lord Chief Justice of England and Wales.

*Terms of appointment*

4 (1) This paragraph applies–

(a) to a person appointed under paragraph 1(1) or 2(1),

(b) to a transferred-in judge of the Upper Tribunal, and

(c) to a transferred-in other member of the Upper Tribunal.

(2) If the terms of the person's appointment provide that he is appointed on a salaried (as opposed to fee-paid) basis, the person may be removed from office–

(a) only by the Lord Chancellor (and in accordance with paragraph 3), and

(b) only on the ground of inability or misbehaviour.

(2A) If the terms of the person's appointment provide that the person is appointed on a fee-paid basis, the person may be removed from office–

(a) only by the Lord Chancellor (and in accordance with paragraph 3), and

(b) only on–

(i) the ground of inability or misbehaviour, or

(ii) a ground specified in the person's terms of appointment.

(2B) If the period (or extended period) for which the person is appointed ends before–

(a) the day on which the person attains the age of 70, or

(b) if different, the day that for the purposes of section 26 of the Judicial Pensions and Retirement Act 1993 is the compulsory retirement date for the office concerned in the person's case,

then, subject to sub-paragraph (2C), the Lord Chancellor must extend the period of the person's appointment (including a period already extended under this sub-paragraph) before it ends.

(2C) Extension under sub-paragraph (2B)–

(a) requires the person's agreement,

(b) is to be for such period as the Lord Chancellor considers appropriate, and

(c) may be refused on–

(i) the ground of inability or misbehaviour, or

(ii) a ground specified in the person's terms of appointment,

but only with any agreement of a senior judge (see section 46(7)), or a nominee of a senior judge, that may be required by those terms.

(3) Subject to the preceding provisions of this paragraph (but subject in the first place to the Judicial Pensions and Retirement Act 1993 (c. 8)), the person is to hold and vacate office as a judge, or other member, of the Upper Tribunal in accordance with the terms of his appointment, which are to be such as the Lord Chancellor may determine.

### Remuneration, allowances and expenses

5 (1) Sub-paragraph (2) applies–

(a) to a person appointed under paragraph 1(1) or 2(1),

(b) to a transferred-in judge of the Upper Tribunal, and

(c) to a transferred-in other member of the Upper Tribunal.

(2) The Lord Chancellor may pay to a person to whom this sub-paragraph applies such amounts (if any) as the Lord Chancellor may determine by way of–

### Certain judges neither appointed under paragraph 1(1) nor transferred in

6 (1) In this paragraph 'judge by request of the Upper Tribunal' means a person who is a judge of the Upper Tribunal but–

(a) is not the Senior President of Tribunals,

(b) is not a judge of the Upper Tribunal appointed under paragraph 1(1),

(c) is not a transferred-in judge of the Upper Tribunal,

(d) is not a judge of the Upper Tribunal by virtue of section 5(1)(d) (legally qualified member of Asylum and Immigration Tribunal),

(e) is not a deputy judge of the Upper Tribunal, and

(f) is not a Chamber President, or Acting Chamber President or Deputy Chamber President, of a chamber of the Upper Tribunal.

(2) A judge by request of the Upper Tribunal may act as a judge of the Upper Tribunal only if requested to do so by the Senior President of Tribunals.

(3) Such a request made to a person who is a judge of the Upper Tribunal by virtue of section 5(1)(g) may be made only with–

(a) the concurrence of the Lord Chief Justice of England and Wales where the person is–

(i) an ordinary judge of the Court of Appeal in England and Wales,

(ii)    a puisne judge of the High Court in England and Wales,

(iii)   a circuit judge,

(iv)   a district judge in England and Wales,

(v)    a District Judge (Magistrates' Courts),

(vi)   the Master of the Rolls,

(vii)  the President of the Queen's Bench Division of the High Court of England and Wales,

(viii) the President of the Family Division of that court,

(ix)   the Chancellor of that court,

(x)    a deputy judge of that court, or

(xi)   the Judge Advocate General;

(b) the concurrence of the Lord President of the Court of Session where the person is–

(i)   a judge of the Court of Session, or

(ii)  a sheriff;

(c) the concurrence of the Lord Chief Justice of Northern Ireland where the person is–

(i)   a Lord Justice of Appeal in Northern Ireland,

(ii)  a puisne judge of the High Court in Northern Ireland,

(iii) a county court judge in Northern Ireland, or

(iv)  a district judge in Northern Ireland.

(4) The Lord Chancellor may pay to a judge by request of the Upper Tribunal, or a person who is a judge of the Upper Tribunal by virtue of section 5(1)(d), such amounts (if any) as the Lord Chancellor may determine by way of–

(a) remuneration;

(b) allowances;

(c) expenses.

### Deputy judges of the Upper Tribunal

7 (1) The Lord Chancellor may appoint a person to be a deputy judge of the Upper Tribunal for such period as the Lord Chancellor considers appropriate.

(2) A person is eligible for appointment under sub-paragraph (1) only if he is eligible to be appointed under paragraph 1(1) (see paragraph 1(2)).

(3) The following provisions of this paragraph apply–

(a) to a person appointed under sub-paragraph (1), and

(b) to a person who becomes a deputy judge of the Upper Tribunal as a result of provision under section 31(2).

(3A) The person may be removed from office–

(a) only by the Lord Chancellor (and in accordance with paragraph 3), and

(b) only on–

(i)  the ground of inability or misbehaviour, or

(ii) a ground specified in the person's terms of appointment.

(3B) If the period (or extended period) for which the person is appointed ends before–

(a) the day on which the person attains the age of 70, or

(b) if different, the day that for the purposes of section 26 of the Judicial Pensions and Retirement Act 1993 is the compulsory retirement date for the office concerned in the person's case,

then, subject to sub-paragraph (3C), the Lord Chancellor must extend the period of the person's appointment (including a period already extended under this sub-paragraph) before it ends.

(3C) Extension under sub-paragraph (3B)–

(a) requires the person's agreement,

(b) is to be for such period as the Lord Chancellor considers appropriate, and

(c) may be refused on–

(i)  the ground of inability or misbehaviour, or

(ii) a ground specified in the person's terms of appointment,

but only with any agreement of a senior judge (see section 46(7)), or a nominee of a senior judge, that may be required by those terms.

(4) Subject to the previous provisions of this paragraph (but subject in the first place to the Judicial Pensions and Retirement Act 1993), a person is to hold and vacate office as a deputy judge of the Upper Tribunal in accordance with the person's terms of appointment, which are to be such as the Lord Chancellor may determine.

(5) The Lord Chancellor may pay to a person to whom this sub-paragraph applies such amounts (if any) as the Lord Chancellor may determine by way of–
  (a) remuneration;
  (b) allowances;
  (c) expenses.

*Other members neither appointed under paragraph 2(1) nor transferred in*

8 (1) In this paragraph 'ex officio member of the Upper Tribunal' means–
  (a) a person who is a member of the Upper Tribunal by virtue of section 5(2)(c) (member of Employment Appeal Tribunal appointed under section 22(1)(c) of the Employment Tribunals Act 1996).

(2) The Lord Chancellor may pay to an ex officio member of the Upper Tribunal such amounts (if any) as the Lord Chancellor may determine by way of–
  (a) remuneration;
  (b) allowances;
  (c) expenses.

*Training etc.*

9 The Senior President of Tribunals is responsible, within the resources made available by the Lord Chancellor, for the maintenance of appropriate arrangements for the training, guidance and welfare of judges and other members of the Upper Tribunal (in their capacities as such judges and other members).

*Oaths*

10 (1) Sub-paragraph (2) applies to a person ('J')–
  (a) who is appointed under paragraph 1(1), 2(1) or 7(1), or
  (b) who–
    (i) becomes a transferred-in judge, or a transferred-in other member, of the Upper Tribunal, or
    (ii) becomes a deputy judge of the Upper Tribunal as a result of provision under section 31(2),
  and has not previously taken the required oaths after accepting another office.

(2) J must take the required oaths before–
  (a) the Senior President of Tribunals, or
  (b) an eligible person who is nominated by the Senior President of Tribunals for the purpose of taking the oaths from J.

(3) A person is eligible for the purposes of sub-paragraph (2)(b) if any one or more of the following paragraphs applies to him–
  (a) he holds high judicial office (as defined in section 60(2) of the Constitutional Reform Act 2005);
  (b) he holds judicial office (as defined in section 109(4) of that Act);
  (c) he holds (in Scotland) the office of sheriff.

(4) In this paragraph 'the required oaths' means (subject to sub-paragraph (5))–
  (a) the oath of allegiance, and
  (b) the judicial oath,
  as set out in the Promissory Oaths Act 1868.

(5) Where it appears to the Lord Chancellor that J will carry out functions as a judge or other member of the Upper Tribunal wholly or mainly in Northern Ireland, the Lord Chancellor may direct that in relation to J 'the required oaths' means–
  (a) the oath as set out in section 19(2) of the Justice (Northern Ireland) Act 2002, or
  (b) the affirmation and declaration as set out in section 19(3) of that Act.

## SCHEDULE 4: CHAMBERS AND CHAMBER PRESIDENTS: FURTHER PROVISION

### PART 1: CHAMBER PRESIDENTS: APPOINTMENT, DELEGATION, DEPUTIES AND FURTHER PROVISION

*Eligibility for appointment as Chamber President under section 7(7)*

1   A person is eligible for appointment under section 7(7) only if–
(a) he is a judge of the Upper Tribunal, or
(b) he does not fall within paragraph (a) but is eligible to be appointed under paragraph 1(1) of Schedule 3 as a judge of the Upper Tribunal (see paragraph 1(2) of that Schedule).

*Appointment as Chamber President under section 7(7): consultation and nomination*

2 (1) The Senior President of Tribunals must consult the Lord Chancellor before the Senior President of Tribunals appoints under section 7(7) a person within–
section 6(1)(a) (ordinary judge of Court of Appeal in England and Wales), section 6(1)(b) (Lord Justice of Appeal in Northern Ireland),
section 6(1)(c) (judge of the Court of Session), or
section 6(1)(d) (puisne judge of the High Court in England and Wales or Northern Ireland).
(2) If the Senior President of Tribunals, in exercise of his power under section 7(7) in a particular case, wishes that the person appointed should be drawn from among the ordinary judges of the Court of Appeal in England and Wales or the puisne judges of the High Court in England and Wales, the Senior President of Tribunals must first ask the Lord Chief Justice of England and Wales to nominate one of those judges for the purpose.
(3) If the Senior President of Tribunals, in exercise of his power under section 7(7) in a particular case, wishes that the person appointed should be drawn from among the judges of the Court of Session, the Senior President of Tribunals must first ask the Lord President of the Court of Session to nominate one of those judges for the purpose.
(4) If the Senior President of Tribunals, in exercise of his power under section 7(7) in a particular case, wishes that the person appointed should be drawn from among the Lords Justices of Appeal in Northern Ireland or the puisne judges of the High Court in Northern Ireland, the Senior President of Tribunals must first ask the Lord Chief Justice of Northern Ireland to nominate one of those judges for the purpose.
(4A) The Senior President of Tribunals may make a request under subparagraph (2), (3) or (4) only with the Lord Chancellor's concurrence.
(5) If a judge is nominated under sub-paragraph (2), (3) or (4) in response to a request under that sub-paragraph, the Senior President of Tribunals must appoint the nominated judge as Chamber President of the chamber concerned.

*Chamber Presidents: duration of appointment, remuneration etc.*

3 (1) A Chamber President is to hold and vacate office as a Chamber President in accordance with the terms of his appointment as a Chamber President but subject to paragraph 5A (and subject in the first place to the Judicial Pensions and Retirement Act 1993 (c. 8) ), and those terms are to be such as the Lord Chancellor may determine.
(2) The Lord Chancellor may pay to a Chamber President such amounts (if any) as the Lord Chancellor may determine by way of–
(a) remuneration;
(b) allowances;
(c) expenses.

*Delegation of functions by Chamber Presidents*

4 (1) The Chamber President of a chamber of the First-tier Tribunal or Upper Tribunal may delegate any function he has in his capacity as the Chamber President of the chamber–

(a) to any judge, or other member, of either of those tribunals;

(b) to staff appointed under section 40(1).

(2) A delegation under sub-paragraph (1) is not revoked by the delegator's becoming incapacitated.

(3) Any delegation made by a person under sub-paragraph (1) that is in force immediately before the person ceases to be the Chamber President of a chamber continues in force until subsequently varied or revoked by another holder of the office of Chamber President of that chamber.

(4) The delegation under sub-paragraph (1) of a function shall not prevent the exercise of the function by the Chamber President of the chamber concerned.

(5) In this paragraph 'delegate' includes further delegate.

*Deputy Chamber Presidents*

5 (1) The Senior President of Tribunals may appoint a person who is not a Deputy Chamber President of a chamber to be a Deputy Chamber President of a chamber.

(2) The Senior President of Tribunals may appoint a person who is a Deputy Chamber President of a chamber to be instead, or to be also, a Deputy Chamber President of another chamber.

(3) The power under sub-paragraph (1) is exercisable in any particular case only if the Senior President of Tribunals–

(a) has consulted the Lord Chancellor about whether a Deputy Chamber President should be appointed for the chamber concerned, and

(b) considers, in the light of the consultation, that a Deputy Chamber President of the chamber should be appointed.

(4) A person is eligible for appointment under sub-paragraph (1) only if–

(a) he is a judge of the Upper Tribunal by virtue of appointment under paragraph 1(1) of Schedule 3,

(b) he is a transferred-in judge of the Upper Tribunal (see section 31(2)),

(c) he is a judge of the Upper Tribunal by virtue of–

section 5(1)(e) (Social Security Commissioner for Northern Ireland),

section 5(1)(g) (certain judges of courts in the United Kingdom), or

section 5(1)(h) (deputy judge of the Upper Tribunal), or

(d) he falls within none of paragraphs (a) to (c) but is eligible to be appointed under paragraph 1(1) of Schedule 3 as a judge of the Upper Tribunal (see paragraph 1(2) of that Schedule).

(5) If the Senior President of Tribunals, in exercise of his power under sub-paragraph (1) in a particular case, wishes that the person appointed should be drawn from among the ordinary judges of the Court of Appeal in England and Wales or the puisne judges of the High Court in England and Wales, the Senior President of Tribunals must first ask the Lord Chief Justice of England and Wales to nominate one of those judges for the purpose.

(6) If the Senior President of Tribunals, in exercise of his power under sub-paragraph (1) in a particular case, wishes that the person appointed should be drawn from among the judges of the Court of Session, the Senior President of Tribunals must first ask the Lord President of the Court of Session to nominate one of those judges for the purpose.

(7) If the Senior President of Tribunals, in exercise of his power under sub-paragraph (1) in a particular case, wishes that the person appointed should be drawn from among the Lords Justices of Appeal in Northern Ireland or the puisne judges of the High Court in Northern Ireland, the Senior President of Tribunals must first ask the Lord Chief Justice of Northern Ireland to nominate one of those judges for the purpose.

(7A) The Senior President of Tribunals may make a request under subparagraph (5), (6) or (7) only with the Lord Chancellor's concurrence.

(8) If a judge is nominated under sub-paragraph (5), (6) or (7) in response to a request under that sub-paragraph, the Senior President of Tribunals must appoint the nominated judge as a Deputy Chamber President of the chamber concerned.

(9) A Deputy Chamber President is to hold and vacate office as a Deputy Chamber President in accordance with the terms of his appointment but subject to paragraph

5A (and subject in the first place to the Judicial Pensions and Retirement Act 1993), and those terms are to be such as the Lord Chancellor may determine.

(10) The Lord Chancellor may pay to a Deputy Chamber President such amounts (if any) as the Lord Chancellor may determine by way of–
   (a) remuneration;
   (b) allowances;
   (c) expenses.

(11) In sub-paragraphs (1) and (2) 'chamber' means chamber of the First-tier Tribunal or chamber of the Upper Tribunal.

*Chamber Presidents and Deputies: removal from office and extension of appointment*

5A(1) This paragraph applies to a person–
   (a) appointed under section 7(6) or (7) as a Chamber President, or
   (b) appointed under paragraph 5(1) or (2) as a Deputy Chamber President of a chamber.

(2) If the terms of the person's appointment provide that the person is appointed otherwise than on a fee-paid basis, the person may be removed from office–
   (a) only by the Lord Chancellor with the concurrence of the Senior President of Tribunals, and
   (b) only on the ground of inability or misbehaviour.

(3) If the terms of the person's appointment provide that the person is appointed on a fee-paid basis, the person may be removed from office–
   (a) only by the Lord Chancellor with the concurrence of the Senior President of Tribunals, and
   (b) only on–
      (i) the ground of inability or misbehaviour, or
      (ii) a ground specified in the person's terms of appointment.

(4) If the period (or extended period) for which the person is appointed ends before–
   (a) the day on which the person attains the age of 70, or
   (b) if different, the day that for the purposes of section 26 of the Judicial Pensions and Retirement Act 1993 is the compulsory retirement date for the office concerned in the person's case,
   then, subject to sub-paragraph (5), the Lord Chancellor must extend the period of the person's appointment (including a period already extended under this sub-paragraph) before it ends.

(5) Extension under sub-paragraph (4)–
   (a) requires the person's agreement,
   (b) is to be for such period as the Lord Chancellor considers appropriate, and
   (c) may be refused on–
      (i) the ground of inability or misbehaviour, or
      (ii) a ground specified in the person's terms of appointment,
   but only with any agreement of a senior judge (see section 46(7)), or a nominee of a senior judge, that may be required by those terms.

*Acting Chamber Presidents*

6 (1) If in the case of a particular chamber of the First-tier Tribunal or Upper Tribunal there is no-one appointed under section 7 to preside over the chamber, the Senior President of Tribunals may appoint a person to preside over the chamber during the vacancy.

(2) A person appointed under sub-paragraph (1) is to be known as an Acting Chamber President.

(3) A person who is the Acting Chamber President of a chamber is to be treated as the Chamber President of the chamber for all purposes other than–
   (a) the purposes of this paragraph of this Schedule, and
   (b) the purposes of the Judicial Pensions and Retirement Act 1993.

(4) A person is eligible for appointment under sub-paragraph (1) only if he is eligible for appointment as a Chamber President.

(5) An Acting Chamber President is to hold and vacate office as an Acting Chamber President in accordance with the terms of his appointment.

(6) The Lord Chancellor may pay to an Acting Chamber President such amounts (if any) as the Lord Chancellor may determine by way of–

    (a) remuneration;

    (b) allowances;

    (c) expenses.

### Guidance

7    The Chamber President of a chamber of the First-tier Tribunal or the Upper Tribunal is to make arrangements for the issuing of guidance on changes in the law and practice as they relate to the functions allocated to the chamber.

### Oaths

8 (1) Sub-paragraph (2) applies to a person ('the appointee')–

    (a) appointed under section 7(7) as a Chamber President,

    (b) appointed under paragraph 5(1) as a Deputy Chamber President of a chamber, or

    (c) appointed as an Acting Chamber President.

(2) The appointee must take the required oaths before–

    (a) the Senior President of Tribunals, or

    (b) an eligible person who is nominated by the Senior President of Tribunals for the purpose of taking the oaths from the appointee.

(3) A person is eligible for the purposes of sub-paragraph (2)(b) if any one or more of the following paragraphs applies to him–

    (a) he holds high judicial office (as defined in section 60(2) of the Constitutional Reform Act 2005);

    (b) he holds judicial office (as defined in section 109(4) of that Act);

    (c) he holds (in Scotland) the office of sheriff.

(4) Sub-paragraph (2) does not apply to the appointee if he has previously taken the required oaths in compliance with a requirement imposed on him under paragraph 9 of Schedule 2 or paragraph 10 of Schedule 3.

(5) In this paragraph 'the required oaths' means (subject to sub-paragraph (6))–

    (a) the oath of allegiance, and

    (b) the judicial oath,

as set out in the Promissory Oaths Act 1868.

(6) Where it appears to the Lord Chancellor that the appointee will carry out functions under his appointment wholly or mainly in Northern Ireland, the Lord Chancellor may direct that in relation to the appointee 'the required oaths' means–

    (a) the oath as set out in section 19(2) of the Justice (Northern Ireland Act 2002, or

    (b) the affirmation and declaration as set out in section 19(3) of that Act.

## PART 2: JUDGES AND OTHER MEMBERS OF CHAMBERS: ASSIGNMENT AND JURISDICTION

### Assignment is function of Senior President of Tribunals

9 (1) The Senior President of Tribunals has–

    (a) the function of assigning judges and other members of the First-tier Tribunal (including himself) to chambers of the First-tier Tribunal, and

    (b) the function of assigning judges and other members of the Upper Tribunal (including himself) to chambers of the Upper Tribunal.

(2) The functions under sub-paragraph (1) are to be exercised in accordance with the following provisions of this Part of this Schedule.

### Deemed assignment of Chamber Presidents and Deputy Chamber Presidents

10 (1) The Chamber President, or a Deputy Chamber President, of a chamber–

    (a) is to be taken to be assigned to that chamber;

    (b) may be assigned additionally to one or more of the other chambers;

    (c) may be assigned under paragraph (b) to different chambers at different times.

(2) Paragraphs 11(1) and (2) and 12(2) and (3) do not apply to assignment of a person who is a Chamber President or a Deputy Chamber President.

(3) In sub-paragraph (1) 'chamber' means chamber of the First-tier Tribunal or the Upper Tribunal.

### Assigning members of First-tier Tribunal to its chambers

11 (1) Each person who is a judge or other member of the First-tier Tribunal by virtue of appointment under paragraph 1(1) or 2(1) of Schedule 2 or who is a transferred-in judge, or transferred-in other member, of the First-tier Tribunal–

(a) is to be assigned to at least one of the chambers of the First-tier Tribunal, and

(b) may be assigned to different chambers of the First-tier Tribunal at different times.

(2) A judge or other member of the First-tier Tribunal to whom sub-paragraph (1) does not apply–

(a) may be assigned to one or more of the chambers of the First-tier Tribunal, and

(b) may be assigned to different chambers of the First-tier Tribunal at different times.

(3) The Senior President of Tribunals may assign a judge or other member of the First-tier Tribunal to a particular chamber of the First-tier Tribunal only with the concurrence–

(a) of the Chamber President of the chamber, and

(b) of the judge or other member.

(4) The Senior President of Tribunals may end the assignment of a judge or other member of the First-tier Tribunal to a particular chamber of the First-tier Tribunal only with the concurrence of the Chamber President of the chamber.

(5) Sub-paragraph (3)(a) does not apply where the judge, or other member, concerned is not assigned to any of the chambers of the First-tier Tribunal.

(6) Sub-paragraphs (3)(a) and (4) do not apply where the judge concerned is within section 6(1)(a) to (d) (judges of Courts of Appeal, Court of Session and High Courts).

(7) Sub-paragraphs (3) and (4) do not apply where the judge concerned is the Senior President of Tribunals himself.

### Assigning members of Upper Tribunal to its chambers

12 (1) Sub-paragraph (2) applies to a person if–

(a) he is a judge of the Upper Tribunal by virtue of appointment under paragraph 1(1) of Schedule 3, or

(b) he is a transferred-in judge of the Upper Tribunal, or

(c) he is a deputy judge of the Upper Tribunal, or

(d) he is a member of the Upper Tribunal by virtue of appointment under paragraph 2(1) of Schedule 3, or

(e) he is a transferred-in other member of the Upper Tribunal.

(2) Each person to whom this sub-paragraph applies–

(a) is to be assigned to at least one of the chambers of the Upper Tribunal, and

(b) may be assigned to different chambers of the Upper Tribunal at different times.

(3) A judge or other member of the Upper Tribunal to whom sub-paragraph (2) does not apply–

(a) may be assigned to one or more of the chambers of the Upper Tribunal, and

(b) may be assigned to different chambers of the Upper Tribunal at different times.

(4) The Senior President of Tribunals may assign a judge or other member of the Upper Tribunal to a particular chamber of the Upper Tribunal only with the concurrence–

(a) of the Chamber President of the chamber, and

(b) of the judge or other member.

(5) The Senior President of Tribunals may end the assignment of a judge or other member of the Upper Tribunal to a particular chamber of the Upper Tribunal only with the concurrence of the Chamber President of the chamber.

(6) Sub-paragraph (4)(a) does not apply where the judge, or other member, concerned is not assigned to any of the chambers of the Upper Tribunal.

(7) Sub-paragraphs (4)(a) and (5) do not apply where the judge concerned is within section 6(1)(a) to (d) (judges of Courts of Appeal, Court of Session and High Courts).

(8) Sub-paragraphs (4) and (5) do not apply where the judge concerned is the Senior President of Tribunals himself.

*Policy of Senior President of Tribunals as respects assigning members to chambers etc.*

13 (1) The Senior President of Tribunals must publish a document recording the policy adopted by him in relation to–

(a) the assigning of persons to chambers in exercise of his functions under paragraph 9, and

(c) the nominating of persons to act as members of panels of members of employment tribunals in exercise of his functions under any such provision as is mentioned in section 5D(1) of the Employment Tribunals Act 1996.

(2) That policy must be such as to secure–

(a) that appropriate use is made of the knowledge and experience of the judges and other members of the First-tier Tribunal and Upper Tribunal, and

(b) that, in the case of a chamber (of the First-tier Tribunal or Upper Tribunal) whose business consists of, or includes, cases likely to involve the application of the law of Scotland or Northern Ireland, sufficient knowledge and experience of that law is to be found among persons assigned to the chamber.

(3) No policy may be adopted by the Senior President of Tribunals for the purposes of sub-paragraph (1) unless the Lord Chancellor concurs in the policy.

(4) The Senior President of Tribunals must keep any policy adopted for the purposes of sub-paragraph (1) under review.

*Choosing members to decide cases*

14 (1) The First-tier Tribunal's function, or the Upper Tribunal's function, of deciding any matter in a case before the tribunal is to be exercised by a member or members of the chamber of the tribunal to which the case is allocated.

(2) The member or members must be chosen by the Senior President of Tribunals.

(3) A person choosing under sub-paragraph (2)–

(a) must act in accordance with any provision under paragraph 15;

(b) may choose himself.

(4) In this paragraph 'member', in relation to a chamber of a tribunal, means a judge or other member of the tribunal who is assigned to the chamber.

*Composition of tribunals*

15 (1) The Lord Chancellor must by order make provision, in relation to every matter that may fall to be decided by the First-tier Tribunal or the Upper Tribunal, for determining the number of members of the tribunal who are to decide the matter.

(2) Where an order under sub-paragraph (1) provides for a matter to be decided by a single member of a tribunal, the order–

(a) must make provision for determining whether the matter is to be decided by one of the judges, or by one of the other members, of the tribunal, and

(b) may make provision for determining, if the matter is to be decided by one of the other members of the tribunal, what qualifications (if any) that other member must have.

(3) Where an order under sub-paragraph (1) provides for a matter to be decided by two or more members of a tribunal, the order–

(a) must make provision for determining how many (if any) of those members are to be judges of the tribunal and how many (if any) are to be other members of the tribunal, and

(b) may make provision for determining–

(i) if the matter is to be decided by persons who include one or more of the other members of the tribunal, or

(ii) if the matter is to be decided by two or more of the other members of the tribunal,

what qualifications (if any) that other member or any of those other members must have.

(4) A duty under sub-paragraph (1), (2) or (3) to provide for the determination of anything may be discharged by providing for the thing to be determined by the Senior President of Tribunals, or a Chamber President, in accordance with any provision made under that sub-paragraph.

(5) Power under paragraph (b) of sub-paragraph (2) or (3) to provide for the determination of anything may be exercised by giving, to the Senior President of Tribunals or a Chamber President, power to determine that thing in accordance with any provision made under that paragraph.

(6) Where under sub-paragraphs (1) to (4) a matter is to be decided by two or more members of a tribunal, the matter may, if the parties to the case agree, be decided in the absence of one or more (but not all) of the members chosen to decide the matter.

(7) Where the member, or any of the members, of a tribunal chosen to decide a matter does not have any qualification that he is required to have under sub-paragraphs (2)(b), or (3)(b), and (5), the matter may despite that, if the parties to the case agree, be decided by the chosen member or members.

(8) Before making an order under this paragraph, the Lord Chancellor must consult the Senior President of Tribunals.

(9) In this paragraph 'qualification' includes experience.

## SCHEDULE 5: PROCEDURE IN FIRST-TIER TRIBUNAL AND UPPER TRIBUNAL

### PART 1: TRIBUNAL PROCEDURE RULES

*Introductory*

1 (1) This Part of this Schedule makes further provision about the content of Tribunal Procedure Rules.

(2) The generality of section 22(1) is not to be taken to be prejudiced by–
   (a) the following paragraphs of this Part of this Schedule, or
   (b) any other provision (including future provision) authorising or requiring the making of provision by Tribunal Procedure Rules.

(3) In the following paragraphs of this Part of this Schedule 'Rules' means Tribunal Procedure Rules.

*Concurrent functions*

2  Rules may make provision as to who is to decide, or as to how to decide, which of the First-tier Tribunal and Upper Tribunal is to exercise, in relation to any particular matter, a function that is exercisable by the two tribunals on the basis that the question as to which of them is to exercise the function is to be determined by, or under, Rules.

*Delegation of functions to staff*

3 (1) Rules may provide for functions–
   (a) of the First-tier Tribunal, or
   (b) of the Upper Tribunal,
   to be exercised by staff appointed under section 40(1).

(2) In making provision of the kind mentioned in sub-paragraph (1) in relation to a function, Rules may (in particular)–
   (a) provide for the function to be exercisable by a member of staff only if the member of staff is, or is of a description, specified in exercise of a discretion conferred by Rules;
   (b) provide for the function to be exercisable by a member of staff only if the member of staff is approved, or is of a description approved, for the purpose by a person specified in Rules.

### Time limits

4    Rules may make provision for time limits as respects initiating, or taking any step in, proceedings before the First-tier Tribunal or the Upper Tribunal.

### Repeat applications

5    Rules may make provision restricting the making of fresh applications where a previous application in relation to the same matter has been made.

### Tribunal acting of its own initiative

6    Rules may make provision about the circumstances in which the First-tier Tribunal, or the Upper Tribunal, may exercise its powers of its own initiative.

### Hearings

7    Rules may–
   (a) make provision for dealing with matters without a hearing;
   (b) make provision as respects allowing or requiring a hearing to be in private or as respects allowing or requiring a hearing to be in public.

### Proceedings without notice

8    Rules may make provision for proceedings to take place, in circumstances described in Rules, at the request of one party even though the other, or another, party has had no notice.

### Representation

9    Rules may make provision conferring additional rights of audience before the First-tier Tribunal or the Upper Tribunal.

### Evidence, witnesses and attendance

10 (1) Rules may make provision about evidence (including evidence on oath and administration of oaths).
   (2) Rules may modify any rules of evidence provided for elsewhere, so far as they would apply to proceedings before the First-tier Tribunal or Upper Tribunal.
   (3) Rules may make provision, where the First-tier Tribunal has required a person–
   (a) to attend at any place for the purpose of giving evidence,
   (b) otherwise to make himself available to give evidence,
   (c) to swear an oath in connection with the giving of evidence,
   (d) to give evidence as a witness,
   (e) to produce a document, or
   (f) to facilitate the inspection of a document or any other thing (including any premises),
   for the Upper Tribunal to deal with non-compliance with the requirement as though the requirement had been imposed by the Upper Tribunal.
   (4) Rules may make provision for the payment of expenses and allowances to persons giving evidence, producing documents, attending proceedings or required to attend proceedings.

### Use of information

11 (1) Rules may make provision for the disclosure or non-disclosure of information received during the course of proceedings before the First-tier Tribunal or Upper Tribunal.
   (2) Rules may make provision for imposing reporting restrictions in circumstances described in Rules.

### Costs and expenses

12 (1) Rules may make provision for regulating matters relating to costs, or (in Scotland) expenses, of proceedings before the First-tier Tribunal or Upper Tribunal.
   (2) The provision mentioned in sub-paragraph (1) includes (in particular)–
   (a) provision prescribing scales of costs or expenses;
   (b) provision for enabling costs to undergo detailed assessment in England and Wales by the county court or the High Court;
   (c) provision for taxation in Scotland of accounts of expenses by an Auditor of Court;

(d) provision for enabling costs to be taxed in Northern Ireland in a county court or the High Court;

(e) provision for costs or expenses–
   (i)  not to be allowed in respect of items of a description specified in Rules;
   (ii) not to be allowed in proceedings of a description so specified;

(f) provision for other exceptions to either or both of subsections (1) and (2) of section 29.

### Set-off and interest

**13** (1) Rules may make provision for a party to proceedings to deduct, from amounts payable by him, amounts payable to him.

(2) Rules may make provision for interest on sums awarded (including provision conferring a discretion or provision in accordance with which interest is to be calculated).

### Arbitration

**14**   Rules may provide for any of the provisions of sections 1 to 15 of and schedule 1 to the Arbitration (Scotland) Act 2010 (which extends to Scotland) or Part 1 of the Arbitration Act 1996 (which extends to England and Wales, and Northern Ireland, but not Scotland) not to apply, or not to apply except so far as is specified in Rules, where the First-tier Tribunal, or Upper Tribunal, acts as arbitrator.

### Correction of errors and setting-aside of decisions on procedural grounds

**15** (1) Rules may make provision for the correction of accidental errors in a decision or record of a decision.

(2) Rules may make provision for the setting aside of a decision in proceedings before the First-tier Tribunal or Upper Tribunal–

(a) where a document relating to the proceedings was not sent to, or was not received at an appropriate time by, a party to the proceedings or a party's representative,

(b) where a document relating to the proceedings was not sent to the First-tier Tribunal or Upper Tribunal at an appropriate time,

(c) where a party to the proceedings, or a party's representative, was not present at a hearing related to the proceedings, or

(d) where there has been any other procedural irregularity in the proceedings.

(3) Sub-paragraphs (1) and (2) shall not be taken to prejudice, or to be prejudiced by, any power to correct errors or set aside decisions that is exercisable apart from rules made by virtue of those sub-paragraphs.

### Ancillary powers

**16**   Rules may confer on the First-tier Tribunal, or the Upper Tribunal, such ancillary powers as are necessary for the proper discharge of its functions.

### Rules may refer to practice directions

**17**   Rules may, instead of providing for any matter, refer to provision made or to be made about that matter by directions under section 23.

### Presumptions

**18**   Rules may make provision in the form of presumptions (including, in particular, presumptions as to service or notification).

### Differential provision

**19**   Rules may make different provision for different purposes or different areas.

## PART 2: TRIBUNAL PROCEDURE COMMITTEE

### Membership

**20**   The Tribunal Procedure Committee is to consist of–

(a) the Senior President of Tribunals or a person nominated by him,

(b) the persons currently appointed by the Lord Chancellor under paragraph 21,

(c) the persons currently appointed by the Lord Chief Justice of England and Wales under paragraph 22,

(d) the person currently appointed by the Lord President of the Court of Session under paragraph 23, and

(e) any person currently appointed under paragraph 24 at the request of the Senior President of Tribunals.

### Lord Chancellor's appointees

21 (1) The Lord Chancellor must appoint–

    (a) three persons each of whom must be a person with experience of–

        (i)  practice in tribunals, or

        (ii) advising persons involved in tribunal proceedings.

  (2) Before making an appointment under sub-paragraph (1), the Lord Chancellor must consult the Lord Chief Justice of England and Wales.

### Lord Chief Justice's appointees

22 (1) The Lord Chief Justice of England and Wales must appoint–

    (a) one of the judges of the First-tier Tribunal,

    (b) one of the judges of the Upper Tribunal, and

    (c) one person who is a member of the First-tier Tribunal, or is a member of the Upper Tribunal, but is not a judge of the First-tier Tribunal and is not a judge of the Upper Tribunal.

  (2) Before making an appointment under sub-paragraph (1), the Lord Chief Justice of England and Wales must consult the Lord Chancellor.

### Lord President's appointee

23 (1) The Lord President of the Court of Session must appoint one person with experience in and knowledge of the Scottish legal system.

  (2) Before making an appointment under sub-paragraph (1), the Lord President of the Court of Session must consult the Lord Chancellor.

### Persons appointed at request of Senior President of Tribunals

24 (1) At the request of the Senior President of Tribunals, an appropriate senior judge may appoint a person or persons with experience in and knowledge of–

    (a) a particular issue, or

    (b) a particular subject area in relation to which the First-tier Tribunal or the Upper Tribunal has, or is likely to have, jurisdiction,

for the purpose of assisting the Committee with regard to that issue or subject area.

  (2) In sub-paragraph (1) 'an appropriate senior judge' means any of–

    (a) the Lord Chief Justice of England and Wales,

    (b) the Lord President of the Court of Session, and

    (c) the Lord Chief Justice of Northern Ireland.

  (3) The total number of persons appointed at any time under sub-paragraph (1) must not exceed four.

  (4) Before making an appointment under sub-paragraph (1), the person making the appointment must consult the Lord Chancellor.

  (5) The terms of appointment of a person appointed under sub-paragraph (1) may (in particular) authorise him to act as a member of the Committee only in relation to matters specified by those terms.

### Power to amend paragraphs 20 to 24

25 (1) The Lord Chancellor may by order–

    (a) amend any of paragraphs 20, 21(1), 22(1), 23(1) and 24(1), and

    (b) make consequential amendments in any other provision of paragraphs 21 to 24 or in paragraph 28(7).

  (2) The making of an order under this paragraph–

    (a) requires the concurrence of the Lord Chief Justice of England and Wales,

    (b) if the order amends paragraph 23(1), requires also the concurrence of the Lord President of the Court of Session, and

    (c) if the order amends paragraph 24(1), requires also the concurrence of the Lord President of the Court of Session and the Lord Chief Justice of Northern Ireland.

### Committee members' expenses

26    The Lord Chancellor may reimburse members of the Tribunal Procedure Committee their travelling and out-of-pocket expenses.

## PART 3: MAKING OF TRIBUNAL PROCEDURE RULES BY TRIBUNAL PROCEDURE COMMITTEE

### Meaning of 'Rules' and 'the Committee'

27    In the following provisions of this Part of this Schedule–
'the Committee' means the Tribunal Procedure Committee;
'Rules' means Tribunal Procedure Rules.

### Process for making Rules

28 (1) Before the Committee makes Rules, the Committee must–
   (a) consult such persons (including such of the Chamber Presidents) as it considers appropriate,
   (b) consult the Lord President of the Court of Session if the Rules contain provision relating to proceedings in Scotland, and
   (c) meet (unless it is inexpedient to do so).

   (2) Rules made by the Committee must be–
   (a) signed by a majority of the members of the Committee, and
   (b) submitted to the Lord Chancellor.

   (3) The Lord Chancellor may allow or disallow Rules so made.

   (4) If the Lord Chancellor disallows Rules so made, he must give the Committee written reasons for doing so.

   (5) Rules so made and allowed–
   (a) come into force on such day as the Lord Chancellor directs, and
   (b) are to be contained in a statutory instrument to which the Statutory Instruments Act 1946 applies as if the instrument contained rules made by a Minister of the Crown.

   (6) A statutory instrument containing Rules made by the Committee is subject to annulment in pursuance of a resolution of either House of Parliament.

   (7) In the case of a member of the Committee appointed under paragraph 24, the terms of his appointment may (in particular) provide that, for the purposes of sub-paragraph (2)(a), he is to count as a member of the Committee only in relation to matters specified in those terms.

### Power of Lord Chancellor to require Rules to be made

29 (1) This paragraph applies if the Lord Chancellor gives the Committee written notice that he thinks it is expedient for Rules to include provision that would achieve a purpose specified in the notice.

   (2) The Committee must make such Rules, in accordance with paragraph 28, as it considers necessary to achieve the specified purpose.

   (3) Those Rules must be made–
   (a) within such period as may be specified by the Lord Chancellor in the notice, or
   (b) if no period is so specified, within a reasonable period after the Lord Chancellor gives the notice to the Committee.

## PART 4: POWER TO AMEND LEGISLATION IN CONNECTION WITH TRIBUNAL PROCEDURE RULES

### Lord Chancellor's power

30 (1) The Lord Chancellor may by order amend, repeal or revoke any enactment to the extent he considers necessary or desirable–
   (a) in order to facilitate the making of Tribunal Procedure Rules, or
   (b) in consequence of–
      (i) section 22,
      (ii) Part 1 or 3 of this Schedule, or
      (iii) Tribunal Procedure Rules.

(2) In this paragraph 'enactment' means any enactment whenever passed or made, including an enactment comprised in subordinate legislation (within the meaning of the Interpretation Act 1978).

## SCHEDULE 6 : TRIBUNALS FOR THE PURPOSES OF SECTIONS 30 TO 36

### PART 1: TRIBUNALS FOR THE PURPOSES OF SECTIONS 30, 35 AND 36

| Tribunal | Enactment |
|---|---|
| Agricultural Land Tribunals for areas in England | Section 73 of the Agriculture Act 1947 |
| Appeal tribunal | Chapter 1 of Part 1 of the Social Security Act 1998 |
| Child Support Commissioner | Section 22 of the Child Support Act 1991 |
| The Secretary of State as respects his function of deciding appeals under: | Section 41 of the Consumer Credit Act 1974 |
| The Secretary of State as respects his function of deciding appeals under: | Section 7(1) of the Estate Agents Act 1979 |
| Foreign Compensation Commission | Section 1 of the Foreign Compensation Act 1950 |
| Commissioner for the general purposes of the income tax | Section 2 of the Taxes Management Act 1970 |
| Information Tribunal | Section 6 of the Data Protection Act 1998 |
| Meat Hygiene Appeals Tribunal | Regulation 6 of the Fresh Meat (Hygiene and Inspection) Regulations 1995 (SI 1995/539) |
| Meat Hygiene Appeals Tribunal | Regulation 6 of the Poultry Meat, Farmed Game Bird Meat and Rabbit Meat (Hygiene and Inspection) Regulations 1995 (SI 1995/540) |
| Meat Hygiene Appeals Tribunal | Regulation 5 of the Wild Game Meat (Hygiene and Inspection) Regulations 1995 (SI 1995/2148) |
| Mental Health Review Tribunal for a region of England | Section 65(1) and (1A)(a) of the Mental Health Act 1983 |
| Reinstatement Committee | Paragraph 1 of Schedule 2 to the Reserve Forces (Safeguard of Employment) Act 1985 |
| Rent assessment committees for areas on England | Section 65 of, and Schedule 10 to, the Rent Act 1977 |

| Tribunal | Enactment |
|---|---|
| Reserve forces appeal tribunal | Section 88 of the Reserve Forces Act 1996 |
| Sea Fish Licence Tribunal | Section 4AA of the Sea Fish (Conservation) Act 1967 |
| Social Security Commissioner | Schedule 4 to the Social Security Act 1998 |
| Special Educational Needs and Disability Tribunal | Section 333 of the Education Act 1996 |
| Transport Tribunal | Schedule 4 to the Transport Act 1985 |
| Umpire or deputy umpire | Paragraph 5 of Schedule 2 to the Reserve Forces (Safeguard of Employment) Act 1985 |
| VAT and duties tribunal | Schedule 12 to the Value Added Tax Act 1994 |

## PART 2: TRIBUNALS FOR THE PURPOSES OF SECTIONS 30 AND 35

| Tribunal | Enactment |
|---|---|
| Adjudicator | Section 5 of the Criminal Injuries Compensation Act 1995 |

## PART 3: TRIBUNALS FOR THE PURPOSES OF SECTIONS 30 AND 36

| Tribunal | Enactment |
|---|---|
| Adjudicator to Her Majesty's Land Registry | Section 107 of the Land Registration Act 2002 |
| Charity Tribunal | Section 2A of the Charities Act 1993 |
| Consumer Credit Appeals Tribunal | Section 40A of the Consumer Credit Act 1974 |
| Gambling Appeals Tribunal | Section 140 of the Gambling Act 2005 |
| Immigration Services Tribunal | Section 87 of the Immigration and Asylum Act 1999 |
| Lands Tribunal | Section 1(1)(b) of the Lands Tribunal Act 1949 |
| Pensions Appeal Tribunal in England and Wales | Paragraph 1(1) of the Schedule to the Pensions Appeal Tribunals Act 1943 |
| Pensions Regulator Tribunal | Section 102 of the Pensions Act 2004 |

| Tribunal | Enactment |
|---|---|
| Commissioner for the special purposes of the Income Tax Acts | Section 4 of the Taxes Management Act 1970 |

## PART 4: TRIBUNALS FOR THE PURPOSES OF SECTION 30

| Tribunal | Enactment |
|---|---|
| Antarctic Act Tribunal | Regulation 11 of the Antarctic Regulations 1995 (SI 1995/490) |
| Appeal tribunal | Part 2 of Schedule 9 to the Scheme set out in Schedule 2 to the Firefighters' Pension Scheme Order 1992 (SI 1992/129) |
| Asylum and Immigration Tribunal | Section 81 of the Nationality, Immigration and Asylum Act 2002 |
| Asylum Support Adjudicator | Section 102 of the Immigration and Asylum Act 1999 |
| Case tribunal, or interim case tribunal, drawn from the Adjudication Panel for England | Section 76 of the Local Government Act 2000 |
| Claims Management Services Tribunal | Section 12 of the Competition Act 2006 |
| Family Health Services Appeal Authority | Section 49S of the National Health Service Act 1977 |
| Gender Recognition Panel | Section 1(3) of the Gender Recognition Act 2004 |
| Insolvency Practitioners Tribunal | Section 396(1) of the Insolvency Act 1986 |
| Appeals Tribunal | Part 3 of the Local Authorities (Code of Conduct) (Local Determination) Regulations 2003 (SI 2003/1483) |
| Panel | Section 189(6) of the Greater London Authority Act 1999 |
| Plant Varieties and Seeds Tribunal | Section 42 of the Plant Varieties Act 1997 |
| Tribunal | Rule 6 of the model provisions with respect to appeals as applied with modifications by the Chemical Weapons (Licence Appeal Provisions) Order 1996 (SI 1996/3030) |

| Tribunal | Enactment |
|---|---|
| Tribunal | Health Service Medicines (Price Control Appeals) Regulations 2000 (SI 2000/124) |
| Tribunal | Section 704 of the Income Tax Act 2007 |
| Tribunal | Section 706 of the Income and Corporation Taxes Act 1988 |
| Tribunal | Section 150 of the Mines and Quarries Act 1954 |
| Tribunal | Part 1 of Schedule 3 to the Misuse of Drugs Act 1971 |
| Tribunal | Regulation H6(3) of the Police Pensions Regulations 1987 (SI 1987/257) |
| Tribunal | Section 9 of the Protection of Children Act 1999 |

## PART 5: TRIBUNALS FOR THE PURPOSES OF SECTIONS 35 AND 36

| Tribunal | Enactment |
|---|---|
| Employment Appeal Tribunal | Section 20 of the Employment Tribunals Act 1996 |

## PART 6: TRIBUNALS FOR THE PURPOSES OF SECTION 35

| Tribunal | Enactment |
|---|---|
| Employment tribunal | Section 1 of the Employment Tribunals Act 1996 |

## PART 7: TRIBUNALS FOR THE PURPOSES OF SECTION 32(3)

| Tribunal | Enactment |
|---|---|
| Case tribunal, or interim case tribunal, drawn from the Adjudication Panel for Wales | Section 76 of the Local Government Act 2000 |
| Agricultural Land Tribunal for Wales | Agricultural Land Tribunal for Wales |
| Appeals Tribunal | Local Government Investigations (Functions of Monitoring Officers and Standards Committees) (Wales) Regulations 2001 (SI 2001/2281) |

| Tribunal | Enactment |
|---|---|
| Mental Health Review Tribunal for Wales | Section 65(1) and (1A)(b) of the Mental Health Act 1983 |
| Rent assessment committees for areas in Wales | Rent assessment committees for areas in Wales |
| Special Educational Needs Tribunal for Wales | Section 336ZA of the Education Act |
| Tribunal | Section 27 of, and Schedule 3 to, the Education Act 2005 |

## SCHEDULE 9 : TRIBUNALS: TRANSITIONAL PROVISION

### PART 1: GENERAL AND MISCELLANEOUS

*Introductory*

1    The following provisions of this Schedule are to be taken not to prejudice the generality of sections 31(9) and 145(1).

*Membership of Tribunal Procedure Committee*

2 (1) The Lord Chancellor may by order make provision for a person–
    (a) who is a scheduled tribunal, or
    (b) who is a member of a scheduled tribunal,
    to be treated for the purposes of sub-paragraph (1) of paragraph 22 of Schedule 5 as falling within paragraph (a), (b) or (c) of that subparagraph.
  (2) In sub-paragraph (1) 'scheduled tribunal' means a tribunal in a list in Schedule 6 that has effect for the purposes of section 30.
  (3) The power under sub-paragraph (1) may not be exercised so as to provide for the Secretary of State to be treated as mentioned in that subparagraph.

### PART 2: JUDGES AND OTHER MEMBERS OF FIRST-TIER AND UPPER TRIBUNALS: RETIREMENT DATES

*Interpretation of Part 2 of Schedule*

3 (1) For the purposes of this Part of this Schedule–
    (a) 'relevant judicial office' means–
        (i)   the office of transferred-in judge, or transferred-in other member, of the First-tier Tribunal or of the Upper Tribunal (see section 31(2)),
        (ii)  an office to which a person is appointed under paragraph 1(1) or 2(1) of Schedule 2 or 3 (judge, or other member, of the First-tier Tribunal or of the Upper Tribunal), Deputy Chamber President of a chamber of the First-tier Tribunal, or of a chamber of the Upper Tribunal, but not where appointed in accordance with paragraph 5(5) to (8) of Schedule 4 to the Tribunals, Courts and Enforcement Act 2007 Paragraph 5(1) of Schedule 4 to the Tribunals, Courts and Enforcement Act 2007
        (iii) the office of deputy judge of the Upper Tribunal (whether under section 31(2) or under paragraph 7 of Schedule 3),
        (iv)  the office of Chamber President, or Deputy Chamber President, of a chamber of the First-tier Tribunal or of the Upper Tribunal, or
        (v)   the office of Senior President of Tribunals;
    (b) 'relevant day', in relation to a person who holds a relevant judicial office, means the day when he was appointed to that office or, if he holds that office as the latest in an unbroken succession of different relevant judicial offices, the day when he was appointed to the first of the offices in that succession;

(c) an office is a 'qualifying office' at any particular time (but see subparagraph (2)) if–
  (i)   the office is that of member of a tribunal which at that time is in a list in Schedule 6, or
  (ii)  the office itself is at that time in a list in Schedule 6,
  and (in either case) the list has effect at that time for the purposes of section 30;

(d) 'the 1993 Act' means the Judicial Pensions and Retirement Act.

(2) Where–
  (a) a person held two or more qualifying offices ('the actual offices') immediately before the relevant day, and
  (b) at that time the person held at least one of the actual offices on a salaried basis and held at least one of the actual offices on a nonsalaried basis,
  the person shall be treated for the purposes of paragraphs 6 and 7 as not having held immediately before the relevant day any of the actual offices that the person held on a non-salaried basis at that time.

(3) For the purposes of sub-paragraph (2)–
  (a) a person holds an office on a salaried basis at any particular time if, at that time, the person's service in the office is remunerated by payment of a salary, and
  (b) a person holds an office on a non-salaried basis at any particular time if, at that time, the person's service in the office–
    (i)   is remunerated by the payment of fees,
    (ii)  is remunerated by the payment of a supplement to the salary payable to him in respect of his service in another office, or
    (iii) is unremunerated.

*Retirement from First-tier and Upper Tribunals: application of paragraphs 5 to 8*

4    Paragraphs 5 to 8 apply where a person holds a relevant judicial office.

*Retirement later than age 70 in certain cases where office previously held in another tribunal*

5 (1) Subject to paragraph 8(1) (persons who held certain judicial offices on 30th. March 1995), sub-paragraphs (3) and (4) apply where the person has a personal retirement date under either or both of paragraphs 6 and 7.

(2) In sub-paragraphs (3) and (4) and paragraph 8(1) and (2)–
  (a) if the person has a personal retirement date under just one of paragraphs 6 and 7 or has the same personal retirement date under each of those paragraphs, 'the special date' means that date;
  (b) if the person has a personal retirement date under each of those paragraphs and those dates are different, 'the special date' means the later of those dates.

(3) Subsection (1) of section 26 of the 1993 Act shall have effect (subject to the following provisions of that section) as if it provided for the person to vacate the relevant judicial office on the special date.

(4) The special date is to be taken for the purposes of that section to be the compulsory retirement date for the relevant judicial office in the person's case.

*Cases where retirement from existing office would be after age 70*

6 (1) Sub-paragraphs (2) and (3) apply where, immediately before the relevant day, the person–
  (a) held a qualifying office, and
  (b) was required to vacate the qualifying office on a day later than the day on which he attains the age of 70.

(2) The person's personal retirement date under this paragraph is the later day mentioned in sub-paragraph (1)(b), subject to sub-paragraph (3).

(3) If–
  (a) there are two or more qualifying offices each of which is one that, immediately before the relevant day, the person–
    (i)  held, and

   (ii) was required to vacate on a day later than the day on which he attains the age of 70, and

  (b) the later day mentioned in paragraph (a)(ii) is not the same for each of those offices,

the person's personal retirement date under this paragraph is the latest (or later) of those later days.

*Cases where no requirement to retire from existing office*

**7** (1) Sub-paragraph (2) applies where–

  (a) immediately before the relevant day, the person held, on an unlimited basis, a qualifying office or two or more qualifying offices, and

  (b) the relevant day falls after the day on which the person attains the age of 69.

 (2) The person's personal retirement date under this paragraph is the last day of the 12 months beginning with the day after the relevant day.

 (3) For the purposes of this paragraph, a person holds an office on an unlimited basis at a particular time if at that time he is not required to vacate the office at any particular later time.

*Interaction between rules under paragraph 5, and rules under Schedule 7 to the 1993 Act, in cases where office held on 30th March 1995*

**8** (1) If–

  (a) sub-paragraph (2) of paragraph 2 of Schedule 7 to the 1993 Act (transitional provision where person held salaried relevant office on 30th March 1995) has effect in relation to retirement from the relevant judicial office in the person's case, and

  (b) the date that, for the purposes of that paragraph, is the person's potential retirement date by reference to his pre-commencement office ('the retirement date preserved in 1995') is the same as, or later than, the special date, paragraph 5(3) and (4) do not apply.

 (2) If the special date is later than the retirement date preserved in 1995, paragraph 2(2)(b) of Schedule 7 to the 1993 Act does not have effect in relation to the relevant judicial office in the person's case.

 (3) Accordingly, in paragraph 1 of Schedule 7 to the 1993 Act, after subparagraph (5) insert–

  '(6) Paragraph 2(2) has effect subject to paragraph 8(2) of Schedule 9 to the Tribunals, Courts and Enforcement Act 2007 (certain cases where the post-commencement office is that of judge, or other member, of the First-tier Tribunal or the Upper Tribunal).'

*Eligibility for appointment after having attained age of 70*

**9** (1) Sub-paragraph (3) applies in respect of a person on each day that–

  (a) is, or is later than, the day on which the person attains the age of 70,

  (b) is a day on which the person holds a qualifying office, and

  (c) is earlier than the day on which the person is required to vacate the qualifying office.

 (2) Sub-paragraph (3) also applies in respect of a person on each day that–

  (a) is, or is later than, the day on which the person attains the age of 70, and

  (b) is a day on which the person holds, on an unlimited basis, a qualifying office.

 (3) Where this sub-paragraph applies in respect of a person on a day, the fact that the person has attained the age of 70 shall not (by itself) render him ineligible for appointment (or re-appointment) on that day to a relevant judicial office.

 (4) For the purposes of this paragraph, a person holds an office on an unlimited basis at a particular time if at that time he is not required to vacate the office at any particular later time.

## PART 3: JUDGES AND OTHER MEMBERS OF FIRST-TIER AND UPPER TRIBUNALS: PENSIONS WHERE OFFICE ACQUIRED UNDER SECTION 31(2)

*Interpretation of Part 3 of Schedule*

10　For the purposes of this Part of this Schedule–

(a) 'new office' means–

    (i)　the office of judge of the First-tier Tribunal by virtue of being a transferred-in judge of the First-tier Tribunal,

    (ii)　the office of other member of the First-tier Tribunal by virtue of being a transferred-in other member of the First-tier Tribunal,

    (iii)　the office of judge of the Upper Tribunal by virtue of being a transferred-in judge of the Upper Tribunal, and

    (iv)　the office of other member of the Upper Tribunal by virtue of being a transferred-in other member of the Upper Tribunal;

(b) a person holds an office 'on a salaried basis' if and so long as, and to the extent that–

    (i)　the person's service in the office is remunerated by payment of a salary, and

    (ii)　the salary is not subject to terms which preclude rights to pensions and other benefits accruing by reference to it;

(c) a person shall be regarded as holding 'qualifying judicial office' at any time when he holds, on a salaried basis, any one or more of the offices specified in Schedule 1 to the 1993 Act, and any reference to a 'qualifying judicial office' is a reference to any office specified in that Schedule if it is held on a salaried basis;

(d) 'the 1993 Act' means the Judicial Pensions and Retirement Act.

*Right to opt in to Part 1 of the 1993 Act where qualifying judicial office not previously held*

11 (1) Sub-paragraphs (2) and (3) apply where–

(a) a person becomes, as a result of provision under section 31(2), the holder of a new office,

(b) before that, the person has never held qualifying judicial office, and

(c) the person, on becoming the holder of the new office, holds the new office on a salaried basis.

(2) Section 1(1)(a) of the 1993 Act (Part 1 of the 1993 Act applies to a person who first holds qualifying judicial office on or after 31st March 1995) does not have effect in relation to the person.

(3) The person is entitled, subject to paragraph 12, to elect for Part 1 of the 1993 Act (judicial pensions) to apply to him.

(4) Part 1 of the 1993 Act applies to a person who makes an election under sub-paragraph (3).

(5) Sub-paragraph (4) is subject to sections 1(5) and 13 of the 1993 Act (where person has opted out of Part 1 of the 1993 Act then, except as provided by section 13 of that Act, that Part does not apply to the person).

*Election under paragraph 11(3) for pension under Part 1 of the 1993 Act*

12 (1) In this paragraph 'opt-in election' means an election under paragraph 11(3).

(2) An opt-in election may be made only in such circumstances, within such time and in such manner as the Lord Chancellor may by regulations prescribe.

(3) An opt-in election is irrevocable.

(4) Regulations under sub-paragraph (2) may permit the making of an opt-in election even though the person in respect of whom the opt-in election is made–

(a) has ceased (whether by virtue of dying or otherwise) to hold the office mentioned in paragraph 11(1)(a), or

(b) has ceased to hold that office on a salaried basis without having ceased to hold that office.

(5) Where regulations under sub-paragraph (2) permit the making of an opt-in election

in respect of a person who has died, the right to make that election is exercisable by the person's personal representatives.

(6) The Lord Chancellor may by regulations provide for a person in respect of whom an opt-in election is made to be treated for such purposes as may be prescribed by the regulations as if the person had, at such times as may be prescribed by the regulations, been a person to whom Part 1 of the 1993 Act applies.

(7) An opt-in election may not be made in respect of a person at any time when an election made under section 13 of the 1993 Act (election to opt out of Part 1 of the 1993 Act) is in force in respect of the person.

*Continuation of existing public service pension arrangements in certain cases*

13 (1) Sub-paragraph (2) applies if–

    (a) a person, as a result of provision under section 31(2), becomes the holder of a new office,

    (b) either–

       (i) the person held qualifying judicial office immediately before 31st March 1995, or

      (ii) before becoming the holder of the new office, the person has never held qualifying judicial office,

    (c) immediately before the person becomes the holder of the new office–

       (i) the person holds an office within paragraph (a), (b) or (c) of section 31(2) (the 'old office'), and

      (ii) the person's service in the old office is subject to a public service pension scheme,

    (d) the person, on becoming the holder of the new office, holds the new office on a salaried basis, and

    (e) immediately after the person becomes the holder of the new office, the person–

       (i) is not a person to whom Part 1 of the 1993 Act applies, and

      (ii) is not a person to whom that Part would apply but for section 13 of that Act.

(2) The person's service in the new office, so far as it is service during the continuity period–

    (a) shall be subject to that public service pension scheme, and

    (b) shall be subject to that scheme in a way that corresponds to the way in which the person's service in the old office was subject to that scheme.

(3) In sub-paragraph (2) 'the continuity period' means the period–

    (a) that begins when the person becomes the holder of the new office on a salaried basis, and

    (b) that ends with whichever of the following first happens after that–

       (i) the person's ceasing to hold the new office,

      (ii) the person's ceasing to hold the new office on a salaried basis without ceasing to hold the new office,

     (iii) the person's becoming a person to whom Part 1 of the 1993 Act applies, and

     (iv) the person's becoming a person to whom Part 1 of the 1993 Act would apply but for section 13 of that Act.

(4) For the purposes of sub-paragraph (1)(c)(ii), the person's service in the old office is not to be treated as subject to a public service pension scheme at a time when the scheme does not apply to him as a result of his having exercised a right to elect for the scheme not to apply to him.

(5) A public service pension scheme which, apart from sub-paragraph (2), would not be a judicial pension scheme for the purposes of the 1993 Act does not become a judicial pension scheme for those purposes if it is only as a result of sub-paragraph (2) that pensions and other benefits are payable under the scheme in respect of service in qualifying judicial office.

(6) In this paragraph 'public service pension scheme' means any public service pension scheme, as defined in–

(a)  section 1 of the Pension Schemes Act 1993, or

(b)  section 1 of the Pension Schemes (Northern Ireland) Act 1993.

## PART 4: AMENDMENTS TO THE JUDICIAL PENSIONS AND RETIREMENT ACT 1993

**14**    The Judicial Pensions and Retirement Act 1993 is amended as follows.

**15** (1)  Section 1 (application of Part 1: judicial pensions) is amended as follows.

   (2)  In subsection (1) (persons to whom Part 1 of the 1993 Act applies), after paragraph (d) insert 'and (e) to any person appointed to a qualifying judicial office in circumstances falling within subsection (4A) below;'.

   (3)  In subsection (1), after 'but this subsection is subject to the following provisions of this Act' insert 'and to Part 3 of Schedule 9 to the Tribunals, Courts and Enforcement Act 2007 (transitional arrangements for pensions of certain judges and other members of the First-tier Tribunal and Upper Tribunal)'.

   (4)  After subsection (4) insert–

> '(4A)  The circumstances of a person's appointment to a qualifying judicial office ('the subsequent office') fall within this subsection if–
>> (a)  the person, immediately before being appointed to the subsequent office, holds an office within subsection (4B) below ('the replacement tribunal office');
>> (b)  the person held the replacement tribunal office on a salaried basis from when he became its holder until immediately before being appointed to the subsequent office; and
>> (c)  the person, before becoming the holder of the replacement tribunal office, had never held qualifying judicial office.
> (4B)  The offices within this subsection are–
>> (a)  the office of judge of the First-tier Tribunal by virtue of being a transferred-in judge of the First-tier Tribunal,
>> (b)  the office of other member of the First-tier Tribunal by virtue of being a transferred-in other member of the First-tier Tribunal,
>> (c)  the office of judge of the Upper Tribunal by virtue of being a transferred-in judge of the Upper Tribunal, and
>> (d)  the office of other member of the Upper Tribunal by virtue of being a transferred-in other member of the Upper Tribunal.'

**16**    In section 9(4) (contribution towards cost of surviving spouse's, surviving civil partner's and surviving children's pension), for 'or (d) above,' substitute ', (d) or (e) above or in the case of persons to whom this Part applies by virtue of paragraph 11(4) of Schedule 9 to the Tribunals, Courts and Enforcement Act 2007,'.

**17** (1)  In section 12(1) (transfer of accrued benefits under judicial pension schemes in certain cases where person held qualifying judicial office before 31st March 1995)–

   (a)  for 'or (d)' substitute ', (d) or (e)',

   (b)  after 'of section 1(1) above' insert 'or by virtue of paragraph 11(4) of Schedule 9 to the Tribunals, Courts and Enforcement Act 2007', and

   (c)  omit paragraph (b) (which is superseded by the new section 12B inserted by this Part of this Schedule).

   (2)  In the sidenote to section 12, for the words after 'Transfer of rights' substitute 'under judicial pension schemes'.

**18**    After section 12 insert–

> '**12A Transfer of rights under other public service pension schemes**
> (1)  Where this Part–
>> (a)  begins, on or after the day on which this section comes into force, to apply to a person by virtue of section 1(1)(d) above, or
>> (b)  begins to apply to a person–
>>> (i)   by virtue of section 1(1)(e) above, or
>>> (ii)  by virtue of paragraph 11(4) of Schedule 9 to the Tribunals, Courts and Enforcement Act 2007,

any relevant public service pension rights of his shall be transferred to the scheme constituted by this Part.

(2) Where a person's rights under a public service pension scheme are transferred under subsection (1) above–
  (a) that scheme shall no longer have effect in relation to him, and
  (b) no pension or lump sum under the scheme shall be paid to or in respect of him.

(3) Regulations may make provision–
  (a) for calculating, whether by actuarial assessment or otherwise, the amount or value of the rights transferred under subsection (1) above, and
  (b) prescribing the manner in which those rights are to be given effect under this Part.

(4) Without prejudice to the generality of paragraph (b) of subsection (3) above, regulations under that paragraph may provide for rights transferred under subsection (1) above to be given effect by crediting the person in question with such service, on or after the day on which this Part first applies to the person, as may be prescribed.

(5) For the purposes of this section, a persons's 'relevant public service pension rights' are the person's accrued rights to benefit under any public service pension scheme, but this is subject to subsections (6) to (8) below.

(6) A person's rights under a public service pension scheme are not 'relevant public service pension rights' if the scheme is a judicial pension scheme other than–
  (a) the principal civil service pension scheme, or
  (b) the principal civil service pension scheme for the civil service of Northern Ireland.

(7) A person's rights–
  (a) under the principal civil service pension scheme, or
  (b) under the principal civil service pension scheme for the civil service of Northern Ireland,
  are not 'relevant public service pension rights' if they are transferred under section 12 above.

(8) A person's rights under a public service pension scheme are not 'relevant public service pension rights' unless at least some of his service which was subject to the scheme was qualifying tribunal service and, in that event, all of his rights under the scheme shall be regarded as relevant public service pension rights.

(9) In this section–
  'prescribe' means prescribe in regulations;
  'public service pension scheme' means any public service pension scheme, as defined in–
    (a) section 1 of the Pension Schemes Act 1993, or
    (b) section 1 of the Pension Schemes (Northern Ireland) Act 1993;
  'qualifying tribunal service' means–
    (a) service as, or as a member of, a tribunal specified in a list in Schedule 6 to the Tribunals, Courts and Enforcement Act 2007 that has effect for the purposes of section 30 of that Act, or
    (b) service as an authorised decision-maker for a tribunal, within the meaning given by section 31(4) of that Act;
  'regulations' means regulations made by the Lord Chancellor with the concurrence of the Treasury.

**12B Rate of pension etc. where rights transferred under section 12 or 12A**
Entitlement to, and the rate or amount of, any judicial pension or derivative benefit payable under this Part to or in respect of a person whose rights are transferred under section 12 or 12A above shall be determined by reference to–

(a) any rights of his that are transferred under section 12 above,

(b) any rights of his that are transferred under section 12A above, and

(c) his service in qualifying judicial office on or after the day on which this Part first applies to him.'

19   In section 23 (which provides that Schedule 2 does not apply to transfers under section 12), after 'section 12' insert 'or 12A'.

# The Tribunal Procedure (Upper Tribunal) Rules 2008[1]

---

1   © Crown Copyright. SI No 2698. These Rules are reproduced as amended up to date to 1 October 2014. Substitutions, insertions and omissions made by Tribunal Procedure (Amendment) Rules 2009 (SI No 274), Tribunal Procedure (Amendment No 2) Rules 2009 (SI No 1975), Tribunal Procedure (Amendment) Rules 2010 (SI No 43), Tribunal Procedure (Amendment No 2) Rules 2010 (SI No 44), Tribunal Procedure (Upper Tribunal) (Amendment) Rules 2010 (SI No 747), Tribunal Procedure (Amendment No 3) Rules 2010 (SI No 2653), Tribunal Procedure (Amendment) Rules 2011 (SI No 651), Tribunal Procedure (Upper Tribunal) (Amendment) Rules 2011 (SI No 2343, Tribunal Procedure (Amendment) Rules 2012 (SI No 500), Public Bodies (Child Maintenance and Enforcement Commission: Abolition and Transfer of Functions) Order 2012 (SI No 2007), Tribunal Procedure (Amendment No 2) Rules 2012 (SI No 1363), Tribunal Procedure (Upper Tribunal) (Amendment) Rules 2012 (SI No 2890), Tribunal Procedure (Amendment) Rules 2013 (SI No 477), Tribunal Procedure (Amendment No 2) Rules 2013 (SI No 606), Tribunal Procedure (Amendment No 4) Rules 2013 (SI No 2067), Tribunal Procedure (Amendment) Rules 2014 (SI No 514), Tribunal Procedure (Amendment No 2) Rules 2014 (SI No 1505) and Tribunal Procedure (Amendment No 3) Rules 2014 (SI No 2128).

## PART 1: Introduction

### Citation, commencement, application and interpretation

1 (1) These Rules may be cited as the Tribunal Procedure (Upper Tribunal) Rules 2008 and come into force on 3rd November 2008.

(2) These Rules apply to proceedings before the Upper Tribunal except proceedings in the Lands Chamber.

(3) In these Rules–

'the 2007 Act' means the Tribunals, Courts and Enforcement Act 2007;

'appellant' means–

(a) a person who makes an appeal, or applies for permission to appeal, to the Upper Tribunal;

(b) in proceedings transferred or referred to the Upper Tribunal from the First-tier Tribunal, a person who started the proceedings in the First-tier Tribunal; or

(c) a person substituted as an appellant under rule 9(1) (substitution and addition of parties);

'applicant' means–

(a) a person who applies for permission to bring, or does bring, judicial review proceedings before the Upper Tribunal and, in judicial review proceedings transferred to the Upper Tribunal from a court, includes a person who was a claimant or petitioner in the proceedings immediately before they were transferred;

(b) a person who refers a financial services case or a wholesale energy case to the Upper Tribunal;

'appropriate national authority' means, in relation to an appeal, the Secretary of State, the Scottish Ministers, the Department of the Environment in Northern Ireland or the Welsh Ministers, as the case may be;

'asylum case' means proceedings before the Upper Tribunal on appeal against a decision in proceedings under section 82, 83 or 83A of the Nationality, Immigration and Asylum Act 2002 in which a person claims that removal from, or a requirement to leave, the United Kingdom would breach the United Kingdom's obligations under the Convention relating to the Status of Refugees done at Geneva on 28 July 1951 and the Protocol to the Convention;

'authorised person' means–

(a) an examiner appointed by the Secretary of State under section 66A of the Road Traffic Act 1988;

(b) an examiner appointed by the Department of the Environment in Northern Ireland under Article 74 of the Road Traffic (Northern Ireland) Order 1995; or

(c) any person authorised in writing by the Department of the Environment in Northern Ireland for the purposes of the Goods Vehicles (Licensing of Operators) Act (Northern Ireland) 2010;

and includes a person acting under the direction of such an examiner or other authorised person, who has detained the vehicle to which an appeal relates;

'disability discrimination in schools case' means proceedings concerning discrimination in the education of a child or young person or related matters;

'dispose of proceedings' includes, unless indicated otherwise, disposing of a part of the proceedings;

'document' means anything in which information is recorded in any form, and an obligation under these Rules or any practice direction or direction to provide or allow access to a document or a copy of a document for any purpose means, unless the Upper Tribunal directs otherwise, an obligation to provide or allow access to such document or copy in a legible form or in a form which can be readily made into a legible form;

'fast-track case' means an asylum case or an immigration case where the person who appealed to the First-tier Tribunal–

(a) was detained under the Immigration Acts at a place specified in rule 2(3) of the Schedule to the Tribunal Procedure (First-tier Tribunal) (Immigration

and Asylum Chamber) Rules 2014 when the notice of decision that was the subject of the appeal to the First-tier Tribunal was served on the appellant;
  (b) remains so detained; and
  (c) the First-tier Tribunal or the Upper Tribunal has not directed that the case cease to be treated as a fast-track case;
'financial services case' means a reference to the Upper Tribunal in respect of–
  (a) a decision of the Financial Conduct Authority;
  (aa) a decision of the Prudential Regulation Authority;
  (b) a decision of the Bank of England;
  (c) a decision of the Pensions Regulator;
  (d) a decision of a person relating to the assessment of any compensation or consideration under the Banking (Special Provisions) Act 2008 or the Banking Act 2009; or
  (e) any determination, calculation or dispute which may be referred to the Upper Tribunal under the Financial Services and Markets Act 2000 (Contribution to Costs of Special Resolution Regime) Regulations 2010 (and in these Rules a decision in respect of which a reference has been made to the Upper Tribunal in a financial services case includes any such determination, calculation or, except for the purposes of rule 5(5), dispute relating to the making of payments under the Regulations;
'hearing' means an oral hearing and includes a hearing conducted in whole or in part by video link, telephone or other means of instantaneous two-way electronic communication;
'immigration case' means proceedings before the Upper Tribunal on appeal against a decision in proceedings under section 40A of the British Nationality Act 1981(c), section 82 of the Nationality, Immigration and Asylum Act 2002, or regulation 26 of the Immigration (European Economic Area) Regulations 2006 that are not an asylum case;
'immigration judicial review proceedings' means judicial review proceedings which are designated as an immigration matter–
  (a) in a direction made in accordance with Part 1 of Schedule 2 to the Constitutional Reform Act 2005 specifying a class of case for the purposes of section 18(6) of the 2007 Act; or
  (b) in an order of the High Court in England and Wales made under section 31A(3) of the Senior Courts Act 1981(a), transferring to the Upper Tribunal an application of a kind described in section 31A(1) of that Act;
'interested party' means–
  (a) a person who is directly affected by the outcome sought in judicial review proceedings, and has been named as an interested party under rule 28 or 29 (judicial review), or has been substituted or added as an interested party under rule 9 (substitution and addition of parties); and
  (b) in judicial review proceedings transferred to the Upper Tribunal under section 25A(2) or (3) of the Judicature (Northern Ireland) Act 1978 or section 31A(2) or (3) of the Senior Courts Act 1981, a person who was an interested party in the proceedings immediately before they were transferred to the Upper Tribunal;
  (c) in a financial services case or a wholesale energy case, any person other than the applicant who could have referred the case to the Upper Tribunal and who has been added or substituted as an interested party under rule 9 (addition, substitution and removal of parties);
'judicial review proceedings' means proceedings within the jurisdiction of the Upper Tribunal pursuant to section 15 or 21 of the 2007 Act, whether such proceedings are started in the Upper Tribunal or transferred to the Upper Tribunal;
'mental health case' means proceedings before the Upper Tribunal on appeal against a decision in proceedings under the Mental Health Act 1983 or paragraph 5(2) of the Schedule to the Repatriation of Prisoners Act 1984;
'national security certificate appeal' means an appeal under section 28 of the Data

Protection Act 1998 or section 60 of the Freedom of Information Act 2000 (including that section as applied and modified by regulation 18 of the Environmental Information Regulations 2004);

'party' means a person who is an appellant, an applicant, a respondent or an interested party in proceedings before the Upper Tribunal, a person who has referred a question or matter to the Upper Tribunal or, if the proceedings have been concluded, a person who was an appellant, an applicant, a respondent or an interested party when the Upper Tribunal finally disposed of all issues in the proceedings;

'permission' includes leave in cases arising under the law of Northern Ireland;

'practice direction' means a direction given under section 23 of the 2007 Act;

'reference', in a financial services case, includes an appeal;

'relevant minister' means the Minister or designated person responsible for the signing of the certificate to which a national security certificate appeal relates;

'respondent' means–

    (a) in an appeal, or application for permission to appeal, against a decision of another tribunal, any person other than the appellant who–

        (i)   was a party before that other tribunal;

           . . . or

        (iii) otherwise has a right of appeal against the decision of the other tribunal and has given notice to the Upper Tribunal that they wish to be a party to the appeal;

    (b) in an appeal other than a road trasport case, the person who made the decision;

    (c) in judicial review proceedings–

        (i)   in proceedings started in the Upper Tribunal, the person named by the applicant as the respondent;

        (ii)  in proceedings transferred to the Upper Tribunal under section 25A(2) or (3) of the Judicature (Northern Ireland) Act 1978 or section 31A(2) or (3) of the Senior Courts Act 1981, a person who was a defendant in the proceedings immediately before they were transferred;

        (iii) in proceedings transferred to the Upper Tribunal under section 20(1) of the 2007 Act, a person to whom intimation of the petition was made before the proceedings were transferred, or to whom the Upper Tribunal has required intimation to be made;

  (ca) in proceedings transferred or referred to the Upper Tribunal from the First-tier Tribunal, a person who was a respondent in the proceedings in the First-tier Tribunal;

    (d) in a reference under the Forfeiture Act 1982, the person whose eligibility for a benefit or advantage is in issue; or

  (da) in a financial services case–

        (i)   where the case is a multiple regulator case, both the primary and secondary regulator as defined in Schedule 3 to these rules (but subject to the operation of paragraph 4A(3) of that Schedule);

        (ii)  where the case is a single regulator case, the maker of the decision in respect of which a reference has been made; or

  (db) in a wholesale energy case, in relation to Great Britain, the Gas and Electricity Markets Authority or, in relation to Northern Ireland, the Northern Ireland Authority for Utility Regulation; or

    (e) a person substituted or added as a respondent under rule 9 (substitution and addition of parties);

'road transport case' means an appeal against a decision of a traffic commissioner or the Department of the Environment in Northern Ireland;

'special educational needs case' means proceedings concerning the education of a child or young person who has or may have special educational needs, including proceedings relating to–

    (a) an EHC needs assessment within the meaning of section 36(2) of the Children and Families Act 2014; or

(b) an EHC plan within the meaning of section 37(2) of that Act,

of such a child or young person;

'tribunal' does not include a traffic commissioner;

'wholesale energy case' means a reference to the Upper Tribunal in respect of a decision of–

    (a) in relation to Great Britain, the Gas and Electricity Markets Authority under the Electricity and Gas (Market Integrity and Transparency) (Enforcement etc.) Regulations 2013; or

    (b) in relation to Northern Ireland, the Northern Ireland Authority for Utility Regulation under the Electricity and Gas (Market Integrity and Transparency) (Enforcement etc.) Regulations (Northern Ireland) 2013;

'working day' means any day except a Saturday or Sunday, Christmas Day, Good Friday or a bank holiday under section 1 of the Banking and Financial Dealings Act 1971;

'young person' means, in relation to a special educational needs case or a disability discrimination in schools case, a person over compulsory school age but under 25.

### Overriding objective and parties' obligation to co-operate with the Upper Tribunal

2 (1) The overriding objective of these Rules is to enable the Upper Tribunal to deal with cases fairly and justly.

(2) Dealing with a case fairly and justly includes–

    (a) dealing with the case in ways which are proportionate to the importance of the case, the complexity of the issues, the anticipated costs and the resources of the parties;

    (b) avoiding unnecessary formality and seeking flexibility in the proceedings;

    (c) ensuring, so far as practicable, that the parties are able to participate fully in the proceedings;

    (d) using any special expertise of the Upper Tribunal effectively; and

    (e) avoiding delay, so far as compatible with proper consideration of the issues.

(3) The Upper Tribunal must seek to give effect to the overriding objective when it–

    (a) exercises any power under these Rules; or

    (b) interprets any rule or practice direction.

(4) Parties must–

    (a) help the Upper Tribunal to further the overriding objective; and

    (b) co-operate with the Upper Tribunal generally.

### Alternative dispute resolution and arbitration

3 (1) The Upper Tribunal should seek, where appropriate–

    (a) to bring to the attention of the parties the availability of any appropriate alternative procedure for the resolution of the dispute; and

    (b) if the parties wish and provided that it is compatible with the overriding objective, to facilitate the use of the procedure.

(2) Part 1 of the Arbitration Act 1996 does not apply to proceedings before the Upper Tribunal.

### PART 2: General powers and provisions

### Delegation to staff

4 (1) Staff appointed under section 40(1) of the 2007 Act (tribunal staff and services) may, with the approval of the Senior President of Tribunals, carry out functions of a judicial nature permitted or required to be done by the Upper Tribunal.

(2) The approval referred to at paragraph (1) may apply generally to the carrying out of specified functions by members of staff of a specified description in specified circumstances.

(3) Within 14 days after the date on which the Upper Tribunal sends notice of a decision made by a member of staff under paragraph (1) to a party, that party may apply in writing to the Upper Tribunal for that decision to be considered afresh by a judge.

**Case management powers**

5 (1) Subject to the provisions of the 2007 Act and any other enactment, the Upper Tribunal may regulate its own procedure.

(2) The Upper Tribunal may give a direction in relation to the conduct or disposal of proceedings at any time, including a direction amending, suspending or setting aside an earlier direction.

(3) In particular, and without restricting the general powers in paragraphs (1) and (2), the Upper Tribunal may–

  (a) extend or shorten the time for complying with any rule, practice direction or direction;

  (b) consolidate or hear together two or more sets of proceedings or parts of proceedings raising common issues, or treat a case as a lead case;

  (c) permit or require a party to amend a document;

  (d) permit or require a party or another person to provide documents, information, evidence or submissions to the Upper Tribunal or a party;

  (e) deal with an issue in the proceedings as a preliminary issue;

  (f) hold a hearing to consider any matter, including a case management issue;

  (g) decide the form of any hearing;

  (h) adjourn or postpone a hearing;

  (i) require a party to produce a bundle for a hearing;

  (j) stay (or, in Scotland, sist) proceedings;

  (k) transfer proceedings to another court or tribunal if that other court or tribunal has jurisdiction in relation to the proceedings and–

    (i) because of a change of circumstances since the proceedings were started, the Upper Tribunal no longer has jurisdiction in relation to the proceedings; or

    (ii) the Upper Tribunal considers that the other court or tribunal is a more appropriate forum for the determination of the case;

  (l) suspend the effect of its own decision pending an appeal or review of that decision;

  (m) in an appeal, or an application for permission to appeal, against the decision of another tribunal, suspend the effect of that decision pending the determination of the application for permission to appeal, and any appeal;

  (n) require any person, body or other tribunal whose decision is the subject of proceedings before the Upper Tribunal to provide reasons for the decision, or other information or documents in relation to the decision or any proceedings before that person, body or tribunal.

(4) The Upper Tribunal may direct that a fast-track case cease to be treated as a fast-track case if–

  (a) all the parties consent; or

  (b) the Upper Tribunal is satisfied that the appeal or application could not be justly determined if it were treated as a fast-track case.

(5) In a financial services case, the Upper Tribunal may direct that the effect of the decision in respect of which the reference has been made is to be suspended pending the determination of the reference, if it is satisfied that to do so would not prejudice–

  (a) the interests of any persons (whether consumers, investors or otherwise) intended to be protected by that notice;

  (b) the smooth operation or integrity of any market intended to be protected by that notice; or

  (c) the stability of the financial system of the United Kingdom.

(6) Paragraph (5) does not apply in the case of a reference in respect of a decision of the Pensions Regulator.

(7) In a wholesale energy case, the Upper Tribunal may direct that the effect of the decision in respect of which the reference has been made is to be suspended pending the determination of the reference.

### Procedure for applying for and giving directions

**6** (1) The Upper Tribunal may give a direction on the application of one or more of the parties or on its own initiative.

(2) An application for a direction may be made–

    (a) by sending or delivering a written application to the Upper Tribunal; or

    (b) orally during the course of a hearing.

(3) An application for a direction must include the reason for making that application.

(4) Unless the Upper Tribunal considers that there is good reason not to do so, the Upper Tribunal must send written notice of any direction to every party and to any other person affected by the direction.

(5) If a party or any other person sent notice of the direction under paragraph (4) wishes to challenge a direction which the Upper Tribunal has given, they may do so by applying for another direction which amends, suspends or sets aside the first direction.

### Failure to comply with rules etc.

**7** (1) An irregularity resulting from a failure to comply with any requirement in these Rules, a practice direction or a direction, does not of itself render void the proceedings or any step taken in the proceedings.

(2) If a party has failed to comply with a requirement in these Rules, a practice direction or a direction, the Upper Tribunal may take such action as it considers just, which may include–

    (a) waiving the requirement;

    (b) requiring the failure to be remedied;

    (c) exercising its power under rule 8 (striking out a party's case); or

    (d) except in a mental health case, an asylum case or an immigration case, restricting a party's participation in the proceedings.

(3) Paragraph (4) applies where the First-tier Tribunal has referred to the Upper Tribunal a failure by a person to comply with a requirement imposed by the First-tier Tribunal–

    (a) to attend at any place for the purpose of giving evidence;

    (b) otherwise to make themselves available to give evidence;

    (c) to swear an oath in connection with the giving of evidence;

    (d) to give evidence as a witness;

    (e) to produce a document; or

    (f) to facilitate the inspection of a document or any other thing (including any premises).

(4) The Upper Tribunal may exercise its power under section 25 of the 2007 Act (supplementary powers of the Upper Tribunal) in relation to such non-compliance as if the requirement had been imposed by the Upper Tribunal.

### Striking out a party's case

**8**(1A) Except for paragraph (2), this rule does not apply to an asylum case or an immigration case.

(1) The proceedings, or the appropriate part of them, will automatically be struck out–

    (a) if the appellant or applicant has failed to comply with a direction that stated that failure by the appellant or applicant to comply with the direction would lead to the striking out of the proceedings or that part of them; or

    (b) in immigration judicial review proceedings, when a fee has not been paid, as required, in respect of an application under rule 30(4) or upon the grant of permission.

(2) The Upper Tribunal must strike out the whole or a part of the proceedings if the Upper Tribunal–

    (a) does not have jurisdiction in relation to the proceedings or that part of them; and

    (b) does not exercise its power under rule 5(3)(k)(i) (transfer to another court or tribunal) in relation to the proceedings or that part of them.

(3) The Upper Tribunal may strike out the whole or a part of the proceedings if–
  (a) the appellant or applicant has failed to comply with a direction which stated that failure by the appellant or applicant to comply with the direction could lead to the striking out of the proceedings or part of them;
  (b) the appellant or applicant has failed to co-operate with the Upper Tribunal to such an extent that the Upper Tribunal cannot deal with the proceedings fairly and justly; or
  (c) in proceedings which are not an appeal from the decision of another tribunal or judicial review proceedings, the Upper Tribunal considers there is no reasonable prospect of the appellant's or the applicant's case, or part of it, succeeding.
(4) The Upper Tribunal may not strike out the whole or a part of the proceedings under paragraph (2) or (3)(b) or (c) without first giving the appellant or applicant an opportunity to make representations in relation to the proposed striking out.
(5) If the proceedings have been struck out under paragraph (1) or (3)(a), the appellant or applicant may apply for the proceedings, or part of them, to be reinstated.
(6) An application under paragraph (5) must be made in writing and received by the Upper Tribunal within 1 month after the date on which the Upper Tribunal sent notification of the striking out to the appellant or applicant.
(7) This rule applies to a respondent or an interested party as it applies to an appellant or applicant except that–
  (a) a reference to the striking out of the proceedings is to be read as a reference to the barring of the respondent or interested party from taking further part in the proceedings; and
  (b) a reference to an application for the reinstatement of proceedings which have been struck out is to be read as a reference to an application for the lifting of the bar on the respondent or interested party taking further part in the proceedings.
(8) If a respondent or an interested party has been barred from taking further part in proceedings under this rule and that bar has not been lifted, the Upper Tribunal need not consider any response or other submission made by that respondent or interested party, and may summarily determine any or all issues against that respondent or interested party.

### Addition, substitution and removal of parties

9 (1) The Upper Tribunal may give a direction adding, substituting or removing a party as an appellant, a respondent or an interested party.
(2) If the Upper Tribunal gives a direction under paragraph (1) it may give such consequential directions as it considers appropriate.
(3) A person who is not a party may apply to the Upper Tribunal to be added or substituted as a party.
(4) If a person who is entitled to be a party to proceedings by virtue of another enactment applies to be added as a party, and any conditions applicable to that entitlement have been satisfied, the Upper Tribunal must give a direction adding that person as a respondent or, if appropriate, as an appellant.
(5) In an asylum case, the United Kingdom Representative of the United Nations High Commissioner for Refugees ('the United Kingdom Representative') may give notice to the Upper Tribunal that the United Kingdom Representative wishes to participate in the proceedings.
(6) If the United Kingdom Representative gives notice under paragraph (5)–
  (i) the United Kingdom Representative is entitled to participate in any hearing; and
  (ii) all documents which are required to be sent or delivered to parties must be sent or delivered to the United Kingdom Representative.

### Orders for costs

10 (1) The Upper Tribunal may not make an order in respect of costs (or, in Scotland, expenses) in proceedings transferred or referred by, or on appeal from, another tribunal except–
  (aa) in a national security certificate appeal, to the extent permitted by paragraph (1A);

    (a) in proceedings transferred by, or on appeal from, the Tax Chamber of the First-tier Tribunal; or

    (b) to the extent and in the circumstances that the other tribunal had the power to make an order in respect of costs (or, in Scotland, expenses).

(1A) In a national security certificate appeal–

    (a) the Upper Tribunal may make an order in respect of costs or expenses in the circumstances described at paragraph (3)(c) and (d);

    (b) if the appeal is against a certificate, the Upper Tribunal may make an order in respect of costs or expenses against the relevant Minister and in favour of the appellant if the Upper Tribunal allows the appeal and quashes the certificate to any extent or the Minister withdraws the certificate;

    (c) if the appeal is against the application of a certificate, the Upper Tribunal may make an order in respect of costs or expenses–

      (i) against the appellant and in favour of any other party if the Upper Tribunal dismisses the appeal to any extent; or

      (ii) in favour of the appellant and against any other party if the Upper Tribunal allows the appeal to any extent.

(2) The Upper Tribunal may not make an order in respect of costs or expenses under section 4 of the Forfeiture Act 1982.

(3) In other proceedings, the Upper Tribunal may not make an order in respect of costs or expenses except–

    (a) in judicial review proceedings;

    (c) under section 29(4) of the 2007 Act (wasted costs) and costs incurred in applying for such costs; or

    (d) if the Upper Tribunal considers that a party or its representative has acted unreasonably in bringing, defending or conducting the proceedings; or

    (e) if, in a financial services case or a wholesale energy case, the Upper Tribunal considers that the decision in respect of which the reference was made was unreasonable.

(4) The Upper Tribunal may make an order for costs (or, in Scotland, expenses) on an application or on its own initiative.

(5) A person making an application for an order for costs or expenses must–

    (a) send or deliver a written application to the Upper Tribunal and to the person against whom it is proposed that the order be made; and

    (b) send or deliver with the application a schedule of the costs or expenses claimed sufficient to allow summary assessment of such costs or expenses by the Upper Tribunal.

(6) An application for an order for costs or expenses may be made at any time during the proceedings but may not be made later than 1 month after the date on which the Upper Tribunal sends–

    (a) a decision notice recording the decision which finally disposes of all issues in the proceedings; or

    (b) notice under rule 17(5) that a withdrawal which ends the proceedings has taken effect.

(7) The Upper Tribunal may not make an order for costs or expenses against a person (the 'paying person') without first–

    (a) giving that person an opportunity to make representations; and

    (b) if the paying person is an individual and the order is to be made under paragraph (3)(a), (b) or (d), considering that person's financial means.

(8) The amount of costs or expenses to be paid under an order under this rule may be ascertained by–

    (a) summary assessment by the Upper Tribunal;

    (b) agreement of a specified sum by the paying person and the person entitled to receive the costs or expenses ('the receiving person'); or

    (c) assessment of the whole or a specified part of the costs or expenses, including the costs or expenses of the assessment, incurred by the receiving person, if not agreed.

(9) Following an order for assessment under paragraph (8)(c), the paying person or the receiving person may apply–

    (a) in England and Wales, to the High Court or the Costs Office of the Supreme Court (as specified in the order) for a detailed assessment of the costs on the standard basis or, if specified in the order, on the indemnity basis; and the Civil Procedure Rules 1998 shall apply, with necessary modifications, to that application and assessment as if the proceedings in the tribunal had been proceedings in a court to which the Civil Procedure Rules 1998 apply;

    (b) in Scotland, to the Auditor of the Court of Session for the taxation of the expenses according to the fees payable in that court; or

    (c) in Northern Ireland, to the Taxing Office of the High Court of Northern Ireland for taxation on the standard basis or, if specified in the order, on the indemnity basis.

(10) Upon making an order for the assessment of costs, the Tribunal may order an amount to be paid on account before the costs or expenses are assessed.

### Representatives

**11** (1) Subject to paragraph 5A, a party may appoint a representative (whether a legal representative or not) to represent that party in the proceedings save that a party in an asylum or immigration case may not be represented by any person prohibited from representing by section 84 of the Immigration and Asylum Act 1999.

  (2) If a party appoints a representative, that party (or the representative if the representative is a legal representative) must send or deliver to the Upper Tribunal written notice of the representative's name and address.

(2A) If the Upper Tribunal receives notice that a party has appointed a representative under paragraph (2), it must send a copy of that notice to each other party.

  (3) Anything permitted or required to be done by a party under these Rules, a practice direction or a direction may be done by the representative of that party, except signing a witness statement.

  (4) A person who receives due notice of the appointment of a representative–

    (a) must provide to the representative any document which is required to be provided to the represented party, and need not provide that document to the represented party; and

    (b) may assume that the representative is and remains authorised as such until they receive written notification that this is not so from the representative or the represented party.

  (5) Subject to paragraph 5B, at a hearing a party may be accompanied by another person whose name and address has not been notified under paragraph (2) but who, subject to paragraph (8) and with the permission of the Upper Tribunal, may act as a representative or otherwise assist in presenting the party's case at the hearing.

(5A) In immigration judicial review proceedings, a party may appoint as a representative only a person authorised under the Legal Services Act 2007 to undertake the conduct of litigation in the High Court.

(5B) At a hearing of immigration judicial review proceedings, rights of audience before the Upper Tribunal are restricted to persons authorised to exercise those rights in the High Court under the Legal Services Act 2007.

  (6) Paragraphs (2) to (4) do not apply to a person who accompanies a party under paragraph (5).

  (7) In a mental health case if the patient has not appointed a representative the Upper Tribunal may appoint a legal representative for the patient where–

    (a) the patient has stated that they do not wish to conduct their own case or that they wish to be represented; or

    (b) the patient lacks the capacity to appoint a representative but the Upper Tribunal believes that it is in the patient's best interests for the patient to be represented.

  (8) In a mental health case a party may not appoint as a representative, or be represented or assisted at a hearing by–

    (a) a person liable to be detained or subject to guardianship or after-care under supervision, or who is a community patient, under the Mental Health Act 1983; or

(b) a person receiving treatment for mental disorder at the same hospital or home as the patient.

(9) In this rule "legal representative" means a person who, for the purposes of the Legal Services Act 2007, is an authorised person in relation to an activity which constitutes the exercise of a right of audience or the conduct of litigation within the meaning of that Act, a qualified person as defined in section 84(2) of the Immigration and Asylum Act 1999, an advocate or solicitor in Scotland or a barrister or solicitor in Northern Ireland.

(10) In an asylum case or an immigration case, an appellant's representative before the First-tier Tribunal will be treated as that party's representative before the Upper Tribunal, unless the Upper Tribunal receives notice–

(a) of a new representative under paragraph (2) of this rule; or

(b) from the appellant stating that they are no longer represented.

### Calculating time

**12** (1) An act required by these Rules, a practice direction or a direction to be done on or by a particular day must be done by 5pm on that day.

(2) If the time specified by these Rules, a practice direction or a direction for doing any act ends on a day other than a working day, the act is done in time if it is done on the next working day.

(3) In a special educational needs case or a disability discrimination in schools case, the following days must not be counted when calculating the time by which an act must be done–

(a) 25th December to 1st January inclusive; and

(b) any day in August.

(3A) In an asylum case or an immigration case, when calculating the time by which an act must be done, in addition to the days specified in the definition of "working days" in rule 1 (interpretation), the following days must also not be counted as working days–

(a) 27th to 31st December inclusive.

(4) Paragraph (3) or (3A) does not apply where the Upper Tribunal directs that an act must be done by or on a specified date.

### Sending and delivery of documents

**13** (1) Any document to be provided to the Upper Tribunal under these Rules, a practice direction or a direction must be–

(a) sent by pre-paid post or by document exchange or delivered by hand to the address specified for the proceedings;

(b) sent by fax to the number specified for the proceedings; or

(c) sent or delivered by such other method as the Upper Tribunal may permit or direct.

(2) Subject to paragraph (3), if a party provides a fax number, email address or other details for the electronic transmission of documents to them, that party must accept delivery of documents by that method.

(3) If a party informs the Upper Tribunal and all other parties that a particular form of communication, other than pre-paid post or delivery by hand, should not be used to provide documents to that party, that form of communication must not be so used.

(4) If the Upper Tribunal or a party sends a document to a party or the Upper Tribunal by email or any other electronic means of communication, the recipient may request that the sender provide a hard copy of the document to the recipient. The recipient must make such a request as soon as reasonably practicable after receiving the document electronically.

(5) The Upper Tribunal and each party may assume that the address provided by a party or its representative is and remains the address to which documents should be sent or delivered until receiving written notification to the contrary.

(6) Subject to paragraph (7), if a document submitted to the Upper Tribunal is not written in English, it must be accompanied by an English translation.

(7) In proceedings that are in Wales or have a connection with Wales, a document or translation may be submitted to the Upper Tribunal in Welsh.

### Use of documents and information

**14** (1) The Upper Tribunal may make an order prohibiting the disclosure or publication of–

(a) specified documents or information relating to the proceedings; or

(b) any matter likely to lead members of the public to identify any person whom the Upper Tribunal considers should not be identified.

(2) The Upper Tribunal may give a direction prohibiting the disclosure of a document or information to a person if–

(a) the Upper Tribunal is satisfied that such disclosure would be likely to cause that person or some other person serious harm; and

(b) the Upper Tribunal is satisfied, having regard to the interests of justice, that it is proportionate to give such a direction.

(3) If a party ('the first party') considers that the Upper Tribunal should give a direction under paragraph (2) prohibiting the disclosure of a document or information to another party ('the second party'), the first party must–

(a) exclude the relevant document or information from any documents that will be provided to the second party; and

(b) provide to the Upper Tribunal the excluded document or information, and the reason for its exclusion, so that the Upper Tribunal may decide whether the document or information should be disclosed to the second party or should be the subject of a direction under paragraph (2).

(5) If the Upper Tribunal gives a direction under paragraph (2) which prevents disclosure to a party who has appointed a representative, the Upper Tribunal may give a direction that the documents or information be disclosed to that representative if the Upper Tribunal is satisfied that–

(a) disclosure to the representative would be in the interests of the party; and

(b) the representative will act in accordance with paragraph (6).

(6) Documents or information disclosed to a representative in accordance with a direction under paragraph (5) must not be disclosed either directly or indirectly to any other person without the Upper Tribunal's consent.

(7) Unless the Upper Tribunal gives a direction to the contrary, information about mental health cases and the names of any persons concerned in such cases must not be made public.

(8) The Upper Tribunal may, on its own initiative or on the application of a party, give a direction that certain documents or information must or may be disclosed to the Upper Tribunal on the basis that the Upper Tribunal will not disclose such documents or information to other persons, or specified other persons.

(9) A party making an application for a direction under paragraph (8) may withhold the relevant documents or information from other parties until the Upper Tribunal has granted or refused the application.

(10) In a case involving matters relating to national security, the Upper Tribunal must ensure that information is not disclosed contrary to the interests of national security.

(11) The Upper Tribunal must conduct proceedings and record its decision and reasons appropriately so as not to undermine the effect of an order made under paragraph (1), a direction given under paragraph (2) or (8) or the duty imposed by paragraph (10).

### Evidence and submissions

**15** (1) Without restriction on the general powers in rule 5(1) and (2) (case management powers), the Upper Tribunal may give directions as to–

(a) issues on which it requires evidence or submissions;

(b) the nature of the evidence or submissions it requires;

(c) whether the parties are permitted or required to provide expert evidence, and

if so whether the parties must jointly appoint a single expert to provide such evidence;
   (d) any limit on the number of witnesses whose evidence a party may put forward, whether in relation to a particular issue or generally;
   (e) the manner in which any evidence or submissions are to be provided, which may include a direction for them to be given–
      (i) orally at a hearing; or
      (ii) by written submissions or witness statement; and
   (f) the time at which any evidence or submissions are to be provided.
(2) The Upper Tribunal may–
   (a) admit evidence whether or not–
      (i) the evidence would be admissible in a civil trial in the United Kingdom; or
      (ii) the evidence was available to a previous decision maker; or
   (b) exclude evidence that would otherwise be admissible where–
      (i) the evidence was not provided within the time allowed by a direction or a practice direction;
      (ii) the evidence was otherwise provided in a manner that did not comply with a direction or a practice direction; or
      (iii) it would otherwise be unfair to admit the evidence.
(2A) In an asylum case or an immigration case–
   (a) if a party wishes the Upper Tribunal to consider evidence that was not before the First-tier Tribunal, that party must send or deliver a notice to the Upper Tribunal and any other party–
      (i) indicating the nature of the evidence; and
      (ii) explaining why it was not submitted to the First-tier Tribunal; and
   (b) when considering whether to admit evidence that was not before the First-tier Tribunal, the Upper Tribunal must have regard to whether there has been unreasonable delay in producing that evidence.
(3) The Upper Tribunal may consent to a witness giving, or require any witness to give, evidence on oath, and may administer an oath for that purpose.

### Summoning or citation of witnesses and orders to answer questions or produce documents

**16** (1) On the application of a party or on its own initiative, the Upper Tribunal may–
   (a) by summons (or, in Scotland, citation) require any person to attend as a witness at a hearing at the time and place specified in the summons or citation; or
   (b) order any person to answer any questions or produce any documents in that person's possession or control which relate to any issue in the proceedings.
(2) A summons or citation under paragraph (1)(a) must–
   (a) give the person required to attend 14 days' notice of the hearing or such shorter period as the Upper Tribunal may direct; and
   (b) where the person is not a party, make provision for the person's necessary expenses of attendance to be paid, and state who is to pay them.
(3) No person may be compelled to give any evidence or produce any document that the person could not be compelled to give or produce on a trial of an action in a court of law in the part of the United Kingdom where the proceedings are due to be determined.
(4) A person who receives a summons, citation or order may apply to the Upper Tribunal for it to be varied or set aside if they did not have an opportunity to object to it before it was made or issued.
(5) A person making an application under paragraph (4) must do so as soon as reasonably practicable after receiving notice of the summons, citation or order.
(6) A summons, citation or order under this rule must–
   (a) state that the person on whom the requirement is imposed may apply to the Upper Tribunal to vary or set aside the summons, citation or order, if they did not have an opportunity to object to it before it was made or issued; and
   (b) state the consequences of failure to comply with the summons, citation or order.

**Withdrawal**

**17** (1) Subject to paragraph (2), a party may give notice of the withdrawal of its case, or any part of it–

(a) at any time by sending or delivering to the Upper Tribunal a written notice of withdrawal; or

(b) orally at a hearing.

(2) Notice of withdrawal will not take effect unless the Upper Tribunal consents to the withdrawal except in relation to an application for permission to appeal.

(3) A party which has withdrawn its case may apply to the Upper Tribunal for the case to be reinstated.

(4) An application under paragraph (3) must be made in writing and be received by the Upper Tribunal within 1 month after–

(a) the date on which the Upper Tribunal received the notice under paragraph (1)(a); or

(b) the date of the hearing at which the case was withdrawn orally under paragraph (1)(b).

(5) The Upper Tribunal must notify each party in writing that a withdrawal has taken effect under this rule.

(6) Paragraph (3) does not apply to a financial services case other than a reference against a penalty.

**Appeal treated as abandoned or finally determined in an asylum case or an immigration case**

**17A**(1) A party to an asylum case or an immigration case before the Upper Tribunal must notify the Upper Tribunal if they are aware that–

(a) the appellant has left the United Kingdom;

(b) the appellant has been granted leave to enter or remain in the United Kingdom;

(c) a deportation order has been made against the appellant; or

(d) a document listed in paragraph 4(2) of Schedule 2 to the Immigration (European Economic Area) Regulations 2006 has been issued to the appellant.

(2) Where an appeal is treated as abandoned pursuant to section 104(4) or (4A) of the Nationality, Immigration and Asylum Act 2002 or paragraph 4(2) of Schedule 2 to the Immigration (European Economic Area) Regulations 2006, or as finally determined pursuant to section 104(5) of the Nationality, Immigration and Asylum Act 2002, the Upper Tribunal must send the parties a notice informing them that the appeal is being treated as abandoned or finally determined.

(3) Where an appeal would otherwise fall to be treated as abandoned pursuant to section 104(4A) of the Nationality, Immigration and Asylum Act 2002, but the appellant wishes to pursue their appeal, the appellant must send or deliver a notice, which must comply with any relevant practice directions, to the Upper Tribunal and the respondent so that it is received within thirty days of the date on which the notice of the grant of leave to enter or remain in the United Kingdom was sent to the appellant.

(4) Where a notice of grant of leave to enter or remain is sent electronically or delivered personally, the time limit in paragraph (3) is twenty eight days.

(5) Notwithstanding rule 5(3)(a) (case management powers) and rule 7(2) (failure to comply with rules etc.), the Upper Tribunal must not extend the time limits in paragraph (3) and (4).

**Notice of funding of legal services**

**18**   If a party is granted funding of legal services at any time, that party must as soon as practicable–

(a) (i) if civil legal services (within the meaning of section 8 of the Legal Aid, Sentencing and Punishment of Offenders Act 2012) are provided under arrangements made for the purposes of Part 1 of that Act or by the Northern Ireland Legal Services Commission, send a copy of the certificate or funding notice to the Upper Tribunal; or

(ii) if funding is granted by the Scottish Legal Aid Board, send a copy of the
legal aid certificate to the Upper Tribunal; and

(b) notify every other party in writing that funding has been granted.

### Confidentiality in social security and child support cases

**19** (1) Paragraph (4) applies to an appeal against a decision of the First-tier Tribunal–

(a) in proceedings under the Child Support Act 1991 in the circumstances described
in paragraph (2), other than an appeal against a reduced benefit decision (as
defined in section 46(10)(b) of the Child Support Act 1991, as that section had
effect prior to the commencement of section 15(b) of the Child Maintenance
and Other Payments Act 2008); or

(b) in proceedings where the parties to the appeal include former joint claimants who are no longer living together in the circumstances described in
paragraph (3).

(2) The circumstances referred to in paragraph (1)(a) are that–

(a) in the proceedings in the First-tier Tribunal in respect of which the appeal has
been brought, there was an obligation to keep a person's address confidential;
or

(b) an absent parent, non-resident parent or person with care would like their
address or the address of the child to be kept confidential and has given notice
to that effect to the Upper Tribunal–

(i)   in an application for permission to appeal or notice of appeal;

(ii)  within 1 month after an enquiry by the Upper Tribunal; or

(iii) when notifying any subsequent change of address after proceedings have
been started.

(3) The circumstances referred to in paragraph (1)(b) are that–

(a) in the proceedings in the First-tier Tribunal in respect of which the appeal has
been brought, there was an obligation to keep a person's address confidential;
or

(b) one of the former joint claimants would like their address to be kept confidential and has given notice to that effect to the Upper Tribunal–

(i)   in an application for permission to appeal or notice of appeal;

(ii)  within 1 month after an enquiry by the Upper Tribunal; or

(iii) when notifying any subsequent change of address after proceedings have
been started.

(4) Where this paragraph applies, the Secretary of State or other decision maker and
the Upper Tribunal must take appropriate steps to secure the confidentiality of the
address and of any information which could reasonably be expected to enable a
person to identify the address, to the extent that the address or that information is
not already known to each other party.

(5) In this rule–

'absent parent', 'non-resident parent' and 'person with care' have the meanings set
out in section 3 of the Child Support Act 1991;

'joint claimants' means the persons who made a joint claim for a jobseeker's allowance under the Jobseekers Act 1995, a tax credit under the Tax Credits Act 2002
or in relation to whom an award of universal credit is made under Part 1 of the
Welfare Reform Act 2012.'

### Power to pay expenses and allowances

**20** (1) In proceedings brought under section 4 of the Safeguarding Vulnerable Groups
Act 2006, the Secretary of State may pay such allowances for the purpose of or in
connection with the attendance of persons at hearings as the Secretary of State
may, with the consent of the Treasury, determine.

(2) Paragraph (3) applies to proceedings on appeal from a decision of–

(a) the First-tier Tribunal in proceedings under the Child Support Act 1991, section 12 of the Social Security Act 1998 or paragraph 6 of Schedule 7 to the Child
Support, Pensions and Social Security Act 2000;

(b) the First-tier Tribunal in a war pensions and armed forces case (as defined in the Tribunal Procedure (First-tier Tribunal) (War Pensions and Armed Forces Compensation Chamber) Rules 2008); or

(c)  a Pensions Appeal Tribunal for Scotland or Northern Ireland.

(3) The Lord Chancellor (or, in Scotland, the Secretary of State) may pay to any person who attends any hearing such travelling and other allowances, including compensation for loss of remunerative time, as the Lord Chancellor (or, in Scotland, the Secretary of State) may determine.

## Procedure for applying for a stay of a decision pending an appeal

20A(1) This rule applies where another enactment provides in any terms for the Upper Tribunal to stay or suspend, or to lift a stay or suspension of, a decision which is or may be the subject of an appeal to the Upper Tribunal ('the substantive decision') pending such appeal.

(2) A person who wishes the Upper Tribunal to decide whether the substantive decision should be stayed or suspended must make a written application to the Upper Tribunal which must include–

(a)  the name and address of the person making the application;

(b)  the name and address of any representative of that person;

(c)  the address to which documents for that person should be sent or delivered;

(d)  the name and address of any person who will be a respondent to the appeal;

(e)  details of the substantive decision and any decision as to when that decision is to take effect, and copies of any written record of, or reasons for, those decisions; and

(f)  the grounds on which the person making the application relies.

(3) In the case of an application under paragraph (2) in a road transport case–

(a)  the person making the application must notify the decision maker when making the application;

(b)  within 7 days of receiving notification of the application the decision maker must send or deliver written reasons for refusing or withdrawing the stay–

(i)  to the Upper Tribunal; and

(ii)  to the person making the application, if the decision maker has not already done so.

(4) If the Upper Tribunal grants a stay or suspension following an application under this rule–

(a)  the Upper Tribunal may give directions as to the conduct of the appeal of the substantive decision; and

(b)  the Upper Tribunal may, where appropriate, grant the stay or suspension subject to conditions.

(5) Unless the Upper Tribunal considers that there is good reason not to do so, the Upper Tribunal must send written notice of any decision made under this rule to each party.

## PART 3: Procedure for cases in the Upper Tribunal

## Application to the Upper Tribunal for permission to appeal

21   . . .

(2) A person may apply to the Upper Tribunal for permission to appeal to the Upper Tribunal against a decision of another tribunal only if–

(a)  they have made an application for permission to appeal to the tribunal which made the decision challenged; and

(b)  that application has been refused or has not been admitted or has been granted only on limited grounds.

(3) An application for permission to appeal must be made in writing and received by the Upper Tribunal no later than–

(a)  in the case of an application under section 4 of the Safeguarding Vulnerable Groups Act 2006, 3 months after the date on which written notice of the decision being challenged was sent to the appellant;

(aa)  in an asylum case or an immigration case where the appellant is in the United Kingdom at the time that the application is made–

(i) 14 days after the date on which notice of the First-tier Tribunal's refusal of permission was sent to the appellant; or

(ii) if the case is a fast-track case, four working days after the date on which notice of the First-tier Tribunal's refusal of permission was sent to the appellant;

(b) otherwise, a month after the date on which the tribunal that made the decision under challenge sent notice of its refusal of permission to appeal, or refusal to admit the application for permission to appeal, to the appellant.

(4) The application must state–

(a) the name and address of the appellant;

(b) the name and address of the representative (if any) of the appellant;

(c) an address where documents for the appellant may be sent or delivered;

(d) details (including the full reference) of the decision challenged;

(e) the grounds on which the appellant relies; and

(f) whether the appellant wants the application to be dealt with at a hearing.

(5) The appellant must provide with the application a copy of–

(a) any written record of the decision being challenged;

(b) any separate written statement of reasons for that decision; and

(c) if the application is for permission to appeal against a decision of another tribunal, the notice of refusal of permission to appeal, or notice of refusal to admit the application for permission to appeal, from that other tribunal.

(6) If the appellant provides the application to the Upper Tribunal later than the time required by paragraph (3) or by an extension of time allowed under rule 5(3)(a) (power to extend time)–

(a) the application must include a request for an extension of time and the reason why the application was not provided in time; and

(b) unless the Upper Tribunal extends time for the application under rule 5(3)(a) (power to extend time) the Upper Tribunal must not admit the application.

(7) If the appellant makes an application to the Upper Tribunal for permission to appeal against the decision of another tribunal, and that other tribunal refused to admit the appellant's application for permission to appeal because the application for permission or for a written statement of reasons was not made in time–

(a) the application to the Upper Tribunal for permission to appeal must include the reason why the application to the other tribunal for permission to appeal or for a written statement of reasons, as the case may be, was not made in time; and

(b) the Upper Tribunal must only admit the application if the Upper Tribunal considers that it is in the interests of justice for it to do so.

(8) In this rule, a reference to notice of a refusal of permission to appeal is to be taken to include a reference to notice of a grant of permission on limited grounds.

### Decision in relation to permission to appeal

22 (1) Except where rule 22A (special procedure for providing notice of a refusal of permission to appeal in an asylum case) applies, if the Upper Tribunal refuses permission to appeal or refuses to admit a late application for permission, it must send written notice of the refusal and of the reasons for the refusal to the appellant.

(2) If the Upper Tribunal gives permission to appeal–

(a) the Upper Tribunal must send written notice of the permission, and of the reasons for any limitations or conditions on such permission, to each party;

(b) subject to any direction by the Upper Tribunal, the application for permission to appeal stands as the notice of appeal and the Upper Tribunal must send to each respondent a copy of the application for permission to appeal and any documents provided with it by the appellant; and

(c) the Upper Tribunal may, with the consent of the appellant and each respondent, determine the appeal without obtaining any further response.

(3) Paragraph (4) applies where the Upper Tribunal, without a hearing, determines an application for permission to appeal–

(a) against a decision of–

(i)   the Tax Chamber of the First-tier Tribunal;
(ii)  the Health, Education and Social Care Chamber of the First-tier Tribunal;
(iia) the General Regulatory Chamber of the First-tier Tribunal;
(iib) the Property Chamber of the First-tier Tribunal;
(iii) the Mental Health Review Tribunal for Wales; or
(iv)  the Special Educational Needs Tribunal for Wales; or
(b) under section 4 of the Safeguarding Vulnerable Groups Act 2006.
(4) In the circumstances set out at paragraph (3) the appellant may apply for the decision to be reconsidered at a hearing if the Upper Tribunal–
  (a) refuses permission to appeal or refuses to admit a late application for permission; or
  (b) gives permission to appeal on limited grounds or subject to conditions.
(5) An application under paragraph (4) must be made in writing and received by the Upper Tribunal within 14 days after the date on which the Upper Tribunal sent written notice of its decision regarding the application to the appellant.

### Special procedure for providing notice of a refusal of permission to appeal in an asylum case

22A(1) This rule applies to a decision in an asylum case to refuse permission to appeal or to refuse to admit a late application for permission to appeal, where–
  (a) the appellant is not the Secretary of State;
  (b) at the time the application is made the appellant is in the United Kingdom; and
  (c) the decision is not made in a fast-track case.
(2) The Upper Tribunal must provide written notice of the refusal and of the reasons for the refusal ('the notice') to the Secretary of State as soon as reasonably practicable.
(3) The Secretary of State must–
  (a) send the notice to the appellant not later than 30 days after the Upper Tribunal provided it to the Secretary of State; and
  (b) as soon as practicable after doing so, inform the Upper Tribunal of the date on which, and the means by which, it was sent.
(4) If the Secretary of State does not give the Upper Tribunal the information required by paragraph (3)(b) within 31 days after the notice was provided to the Secretary of State, the Upper Tribunal must send the notice to the appellant as soon as reasonably practicable.

### Notice of appeal

23 (1) This rule applies–
  (a) to proceedings on appeal to the Upper Tribunal for which permission to appeal is not required, except proceedings to which rule 26A or 26B applies;
  (b) if another tribunal has given permission for a party to appeal to the Upper Tribunal; or
  (c) subject to any other direction by the Upper Tribunal, if the Upper Tribunal has given permission to appeal and has given a direction that the application for permission to appeal does not stand as the notice of appeal.
(1A) In an asylum case or an immigration case in which the First-tier tribunal has given permission to appeal, subject to any direction of the First-tier Tribunal or the Upper Tribunal, the application for permission to appeal sent or delivered to the First-tier Tribunal stands as the notice of appeal and accordingly paragraphs (2) to (6) of this rule do not apply.
(2) The appellant must provide a notice of appeal to the Upper Tribunal so that it is received within 1 month after–
  (a) the date that the tribunal that gave permission to appeal sent notice of such permission to the appellant; or
  (b) if permission to appeal is not required, the date on which notice of decision to which the appeal relates was sent to the appellant.
(3) The notice of appeal must include the information listed in rule 21(4)(a) to (e)

(content of the application for permission to appeal) and, where the Upper Tribunal has given permission to appeal, the Upper Tribunal's case reference.

(4) If another tribunal has granted permission to appeal, the appellant must provide with the notice of appeal a copy of–

   (a) any written record of the decision being challenged;

   (b) any separate written statement of reasons for that decision; and

   (c) the notice of permission to appeal.

(5) If the appellant provides the notice of appeal to the Upper Tribunal later than the time required by paragraph (2) or by an extension of time allowed under rule 5(3)(a) (power to extend time)–

   (a) the notice of appeal must include a request for an extension of time and the reason why the notice was not provided in time; and

   (b) unless the Upper Tribunal extends time for the notice of appeal under rule 5(3)(a) (power to extend time) the Upper Tribunal must not admit the notice of appeal.

(6) When the Upper Tribunal receives the notice of appeal it must send a copy of the notice and any accompanying documents–

   (a) to each respondent; or

   (b) in road transport case, to–

      (i)   the decision maker;

      (ii)  the appropriate national authority; and

      (iii) in a case relating to the detention of a vehicle, the authorised person.

### Response to the notice of appeal

**24** (1) This rule and rule 25 do not apply to a road transport case, in respect of which Schedule 1 makes alternative provision.

(1A) Subject to any direction given by the Upper Tribunal, a respondent may provide a response to a notice of appeal.

(2) Any response provided under paragraph (1A) must be in writing and must be sent or delivered to the Upper Tribunal so that it is received–

   (a) if an application for permission to appeal stands as the notice of appeal, no later than one month after the date on which the respondent was sent notice that permission to appeal had been granted; or

   (aa) in a fast-track case, two days before the hearing of the appeal; or

   (b) in any other case, no later than 1 month after the date on which the Upper Tribunal sent a copy of the notice of appeal to the respondent.

(3) The response must state–

   (a) the name and address of the respondent;

   (b) the name and address of the representative (if any) of the respondent;

   (c) an address where documents for the respondent may be sent or delivered;

   (d) whether the respondent opposes the appeal;

   (e) the grounds on which the respondent relies, including (in the case of an appeal against the decision of another tribunal) any grounds on which the respondent was unsuccessful in the proceedings which are the subject of the appeal, but intends to rely in the appeal; and

   (f) whether the respondent wants the case to be dealt with at a hearing.

(4) If the respondent provides the response to the Upper Tribunal later than the time required by paragraph (2) or by an extension of time allowed under rule 5(3)(a) (power to extend time), the response must include a request for an extension of time and the reason why the response was not provided in time.

(5) When the Upper Tribunal receives the response it must send a copy of the response and any accompanying documents to the appellant and each other party.

### Appellant's reply

**25** (1) Subject to any direction given by the Upper Tribunal, the appellant may provide a reply to any response provided under rule 24 (response to the notice of appeal).

(2) Subject to paragraph (2A), any reply provided under paragraph (1) must be in writing and must be sent or delivered to the Upper Tribunal so that it is received within

one month after the date on which the Upper Tribunal sent a copy of the response to the appellant.

(2A) In an asylum case or an immigration case, the time limit in paragraph (2) is–

    (a) one month after the date on which the Upper Tribunal sent a copy of the response to the appellant, or five days before the hearing of the appeal, which-ever is the earlier; and

    (b) in a fast-track case, the day of the hearing.

(3) When the Upper Tribunal receives the reply it must send a copy of the reply and any accompanying documents to each respondent.

### References under the Forfeiture Act 1982

26 (1) If a question arises which is required to be determined by the Upper Tribunal under section 4 of the Forfeiture Act 1982, the person to whom the application for the relevant benefit or advantage has been made must refer the question to the Upper Tribunal.

(2) The reference must be in writing and must include–

    (a) a statement of the question for determination;

    (b) a statement of the relevant facts;

    (c) the grounds upon which the reference is made; and

    (d) an address for sending documents to the person making the reference and each respondent.

(3) When the Upper Tribunal receives the reference it must send a copy of the refer-ence and any accompanying documents to each respondent.

(4) Rules 24 (response to the notice of appeal) and 25 (appellant's reply) apply to a reference made under this rule as if it were a notice of appeal.

### Cases transferred or referred to the Upper Tribunal, applications made directly to the Upper Tribunal and proceedings without notice to a respondent

26A(1) Paragraphs (2) and (3) apply to–

    (a) a case transferred or referred to the Upper Tribunal from the First-tier Tribunal; or

    (b) a case, other than an appeal or a case to which rule 26 (references under the Forfeiture Act 1982) applies, which is started by an application made directly to the Upper Tribunal.

(2) In a case to which this paragraph applies–

    (a) the Upper Tribunal must give directions as to the procedure to be followed in the consideration and disposal of the proceedings;

    (aa) in a reference under Schedule 1D of the Charities Act 1993, the Upper Tribu-nal may give directions providing for an application to join the proceedings as a party and the time within which it may be made; and

    (b) the preceding rules in this Part will only apply to the proceedings to the extent provided for by such directions.

(3) If a case or matter to which this paragraph applies is to be determined without notice to or the involvement of a respondent–

    (a) any provision in these Rules requiring a document to be provided by or to a respondent; and

    (b) any other provision in these Rules permitting a respondent to participate in the proceedings

does not apply to that case or matter.

(4) Schedule 2 makes further provision for national security certificate appeals trans-ferred to the Upper Tribunal.

### Financial services cases and wholesale energy cases

26B   Schedule 3 makes provision for financial services cases and wholsale energy cases.

## PART 4: Judicial review proceedings in the Upper Tribunal

### Application of this Part to judicial review proceedings transferred to the Upper Tribunal

27 (1) When a court transfers judicial review proceedings to the Upper Tribunal, the Upper Tribunal–

    (a) must notify each party in writing that the proceedings have been transferred to the Upper Tribunal; and

    (b) must give directions as to the future conduct of the proceedings.

  (2) The directions given under paragraph (1)(b) may modify or disapply for the purposes of the proceedings any of the provisions of the following rules in this Part.

  (3) In proceedings transferred from the Court of Session under section 20(1) of the 2007 Act, the directions given under paragraph (1)(b) must–

    (a) if the Court of Session did not make a first order specifying the required intimation, service and advertisement of the petition, state the Upper Tribunal's requirements in relation to those matters;

    (b) state whether the Upper Tribunal will consider summary dismissal of the proceedings; and

    (c) where necessary, modify or disapply provisions relating to permission in the following rules in this Part.

### Applications for permission to bring judicial review proceedings

28 (1) A person seeking permission to bring judicial review proceedings before the Upper Tribunal under section 16 of the 2007 Act must make a written application to the Upper Tribunal for such permission.

  (2) Subject to paragraph (3), an application under paragraph (1) must be made promptly and, unless any other enactment specifies a shorter time limit, must be sent or delivered to the Upper Tribunal so that it is received no later than 3 months after the date of the decision, action or omission to which the application relates.

  (3) An application for permission to bring judicial review proceedings challenging a decision of the First-tier Tribunal may be made later than the time required by paragraph (2) if it is made within 1 month after the date on which the First-tier Tribunal sent–

    (a) written reasons for the decision; or

    (b) notification that an application for the decision to be set aside has been unsuccessful, provided that that application was made in time.

  (4) The application must state–

    (a) the name and address of the applicant, the respondent and any other person whom the applicant considers to be an interested party;

    (b) the name and address of the applicant's representative (if any);

    (c) an address where documents for the applicant may be sent or delivered;

    (d) details of the decision challenged (including the date, the full reference and the identity of the decision maker);

    (e) that the application is for permission to bring judicial review proceedings;

    (f) the outcome that the applicant is seeking; and

    (g) the facts and grounds on which the applicant relies.

  (5) If the application relates to proceedings in a court or tribunal, the application must name as an interested party each party to those proceedings who is not the applicant or a respondent.

  (6) The applicant must send with the application–

    (a) a copy of any written record of the decision in the applicant's possession or control; and

    (b) copies of any other documents in the applicant's possession or control on which the applicant intends to rely.

  (7) If the applicant provides the application to the Upper Tribunal later than the time required by paragraph (2) or (3) or by an extension of time allowed under rule 5(3)(a) (power to extend time)–

    (a) the application must include a request for an extension of time and the reason why the application was not provided in time; and

(b) unless the Upper Tribunal extends time for the application under rule 5(3)(a) (power to extend time) the Upper Tribunal must not admit the application.

(8) Except where rule 28A(2)(a) (special provisions for immigration judicial review proceedings) applies, when the Upper Tribunal receives the application it must send a copy of the application and any accompanying documents to each person named in the application as a respondent or interested party.

### Special provisions for immigration judicial review proceedings

28A(1) The Upper Tribunal must not accept an application for permission to bring immigration judicial review proceedings unless it is either accompanied by any required fee or the Upper Tribunal accepts an undertaking that the fee will be paid.

(2) Within 9 days of making an application referred to in paragraph (1), an applicant must provide–
    (a) a copy of the application and any accompanying documents to each person named in the application as a respondent or an interested party; and
    (b) the Upper Tribunal with a written statement of when and how this was done.

### Acknowledgment of service

29 (1) A person who is sent or provided with a copy of an application for permission under rule 28(8) (application for permission to bring judicial review proceedings) or rule 28A(2)(a) (special provisions for immigration judicial review proceedings) and wishes to take part in the proceedings must provide to the Upper Tribunal an acknowledgment of service so that it is received no later than 21 days after the date on which the Upper Tribunal sent, or in immigration judicial review proceedings the applicant provided, a copy of the application to that person.

(2) An acknowledgment of service under paragraph (1) must be in writing and state–
    (a) whether the person intends to support or oppose the application for permission;
    (b) their grounds for any support or opposition under sub-paragraph (a), or any other submission or information which they consider may assist the Upper Tribunal; and
    (c) the name and address of any other person not named in the application as a respondent or interested party whom the person providing the acknowledgment considers to be an interested party.

(2A) In immigration judicial review proceedings, a person who provides an acknowledgement of service under paragraph (1) must also provide a copy to–
    (a) the applicant; and
    (b) any other person named in the application under rule 28(4)(a) or acknowledgement of service under paragraph (2)(c) no later than the time specified in paragraph (1).

(3) A person who is provided with a copy of an application for permission under rule 28(8) or rule 28A(2)(a) but does not provide an acknowledgment of service to the Upper Tribunal may not take part in the application for permission unless allowed to do so by the Upper Tribunal, but may take part in the subsequent proceedings if the application is successful.

### Decision on permission or summary dismissal, and reconsideration of permission or summary dismissal at a hearing

30 (1) The Upper Tribunal must send to the applicant, each respondent and any other person who provided an acknowledgment of service to the Upper Tribunal, and may send to any other person who may have an interest in the proceedings, written notice of–
    (a) its decision in relation to the application for permission; and
    (b) the reasons for any–
        (i) refusal of the application or refusal to admit the late application, or
        (ii) limitations or conditions on permission.

(2) In proceedings transferred from the Court of Session under section 20(1) of the 2007 Act, where the Upper Tribunal has considered whether summarily to dismiss of the proceedings, the Upper Tribunal must send to the applicant and each

respondent, and may send to any other person who may have an interest in the proceedings, written notice of–

   (a) its decision in relation to the summary dismissal of proceedings; and

   (b) the reasons for any decision summarily to dismiss part or all of the proceedings, or any limitations or conditions on the continuation of such proceedings.

(3) Paragraph (4) applies where the Upper Tribunal, without a hearing–

   (a) determines an application for permission to bring judicial review proceedings and either refuses permission, or gives permission on limited grounds or subject to conditions; or

   (b) in proceedings transferred from the Court of Session, summarily dismisses part or all of the proceedings, or imposes any limitations or conditions on the continuation of such proceedings.

(4) Subject to paragraph (4A), in the circumstances specified in paragraph (3) the applicant may apply for the decision to be reconsidered at a hearing.

(4A) Where the Upper Tribunal refuses permission to bring immigration judicial review proceedings or refuses to admit a late application for permission to bring such proceedings and considers the application to be totally without merit, it shall record that fact in its decision notice and, in those circumstances, the applicant may not request the decision to be reconsidered at a hearing.

(5) An application under paragraph (4) must be made in writing and must be sent or delivered to the Upper Tribunal so that it is received within 14 days, or in immigration judicial review proceedings 9 days, after the date on which the Upper Tribunal sent written notice of its decision regarding the application to the applicant.

### Responses

**31** (1) Any person to whom the Upper Tribunal has sent notice of the grant of permission under rule 30(1) (notification of decision on permission), and who wishes to contest the application or support it on additional grounds, must provide detailed grounds for contesting or supporting the application to the Upper Tribunal.

   (2) Any detailed grounds must be provided in writing and must be sent or delivered to the Upper Tribunal so that they are received not more than 35 days after the Upper Tribunal sent notice of the grant of permission under rule 30(1).

### Applicant seeking to rely on additional grounds

**32**   The applicant may not rely on any grounds, other than those grounds on which the applicant obtained permission for the judicial review proceedings, without the consent of the Upper Tribunal.

### Right to make representations

**33**   Each party and, with the permission of the Upper Tribunal, any other person, may–

   (a) submit evidence, except at the hearing of an application for permission;

   (b) make representations at any hearing which they are entitled to attend; and

   (c) make written representations in relation to a decision to be made without a hearing.

### Amendments and additional grounds resulting in transfer of proceedings to the High Court in England and Wales

**33A**(1) This rule applies only to judicial review proceedings arising under the law of England and Wales.

   (2) In relation to such proceedings–

   (a) the powers of the Upper Tribunal to permit or require amendments under rule 5(3)(c) extend to amendments which would, once in place, give rise to an obligation or power to transfer the proceedings to the High Court in England and Wales under section 18(3) of the 2007 Act or paragraph (3);

   (b) except with the permission of the Upper Tribunal, additional grounds may not be advanced, whether by an applicant or otherwise, if they would give rise to an obligation or power to transfer the proceedings to the High Court in England and Wales under section 18(3) of the 2007 Act or paragraph (3).

(3) Where the High Court in England and Wales has transferred judicial review proceedings to the Upper Tribunal under any power or duty and subsequently the proceedings are amended or any party advances additional grounds–

(a) if the proceedings in their present form could not have been transferred to the Upper Tribunal under the relevant power or duty had they been in that form at the time of the transfer, the Upper Tribunal must transfer the proceedings back to the High Court in England and Wales;

(b) subject to sub-paragraph (a), where the proceedings were transferred to the Upper Tribunal under section 31A(3) of the Senior Courts Act 1981(a)(power to transfer judicial review proceedings to the Upper Tribunal), the Upper Tribunal may transfer proceedings back to the High Court in England and Wales if it appears just and convenient to do so.

## PART 5: Hearings

### Decision with or without a hearing

34 (1) Subject to paragraphs (2) and (3), the Upper Tribunal may make any decision without a hearing.

(2) The Upper Tribunal must have regard to any view expressed by a party when deciding whether to hold a hearing to consider any matter, and the form of any such hearing.

(3) In immigration judicial review proceedings, the Upper Tribunal must hold a hearing before making a decision which disposes of proceedings.

(4) Paragraph (3) does not affect the power of the Upper Tribunal to–

(a) strike out a party's case, pursuant to rule 8(1)(b) or 8(2);

(b) consent to withdrawal, pursuant to rule 17;

(c) determine an application for permission to bring judicial review proceedings, pursuant to rule 30; or

(d) make a consent order disposing of proceedings, pursuant to rule 39,

without a hearing.

### Entitlement to attend a hearing

35 (1) Subject to rule 37(4) (exclusion of a person from a hearing), each party is entitled to attend a hearing.

(2) In a national security certificate appeal the relevant Minister is entitled to attend any hearing.

### Notice of hearings

36 (1) The Upper Tribunal must give each party entitled to attend a hearing reasonable notice of the time and place of the hearing (including any adjourned or postponed hearing) and any change to the time and place of the hearing.

(2) The period of notice under paragraph (1) must be at least 14 days except that–

(a) in applications for permission to bring judicial review proceedings, the period of notice must be at least 2 working days; and

(aa) in a fast-track case the period of notice must be at least one working day; and

(b) in any case other than a fast-track case the Upper Tribunal may give shorter notice–

(i) with the parties' consent; or

(ii) in urgent or exceptional cases.

### Special time limits for hearing an appeal in a fast-track case

36A(1) Subject to rule 36(2)(aa) (notice of hearings) and paragraph (2) of this rule, where permission to appeal to the Upper Tribunal has been given in a fast-track case, the Upper Tribunal must start the hearing of the appeal not later than–

(a) five working days after the date on which the First-tier Tribunal or the Upper Tribunal sent notice of its grant of permission to appeal to the appellant; or

(b) where the notice of its grant of permission to appeal is sent electronically or delivered personally, two working days after the date on which the First-tier Tribunal or the Upper Tribunal sent notice of its grant of permission to appeal to the appellant.

(2) If the Upper Tribunal is unable to arrange for the hearing to start within the time specified in paragraph (1), it must set a date for the hearing as soon as is reasonably practicable.

### Public and private hearings

37 (1) Subject to the following paragraphs, all hearings must be held in public.

(2) The Upper Tribunal may give a direction that a hearing, or part of it, is to be held in private.

(2A) In a national security certificate appeal, the Upper Tribunal must have regard to its duty under rule 14(10) (no disclosure of information contrary to the interests of national security) when considering whether to give a direction that a hearing, or part of it, is to be held in private.

(3) Where a hearing, or part of it, is to be held in private, the Upper Tribunal may determine who is entitled to attend the hearing or part of it.

(4) The Upper Tribunal may give a direction excluding from any hearing, or part of it–

(a) any person whose conduct the Upper Tribunal considers is disrupting or is likely to disrupt the hearing;

(b) any person whose presence the Upper Tribunal considers is likely to prevent another person from giving evidence or making submissions freely;

(c) any person who the Upper Tribunal considers should be excluded in order to give effect to the requirement at rule 14(11) (prevention of disclosure or publication of documents and information);

(d) any person where the purpose of the hearing would be defeated by the attendance of that person; or

(e) a person under 18, other than a young person who is a party in a special educational needs case or a disability discrimination in schools case.

(5) The Upper Tribunal may give a direction excluding a witness from a hearing until that witness gives evidence.

### Hearings in a party's absence

38     If a party fails to attend a hearing, the Upper Tribunal may proceed with the hearing if the Upper Tribunal–

(a) is satisfied that the party has been notified of the hearing or that reasonable steps have been taken to notify the party of the hearing; and

(b) considers that it is in the interests of justice to proceed with the hearing.

## PART 6: Decisions

### Consent orders

39 (1) The Upper Tribunal may, at the request of the parties but only if it considers it appropriate, make a consent order disposing of the proceedings and making such other appropriate provision as the parties have agreed.

(2) Notwithstanding any other provision of these Rules, the Upper Tribunal need not hold a hearing before making an order under paragraph (1).

### Decisions

40 (1) The Upper Tribunal may give a decision orally at a hearing.

(2) Except where rule 22 (decision in relation to permission to appeal) or rule 22A (special procedure for providing notice of a refusal of permission to appeal in an asylum case) applies, the Upper Tribunal must provide to each party as soon as reasonably practicable after making a decision (other than a decision under Part 7) which finally disposes of all issues in the proceedings or of a preliminary issue dealt with following a direction under rule 5(3)(e)–

(a) a decision notice stating the Upper Tribunal's decision; and

(b) notification of any rights of review or appeal against the decision and the time and manner in which such rights of review or appeal may be exercised.

(3) Subject to rule 14(11) (prevention of disclosure or publication of documents and information), the Upper Tribunal must provide written reasons for its decision with a decision notice provided under paragraph (2)(a) unless–

(a) the decision was made with the consent of the parties; or

(b) the parties have consented to the Upper Tribunal not giving written reasons.

(4) The Upper Tribunal may provide written reasons for any decision to which paragraph (2) does not apply.

(5) In a national security certificate appeal, when the Upper Tribunal provides a notice or reasons to the parties under this rule, it must also provide the notice or reasons to the relevant Minister and the Information Commissioner, if they are not parties.

## PART 7: Correcting, setting aside, reviewing and appealing decisions of the Upper Tribunal

### Interpretation

41    In this Part–

'appeal', except in rule 44(2) (application for permission to appeal), means the exercise of a right of appeal under section 13 of the 2007 Act; and 'review' means the review of a decision by the Upper Tribunal under section 10 of the 2007 Act.

### Clerical mistakes and accidental slips or omissions

42    The Upper Tribunal may at any time correct any clerical mistake or other accidental slip or omission in a decision or record of a decision by–

(a) sending notification of the amended decision, or a copy of the amended record, to all parties; and

(b) making any necessary amendment to any information published in relation to the decision or record.

### Setting aside a decision which disposes of proceedings

43 (1) The Upper Tribunal may set aside a decision which disposes of proceedings, or part of such a decision, and re-make the decision or the relevant part of it, if–

(a) the Upper Tribunal considers that it is in the interests of justice to do so; and

(b) one or more of the conditions in paragraph (2) are satisfied.

(2) The conditions are–

(a) a document relating to the proceedings was not sent to, or was not received at an appropriate time by, a party or a party's representative;

(b) a document relating to the proceedings was not sent to the Upper Tribunal at an appropriate time;

(c) a party, or a party's representative, was not present at a hearing related to the proceedings; or

(d) there has been some other procedural irregularity in the proceedings.

(3) Except where paragraph (4) applies, a party applying for a decision, or part of a decision, to be set aside under paragraph (1) must make a written application to the Upper Tribunal so that it is received no later than 1 month after the date on which the Tribunal sent notice of the decision to the party.

(4) In an asylum case or an immigration case, the written application referred to in paragraph (3) must be sent or delivered so that it is received by the Upper Tribunal–

(a) where the person who appealed to the First-tier Tribunal is in the United Kingdom at the time that the application is made, no later than twelve days after the date on which the Upper Tribunal or, as the case may be in an asylum case, the Secretary of State for the Home Department, sent notice of the decision to the party making the application; or

(b) where the person who appealed to the First-tier Tribunal is outside the United Kingdom at the time that the application is made, no later than thirty eight days after the date on which the Upper Tribunal sent notice of the decision to the party making the application.

(5) Where a notice of decision is sent electronically or delivered personally, the time limits in paragraph (4) are ten working days.

### Application for permission to appeal

**44** (1) Subject to paragraphs (4A) and (4B), a person seeking permission to appeal must make a written application to the Upper Tribunal for permission to appeal.

(2) Paragraph (3) applies to an application under paragraph (1) in respect of a decision–

   (a) on an appeal against a decision in a social security and child support case (as defined in the Tribunal Procedure (First-tier Tribunal) (Social Entitlement Chamber) Rules 2008);

   (b) on an appeal against a decision in proceedings in the War Pensions and Armed Forces Compensation Chamber of the First-tier Tribunal;

   (ba) on an appeal against a decision of a Pensions Appeal Tribunal for Scotland or Northern Ireland; or

   (c) in proceedings under the Forfeiture Act 1982.

(3) Where this paragraph applies, the application must be sent or delivered to the Upper Tribunal so that it is received within 3 months after the date on which the Upper Tribunal sent to the person making the application–

   (a) written notice of the decision;

   (b) notification of amended reasons for, or correction of, the decision following a review; or

   (c) notification that an application for the decision to be set aside has been unsuccessful.

(3A) An application under paragraph (1) in respect of a decision in an asylum case or an immigration case must be sent or delivered to the Upper Tribunal so that it is received within the appropriate period after the Upper Tribunal or, as the case may be in an asylum case, the Secretary of State for the Home Department, sent any of the documents in paragraph (3) to the party making the application.

(3B) The appropriate period referred to in paragraph (3A) is as follows–

   (a) where the person who appealed to the First-tier Tribunal is in the United Kingdom at the time that the application is made–

   (i) twelve working days; or

   (ii) if the party making the application is in detention under the Immigration Acts, seven working days; and

   (b) where the person who appealed to the First-tier Tribunal is outside the United Kingdom at the time that the application is made, thirty eight days.

(3C) Where a notice of decision is sent electronically or delivered personally, the time limits in paragraph (3B) are–

   (a) in sub-paragraph (a)(i), ten working days;

   (b) in sub-paragraph (a)(ii), five working days; and

   (c) in sub-paragraph (b), ten working days.

(3D) An application under paragraph (1) in respect of a decision in a financial services case must be sent or delivered to the Upper Tribunal so that it is received within 14 days after the date on which the Upper Tribunal sent to the person making the application–

   (a) written notice of the decision;

   (b) notification of amended reasons for, or correction of, the decision following a review; or

   (c) notification that an application for the decision to be set aside has been unsuccessful.

(4) Where paragraph (3), (3A), (3D) or (4C) does not apply, an application under paragraph (1) must be sent or delivered to the Upper Tribunal so that it is received within 1 month after the latest of the dates on which the Upper Tribunal sent to the person making the application–

   (a) written reasons for the decision;

   (b) notification of amended reasons for, or correction of, the decision following a review; or

   (c) notification that an application for the decision to be set aside has been unsuccessful.

(4A) Where a decision that disposes of immigration judicial review proceedings is given at a hearing, a party may apply at that hearing for permission to appeal, and the Upper Tribunal must consider at the hearing whether to give or refuse permission to appeal.

(4B) Where a decision that disposes of immigration judicial review proceedings is given at a hearing and no application for permission to appeal is made at that hearing–

  (a) the Upper Tribunal must nonetheless consider at the hearing whether to give or refuse permission to appeal; and

  (b) if permission to appeal is given to a party, it shall be deemed for the purposes of section 13(4) of the 2007 Act to be given on application by that party.

(4C) Where a decision that disposes of immigration judicial review proceedings is given pursuant to rule 30 and the Upper Tribunal records under rule 30(4A) that the application is totally without merit, an application under paragraph (1) must be sent or delivered to the Upper Tribunal so that it is received within 7 days after the later of the dates on which the Upper Tribunal sent to the applicant–

  (a) written reasons for the decision; or

  (b) notification of amended reasons for, or correction of, the decision following a review.

 (5) The date in paragraph (3)(c) or (4)(c) applies only if the application for the decision to be set aside was made within the time stipulated in rule 43 (setting aside a decision which disposes of proceedings) or any extension of that time granted by the Upper Tribunal.

 (6) If the person seeking permission to appeal provides the application to the Upper Tribunal later than the time required by paragraph (3), (3A) (3D) or (4), or by any extension of time under rule 5(3)(a) (power to extend time)–

  (a) the application must include a request for an extension of time and the reason why the application notice was not provided in time; and

  (b) unless the Upper Tribunal extends time for the application under rule 5(3)(a) (power to extend time) the Upper Tribunal must refuse the application.

 (7) An application under paragraph (1) or (4A)(a) must–

  (a) identify the decision of the Upper Tribunal to which it relates;

  (b) identify the alleged error or errors of law in the decision; and

  (c) state the result the party making the application is seeking.

### Upper Tribunal's consideration of application for permission to appeal

45 (1) On receiving an application for permission to appeal the Upper Tribunal may review the decision in accordance with rule 46 (review of a decision), but may only do so if–

  (a) when making the decision the Upper Tribunal overlooked a legislative provision or binding authority which could have had a material effect on the decision; or

  (b) since the Upper Tribunal's decision, a court has made a decision which is binding on the Upper Tribunal and which, had it been made before the Upper Tribunal's decision, could have had a material effect on the decision.

 (2) If the Upper Tribunal decides not to review the decision, or reviews the decision and decides to take no action in relation to the decision or part of it, the Upper Tribunal must consider whether to give permission to appeal in relation to the decision or that part of it.

 (3) The Upper Tribunal must provide a record of its decision to the parties as soon as practicable.

 (4) If the Upper Tribunal refuses permission to appeal it must provide with the record of its decision–

  (a) a statement of its reasons for such refusal; and

  (b) notification of the right to make an application to the relevant appellate court for permission to appeal and the time within which, and the method by which, such application must be made.

 (5) The Upper Tribunal may give permission to appeal on limited grounds, but must comply with paragraph (4) in relation to any grounds on which it has refused permission.

**Review of a decision**

46 (1) The Upper Tribunal may only undertake a review of a decision pursuant to rule 45(1) (review on an application for permission to appeal).

(2) The Upper Tribunal must notify the parties in writing of the outcome of any review and of any rights of review or appeal in relation to the outcome.

(3) If the Upper Tribunal decides to take any action in relation to a decision following a review without first giving every party an opportunity to make representations, the notice under paragraph (2) must state that any party that did not have an opportunity to make representations may apply for such action to be set aside and for the decision to be reviewed again.

**Setting aside a decision in proceedings under the Forfeiture Act 1982**

47 (1) A person who referred a question to the Upper Tribunal under rule 26 (references under the Forfeiture Act 1982) must refer the Upper Tribunal's previous decision in relation to the question to the Upper Tribunal if they–

(a) consider that the decision should be set aside or re-made under this rule; or

(b) have received a written application for the decision to be set aside or re-made under this rule from the person to whom the decision related.

(2) The Upper Tribunal may set aside the decision, either in whole or in part, or re-make it if–

(b) the decision was made in ignorance of, or was based on a mistake as to, some material fact; or

(c) there has been a relevant change in circumstances since the decision was made.

(3) Rule 26(2) to (4), Parts 5 and 6 and this Part apply to a reference under this rule as they apply to a reference under rule 26(1).

**Power to treat an application as a different type of application**

48 The Upper Tribunal may treat an application for a decision to be corrected, set aside or reviewed, or for permission to appeal against a decision, as an application for any other one of those things.

## SCHEDULE 1: PROCEDURE AFTER THE NOTICE OF APPEAL IN ROAD TRANSPORT CASES

**Rule 24(1)**

1. This Schedule applies to road transport cases.

2. The only parties to the appeal are the appellant and any person added as a party under rule 9 (addition, substitution and removal of parties).

3. On receipt of a copy of a notice of appeal under rule 23(6)(b), the decision maker must send to the Upper Tribunal a copy (and, on request, further copies) of–

(a) a written record of the decision appealed against and reasons for the decision;

(b) all documents produced to the decision maker in connection with the decision;

(c) if a public inquiry was held, the transcript of the inquiry or, if no such transcript was produced, the decision maker's note of the inquiry; and

(d) in an appeal under–

(i) section 50 of the Public Passenger Vehicles Act 1981 or section 37 of the Goods Vehicles (Licensing of Operators) Act 1995, or

(ii) section 35 of the Goods Vehicles (Licensing of Operators) Act (Northern Ireland) 2010

a list of the names and addresses of objectors and representors.

4. On receipt of a list under paragraph 3(d) the Upper Tribunal must send a copy of the notice of appeal–

(a) where the appellant had applied for, or for the variation of, an operator's licence, to each person who made an objection to the application;

(b) where the appellant had made an objection to an application for, or (in the case of a goods vehicle operator's licence) for the variation of, an operator's licence, to the person who made the application and to every other person who made an objection to the application;

(c) in an appeal under section 37(5) of the Goods Vehicles (Licensing of Operators) Act 1995, to each person who made representations under section 12(4) or 19(2) of that Act against the application for, or for the variation of, the operator's licence in question;

(d) in an appeal under section 35(5) of the Goods Vehicles (Licensing of Operators) Act (Northern Ireland) 2010, to each person who made representations under section 11(4) or 18(2) of that Act.

5. The appropriate national authority and any person to whom the Upper Tribunal has sent a copy of the notice of appeal under paragraph 4 may apply for a direction under rule 9(2) adding them as a respondent.

6. An application under paragraph 5 must be sent or delivered to the Upper Tribunal so that it is received within 14 days of the date that the Upper Tribunal sent a copy of the notice of appeal to the person making the application.

7. If a person makes an application in accordance with paragraphs 5 and 6, the Upper Tribunal must give a direction under rule 9(2) adding that person as a respondent.

. . .

9. The Upper Tribunal must notify each other party of any application under paragraph 3 and the Upper Tribunal's decision in respect of each such application.

10. Any party may make a request to the Upper Tribunal for copies of specified documents provided by the decision maker under paragraph 3.

11. On receiving a request under paragraph 10 the Upper Tribunal–
   (a) must provide the requested copies unless it considers the request unreasonable; and
   (b) if it considers the request unreasonable, give details of why it considers the request unreasonable.

## SCHEDULE 2: ADDITIONAL PROCEDURE IN NATIONAL SECURITY CERTIFICATE CASES

**Rule 26A(4)**

1. This Schedule applies only to national security certificate appeals.

2. Following the transfer of the appeal from the First-tier Tribunal, the Upper Tribunal must provide a copy of the notice of appeal to the respondent, the relevant Minister and the Information Commissioner.

3. The relevant Minister must send or deliver to the Upper Tribunal a copy of the certificate to which the appeal relates, and a response to the notice of appeal, not later than 42 days after the date on which the relevant Minister received a copy of the notice of appeal.

4. In an appeal under section 28(4) of the Data Protection Act 1998 or section 60(1) of the Freedom of Information Act 2000 (including that subsection as applied and modified by regulation 18 of the Environmental Information Regulations 2004), the relevant Minister's response must state whether the relevant Minister intends to oppose the appeal and, if so set out–
   (a) a summary of the circumstances relating to the issue of the certificate;
   (b) the reason for the issue of the certificate;
   (c) the grounds on which the relevant Minister relies in opposing the appeal; and
   (d) a statement of the evidence on which the relevant Minister relies in support of those grounds.

5. In an appeal under section 28(6) of the Data Protection Act 1998 or section 60(4) of the Freedom of Information Act 2000 (including that subsection as applied and modified by regulation 18 of the Environmental Information Regulations 2004), the relevant Minister's response must state whether the relevant Minister intends to make representations in relation to the appeal and, if so set out–
   (a) the extent to which the relevant Minister intends to support or oppose the appeal;

(b) the grounds on which the relevant Minister relies in supporting or opposing the appeal; and

(c) a statement of the evidence on which the relevant Minister relies in support of those grounds.

6. The Upper Tribunal must–

(a) subject to paragraph 11, provide the relevant Minister's response and any other response to the appellant, the Information Commissioner and any respondent; and

(b) send a copy of any other response to the relevant Minister.

7. On grounds of the need to ensure that information is not disclosed contrary to the interests of national security, the relevant Minster may–

(a) object to the disclosure of the relevant Minister's response to the appellant, the Information Commissioner or any respondent, by sending a notice to the Upper Tribunal with the response; or

(b) object to the disclosure of any other response to the Information Commissioner or any respondent, by sending a notice to the Upper Tribunal within 42 days of the date on which the relevant Minister received a copy of the response.

8. A notice under paragraph 7 must–

(a) state the reason for the objection; and

(b) in the case of a notice under paragraph 7(a) and to the extent that it is possible to do so, be accompanied by a version of the relevant Minister's response in a form that can be shown to the appellant, the Commissioner or, as the case may be, a respondent.

9. Before the Upper Tribunal gives a direction, issues a summons or citation, or produces or publishes a written record of, or reasons for, a decision–

(a) the Upper Tribunal must notify the relevant Minister of the proposed action; and

(b) if the relevant Minister considers that the proposal would cause information that is or would be exempt by virtue of a provision in Part 2 of the Freedom of Information Act 2000 to be disclosed, the relevant Minister may object to the proposal by sending a notice to the Upper Tribunal so that the Upper Tribunal receives the notice within 14 days of the date that the Minister received notice of the proposal.

10. When deciding whether to uphold an objection made by the relevant Minister–

(a) any hearing must take place in the absence of the parties;

(b) if the Upper Tribunal is minded to overrule the relevant Minister's objection, or to require the relevant Minister to provide a version of the relevant Minister's response in a form other than one provided under paragraph 8(b) above, the Upper Tribunal must invite the relevant Minister to make representations; and

(c) if the Upper Tribunal overrules an objection in relation to the disclosure of a response, the Upper Tribunal must not disclose, or require the relevant Minister to disclose, any material the subject of the objection unless the relevant Minister relies upon that material in opposing the appeal.

11. Where the relevant Minister may object to the disclosure of a response or proposed action by the Upper Tribunal, the Upper Tribunal may not proceed with that disclosure or that proposed action unless–

(a) the time for the relevant Minister to object has expired; and

(b) the relevant Minister has not objected, or the Upper Tribunal has overruled the relevant Minister's objection and, in the case of the disclosure of a response, may proceed with the disclosure under paragraph 10(c).

## SCHEDULE 3: PROCEDURE IN FINANCIAL SERVICES CASES AND WHOLESALE ENERGY CASES

**Rule 26B**

### Interpretation
1.   In this Schedule–
'further material' means–
  (a) in a single regulator case, documents which–
    (i)  were considered by the respondent in reaching or maintaining the deci-
sion to give the notice in respect of which the reference has been made;
or
    (ii) were obtained by the respondent in connection with the matter to which
that notice relates (whether they were obtained before or after giving the
notice) but which were not considered by it in reaching or maintaining
that decision;
  but does not include documents on which the respondent relies in support
of the referred action;
  (b) in a multiple regulator case–
    (i)  in relation to a respondent who is the primary regulator, documents
which–
      (aa) were considered by that regulator in reaching or maintaining its
decision to give the notice in respect of which the reference has
been made; or
      (bb) were obtained by that regulator in connection with the matter to
which that notice relates (whether they were obtained before or
after the notice was given) but which were not considered by that
regulator in reaching or maintaining its decision;
    (ii) in relation to a respondent who is the secondary regulator, documents
which–
      (aa) were considered by that regulator in reaching or maintaining its
decision to take the secondary regulator action in relation to the
notice in respect of which the reference has been made; or
      (bb) were obtained by that regulator in connection with the matter to
which that notice relates (whether they were obtained before or
after the notice was given) but which were not considered by that
regulator in reaching or maintaining its decision;
  but does not include documents on which either the primary regulator or
the secondary regulator relies;
'multiple regulator case' means a case where–
  (a) any of the Financial Conduct Authority, the Prudential Regulation Authority or the Bank of England has given the notice in respect of which the reference has been made; and
  (b) such notice stated that another of those regulators had decided to take one
of the following actions–
    (i)  to refuse a consent where such consent is required under the 2000
Act;
    (ii) to give a conditional consent under the 2000 Act; or
    (iii) to direct another regulator to take an action or not to take an action
under the 2000 Act;'
'primary regulator' means, in a multiple regulator case, the regulator giving the
notice;
'reference notice' means the written notice required in making a reference in a
financial services case or a wholesale energy case;
'referred action' means–
  (a) in a single regulator case, the act (or proposed act) on the part of the respondent that gave rise to the reference; and
  (b) in a multiple regulator case, the act (or proposed act) on the part of the primary regulator that gave rise to the reference;

'secondary regulator action' means an action taken by a secondary regulator, as stated in the notice given by the primary regulator;

'secondary regulator' means, in a multiple regulator case, a regulator specified in the notice other than the primary regulator;

'single regulator case' means a case that is not a multiple regulator case;

'the 2000 Act' means the Financial Services and Markets Act 2000;

'the 2013 Regulations' means the Electricity and Gas (Market Integrity and Transparency) (Enforcement etc.) Regulations 2013;

'the 2013 (NI) Regulations' means the Electricity and Gas (Market Integrity and Transparency) (Enforcement etc.) Regulations (Northern Ireland) 2013.

### Reference notice

2. (1) A reference notice must be signed by or on behalf of the applicant and sent or delivered by the applicant to the Upper Tribunal.

(2) A reference notice must be received by the Upper Tribunal no later than 28 days after notice was given of the decision in respect of which the reference is made.

(3) The reference notice must state–
   (a) the name and address of the applicant;
   (b) the name and address of the applicant's representative (if any);
   (c) if no representative is named under sub-paragraph (b), an address where documents for the applicant may be sent or delivered; and
   (d) the issues that the applicant wishes the Upper Tribunal to consider.

(4) The applicant must send or deliver to the Upper Tribunal with the reference notice a copy of the notice of the decision in respect of which the reference has been made.

(5) At the same time the applicant must send a copy of the reference notice–
   (a) in a single regulator case, to the respondent; and
   (b) in a multiple regulator case, to each of the primary and secondary regulators.

### Register of references and decisions

3. (1) The Upper Tribunal must keep a register of references and decisions in financial services cases and wholesale energy cases.

(2) The register must be open to inspection by any person without charge and at all reasonable hours.

(3) The Upper Tribunal may direct that the register is not to include particulars of a reference if it is satisfied that it is necessary to do so having regard in particular to–
   (a) any unfairness to the applicant or, except as regards a reference in respect of a decision of the Prudential Regulation Authority, any prejudice to the interests of consumers that might otherwise result;
   (b) as regards a reference in respect of a decision of the Financial Conduct Authority, any detriment to the stability of the UK financial system;
   (c) as regards a reference in respect of a decision of the Prudential Regulation Authority, any prejudice to the safety and soundness of persons authorised by it, or where section 2C of the 2000 Act applies, any prejudice to securing the appropriate degree of protection for policy holders; or
   (d) as regards a reference under the 2013 Regulations or the 2013 (NI) Regulations any detriment to the stability of the wholesale energy market as defined in those Regulations.

(4) Upon receiving a reference notice, the Upper Tribunal must–
   (a) subject to any direction given under sub-paragraph (3), enter particulars of the reference in the register; and
   (b) notify the parties either that it has done so or that it will not include particulars in the register, as the case may be.

(5) In a multiple regulator case, notification under sub-paragraph (4)(b) must be given to each of the primary and secondary regulators.

### Respondent's statement of case in a single regulator case

4. (1) The respondent in a single regulator case must send or deliver a written statement

('a statement of case') in support of the referred action so that it is received by the Upper Tribunal no later than 28 days after the day on which the respondent received from the Upper Tribunal the notification required by paragraph 3(4)(b).

(2) The statement of case must–

    (a) identify the statutory provisions providing for the referred action;

    (b) state the reasons for the referred action; and

    (c) set out all the matters and facts upon which the respondent relies to support the referred action.

(3) The respondent must provide with the statement of case a list of–

    (a) any documents on which the respondent relies in support of the referred action; and

    (b) any further material which in the opinion of the respondent might undermine the decision to take action.

(4) At the same time as it sends or delivers the statement of case, the respondent must send to the applicant a copy of the statement of case and of the list referred to in subparagraph (3).

### Respondents' statements of case in a multiple regulator case

4A. (1) This paragraph applies in a multiple regulator case.

    (2) The primary regulator must send or deliver either–

        (a) a written statement (a "statement of case") in support of the referred action; or

        (b) a written notification that it does not itself advance a case in support of the referred action,

    so that it is received by the Upper Tribunal no later than 28 days after the day on which the primary regulator received from the Upper Tribunal the notification required by paragraph 3(4)(b).

    (3) A primary regulator providing a written notification under sub-paragraph (2)(b) must send or deliver a copy to the secondary regulator and the applicant and upon so doing–

        (a) the primary regulator shall not be required to take further steps in the proceedings unless the Upper Tribunal gives a direction to the contrary under rule 6; and

        (b) the respondent shall be the secondary regulator unless the Upper Tribunal orders otherwise.

    (4) The secondary regulator must send or deliver a written statement ("a statement of case") in support of its decision to take the secondary regulator action so that it is received by the Upper Tribunal no later than 28 days after the day on which the secondary regulator received from the Upper Tribunal the notification required by paragraph 3(4)(b).

    (5) A statement of case must–

        (a) identify the statutory provisions providing for the referred action;

        (b) state the reasons in support for the referred action; and

        (c) set out all the matters and facts upon which the regulator relies to support the referred action.

    (6) A regulator must provide with the statement of case a list of–

        (a) all documents on which it relies in support of the referred action;

        (b) any further material which, in the opinion of the regulator, might undermine its decision to–

            (i) in the case of a primary regulator; take the referred action; and

            (ii) in the case of a secondary regulator; take the secondary regulator action.

    (7) The primary regulator and the secondary regulator must send to the applicant and the other regulator a copy of any statement of case required by sub-paragraphs (2) and (4) above and of the list referred to in sub-paragraph (6).

### Applicant's reply

5. (1) The applicant must send or deliver a written reply so that it is received by the Upper Tribunal no later than 28 days after–

    (a) in a single regulator case, on the date on which the applicant received a copy of the statement of case;

    (aa) in a multiple regulator case, on the first date on which the applicant was in receipt of all the statements and, where relevant, notifications required under paragraphs 4A(2) and 4A(4); or

    (b) if a respondent amends its statement of case, the date on which the applicant received a copy of the amended statement of case.

(2) The reply must–

    (a) state the grounds on which the applicant relies in the reference;

    (b) identify all matters contained in the respondent's statement of case (or, where applicable, respondents' statements of case) which are disputed by the applicant;

    (c) state the applicant's reasons for disputing them.

(3) The applicant must send with the reply a list of all the documents on which the applicant relies in support of his case.

(4) At the same time the applicant must send to all other parties a copy of the reply and of the list referred to in sub-paragraph (3).

(5) Where the primary regulator has provided a written notification under paragraph 4A(2)(b), if the applicant wishes the Tribunal to direct that further steps in the proceedings be taken by the primary regulator, an application must be made at the time of sending the reply.

### Secondary disclosure by a respondent

6. (1) After the applicant's reply has been sent or delivered, if there is any further material which might reasonably be expected to assist the applicant's case as disclosed by the applicant's reply and which is not listed in the list (or lists) provided in accordance with paragraph 4(3) (or paragraph 4A(6) where applicable), the respondent (or the respondents) must send or deliver to the Upper Tribunal a list (or lists) of such further material.

(2) Any list required to be sent or delivered by sub-paragraph (1) must be sent or delivered so that it is received no later than 14 days after the day on which the respondent in question received the applicant's reply.

(3) At the same time as it sends or delivers any list required by sub-paragraph (1) a respondent must send a copy to the applicant (and where applicable the other parties).

### Exceptions to disclosure

7. (1) A list provided in accordance with paragraph 4(3), 4A(6) or 6(1) need not include any document that relates to a case involving a person other than the applicant which was taken into account by the respondent providing the list in the applicant's case only for the purposes of comparison with other cases.

(2) A list provided in accordance with paragraph 4(3), 4A(6), 5(3) or 6(1) need not include any document that is material the disclosure of which for the purposes of or in connection with any legal proceedings is prohibited by section 17 of the Regulation of Investigatory Powers Act 2000.

(3) A list provided in accordance with paragraph 4(3), 4A(6), 5(3) or 6(1) need not include any document in respect of which an application has been or is being made under sub-paragraph (4).

(4) A party may apply to the Upper Tribunal (without giving notice to any other party) for a direction authorising the party making the application not to include in the list required by paragraph 4(3), 4A(6), 5(3) or 6(1) a document on the ground that disclosure of the document–

    (a) would not be in the public interest; or

    (b) would not be fair, having regard to–

        (i) the likely significance of the document to the applicant in relation to the matter referred to the Upper Tribunal; and

        (ii) the potential prejudice to the commercial interests of a person other than the applicant which would be caused by disclosure of the document.

(5) For the purpose of deciding an application by a party under sub-paragraph (4), the Upper Tribunal may–

    (a) require the document to be produced to the Upper Tribunal together with a statement of the reasons why its inclusion in the list would–

        (i) in the case of an application under sub-paragraph (4)(a), not be in the public interest; or

        (ii) in the case of an application under sub-paragraph (4)(b), not be fair; and

    (b) invite any other party to make representations.

(6) If the Upper Tribunal refuses an application under sub-paragraph (4), it must direct the part–

    (a) to revise its list so as to include the document; and

    (b) to send or deliver a copy of the revised list to the Upper Tribunal and to any other party.

(7) A party ('P') who has sent or delivered a list under paragraph 4(3), 4A(6), 5(3) or 6(1) must, upon the request of another party, provide that other party with a copy of any document which P has which is specified in the list, or make it available for inspection or copying, and if P does not have it, tell the other party where to the best of P's knowledge and belief it may be found.

(8) Sub-paragraph (7) does not apply to any document that is a protected item.

(9) In this paragraph "protected item" has the meaning provided by section 413 of the 2000 Act, section 311(2) of the Pensions Act 2004 or article 283(2) of the Pensions (Northern Ireland) Order 2005 or regulation 52(2) of the 2013 Regulations or regulation 51(2) of the 2013 (NI) Regulations.

### Subsequent notices in relation to the referred action

8.    Where, after a reference notice has been sent or delivered, a respondent gives the applicant any further, amended or supplementary notice in relation to the referred action, that respondent must without delay send or deliver a copy of that notice to the Upper Tribunal.

### References by third parties

9. (1) In the case of any reference made by an applicant under section 393 of the 2000 Act, regulation 40 of the 2013 Regulations or regulation 40 of the 2013 (NI) Regulations (third party rights) these rules apply subject to the modifications set out in this paragraph.

(2) In this paragraph–

    (a) if the reference was made under section 393(9) of the 2000 Act, regulation 40(9) of the 2013 Regulations or regulation 40(9) of the 2013 (NI) Regulations (reference to the Upper Tribunal by a third party to whom a decision notice was copied), the notice of the decision in respect of which the reference has been made is the decision notice which was copied to the applicant by the respondent that gave the notice; and

    (b) if the reference was made under section 393(11) of the 2000 Act, regulation 40(11) of the 2013 Regulations or regulation 40(11) of the 2013 (NI) Regulations (reference to the Upper Tribunal by a third party who alleges that they were not given a copy of a decision notice), the notice of the decision in respect of which the reference has been made is the decision notice which the applicant alleges was not copied to them.

(3) If the reference was made under section 393(11) of the 2000 Act, regulation 40(11) of the 2013 Regulations or regulation 40(11) of the 2013 (NI) Regulations, paragraph 2(4) does not apply.

(4) The duties of the respondent to–

    (a) set out information under paragraph 4(2), 4A(2), 4A(4) or 4A(5); or

    (b) list material under paragraph 4(3), 4A(6) or 6(1)

apply only to information or material which relate to the matters referred to the Upper Tribunal in accordance with section 393(9) or (as the case may be) section 393(11) of the 2000 Act, regulation 40(9), or as the case may be, regulation 40(11) of the 2013 Regulations or regulation 40(9), or as the case may be, regulation 40(11) of the 2013 (NI) Regulations.

# Articles in *Tribunals*

**TRIBUNALS** is a journal published by the Judicial College and issued to all members of tribunals. Its articles contain a wealth of practical guidance on many matters of practice and procedure. The relevant articles are listed here.

## Nature of tribunals and tribunal adjudication
Adjudication, Martin Partington (1994) 1(1) 12

## Procedure
Evolution rather than revolution, Kris Gledhill (Autumn 2009) 10
Giving effect to the overriding objective, Charles Blake (Spring 2010) 7

## Preparing for the hearing
Reading the papers, Mark Ockelton (1999) 6(1) 10

## The hearing
Handling hostility in tribunals: some experiences from the CSAT, Mary Holmes
    (1997) 4(1) 3
Adjournments in tribunals, David Pearl (1998) 5(2) 9
The tribunal introduction, Mungo Deans (1998) 5(2) 11
Sitting alone, Jenny Waine (1999) 6(2) 13
When delay is no excuse, Tim Eicke, Stuart Vernon and Nuala Brice (2003)
    10(1) 17
When contact can be crucial, Godfrey Cole (Autumn 2005) 18
Delivering fair hearings, Hazel Genn (Spring 2006) 10
Listening to a range of views, Genevra Richardson (Spring 2006) 18
Choosing to get personal, John Raine and Eileen Dunstan (Spring 2006) 21
You are in charge, Mary Kane (Summer 2006) 12
Is the mouse mightier than the pen?, Leslie Cuthbert (Summer 2008) 11
How to handle the unexpected, Julia O'Hara (Spring 2011) 4

*The enabling and inquisitorial role*
The unrepresented tribunal applicant, Hazel Genn (1994) 1(1) 8
Dealing with an unrepresented appellant, Martin Partington (1997) 4(2) 9
The unrepresented appellant: principles and advice from Australia, Stuart Vernon
    (1999) 6(1) 19
Helping the under-represented appellant, Michael Johnson (2000) 7(1) 5
What users want, Michael Adler and Jackie Gulland (2003) 10(2) 17
Creating the right conditions, Andrew Bano (Spring 2006) 2
Walking a tightrope to a solution, Melanie Lewis (Summer 2009) 12
A special group of tribunal users, Andrew Bano (Summer 2010) 8
From intervention to interfering, Leslie Cuthburt (Spring 2011) 2
No need for fussing and fighting, Nick Warren (Summer 2011) 6
Fundamentally different from courts, Andrew Bano (Summer 2011) 16
Intervention: a delicate feat of balance, Andrew Bano (Spring 2012) 9

*Diversity*
Getting the best from interpreters, Godfrey Cole (2001) 8(1) 14
Bridging the gap in understanding, Sarah de Mas (1996) 3(1) 4

## Enforcement

## Alternative dispute resolution and avoidance

## Assessing performance

## Representation

# Index